T0211674

More information about this subseries at http://www.springer.com/series/1244

Lecture Notes in Artificial Intelligence   12838

Subseries of Lecture Notes in Computer Science

Pufeng Du

Atif Mehmood

Jonggeun Kim

Eun Kyeong Kim

Hansoo Lee

Yiqiao Cai

Wuritu Yang

Weitao Sun

Guihua Tao

Jinzhong Zhang

Wenjie Yi

Lingyun Huang

Chao Chen

Jiangping He

Wei Wang

Jin Ma

Liang Xu

Vitoantonio Bevilacqua

Huan Liu

Lei Deng

Di Liu

Zhongrui Zhang

Qinhu Zhang

Yanyun Qu

Jinxing Liu

Shravan Sukumar

Long Gao

Yifei Wu

Tianhua Jiang

Lixiang Hong

Tingzhong Tian

Yijie Ding

Junwei Wang

Zhe Yan

Rui Song

S. A. K. Bangyal

Giansalvo Cirrincione

Xiancui Xiao

X. Zheng

Vincenzo Randazzo

Huijuan Zhu

Dongyuan Li

Jingbo Xia

Boya Ji

Manilo Monaco

Xiaohua Yu

Zuguo Yu

Jun Yuan

Punam Kumari

Bowei Zhao

X. J. Chen

Takashi Kurmeoto

Pallavi Pandey

Yan Zhou

Mascot Wang

Chenhui Qiu

Haizhou Wu

Lulu Zuo

Juan Wang

Rafal Kozik

Wenyan Gu

Shiyin Tan

Yaping Fang

Alexander Moopenn

Xiuxiu Ren

Aniello Castiglionc

Qiong Wu

Junyi Chen

Meineng Wang

Xiaorui Su

Jianping Yu

Lizhi Liu

Junwei Luo

Yuanyuan Wang

Xiaolei Zhu

Jiafan Zhu

Yongle Li

Xiaoyin Xu

Shiwei Sun

Hongxuan Hua

Shiping Zhang

Xiangtian Yu

Angelo Riccio

Yuanpeng Xiong

Jing Xu

Chienyuan Lai

Guo-Feng Fan

Zheng Chen

Renzhi Cao

Ronggen Yang

Zhongming Zhao

Yongna Yuan

Chuanxing Liu

Panpan Song

Joao Sousa

Wenying He

Ming Chen

Puneet Gupta

Ziqi Zhang

Davide Nardone

Liangxu Liu

Huijian Han

Qingjun Zhu

Hongluan Zhao

Rey-Sern Lin

Hung-Chi Su

Conghua Xie

Caitong Yue

Li Yan

Tuozhong Yao

Xuzhao Chai

Zhenhu Liang

Yu Lu

Jing Sun

Hua Tang

Liang Cheng

Puneet Rawat

Kulandaisamy A.

Jun Zhang

Egidio Falotico

Peng Chen

Cheng Wang

Jing Li

He Chen

Giacomo Donato Cascarano

Shaohua Wan

Cheng Chen

Jie Li

Ruxin Zhao

Jiazhou Chen

Guoliang Xu

Congxu Zhu

Deng Li

Piyush Joshi

Syed Sadaf Ali

Kuan Li

Teng Wan

Hao Liu

Dong Wang	University of Jinan, China
Gai-Ge Wang	Ocean University of China, China
Yunhai Wang	Shandong University, China
Ka-Chun Wong	City University of Hong Kong, Hong Kong, China
Hongjie Wu	Suzhou University of Science and Technology, China
Junfeng Xia	Anhui University, China
Shunren Xia	Zhejiang University, China
Yi Xiong	Shanghai Jiao Tong University, China
Zhenyu Xuan	University of Texas at Dallas, USA
Bai Xue	Institute of Software, CAS, China
Shen Yin	Harbin Institute of Technology, China
Xiao-Hua Yu	California Polytechnic State University, USA
Naijun Zhan	Institute of Software, CAS, China
Bohua Zhan	Institute of Software, CAS, China
Fa Zhang	Institute of Computing Technology, CAS, China
JunQi Zhang	Tongji University, China
Le Zhang	Sichuan University, China
Wen Zhang	Huazhong Agricultural University, China
Zhihua Zhang	Beijing Institute of Genomics, CAS, China
Shixiong Zhang	Xidian University, China
Qi Zhao	University of Science and Technology of Liaoning, China
Yongquan Zhou	Guangxi University for Nationalities, China
Fengfeng Zhou	Jilin University, China
Shanfeng Zhu	Fudan University, China
Quan Zou	University of Electronic Science and Technology of China, China

Additional Reviewers

Nureize Arbaiy	Shutao Mei	Na Cheng
Shingo Mabu	Jing Jiang	Menglu Li
Farid Garcia Lamont	Yuelin Sun	Zhenhao Guo
Lianming Zhang	Haicheng Yi	Limin Jiang
Xiao Yu	Suwen Zhao	Kun Zhan
Shaohua Li	Xin Hong	Cheng-Hsiung Chiang
Yuntao Wei	Ziyi Chen	Yuqi Wang
Jinglong Wu	Hailin Chen	Bahattin Karakaya
Weichiang Hong	Xiwei Tang	Tejaswini Mallavarapu
Sungshin Kim	Shulin Wang	Jun Li
Chen Li	Di Zhang	Sheng Yang
Tianhua Guan	Sijia Zhang	Laurent Heutte

De-Shuang Huang · Kang-Hyun Jo ·
Jianqiang Li · Valeriya Gribova ·
Prashan Premaratne (Eds.)

Intelligent Computing Theories and Application

17th International Conference, ICIC 2021
Shenzhen, China, August 12–15, 2021
Proceedings, Part III

 Springer

Editors
De-Shuang Huang
Tongji University
Shanghai, China

Jianqiang Li
Shenzhen University
Shenzhen, China

Prashan Premaratne
University of Wollongong
North Wollongong, NSW, Australia

Kang-Hyun Jo
University of Ulsan
Ulsan, Korea (Republic of)

Valeriya Gribova
Far Eastern Branch of the Russian Academy
of Sciences
Vladivostok, Russia

ISSN 0302-9743   ISSN 1611-3349 (electronic)
Lecture Notes in Artificial Intelligence
ISBN 978-3-030-84531-5   ISBN 978-3-030-84532-2 (eBook)
https://doi.org/10.1007/978-3-030-84532-2

LNCS Sublibrary: SL7 – Artificial Intelligence

This Springer imprint is published by the registered company Springer Nature Switzerland AG
The registered company address is: Gewerbestrasse 11, 6330 Cham, Switzerland

Preface

The International Conference on Intelligent Computing (ICIC) was started to provide an annual forum dedicated to the emerging and challenging topics in artificial intelligence, machine learning, pattern recognition, bioinformatics, and computational biology. It aims to bring together researchers and practitioners from both academia and industry to share ideas, problems, and solutions related to the multifaceted aspects of intelligent computing.

ICIC 2021, held in Shenzhen, China, during August 12–15, 2021, constituted the 17th International Conference on Intelligent Computing. It built upon the success of ICIC 2020 (Bari, Italy), ICIC 2019 (Nanchang, China), ICIC 2018 (Wuhan, China), ICIC 2017 (Liverpool, UK), ICIC 2016 (Lanzhou, China), ICIC 2015 (Fuzhou, China), ICIC 2014 (Taiyuan, China), ICIC 2013 (Nanning, China), ICIC 2012 (Huangshan, China), ICIC 2011 (Zhengzhou, China), ICIC 2010 (Changsha, China), ICIC 2009 (Ulsan, South Korea), ICIC 2008 (Shanghai, China), ICIC 2007 (Qingdao, China), ICIC 2006 (Kunming, China), and ICIC 2005 (Hefei, China).

This year, the conference concentrated mainly on the theories and methodologies as well as the emerging applications of intelligent computing. Its aim was to unify the picture of contemporary intelligent computing techniques as an integral concept that highlights the trends in advanced computational intelligence and bridges theoretical research with applications. Therefore, the theme for this conference was "Advanced Intelligent Computing Technology and Applications". Papers that focused on this theme were solicited, addressing theories, methodologies, and applications in science and technology.

ICIC 2021 received 458 submissions from authors in 21 countries and regions. All papers went through a rigorous peer-review procedure and each paper received at least three review reports. Based on the review reports, the Program Committee finally selected 192 high-quality papers for presentation at ICIC 2021, which are included in three volumes of proceedings published by Springer: two volumes of *Lecture Notes in Computer Science* (LNCS) and one volume of *Lecture Notes in Artificial Intelligence* (LNAI).

This volume of LNAI includes 59 papers.

The organizers of ICIC 2021, including Tongji University and Shenzhen University, China, made an enormous effort to ensure the success of the conference. We hereby would like to thank all the ICIC 2021 organizers, the members of the Program Committee, and the referees for their collective effort in reviewing and soliciting the papers. We would like to thank Ronan Nugent, executive editor from Springer, for his frank and helpful advice and guidance throughout as well as his continuous support in publishing the proceedings. In particular, we would like to thank all the authors for contributing their papers. Without the high-quality submissions from the authors, the success of the conference would not have been possible. Finally, we are especially grateful to the International Neural Network Society and the National Science Foundation of China for their sponsorship.

August 2021   De-Shuang Huang
                                                     Kang-Hyun Jo
                                                     Jianqiang Li
                                                     Valeriya Gribova
                                                     Prashan Premaratne

Organization

General Co-chairs

De-Shuang Huang   Tongji University, China
Zhong Ming   Shenzhen University, China

Program Committee Co-chairs

Kang-Hyun Jo   University of Ulsan, South Korea
Jianqiang Li   Shenzhen University, China
Valeriya Gribova   Far Eastern Branch of Russian Academy of Sciences, Russia

Organizing Committee Co-chairs

Qiuzhen Lin   Shenzhen University, China
Cheng Wen Luo   Shenzhen University, China

Organizing Committee Members

Lijia Ma   Shenzhen University, China
Jie Chen   Shenzhen University, China
Jia Wang   Shenzhen University, China
Changkun Jiang   Shenzhen University, China
Junkai Ji   Shenzhen University, China
Zun Liu   Shenzhen University, China

Award Committee Co-chairs

Ling Wang   Tsinghua University, China
Abir Hussain   Liverpool John Moores University, UK

Tutorial Co-chairs

Kyungsook Han   Inha University, South Korea
Prashan Premaratne   University of Wollongong, Australia

Publication Co-chairs

Vitoantonio Bevilacqua Polytechnic of Bari, Italy
Phalguni Gupta   Indian Institute of Technology Kanpur, India

Special Session Co-chairs

Michal Choras	University of Science and Technology in Bydgoszcz, Poland
Hong-Hee Lee	University of Ulsan, South Korea

Special Issue Co-chairs

M. Michael Gromiha	Indian Institute of Technology Madras, India
Laurent Heutte	Université de Rouen, France
Hee-Jun Kang	University of Ulsan, South Korea

International Liaison Co-chair

Prashan Premaratne	University of Wollongong, Australia

Workshop Co-chairs

Yoshinori Kuno	Saitama University, Japan
Jair Cervantes Canales	Autonomous University of Mexico State, Mexico

Publicity Co-chairs

Chun-Hou Zheng	Anhui University, China
Dhiya Al-Jumeily	Liverpool John Moores University, UK

Exhibition Contact Co-chairs

Qiuzhen Lin	Shenzhen University, China

Program Committee

Mohd Helmy Abd Wahab	Universiti Tun Hussein Onn Malaysia, Malaysia
Nicola Altini	Polytechnic University of Bari, Italy
Waqas Bangyal	University of Gujrat, Pakistan
Wenzheng Bao	Xuzhou University of Technology, China
Antonio Brunetti	Polytechnic University of Bari, Italy
Domenico Buongiorno	Politecnico di Bari, Italy
Hongmin Cai	South China University of Technology, China
Nicholas Caporusso	Northern Kentucky University, USA
Jair Cervantes	Autonomous University of Mexico State, Mexico
Chin-Chih Chang	Chung Hua University, Taiwan, China
Zhanheng Chen	Shenzhen University, China
Wen-Sheng Chen	Shenzhen University, China
Xiyuan Chen	Southeast University, China

Wei Chen	Chengdu University of Traditional Chinese Medicine, China
Michal Choras	University of Science and Technology in Bydgoszcz, Poland
Angelo Ciaramella	Università di Napoli, Italy
Guojun Dai	Hangzhou Dianzi University, China
Weihong Deng	Beijing University of Posts and Telecommunications, China
YanRui Ding	Jiangnan University, China
Pu-Feng Du	Tianjing University, China
Jianbo Fan	Ningbo University of Technology, China
Zhiqiang Geng	Beijing University of Chemical Technology, China
Lejun Gong	Nanjing University of Posts and Telecommunications, China
Dunwei Gong	China University of Mining and Technology, China
Wenyin Gong	China University of Geosciences, China
Valeriya Gribova	Far Eastern Branch of Russian Academy of Sciences, Russia
Michael Gromiha	Indian Institute of Technology Madras, India
Zhi-Hong Guan	Huazhong University of Science and Technology, China
Ping Guo	Beijing Normal University, China
Fei Guo	Tianjin University, China
Phalguni Gupta	Indian Institute of Technology Kanpur, India
Kyungsook Han	Inha University, South Korea
Fei Han	Jiangsu University, China
Laurent Heutte	Université de Rouen Normandie, France
Jian Huang	University of Electronic Science and Technology of China, China
Chenxi Huang	Xiamen University, China
Abir Hussain	Liverpool John Moores University, UK
Qinghua Jiang	Harbin Institute of Technology, China
Kanghyun Jo	University of Ulsan, South Korea
Dah-Jing Jwo	National Taiwan Ocean University, Taiwan, China
Seeja K R	Indira Gandhi Delhi Technical University for Women, India
Weiwei Kong	Xi'an University of Posts and Telecommunications, China
Yoshinori Kuno	Saitama University, Japan
Takashi Kuremoto	Nippon Institute of Technology, Japan
Hong-Hee Lee	University of Ulsan, South Korea
Zhen Lei	Institute of Automation, CAS, China
Chunquan Li	Harbin Medical University, China
Bo Li	Wuhan University of Science and Technology, China
Xiangtao Li	Jilin University, China

Hao Lin	University of Electronic Science and Technology of China, China
Juan Liu	Wuhan University, China
Chunmei Liu	Howard University, USA
Bingqiang Liu	Shandong University, China
Bo Liu	Academy of Mathematics and Systems Science, CAS, China
Bin Liu	Beijing Institute of Technology, China
Zhi-Ping Liu	Shandong University, China
Xiwei Liu	Tongji University, China
Haibin Liu	Beijing University of Technology, China
Jin-Xing Liu	Qufu Normal University, China
Jungang Lou	Huzhou University, China
Xinguo Lu	Hunan University, China
Xiaoke Ma	Xidian University, China
Yue Ming	Beijing University of Posts and Telecommunications, China
Liqiang Nie	Shandong University, China
Ben Niu	Shenzhen University, China
Marzio Pennisi	University of Eastern Piedmont Amedeo Avogadro, Italy
Surya Prakash	IIT Indore, India
Prashan Premaratne	University of Wollongong, Australia
Bin Qian	Kunming University of Science and Technology, China
Daowen Qiu	Sun Yat-sen University, China
Mine Sarac	Stanford University, USA
Xuequn Shang	Northwestern Polytechnical University, China
Evi Sjukur	Monash University, Australia
Jiangning Song	Monash University, Australia
Chao Song	Harbin Medical University, China
Antonino Staiano	Parthenope University of Naples, Italy
Fabio Stroppa	Stanford University, USA
Zhan-Li Sun	Anhui University, China
Xu-Qing Tang	Jiangnan University, China
Binhua Tang	Hohai University, China
Joaquin Torres-Sospedra	UBIK Geospatial Solutions S.L., Spain
Shikui Tu	Shanghai Jiao Tong University, China
Jian Wang	China University of Petroleum, China
Ling Wang	Tsinghua University, China
Ruiping Wang	Institute of Computing Technology, CAS, China
Xuesong Wang	China University of Mining and Technology, China
Rui Wang	National University of Defense Technology, China
Xiao-Feng Wang	Hefei University, China
Shitong Wang	Jiangnan University, China
Bing Wang	Anhui University of Technology, China
Jing-Yan Wang	New York University Abu Dhabi, Abu Dhabi

Yexian Zhang	Lianrong Pu	Zhenqing Ye
Xu Qiao	Di Wang	Zijing Wang
Lingchong Zhong	Fangping Wan	Lida Zhu
Wenyan Wang	Renmeng Liu	Xionghui Zhou
Xiaoyu Ji	Jiancheng Zhong	Jia-Xiang Wang
Weifeng Guo	Yinan Guo	Gongxin Peng
Yuchen Jiang	Lujie Fang	Junbo Liang
Van-Dung Hoang	Ying Zhang	Linjing Liu
Yuanyuan Huang	Yinghao Cao	Xiangeng Wang
Zaixing Sun	Xhize Wu	Y. M. Nie
Honglin Zhang	Chao Wu	Sheng Ding
Yu-Jie He	Ambuj Srivastava	Laksono Kurnianggoro
Rong Hu	Prabakaran R.	Minxia Cheng
Youjie Yao	Xingquan Zuo	Meiyi Li
Naikang Yu	Jiabin Huang	Qizhi Zhu
Giulia Russo	Jingwen Yang	Pengchao Li
Dian Liu	Qianying Liu	Ming Xiao
Cheng Liang	Tongchi Zhou	Guangdi Liu
Iyyakutti Iyappan Ganapathi	Xinyan Liang	Jing Meng
Mingon Kang	Xiaopeng Jin	Kang Xu
Xuefeng Cui	Yumeng Liu	Cong Feng
Hao Dai	Junliang Shang	Arturo Yee
Geethan Mendiz	Shanghan Li	Kazunori Onoguchi
Brendan Halloran	Jianhua Zhang	Hotaka Takizawa
Yue Li	Wei Zhang	Suhang Gu
Qianqian Shi	Han-Jing Jiang	Zhang Yu
Zhiqiang Tian	Kunikazu Kobayashi	Bin Qin
Ce Li	Shenglin Mu	Yang Gu
Yang Yang	Jing Liang	Zhibin Jiang
Jun Wang	Jialing Li	Chuanyan Wu
Ke Yan	Zhe Sun	Wahyono Wahyono
Hang Wei	Wentao Fan	Kaushik Deb
Yuyan Han	Wei Lan	Alexander Filonenko
Hisato Fukuda	Josue Espejel Cabrera	Van-Thanh Hoang
Yaning Yang	José Sergio Ruiz Castilla	Ning Guo
Lixiang Xu	Rencai Zhou	Deng Chao
Yuanke Zhou	Moli Huang	Jian Liu
Shihui Ying	Yong Zhang	Sen Zhang
Wenqiang Fan	Joaquín Torres-Sospedra	Nagarajan Raju
Zhao Li	Xingjian Chen	Kumar Yugandhar
Zhe Zhang	Saifur Rahaman	Anoosha Paruchuri
Xiaoying Guo	Olutomilayo Petinrin	Lei Che
Zhuoqun Xia	Xiaoming Liu	Yujia Xi
Na Geng	Lei Wang	Ma Haiying
Xin Ding	Xin Xu	Huanqiang Zeng
Balachandran Manavalan	Najme Zehra	Hong-Bo Zhang

Yewang Chen
Sama Ukyo
Akash Tayal
Ru Yang
Junning Gao
Jianqing Zhu
Haizhou Liu
Nobutaka Shimada
Yuan Xu
Shuo Jiang
Minghua Zhao
Jiulong Zhang
Shui-Hua Wang
Sandesh Gupta
Nadia Siddiqui
Syeda Shira Moin
Ruidong Li
Mauro Castelli
Ivanoe De Falco
Antonio Della Cioppa
Kamlesh Tiwari
Luca Tiseni
Ruizhi Fan
Grigorios Skaltsas
Mario Selvaggio
Xiang Yu
Huajuan Huang
Vasily Aristarkhov
Zhonghao Liu
Lichuan Pan
Zhongying Zhao
Atsushi Yamashita
Ying Xu
Wei Peng
Haodi Feng
Jin Zhao
Shunheng Zhou
Changlong Gu
Xiangwen Wang
Zhe Liu
Pi-Jing Wei
Haozhen Situ
Xiangtao Chen
Hui Tang
Akio Nakamura
Antony Lam

Weilin Deng
Xu Zhou
Shuyuan Wang
Rabia Shakir
Haotian Xu
Zekang Bian
Shuguang Ge
Hong Peng
Thar Baker
Siguo Wang
Jianqing Chen
Chunhui Wang
Xiaoshu Zhu
Yongchun Zuo
Hyunsoo Kim
Areesha Anjum
Shaojin Geng
He Yongqiang
Mario Camana
Long Chen
Jialin Lyu
Zhenyang Li
Tian Rui
Duygun Erol Barkana
Huiyu Zhou
Yichuan Wang
Eray A. Baran
Jiakai Ding
Dehua Zhang
Insoo Koo
Yudong Zhang
Zafaryab Haider
Vladimir Shakhov
Daniele Leonardis
Byungkyu Park
Elena Battini
Radzi Ambar
Noraziah Chepa
Liang Liang
Ling-Yun Dai
Xiongtao Zhang
Sobia Pervaiz Iqbal
Fang Yang
Si Liu
Natsa Kleanthous
Zhen Shen

Chunyan Fan
Jie Zhao
Yuchen Zhang
Jianwei Yang
Wenrui Zhao
Di Wu
Chao Wang
Fuyi Li
Guangsheng Wu
Yuchong Gong
Weitai Yang
Yanan Wang
Bo Chen
Binbin Pan
Chunhou Zheng
Bowen Song
Guojing Wu
Weiping Liu
Laura Jalili
Xing Chen
Xiujuan Lei
Marek Pawlicki
Hao Zhu
Wang Zhanjun
Mohamed Alloghani
Yu Hu
Baohua Wang
Hanfu Wang
Hongle Xie
Guangming Wang
Fuchun Liu
Farid Garcia-Lamont
Hengyue Shi
Po Yang
Wen Zheng Ma
Jianxun Mi
Michele Scarpiniti
Yasushi Mae
Haoran Mo
Gaoyuan Liang
Pengfei Cui
Yoshinori Kobayashi
Kongtao Chen
Feng Feng
Wenli Yan
Zhibo Wang

Ying Qiao

Qiyue Lu

Dong Li

Heqi Wang

Tony Hao

Chenglong Wei

My Ha Le

Yu Chen

Naida Fetic

Bing Sun

Zhenzhong Chu

Meijing Li

Wentao Chen

Mingpeng Zheng

Zhihao Tang

Li Keng Liang

Alberto Mazzoni

Liang Chen

Meng-Meng Yin

Yannan Bin

Wasiq Khan

Yong Wu

Juanjuan Shi

Shiting Sun

Xujing Yao

Wenming Wu

Na Zhang

Anteneh Birga

Yipeng Lv

Qiuye Wang

Adrian Trueba

Ao Liu

Bifang He

Jun Pang

Jie Ding

Shixuan Guan

Boheng Cao

Bingxiang Xu

Lin Zhang

Mengya Liu

Xueping Lv

Hee-Jun Kang

Yuanyuan Zhang

Jin Zhang

Lin Chen

Runshan Xie

Zichang Tan

Fengcui Qian

Xianming Li

Jing Wang

Yuexin Zhang

Fan Wang

Yanyu Li

Qi Pan

Jiaxin Chen

Yuhan Hao

Xiaokang Wang

Jiekai Tang

Wen Jiang

Nan Li

Zhengwen Li

Yuanyuan Yang

Wenbo Chen

Wenchong Luo

Jiang Xue

Xuanying Zhang

Lianlian Zhong

Liu Xiaolin

Difei Liu

Bowen Zhao

Bowen Xue

Churong Zhang

Xing Xing Zhang

Yang Guo

Lu Yang

Jinbao Teng

Yupei Zhang

Keyu Zhong

Mingming Jiang

Chen Yong

Haidong Shao

Weizhong Lin

Leyi Wei

Ravi Kant Kumar

Jogendra Garain

Teressa Longjam

Zhaochun Xu

Zhirui Liao

Qifeng Wu

Nanxuan Zhou

Song Gu

Bin Li

Xiang Li

Yuanpeng Zhang

Dewu Ding

Jiaxuan Liu

Zhenyu Tang

Zhize Wu

Zhihao Huang

Yu Feng

Chen Zhang

Min Liu

Baiying Lei

Jiaming Liu

Xiaochuan Jing

Francesco Berloco

Shaofei Zang

Shenghua Feng

Xiaoqing Gu

Jing Xue

Junqing Zhu

Wenqiang Ji

Muhamad Dwisnanto Putro

Li-Hua Wen

Zhiwen Qiang

Chenchen Liu

Juntao Liu

Yang Miao

Yan Chen

Xiangyu Wang

Cristina Juárez

Ziheng Rong

Jing Lu

Lisbeth Rodriguez Mazahua

Rui Yan

Yuhang Zhou

Huiming Song

Li Ding

Alma Delia Cuevas

Zixiao Pan

Yuchae Jung

Chunfeng Mi

Guixin Zhao

Yuqian Pu

Hongpeng Ynag

Yan Pan

Rinku Datta Rakshit

Ming-Feng Ge

Mingliang Xue

Fahai Zhong

Shan Li

Qingwen Wu

Tao Li

Liwen Xie

Daiwei Li

Yuzhen Han

Fengqiang Li

Chenggang Lai

Shuai Liu

Cuiling Huang

Wenqiang Gu

Haitao Du

Bingbo Cui

Yang Lei

Xiaohan Sun

Inas Kadhim

Jing Feng

Xin Juan

Hongguo Zhao

Masoomeh Mirrashid

Jialiang Li

Yaping Hu

Xiangzhen Kong

Mixiao Hou

Zhen Cui

Na Yu

Meiyu Duan

Baoping Yuan

Umarani Jayaraman

Guanghui Li

Lihong Peng

Fabio Bellavia

Giosue' Lo Bosco

Zhen Chen

Jiajie Xiao

Chunyan Liu

Yue Zhao

Yuwen Tao

Nuo Yu

Liguang Huang

Duy-Linh Nguyen

Kai Shang

Wu Hao

Jiatong Li

Enda Jiang

Yichen Sun

Yanyuan Qin

Chengwei Ai

Kang Li

Jhony Heriberto Giraldo Zuluaga

Waqas Haider Bangyal

Tingting Dan

Haiyan Wang

Dandan Lu

Bin Zhang

Cuco Cristanno

Antonio Junior Spoleto

Zhenghao Shi

Ya Wang

Shuyi Zhang

Xiaoqing Li

Yajun Zou

Chuanlei Zhang

Berardino Prencipe

Feng Liu

Yongsheng Dong

Rong Fei

Zhen Wang

Jun Sang

Jun Wu

Xiaowen Chen

Hong Wang

Daniele Malitesta

Fenqiang Zhao

Xinghuo Ye

Hongyi Zhang

Xuexin Yu

Xujun Duan

Xing-Ming Zhao

Jiayan Han

Weizhong Lu

Frederic Comby

Taemoon Seo

Sergio Cannata

Yong-Wan Kwon

Heng Chen

Min Chen

Qing Lei

Francesco Fontanella

Rahul Kumar

Alessandra Scotto di Freca

Nicole Cilia

Annunziata Paviglianiti

Jacopo Ferretti

Pietro Barbiero

Seong-Jae Kim

Jing Yang

Dan Yang

Dongxue Peng

Wenting Cui

Wenhao Chi

Ruobing Liang

Feixiang Zhou

Jijia Kang

Huawei Huang

Peng Li

Yunfeng Zhao

Xiaoyan Hu

Li Guo

Lei Du

Xia-An Bi

Xiuquan Du

Ping Zhu

Young-Seob Jeong

Han-Gyu Kim

Dongkun Lee

Jonghwan Hyeon

Chae-Gyun Lim

Dingna Duan

Shiqiang Ma

Mingliang Dou

Jansen Woo

Shanshan Hu

Hai-Tao Li

Francescomaria Marino

Jiayi Ji

Jun Peng

Shirley Meng

Lucia Ballerini

Haifeng Hu

Jingyu Hou

Contents – Part III

Complex Diseases Informatics

Gene Regulation Modeling and Analysis

Intelligent Computing in Computational Biology

Protein Structure and Function Prediction

Artificial Intelligence in Real World Applications

Task-Oriented Snapshot Network Construction of Stock Market

Jiancheng Sun[1](✉), Yunfan Hu[2], Zhinan Wu[3,4], Huimin Niu[1], and Si Chen[1]

[1] School of Software and Internet of Things Engineering,
Jiangxi University of Finance and Economics, Nanchang 330013, China
`sunjc@jxufe.edu.cn`
[2] Glasgow College, University of Electronic Science and Technology of China,
Chengdu 611731, China
[3] School of Information Management, Jiangxi University of Finance and Economics,
Nanchang 330013, China
[4] School of Mathematics and Computer Science, Yichun University, Yichun 336000, China

Abstract. The stock market is a dynamic and complex system in which individual stocks interact with each other and thus influence the rules of the market as a whole. Moreover, we usually want to know how individual stocks and their interactions affect a particular economic indicator. In this paper, for a task, we use eXtreme Gradient Boosting and SHapley Additive exPlanations to construct snapshot networks of the stock market. The snapshot network gives a quantitative explanation of the target output at each moment in terms of the stocks themselves and their interactions. We take the stocks contained in Dow Jones Industrial Average (DJIA) as an example and DJIA itself as the task to construct the snapshot networks. The experimental results show that the snapshot networks can explain the tasks from three aspects: dynamic evolution, stocks themselves and their interactions.

Keywords: Snapshot network · Stock market · Time series

1 Introduction

Complex systems are usually natural or social systems made up of a large number of interacting elements, and the financial markets are no exception. Therefore, studying financial markets from the perspective of complex networks is a viable direction and has therefore received a great deal of research [1–4]. The motivation to study financial markets in the form of networks is based on the interactions between financial entities, e.g., stocks in the same sector may will have similar up and down trends. Using theoretical and statistical techniques in complex networks, some special or hidden network topologies may be discovered that will help us understand and explain how markets work.

In previous studies, the usual approach has focused on the process of first finding correlations between each pair of stock price time series and the subsequent creation of a network based on the level of correlations, thus linking the individual stocks [3–5].

D.-S. Huang et al. (Eds.): ICIC 2021, LNAI 12838, pp. 3–11, 2021.
https://doi.org/10.1007/978-3-030-84532-2_1

Depending on the need of the observation time interval, correlation is usually obtained by calculating the similarity between the time series within the interval. This means that usually such methods have a low temporal resolution, i.e., the entire observation interval. Therefore, these types of methods are generally used to analyze the characteristics of the network globally or over a region of time. If the evolution and dynamics of the network are to be studied, they generally rely on sliding window to intercept the time series, in which case the time resolution is the width of the sliding window [6–8].

The above literature is based on the data itself for network construction, which means that it is not associated with a task. In many cases, we typically use financial data to solve critical problems, such as stock price prediction and financial fraud [9, 10]. In these tasks, we usually want to know what factors determine these outcomes. Therefore, it is essential to study the network structure associated with the task.

To address the above problems, in this paper we construct the snapshot networks of stock markets oriented to a task. Our contribution is twofold: (1) on the one hand, we construct a stock market network, or snapshot network, at each time stamp. Finally, a series of networks are formed along the time direction. Thus, the temporal resolution of the snapshot network is the interval between two timestamps. (2) Another aspect is that, based on the constructed model, we can give an explanation of the causes of a given task. For example, we can give which stocks and which interactions between them are mainly responsible for the task. To the best of our knowledge, no previous work has attempted to construct a task-oriented snapshot network for the stock market.

2   Methods of Snapshot Network Construction

We first formulate the task-oriented problem, then use eXtreme Gradient Boosting (XGBoost) [11] to solve the regression problem, and finally construct the network based on SHapley Additive exPlanations (SHAP) [12].

2.1   Formulation of Task-Oriented Problem

Task-oriented problems are explained in machine learning terms as supervised learning and can generally be attributed to either classification or regression problems. Classification and regression problems are usually solved in a similar way, and this paper focuses only on the regression problem. Assume that given a training dataset on a feature space:

$$T = \{(x_1, y_1), (x_2, y_2), \cdots, (x_N, y_N)\} \tag{1}$$

where $x_t \in \mathcal{X} = \mathbb{R}^M$ is the t-th feature vector, $y_t \in \mathcal{Y} = \mathbb{R}$ is the observed response value for the task corresponding to x_t, and the data pair (x_t, y_t) is called a sample point. The goal of model training is to find a function $f(\cdot)$ in the feature space such that $y = f(x)$.

In the case of the stock market, the i-th element $x_{t,i}$ of vector x_t is the price of stock i at moment t. Thus, x_t can also be called a snapshot vector. The task observation y, in turn, depends on the problem being solved, and in this paper we use the Dow Jones Industrial Average (DJIA) as the task observation. In addition, we use XGBoost to solve the regression problem. The reason for using XGBoost is that it is essentially a decision tree boosting model with interpretability.

2.2 Snapshot Network Construction with SHAP

To construct the network, for a particular y_t, we need to find the importance of each element (stock) of x_t and interactions between the elements. Each network corresponds to a moment, hence we call it a snapshot network. In the network, nodes represent individual features (stocks), and the interactions between stocks act as connected edges. Here we use SHAP to extract the importance of each feature and the strength of interaction between features.

SHAP is an additive explanatory model inspired by cooperative game theory to give an explanation for the output of the machine learning model. For each training sample, the model generates a predictive value, SHAP value being the value assigned to each feature in that sample. Assuming that the t-th sample is x_t, the i-th feature of the x_t is $x_{t,i}$, the model's predictive value for that sample is y_t, and the baseline of the entire model (usually the mean of the target variables for all samples) is ϕ_0, then the SHAP value obeys the following equation [13]:

$$y_t = \phi_0 + \sum_{i=1}^{M} \phi_i(x_{t,i}) \tag{2}$$

where M is the number of the features and $\phi_i(x_{t,i})$ is the SHAP value of $x_{t,j}$. Intuitively, $\phi_1(x_{t,1})$ is the contribution of the 1st feature in the t-th sample to the final predicted value of y_t, and when $\phi_1(x_{t,1}) > 0$, it means that the feature raises the predicted value and therefore has a positive effect; conversely, it indicates that the feature makes the predicted value lower and has the opposite effect. The SHAP value $\phi_i(x_{t,i})$ is defined as [13]:

$$\phi_i(x_{t,i}) = \sum_{S \subseteq \{x_{t,1},...,x_{t,M}\} \setminus \{x_{t,i}\}} \frac{|S|!(M - |S| - 1)!}{M!} \left(f\left(S \cup \{x_{t,i}\}\right) - f(S) \right) \tag{3}$$

where $\{x_{t,1}, \ldots, x_{t,M}\}$ is the set of all the input features, $\{x_{t,1}, \ldots, x_{t,M}\} \setminus \{x_{t,i}\}$ is the set of all input features excluding $\{x_{t,i}\}$, and $f(S)$ is the prediction of feature subset S. Traditional feature importance can only tell us globally which feature is important, but we don't know how that feature of an individual sample affects prediction of the results. The most striking advantage of the SHAP value is that it not only reflects the influence of the features in each sample, and being able to show the positive and negative impact.

A network can usually be represented as a graph (here we only focus on the undirected simple graph), which is a data pair $G = (V, E)$, where V is a set of vertices and $E \subseteq \{\{p, q\} | (p, q) \in V^2 \wedge p \neq q\}$ is a set of edges. Once V is defined, the next step is to complete the network construction by obtaining E. Here we use a combination of SHAP and XGBoost to obtain E, i.e., we use SHAP to compute the interaction values between features. The interaction value $\phi_{i,j}(x_{t,i}, x_{t,j})$ between feature $x_{t,i}$ and $x_{t,j}$ is defined as [13]:

$$\phi_{i,j}(x_{t,i}, x_{t,j}) = \sum_{S \subseteq \{x_{t,1},...,x_{t,M}\} \setminus \{x_{t,i}, x_{t,j}\}} \frac{|S|!(M - |S| - 2)!}{2(M - 1)!} \delta_{i,j}(S) \tag{4}$$

when $i \neq j$, and

$$\delta_{i,j}(S) = f\left(S \cup \{x_{t,i}, x_{t,j}\}\right) - f\left(S \cup \{x_{t,i}\}\right) - f\left(S \cup \{x_{t,j}\}\right) + f(S) \tag{5}$$

The interactions form an $M \times M$ matrix $A_t = (a_{i,j})$ which is the mathematical expression for E, where $a_{i,j} = \phi_{i,j}(x_{t,i}, x_{t,j})$ represents the interaction between features $x_{t,i}$ and $x_{t,j}$. The matrix A_t can be viewed as a weighted adjacency matrix, which we use to form a snapshot network for moment t.

3 Experiments and Results

Here we use the DJIA as our research objective, which is a stock market index that measures the stock performance of 30 large companies listed on U.S. stock exchanges. DJIA measures industrial development on the U.S. stock market and is one of the most credible U.S. market indices. To this day, the DJAI includes thirty of the best-known publicly traded companies in the United States. Although the word "industrial" is mentioned in the name, most of the 30 constituent companies are no longer associated with heavy industry. INDJ reflects the sum of the prices of one share of all components, divided by the divisor, which is defined as

$$DJIA\ Price = SUM\ (Component\ stock\ prices)/Dow\ divisor \tag{6}$$

However, calculating DJIA is not as simple as adding up the prices of 30 stocks and dividing by 30. Operations such as mergers, splits, stock splits, etc. complicate the arithmetic and require the determination of a dynamic "Dow divisor". We use the daily closing price data from 2012 to 2018 and the corresponding DJIA as training data. In order to remove the trend and periodic terms, we apply a first-order difference operation to each stock's closing price to generate the training series (x_t, y_t) as

$$\begin{aligned} x_{t,i} &= p_{t,i} - p_{t-1,i} \\ y_t &= d_t - d_{t-1} \end{aligned} \tag{7}$$

where, $p_{t,i}$ is the closing price of stock i at moment t, d_t is the value of DJIA at moment t, $t = 1, 2, \ldots, N, i = 1, 2, \ldots, M$ ($N = 1150$ and $M = 30$ are the number of samples and features, respectively). So far, the training data pairs $\{(x_1, y_1), (x_2, y_2), \cdots, (x_N, y_N)\}$ are in place. For the sake of clarity, in the following description we will use feature and stock alternately to refer to the element $x_{t,i}$ of vector x_t, depending on the context.

We used the first 1000 data and the subsequent 150 data as training and test data, respectively. Training was conducted using XGBoost, and Fig. 1 shows the prediction results of the model on the test set. It can be seen from Fig. 1 that the regression curves basically overlap with the real curves. Good regression performance is a prerequisite for subsequent network construction, this is because only if the regression performance is within an acceptable range, the network is likely to correctly expresses the relationship between features. Also note that we use XGBoost here for two reasons, one is its excellent regression performance and the other is that it is a tree-based method. The tree-based approach can provide the importance of the interactions between features, which is the

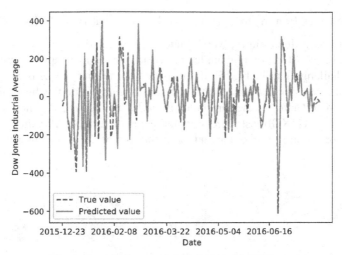

Fig. 1. Regression results for DJIA with XGBoost

reason why the tree-based explanatory model in the SHAP method can give the feature interactions.

We selected the data pairs (x_t, y_t) at January 1, 2012 as an example and plotted Fig. 2 based on Eq. (2). For individual DJIA, Fig. 2 shows the impact and contribution of each stock's price to DJIA. Positive and negative SHAP values are shown in red and blue, respectively, while the length of the corresponding color bars represents the absolute value of the SHAP. As can be seen in Fig. 2, each stock has its own contribution to the target. Positive and negative SHAP values contribute positively (increase) and negatively (decrease) to the model's output, respectively, and finally drive the model's predictions from base value ϕ_0 to the final value y_t (model output). It should be noted here that the tick on the coordinates represents the value of the target, while the red and blue bars are the differential values of the different stocks. Overall, Fig. 2 provides a quantitative explanation of how each stock affects the target output in terms of direction and intensity.

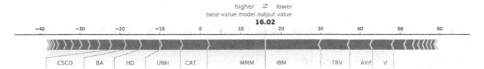

Fig. 2. The impact and contribution of each stock to the individual target value. The text below the color bar is the abbreviation of the stock, and the output value of the target is 16.02, with red and blue stocks pushing up and pulling down the model output value respectively.

So far, we have given the contribution of each stock itself to the task output. But to form a network, the connected edges of the network, i.e. the adjacency matrix $A_t = (a_{i,j})$, need to be given. As described in Sect. 2.2, we use SHAP combined with XGBoost to generate the set $\mathcal{A} = \{A_1, A_2, \ldots, A_N\}$. Therefore, we get an adjacency matrix at each moment, *i.e.*, a snapshot network. To highlight the topology of the network, we need to remove some edges from A_t to form a new adjacency matrix $A'_t = \left(a'_{i,j} \right)$. The usual approach is to set a threshold r_c, which yields $a'_{i,j} = a_{i,j}$ if $|a_{i,j}| \geq r_c$, and $a'_{i,j} = 0$ otherwise. In the construction of complex networks, choosing an appropriate threshold is usually a challenging task [14, 15]. In this paper, our primary focus is on the method of constructing snapshot networks, so we are simply going to do this by retaining 20% of the edges in order to set the threshold. In addition, the snapshot network mainly consists of two parts, XGBoost regression and estimation of SHAP values. Therefore, the computational complexity of the method is the sum of these two algorithms.

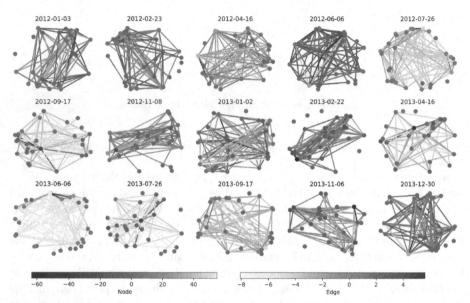

Fig. 3. Snapshot networks at different moments. The corresponding moments of the network are given on top of the network, arranged in the order of first from left to right, then from top to bottom. The two color bars below identify the degree to which the stocks (nodes) themselves and their interactions (edges) affect the target. (Color figure online)

We selected a number of snapshot networks in chronological order to display in Fig. 3. The figure provides information on three aspects: first, the dynamic evolution of the network; second, the contribution of each stock to the target output; and third, the impact of edges on the target output. Three types of information can be used to interpret the target output from different perspectives. The dynamic snapshot network can be used to study the evolution of the topology of the network and the correspondence between it and the changes in the target. Moreover, as can be seen in Fig. 3, using the snapshot network at a particular moment, we can give an interpretation of the target output in terms of both the stocks themselves and their interactions with each other at the same time. For example, the diagram shows that the stocks themselves usually have a greater effect on the goal than the interactions with each other.

To study the evolution of snapshot networks, we visualize them through dimension reduction [16]. Because of the invisibility of the high-dimensional space, we first transform the adjacency matrix A_t into a vector in Euclidean space [17, 18] and then apply the Multidimensional scaling (MDS) perform dimension reduction [19]. We reduced the snapshot networks of training data to two dimensions and displayed them in Fig. 4. The horizontal and vertical coordinates are the two components of the reduced dimension respectively. Each point in the figure corresponds to a snapshot network, as in the example at the top left of the figure. In a rough overall view, the network of snapshots from each moment is mixed together. This phenomenon suggests that there are similarities in the topology of the network at different moments, or that history may repeat itself. However, in local detail, networks over short time periods tend to cluster together, as in the region identified by the ellipse in the figure. This situation indicates that the networks have some similarity in continuous time, which is consistent with our common sense.

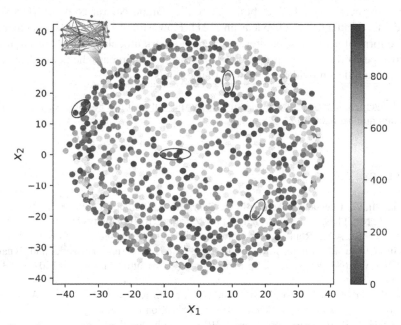

Fig. 4. Snapshot networks after dimension reduction. The order of the sample points is color-coded, with a zero on the color bar representing the first sample point.

4 Discussion and Conclusions

The work in this paper focuses on two main aspects, one is the snapshot network construction of the individual sample, and the other is the use of the constructed network on the particular task to make an interpretation. Taking the example of the stocks included in the DJIA, the snapshot network is able to give an interpretation of the DJIA values in terms of direction (positive or negative action) and strength. In the field of time series analysis, as mentioned in Sect. 1, classical methods tend to compute similarities between two time series rather than for the individual samples [20]. Thus, the snapshot network of individual sample not only greatly improves the temporal resolution (for each moment), but also provides new means and data structures for analyzing the dynamic characteristics of the network. One of the future works is to construct networks of individual data by linear classification or regression methods using self-learning strategies. Self-learning algorithms have the advantage of being label-independent and constructing networks based on the implicit properties of the data.

In this paper, the task of the model is relatively simple and the main objective is to highlight methods for the construction and analysis of snapshot networks. In fact, due to the power of the tree-based models, they can be used to solve more complex tasks and will be used well in many areas. For example, in the field of meteorology, we can use snapshot networks to dynamically analyze the causes of climate extremes. As another example, in the field of brain science, snapshot networks can give explanations for the dynamic cognition of the human brain. Recently, Graph Neural Network (GNN) has received a lot of attention in deep learning [21]. However, most of the data is inherently not in the form of network structures, so graph network models cannot be used directly to improve performance. The proposed method is able to prepare the network structure for the data and thus provides a new way to use GNN.

Acknowledgements. This research was funded by the National Natural Science Foundation of China, grant number 62066017.

References

1. Caldarelli, G., Chessa, A., Pammolli, F., Gabrielli, A., Puliga, M.: Reconstructing a credit network. Nat. Phys. **9**, 125–126 (2013). https://doi.org/10.1038/nphys2580
2. D'Arcangelis, A.M., Rotundo, G.: Complex Networks in Finance. In: Commendatore, P., Matilla-García, M., Varela, L.M., Cánovas, J.S. (eds.) Complex networks and dynamics. LNEMS, vol. 683, pp. 209–235. Springer, Cham (2016). https://doi.org/10.1007/978-3-319-40803-3_9
3. Esmaeilpour Moghadam, H., Mohammadi, T., Feghhi Kashani, M., Shakeri, A.: Complex networks analysis in Iran stock market: the application of centrality. Phys. A Stat. Mech. Appl. **531**, 121800 (2019). https://doi.org/10.1016/j.physa.2019.121800
4. Li, S., Yang, Y., Li, C., Li, L., Gui, X.: Stock correlation analysis based on complex network. In: 2016 6th International Conference on Electronics Information and Emergency Communication (ICEIEC), pp. 174–177. IEEE (2016). https://doi.org/10.1109/ICEIEC.2016.7589713
5. Li, X., Wang, Q., Jia, S.: Analysis of topological properties of complex network of Chinese stock based on Copula tail correlation. In: 2017 International Conference on Service Systems and Service Management, pp. 1–6. IEEE (2017). https://doi.org/10.1109/ICSSSM.2017.7996279
6. Dong, Z., An, H., Liu, S., Li, Z., Yuan, M.: Research on the time-varying network structure evolution of the stock indices of the BRICS countries based on fluctuation correlation. Int. Rev. Econ. Finance **69**, 63–74 (2020). https://doi.org/10.1016/j.iref.2020.04.008

7. Cao, G., Shi, Y., Li, Q.: Structure characteristics of the international stock market complex network in the perspective of whole and part. Discrete Dyn. Nat. Soc. **2017**, 1–11 (2017). https://doi.org/10.1155/2017/9731219
8. Jiang, M., Gao, X., An, H., Li, H., Sun, B.: Reconstructing complex network for characterizing the time-varying causality evolution behavior of multivariate time series. Sci. Rep. **7**, 10486 (2017). https://doi.org/10.1038/s41598-017-10759-3
9. Zhou, X., Pan, Z., Hu, G., Tang, S., Zhao, C.: Stock market prediction on high-frequency data using generative adversarial nets. Math. Probl. Eng. **2018**, 1–11 (2018). https://doi.org/10.1155/2018/4907423
10. Mishra, A., Ghorpade, C.: Credit card fraud detection on the skewed data using various classification and ensemble techniques. In: 2018 IEEE International Students' Conference on Electrical, Electronics and Computer Science (SCEECS), pp. 1–5. IEEE (2018). https://doi.org/10.1109/SCEECS.2018.8546939.
11. Chen, T., Guestrin, C.: XGBoost: a scalable tree boosting system. In: Proceedings of the 22nd ACM SIGKDD International Conference on Knowledge Discovery and Data Mining, pp. 785–794. ACM, New York (2016). https://doi.org/10.1145/2939672.2939785
12. Scott, M., Lundberg, L.S.-I.: A unified approach to interpreting model predictions. In: Advances in Neural Information Processing Systems 30 (NIPS 2017), Long Beach, CA, USA, pp. 1–10 (2017)
13. Lundberg, S.M., et al.: From local explanations to global understanding with explainable AI for trees. Nat. Mach. Intell. **2**, 56–67 (2020). https://doi.org/10.1038/s42256-019-0138-9
14. Perkins, A.D., Langston, M.A.: Threshold selection in gene co-expression networks using spectral graph theory techniques. BMC Bioinform. **10**, S4 (2009). https://doi.org/10.1186/1471-2105-10-S11-S4
15. Langer, N., Pedroni, A., Jäncke, L.: The problem of thresholding in small-world network analysis. PLoS ONE **8**, e53199 (2013). https://doi.org/10.1371/journal.pone.0053199
16. van den Elzen, S., Holten, D., Blaas, J., van Wijk, J.J.: Reducing snapshots to points: a visual analytics approach to dynamic network exploration. IEEE Trans. Vis. Comput. Graph. **22**, 1 (2016). https://doi.org/10.1109/TVCG.2015.2468078
17. Sun, J., Yang, Y., Xiong, N.N., Dai, L., Peng, X., Luo, J.: Complex network construction of multivariate time series using information geometry. IEEE Trans. Syst. Man Cybern. Syst. **49**, 107–122 (2019). https://doi.org/10.1109/TSMC.2017.2751504
18. Sun, J., Yang, Y., Liu, Y., Chen, C., Rao, W., Bai, Y.: Univariate time series classification using information geometry. Pattern Recognit. **95**, 24–35 (2019). https://doi.org/10.1016/j.patcog.2019.05.040
19. Borg, I., Groenen, P.: Modern Multidimensional Scaling: Theory and Applications. Springer, New York (2005). https://doi.org/10.1007/0-387-28981-X
20. Zou, Y., Donner, R.V., Marwan, N., Donges, J.F., Kurths, J.: Complex network approaches to nonlinear time series analysis. Phys. Rep. **787**, 1–97 (2019). https://doi.org/10.1016/j.physrep.2018.10.005
21. Battaglia, P.W., et al.: Relational inductive biases, deep learning, and graph networks. arXiv: 1806.01261 (2018)

Analysis of Elimination Algorithm Based on Curve Self-intersection

Qingyue Bai[✉] and Junrui Yue[✉]

School of Computer and Information Engineering, Shanxi Technology and Business College, Taiyuan 030000, Shanxi, China

Abstract. In this paper, the algebraic elimination algorithm is used to investigate the self-intersection problem of a class of irregular curves. This paper analyzes the curve equation of self-intersection expression $C(u) - C(v) = 0$ and structure curve expression in the form of binary Bezier function. By eliminating the common parameter terms, not only is the order of the expression reduced formally, but the self-intersection region is also determined, so as to realize the purpose of self-intersection.

Keywords: Irregular · Self-intersection · Elimination algorithm

1 Introduction

The offset curves and surfaces are applied in model brushes, special processing of images and removal techniques of control point. Since they have many kinds of geometric structure, such offset curves and surfaces often appear in the modeling applications of CAD/CAM, such as the application of Rhinoceros software [1]. In the modeling process, it is easy to produce a kind of very complex self-intersection phenomenon where the curve appears to bend [2].

In the early time, Pham B and some other scholars had carried out some researches on the curve theory [3]. Because the variable offset curve is more special than the equidistant offset curve in the distance, domestic scholars have encountered great difficulties in the field of self-intersection [4], such as in the process of the realization of self-intersection; consequently, all the self-intersecting points can not be found [5]. In order to solve above-mentioned problem, this paper will analyze parametric equation of the offset curve to find and remove all the self-intersecting points [6]. Given the problems existing in the process of removing the self-intersecting region, this paper proposes an algebraic elimination algorithm. It provides a new thought for the study of de-self-intersection of curves and surfaces [7].

2 Parametric Representation of the Offset Curve

Offset curves can be divided into equidistant offset curves and variable distance offset curves, and the biggest difference between them lies in the difference in the offset distance

© Springer Nature Switzerland AG 2021
D.-S. Huang et al. (Eds.): ICIC 2021, LNAI 12838, pp. 12–23, 2021.
https://doi.org/10.1007/978-3-030-84532-2_2

[8]. The distance function of the equidistant offset curve is a fixed constant function, while the distance function of the variable distance offset curve is a very flexible function. In this paper, the offset curve is mainly expressed by parameters. It is worth mentioning that there is always a deviation between the original base curve and the offset curve generated after bias, which can be accurately quantified. Based on this, the algebraic distance is generally taken as the measurement standard in CAD/CAM research, which is the offset curve approximation theory in a sense [9] (Fig. 1).

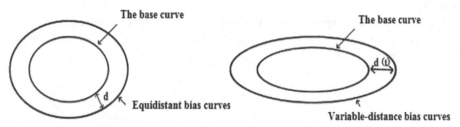

Fig. 1. Equidistant and variable-distance bias curves

2.1 Equidistant Offset Curves

The equidistant offset curve is a curve which is generated by the point of a given curve moving a fixed distance along its normal direction [10].

Definition 1. Given a free rational basis curve $C_0(t)$ (t is arc length parameter), the equidistant offset curve with the offset distance d is $C_d(t)$, and where $d > 0$ (Make counterclockwise offset distance is positive and clockwise offset distance is negative); then, we get the representation of the equidistant offset curve, which is as follows:

$$C_d(t) = C_0(t) + N(t)d \tag{1}$$

Where, $N(t)$ is the normal of the curve $C_0(t)$, d is the offset distance, since the unit normal vector $N(t)$ is generally irrational, the bias curve $C_d(t)$ is also irrational, which cannot be effectively dealt with in computer aided geometric design. Therefore, it is necessary to approximate it by means of a rational curve. Let the approximation error is ε, then the approximation to a rational curve is denoted as $C_d^\varepsilon(t)$[11].

2.2 Variable Offset Curves

The variable offset curve is a generalized form of equidistant offset curve.

Definition 2. When the offset distance in an equidistant offset curve changes from a constant $d > 0$ to a function $d(t)$, and $d(t) > 0$, such a curve is called a variable offset curve. Its representation is as follows:

$$C_d(t) = C_0(t) + d(t)N(t) \tag{2}$$

3 The Self-intersection Detection of Offset Curves

In the practical application of the offset curve, once the curve is bent, there will be the situation of large curvature bending and a small distance between two points on the base curve, which is the self-intersection of the irregular problem. The self-intersection problem of equidistant offset curve and variable distance offset curve cannot be used to remove the self-intersection by the same method. This paper attempts to use an elimination algorithm to solve the self-intersection problem of variable distance offset curve [12].

If a free curve $C(t)$ appears to $C_1(u) = C_2(v)$, it is called the intersection of the curve, and if $C(u) = C(v)$, and $u \neq v$, this phenomenon is called the self-intersection of the curve (Figs. 2 and 3).

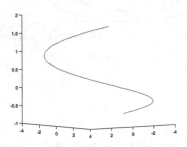

Fig. 2. Spatial free curve

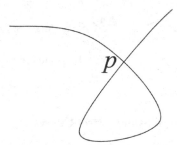

Fig. 3. Self-intersecting curve

3.1 Intersecting Problem of Offset Curves

According to the analysis of the self-intersection problem of the curve, the algorithm is now used to accurately find the intersection position of the two curves. The parametric form of the equation is given as follows:

$$C_1(u) = C_2(v) \tag{3}$$

We know from (3) that if (x_i, y_i) $(i = 1, 2)$ is the components of the unknown quantity (x, y) in the curve C_i, then

$$\begin{cases} x_1(u) = x_2(v) \\ y_1(u) = y_2(v) \end{cases} \tag{4}$$

Clearly, it can be determined that C_1 and C_2 have intersected with these two free curves.

However, as u, v are two independent parameter variables, if $u \neq v$, we have the following two forms

$$C(u) = C(v) \tag{5}$$

and

$$\begin{cases} x(u) = x(v) \\ y(u) = y(v) \end{cases}$$

When this relationship happens to the curve $C(t)$, the two parts of one curve are said to have self-intersected (Figs. 4 and 5).

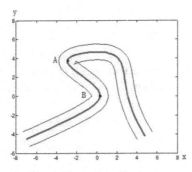

Fig. 4. Irregular offset curve

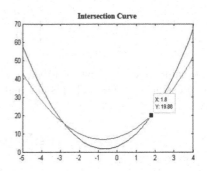

Fig. 5. Intersection curve

3.2   The solution of the Self-intersection Problem of Curves

In this section, the self-intersection equation of the curve is solved by elimination algorithm, and the self-intersection point is found.

Power Basis Representation of Self-intersection. When it is possible for free curve $C(u)$ and $C(v)$ to intersect, we can use the following expression to judge the intersection [13].

Definition 3. Let $C(t) = \sum\limits_{i=0}^{n} a_i t^i$, $t \in [0, 1]$. u and v are two mutually independent parameters, and the following is the self intersection equation of the curve.

$$I(u, v) = C(u) - C(v)$$
$$= \sum_{i=1}^{n} a_i u^i - \sum_{i=0}^{n} a_i v^i$$
$$= \sum_{i=1}^{n} a_i (u^i - v^i) \tag{6}$$

When $i \neq 0$, since $(u^i - v^i)$ is unknown, the Eq. (6) is unknown; when $i = 0$, that determined value of the Eq. (6) is 0, which is also a self-intersection situation.

In the case of non-trivial solutions, we observe the self-intersection expression and find the parameter term $(u - v)$ which always appears. This discovery not only proves the possibility of solving the self-intersection point, but also greatly reduces the complexity of finding the self-intersection position.

The Bernstein Basis Representation of the Self-intersection Equation. For the Eq. (6), rewrite the parameter form as $u^i = B_i^n = C_n^i t^i (1 - t)^{n-i}$, here B_i^n called Bernstein basis, and the binomial coefficient of the equation is

$$C_n^i = \begin{cases} \dfrac{n!}{i!(n-i)!}, & 0 \le i \le n \\ 0, & 其他 \end{cases} \tag{7}$$

At the same time $I(u, v) = (u - v)\hat{I}(u, v)$. Moreover, if the self-intersecting expression is an expression with a basis Bernstein, and then the parametric curve is called the Bezier curve.

$$C(t) = \sum_{i=0}^{n} b_i B_i^n(t), \quad t \in [0, 1]$$

Where b_i is the control vertex of the Bezier curve control polygon, it is called Bezier coefficient for short

$$\begin{aligned} I(u, v) &= C(u) - C(v) \\ &= \sum_{k=0}^{m} b_k B_k^m(u) - \sum_{l=0}^{n} b_l B_l^n(v) \\ &= \sum_{k=0}^{m} \sum_{l=0}^{n} q_{kl} B_k^m(u) B_l^n(v) \end{aligned} \tag{8}$$

Definition 4. Since a mixed curve consisting of two free Bezier curves is still a Bezier curve, it may be assumed $I(u, v)$ that it is a binary function with parameter terms $(u - v)$. Then there are expressions of the lower order $\hat{I}(u, v)$, and the solution of the equation is equivalent to the solution of the self-intersecting equation.

$$\begin{aligned} I(u, v) &= (u - v)\hat{I}(u, v) \\ &= (u - v) \sum_{i=0}^{m-1} \sum_{j=0}^{n-1} p_{ij} \theta_i^{m-1}(u) \theta_j^{n-1}(v) \\ &= \sum_{k=0}^{m} \sum_{l=0}^{n} q_{kl} \theta_k^m(u) \theta_l^n(v) \end{aligned} \tag{9}$$

among them, the term

$$\theta_i^{m-1}(u) = C_{m-1}^i u^i (1 - u)^{m-1-i}$$
$$\theta_j^{n-1}(v) = C_{n-1}^j v^j (1 - v)^{n-1-j}$$

Where, p_{ij} is the coefficient of the low-order Bezier curve $\hat{I}(u, v)$; q_{kl} is the Bezier coefficient of the mixture curve $I(u, v)$.

Obviously, the problem of finding all the self-intersection points by solving the solution of the formula $I(u, v) = 0$ is transformed into the solution of the equation

$$\hat{I}(u, v) = 0$$

$$I(u, v) = (u - v)\hat{I}(u, v) \tag{10}$$

Proof.

$$(u - v) \sum_{i=0}^{m-1} \sum_{j=0}^{n-1} p_{ij}\theta_i^{m-1}(u)\theta_j^{n-1}(v)$$

$$= \sum_{i=0}^{m-1} \sum_{j=0}^{n-1} p_{ij}u\theta_i^{m-1}(u)\theta_j^{n-1}(v) - \sum_{i=0}^{m-1} \sum_{j=0}^{n-1} p_{ij}\theta_i^{m-1}(u)v\theta_j^{n-1}(v)$$

$$= \sum_{i=0}^{m-1} \sum_{j=0}^{n-1} p_{ij}C_{m-1}^i u^{i+1}(1-u)^{m-1-i}\theta_j^{n-1}(v) - \sum_{i=0}^{m-1} \sum_{j=0}^{n-1} p_{ij}\theta_i^{m-1}(u)C_{n-1}^j v^{j+1}(1-v)^{n-1-j}$$

$$= \sum_{i=1}^{m} \sum_{j=0}^{n-1} p_{i-1,j}C_{m-1}^{i-1} u^i(1-u)^{m-i}\theta_j^{n-1}(v) - \sum_{i=0}^{m-1} \sum_{j=1}^{n} p_{i,j-1}\theta_i^{m-1}(u)C_{n-1}^{j-1} v^j(1-v)^{n-j}$$

$$\tag{11}$$

The idea of back substitution is adopted for the above formula to change the expression of some items, such as:

$$C_{m-1}^{i-1} u^i(1-u)^{m-i} = \frac{i}{m}C_m^i u^i(1-u)^{m-i}$$

$$= \frac{i}{m}\theta_i^m(u) \tag{12}$$

In a similar way

$$C_{n-1}^{j-1} v^j(1-v)^{n-j} = \frac{j}{n}\theta_j^n(v) \tag{13}$$

Substituting (12), (13) into (11)

$$C_{n-1}^{j-1} v^j(1-v)^{n-j} = \sum_{i=1}^{m} \sum_{j=0}^{n-1} p_{i-1,j}\frac{i}{m}\theta_i^m(u)\theta_j^{n-1}(v) - \sum_{i=0}^{m-1} \sum_{j=1}^{n} p_{i,j-1}\theta_i^{m-1}(u)\frac{j}{n}\theta_j^n(v)$$

$$= \sum_{i=0}^{m} \sum_{j=0}^{n-1} \frac{i}{m}p_{i-1,j}\theta_i^m(u)\theta_j^{n-1}(v) - \sum_{i=0}^{m-1} \sum_{j=0}^{n} \frac{j}{n}p_{i,j-1}\theta_i^{m-1}(u)\theta_j^n(v)$$

$$\tag{14}$$

and

$$\sum_{i=0}^{m}\sum_{j=0}^{n-1} p_{i-1,j} = \sum_{i=0}^{m}\sum_{j=0}^{n-1} (\frac{j}{n}p_{i-1,j} + \frac{n-j}{n}p_{i-1,j})$$

$$= \sum_{i=0}^{m}\sum_{j=0}^{n-1} \frac{j}{n}p_{i-1,j} + \sum_{i=0}^{m}\sum_{j=0}^{n-1} \frac{n-j}{n}p_{i-1,j}$$

$$= \sum_{i=0}^{m} (\frac{1}{n}p_{i-1,1} + \frac{2}{n}p_{i-1,2} + \cdots + \frac{n-1}{n}p_{i-1,n-1})$$

$$+ \sum_{i=0}^{m} (p_{i-1,0} + \frac{n-1}{n}p_{i-1,1} + \cdots + \frac{n-(n-1)}{n}p_{i-1,n-1})$$

$$= \sum_{i=0}^{m} (\frac{1}{n}p_{i-1,1} + \frac{2}{n}p_{i-1,2} + \cdots + \frac{n-1}{n}p_{i-1,n-1} + \frac{n}{n}p_{i-1,n} - \frac{n}{n}p_{i-1,n})$$

$$+ \sum_{i=0}^{m} (p_{i-1,0} + \frac{n-1}{n}p_{i-1,1} + \cdots + \frac{1}{n}p_{i-1,n-1})$$

$$= \sum_{i=0}^{m}\sum_{j=0}^{n} \frac{j}{n}p_{i-1,j-1} + \sum_{i=0}^{m}\sum_{j=0}^{n} \frac{n-j}{n}p_{i-1,j} \tag{15}$$

Similarly,

$$\sum_{i=0}^{m-1}\sum_{j=0}^{n} p_{i,j-1} = \sum_{i=0}^{m}\sum_{j=0}^{n} (\frac{i}{m}p_{i-1,j-1} + \frac{m-i}{m}p_{i,j-1}) \tag{16}$$

Substituting (15), (16) into (14), we have

$$C_{n-1}^{j-1} v^{j}(1-v)^{n-j} = \sum_{i=0}^{m}\sum_{j=0}^{n} \frac{i}{m}(\frac{j}{n}p_{i-1,j-1} + \frac{n-j}{n}p_{i-1,j})\theta_i^m(u)\theta_j^n(v)$$

$$- \sum_{i=0}^{m}\sum_{j=0}^{n} \frac{j}{n}(\frac{i}{m}p_{i-1,j-1} + \frac{m-i}{m}p_{i,j-1})\theta_i^m(u)\theta_j^n(v)$$

$$= \sum_{i=0}^{m}\sum_{j=0}^{n} (\frac{i}{m}\frac{n-j}{n}p_{i-1,j-1} - \frac{j}{n}\frac{m-i}{m}p_{i,j-1})\theta_i^m(u)\theta_j^n(v). \tag{17}$$

Let

$$q_{0j} = -\frac{j(m-0)}{nm}p_{0,j-1},$$

$$q_{ij} = \frac{i}{m}\frac{n-j}{n}p_{i-1,j-1} - \frac{j}{n}\frac{m-i}{m}p_{i,j-1}$$

then

$$p_{0,j-1} = -\frac{n}{j}q_{0j},$$

$$p_{i,j-1} = \frac{i}{j}\frac{n-j}{m-i}p_{i-1,j} - \frac{n}{j}\frac{m}{m-i}q_{ij}$$

By solving the above self intersection equation, it is found that as long as the factor $(u - v)$ is eliminated, the operation performance of finding the self-intersection position is greatly improved. As long as $\hat{I}(u, v) = 0$, the self-intersection problem in the case of Bezier polynomial can be effectively solved [14].

4 Examples

Bezier curve is a B spline curve whose order is the same as the number of poles. The order of the spline curve is determined by the adjacent continuous segments of the control polygon, which is called several order spline, and the most commonly used ones are quadratic and cubic spline.

4.1 Example Analysis of Power Base Representation

In this paper, the feasibility of finding the self intersection locations of two different curves is demonstrated by the elimination algorithm. The following examples are used to verify it, which is convenient for further research.

Let $n = 3$, the self-intersection expression of curves is as follows

$$C(u) - C(v) = a_0(u^0 - v^0) + a_1(u^1 - v^1) + a_2(u^2 - v^2) + a_3(u^3 - v^3)$$

$$= (u - v)[a_1 + a_2(u + v) + a_3(u^2 + uv + v^2)]$$

$$I(u, v) = (u - v)\hat{I}(u, v)$$

$$\hat{I}(u, v) = a_1 + a_2(u + v) + a_3(u^2 + uv + v^2)$$

Finally, the problem of finding the self-intersection point is transformed into solving the equation $\hat{I}(u, v)=0$.

For this example, let $a_1 = 1$, $a_2 = 2$, $a_3 = 3$, the results are as follows.

$$u_1 = -1/4 + \frac{\sqrt{3}}{4}i, \; u_2 = -1/4 - \frac{\sqrt{3}}{4}i.$$

$$v_1 = -1/4 - \frac{\sqrt{3}}{4}i, \; v_2 = -1/4 + \frac{\sqrt{3}}{4}i.$$

It shows that both (u_1, v_1) and (u_2, v_2) are self-intersecting points.

4.2 Example Analysis of Bezier Base Representation

According to the foregoing analysis, we get a method to remove the self intersection points of curves. Whether it is intersection or self intersection, we firstly find the self intersection points, and then find all the special points and remove them. Therefore, this algorithm is to prove the equation after given specific data.

$$I(u, v) = (u - v)\hat{I}(u, v).$$

that is.

$$\sum_{k=0}^{m} \sum_{l=0}^{n} q_{kl}\theta_k^m(u)\theta_l^n(v) = (u - v) \sum_{i=0}^{m-1} \sum_{j=0}^{n-1} p_{ij}\theta_i^{m-1}(u)\theta_j^{n-1}(v).$$

Because

$$\theta_i^{m-1}(u) = C_{m-1}^i u^i (1 - u)^{m-1-i}, \theta_j^{n-1}(v) = C_{n-1}^j v^j (1 - v)^{n-1-j}$$

$$q_{0j} = -\frac{j}{n} p_{0,j-1}, q_{ij} = \frac{i}{m} \frac{n-j}{n} p_{i-1,j-1} - \frac{j}{n} \frac{m-i}{m} p_{i,j-1}.$$

Let $m = 3, n = 2$

$$I(u, v) = \sum_{k=0}^{3} \sum_{l=0}^{2} q_{kl}\theta_k^3(u)\theta_l^2(v)$$

$$= \sum_{k=0}^{3} [q_{k0}\theta_k^3(u)\theta_0^2(v) + q_{k1}\theta_k^3(u)\theta_1^2(v) + q_{k2}\theta_k^3(u)\theta_2^2(v)]$$

$$= q_{00}\theta_0^3(u)\theta_0^2(v) + q_{01}\theta_0^3(u)\theta_1^2(v) + q_{02}\theta_0^3(u)\theta_2^2(v)$$
$$+ q_{10}\theta_1^3(u)\theta_0^2(v) + q_{11}\theta_1^3(u)\theta_1^2(v) + q_{12}\theta_1^3(u)\theta_2^2(v)$$
$$+ q_{20}\theta_2^3(u)\theta_0^2(v) + q_{21}\theta_2^3(u)\theta_1^2(v) + q_{22}\theta_2^3(u)\theta_2^2(v)$$
$$+ q_{30}\theta_3^3(u)\theta_0^2(v) + q_{31}\theta_3^3(u)\theta_1^2(v) + q_{32}\theta_3^3(u)\theta_2^2(v)$$

$$= \begin{pmatrix} q_{00} & q_{01} & q_{02} \\ q_{10} & q_{11} & q_{12} \\ q_{20} & q_{21} & q_{22} \\ q_{30} & q_{31} & q_{32} \end{pmatrix} \begin{pmatrix} \theta_0^3(u)\theta_0^2(v) & \theta_1^3(u)\theta_0^2(v) & \theta_2^3(u)\theta_0^2(v) & \theta_3^3(u)\theta_0^2(v) \\ \theta_0^3(u)\theta_1^2(v) & \theta_1^3(u)\theta_1^2(v) & \theta_2^3(u)\theta_1^2(v) & \theta_3^3(u)\theta_1^2(v) \\ \theta_0^3(u)\theta_2^2(v) & \theta_1^3(u)\theta_2^2(v) & \theta_2^3(u)\theta_2^2(v) & \theta_3^3(u)\theta_2^2(v) \end{pmatrix}$$

$$\hat{I}(u, v) = \sum_{i=0}^{2} \sum_{j=0}^{1} p_{ij}\theta_i^2(u)\theta_j(v)$$

$$= \sum_{i=0}^{2} [p_{i0}\theta_i^2(u)\theta_0(v) + p_{i1}\theta_i^2(u)\theta_1(v)]$$

$$= p_{00}\theta_0^2(u)\theta_0(v) + p_{01}\theta_0^2(u)\theta_1(v)$$
$$+ p_{10}\theta_1^2(u)\theta_0(v) + p_{11}\theta_1^2(u)\theta_1(v)$$
$$+ p_{20}\theta_2^2(u)\theta_0(v) + p_{21}\theta_2^2(u)\theta_1(v)$$

$$= \begin{pmatrix} p_{00} & p_{01} \\ p_{10} & p_{11} \\ p_{20} & p_{21} \end{pmatrix} \begin{pmatrix} \theta_0^2(u)\theta_0(v) & \theta_1^2(u)\theta_0(v) & \theta_2^2(u)\theta_0(v) \\ \theta_0^2(u)\theta_1(v) & \theta_1^2(u)\theta_1(v) & \theta_2^2(u)\theta_1(v) \end{pmatrix}.$$

then

$$p_{00} = -2q_{01}, \qquad p_{01} = -q_{02};$$

$$p_{10} = \frac{1}{2}p_{01} - 3q_{11}, \qquad p_{11} = -\frac{3}{2}q_{12};$$

$$p_{20} = 2p_{11} - 6q_{21}, \qquad p_{21} = -3q_{22}.$$

Therefore

$$I(u, v) = \begin{pmatrix} q_{00} & q_{01} & q_{02} \\ q_{10} & q_{11} & q_{12} \\ q_{20} & q_{21} & q_{22} \\ q_{30} & q_{31} & q_{32} \end{pmatrix} \begin{pmatrix} \theta_0^3(u)\theta_0^2(v) & \theta_1^3(u)\theta_0^2(v) & \theta_2^3(u)\theta_0^2(v) & \theta_3^3(u)\theta_0^2(v) \\ \theta_0^3(u)\theta_1^2(v) & \theta_1^3(u)\theta_1^2(v) & \theta_2^3(u)\theta_1^2(v) & \theta_3^3(u)\theta_1^2(v) \\ \theta_0^3(u)\theta_2^2(v) & \theta_1^3(u)\theta_2^2(v) & \theta_2^3(u)\theta_2^2(v) & \theta_3^3(u)\theta_2^2(v) \end{pmatrix}$$

$$= (u - v)\begin{pmatrix} -2q_{01} & -q_{02} \\ \frac{1}{2}p_{01} - 3q_{11} & -\frac{3}{2}q_{12} \\ 2p_{11} - 6q_{21} & -3q_{22} \end{pmatrix} \begin{pmatrix} \theta_0^2(u)\theta_0(v) & \theta_1^2(u)\theta_0(v) & \theta_2^2(u)\theta_0(v) \\ \theta_0^2(u)\theta_1(v) & \theta_1^2(u)\theta_1(v) & \theta_2^2(u)\theta_1(v) \end{pmatrix}$$

$$= (u - v)\hat{I}(u, v).$$

The above proposition proves that the application of the algorithm in the example is effective. As long as $\hat{I}(u, v) = 0$, the final solution of the equation is equivalent to the determination of the self-intersection point [15].

If let $p_{00} = 1$, $p_{01} = 2$; $p_{10} = 3$, $p_{11} = 4$; $p_{20} = 5$, $p_{21} = 6$. The results are as follows

$$\left\{ (u, v) | u = c, 1, c, 0, 1, 0, 1, v = 1, c, -\frac{1}{2}, 1, 1, -\frac{1}{2}, -\frac{1}{2} \right\}$$

Because of the parameters $u, v \in [0, 1]$, the self-intersection point occurs only at $(1, 1)$ after parameterization is specified.

Figure 6 it is a schematic diagram of the intersection of a straight line and a curve, where the intersection points A (-2.7), B $(0.5, 23.5)$ and C $(2.3, 61.3)$ indicate the intersection. Figure 7 it is the effect drawing after removing the self-intersection points.

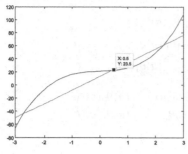

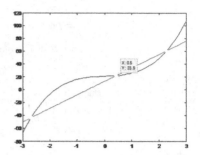

Fig. 6. The line intersects the curve   **Fig. 7.** Remove self-intersection schematic

5 Summary and Prospect

Based on the theory of equidistant offset curves and variable-distance offset curves, this paper mainly focuses on the self-intersection of curves and surfaces, and proposes an elimination algorithm for the problem of self-intersection of the curve. Firstly, the algorithm parameterizes the representation of free-intersection curves, and then it optimizes the algorithm and solves the problem by eliminating the common item factor. We will further explore and study the surface field, and promote the application of algorithm.

Acknowledgement. This work is supported by the funding project: The Research on Process Assessment System of Students under Mixed Teaching Mode" (HLW-20139), 2020 Annual Project of Educational Science of Shanxi Province "13th Five-Year Plan".

References

1. Zhu, C.G., Zhao, X.Y.: Self-intersections of rational Bezier curves. Gr. Models **76**(5), 312–320 (2014)
2. Pekermana, D., Elberb, G., Kim, M.-S.: Self-intersection detection and elimination in free form curves and surfaces. Comput. Aided Des. **40**(2), 150–159 (2008)
3. Jia, X., Chen, F., Deng, J.: Computing self-intersection curves of rational ruled surfaces. Comput. Aided Geom. Des. **26**(3), 287–299 (2009)
4. Seong, J.-K., Elber, G., Kim, M.-S.: Trimming local and global self-intersections in offset curves/surfaces using distance maps. Comput. Aided Des. **38**(3), 183–193 (2006)
5. Gustavson, R., Ovchinnikov, A., Pogudin, G.: New order bounds in differential elimination algorithms. J. Symb. Comput. **85**, 128–147 (2018)
6. Dorado, R.: Medial axis of a planar region by offset self-intersections. Comput. Aided Des. **41**(12), 1050–1059 (2009)
7. Farouki, R.T.: Reduced difference polynomials and self-intersection computations. Appl. Math. Comput. **324**(1), 174–190 (2018)
8. Xu, J., Sun, Y., Zhang, L.: A mapping-based approach to eliminating self-intersection of offset paths on mesh surfaces for CNC machining. Comput. Aided Des. **62**, 131–142 (2015)
9. Maekawa, T.: An overview of offset curves and surfaces. Comput. Aided Des. **31**(3), 165–173 (1999)
10. Elber, G., Grandine, T., Kim, M.-S.: Surface self-intersection computation via algebraic decomposition. Comput. Aided Des. **41**(12), 1060–1066 (2009)

11. Danaee, E., Geravand, A., Danaie, M.: Wide-band low cross-talk photonic crystal wave guide intersections using self-collimation phenomenon. Opt. Commun. **431**(15), 216–228 (2019)
12. Len, Y., Satriano, M.: Lifting tropical self intersections. J. Comb. Theory Ser. A **170**, 105–138 (2020)
13. Hescock, J., Newman, C., Agioutantis, Z.: Development of a new algorithm for implementing the edge effect offset for subsidence calculations. Int. J. Min. Sci. Technol. **28**(1), 61–66 (2018)
14. Ahn, Y.J., Hoffmann, C., Rosen, P.: Geometric constraints on quadratic Bézier curves using minimal length and energy. J. Comput. Appl. Math. **255**(1), 887–897 (2014)
15. Ahn, Y.J., Kim, Y., Shin, Y.: Approximation of circular arcs and offset curves by Bézier curves of high degree. J. Comput. Appl. Math. **167**(2), 405–416 (2004)

Towards AI-Based Reaction and Mitigation for e-Commerce - the ENSURESEC Engine

Marek Pawlicki[1,2(✉)], Rafał Kozik[1,2], Damian Puchalski[1], and Michał Choraś[1,2]

[1] ITTI Sp. z o.o., Poznań, Poland
mpawlicki@itti.com.pl
[2] UTP University of Science and Technology, Bydgoszcz, Poland

Abstract. E-commerce services have expanded tremendously in the recent years, with market value estimations for cross-border trade reaching well over a hundred billion euro just in the European Union. At the same time, e-commerce-related fraud rate and cybersecurity issues are staggering. With e-commerce clearly gaining the critical infrastructure status, any significant disruptions could potentially ripple all across the society. Thus, new security tools address the full spectrum of threats, offering the complete response and mitigation process. This paper introduces a comprehensive analysis, detection, response, mitigation, and cyberthreat knowledge-building pipeline.

Keywords: Mitigation · Cybersecurity · Reaction · e-commerce

1 Context and Motivation

In recent years, e-commerce services have become one of the key pillars of the European Digital Single Market. According to the European E-commerce 2019 report, the market is constantly growing. E-commerce sales in Europe reached €621 billion in 2019 and were expected to reach €717 billion at the end of 2020.This means an increase of almost 13% in comparison to the previous year [1]. According to the report, the COVID-19 pandemic outbreak has changed the preferences of the online consumers; however, the full impact of the pandemic on the market will be visible in 2021.

In the majority of countries in Western Europe, the share of the consumers using the Internet for online shopping exceeds 70%. It is also worth mentioning that cross-border e-commerce market is worth €143 billion, despite the fact that in many European countries consumers prefer local or national e-commerce providers, while the international marketplaces such as Amazon are less popular [2].

Due to the market size and the general trend of growth of e-services across Europe, the e-commerce ecosystem has evolved into a highly distributed critical infrastructure involving the majority of actors at different levels – including citizens/customers, technical vendors, and sub-services such as supplies, online payment processing platforms, physical delivery, etc. This poses numerous cyber and physical threats at different stages

© Springer Nature Switzerland AG 2021
D.-S. Huang et al. (Eds.): ICIC 2021, LNAI 12838, pp. 24–31, 2021.
https://doi.org/10.1007/978-3-030-84532-2_3

of the online shopping process. In addition, it makes protecting the process be exceptionally complex, in particular due to a large attack surface and limited visibility of the entities involved in thee-commerce value chains. At the same time, e-commerce services are extremely attractive to cyber-criminals, due to the fact that they involve sensitive data such as the payment card numbers and PIN codes. One of the examples of this vulnerability is the fact that the e-commerce fraud is currently about 50% of total card fraud losses in the UK (over £300 million), while the whole EU suffered over €1.3 billion of such fraud losses last year [3, 4]. In addition to monetary impacts, such as operational costs, there is a list of non-monetary repercussions, including loss of reputation, harm to people and damage to the environment [5].

The intricacy of the e-commerce market and a massive increase in the e-commerce user base continue to inflate the emerging cybersecurity challenges. The fast expansion and the constant emergence of new e-commerce solutions has the potential of creating new, vast attack surfaces. According to [6], the intricacy of the threat scene, mixed with constantly fluctuating standards, legislation and privacy issues, render creating effective security solutions more and more troublesome. Contemporary cyberthreat landscape is too complex to allow a reactive approach to threats. Only the companies which switch to a proactive approach, i.e., one leveraging cyberthreat intelligence, can hope to keep up with the current cyber-arms race. Not participating in the cyberthreat intelligence community leaves an organization vulnerable. The authors of [7] list some recent threat modelling and cyberthreat intelligence solutions as they propose their own tool in the energy cloud environment. They noticed a trend of balancing the cost and efficiency of each action in the relation between the malicious actor and the protected asset with the use of game theoretic approaches. The approach could be used as a way to motivate organizations to share CTI [8].

There is a gap to be filled by the security solutions which focus on granting protection of both the legacy and new e-commerce platforms. The H2020 ENSURESEC project aims at filling that gap, by fully recognizing e-commerce as critical infrastructure, and balancing physical, cyber-physical and cyberthreat protection. The H2020 ENSURESEC addresses the problem of accurately assessing the threat level of a malicious action, operating with the realization that no organization can have full knowledge, or even access to all the relevant circumstances of an attack. The cyberthreat landscape has reached the level of maturity in which no single organization can hope to maintain the pace on its own. Only congregations sharing actionable intel can maintain the risk levels sufficiently low. Despite the numerous benefits for single organizations and whole communities, the adoption of CTI exchange is still not widespread enough [9]. For these reasons, the project leverages the cyberthreat intelligence sharing and integrations with CTI platforms to form an actionable knowledge base and indicate adequate response and mitigation measures in cybersecurity of e-commerce.

However, as noted by [10], despite its quick growth, the state of affairs in the cyberthreat intelligence leaves a lot to be desired. A multitude of services, architectures and technological solutions produce unhomogenized data, which necessitates standardization. There are standards proposed for exactly this situation - like STIX [11], TAXII [12] or CybOX [13], but the adoption is not as wide as it should be at this stage. In [14], the author argues that the domain needs incident response data formats and integration into existing CTI formats - like STIX. At the same time, with the rapid expansion of the CTI field there is work towards establishing a methodology to evaluate standards and platforms within CTI [15]. In the same paper, the authors evaluate the existing CTI frameworks, concluding that STIX is the most consolidated standard, and MISP is the most complete and flexible platform.

The literature and situational analysis of the domain clearly show that the field needs to progress in the direction of adopting reliable information exchange standards, utilization of dependable, flexible CTI platforms, emphasizing the benefits of information sharing for both individual organizations and the community, and the development of adequate incident response, reaction, and mitigation systems. The ENSURESEC Response and Mitigation Engine aims to accomplish all those objectives.

This paper is structured as follows. In Sect. 2, the vision of the detection, information sharing, and automated reaction suite of tools is provided. Section 3 presents a brief analysis of the existing solutions. Section 4 details the technical implementation. In Sect. 5, conclusions and ideas for future work are disclosed.

2 Vision of the Proposed Tool

The three main pillars of the proposed tool are: detection of an incident, information sharing, and automated reaction tailored to the given context (infrastructure, category of an attack, its severity, etc.). The main goal is to counter attacks such as Botnets, infection assets by malware, attacks on application layer and general malicious/anomalous activities, such as SPAM.

The goal of the development of an engine for the e-commerce cybersecurity is to provide the owners of the e-commerce infrastructure and their business partners a tool able to perform online analysis, and to suggest an adequate response and mitigation strategy in case of an attack. The assumption is that the incident is firstly detected with all the relevant information about an attack collected. The mitigation engine employs innovative machine learning techniques to optimize the selection of mitigation strategies that are later executed by matching the characteristics of the detected or suspected incident with the knowledge base of such incidents. Based on the historical data, such as potential mitigation plans for specific threats, and root cause analyses, the tools adapt ML-based recommendation methods to provide a suggestion that would be the most accurate in the current context. The reactions triggered by the reaction module can be categorized as follows:

- Level 0 - automatic blocking the communication coming from an attacker, e.g., blocking by IP address, domain name, hash values, etc., to stop the attack in its initial phase.
- Level 1 - blocking the communication based on signatures matching the packet/request content (e.g., based on OWASP CRS).
- Level 2 - anomaly-based detection with the use of models that can be trained on the fly or be pre-trained in a batch mode.
- Level 3 - deep analysis of historical (collected) traffic in order to produce knowledge or new detection mechanisms.

The solution will also be able to share the incident information with business partners and their users, initiating a desired mitigation strategy. Furthermore, the tool implements innovative diagnostic methods to quickly determine the dependencies of the incident so that all the related business partners and users are informed about the event. The tool also shares the exact cause of the event with the mitigation engine so that an appropriate mitigation plan can be executed.

The information flow and dependencies between detection, reaction and information sharing are presented in Fig. 1.

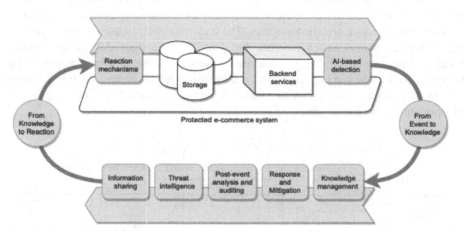

Fig. 1. The information flow and dependencies between detection, reaction, and information sharing.

3 Competitive Solutions

There is a number of market solutions focusing on real-time, automated reaction and mitigation in case of cyber incident. Solutions such as FortiEDR [16], IBM Resilient Security Orchestration, Automation and Response [17], Vectra Cognito Platform [18], Checkpoint Software Event Management: SmartEvent [19] are general purpose tools to respond to and remediate an attack. Providers of such tools, such as The Hive [20] combined with Cortex [21] or Stealthbits [22], advertise their capabilities related to incident information sharing to facilitate collaboration. Also, part of the tools can be integrated with MISP (Malware Information Sharing Platform) [23]. The advantage of the presented engine in relation to market solutions is the use of machine learning techniques for selection to the most optimal way of reaction by matching an ongoing incident with the past cases.

4 Technical Implementation

The most important element in the environment is the e-commerce system. It is the source of inputs to the proposed tools. The data from the e-commerce system is processed by the suite, and suitable recovery and mitigation are proposed. The processed inputs also feed the post-event analysis module.

4.1   Input Data and Machine Learning Based Detection

The data coming from the e-commerce system is passed through adequate monitoring systems and detector which produce the data for the response and mitigation engine. The detectors send events that are related to abnormal behavior of the observed system or violate certain policies, emphasizing the cases displaying the symptoms of being malicious. An example of these kinds of anomalies are intrusion detection alerts, coming from network intrusion detection modules. The traffic is collected using network probes, then adequate features are engineered. Based on those features, ML-based anomaly detection is performed [24–26]. The detection pipeline (as well as the input gathering for this situation) is shown in Fig. 2. For network intrusion detection, the anomaly detectors operate on both application and network layers, having the capability of intercepting the full spectrum of network attacks.

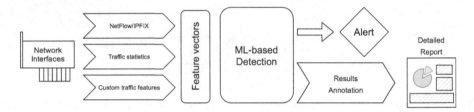

Fig. 2. ML-based detection pipeline

4.2   Response and Mitigation Leveraging the Accumulated Knowledge

The data coming from the detectors is further processed to ensure a standardized format of incident and observation description. The data contains information that is relevant and uniquely describes the incident or the observation.

The data identifies the origin of the observation, be it host name or session ID, username, IP address etc., simply put, an identifier that makes it possible to pinpoint a specific event. The data describes the reason why the alert was raised, including the severity. These are the indicators of compromise (IoC) - any behavior flagged as anomalous in the given context, like unusual network traffic, deviant DNS requests or strange HTML response sizes, etc.

To facilitate knowledge building and both the internal communication with the detection tools and the external communication with cyberthreat intelligence (CTI) services, the STIX format is used [11]. Knowledge building is crucial for the purposes of response and mitigation, as it is used to support decisions made by the engine. Knowledge accumulation is also necessary from the post-event analysis standpoint. The STIX format allows getting the data that is provided by and available in the cyberthreat intelligence community and form a basis for building knowledge about the system and about the observed incident. Most importantly, STIX facilitates the utilization of the MISP platform and similar CTI communities. CTI communities share the identified malicious activities, with MISP being the industry standard. The proposed solution is directly connected to the CTI ecosystem; they both share the identified attacks and leveraging community knowledge. This exchange allows to build full awareness of the detected threat based on partial information gathered from the e-commerce system.

The response and mitigation engine uses the detection results and accumulated knowledge to propose and conduct a suitable and smart countermeasure. Threat symptoms of high enough severity are mapped to necessary reactions, reducing the consequences of the detected malicious actions. The engine relies on automation scripts that can lock in to a given service and perform a range of response and mitigation actions, like updating rules, configurations, closing the connections, blocking specific requests, or produce a detailed suggestion for the operator in the security team, etc.

4.3 Maintaining Business Processes Intact

In cases where malicious activity is apparent, the reaction is relatively straight-forward - if a file is malicious, anything related to the hash of that file can be blocked. The connection to the machine where the file originated can be blocked as well; so can be the associated user names. Any connection trying to reach the compromised machine, and any leaked credentials can be blocked. Compromised DNS can be blackholed. Lastly, any activity which expresses, with full certainly, the symptoms of an attack pattern or malicious activity, may be blocked, too. Blocking users and disabling services do not pose significant difficulty from the technological standpoint. However, actions of this sort have the potential of being a significant disruption for the business processes of e-commerce.

From the business point of view, removing vulnerabilities and restoring the full functionality has the highest priority. The processes of response, mitigation and recovery could be fully automated, but for the sake of the safety of business operations, maintaining a human in the loop allows to dampen the possible dangers. Having a human in the loop necessitates a notification system that is understandable to the security operations officers, providing explanation as to what happened, what the source of the problem was and what the identified risk is. That kind of information is retrieved from the knowledge base. The engine, after consulting the knowledge base, provides further information on the related or connected elements, and then the scope of an attack.

The current Response and Mitigation tool prototype is on its way to testing with the ENSURESEC pilot partners, capable of responding to prompts from real-time network intrusion detection [27].

5 Conclusions and Future Work

The plan for further development of the AI-based response and mitigation engine is to propose better reactions using deep(er) inspection of the knowledge stored in MISP. For this purpose, it has been planned to use collaborative filtering to better contextualize the reaction to a given context (installed assets, applied countermeasures, network topology, etc.). In addition, there is the intention of developing a new mechanism for automation regarding data collection and analysis.

Acknowledgment. This work is supported by the Ensuresec project, which has received funding from the European Union's Horizon 2020 research and innovation programme under grant agreement No. 883242.

References

1. European ecommerce report 2019. https://tinyurl.com/4wpmrv52. Accessed 04 May 2021
2. Ecommerce in Europe: €717 billion in 2020. https://tinyurl.com/hy3x8kwa. Accessed 04 May 2021
3. Fraud losses in e-commerce on UK-issued credit cards-2019 — Statista. https://tinyurl.com/9bx7dr3n. Accessed 04 May 2021
4. Survey on "scams and fraud experienced by consumers". Final report. https://tinyurl.com/e6n97hf2. Accessed 04 May 2021
5. Couce-Vieira, A., Insua, D.R., Kosgodagan, A.: Assessing and forecasting cyber-security impacts. Decis. Anal. **17**(4), 356–374 (2020)
6. 2020 global threat intelligence report the nature of security: be resilient to thrive. https://tinyurl.com/4ayv32xx. Accessed 04 May 2021
7. Gong, S., Lee, C.: Cyber threat intelligence framework for incident response in an energy cloud platform. Electronics **10**(3), 239 (2021)
8. Xie, W., Yu, X., Zhang, Y., Wang, H.: An improved shapley value benefit distribution mechanism in cooperative game of cyber threat intelligence sharing. In: IEEE INFOCOM 2020 - IEEE Conference on Computer Communications Workshops (INFOCOM WKSHPS), pp. 810–815 (2020). https://doi.org/10.1109/INFOCOMWKSHPS50562.2020.91627399
9. Alkalabi, W., Simpson, L., Morarji, H.: Barriers and incentives to cybersecurity threat information sharing in developing countries: a case study of Saudi Arabia. In: 2021 Australasian Computer Science Week Multiconference. ACSW 2021, Association for Computing Machinery, NewYork, NY, USA (2021). https://doi.org/10.1145/3437378.3437391
10. Ramsdale, A., Shiaeles, S., Kolokotronis, N.: A comparative analysis of cyber-threat intelligence sources, formats and languages. Electronics **9**(5), 824 (2020)
11. Stix - structured threat information expression (archive) — stix project documentation. https://stixproject.github.io/. Accessed 04 May 2021
12. Connolly, J., Davidson, M., Schmidt, C.: The trusted automated exchange of indicator information (TAXII). The MITRE Corporation, pp. 1–20 (2014)
13. Barnum, S., Martin, R., Worrell, B., Kirillov, I.: The cybox language specification. The MITRE Corporation (2012)
14. Schlette, D.: Cyber threat intelligence (2021)
15. de Melo e Silva, A., Costa Gondim, J.J., de Oliveira Albuquerque, R., Garcia Villalba, L.J.: A methodology to evaluate standards and platforms within cyber threat intelligence. Future Internet **12**(6), 108 (2020)
16. Endpoint detection & response (EDR) security solutions. https://www.fortinet.com/products/endpoint-security/fortiedr. Accessed 04 May 2021
17. Resilient security orchestration, automation and response platform - Egypt — IBM. https://tinyurl.com/8ewe7usx. Accessed 04 May 2021
18. Network threat detection & response platform—vectraai. https://www.vectra.ai/products/cognito-platform. Accessed 04 May 2021

19. Event management for full threat visibility — check point software. https://www.checkpoint. com/products/event-management/. Accessed 04 May 2021
20. The hive project. https://thehive-project.org/. Accessed 04 May 2021
21. Cortex XDR - extended detection and response - Palo Alto networks. https://www.paloalton etworks.com/cortex/cortex-xdr. Accessed 04 May 2021
22. Data access governance — active directory security — privileged access management — stealthbits. https://stealthbits.com/. Accessed 04 May 2021
23. Misp - open source threat intelligence platform & open standards for threat information sharing (formerly known as malware information sharing platform). https://www.misp-pro ject.org/. Accessed 04 May 2021
24. Choraś, M., Pawlicki, M.: Intrusion detection approach based on optimised artificial neural network. Neurocomputing (2021)
25. Dutta, V., Choraś, M., Pawlicki, M., Kozik, R.: A deep learning ensemble for network anomaly and cyber-attack detection. Sensors **20**(16), 4583 (2020)
26. Komisarek, M., Choraś, M., Kozik, R., Pawlicki, M.: Real-time stream processing tool for detecting suspicious network patterns using machine learning. In: Proceedings of the 15th International Conference on Availability, Reliability and Security, pp. 1–7 (2020)
27. Kozik, R., Choraś, M., Flizikowski, A., Theocharidou, M., Rosato, V., Rome, E.: Advanced services for critical infrastructures protection. J. Ambient. Intell. Humaniz. Comput. **6**(6), 783–795 (2015). https://doi.org/10.1007/s12652-015-0283-x

Arabic Light Stemmer Based on ISRI Stemmer

Dhafar Hamed Abd[1], Wasiq Khan[2(✉)], Khudhair Abed Thamer[1], and Abir J. Hussain[2]

[1] Department of Computer Science, Al-Maarif University College, Ramadi, Al-Anbar, Iraq
[2] Department of Computer Science, Liverpool John Moores University, Liverpool L33AF, UK
{W.Khan,A.Hussain}@ljmu.ac.uk

Abstract. The process of stemming is considered as one of the most essential steps in natural language processing and retrieving information. Nevertheless, in Arabic language, the task of stemming remains a major challenge due to the fact that Arabic language has a particular morphology, thereby making it different from other languages. Majority of existing algorithms are limited to a given number of words, create ambiguity between original letters and affixes, and often make use of dictionary patterns or words. We therefore, for the first time, present a design and implementation of Arabic light stemmer based on Information Science Research Institute algorithm. The algorithm is evaluated empirically using a newly created Arabic dataset which was created using data from different Arabic websites with contents that have been written in modern Arabic language. The experimental results indicated that the proposed method outperforms when benchmarked with existing methods.

Keywords: Light stemmer · Root stemmer · Information Science Research Institute's (ISRI) · Political Arabic article

1 Introduction

The main purpose of stemming is to reduce different words to their origin word stem by extracting affixes and suffixes. Stemming processes are used in the execution of many tasks that require text preprocessing [1], such as text categorization [2, 3], summarization [4], retrieval [5], etc. There are different kinds of stemming approaches that have been proposed for many languages such as English [6], French [7], Indian [8] and Malay [9]. Obviously, in every natural language the addition of derivational morphemes like suffixes or affixes have been made, and this addition can change the meaning of existing words, thereby changing the way they are understood by humans.

Arabic language is a very complex language that needs a strong stemming to process its complex morphology. In this regard, there are two types of stemming used for Arabic language [10, 11] including, root approach stemming [12] and light approach stemming [13]; these two types of stemming are only used in Arabic language, and not in other language like English, German, French, etc. The Root approach involves the use of morphological analysis to find Arabic word root. Many researchers have proposed root stemmer algorithms such as, Information Science Research Institute's (ISRI) [14] and Khoja [12]. The main purpose of the light approach is to eliminate the most frequent

© Springer Nature Switzerland AG 2021
D.-S. Huang et al. (Eds.): ICIC 2021, LNAI 12838, pp. 32–45, 2021.
https://doi.org/10.1007/978-3-030-84532-2_4

prefixes and suffixes as explained in [15]. There is almost no standard algorithm for Arabic light stemming, and as such, all trials in this field were a set of rules to strip off a small set of suffixes and prefixes.

So far, the two most successful approaches for Arabic stemming, are Koja [12] and ISRI stemmer [14]. ISRI stemmer was introduced in 2005 by Kazem et al. [14], and according to Ezzelding and Shaheed [16]. There are so many features that are common in both ISRI stemmer and Khoja stemmer, but the ISRI makes no use of a root dictionary. By virtue of these features, the capability of the ISRI in terms of stemming uncommon and new words is enhanced. In addition, if a word cannot be rooted, it is normalized and has more stemming patterns and more than 60 stop words. ISRI has demonstrated superior performance as compared with other algorithms proposed in [17, 18]. The ISRI stemmer has demonstrated a strong ability to improve document clustering [19].

In this paper, an Arabic light stemmer is introduced to enable the removal of prefixes, waw, and suffixes. Also, to the best of our knowledge, this work is the first of its kind, as it is based on ISRI stemming algorithm for Arabic language. An Arabic dataset was constructed using data from various Arabic websites so as to study the efficacy of the light stemming algorithm. However, the dataset is accompanied by two main challenges including, how to specify the Arabic language, and how to deal with the text corruption. After that, a comparison is done between the light stemmer that has been proposed in this study and ISRI root stemming using the same dataset and conditions.

This rest of the paper is organized as follows: Sect. 2 presents some previous related works. In Sect. 3, the proposed stemmer algorithm is introduced. Section 4 describes the Arabic dataset and presents the experimental results. Finally, the conclusion and future works are presented in Sect. 6.

2 Literature Review

Many researchers worked with Arabic stemming in different fields including text mining. Most of these researchers aimed to enhance the stemming process to be applied in training various applications such as search engines, machine learning, translation, etc. The studies reviewed are selected based on their relationship with the current study. The following is a review of the most related works about light stemming with a summary, in which the limitations in the related literature are stated.

Zeroual et al. [20], the authors improved Arabic light stemming using linguistic resources based on Kohja stemmer. Two important phases were proposed; in the first phase all possible clitics and checking for correct stem are eliminated, while in the second phase, dictionary of Arabic linguistic resources such as pattern, proper nouns, and utilities words were used. Clitics which are linguistic unit attached to stem, are pronounced and written as an affix. The Alkhalil morphological analyzer contains a list of clitics [21], which have been extended by another clitics such as Mujam Al-Arab being an important reference for Arabic grammar. The application of this method was applied on Quranic corpus in order to remove prefix and suffix, and the results showed that the proposed method outperformed Kohja.

A novel approach was introduced by Aldabbas et al. [22] based on the regular expression with the aim of checking if a word is related to its text or not. This method involves two phases which are, regular expression and Microsoft word dictionary. The proposed approach achieved between 73.3 and 79.6 in term of accuracy. The dictionary was used to find words' meaning, and to also check if there is a similarity between words and patterns. Another light stemming was proposed by Khedr et al. [23] for the enhancement of the process of search in the Arabic language during data mining based on rules. Furthermore, the authors extended the stemming approach proposed by El-Beltagy et al. [24] with the aim of improving the accuracy. The result of their study indicated improved accuracy (by 10% on average). This algorithm has two phases; the first phase involves the creation of a dictionary belonging to a domain, while the second phase performs the stemming task. Their experimental results showed that the proposed algorithm achieved high accuracy because it works with a special domain (e.g., politics, sports etc.) and has a dictionary.

Abainia et al. [25] proposed a new approach for Arabic light stemming based on rules building for the removal of prefix, suffix, and affix. The proposed approach deals with Arabic infixes by considering irregular rules. A comparative analysis was carried based on a number of parameters including, stemming weight (SW), under stemming index (UI), and over stemming index (OI). There are six steps involved in the proposed algorithm; normalization, prefix, suffix, plural to the singular form, feminine to the masculine form, and verb stems. Basically, this work focused in Arabic infixes, as well as the evaluation of works dealing with Arabic infixes. The new Arabic dataset (ARASTEM) was used for the evaluation.

In 2018 two researchers proposed two methods using light stemming. The first method which was proposed by Al-Lahham et al. [26], makes use of light-10 stemming to remove prefix and suffix from a word. The authors made addition of affixes in light-10 so as to make it three words attachments, prefix, suffix and affixes. However, this method adds extra words for prefix and suffix, while creating a list of affix words. This method demonstrated better precision than light-10 stemming. The second method, which was proposed by Al-Abweeny et al. [27], is an improved Arabic stemming for text retrieval using stemming rules. The word was matched with suitable rules based on some characters in order to return all roots of the word. This method returns the word which belongs to rule roots such as 3, 4, 5, and 6. In addition, this method removes prefix, suffix and infixes from the word.

Mustafa et al. [28] proposed two different methods of stemming. The first, being light-10, involves the addition of extra prefix and suffix to verbs. The second one which is linguistic with different patterns, has been used for different parts of speech. In this work, this proposed work classified into verb and nouns. In an event that failure occurs in the classification, the part of speech is used. For verb, the Khoja algorithm is employed, while for noun, the proposed methods are used. The proposed method has different patterns with the extra character for suffix and prefix. Table 1 contains a summary of light Arabic stemming.

One of the limitations of the first three methods is the deployment of a dictionary that is limited for a specific domain. Moreover, building and managing the dictionary takes time, before using the dictionary and during using it for stemming. The Abainia et al. [25] method has many parameters, and all these parameters need to be configured for the relevant domain because of the fact that it deals with noisy texts. Al-Lahham

Table 1. Summary of light Arabic stemming

Author	Preprocessing	Dataset	Method
Zeroual et al. [20]	Yes	Quranic	This algorithm is based on khoja stemming and dictionary
Aldabbas et al. [22]	Yes	1000 words extract them from articles	Used regular expression with Microsoft word dictionary
Khedr et al. [23]	Yes	Elixir and Arabic Wikipedia	This algorithm is based on El-Beltagy et al. [24] algorithm with dictionary belonging to domain
Abainia et al. [25]	Yes	ARASTEM	Based on rules for removing prefixes, suffixes, and infixes
Al-Lahham et al. [26]	Yes	TREC2002	Based on light-10 stemming, with addition of some prefix and suffix. This work focused on the removal of prefix, suffix, and affix
Al-Abweeny et al. [27]	Yes	Almojaz and Alshamel	Based on the root stemming, and it removes suffixes, prefixes, and infixes
Mustafa et al. [28]	Yes	TREC2001	Based on light-10 stemming and adding into prefixes and suffix. POS is used for nouns and Khoja stem is used for the verb

et al. [26] was based on light-10 method adding the infix as an extra character to a prefix and suffix. Although the addition of infixes to the method was helpful in word stemming, infixes result in confusing many words while stemming them. Furthermore, the proposed method added more prefixes and suffixes, which results in more word deconstruction that might lead to missing the intended meaning. Al-Abweeny et al. [27] utilized stemming rules extracted from roots stemming. They established many patterns to delete the suffixes, prefixes and infixes. Yet, these patterns require too many steps in performing the stemming process. As it was the case in Al-Lahham et al. [26], this method resulted in more words deconstruction and consequently the risk of missing the intended meaning is too high. Mustafa et al. [28] extended light-10 stemming, and used linguistic to enhance the stemming process. The proposed method was accurate;

however, it was time consuming with too many steps. Besides, this method was difficult to apply as it includes several operation techniques.

3   Proposed Methods

In the field of stemming, Arabic is one of the languages that has high level of privacy. Due to the fact that it is a robust language characterized by great number of synonyms and rich vocabulary, alongside several grammar rules, it requires special rules on how to handle the addition that is made on the word of suffixes and prefixes. By so doing, all the words that have been obtained from one origin can be returned to the original, and then represented in one form. More so, when this stemmer is implemented, it results in the reduction of both space and time complexity, thereby decreasing the performance and efficiency of all rules. In this study, the authors have presented an Arabic Light stemmer through the modification of ISRI, which is number of rules that ascertain the manner in which the stemming can be applied on a certain word or not, the pre-processing steps, elimination of waw, suffixes and prefixes in Arabic Light Stemmer as illustrated in Fig. 1.

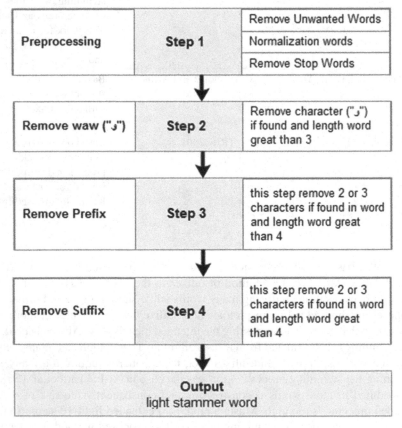

Fig. 1. Proposed model

3.1 Preprocessing

Generally, text contains a lot of noise data like punctuation, numbers, non-Arabic word, Arabic diacritics, and other types of noises. These noisy data may make the extraction of influential words from text difficult. Therefore, it is necessary to apply a preprocessing method to enable the elimination of these data, since they are not meaningful [29]. This removes unwanted words involves many unnecessary words such as punctuation marks, Arabic or English numbers, non-Arabic characters or words, etc. This can be achieved by several of regular expressions [30].

Arabic text normalization is the process through which textual contents are remodeled into one canonical structure. In this work, text has been normalized and transformed into a single form, because Arabic words have many shapes that make it highly dimensional and reduces accuracy. The normalization process involves three steps including, removal of diacritics, removal of tatweel, normalization of letters [31, 32]. In order to eliminate the Arabic, stop word, the words will have to be matched with the Arabic stop words list, and then filtered out. The stop words list is a built-in NLTK library where all words (i.e. 243 words) are sign words [33]. The following algorithm shown steps of preprocessing [34].

Algorithm 1: Preprocessing

Input: list of Words
$W = \{w_1, w_2, w_3, \dots, w_r\}$, where r number of words
$SW = \{sw_1, sw_2, sw_3, \dots, sw_m\}$, list of stop words
$U = \{u_1, u_2, u_3, \dots, u_r\}$, apply regular expression on W
$N = \{n_1, n_2, n_3, \dots, n_r\}$, apply normalization on U
$S = \{\ \}$, new words list
Procedure
    For $n_i \in N$ do
      For $sw_j \in SW$ do
        If n_i not in sw_j then
          S. append (n_i)
        Else
          Continue
      End For
    End For
Output:
  S, new word list

B) Step 2
In this step, waw (" و") is removed; the presence or absence waw (" و") letter depends on the length of the word, as shown in formula (1).

$$word + \ waw(و) = \begin{cases} word & if \ length \ (word) \geq 4 \\ word + waw(و) & else \end{cases} \tag{1}$$

C) Step 3

The presence or absence of prefix depends on the length of the word and the number of letters as shown in formula (2). The letter for matching patterns is shown in Table 2.

$$word + prefix = \begin{cases} word & if \ (length(word) \geq 5) \ and \ (letter == 2) \\ word & if \ (length(word) \geq 6) \ and \ (letter == 3) \\ word + prefix & else \end{cases} \quad (2)$$

Table 2. Prefix letter

Length of word	Letter Removed from word	Letters
p>=5	2	ال , لل
p>=6	3	كال , بال , ولل , وال

D) Step 4

The final step involves the removal of the common suffixes, but only if the remaining word has a minimum of five characters, as shown in formula (3). Table 3 shows the letter.

$$word + suffix = \begin{cases} word & if \ (length(word) \geq 5) \ and \ (letter == 2) \\ word & if \ (length(word) \geq 6) \ and \ (letter == 3) \\ word + suffix & else \end{cases} \quad (3)$$

Table 3. Suffix letter

Length of word	Letter Removed from word	Letters
s>=5	2	ون , ات , ان , ين , تن , كم , هن , نا , يا , ها , تم , كن, ني, وا , مارهم
s>=6	3	تمل , همل , تان , كمل , تين

The proposed stemmer consists of several steps as shown in algorithm 2.

Algorithm 2: Light stemmer

Input: list of words

$S = \{s_1, s_2, s_3, \dots, s_i\}$, list of words from preprocessing step

$LS = \{ \ \}$, list of light stem word

Procedure

For s_i in S do

    a) Using formula (1) for removing ("ال")

    b) Using formula (2) for removing prefix

    c) Using formula (3) for removing suffix

  $LS.\,appeand(s_i)$

Output:

  LS, list of light stemming words

---

4 Experimental Results

4.1 Dataset Description

To evaluate the proposed light stemming algorithm, a new dataset known as political Arabic article dataset (PAAD) was created [35]. This dataset will be released under an open-source license and will be freely available for download at Mendeley repository.[1] The Political Arabic dataset includes 206 Arabic articles with different lengths that can be categorised into 3 categories, including Reform, Conservative and Revolutionary as shown in Table 4.

Table 4. Dataset description

Article number	Arabic label	English label
80	تيار اصلاحي	Reform
58	تيار محافظ	Conservative
68	تيار ثوري	Revolutionary

The text articles are related to three topics of different lengths. Table 5 shows the statistic for each class.

Table 5. The different statistics for each class of dataset

Statistical	Conservative	Reform	Revolutionary	Total
Number of all word	14111	29607	23853	67571
Number of English words	65	110	7	182
Number of punctuations	704	1478	1265	3447

4.2 Experiments and Result

In Fig. 2, Arabic texts may contain punctuations, numbers, or English words. So, such words have been removed from the text. Upon completion of pre-processing operation, a list of words is automatically extracted from each text based on white spaces. Subsequently, stop words are removed from the text as shown in Fig. 3. Lastly, the final lists of words are kept and saved in list S.

Upon completion of the pre-processing step, three rules of light stemming are applied and the output is presented in Fig. 4. The number of words in Fig. 2 is 120, but after preprocessing it can be seen from Fig. 3 that the number of words becomes 84. The Fig. 4 shows the light stemming, while Fig. 5 shows the root stemming.

---

[1] https://data.mendeley.com/datasets/spvbf5bgjs.

أن المشكلة الأساسية في العراق تكمن في انحراف العملية السياسية في العراق من حيث بنية النظام السياسي والخلل القائم في بنية النظام   (المحاصصة الطائفية والقومية) الذي يمثل الركيزة الأساسية في النظام السياسي العراقي بعد عام 2003 والذي أدى إلى تدهور الأوضاع وساعد على تعميق الأزمات بدلاً من حلها . فقد بات من الضروري العمل على إجراء عملية إصلاح شامل في بنية النظام السياسي العراقي. لان النظام أُسس في ظروفٍ استثنائية، يشوبها الكثير من الأخطاء وعلامات الاستفهام , كذلك القول أن المتابع لأي مجتمع من المجتمعات البشرية يجد أن عملية بناء المجتمع واتجاهه نحو بناء نفسه وتكامله لا يمكن أن تتم إلا عن طريق الإصلاح أي من خلال مجموعة من الحركات الإصلاحية الهادفة إلى تقويم مسار هذه المجتمعات .

Fig. 2. Original Arabic article

المشكله الاساسيه العراق تكمن انحراف العمليه السياسيه العراق حيث بنيه النظام السياسي والخلل القائم بنيه النظام المحاصصه الطائفيه والقوميه يمثل الركيزه الاساسيه النظام السياسي العراقي عام ادي تدهور الاوضاع وساعد تعميق الازمات بدلا حلها فقد بات الضروري العمل اجراء عمليه اصلاح شامل بنيه النظام السياسي العراقي لان النظام اسس ظروف يشوبها الكثير الاخطاء وعلامات الاستفهام القول المتابع لاي مجتمع المجتمعات البشريه يجد عمليه بناء المجتمع واتجاهه نحو بناء نفسه وتكاملها لا يمكن تتم الا طريق الاصلاح خلال مجموعه الحركات الاصلاحيه الهادفه تقويم مسار المجتمعات

Fig. 3. Preprocessing on Arabic article

مشكله اساسيه عراق تكمن انحراف عمليه سياسيه عراق حيث بنيه نظام سياسي خلال قاعم بنيه نظام محاصصه طاءفيه قوميه يمثل ركيزه اساسيه نظام سياسي عراقي عام ادي تدهور اوضاع ساعد تعميق ازم بدلا حلها فقد بات ضروري عمل اجراء عمليه اصلاح شامل بنيه نظام سياسي عراقي لان نظام اسس ظروف يشوب كثير اخطاء علام استفهام قول متابع لاي مجتمع مجتمع بشريه يجد عمليه بناء مجتمع اتجاهه نحو بناء نفسه تكامل لا يمكن تتم الا طريق اصلاح خلال مجموعه حرك اصلاحيه هادفه تقويم مسار مجتمع.

Fig. 4. Arabic light stemming

ان شكل سسي في عرق تكم في حرف عمل سيس في عرق من حيث بنة نظم سيس خلل قنم في بنة نظم (حصص طنف قوم) الذي مثل ركز سسي في نظم سيس عرق بعد عام 2003 والذي ادى الى دهر وضع سعد على عمق ازم بدل من حله . فقد بات من ضرر عمل على جرء عمل صلح شمل في بنة نظم سيس عراقي. لان نظم اسس في ظرف استثنائية، يشب كثر من خطء علم ءلم فهم , كذلك قول ان تبع لأي جمع من جمع بشر يجد ان عمل بنء جمع وتج نحو بنء نفس كمل لا يمكن ان تتم الا عن طرق صلح اي من خلال جمع من حرك صلح هدف الى

Fig. 5. Arabic root stemming

As it can be seen in Fig. 4, the number of words is 84, and Fig. 5 shows the root stemming with 120 words. Table 6 shows the comparison between the original ISRI, and proposed light algorithm.

4.3 Comparative Analysis

Table 6 shows the number of words, these words compared between root stemming (original) and light stemming (based on original stemming). In this case used different words from PAAD to give more explanation between these two methods.

Table 6. Comparison between light and root stemming

No	Word	Correct meaning	ISRI root stem	ISRI light stem (proposed method)	
1	الاصلاح	اصلاح	صلح	اصلاح	Step 3
2	اصلاح	اصلاح	صلح	اصلاح	-
3	ثوره	ثوره	ثور	ثوره	-
4	الثوره	ثوره	ثور	ثوره	Step 3
5	الثورات	ثوره	ثور	ثور	Step 3 and Step 4
6	سياسه	سياسه	سيس	سياسه	-
7	السياسه	سياسه	سيس	سياسه	Step 3
8	محافظ	محافظ	حفظ	محافظ	-
9	المحافظون	محافظ	حفظ	محافظ	Step 3 and Step 4
10	والمحافظون	محافظ	حفظ	محافظ	Step 2, Step 3, and Step 4
11	حزب	حزب	حزب	حزب	-
12	الاحزاب	حزب احزاب	حزب	احزاب	Step 3
Similarity number			5 words	7 words	

It can be observed that there are 12 words in the Table 6, so repeated words are removed using the root stemmer. Afterwards, the words are reduced to 5, but when a light stemmer is used, the words become 7. As seen, the word for human is very clear in light stemmer, only the word (" ثور ") becomes (" سياسه "). Root stemmer uses infix that is why a word such as (" سيس ") becomes (" سيس "), therefore, losing its meaning. Table 7 shows the number of words in each class for PAAD dataset in both root and light stemming.

Table 7. Comparison between root and light stemming

Corpus	Numbers of words		
	Conservative	Reform	Revolutionary
Root stemming	13259	27617	22375
Light stemming	9428	19834	16298

The Table 7 *shows* the number of words in each class for PAAD dataset. It can be seen that the application of pre-processing steps to the dataset is very effective in increasing the number of words. As we can see the root stemmer has the higher number of words than light stemmer. In the table above, it can be seen that if there are three same words, then all the words should be counted as three. Root stemming works very well with machine learning, but if working with lexicon it becomes problematic. This is also the same for semantic, because it is difficult for humans to read and understand root stemming.

4.4 Comparison Between Proposed and Existing Light Stemming Methods

Arabic stemmers are widely used in many text processing tasks such as text categorization, information extraction, text summarization and search engine indexing. Therefore, evaluating and benchmarking these stemmers are crucial for researchers to select the best stemmer that suits their needs in a given context. In addition, authors are generally supposed to compare their stemmers with other works in order to demonstrate their contributions and enhancements. That is to say, NLP community should have common tools and resources to make fair evaluations of stemmers. In this study we compared our method (ISRL light stem) with four Arabic light stems as shown in Table 8.

Table 8. Comparison between proposed and other light stemming method

No	Word	Proposed method	Tashaphyne [36]	Snow-ball[37]	Assem's[38]	ARLSTem [25]	Correct meaning	Win
1	الاصلاح	اصلاح	اصلاح	اصلاح	اصلاح	صلح	اصلاح	√
2	اصلاح	اصلاح	صلاح	اصلاح	اصلاح	صلح	اصلاح	√
3	ثوره	ثوره	ثور	ثور	ثور	ثور	ثوره	√
4	الثوره	ثوره	ثور	ثور	ثور	ثور	ثوره	√
5	الثورات	ثور	ثور	ثور	ثور	ثور	ثوره	×
6	سياسه	سياسه	سياس	سياس	سياس	سياس	سياسه	√
7	السياسه	سياسه	سياس	سياس	سياس	سياسة	سياسه	√
8	محافظ	محافظ	محافظ	محافظ	محافظ	محافظ	محافظ	√
9	المحافظون	محافظ	محافظ	محافظ	محافظ	محافظ	محافظ	√
10	والمحافظون	محافظ	محافظ	والمحافظ	محافظ	محافظ	محافظ	√
11	حزب	حزب	حزب	حزب	حزب	حزب	حزب	√
12	الاحزاب	احزاب	احزاب	احزاب	احزاب	حزب	حزب احزاب	√
Total stem words	7	6	7	6	6			

As shown in Table 8 our method and Snowball are total stem words 7 and others work achieved 6. As shown our method still the words have same meaning as see in column correct meaning but others work the meaning different.

5 Discussion

In this study, the focus was on the problem of Arabic light stemming with the main aim of reducing the dimensionality of data while regrouping the words that are semantically and morphologically related. The major uniqueness of this study lies in the focus on Arabic language, which is quite different from several other languages. In this work, a light stemming has been proposed based on ISRI stemming algorithm, particularly for Arabic language. The proposed Arabic language light stemming does not require any dictionary of patterns or words. The proposed stemmer is considered as original because it induces some smart rules and stripping waw, prefixes or suffixes from the word. It also tries to minimize the confusion with original letters as much as possible. In this research, a comparative analysis was done between the proposed stemmer and ISRI stemmer. Therefore, a wide range of experiments were conducted on the newly created Arabic dataset, containing Arabic discussion preprocessing. In addition, three pre-processing steps have been proposed. More so, a list of stop words containing 25 stop words have been presented in this work, and the list is particularly tailored for discussion pre-processing texts.

6 Conclusion

Based on the results of the experiments, it can be concluded that the Arabic light stemmer proposed in this study is better than the ISRL stemming which was investigated. More so, the proposed light stemmer has demonstrated consistently good performance. However, despite the fact that the proposed stemmer demonstrated superior performance with encouraging results in terms of forum genre, it cannot be argued that it will stile demonstrate the same performance in every text genre. Consequently, it becomes crucial to determine the reliability of the proposed stemming by evaluating the performance of a wide variety of genres. This will help in ascertaining the most appropriate stemmer that should be used in each genre. For future works, an in-depth analyses of the Arabic word morphology will be carried out, focusing on the word infixes with the aim of further improving the efficiency of the stemmer.

References

1. Singh, J., Gupta, V.: Text stemming: approaches, applications, and challenges. ACM Comput. Surv. **49**(03), 1–46 (2016)
2. Harrag, F., El-Qawasmah, E., Al-Salman, A.M.S.: Stemming as a feature reduction technique for Arabic text categorization. İn: 2011 10th International Symposium on Programming and Systems, pp. 128–133 (2011)
3. Al-Anzi, F.S., AbuZeina, D.: Stemming impact on Arabic text categorization performance: a survey. İn: 2015 5th International Conference on Information & Communication Technology and Accessibility (ICTA), pp. 1–7. IEEE (2015)
4. Al-Abdallah, R.Z., Al-Taani, A.T.: Arabic text summarization using firefly algorithm. İn: 2019 Amity International Conference on Artificial Intelligence (AICAI), pp. 61–65. IEEE (2019)
5. Mansour, N., Haraty, R.A., Daher, W., Houri, M.: An auto-indexing method for Arabic text. Inform. Process. Manage. **44**(4), 1538–1545 (2008)
6. Utomo, M.R.A., Sibaroni, Y.: Text classification of British English and American English using support vector machine. In: 7th International Conference on Information and Communication Technology (ICoICT), pp. 1–6. IEEE (2019)
7. Savoy, J.: A stemming procedure and stopword list for general French corpora. J. Am. Soc. Inform. Sci. **50**(10), 944–952 (1999)

8. Gupta, V., Joshi, N., Mathur, I.: Advanced Machine Learning Techniques in Natural Language Processing for Indian Languages. In: Mishra, M.K., Mishra, B.S.P., Patel, Y.S., Misra, R. (eds.) Smart Techniques for a Smarter Planet. SFSC, vol. 374, pp. 117–144. Springer, Cham (2019). https://doi.org/10.1007/978-3-030-03131-2_7

9. Kassim, M., Jali, S., Maarof, M., Zainal, A.: Towards stemming error reduction for Malay texts. Presented at the (2019). https://doi.org/10.1007/978-981-13-2622-6_2

10. Otair, M.A.: Comparative analysis of Arabic stemming algorithms. Int. J. Manag. Inform. Technol. **5**(2), 1–13 (2013)

11. Abooraig, R., Al-, S., Kanan, T., Hawashin, B., Al , M., Hmeidi, I.: Automatic categorization of Arabic articles based on their political orientation. Digital Invest. **25**, 24–41 (2018)

12. Khoja, S., Garside, R.: Stemming Arabic Text. Computing Department, Lancaster University, Lancaster, UK (1999)

13. Larkey, L.S., Ballesteros, L., Connell, M.E.: Improving stemming for Arabic information retrieval: light stemming and co-occurrence analysis. İn: Proceedings of the 25th Annual İnternational ACM SIGIR Conference on Research and Development in İnformation Retrieval, pp. 275–282 (2002)

14. Taghva, K., Elkhoury, R., Coombs, J.: Arabic stemming without a root dictionary. İn: International Conference on Information Technology: Coding and Computing (ITCC2005)-Volume II, vol.1, pp. 152–157. IEEE (2005)

15. Khan, W., Kuru, K.: An intelligent system for spoken term detection that uses belief combination. IEEE Intell. Syst. **32**, 70–79 (2017)

16. Ezzeldin, A.M., Shaheen, M.: A survey of Arabic question answering: challenges, tasks, approaches, tools, and future trends. İn: Proceedings of The 13th International Arab Conference on Information Technology (ACIT 2012), pp. 1–8 (2012)

17. Oraby, S., El-Sonbaty, Y., El-Nasr, M.A.: Exploring the effects of word roots for arabic sentiment analysis. İn: Proceedings of the Sixth International Joint Conference on Natural Language Processing, pp. 471–479 (2013)

18. Ezzeldin, A., El-, A., Kholief, M.: Exploring the Effects of Root Expansion. College of Computing and Information Technology, AASTMT, Alexandria, Egypt (2013)

19. Kreaa, A.H., Ahmad, A.S., Kabalan, K.: Arabic words stemming approach using Arabic WordNet. Int. J. Data Mining Knowl. Manage. Process. **4**(6), 1–14 (2014)

20. Zeroual, I., Boudchiche, M., Mazroui, A., Lakhouaja, A.: Improving Arabic light stemming algorithm using linguistic resources. In: The Second National Doctoral Symposium on Arabic Language Engineering (JDILA2015). Fez, Morocco (2015)

21. Boudchiche, M., Mazroui A., Bebah, A., Lakhouaja, A., Boudlal, A.: L'Analyseur Morphosyntaxique AlKhalil Morpho Sys 2. İn: 1ère Journée Doctorale Nationale sur l'Ingénierie de la Langue Arabe (JDILA2014), pp. 1–5 (2014)

22. Aldabbas, O., Al-Shalabi, R., Kanan, G., Shehabd, M.A.: Arabic light stemmer based on regular expression. İn: Proceedings of the International Computer Sciences and Informatics Conference (ICSIC 2016), pp. 1–9 (2016)

23. Khedr, S., Sayed, D., Hanafy, A.: Arabic light stemmer for better search accuracy. Int. J. Cognit. Lang. Sci. **10**(11), 3587–3595 (2016)

24. El-, S.R., Rafea, R.: An accuracy-enhanced light stemmer for Arabic text. ACM Trans. Speech Lang. Process. **7**(02), 1–22 (2010)

25. Abainia, K., Ouamour, S., Sayoud, H.: A novel robust Arabic light stemmer. J. Exp. Theor. Artif. Intell. **29**(03), 557–573 (2017)

26. Al-, Y.A., Matarneh, K., Hasan, M.: Conditional Arabic light stemmer: condlight. Int. Arab J. Inform. Technol. **15**(03), 559–564 (2018)

27. Al-, W.W., Zaid, N.A.: Arabic stemmer system based on rules of roots. Int. J. Inform. Technol. Lang. Stud. **2**(1), 19–26 (2018)

28. Mustafa, M., Aldeen, A., Zidan, M., Ahmed, R., Eltigani, Y.: Developing two different novel techniques for Arabic text stemming. Intell. Inform. Manage. **11**(01), 1–23 (2019). https://doi.org/10.4236/iim.2019.111001

29. Abd, D.H., Abbas, A.R., Sadiq, A.T.: Analyzing sentiment system to specify polarity by lexicon-based. Bull. Electr. Eng. Inform. **10**(1), 283–289 (2020)

30. Abd, D., Sadiq, A., Abbas, A.: Political Articles Categorization Based on Different Naïve Bayes Models. In: Khalaf, M.I., Al-Jumeily, D., Lisitsa, A. (eds.) Applied Computing to Support Industry: Innovation and Technology: First International Conference, ACRIT 2019, Ramadi, Iraq, September 15–16, 2019, Revised Selected Papers, pp. 286–301. Springer International Publishing, Cham (2020). https://doi.org/10.1007/978-3-030-38752-5_23

31. Abd, D., Sadiq, A., Abbas, A.: Classifying Political Arabic Articles Using Support Vector Machine with Different Feature Extraction. In: Khalaf, M.I., Al-Jumeily, D., Lisitsa, A. (eds.) ACRIT 2019. CCIS, vol. 1174, pp. 79–94. Springer, Cham (2020). https://doi.org/10.1007/978-3-030-38752-5_7

32. Alwan, J.K., Hussain, J., Abd, D.H., Sadiq, A.T., Khalaf, M., Liatsis, P.: Political Arabic articles orientation using rough set theory with sentiment lexicon. IEEE Access **09**, 24475–24484 (2021)

33. Hardeniya, N., Perkins, J., Chopra, D., Joshi, N., Mathur, I.: Natural Language Processing: Python and NLTK. Packt Publishing Ltd (2016)

34. Abd, D.H., Sadiq, A.T., Abbas, A.R.: Political Arabic articles classification based on machine learning and hybrid vector. In: 2020 5th International Conference on Innovative Technologies in Intelligent Systems and Industrial Applications (CITISIA), pp. 1–7. IEEE (2020)

35. Abbas, A.R., Sadiq, A.T., Abd, D.H.: PAAD: political Arabic articles dataset for automatic text categorization. Iraq. J. Comput. Inform. **46**(01), 1–11 (2020)

36. Jaafar, Y., Bouzoubaa, K.: A survey and comparative study of Arabic NLP architectures. In: Shaalan, K., Hassanien, A.E., Tolba, F. (eds.) Intelligent Natural Language Processing: Trends and Applications. SCI, vol. 740, pp. 585–610. Springer, Cham (2018). https://doi.org/10.1007/978-3-319-67056-0_28

37. Porter, M.F.: Snowball: A Language for Stemming Algorithms, https://snowballstem.org/credits.html (2001)

38. Chelli, A.: Assem's Arabic Stemmer. https://arabicstemmer.com/ (2018)

Biomedical Informatics Theory
and Methods

Predicting miRNA-Disease Associations via a New MeSH Headings Representation of Diseases and eXtreme Gradient Boosting

Bo-Ya Ji[1,2,3], Zhu-Hong You[1,2,3(✉)], Lei Wang[1,3], Leon Wong[1,2,3], Xiao-Rui Su[1,2,3], and Bo-Wei Zhao[1,2,3]

[1] Xinjiang Technical Institutes of Physics and Chemistry, Chinese Academy of Sciences, Urumqi 830011, China
zhuhongyou@ms.xjb.ac.cn
[2] University of Chinese Academy of Sciences, Beijing 100049, China
[3] Xinjiang Laboratory of Minority Speech and Language Information Processing, Urumqi, China

Abstract. Taking into account the intrinsic high cost and time-consuming in traditional Vitro studies, a computational approach that can enable researchers to easily predict the potential miRNA-disease associations is imminently required. In this paper, we propose a computational method to predict potential associations between miRNAs and diseases via a new MeSH headings representation of diseases and eXtreme Gradient Boosting algorithm. Particularly, a novel MeSH-Heading2vec method is first utilized to obtain a higher-quality MeSH heading representation of diseases, and then it is fused with miRNA functional similarity, disease semantic similarity and Gaussian interaction profile kernel similarity information to efficiently represent miRNA-disease pairs. Second, the deep auto-encoder neural network is adopted to extract the more representative feature subspace from the initial feature set. Finally, the eXtreme Gradient Boosting (XGBoost) algorithm is implemented for training and prediction. In the 5-fold cross-validation experiment, our method obtained average accuracy and AUC of 0.8668 and 0.9407, which performed better than many existing works.

Keywords: miRNA-disease associations · Multiple similarities fusion · MeSH headings representation · Deep auto-encoder neural network · eXtreme Gradient Boosting

1 Introduction

Multiple experiments continue to prove the essential roles of miRNAs in various biologic processes, such as proliferation [1], metabolism [2], apoptosis [3], viral infection [4] and cell development [5]. As reported by previous researches, miRNAs are being therapeutic/diagnostic instruments for diseases and also possible prognostic biomarkers. For instance, the level of expression of hsa-mir-21 is correlated to more than 125 diseases and miR-185 plays a key function in breast cancer [6]. Consequently, detecting potential

© Springer Nature Switzerland AG 2021
D.-S. Huang et al. (Eds.): ICIC 2021, LNAI 12838, pp. 49–56, 2021.
https://doi.org/10.1007/978-3-030-84532-2_5

relationships between miRNAs and diseases is valuable for the diagnosis and treatment of complex human diseases. Nevertheless, considering the massive time-consuming and high cost we have to invest in conducting traditional experiments to confirm a single miRNA-disease association, it is difficult to confirm the potential associations one by one. Thereby, it is appropriate and meaningful to select the most possible associations to confirm in the biological labs first. Furthermore, there are several confirmed miRNA-disease databases that can be used as resources for prediction, we can build computational models to forecast possible miRNA-disease associations. Depended on the hypothesis that miRNAs that have similar functionalities seem to be more probably to have associations with diseases that have similar phenotypes, different computational approaches have been employed in the field of possible miRNA-disease association prediction [7–11]. For instance, You et al. [12] proposed a prediction method of path-based miRNA-disease association (PBMDA) by combining the semantic similarity of diseases, Gaussian interaction profile kernel similarity, known human miRNA-disease associations, and functional similarity of miRNAs. They firstly developed a heterogeneous network composed of three interconnected sub-networks, and then the depth-first search (DFS) method was adopted. Motivated by the successful implementation of machine learning methods in the bioinformatics field, several researchers utilized supervised machine learning algorithms for inferring underlying miRNA-disease associations [13–17]. For instance, Wang et al. [18] introduced a logistic tree method to identify miRNA-disease associations (LMTRDA). They first combined a variety of information, including miRNA sequence information, known miRNA-disease associations, miRNA functional similarity and disease semantic similarity. Then, a logical model tree classifier was applied for training and prediction. In this article, we propose a new computational method for predicting potential miRNA-disease associations via a new MeSH headings representation of diseases and eXtreme Gradient Boosting algorithm.

2 Methods and Materials

2.1 Human miRNA-Disease Associations

In this article, we evaluate our proposed model utilizing the Human microRNA Disease Database (HMDD) v3.0 [19], which contains 32281 miRNA-disease associations from 17412 papers, including 1102 miRNAs and 850 diseases. Then, we removed some miRNAs because the public database miRBase deemed their information unreliable. Finally, 32226 miRNA-disease associations including 1057 miRNAs and 850 diseases were used as the positive dataset for our experiment. For the negative dataset, we randomly picked 32226 miRNA-disease associations from all possible miRNA-disease pairs which have removed the positive dataset.

2.2 MiRNA Functional Similarity

Wang et al. [20] calculated the functional similarity among various miRNAs depended on the hypothesis that miRNAs that have similar functionalities seem to be more probably to have associations with diseases that have similar phenotypes. In this work, we selected this functional similarity score matrix as the miRNA function similarity information (MF), which can be obtained at http://www.cuilab.cn/files/images/cuilab/misim.zip. For the element in the matrix, $MF(m_1, m_2)$ means the similarity score between the miRNA m_1 and the miRNA m_2.

2.3 Gaussian Interaction Profile (GIP) Kernel Similarity for miRNA and Disease

Depended on the hypothesis that miRNAs that have similar functionalities seem to be more probably to have associations with diseases that have similar phenotypes and vice versa, we further calculated the GIP kernel similarity for diseases and miRNAs [21]. Particularly, we first built the miRNA-disease adjacency matrix (MD), which has 1057 columns and 850 rows, related to 1057 miRNAs and 850 diseases. For the element in the matrix, if miRNA m_i is associated with disease d_j on HMDD v3.0 database, $MD(m_i, d_j)$ of the adjacency matrix is equal to 1, otherwise, it is equal to 0. On this basis, the interaction profiles of miRNA mi can be represented by the binary vector $MD(m_i)$, which is the i-row vector of the adjacency matrix MD. The Gaussian interaction profile kernel similarity between miRNA m_i and miRNA m_j was calculated by:

$$GM(m_i, m_j) = \exp(-\delta_m \|MD(m_i) - MD(m_j)\|^2) \tag{1}$$

where δ_m is the bandwidth of kernel that can be obtained through normalizing the original parameter:

$$\delta_m = \frac{1}{m} \sum_{i=1}^{m} \|MD(m_i)\|^2 \tag{2}$$

where m is the total number of rows in the adjacency matrix MD.

Similarly, GIP kernel similarity between disease d_i and disease d_j can be obtained by:

$$GD(d_i, d_j) = \exp(-\delta_d \|MD(d_i) - MD(d_j)\|^2) \tag{3}$$

$$\delta_d = \frac{1}{d} \sum_{i=1}^{d} \|MD(d_i)\|^2 \tag{4}$$

where $MD(d_i)$ and d respectively are the i-column vector and the total number of columns in the adjacency matrix MD.

2.4 Disease Semantic Similarity

The Medical Subject Heading (MeSH) database is a specific disease classification system, available from the U.S. National Library of Medicine (https://www.nlm.nih.gov/). On this basis, each disease can be described by a Directed Acyclic Graph (DAG). For instance, a disease i can be defined as $DAG(i) = (i, T(i), E(i))$, in which $T(i)$ is composed of node i and its ancestor nodes, $E(i)$ composed of their relevant edges. Besides, the contribution of disease d in DAG(i) to the semantic value of disease i was described as:

$$DV(i) = \sum_{d \in T(i)} D_i(d) \tag{5}$$

$$\begin{cases} D_i(d) = 1 & \text{if } d = i \\ D_i(d) = \max\{\Delta * D_i(d') | d' \in \text{children of } d\} & \text{if } d \neq i \end{cases} \tag{6}$$

where Δ is the semantic contribution factor. It can be observed that two diseases have higher similarity scores if they have a larger shared portion. Therefore, the semantic similarity score (DS) between two diseases (d_i, d_j) could be obtained by:

$$DS(d_i, d_j) = \frac{\sum_{t \in T(d_i) \cap T(d_j)} (D_{d_i}(t) + D_{d_j}(t))}{DV(d_i) + DV(d_j)} \tag{7}$$

2.5 MeSHHeading2vec Method

In order to get higher-quality representation vectors of diseases, Guo et al. [22] proposed a novel method called MeSHHeading2vec to represent diseases. The new disease representation vector obtained by the MeSHHeading2vec method had a better performance than the semantic similarity obtained based on the DAGs of diseases in the prediction of miRNA-disease associations. Specifically, MeSHHeading2vec firstly connected different Mesh headings to transform the MeSH tree structure of diseases into a relationship network. In the network, the label (category) of each node (MeSH heading) is determined by its corresponding tree number pattern. Secondly, a brief analysis is made on the degree of nodes, the label distribution, and the number of nodes and edges. Thirdly, the network embedding method such as SDNE [23], LINE [24], HOPE [25], DeepWalk [26] and LAP [27] was used on the network to obtain the low-dimensional dense vectors of diseases while preserving the original network structure and node relationship information. In this paper, we utilized the MeSHHeading2vec method to represent the diseases in our dataset, and the LINE method which has a better performance than other network embedding methods was selected to extract the disease features (DM).

2.6 Multi-source Feature Fusion

In this paper, we respectively represented miRNA and disease by fusing multiple features of them to catch their characteristics from different angles. For the feature of miRNAs, we obtained miRNA functional similarity (MF) and miRNA Gaussian interaction profile kernel similarity (GM). In this way, the miRNA feature matrix MFM(m_i, m_j) can be achieved by the formula as follows:

$$MFM(m_i, m_j) = \begin{cases} MF(m_i, m_j), & \text{if } m_i \text{ and } m_j \text{ has functional similarity} \\ GM(m_i, m_j), & \text{Otherwise} \end{cases} \tag{8}$$

For the feature of diseases, we calculated the new Meshheading representation feature (DM), Gaussian interaction profile kernel similarity (GD), and semantic similarity (DS). In this way, the disease feature matrix $DFM(d_i, d_j)$ can be achieved by the formula as follows:

$$DFM(d_i, d_j) = \begin{cases} DM(d_i, d_j) & \text{if } d_i \text{ and } d_j \text{ has Meshheading feature} \\ DS(d_i, d_j) & \text{if } d_i \text{ and } d_j \text{ has no Meshheading feature} \\ GD(d_i, d_j) & \text{otherwise} \end{cases} \quad (9)$$

3 Experimental Results

Cross-validation is a mathematical approach widely employed to measure the skill of machine learning models. Generally, it has a lower bias than other methods in skill estimates, and it is easy to implement and understand. In this work, we applied the 5-fold cross-validation method to verify the predictive ability of our method. Specifically, we randomly shuffle the dataset and then split the dataset into 5 groups. The first group is used as a test dataset, and the model is fit based on the rest of 4 groups. We repeated the experiment five times and recorded six commonly used indicators including accuracy (Acc.), specificity (Spec.), sensitivity (Sen.), matthews correlation coefficient (MCC), precision (Prec.) and the area under the ROC curve (AUC). Furthermore, two diagnostic tools (Receiver Operating Characteristic curves and Precision-Recall curves) were selected to help interpret the classification predictive model. The ROC and PR curves respectively summarize the tradeoffs between the true positive rate and false positive rate, true positive rate and positive predictive value of prediction models using different probability thresholds. Table 1 shows the detailed results of our method in the 5-fold cross-validation experiment. The ROC curves and AUC values, PR curves and AUPR values are respectively shown in Figs. 1 and 2.

Table 1. The detailed results of our method under 5-fold cross-validation

Fold	ACC. (%)	Spec. (%)	Sen. (%)	MCC (%)	Prec. (%)	AUC (%)
0	86.82	86.95	86.69	73.64	86.92	94.16
1	86.99	86.45	87.53	73.98	86.60	94.30
2	86.80	86.52	87.08	73.59	86.59	94.02
3	85.94	85.76	86.13	71.89	85.81	93.70
4	86.86	87.01	86.70	73.72	86.97	94.17
Average	86.68 ± 0.42	86.54 ± 0.50	86.83 ± 0.52	73.36 ± 0.84	86.58 ± 0.46	94.06 ± 0.23

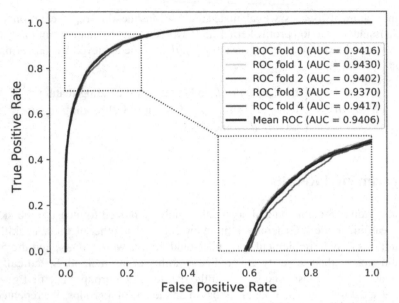

Fig. 1. The ROC curves of our method under 5-fold cross validation

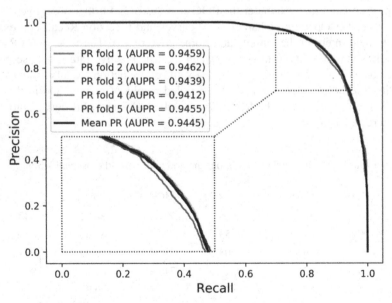

Fig. 2. The ROC curves of our method under 5-fold cross validation

4   Conclusions

Recently, the computational models for inferring underlying associations between miR-NAs and diseases have been the focus of researchers. In this paper, we proposed a new computational method by fusing multi-source features to predict potential miRNA-disease associations. One significant aspect of our method is the utilization of the MeSH-Heading2vec method to represent the MeSH headings of diseases as vectors and fuses it with disease semantic similarities, Gaussian interaction profile kernel similarity of miRNAs and diseases, miRNA functional similarity to construct feature descriptors. On this basis, the deep auto-encoder neural network and XGBoost classifier was respectively selected for feature extraction and prediction. Under the 5-fold cross-validation experiment, our method obtained excellent performance on the HMDD v3.0 dataset, which is better than many existing computational methods.

Funding. This work is supported by the Xinjiang Natural Science Foundation under Grant 2017D01A78 and National Natural Science Foundation of China under Grant NO. 62002297.

Conflict of Interest. The authors declare that they have no conflict of interest.

References

1. Cheng, A.M., et al.: Antisense inhibition of human miRNAs and indications for an involvement of miRNA in cell growth and apoptosis. Nucleic Acids Res. **33**(4), 1290–1297 (2005)
2. Alshalalfa, M., Alhajj, R.: Using context-specific effect of miRNAs to identify functional associations between miRNAs and gene signatures. BMC Bioinform. **14**(S12), S1 (2013)
3. Xu, P., Guo, M., Hay, B.A.: MicroRNAs and the regulation of cell death. Trends Genet. **20**(12), 617–624 (2004)
4. Griffiths-Jones, S.: miRBase: microRNA sequences and annotation. Curr. Protoc. Bioinform. **29**(1), 12.9.1-12.9.10 (2010)
5. Karp, X., Ambros, V.: Encountering microRNAs in cell fate signaling. Science **310**(5752), 1288–1289 (2005)
6. Wang, R., et al.: MiR-185 is involved in human breast carcinogenesis by targeting Vegfa. FEBS Lett. **588**(23), 4438–4447 (2014)
7. Ji, B.-Y., et al.: Predicting miRNA-disease association from heterogeneous information network with GraRep embedding model. Sci. Rep. **10**(1), 1–12 (2020)
8. Guo, Z.-H., You, Z.-H., Wang, Y.-B., Huang, D.-S., Yi, H.-C., Chen, Z.-H.: Bioentity2vec: Attribute- and behavior-driven representation for predicting multi-type relationships between bioentities. GigaScience **9**(6), giaa032 (2020)
9. Guo, Z.-H., et al.: A learning based framework for diverse biomolecule relationship prediction in molecular association network. Commun. Biol. **3**(1), 1–9 (2020)
10. Chen, X., Zhang, D.-H., You, Z.-H.: A heterogeneous label propagation approach to explore the potential associations between miRNA and disease. J. Transl. Med. **16**(1), 348 (2018)
11. Chen, X., et al.: BNPMDA: bipartite network projection for miRNA-disease association prediction. Bioinformatics **34**(18), 3178–3186 (2018)
12. You, Z.-H., et al.: PBMDA: A novel and effective path-based computational model for miRNA-disease association prediction. PLoS Comput. Biol. **13**(3), e1005455 (2017)
13. Zheng, K., et al.: MLMDA: a machine learning approach to predict and validate microRNA-disease associations by integrating of heterogenous information sources. J. Transl. Med. **17**(1), 260 (2019)

14. Xu, J., et al.: Prioritizing candidate disease miRNAs by topological features in the miRNA target-dysregulated network: case study of prostate cancer. Mol. Cancer Ther. **10**(10), 1857–1866 (2011)
15. Zhang, L., Chen, X., Yin, J.: Prediction of potential miRNA-disease associations through a novel unsupervised deep learning framework with variational autoencoder. Cells **8**(9), 1040 (2019)
16. Ji, B.-Y., et al.: NEMPD: a network embedding-based method for predicting miRNA-disease associations by preserving behavior and attribute information. BMC Bioinform. **21**(1), 1–17 (2020)
17. Ji, B.-Y., You, Z.-H., Wang, Y., Li, Z.-W., Wong, L.: DANE-MDA: predicting microRNA-disease associations via deep attributed network embedding. iScience **24**(6), 102455 (2021)
18. Wang, L., et al.: LMTRDA: using logistic model tree to predict miRNA-disease associations by fusing multi-source information of sequences and similarities. PLOS Comput. Biol **15**(3), e1006865 (2019)
19. Huang, Z., et al.: HMDD v3.0: a database for experimentally supported human microRNA–disease associations. Nucleic Acids Res. **47**(D1), D1013–D1017 (2019)
20. Wang, D., et al.: Inferring the human microRNA functional similarity and functional network based on microRNA-associated diseases. Bioinformatics **26**(13), 1644–1650 (2010)
21. van Laarhoven, T., Nabuurs, S.B., Marchiori, E.: Gaussian interaction profile kernels for predicting drug-target interaction. Bioinformatics **27**(21), 3036–3043 (2011)
22. Guo, Z.-H., et al.: MeSHHeading2vec: a new method for representing MeSH headings as vectors based on graph embedding algorithm. Brief. Bioinform. (2020)
23. Wang, D., Cui, P., Zhu, W.: Structural deep network embedding. In: Proceedings of the 22nd ACM SIGKDD International Conference on Knowledge Discovery and Data Mining (2016)
24. Tang, J., et al.: Line: large-scale information network embedding. In: Proceedings of the 24th International Conference on World Wide Web (2015)
25. Ou, M., et al.: Asymmetric transitivity preserving graph embedding. In: Proceedings of the 22nd ACM SIGKDD International Conference on Knowledge Discovery and Data Mining (2016)
26. Perozzi, B., Al-Rfou, R., Skiena, S.: Deepwalk: online learning of social representations. In: Proceedings of the 20th ACM SIGKDD International Conference on Knowledge Discovery and Data Mining (2014)
27. Belkin, M., Niyogi, P.: Laplacian eigenmaps and spectral techniques for embedding and clustering. Advances in Neural Information Processing Systems (2002)

Social Media Adverse Drug Reaction Detection Based on Bi-LSTM with Multi-head Attention Mechanism

Xuqi Wang, Wenzhun Huang, and Shanwen Zhang(✉)

School of Information Engineering, Xijing University, Xi'an 710123, China

Abstract. Social media text contains a large amount of adverse drug reaction (ADR) information, which is an important channel for ADR information extraction. It is difficult to extract the detection features from the social media text by the traditional ADR extraction methods. Convolutional neural network (CNN) and its variants have the disadvantages of low modeling efficiency and space insensitivity when constructing spatial information. An ADR detection method from social media text is proposed based on bidirectional short and long time memory network (Bi-LSTM) with multi-head attention mechanism (MHAM). After pretreatment on corpus to markers of adverse drug reactions, and constructs the distributed word vector features, part-of-speech tags, character vector and each sentence Chinese medicine things and emotional words as the characteristics of the model input, contrast experiments, to solve the lack of space relationship between features in the process of classification and building the model of the problem of low efficiency. Experimental results on SMM4H corpus validate that the proposed method is effective and has good performance in the detection of ADR events in social media. To improve the detection efficiency of ADRs, the multi-head attention mechanism is introduced bi-directional long short-term memory (Bi-LSTM). Experiment results on Social Media Mining for Health (SMM4H-2017) corpus dataset validate the proposed method can significantly improve the recognition and classification performance of ADRs.

Keywords: Adverse drug reactions (ADR) · Social media · Bidirectional short and long time memory (Bi-LSTM) · Multi-headed attention mechanism (MHAM)

1 Introduction

Understanding the appearance of ADRs in patients receiving treatment is important, and may be related to morbidity and mortality. ADRs caused by drugs are potentially life-threatening problems. ADRs have become the fourth leading cause of death in the United States, after heart disease, diabetes, and AIDS [1–3]. The adverse reactions caused by drugs also result in public health problems, millions of deaths and hospitalizations each year, and cost approximately US $7.5 billion per year [4, 5]. With the rapid growth of the number of drug types, it is essential to determine the safety of the drugs that are used.

© Springer Nature Switzerland AG 2021
D.-S. Huang et al. (Eds.): ICIC 2021, LNAI 12838, pp. 57–65, 2021.
https://doi.org/10.1007/978-3-030-84532-2_6

Detecting ADRs through clinical trials takes a large number of experiments and a long period of time. ADR is an important and challenging research in the field of biomedical science and even the society, and has attracted great attention in the world. But in practice it is impossible to investigate all the conditions and environments under which a drug can be used in a clinical trial, so it is also impossible to known all ADRs, then the issue of ADR detection is crucial [6]. Imam et al. [7] aimed to characterize the mechanisms underlying adverse drug reactions due to combination anti-tuberculosis therapy of the Revised National Tuberculosis Control Program (RNTCP). Huang et al. [8] proposed a two-stage method based on support vector machine (SVM) and bidirectional long short term memory network (LSTM). In the method, the positive instances are firstly defined using a feature based binary classifier, and LSTM based classifier is used to classify the positive instances into the specific category. To solve the problems of gradient explosion and disappearance in deep learning models, Kang et al. [9] proposed a research method of adverse drug reactions based on attention mechanism and fusion of emotional information, and constructed a neural network model, Attention based Convolutional neural networks and Bi-directional long short-Term Memory (ACB). With the rapid popularization of the internet and big data, social media such as Twitter has become the main platform for users and patients to share knowledge and exchange emotions [10]. On this platform, users will discuss their experiences and feelings about taking drugs for diseases, including the use of prescription drugs, side effects and therapeutic effects, which can provide with a large amount of data for ADR detection. Compared with traditional medical reports, such information on social media is more adequate, timelier and spread more quickly. Deep Learning has achieved great success in a variety of applications, including ADR detection [11–13].

Although the extension from Multilayer Perceptron (MLP) to Cyclic Neural Networks (RNN) may seem trivial, it has profound implications for sequence learning. Cyclic neural networks (RNN) are used to process sequence data. In the traditional neural network model, layers are fully connected, and nodes between layers are disconnected. But this kind of ordinary neural network can't solve many problems. For example, to predict what will be the next word in a sentence, you usually need to use the word before it, because the word before it is not independent of the word in a sentence. A recurrent neural network (RNN) is a sequence in which the current output is related to the previous output. The specific form is that the network will remember the previous information, save it in the internal state of the network, and apply it to the calculation of the current output, that is, the nodes between the hidden layer are no longer disconnected but linked, and the input of the hidden layer includes not only the output of the input layer but also the output of the previous hidden layer. In theory, the cyclic neural network can process the sequence data of any length, but in practice, in order to reduce the complexity, it often assumes that the current state is only related to the previous states. Deep learning with attention mechanism has recently been successful in a wide variety of tasks [14]. Attention mechanism can help the model assign different weights to each part of the input and extract more critical and important information, so that the model can make more accurate judgments without bringing more overhead to the calculation and storage of the model. This is also the reason why Attention Mechanism is so widely used. The attention mechanism is more suitable for reasoning the complex and difficult to explain mapping relationship between various modes of data [15]. Inspired by attention mechanism and Bi-LSTM, a Bi-LSTM with multi-head Attention Mechanism is proposed for ADR detection, and is test on a related corpus dataset of ADR.

The rest of the paper is organized as follows. Section 2 introduces attention mechanism and CNets. Section 3 presents an improved CNet with attention mechanism in detail. The experiments and results are presented in Sect. 4. Section 5 concludes and recommends future works.

2 Method

2.1 Bi-LSTM

The unit architecture of LSTM is shown in Fig. 1, consisting of forgetting gate, input gate, output gate and one memory unit.

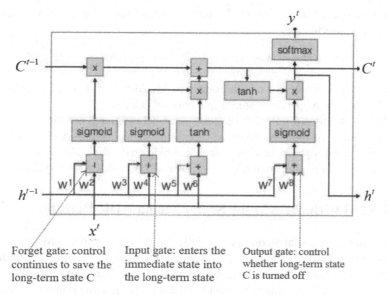

Forget gate: control continues to save the long-term state C

Input gate: enters the immediate state into the long-term state

Output gate: control whether long-term state C is turned off

Fig. 1. The architecture of LSTM

Bi-directional LSTM (BI-LSTM) is a combination of the forward and backward LSTMs. BI-LSTM is often used to model the context information in natural language processing tasks. Compared with LSTM, Bi-LSTM can better capture context information in sentences. For word token x_i, two LSTM layers capture contextual information along the sentence through forward and backward. The outputs of Bi-LSTM at the last time step are concatenated as follows,

$$\overrightarrow{h_i} = LSTM(x_i, \overrightarrow{h_{i-1}}), \overleftarrow{h_i} = LSTM(x_i, \overleftarrow{h_{i-1}}), \widetilde{h_i} = [\overrightarrow{h_i}, \overleftarrow{h_i}] \tag{1}$$

where $\overrightarrow{h_i}$ and $\overleftarrow{h_i}$ are the output of the Bi-LSTM at the last time step i, and $\widetilde{h_i}$ is the concatenated context-sensitive features.

2.2 Multi-head Attention Mechanisms (MDAM)

MDAM utilizes the multiple queries to select in parallel the multi-information from the input [2, 15], each attention focuses on a different part of the input, the information from the different representation subspaces at different positions is jointly introduced to map the Query, Key and Value to multiple parallel heads and then to perform repeated attention computation by different parameter matrix, where each head processes the different information, so that the different parts of sentence sequence can be processed and richer sentence features can be extracted. Finally, the results of multiple attention operations are concatenated with vectors, which is calculated as follows

$$head_i = Attention(Query \cdot W_i^{query}, Key \cdot W_i^{Key}, Value \cdot W_i^{value}) \tag{2}$$

where the weight parameters W_i^{query}, W_i^{Key}, W_i^{value} are learnable parameters for linear calculation.

The output of each head in MDAM is concatenated to obtain a sentence matrix with richer semantic information.

$$Multihead(Query, Key, Value) = W^M [head_1, head_2, \ldots, head_h] \tag{3}$$

where H is the number of parallel heads in MDAM, W^M is used to connect the results of the attention operation of multiple parallel heads.

MDAM is often used to calculate the correlation between each word in a sentence and the rest. GCN based on multi-position self-attention mechanism only needs to assign different weights to the edges in the dependency tree to learn the dependency representation of sentences without paying attention to the position information between nodes.

3 Bi-LSTM with MDAM for Social Media ADR Detection

ADR extraction from social media is essentially a multi-classification problem. Its most important work is feature extraction and classification model selection. The traditional approaches rely on some existing lexical resources (such as WordNet), natural language processing (NLP) systems, and some hand-extracted features. Such methods may lead to the increase of computational complexity, and lexical resources and feature extraction will consume a lot of time and energy, the quality of feature extraction has a great impact on the experimental results. Therefore, a Bi-LSTM with MDAM is proposed for ADR extraction, where MDAM can automatically find the words played a key role for the ADR classification. The model can capture the most important semantic information in each sentence, and does not depend on any external knowledge or NLP system. The model consists of 6 layers of structure, where the input layer inputs the sentence into the model, embedding layer maps each word to a low-dimensional space, Bi-LSTM is used to obtain the classification features from the embedding layer, the MDAM layer generates a weight vector, and by multiplying this weight vector, the lexical-level features in each iteration are merged into sentence-level features, the concatenating layer concatenates the sentence-level feature vectors as a fusion vector, and finally the output layer uses the fusion vectors for ADR classification. Its architecture is shown in Fig. 2.

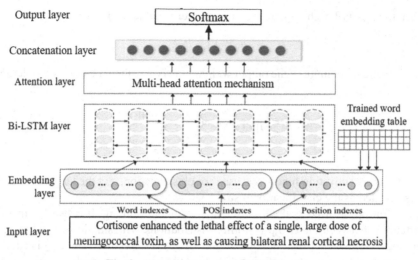

Fig. 2. The architecture of ADR detection

The steps of the proposed method consist of word feature representation in Twitter comments and Twitter classifier. The first part is composed of word vector, character-level vector, POS feature, emotion word and other features. The second part is composed of bidirectional LSTM neural network and capsule network, which can improve the shortcomings of current machine learning and convolutional neural network to a certain extent. The feature representation in this model is composed of CharCNN, word vector, POS marker, drug name and emotion word feature, which provides a good basis for detection of adverse drug reaction events. We store the pre-processed Twitter comments in one, the TXT file is noted as D.

$$D = (T_1, T_2, \ldots, T_n) \tag{4}$$

Where $T_1, T_2, \ldots, T_n$ is each Twitter comment in the document, and the classifier ultimately determines whether the sentence contains a comment about an ADR.

Word2Vec tool has two kinds of working mode: Skip-Gramm model and continuous word bag model (CBOW). In the paper, CBOW is used for model training, randomly initializing, and then the word or words are mapped in the same coordinate system, neural network is used to learn the characteristics, the continuous numeric vectors are gotten, so the vector contains the rich context semantic information play an important role in text classification task, to some extent, it decided to limit classification task. The window of this experiment is set as 5, and the size of the vocabulary is V, then the input layer can be expressed as $\{x_1, x_2, x_3, x_4, x_5\}$, and the output of the hidden layer can be calculated firstly. The output h is the weighted average of the input vector, as follows,

$$h = \frac{1}{C} W \cdot \sum_{i=1}^{C} x_i \tag{5}$$

where W is the weight matrix from the input layer to the hidden layer.

Then the input of each node in the output layer is calculated as follows,

$$u_j = v_{wj}^T \cdot h \tag{6}$$

where v_{wj}^T is the jth column of the output weight matrix W', then the output is calculated as,

$$y_{cj} = p(w_{y,j}|w_1, \cdots, w_c) = \frac{\exp(u_j)}{\sum\limits_{j'}^{V} \exp(u_{j'})} \tag{7}$$

The Softmax activation function is used for classification, and the larger probability value is selected as the classification result.

Cross Entropy is used as the loss function in model training. It is used to measure the difference between the two probability distributions. The smaller the value is, the smaller the difference between the two is, and vice versa. Regularization L_2 is added to the loss function to prevent overfitting. The loss function of the model in this paper is shown as follows:

$$J(\theta) = -\frac{1}{m}\left[\sum_{i=1}^{m}\sum_{j=1}^{k} 1\left\{y^{(i)} = j\right\} \ln \frac{\exp(\theta_j^T x^{(i)})}{\sum_{i=1}^{k} \exp(\theta_i^T x^{(i)})}\right] + \frac{\lambda}{2}\|\theta\|^2 \tag{8}$$

where λ is the coefficient of regularization L_2.

In the optimization process of the model, mini-batch Gradient Descent is used to update the iteration weights, its operation speed is fast, and also solves the randomness of the results, so this paper chooses the small-batch Gradient Descent method to update the superparameters, using the back propagation method to adjust the parameters. That is,

$$\theta = \theta + \mu \frac{\partial \log J(\theta)}{\partial \theta} \tag{9}$$

where μ is the learning rate.

4   Experiments and Results

The proposed method is validated on the SMM4H corpus dataset in 2017, and the training set is extended on the basis of shared task in 2016. In the experiment, the DDIE experiments are conducted on Keras and TensorFlow1.7.0 framework, including LSTM, Ubuntu18.04LTS as the operating system, 32G memory, Intel Core i5-4200U CPU @2.30 GHz, GPU GEFORCE GTX 1080ti, Ubuntu14.0. The experimental parameters are set as follows. For BLSTMCN, the dimension of word embedding is set to 300 and they are initialized as vectors by the GloVe algorithm. Learning rate = 0.001, batch size = 32. The dropout rate is set to 0.5 to prevent possible over-fitting. Dropout is set to 0.1 and batch size = 16. The head number of multi-head attention is set to 3.

Considering that the Twitter ID and the fact that users delete a lot of posts, we crawled to 14,881 Twitter posts. Before the experiment, the dataset of this experiment is analyzed in detail. As for ADR detection, drugs are indispensable. Therefore, the detection of drug names in sentences is a key factor to judge adverse drug reactions. Only when relevant drug names appear in the corpus sentences, they are related to ADRs. In addition, attention should also be paid to the appearance of emotional words, as users often express certain feelings of dissatisfaction, sadness or even despair in comments about adverse drug reactions. For example, "Metormin has made me very ill for a very long time. It feels good to be alive and not taking that fucking poison", it can be clearly seen that the user may be tortured by metformin drugs very painful. SentiwordNet3.0.0 sentiment dictionary and Sider 4.1 medical pharmacopoeia are used to extract the drug name and sentiment words of each tweet in the proposed model, which is another feature of the training model.

The research content of this paper is ADR detection, which is common classification task in natural language processing, so we can use for the system performance accuracy (P), the recall (R) rate to evaluate two parameters, and the value is the comprehensive evaluation index for accuracy and recall rate, choose with F1-value as a parameter to evaluate the experiment.

$$F1 = \frac{2PR}{P+R} \tag{10}$$

where $P = \frac{TP}{TP+FP}$, $R = \frac{TP}{TP+FN}$, TP is the sentences with correct classification of ADRs, FN is the sentences with ADRs predicted as no ADRs, FP is the sentences without ADRs predicted as ADRs, and TN is the sentences without correct prediction of ADRs.

The overall results of the proposed method and 4 comparative methods on the test set are shown in Table 1.

Table 1. The results of 5 methods on the SMM4H corpus dataset

Methods	SVM	CNN	CNN + Attention	LSTM + Attention	Our
F1 (%)	42.32	42.64	45.09	43.51	47.58

From Table 1, it is found that the proposed method outperforms the other methods. By comparative experiments, it is known that the ADR detection based on Bi-LSTM with MDAM is helpful to improve the classification performance compared with one classical SVM and 3 traditional deep learning models. In the process of modeling spatial information, CNN often needs to copy the feature detector, which will reduce the modeling efficiency of the model. Because CNN is insensitive to the spatial position, it is difficult to effectively encode information such as position information and semantic information in text sentences. On the basis of LSTM, Bi-LSTM combines the information of input sequence in both forward and backward directions. For the output at time t, the forward LSTM layer has the information of time t in the input sequence and the time before, and the backward LSTM layer has the information of time t in the input sequence and the time after. Therefore, Bi-LSTM can extract more classification information than LSTM. This validates that MDAM is effective for word embedding and has richer semantic information. Bi-LSTM with MDAM has the highest Precision, which indicates that enables the fusion of multiple word embedding and the use of multichannel word embedding can improve the ADR detection ability.

5 Conclusions

This paper proposed a ADR detected method from Social media based on Bi-LSTM with MDAM. This study belongs to the field of natural language processing and text mining, and the dataset adopted is the dataset in the social media mining for health (SMM4H-2017) shared task to complete the detection task of ADRs. The results paper show that, using social media as the carrier, combined with the feature representation of text classification task and MDAM, the effective detection of ADR can be achieved, which is of great significance to the improvement of human health level. However, the F1-value of the ADR detection methods on the basis of social media is generally low, with the user in the post express the informal and the data set has a lot to do with the positive and negative cases of imbalance of social media, the future research is focused on how the user express standardization and solve the problem of positive and negative cases balance data sets, how to utilize the related characteristics of learning ability of the system model.

Acknowledgement. This work is supported by the National Science Foundation of China (Grants No. 62072378).

References

1. Plumpton, C.O., Roberts, D., Pirmohamed, M., et al.: A systematic review of economic evaluations of Pharmacogenetic testing for prevention of adverse drug reactions. Pharmacoeconomics. **34**(8), 771–793 (2016)
2. Hazell, L., Shakir, S.A.W., et al.: Under-reporting of adverse drug reactions: a systematic review. Drug Saf. **29**(5), 385–396 (2006)
3. Li, H., Guo, X.J., Ye, X.F., et al.: Adverse drug reactions of spontaneous reports in shanghai pediatric population. PLoS ONE **9**(2), 89829 (2014)
4. Fleuranceau-Morel, P.: How do pharmaceutical companies handle consumer adverse drug reaction reports? An overview based on a survey of French drug safety managers and officers. Pharmacoepidemiol. Drug Saf. **11**(1), 37–44 (2010)
5. Margraff, F., Bertram, D.: Adverse drug reaction reporting by patients: an overview of fifty countries. Drug Saf. **37**(6), 409–419 (2014)
6. Olivier-Abbal, P.: Measuring the preventability of adverse drug reactions in France: a 2015 overview. Therapies **71**(2), 195–202 (2016)
7. Imam, F., et al.: Adverse drug reaction prevalence and mechanisms of action of first-line anti-tubercular drugs. Saudi Pharma. J. **28**(3), 316–324 (2020). https://doi.org/10.1016/j.jsps.2020.01.011
8. Huang, D., Jiang, Z.H., Zou, L., et al.: Drug–drug interaction extraction from biomedical literature using support vector machine and long short term memory networks. Inform. Sci. **415–416**, 100–109 (2017)

9. Alvaro, N., Miyao, Y., Collier, N.: Twimed: Twitter and pubmed comparable corpus of drugs, diseases, symptoms, and their relations. JMIR Public Health Surveill. **3**(2), 24 (2017)
10. Liu, J., Zhao, S., Zhang, X.: An ensemble method for extracting adverse drug events from social media. Artif. Intell. Med. **70**(9), 62–76 (2016)
11. Reddy, M., Rana, P.: Biomedical image classification using deep convolutional neural networks – overview. In: IOP Conference Series: Materials Science and Engineering. 1022(1):012020 (2021)
12. Huynh, T., He, Y., Willis, A., et al.: Adverse drug reaction classification with deep neural networks. In: 26th International Conference on Computational Linguistics: Technical Paper. pp. 877–887 (2016)
13. Zhang, Y., Zheng, W., Lin, H., Wang, J., Yang, Z., Dumontier, M.: Drug-drug interaction extraction via hierarchical RNNs on sequence and shortest dependency paths. Bioinformatics **34**(5), 828–835 (2017)
14. Mamo, T., Wang, F.K.: Long short-term memory with attention mechanism for state of charge estimation of lithium-ion batteries. IEEE Access **8**, 94140–94151 (2020)
15. Zhou, P., et al.: Attention-based bidirectional long short-term memory networks for relation classification. In: Meeting of the Association for Computational Linguistics, pp. 207–212. Berlin (2016)

HOMC: A Hierarchical Clustering Algorithm Based on Optimal Low Rank Matrix Completion for Single Cell Analysis

Xiaoqing Cheng[1], Chang Yan[2], Hao Jiang[3(⊠)], and Yushan Qiu[2(⊠)]

[1] School of Mathematics and Statistics, Xi'an Jiaotong University, Xi'an, China
[2] College of Mathematics and Statistics, Shenzhen University, Shenzhen 518000, China
yushan.qiu@szu.edu.cn
[3] School of Mathematics, Renmin University of China, Beijing, China
jiangh@ruc.edu.cn

Abstract. The tremendous development of single-cell RNA sequencing (scRNA-seq) technology offers the promise of addressing cellular heterogeneity problem which cannot be addressed with bulk sequencing technologies. However, scRNA-seq data is noisy and sparse due to the dropout events. In this study, we focused on cellular heterogeneity problem and proposed a hierarchical clustering algorithm based on optimal low rank matrix completion (HOMC). We first applied nonnegative matrix factorization for determining optimal low rank approximation for the original scRNA-seq data. Then we performed hierarchical clustering based on correlation-based distance for grouping those imputed data points, and optimal number of clusters can be determined by integrating three classical measures. Experimental results have showed that HOMC is capable of distinguishing cellular differences and the clustering performance is superior to other state-of-the-art methods.

Keywords: Single cell · Matrix completion · Imputation · Clustering low rank

1 Introduction

The tremendous development of single-cell RNA sequencing (scRNA-seq) technology enables us to quantitatively characterize gene expression in individual cellular [1–3]. Unlike bulk RNA sequencing, scRNA-seq can capture cellular heterogeneity within seemingly similar cells, which offers the promise of addressing a variety of biological problems, such as quantifying differences on gene expression levels between normal and cancer cells [4, 5], discovering new cell types [6] and constructing pseudotrajectory lineages [7, 8].

A large amount of gene expression data would be generated from a scRNA-seq experiment, those data are high-dimensional, noisy, unbalanced and sparse, bringing new challenges for downstream analyses [9]. Among all characteristics, sparsity is one of the most distinctive features. In contrast to bulk RNA sequencing, the fraction of 'zeros' is increasing in a scRNA expression matrix. And there are two interpretations

© Springer Nature Switzerland AG 2021
D.-S. Huang et al. (Eds.): ICIC 2021, LNAI 12838, pp. 66–76, 2021.
https://doi.org/10.1007/978-3-030-84532-2_7

for those 'zeros', part of them are 'true zeros', or biologically observed zeros that means those genes are truly expressed and there is no transcripts. Relatively speaking, there exist 'false zeros', or technical zeros that means transcripts cannot be detected technically. The possible reason is a large number of transcripts failed to get amplified in amplification process and the amount of mRNA is insufficient to be captured [10]. The 'dropout' or 'dropout event' is used to describe those false zeros, indicating that a gene is not detected even it is expressed at high level [10, 11]. The dropout events would greatly impair the clustering performance, thus effective and efficient imputation methods are in great demand.

Recently, many algorithms have been proposed to recover the expression matrix by trying to impute dropouts and keep those true zeros at same time. According to [12], those methods can be classified into three categories: (1) model-based imputation methods, such as scImpute [13], VIPER [14]; (2) smooth-based imputation methods, such as DrImpute [15], MAGIC [16]; (3) data reconstruction methods, such as AutoImpute [17] and mcImpute [18]. ScImpute first estimated each gene's dropout probability in each cell from a mixture probability model [13]. Then it automatically identified dropout events and imputed their value by integrating information of same gene in similar cells. However, a prior information on number of cell subpopulations was needed [19]. The expression level of a target cell could be filled by VIPER through averaging weighed expression value of a sparse set of neighborhood cells [14]. The selection of neighborhood cells was accomplished in a sparse nonnegative regression model and in a progressive manner, which ensured VIPER's robustness and computational scalability. It assumed a zero inflated Poisson model for the gene expression data, but it may not be always true [19]. MAGIC recovered those missing values through sharing information across similar cells based on heat diffusion and the performance highly depended on the structure of data [16]. It performed imputation based on a projected low-dimensional space, which may remove gene expression variability across cells [14]. DrImpute first identified similar cells through clustering and then imputed those dropout values by averaging the expression values of same gene in similar cells [15]. Similar to scImpute, we need to specify the number of sub-populations in prior [19]. AutoImpute learned the inherent distribution of the input data and recovered the dropout values accordingly with minimal modification to those biological zeros [17]. It worked only on the top 1000 differential genes in a data set, and this may not be sufficient [20]. mcImpute was a low-rank matrix completion based technique, by applying soft thresholds iteratively on single values of scRNA-seq data, it can recover the full gene expression matrix. Its advantage is that it did not assume any distributions for gene expression [18]. However, matrices imputed with different rank values may have significant differences. Hence, it is of great importance to give a reasonable estimation on the best rank values for each data set in low rank matrix completion imputations.

Clustering plays a key role on finding new cell types based on similarities of transcriptomes. However, gene expression data are high-dimensional and thus distances between cells become similar due to 'curse of dimensionality'. It is inevitable to reduce dimension so as to eliminate noise and speed up computation. Besides, the existence of dropout events may led to the failure of traditional dimension reduction algorithms, and adding an imputation model may generate more stable results. A variety of clustering methods have been proposed, such as k-means [21] and its extensions [22], hierarchical clustering [23], community-detection-based algorithms, nonnegative matrix factorization (NMF) based [24] and neural-network based algorithms [25–28]. K-means identified k clusters iteratively and then assigned each cell into a cluster according to the distance but it cannot guarantee an optimal solution (or global minimum). SC3 incorporated k-means with consensus clustering, which achieved a higher accuracy compared to many typical clustering methods if an optimal clustering number is given [29]. However, there is no establishing method in identifying the optimal clustering number. It is of significant importance in seeking for such number.

In this paper, we proposed a novel and stable method (HOMC) for single cell clustering. Firstly, we recovered the expression matrix through a low matrix completion method and optimal rank is determined by variance analysis. Then hierarchical clustering with correlation distance is applied to cluster cells into different sub-groups. Our proposed algorithm adopted hierarchical clustering for scRNA-seq data by adding an imputation step, which achieves more stable and robust results. Furthermore, HOMC is capable of determining the optimal number of clusters automatically.

This paper is organized as follows: Sect. 2 presents our main method, Sect. 3 shows the performance of HOMC on three data sets compared to three state-of-the-art algorithms. Finally, Sect. 4 gives a conclusion of this paper.

2   Method

Previous argument states that only a few biophysical functions trigger the functioning of transcription factors, thus generating a highly correlated gene expression data matrix. Hence it is reasonable to assume that gene expression values lie in a low-dimensional linear subspace, with the gene expression data matrix formed as a low-rank matrix. In the case of scRNA-seq data, when gene expression values are used to measure the expressions of single cells, the dropout ratio is quite high. Hence the single cell gene expression data matrix becomes a low-rank, sparse matrix. The high dropout ration in scRNA-seq data is deemed as a matrix completion problem with partially known matrix entries.

2.1   Low Rank Matrix Completion

Assume the single cell data $S \in R^{n \times p}$ a sampled version of the complete expression matrix (without dropout) X, where n is the number of cells, p is the number of gene attributes. Mathematically, it can be formulated in the following formula,

$$S = A(X)$$

Here A is a sub-sampling binary operator that 0's (1's) represent the corresponding entries of expression data unobserved (observed, respectively). Our problem is to recover X based on the observation S and the sub-sampling mask. It is assumed that X is a low-rank matrix.

Optimal Low Rank Matrix Completion. To solve the low rank matrix completion problem, one of the most straightforward methods is to use nonnegative matrix factorization (NMF). NMF is a well-known linear regression technique for part-based representation of the nonnegative high-dimensional data, it aims to find two nonnegative matrices whose product provides a good approximation for the original matrix. Here, we assume the complete matrix X can be represented as a product of two low rank nonnegative matrices: U and V of rank r where $r < \min(n, p)$. Thus, we solve the following optimization problem to get a low rank approximation for the matrix X:

$$\min_X F(X) = \|S - A(X)\|_F^2 = \min_{U \geq 0, V \geq 0} \|S - A(UV)\|_F^2 \tag{1}$$

Majorization minimization (MM) approach [30] have been proposed to solve the problem in an elegant way. The MM algorithm consists of two major steps. In the Majorization step, a surrogate function is constructed to give an upper bound of the target function, and difference between the surrogate function and the target function is minimized at current iterating point. Afterwards, in the Minimization step, the surrogate function is minimized to obtain the next point.

The majorization step decouples the problem (from A), which is to solve the following optimization problem:

$$\min_{U \geq 0, V \geq 0} \|B - UV\|_F^2 \tag{2}$$

It should be noted that due to the non-convexity of $\|B - UV\|_F^2$ in both U and V, the numerical solutions of Eq. (2) may always converge to local minima. We here propose alternating least square algorithm to solve the minimization problem by considering a regularized optimization framework as following:

$$\min_{U \geq 0, V \geq 0} L(U, V) = \min_{U \geq 0, V \geq 0} \sum_{i=1}^n \sum_{j=1}^n \left(B_{ij} - (u_i)^T v_j\right)^2 + \lambda\left(\|u_i\|_2^2 + \|v_j\|_2^2\right)$$

Where $U = \begin{pmatrix} u_1^T \\ \vdots \\ u_n^T \end{pmatrix}$ and $V = \left(v_1 \cdots v_p\right)$.

For a fixed low dimensionality r, the computational complexity of the alternating least square algorithm is of $O\left(2nr^3 + n^2 r^2\right)$. It is worthy to point out that such algorithm does not depend on the attribute dimensionality, hence it is efficient.

Different values of r will result in different factorization results in U and V. Hence it is critical to determine a suitable value for the low dimensionality r in representing the imputed scRNA-seq data. Motivated by this, we propose to use variance analysis to determine the optimal dimensionality r.

We denote the imputed expression profile for gene j across n cells by $(\tilde{x}_{1j}, \ldots, \tilde{x}_{nj})$.

Now assume there are s cell subpopulations and each cell belongs to one and only one subpopulation. We formulate the expected expression value of gene j in cell i by

$$E(\tilde{x}_{ij}) = \alpha_j + \sum_{k=1}^s z_{ik} \beta_k$$

where z_{ik} is a binary membership indicator (i.e., $z_{ik} = 1$ if cell i belongs to subpopulation k, and $z_{ik} = 0$ otherwise). For each gene j, regarding each cell subpopulation as a treatment group, we can defineto characterize the consistency between the expression in gene j and the subpopulation distribution. If the s cell subpopulations are well separated, ratio $_j = \frac{SSB_j}{SST_j}$ is likely to be large, where SST_j denotes total variance, and SSB_j: between-sample variance.

For each imputed scRNA-seq data matrix, $r \in [1, 50]$, we pre-selected a fixed number of m genes by filtering the ones with the largest deviation. We determine a potentially optimal number of rank r under hierarchical clustering by checking the values of $R_r = \sum_{j=1}^{m}$ ratio $_j$ in each data D_r. The optimal rank r is selected when R_r is the largest among all the r values ranging in [1,50].

2.2 Hierarchical Clustering

We use hierarchical clustering on the imputed data with differentially distributed attributes to group cell and investigate cell heterogeneity. Hierarchical clustering is powerful in grouping data by creating a cluster tree or dendrogram. It can not only group cells but also provide a natural way to graphically represent cells in a hierarchical structure, allowing a thorough inspection on the relationships between cells and clusters of cells. The major steps of hierarchical clustering include similarity construction and hierarchical cluster tree construction.

We propose to use Pearson correlation to measure the similarity between cells in the imputed data set. Then we calculate the correlation among the given cells in the data set

$$\text{Sim}(i, j) = \frac{\sum_{k=1}^{p} (\tilde{x}_{ik} - \overline{\tilde{x}}_i)(\tilde{x}_{jk} - \overline{\tilde{x}}_j)}{\sqrt{\sum_{k=1}^{p} (\tilde{x}_{ik} - \overline{\tilde{x}}_i)^2}\sqrt{\sum_{k=1}^{p} (\tilde{x}_{jk} - \overline{\tilde{x}}_i)^2}}$$

Where $\overline{\tilde{x}}_i = \sum_{k=1}^{p} \tilde{x}_{ik}/p$.

Cluster Number Determination. It is significant to determine the optimal number of clusters for hierarchical clustering, then we integrated the following three classical measures to seek for the optimal one: the Calinski-Harabasz index from [31], the Davies-Bouldin index from [32], and the silhouette value from [33]. We conduct clustering on transformed data using diffusion maps over a number of candidate cluster numbers. Then we determine the optimal cluster number based on each index measures. Different index measure would generate different number of cluster, hence we adopt the most frequently appear number among these three index measures as the optimal one.

3   Results

To investigate the performance of our model, we compare our method with several state-of-the-art methods. Firstly, as HOMC is an integrated algorithm, we compare it with CIDR [34], the only integrated algorithm in literature. Secondly, we try to verify if HOMC gives a better estimation of optimal number of cluster k, we compare it with CIDR and SNN-cliq [35]. Finally, we compare our proposed method with SC3, CIDR and SNN-cliq which is used to evaluate the overall clustering performance of HOMC. We run each algorithm for both original expression matrix and imputed expression matrix X.

3.1 Data Materials

We extracted two data sets to estimate the performance of our model as follows:

- **Neuronal Cells.** This data set contains 622 neuronal cells with sensory subtypes: peptidergic nociceptors, nonpeptidergic nociceptors, neurofilament containing and tyrosine hydroxylase containing. It is obtained from mouse dorsal root ganglion, generated using Illumina Genome Analyzer IIx.
- **Pluripotent Cells.** This data set consists of 704 mESCs which includes three different culture conditions. It can be accessed from a stem cell study considering the influence of culture conditions on pluripotent states of mESCs. The data set is available at Array- Express database (http://www.ebi.ac.uk/arrayexpress) under accession number E-MTAB-2600.

3.2 Performance Evaluation

Effect of Rank k in Low Rank Matrix Completion. Low rank matrix completion is used to impute the single cell expression matrix. However, different matrix rank would generate different reconstructed matrix, hence having an important effect on the performance of clustering. To evaluate the imputation performance, we adopted the t-SNE to visualize the clustering results from the considered single-cell expression profiles. Figure 1 depicted the t-SNE results for neuronal cells with imputation of different number of rank ranging from 2 to 50. Due to the page limitation, we showed the the t-SNE results for rank k = 2, 9, 16, 23, 30, 37 and 44 in Fig. 1(a)–(g). In addition, we compare the t-SNE result with our selected optimal rank (i.e., 11) in Fig. 1(h). As we can see from Fig. 1(a) that when the rank is 2, the cell types are mixed and difficult to be distinguished. For other rank values 9, 16, 23, 30, 37, and 44 in Figs. 1(b)–(g), the cells in purple color are not grouped together and divided into 3 subgroups. We can see from Fig. 1(h) that different cell types are well differentiated when the rank value is 11, and the cells in purple color are grouped as one cluster which illustrates the superiority of our proposed method 1.

In Fig. 2, for pluripotent cell data set, the optimal rank we selected is 28. As we can see from the Fig. 2(a) that when rank is 2, the cells are mixed. In this dataset, 704 mESC cells are cultured in 3 different conditions. For other rank values: 9, 16, 23, 30, 37, and 44 shown in Fig. 2(b)–(g), the cells are divided into 3 subgroups. In particular, for rank values 9 and 16 Fig. 2(a)–(b), the cells are distributed less tightly. Besides, when the rank value is 28 Fig. 2(h), different cell types are also well differentiated. We can conclude that when the rank values are 23, 30, 37, 44 and 28 (the selected optimal one), the clustering results are similar.

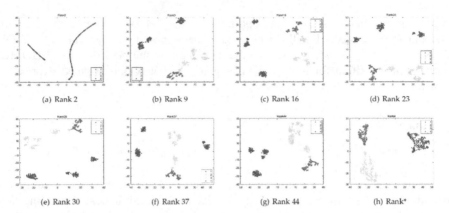

Fig. 1. tsne distribution for different rank values in neuronal cell data (color figure online)

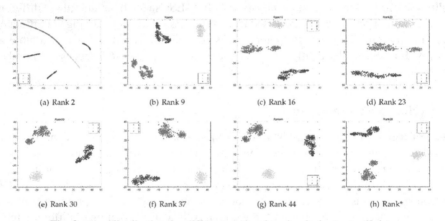

Fig. 2. tsne distribution for different rank values in pluripotent cell data

In order to further investigate the differences among the imputed single cell data sets for different rank values, we conducted clustering analysis on the imputed matrices. We performed hierarchical clustering based on correlation distances on the imputed matrices for the selected single cell data sets. And we used adjusted rand index (ARI) to measure the clustering accuracy. ARI is a measure for the agreement between two partitions with different number of clusters.

Figures 3 and 4 have showed the ARI distribution for different data sets when rank values differ from 2 to 50. The x-axis represents the rank value that ranges from 2 to 50. Hierarchical clustering based on correlation distance was conducted on the imputed data matrix with different rank values ranging from 2 to 50. Hence, each ARI value are shown for 49 clustering results, and the ARI value for selected optimal rank in the considered data set are marker as red star.

Figure 3 have depicted the ARI distribution for neuronal cell data set when hierarchical clustering is conducted on it. The optimal rank we selected is 11, and we can see that the ARI value can achieve up to 98.76% at this rank. Besides, the optimal ARI value

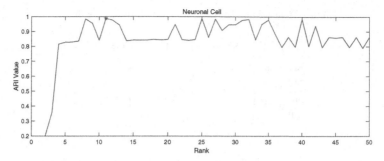

Fig. 3. ARI distribution for different rank values in neuronal cell data

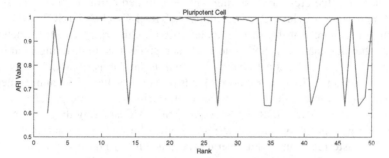

Fig. 4. ARI distribution for different rank values in pluripotent cell data

is 98.77% which is comparable to the one with the selected rank. Hence, our optimal rank selection method can help in finding the rank which is close to the optimal rank. It is almost the best performance among the performances over all the considered rank values.

Figure 4 have illustrated the ARI distribution for pluripotent cell data set. The selected optimal rank is 28, and we can see that at this rank, the performance of clustering is the best whose ARI value is 100%. Hence, our optimal rank selection method is successful in identifying the optimal rank. It is the best performance among the performances over all the considered rank values.

Optimal Cluster Number Comparison. We compare the accuracy on number of clusters for the considered algorithms. SC3 is not considered here since it cannot determine the optimal number of cluster automatically. Table 1 shows details of predicted number of clusters for algorithms: SNN-Cliq, CIDR and our proposed HOMC.

The actual number of clusters in neuronal cell data set, pluripotent cell data set is 4, 3 respectively. We can see from the Table 1 that HOMC can suggest an accurate number of cluster for each data set. In comparison, CIDR cannot provide accurate number of clusters for Pluripotent cells. SNN-Cliq can determine the number of cluster for pluripotent cell data set. And for neuronal cell data set, it over-estimated the number of cluster.

Table 1. Cluster number determined by different methods

	SNN-Cliq	CIDR	HOMC
Neuronal cell	28	4	4
Pluripotent cell	3	5	3

Overall Evaluation in Performance. As we mentioned in Sect. 2, HOMC is an integrated algorithm consisting of two major steps: 1) imputation based on low rank matrix completion and 2) hierarchical clustering with determined optimal cluster number. We choose 3 representative clustering algorithms: CIDR, SNN-cliq and SC3. CIDR is the algorithm in literature that integrates imputation with clustering, and it can determine cluster number automatically. SNN-cliq is chosen since it is a clustering method that can determine cluster number automatically, which is similar as HOMC. SC3 is chosen due to its splendid performance on various kinds of data sets, though it cannot determine cluster number automatically. Comparison of clustering results are performed among the 4 algorithms: HOMC, CIDR, SNN-cliq and SC3. Considering that SC3, as a consensus clustering algorithm cannot determine the number of clusters automatically, we examine the clustering results with several candidate cluster numbers for each data set. SC3* (SC3*-imputed, respectively) represents SC3 method with accurate cluster number as input. SC3$^-$ (SC3$^-$-imputed, respectively) represents SC3 method with cluster number underestimated for each data set. SC3$^+$ (SC3$^+$-imputed, respectively) represents SC3 method with cluster number overestimated for each data set. And results on those experiments are listed in Table 2.

It is obvious to see that the performance of HOMC is superior to CIDR and SNN-Cliq in those three data sets. It is difficult to compare the performance of SC3 and other clustering algorithms that can determine the number of clusters automatically. Hence, we include three variants of SC3 for comparison. It can be seen that there is no dominant algorithm within the three SC3 variants. The clustering accuracy of SC3 highly depends on the input of the cluster number estimated for each data set. We can see from Table 2 that SC3* gives the best performance in an overall manner.

And the performance of SC3$^-$ and SC3$^+$ in pluripotent cell data set is unsatisfactory. Regarding the comparison of SC3 with other algorithms, we can see that the clustering result in SC3*is the best compared to SNN-Cliq. When we compare SC3* with our proposed HOMC, it is easy to see that the performance of SC3* in neuronal cell data set is clearly inferior to HOMC. The performance of HOMC in pluripotent cell data set is the same as that of SC3*. The performance of SC3* in brain cell data set is slightly superior to that of HOMC. Considering clustering accuracy of SC3 highly depends on the input of cluster number while HOMC can give an estimation of optimal number of clusters automatically, we can conclude that HOMC is almost the best among all compared partners.

Table 2. Clustering performance evaluated for different methods

	SNN-Cliq	CIDR	SC3⁻	SC3⁺	SC3*	HOMC
Neuronal cell	0.2442	0.0294	0.8454	0.8505	0.8453	0.9876
Pluripotent cell	0.0096	0.5795	0.6300	0.8328	1	1

4   Conclusion

In this paper, we have proposed a hierarchical clustering algorithm based on optimal low rank matrix completion (HOMC) for single cell analysis. Through determining optimal rank in low rank matrix completion method, we are able to obtain a relatively clear and accurate representation for the original sparse, noisy single cell data. Our hierarchical clustering method with correlation distance further helps to guarantee a robust differentiation on the heterogeneous cells. The experimental results have illustrated the superiority and robustness of our model when compared with other state-of-the-art methods. The HOMC algorithm can estimate the cluster number embedded in the single cell data set, as such it can be applied to various settings of single cell analysis.

Acknowledgments. This work was supported in part by the National Natural Science Foundation of China (Grant nos: 11801434, 11901575, 91730301, 62002234), China Postdoctoral Science Foundation (Grant no: 3115200128), Guangdong Basic and Applied Basic Research Foundation (Grant no: 2019A1515111180). The authors would like to thank the anonymous reviewers for helpful and constructive comments.

References

1. Kalisky, T., Quake, S.R.: Single-cell genomics. Nat. Methods **8**(4), 311–314 (2011)
2. Pelkmans, L.: Using cell-to-cell variability – a new era in molecular biology. Science **336**(6080), 425–426 (2012)
3. Patel, A.P., Tirosh, I., Trombetta, J.J., et al.: Single-cell RNA-seq highlights intratumoral heterogeneity in primary glioblastoma. Science **344**(6190), 1396–1401 (2014)
4. Tirosh, I., et al.: Dissecting the multicellular ecosystem of metastatic melanoma by single-cell rna-seq. Science **352**(6282), 189–196 (2016)
5. Wagner, A., Regev, A., Yosef, N.: Revealing the vectors of cellular identity with single-cell genomics. Nat. Biotechnol. **34**(11), 1145–1160 (2016)
6. Trapnell, C.: Defining cell types and states with single-cell genomics. Genome Res. **25**(10), 1491–1498 (2015)
7. Biase, F.H., Cao, X., Zhong, S.: Cell fate inclination within 2-cell and 4-cell mouse embryos revealed by single-cell rna sequencing. Genome Res. **24**(11), 1787–1796 (2014)
8. Trapnell, C., et al.: Pseudo-temporal ordering of individual cells reveals dynamics and regulators of cell fate decisions. Nat. Biotechnol. **32**(4), 381 (2014)
9. AlJanahi, A.A., Danielsen, M., Dunbar, C.E.: An introduction to the analysis of single-cell rna-sequencing data. Mol. Therapy-Methods Clin. Dev. **10**, 189–196 (2018)
10. Kharchenko, P.V., Silberstein, L., Scadden, D.T.: Bayesian approach to single-cell differential expression analysis. Nat. Methods **11**(7), 740–742 (2014)

11. Tracy, S., Yuan, G.-C., Dries, R.: Rescue: imputing dropout events in single-cell rna-sequencing data. BMC Bioinform. **20**(1), 388 (2019)
12. Hou, W., Ji, Z., Ji, H., Hicks, S.C.: A systematic evaluation of single-cell rna-sequencing imputation methods, bioRxiv (2020)
13. Li, W.V., Li, J.J.: An accurate and robust imputation method scimpute for single-cell rna-seq data. Nat. Commun. **9**(1), 1–9 (2018)
14. Chen, M., Zhou, X.: Viper: variability-preserving imputation for accurate gene expression recovery in single-cell rna sequencing studies. Genome Biol. **19**(1), 1–15 (2018)
15. Gong, W., Kwak, I.-Y., Pota, P., Koyano-Nakagawa, N., Garry, D.J.: Drimpute: imputing dropout events in single cell rna sequencing data. BMC Bioinform. **19**(1), 1–10 (2018)
16. Van Dijk, D., et al.: Recovering gene interactions from single-cell data using data diffusion. Cell **174**(3), 716–729 (2018)
17. Talwar, D., Mongia, A., Sengupta, D., Majumdar, A.: Autoimpute: Autoencoder based imputation of single-cell rna-seq data. Sci. Rep. **8**(1), 1–11 (2018)
18. Mongia, A., Sengupta, D., Majumdar, A.: Mcimpute: Matrix completion based imputation for single cell rna-seq data. Front. Genet. **10**, 9 (2019)
19. Zhu, K., Anastassiou, D.: 2dimpute: imputation in single-cell rna-seq data from correlations in two dimensions. Bioinformatics **36**(11), 3588–3589 (2020)
20. Gunady, M.K., Kancherla, J., Bravo, H.C., Feizi, S.: scgain: Single cell rna-seq data imputation using generative adversarialnetworks, bioRxiv, p. 837302 (2019)
21. Hartigan, J.A., Wong, M.A.: Algorithm as 136: A k-means clustering algorithm. Appl. Stat. **28**(1), 100–108 (1979)
22. Lloyd, S.: Least squares quantization in pcm. IEEE Trans. Inform. Theory **28**(2), 129–137 (1982)
23. Ng, A.Y., Jordan, M.I., Weiss, Y.: On spectral clustering: analysis and an algorithm. In: Advances in Neural Information Processing Systems, pp. 849–856 (2002)
24. Shao, C., Hofer, T.: Robust classification of single-cell transcriptome data by nonnegative matrix factorization. Bioinformatics **33**(2), 235–242 (2017)
25. Lv, D., et al.: Systematic characterization of lncrnas' cell-to-cell expression heterogeneity in glioblastoma cells. Oncotarget **7**(14), 18403 (2016)
26. Kim, D.H., et al.: Single-cell transcriptome analysis reveals dynamic changes in lncrna expression during reprogramming. Cell Stem Cell **16**(1), 88–101 (2015)
27. Camp, J.G., et al.: Multilineage communication regulates human liver bud development from pluripotency. Nature **546**(7659), 533–538 (2017)
28. Peng, T., Nie, Q.: Somsc: self-organization-map for high dimensional single-cell data of cellular states and their transitions, bioRxiv, p. 124693 (2017)
29. Kiselev, V.Y., et al.: Sc3: consensus clustering of single-cell rna-seq data. Nat. Methods **14**(5), 483–486 (2017)
30. Sun, Y., Babu, P., Palomar, D.P.: Majorization minimization algorithms in signal processing, communications, and machine learning. IEEE Trans. Signal Process. **65**(3), 794–816 (2017)
31. Calinski, T., Harabasz, J.: A dendrite method for cluster analysis. Commun. Stat. **3**(1), 1–27 (1974)
32. Davies, D.L., Bouldin, D.W.: A Cluster Separation Measure. IEEE Computer Society (1979)
33. Peter, R.J.: Silhouettes: a graphical aid to the interpretation and validation of cluster analysis. J. Comput. Appl. Math. **20**, 53–65 (1999)
34. Lin, P., Troup, M., Ho, J.W.: Cidr: ultrafast and accurate clustering through imputation for single-cell rna-seq data. Genome Biol. **18**(1), 59 (2017)
35. Xu, C., Su, Z.: Identification of cell types from single-cell transcriptomes using a novel clustering method. Bioinformatics **31**(12), 1974–1980 (2015)
36. Kiselev, V.Y., Kirschner, K., Schaub, M.T., et al.: SC3: consensus clustering of single-cell RNA-seq data. Nat. Methods **14**(5), 483–486 (2017)

mzMD: A New Storage and Retrieval System for Mass Spectrometry Data

Runmin Yang[1], Jingjing Ma[1], Shu Zhang[1], Yu Zheng[1], Lusheng Wang[2], and Daming Zhu[1(✉)]

[1] School of Computer Science and Technology, Shandong University, Qingdao, China
dmzhu@sdu.edu.cn
[2] Department of Computer Science, City University of Hong Kong, Hong Kong, China

Abstract. Viewing peaks in LC–MS data sets always happens in liquid-chromatography mass spectrometry data analysis. It is challenging to develop an LC–MS data storage and retrieval tool that can get some peaks in a data window whose image presented with their intensities in a display window resembles as closely as possible that of all peaks in the data window at a speed of real-time level. We present mzMD, a new storage system that is intended to store a set of mass spectral peaks in multiple database tables with different numbers of peaks selected from the set of peaks. We present an algorithm for visualization applications to query for summaries (representative peak sets) of given data windows. We propose criteria to evaluate the quality of summaries of data windows. Experimental statistics on real LC–MS data sets verified the high speed of mzMD in retrieving high-quality summaries of data windows. The source code is freely available at https://github.com/yrm9837/mzMD-java

Keywords: Mass spectrometry · Data storage · Visualization · Data window · Algorithm

1 Introduction

Liquid chromatography-mass spectrometry (LC–MS) has been widely used in high-throughput protein, lipid and metabolite identification and quantification [1, 12]. Although a majority of LC–MS data analysis functions can be done by software tools [8, 9, 16, 17], manual inspection of LC–MS data is indispensable in the identification and quantification of proteins and other biological molecules. LC–MS data visualization tools have been developed to meet the increasing needs of manual inspection aided LC–MS data analysis [7, 13, 14]. Because of the rapid rise in the volume of LC–MS data, visualization tools play an increasingly important role in MS data analysis [7].

LC–MS experiments generate data sets of mass spectral *peaks*. A basic function in LC–MS data visualization is to draw the MS1 peaks in a data window defined by a retention time interval and an m/z value interval, which often contains millions of peaks. Due to the limitation of speed and memory, only thousands of peaks can be presented without significant delay. To address this problem, some representative peaks

© Springer Nature Switzerland AG 2021
D.-S. Huang et al. (Eds.): ICIC 2021, LNAI 12838, pp. 77–86, 2021.
https://doi.org/10.1007/978-3-030-84532-2_8

in a data window, called a summary of the data window, were proposed for use in LC–MS data visualization [6]. It is a challenging problem to design an efficient storage mode of LC–MS data for retrieving high-quality summaries at as fast a speed as for interactive visualization of LC–MS data. We restrict our attention to LC–MS data storage methodology. We shall mention the phrase LC–MS data as *MS data*.

MS data sets are often stored in files with the mzML [4] or mzXML [11] format. Mass spectra in mzML or mzXML files are stored in the order of retention time. Since peaks in a data window have to be read from consecutive MS scans, it is impossible to quickly extract a summary when the data window covers thousands of scans.

Several other file formats were proposed for MS data storage and retrieval, such as mz5 [15], mzDB [2] and mzTree [6]. mz5 employs HDF5 files to store peaks in an MS data set, which facilitates access to peaks in consecutive scans. It provides faster access to peaks than the XML-based mzML and mzXML format, but is still inefficient for retrieving peaks in specific m/z value intervals. mzDB offers fast access to peaks in a data window. It always reports all peaks instead of a summary of a data window, causing a query for a data window summary to report more peaks than required for real-time data visualization.

mzTree [6] is capable of querying an MS data set for a summary of a data window quickly. It is apt to report summaries with more high-intensity peaks than low-intensity ones. Thus, it tends to report summaries with peaks that are more than needed for visualization, slowing down MS data retrieval in applications.

In this manuscript, we propose mzMD, a new storage and retrieval system for MS data visualization. mzMD stores peaks in an MS data set using multiple subsets of representative peaks of various sizes. We propose algorithms for mzMD to query an MS data set in mzMD format for data window summaries.

To examine the performance of mzMD, we propose two numerical features, called *coverage* and *efficiency* to reflect the quality of data window summaries from respective sides. As conventionally used [5], we combine the coverage and efficiency of a data window summary into a formula called Q-score to indicate the summary quality. The performance of mzMD was examined on a public MS data set of ovarian cancer tumor samples. For an MS data set of 1.8 GB, mzMD reported summaries of data windows whose mean Q-score is 4.5 times higher than that of mzTree. The speed and the speed stability of mzMD for it to query for summaries both surpassed those of mzTree.

2   Methods

A peak in an MS data set is represented by three values: its m/z value, retention time and intensity. A *data window* is defined by a retention time interval and an m/z value interval. A peak is *in a data window* if its retention time and m/z value are in the retention time and the m/z value intervals of the data window, respectively.

A set of peaks is *in a data window* if all peaks in the set are in the data window. A data window is *with respect to an MS data set*, if every time we mention a peak in the data window, the peak is meant in the data window as well as a member in the MS data set. We shall mention a data window without regard to any MS data set, if there is no ambiguity of the MS data set with respect to which the data window is mentioned.

In MS data visualization, all peaks in a data window are ready to show their intensities in a display window. Since there is no need to present in a display window overlapping peaks, it often suffices to show a subset of the peaks in the data window. This will speed up MS data visualization.

Based on this idea, Kyle et al. [6] proposed to store pre-prepared subsets of an MS data set so that the peaks in a data window reported by querying some of them are sufficient to represent the visual feature of all peaks in the data window. A *summary* of a data window refers to a subset of all peaks in the data window. A good summary needs to have the following characteristics [6]:

1. **Integral samples:** Summaries must be samples of real points, not derived points.
2. **Deterministic sub-samples:** Samples must be collected without stochasticity.
3. **Representative sub-samples:** Summaries must visually resemble the underlying data.

mzTree reports summaries with the first two characteristics. Here our study focuses on the representativeness of summaries.

Let $\alpha = [rtMin, rtMax] \times [mzMin, mzMax]$ denote a data window with respect to an MS data set where $[rtMin, rtMax]$ is its retention time interval and $[mzMin, mzMax]$ its m/z value interval. Dividing $[rtMin, rtMax]$ and $[mzMin, mzMax]$ evenly into m and n bins respectively, we partition α into $m \times n$ *cells*. We refer to the set of $m \times n$ cells as the $m \times n$-*partition* of α. We denote by $\alpha[i, j]$ the cell in the $m \times n$-partition of α whose retention time interval is the ith of the m retention time bins and m/z value interval is the jth of the n m/z value bins, $1 \leq i \leq m, 1 \leq j \leq n$.

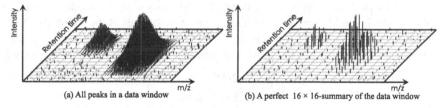

(a) All peaks in a data window   (b) A perfect 16×16-summary of the data window

Fig. 1. Summary of a data window.

A summary of α is called an $m \times n$-*summary* if the summary contains at most one peak in each cell of the data window's $m \times n$-partition. An $m \times n$-summary is a *squared* summary if $m = n$. The *side length* of a $k \times k$-summary is k. A peak in a cell is *representative* if its intensity is the highest in the cell. An $m \times n$-summary of α is *perfect* if it contains one and only one peak in each non-empty cell of α's $m \times n$-partition and each peak is representative in its cell. Figure 1 shows a three-dimensional view of all peaks in a data window as well as a perfect 16×16-summary of the data window.

Assume a display window is capable of presenting at most m spectra and at most n peaks in a mass spectrum. Then a perfect $m \times n$-summary of α tends to achieve the highest visual similarity to that of all peaks in α. So, an $m \times n$-summary of α is the most representative if it is perfect. We focus on how to measure the representativeness of an arbitrary summary of a data window.

Let S denote a summary of α. More than one peak of S may occur in a cell of the $m \times n$-partition of α. Let $X[\alpha]$ denote the set of all peaks in α. Let $H[i,j]$ be the highest intensity of all peaks in $\alpha[i,j]$, and $h[i,j]$ the highest intensity of those peaks in S as well as $\alpha[i,j]$ if the peak is present. The *representative rate* of S with respect to $\alpha[i,j]$ is defined as the following formula.

$$r[i,j] = \begin{cases} \frac{h[i,j]}{H[i,j]} & H[i,j] > 0, \\ 0 & H[i,j] = 0. \end{cases} \tag{1}$$

Let P denote a perfect $m \times n$-summary of α. We refer to the following value as the *coverage* of S.

$$c[S] = \frac{\sum_{i=1}^{m} \sum_{j=1}^{n} r[i,j]}{|P|} \tag{2}$$

Although it is reasonable to express the representativeness of S by its coverage, a summary becomes inefficient when more than one peak occurs in a cell. This asks for another criterion to examine if all peaks in a summary are required to achieve good representativeness. The *efficiency* of S is as the following formula.

$$e[S] = \frac{\sum_{i=1}^{m} \sum_{j=1}^{n} r[i,j]}{|S|} \tag{3}$$

An $m \times n$-summary of a data window is perfect if and only if both the coverage and the efficiency of the summary are 1. The coverage (resp. efficiency) of a summary might be improved by increasing (resp. decreasing) the summary size to include more (resp. less) peaks, which would deprive the efficiency (resp. coverage) of the summary. As by F-measure to combine the *precision* and *recall* for the use of quality evaluation of a data mining solution [5], we refer to the following formula as the Q-score of the summary S.

$$q[S] = \frac{2c[S]e[S]}{c[S] + e[S]}. \tag{4}$$

An $m \times n$-summary of a data window is perfect if and only if the Q-score of the summary is 1.

2.1 Mass Spectrometry Data Storage System

Let F denote an MS data set, M and N the maximum retention time and m/z value over all peaks in F. Then F is *in* the data window $\beta = [0, M] \times [0, N]$. A data window α is in β if its retention time and m/z value intervals are sub-intervals of $[0, M]$ and $[0, N]$ respectively.

Data Density. Since there are usually fewer peaks in a summary of β than in F, querying a summary of β instead of F for an $m \times n$-summary of a given data window will help speed up the time it takes to get the $m \times n$-summary. Here we generate some pre-calculated summaries of β for querying, in which the following metric will be used.

Definition 1. *The data density of an $m \times n$-summary of a data window* $\alpha = [rtMin, rtMax] \times [mzMin, mzMax]$ *is* $\frac{m \times n}{(rtMax - rtMin) \times (mzMax - mzMin)}$.

Let P_β be a perfect $k \times k$-summary of β. Then the data density of P_β is $\frac{k^2}{M \times N}$. Assume α remains a data window in β and we are asked to query F for a perfect $m \times n$-summary of α that is prepared for presentation with their peak intensities in a display window. If the data density of P_β is close to that of an $m \times n$-summary of α, then the $m \times n$-summary of α reported by querying P_β for is expected to admit representativeness close to that of a perfect $m \times n$-summary of α. An $m \times n$-summary of α will be reported by querying P_β for with sufficiently less time and space than by querying F for straight forwardly.

This inspired us to split an MS data set into several perfect squared summaries according to specific data densities so that all such summaries can be pre-stored independently for querying. Then it will be available to query a perfect squared summary whose data density comes closest to that of a given data window's $m \times n$-summary.

Given a data density Φ, the minimum integral side length of a perfect squared summary of β with a data density no less than Φ is $\sqrt{\Phi \times M \times N}$.

MS Data Set Splitting. We aim to split F into perfect squared summaries of β whose data densities are mutually distinct. To do so, we need to decide how many squared summaries F needs to be split into as well as what data densities are used for the summaries. We choose to split F into perfect squared summaries whose data densities scale down geometrically at a fixed rate.

Since there are $|F|$ peaks in β, we choose a perfect squared summary of β to admit the largest data density $\frac{|F|}{M \times N}$. Let B_{min} denote the minimum peak number of a data window summary over those for queries of F to report. Then the data density of a perfect squared summary of β is in no need of less than $\frac{B_{min}}{M \times N}$. It follows that the perfect squared summaries of β with respect to F should admit data densities in the interval $\left[\frac{B_{min}}{M \times N}, \frac{|F|}{M \times N}\right]$. Let γ be a real number with $0 < \gamma < 1$, $K = \left\lfloor \frac{\ln B_{min} - \ln |F|}{\ln \gamma} \right\rfloor + 1$. Then if one would like to split F into squared summaries whose data densities scale down in proportion as γ, it suffices to split F into K squared summaries, whose data densities are as follows: $\frac{|F|}{M \times N}, \frac{|F|\gamma}{M \times N}, \ldots, \frac{|F|\gamma^{K-1}}{M \times N}$. Since in practice, we always select squared summaries of β with integral side lengths, once γ is selected as the proportion following which the summary data densities scale down, the actual side length of the ith perfect squared summary for F to be split into will be set as $\left\lceil \sqrt{|F|\gamma^{i-1}} \right\rceil$, $1 \leq i \leq K$.

Summary Extraction. Let $k[i] = \left\lceil \sqrt{|F|\gamma^{i-1}} \right\rceil$, $1 \leq i \leq K$. Then a perfect $k[i] \times k[i]$ - summary of β can be extracted from F.

Let $S_0 = F$ and S_i for $1 \leq i \leq K$ denote a perfect $k[i] \times k[i]$ - summary of β with respect to F. We can set up $K + 1$ data files to store $S_0, S_1, \ldots, S_K$ respectively. In what follows, we shall mention by *a storage system* of an MS data set to indicate a set of files that are used to store peaks in the MS data set. We name a storage system of F as *mzMD*, if the storage system happens to store such data files as $S_i \subseteq F$ for $0 \leq i \leq K$.

To set up the mzMD format of a storage system of F, we used a SQLite3 table to store an mzMD file. All tables admit the same record format that contains four attribute values: ID, mz, rt and intensity. A table was always set up together with the attributes *rt* and *mz* as a multi-column index. For the purpose of querying the files in the mzMD format of a storage system for a summary of a given data window, we are asked to set up a table to store the data densities of all squared summaries of β. Since the side length of S_i is $k[i]$, the data density of S_i is $\frac{k[i] \times k[i]}{M \times N}$ for $1 \leq i \leq K$. Since so, we have set up a SQLite3 table named as *Information* with K records to store the data density of S_i for $1 \leq i \leq K$. So far, we are ready to focus on how to query the mzMD format of a storage system for a summary of a given data window.

2.2 Query a Data Window for a Summary

Given positive integers m, n and a data window $\alpha = [rtMin, rtMax] \times [mzMin, mzMax]$, then $\Phi_\alpha = \frac{m \times n}{(rtMax-rtMin) \times (mzMax-mzMin)}$ is the data density of an $m \times n$-summary of α. Assume in the mzMD format of a storage system of β, there are $K + 1$ files represented by S_i for $0 \leq i \leq K$, where S_i is a perfect $k[i] \times k[i]$-summary of β with respect to F for $i \geq 1$ and $S_0 = F$.

Let $\Phi[i] = \frac{k[i] \times k[i]}{M \times N}$, $1 \leq i \leq K$. Then the data density of S_i is $\Phi[i]$. We set $\Phi[0] = \infty$ as the data density of F.

Input: A data window $\alpha = [rtMin, rtMax] \times [mzMin, mzMax]$, m and n.
Output: An $m \times n$-summary of α.
1. $\Phi_\alpha \leftarrow \frac{m \times n}{(rtMax-rtMin) \times (mzMax-mzMin)}$.
2. Get x such that $\Phi[x + 1] < \Phi_\alpha \leq \Phi[x]$.
3. $\alpha[S_x] \leftarrow Get(\alpha, x, K)$.
4. Output the $m \times n$-summary of $\alpha[S_x]$.

Fig. 2. The algorithm to get an $m \times n$-summary.

Since $\Phi[i + 1] < \Phi[i]$, $0 \leq i \leq K$, one can always get an integer x such that $\Phi[x + 1] < \Phi_\alpha \leq \Phi[x]$ by the Information table in the storage system. Then S_x instead of F is of what we aim at to query for a summary. Let $\alpha[S_i]$ denote the set of all peaks in α with respect to S_i. We set a subroutine named as $Get(\alpha, x, K)$ that can get $\alpha[S_x]$ from S_x. Then the algorithm to query the storage system for an $m \times n$-summary of α is described in Fig. 2.

3 Results

We downloaded the Java source code of mzTree and implemented mzMD in Java. We downloaded 10 raw files of a public MS data set of ovarian cancer tumor samples (MASSIVE ID: MSV000080257) [10]. The raw files were converted into mzML files in the profile modes by msconvert [3].

The profile mode mzML formats of those 10 files were utilized to assess the performance of mzMD and mzTree for them to convert an MS data set into their formats of a storage system. The eighth of these 10 mzML files which will be denoted as F, contains 67 936 443 peaks and is in size of 1.8 GB. The three formats of storage systems respectively converted from F were used to examine the performance of mzMD and mzTree in querying for data window summaries. All experiments were performed on a MacBook Pro laptop with a 2.3 GHz Intel Core i9 processor and 16 GB 2 400 MHz DDR4 memory.

3.1 Query for Data Window Summaries

We shall denote by F the storage system that stores F when we mention mzMD and mzTree for them to query their formats of a storage system that stores F for a summary. Let $\beta = [0, M] \times [0, N]$ be a data window for F to be in. A data window in β can be generated randomly as follows. Let a_1 and a_2 denote two random real numbers in $[0, 1]$. An m/z value interval can be generated by setting the length of the m/z value interval as $x = (0.9a_1 + 0.1)M$ and the left end of the interval as $mz = a_2(M - x)$. For two random numbers b_1 and b_2 in $[0, 1]$, a retention time interval can be generated by setting the retention time interval length as $y = (0.9b_1 + 0.1)N$ and the left end of the interval as $rt = b_2(N - y)$. Then $[rt, rt + y] \times [mz, mz + x]\$$ is a data window in β. In this way, we generated 1 000 data windows.

We obtained 1 000 perfect 100×100-summaries of the 1 000 randomly generated data windows respectively. Let α denote an arbitrary one of the 1 000 randomly generated data windows and P a perfect 100×100-summary of α. The Q-score of an arbitrary summary S of α can be computed using Formula (4). Then to compare mzTree and mzMD in their summary retrieval performance, we utilized the summaries of these data windows they reported through querying F and the running time for them to query F for summaries of these data windows.

Methods for Comparing mzMD With mzTree. While mzMD reports an $m \times n$-summary for a query with a data window α and two positive integers m and n, mzTree returns a summary of c peaks for a query with a data window α and a positive integer c. To compare mzMD with mzTree, we utilized the following experiment to find out what a value c should be set in mzTree when it runs to query F for a data window summary.

Setting m and n with $m = n = 100$ means that at most 10 000 peaks in a given data window are appropriate to show their intensities without overlaps. The parameter c in mzTree specifies the number of peaks it should report in the summary of a given data window. In practice, we need to set c by a value of about 10 000 to make sure that mzTree can report high-quality summaries. For an arbitrary $c \in \{100 \times i | 1 \leq i \leq 25\}$, there are always 1 000 respective summaries of those randomly generated data windows which were reported by mzTree to query F for data window summaries of c peaks.

When $c = 13000$, the average Q-score of those 1 000 summaries is 0.1664, that achieves the maximum over all values of $c \in \{100 \times i | 1 \leq i \leq 25\}$. We set c to 13000 for mzTree in the experiments.

Summary Quality. Aiming at those 1 000 randomly generated data windows, mzMD and mzTree were respectively invoked to query F for 100×100-summaries and summaries of 13000 peaks. The experimental results imply that mzMD is superior to mzTree in terms of the coverage and efficiency of summaries they reported. The Q-score of those summaries reported by mzMD and mzTree are showed in Fig. 3(a).

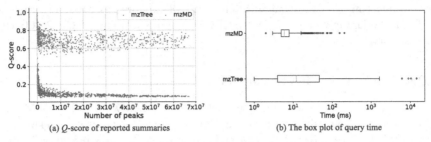

(a) Q-score of reported summaries   (b) The box plot of query time

Fig. 3. Q-score and query time of reported summaries

The average Q-score of the summaries reported by mzMD and mzTree for them to query F are 0.71 and 0.13, respectively. This informs that the summary quality of mzMD is about 4.5 times higher than mzTree.

Summary Query Speed. In Fig. 3(b), we present the running time of mzMD and mzTree for them to query F for summaries of the 1 000 randomly generated data windows. The mean query times of mzTree and mzMD are 65.058 and 8.532, the standard query time variances of them are 351.708 and 11.145. This informs that mzMD can query their formats of storage systems for a data window summary at faster a speed.

Table 1. The distribution of query classes in executions for mzMD and mzTree to query F for summaries of 1 000 randomly generated data windows

Class	Time cost (ms)	mzMD	mzTree
A	≤20	951	629
B	20–100	47	227
C	100–300	2	88
D	300–500	0	17
	500–5000	0	35
	>5000	0	4

The running time stability of querying for data window summaries deeply affects the user experience of an MS data visualization tool. To examine the running time stability of summary queries, we divide the queries into four classes based on their query times: A: ≤20 ms, B: 20–100 ms, C: 100–300 ms and D: >300 ms. A query usually brings an obvious delay in real-time visualization when it takes more than 300 ms. Table 1 presents the distributions of the queries of the three tools. While 95% of mzMD queries were Class-A, only 63% of mzTree queries were Class-A, showing that mzMD is much faster than mzTree.

There were 56 class-D ones in mzTree's queries of F for summaries, while there were no class-D ones in mzMD's queries. Moreover, there were 39 queries of mzTree whose running time are longer than 500 ms. The longest query time of mzTree was 14 451 ms. The longest query time of mzMD was 207 ms.

Data Conversion. We also assessed the performance of mzMD and mzTree for them to convert mzML files into their formats of storage systems. In the experiments for mzMD to do data conversion, we always set $\gamma = 0.5$ and $B_{min} = 1000$. The 10 profile-mode mzML files were used for the performance evaluation of mzTree and mzMD for converting these MS files into their formats of storage systems. Figure 4 shows the running time and disk space usage statistics of the three tools. For the three tools, the storage size increases linearly as the number of peaks in the MS data sets increases. In terms of data conversion speed, mzMD outperformed mzTree.

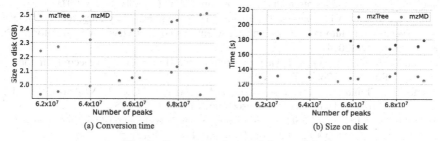

(a) Conversion time   (b) Size on disk

Fig. 4. Conversion time and size on disk

4 Conclusions

We presented a new MS data storage and retrieval system mzMD, that is intended for use in manual inspection aided LC–MS data analysis. We proposed two criteria coverage and efficiency, to reflect the efficient representativeness of a data window summary and, a formula called Q-score, which is synthesized from the coverage and efficiency of a data window summary, to evaluate the summary quality. Experimental statistics demonstrated that mzMD reported better quality summaries and achieved better query time stability than mzTree. In future research, we will further improve the coverage and efficiency of mzMD, especially for small data windows of which high data density summaries are queried for. We look forward to seeing mzMD to be taken for use in MS data visualization applications.

References

1. Aebersold, R., Mann, M.: Mass spectrometry-based proteomics. Nature **422**(6928), 198–207 (2003)
2. Bouyssie, D., et al.: mzdb: a file format using multiple indexing strategies for the efficient analysis of large lc-ms/ms and swath-ms data sets. Mol. Cell. Proteom. **14**(3), 771–781 (2015)

3. Chambers, M.C., et al.: A cross-platform toolkit for mass spectrometry and proteomics. Nat. Biotechnol. **30**(10), 918–920 (2012)
4. Deutsch, E.: Mzml: a single, unifying data format for mass spectrometer output. Proteomics **8**(14), 2776–2777 (2008)
5. Hand, D.J.: Principles of data mining. Drug Saf. **30**(7), 621–622 (2007)
6. Handy, K., Rosen, J., Gillan, A., Smith, R.: Fast, axis-agnostic, dynamically summarized storage and retrieval for mass spectrometry data. PLoS ONE **12**(11), e0188059 (2017)
7. Henning, J., Smith, R.: A web-based system for creating, viewing, and editing precursor mass spectrometry ground truth data. BMC Bioinform. **21**(1), 1–10 (2020)
8. Kou, Q., Xun, L., Liu, X.: Toppic: a software tool for top-down mass spectrometry-based proteoform identification and characterization. Bioinformatics **32**(22), 3495–3497 (2016)
9. Liu, X., et al.: Protein identification using top-down spectra. Mol. Cell. Proteom. **11**(6), (2012)
10. Park, J., et al.: Informed-proteomics: open-source software package for top-down proteomics. Nat. Methods **14**(9), 909–914 (2017)
11. Pedrioli, P.G.A., et al.: A common open representation of mass spectrometry data and its application to proteomics research. Nat. Biotechnol. **22**(11), 1459–1466 (2004)
12. Smith, R., Mathis, A.D., Ventura, D., Prince, J.T.: Proteomics, lipidomics, metabolomics: a mass spectrometry tutorial from a computer scientist's point of view. BMC Bioinform. **15**(7 Supplement), S9 (2014)
13. Sturm, M., Kohlbacher, O.: Toppview: an open-source viewer for mass spectrometry data. J. Proteome Res. **8**(7), 3760–3763 (2009)
14. Tyanova, S., Temu, T., Carlson, A., Sinitcyn, P., Mann, M., Cox, J.: Visualization of LC-MS/MS proteomics data in maxquant. Proteomics **15**(8), 1453–1456 (2015)
15. Wilhelm, M., Kirchner, M., Steen, J.A., Steen, H.: mz5: space-and time-efficient storage of mass spectrometry data sets. Mol. Cell. Proteom., **11**(1), (2012)
16. Wüllems, K., Kolling, J., Bednarz, H., Niehaus, K., Hans, V.H., Nattkemper, T.W.: Detection and visualization of communities in mass spectrometry imaging data. BMC Bioinform. **20**(1), 303 (2019)
17. Yang, R., et al.: A spectrum graph-based protein sequence filtering algorithm for proteoform identification by top-down mass spectrometry. In: 2017 IEEE International Conference on Bioinformatics and Biomedicine (BIBM), pp. 222–229. IEEE (2017)

Drug-Target Interaction Prediction via Multiple Output Graph Convolutional Networks

Qing Ye$^{(\boxtimes)}$, Xiaolong Zhang, and Xiaoli Lin

Hubei Key Laboratory of Intelligent Information Processing and Real-Time Industrial System, School of Computer Science and Technology, Wuhan University of Science and Technology, Wuhan, China
{xiaolong.zhang,linxiaoli}@wust.edu.cn

Abstract. Computational prediction of drug-target interaction (DTI) is very important for the new drug discovery. Currently, graph convolutional networks (GCNs) have been gained a lot of momentum, as its performance on non-Euclidean data. Although drugs and targets are two typical non-Euclidean data, many problems are also existed when use GCNs in DTI prediction. Firstly, most state-of-the-art GCN models are prone to the vanishing gradient problem, which is more serious in DTI prediction, as the number of interactions is limit. Secondly, a suitable graph is hardly defined for GCN in DTI prediction, as the relationship between the samples is not explicitly provided. To overcome the above problems, in this paper, a multiple output graph convolutional network (MOGCN) based DTI prediction method is designed. MOGCN enhances its learning ability with many new designed auxiliary classifier layers and a new designed graph calculation method. Many auxiliary classifier layers can increase the gradient signal that gets propagated back, utilize multi-level features to train the model, and use the features produced by the higher, middle or lower layers in a unified framework. The graph calculation method can use both the label information and the manifold. The conducted experiments validate the effectiveness of our MOGCN.

Keywords: Drug-target interactions · Graph convolutional network · Multiple output deep learning · Auxiliary classifier layer

1 Introduction

The deep learning based DTI prediction method has recently been taken more and more attention, which can be divided into three categories: deep neural networks (DNN) based method, convolutional neural networks (CNN) based method, and graph convolutional networks (GCN) based method.

Many DNN based DTI prediction methods have been proposed. Firstly, different inputs have been designed for DNN [1, 2]. Secondly, different DNN structures have been designed for DTI prediction [3–6]. Thirdly, some researchers used DNN together with other methods [7, 8]. DNN can effectively improve the effect of DTI prediction. However, a large number of parameters need to be trained. CNN is mainly composed of convolutional layers, which can greatly reduce the parameters.

© Springer Nature Switzerland AG 2021
D.-S. Huang et al. (Eds.): ICIC 2021, LNAI 12838, pp. 87–99, 2021.
https://doi.org/10.1007/978-3-030-84532-2_9

Many CNN based DTI prediction methods have been proposed, where the main difference is designing different inputs. Firstly, reshaped the extracted feature vector to generate the input is a popular method [9, 10]. Secondly, the sequence of target and the SMILES of drug are used as the input [7, 11, 12]. However, it's may be difficult for CNN to extract the feature from the drug and the targets, as local features are distributed in different locations in different sequence and SMILES. GCNs have been gained a lot of momentum in the last few years, as the limited performance of CNNs when dealing with the non-Euclidean data. Drugs and targets are two typical non-Euclidean data, and then GCNs could be promising for DTI prediction.

Many GCN based DTI prediction methods have been proposed. Firstly, GCNs have been used to extract features from the drug molecular [13–15]. However, the optimization goal of the GCN and the optimization goal of classifier are independent in Ref. [13, 15], and the graph is constructed by atoms but not by molecules in Ref. [14]. Secondly, GCNs have been used for dimensionality reduction [16, 17]. However, GCN optimization goals and classification optimization goals are also independent in these methods. Thirdly, GCNs has been used for classification [18]. However, the GCN structure contains only one GCN layer, and he graph used by GCN is calculated according to DDI and PPI, which is hardly automatically predicted.

Many problems can be concluded from the above methods: Firstly, goals of GCN optimization and classification optimization are optimized independently [13, 15–17], and then the classification ability of GCN is not utilized. Secondly, a shallow GCN is used for DTI prediction [18]. Thirdly, the graph could be difficult calculated in real application in Ref. [18]. Furthermore, the graph of many methods is calculated by bonds of drugs [13–16] but not the relationships among drug-target pairs.

To overcome the first and second problems, a multiple output graph convolutional network (MOGCN) is designed, which contains many auxiliary classifier layers. These auxiliary classifier layers are distributed in the low, middle and high layers. As a result, MOGCN owns following advantages: losses in different layers can increase the gradient signal that gets propagated back; multi classification regularizations can be used to optimize the MOGCN; the model can be trained by multi-level features; features in different levels can be used for classification in a unified framework. To overcome the third and fourth problems, a DNN and k-nearest neighbor (KNN) based method is designed to calculate the graph, where the calculated graph contains both the manifold and the label information. To further overcome the second problem, two auto-encoders are respectively used to learn low-level features for drugs and targets, which can make that the MOGCN can mainly focus on learning high-level features.

2   Proposed Method

2.1   Problem Description and Notation Definition

The goal of DTI prediction is to learn a model that takes a pair of drug and target and output the interaction. Before introducing our method, many important notations adopted in this paper are provided in Table 1.

Table 1. Notations used in this paper.

Notations	Descriptions
D, T, I, n, m	D and T are drugs and targets features, I is interaction matrix, n and m are number of drugs targets
$\hat{D}, \hat{T}, d_i, t_j$	$\hat{D}$ is output of encoder of SAE of D, $\hat{T}$ is output of encoder of SAE of T, d_i is i-th sample of D, t_j is j-th sample of T
$X, L, X_L, L_L, X_T, L_T, u$	X and L are all samples and labels, X_L and L_L are the training samples and labels, X_T and L_T are the testing samples and labels, u is the number of samples
$\delta(\cdot), \varphi(\cdot)$	$\delta(\cdot)$ is an activation function, where the sigmoid function is used here $\varphi(\cdot)$ is a loss function, where the cross entropy loss function is used here
$A, \tilde{A}, Z$	A is the adjacency matrix, $\tilde{A}$ is the adjacency matrix with add self-loop for A, Z is the graph diagonal degree matrix
$X_g, \tilde{W}g, Og, \hat{O}g, \widehat{W}g, \hat{b}g, Yg, Y_G, G$	X_g is the input of g-th layer, $\tilde{W}g$ is the weight of the GCN sub layer of g-th layer, Og is the output of the GCN sub layer of g-th layer, $\hat{O}g$ is the output of the dropout sub layer, $\widehat{W}g$ is the weight of linear sub layer of g-th layer, $\hat{b}g$ is the bias term of linear sub layer, and Y_g is the output of the linear sub layer of g-th layer, Y_G is the output of the linear layer, G is the number of layers of MOGCN
$k, N_k(y_j), \hat{y}i$	k is number of nearest neighbor, $N_k(y_j)$ is the j-th k nearest neighbor of $\hat{y}i$, $\hat{y}i$ is i-th sample of $\hat{Y}$

2.2 Overview of Our Method

The overview of our method is shown in the Fig. 1, which contains 5 steps, such as feature extraction, low-level features extraction, feature concatenation, graph calculation, and MOGCN. The feature extraction is used to extract the features for drugs and targets. The low-level features extraction is used to learn the low-level features for drugs and targets. The feature concatenation is used to generate the sample of the drug-target pair. The graph calculation is used to calculate the adjacency matrix A for MOGCN. The MOGCN is our newly designed deep learning framework. These steps will be described in detail in the following subsections.

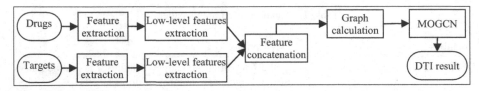

Fig. 1. Overview of our method

2.3 Feature Extraction

Drugs features $D = [d_1, d_2, \cdots, d_n]^T$ and targets features $T = [t_1, t_2, \cdots, t_m]^T$ are respectively calculated by PaDEL [19] and the propy tool [20]. The drug features include 797 descriptors (663 1D, 2D descriptors, and 134 3D descriptors) and 10 types of fingerprints. The total number of the drug features is 15329. The target features include five feature groups such as: amino acid composition, autocorrelation, composition, transition and distribution, quasi-sequence order, pseudo-amino acid composition and so on. The total number of the target features is 9543.

2.4 Low-Level Features Extraction and Feature Concatenation

Training GCN directly on high-dimensional drug features and target features will cause too many parameters to be trained in the first layer. Furthermore, with the larger depth of the network, the ability to propagate gradients back through all the layers in an effective manner was a serious concern, which is more serious for the first few layers. This leads to insufficient extraction of low-level features. To overcome the above problem, low-level features are firstly extracted by the stack auto encoder (SAE). Because the goal of the SAE is to extract the low-level features, the shallow encoder and decoder are used in this paper. The encoder and decoder of the SAE contain two linear layers and two activation layers, where the sigmoid function is used for the activation layer. The output of the encoder is the low-level feature.

After training the encoder for drugs by D, the low-level features $\hat{D}$ of D can be obtained by the encoder. Similarly, the low-level features $\hat{T}$ of T can be obtained by the encoder trained by T. The u samples $X = [x_1, x_2, \cdots, x_u]$ can be generated from $\hat{D}$ and $\hat{T}$, where $xk = [\hat{d}_i, \hat{t}_j]^T$. The corresponding u labels $L = [l_1, l_2, \cdots, l_u]$ can be generated from I, where l_k is the i-th row and j-th column of I.

2.5 Graph Calculation

An adjacency matrix A should be calculated for MOGCN. Many graph calculation methods have been proposed for DTI prediction. Zhao et.al calculated A by DDI and PPI; however, DDI and PPI are also hardly automatically predicted [18]. And many other A are calculated by bonds of drugs [13–17], however, these graphs are only used for extracting features. Analyzed the function of A, A should represent the relationship between samples, especially the classification relationship between samples. However, the labels of testing samples are unknown. As a result, to calculate the A, a DNN and KNN based method is designed.

Given training samples X_L, corresponding label L_L, testing samples X_T, the DNN and KNN based method owns 4 steps. Firstly, a two layers DNN model is trained. And then X_L and X_T are projected to $\hat{Y}_L$ and $\hat{Y}_T$ by the first layer of the trained DNN model. Thirdly, $\hat{Y}$ is calculated by $\hat{Y} = [\hat{Y}_L; \hat{Y}_T]$. In the last, the A can be calculated by Eq. (1).

$$A_{ij} = \begin{cases} 1, & \text{if } \hat{y}_i \in N_k(\hat{y}_j) \text{ and } \hat{y}_j \in N_k(\hat{y}_i) \\ 0, & \text{others} \end{cases} \tag{1}$$

A two layers DNN model is trained here, as DNN is only used to learn a low dimensional space that contains both manifold information or label information. Furthermore, low dimensional space is obtained by the first linear sub layer but not by the second linear sub layer, as the result of second linear sub layer is too much affected by the label but the label of the testing sample is unknown. According to above analyze, the proposed graph calculation method can make that A_{ij} has a greater probability of being set to 1 when x_i and x_j are near with each other or x_i and x_j are with the same labels. As a result, A contains both manifold and label information.

2.6 The Proposed MOGCN Model

Unlike DNN, which are able to take advantage of stacking very deep layers, GCNs suffer from vanishing gradient, over-smoothing and over-fitting issues when going deeper [21]. These challenges are particularly serious in DTI prediction, as the number of interactions is limited in the DTI datasets. Specifically, most interactions focus on only a few targets or a few drugs, which makes that the training samples of most drugs and targets are not enough. As a result, these challenges limit the representation power of GCNs on DTI prediction. For example, Zhao et.al used a GCN structure with one GCN layer [18]. To overcome the above problem, in this paper, a MOGCN for DTI prediction is designed.

Given the training samples X_L, the corresponding labels L_L, and the adjacency matrix A, the MOGCN can be shown in the Fig. 2, which contains an input layer, an output layer, an linear layer, many hidden layers and many auxiliary classifier layers. The hidden layer contains a GCN sub layer, an activation sub layer and a dropout sub layer. The auxiliary classifier layer is a new designed layer, which contains a GCN sub layer, an activation sub layer, a linear sub layer, and a loss function.

Given X_g as the input of the g-th layer, the GCN sub layer can be defined as:

$$Og = Z^{-\frac{1}{2}} \tilde{A} Z^{-\frac{1}{2}} X_g \tilde{W}_g \tag{2}$$

Where $\tilde{A}$ is the graph adjacency matrix with add self-loop for A, Z is the graph diagonal degree matrix which can be calculated from A, $A \in R^{u \times u}$ is a graph adjacency matrix that can be calculated by Algorithm 1.

The definition of the activation and dropout sub layers can be found from [22].

For an auxiliary classifier layer, a linear sub layer and a loss function are existed here, which can be respectively defined as Eq. (3) and Eq. (4):

$$Yg = \widehat{W}_g^{T} \widehat{Og} + \widehat{b}_g \tag{3}$$

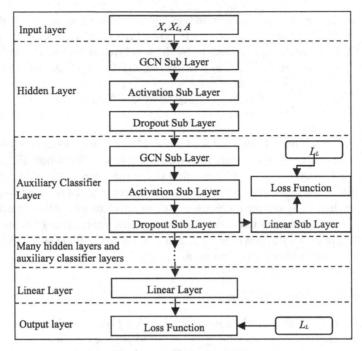

Fig. 2. Overview of MOGCN

$$J_g(W, b, X, L_L) = \varphi(Y_g, L_L) \tag{4}$$

The loss function of the output layer can be defined as:

$$J_G(W, b, X, L_L) = \varphi(Y_G, L_L) \tag{5}$$

W and b can be optimized by minimizing Eq. (6) with the Adam optimizer [25].

$$\min_{W,b} \sum_{g=1}^{G} J_g(W, b, X, L_L) \tag{6}$$

Where $J_g(W, b, X, L_L) = 0$, if g-th layer is a hidden layer.

It can be seen from Fig. 2 and Eq. (6) that the number of layers of propagate gradients back is smaller when g is smaller. And then the effective of $J_g(W, b, X, L_L)$ for calculating W_i and b_i is higher. Furthermore, the stronger performance of relatively shallower networks on this task suggests that the features produced by the layers in the middle of the network should be more discriminative. As a result, by adding these auxiliary classifiers layers connected to these intermediate layers, MOGCN would expect to increase discrimination in the lower stages in the classifier, enhance the gradient signal used for propagated back, and provide additional regularization.

2.7 Architectural Parameter

Many architectural parameters are existed in the low-level features extraction, graph calculation and MOGCN.

In the low-level features extraction, output dimensions of two encoder layers should be set, which are set to 800 and 500. Similarly, the output dimensions of two decoder layers are set to 500 and 800. These output dimensions have little effect on the results in a larger range, as encoder layers is only used for low-level features extraction, so that they are simply set to the above values.

In the graph calculation, the output dimensions of two linear layers should be set, which are respectively set to 100, 2, where 2 is the number of the class. k used in Eq. (4) is set to 10. These values are also have little effect on the results in a larger range, as DNN is only used to learn low dimensional space and k is only used to define the manifold, so that they are simply set to the above values.

In the MOGCN, the layer number G, the output dimensions of the GCN sub layer and the linear sub layer should be set. To simplify the parameter search, the output dimensions of all GCN sub layers are set to 300, as the ability of the MOGCN can also be controlled by depth. The output dimensions of all linear sub layers are set to 2, as the number of the class is 2. The layer number G is set to 1, 3, 5, which is chosen by 5-fold cross validation. G is not chosen from a larger range, as a larger MOGCN structure could be hardly trained when the positive examples is limited.

3 Experiments

3.1 Dataset

Nuclear receptors (NR), G protein coupled receptors (GPCR), ion channels (IC), enzymes (E) [23] and drug bank (DB) [24] are used here. Simple statistics of them are represented in the Table 2. The 2-th to 4-th rows respectively represents the number of drugs, targets and interactions, which shows that the number of interactions is small and the number of drug target pairs is far more than that of interactions.

Table 2. Simple statistics for datasets.

Type	NR	GPCR	IC	E	DB
Drugs	54	223	210	445	5877
Targets	26	95	204	664	3348
Interactions	90	635	1476	2926	12674

3.2 Compared Methods

MOGCN is a GCN based method, so that it is compared with a GCN based method, which is come from MOGCN by replacing each auxiliary classifier layer of MOGCN with a hidden layer. MOGCN is also compared with two DNN structures [3, 5], as these two DNN structures may be good and both DNN and GCN belong to deep learning. These two DNN structures are defined as DNN1 [3] and DNN2 [5].

Furthermore, SAE is used to learn the low level features in this paper. To prove that SAE is benefit for MOGCN, low level features and the original features are respectively inputted to the compared methods. As a result, after defining the original features as SRC and the low level features as SAE, following methods are compared: SRC+DNN1, SRC+DNN2, SRC+GCN, SRC+MOGCN, SAE+DNN1, SAE+DNN2, SAE+GCN and SAE+MOGCN.

3.3 Experimental Setting

In this work, three experimental settings that are shown in the Table 3 are evaluated. CVD and CVT and CVP respectively represent the corresponding DTI values of certain drugs, targets and interactions in the training set are missed but existed in the test sets, where CVD can be used for new drug development, CVT can be used to find effective drugs from known drugs for new targets, CVP can be used to find new interactions from known drugs and known targets.

Table 3. The information of three experimental settings.

Experimental setting	Drugs	Targets	Interactions
CVD	New	Known	New
CVT	Known	New	New
CVP	Known	Known	New

A standard 5-fold cross validation is performed. More precisely, drugs, targets and interactions are respectively divided into 5 parts in *CVD*, *CVT* and *CVP*, where one part is used for testing and other parts are used for training. Furthermore, for the training samples, not all negative samples but five times more negative samples than positive samples are used, as using too more negative samples will make the data imbalance problem too prominent and using too few negative samples will result in too much negative sample information loss. The used negative samples are randomly selected all negative samples. The batch size is set to 128 for DNN1 and DNN2. The batch size is set to 1 for GCN and MOGCN, as GCN based methods trained by the batched training samples is still difficult. Furthermore, two evaluation metrics named AUC and AUPR are used in the experiments, where AUC is the area under the ROC and AUPR is the area under the precision-recall curve.

3.4 The *CVD* Experiments

CVD can be used for new drug development. The experiment results are presented in the Fig. 3. Following concludes can be obtained from the Fig. 3:

Firstly, GCN based methods are better than DNN based methods. It can be seen from Fig. 3 that most evaluation metrics of GCN based methods are higher than that of DNN based methods, and all evaluation metrics of the SRC+MOGCN and SAE + MOGCN are higher than that of the DNN based methods. They show that using GCN based methods to improve the DTI prediction is necessary.

Secondly, the low level features are better than the original features for GCN based methods. It can be seen from Fig. 3 that AUCs and AUPRs of SAE+GCN and SAE+MOGCN are higher than that of SRC+GCN and SRC+MOGCN on IC, GPCR, E and DB, and most evaluation metrics of SAE+MOGCN are higher than that of SRC+MOGCN on NR. They prove that using SAE to learn low level features is benefit for GCN and MOGCN.

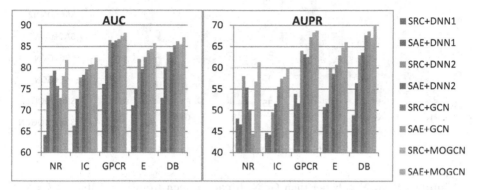

Fig. 3. Results of CVD experiments

Thirdly, MOGCN is better than GCN. It can be seen from Fig. 3 that AUCs and AUPRs of SRC+MOGCN and SAE+MOGCN are higher than that of SRC+GCN and SAE+GCN on all datasets. It shows that using the multiple output graph convolutional network structure can improve the effectiveness of DTI prediction.

Fourthly, SAE+MOGCN is the best. It can be seen from Fig. 3 that most evaluation metrics of SAE+MOGCN are higher than that of the compared methods. Specially, AUCs of SAE+MOGCN are respectively 2.56%, 1.58%, 0.75%, 1.36%, and 0.92% higher than that of the second best methods on datasets. *AUPRs* of SAE+MOGCN are respectively 3.27%, 2.14%, 0.39%, 1.25%, 1.36%, and 1.55% higher than that of the second best methods on datasets. They show that using SAE together with MOGCN is a good method for DTI prediction.

3.5 The *CVT* Experiments

CVT can be used to find effective drugs for new targets. The experiment results are presented in the Fig. 4. Following concludes can be obtained from the Fig. 4:

Firstly, GCN based methods are better than DNN based methods. It can be seen from Fig. 4 that nearly all evaluation metrics of GCN based methods are higher than that of DNN based methods on IC, GPCR, E and DB, where only some evaluation metrics of SRC+GCN lower than that of SRC+DNN2. Furthermore, it can be seen from Fig. 4 that AUCs and AUPRs of the SAE+MOGCN are higher than that of the DNN based methods on NR. They prove that using GCN based methods to improve the DTI prediction is necessary.

Secondly, the low level features are better than the original features for GCN based methods. It can be seen from Fig. 4 that AUCs and AUPRs of SAE+GCN and SAE+MOGCN are all higher than that of SRC+GCN and SRC+MOGCN. It shows that using SAE to learn low level features is benefit for GCN and MOGCN.

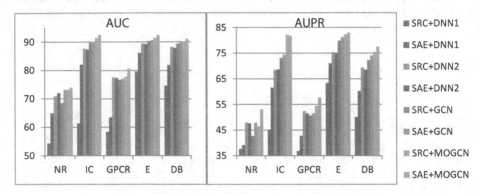

Fig. 4. Results of CVT experiments

Thirdly, MOGCN is better than GCN. It can be seen from Fig. 4 that AUCs and AUPRs of SRC+MOGCN and SAE+MOGCN are higher than that of SRC+GCN and SAE+GCN. It shows that using the multiple output graph convolutional network structure can improve the effectiveness of DTI prediction.

Fourthly, SAE+MOGCN is the best. It can be seen from Fig. 4 that most evaluation metrics of SAE+MOGCN are higher than that of the compared methods. Specially, AUCs of SAE+MOGCN are respectively 0.70%, 1.05%, 2.88%, 1.02% and 0.97% higher than that of the second best methods. AUPRs of SAE+MOGCN are respectively 5.16%, -0.46%, 3.20%, 0.68%, and 2.11% higher than that of the second best methods. They prove that using SAE together with MOGCN is also a good method for DTI prediction.

3.6 The *CVP* Experiments

CVP can be used to find effective drugs from known drugs for new targets. The experiment results of all compared methods are presented in the Fig. 5. Following concludes can be obtained from the Fig. 5:

Firstly, the GCN based methods are better than the DNN based methods. It can be seen from Fig. 5 that the results of all evaluation metrics of GCN based methods are higher than that of DNN based methods. It proves that GCN based methods are better than the DNN based methods.

Secondly, the low level features are better than the original features for GCN based methods. It can be seen from Fig. 5 that most AUCs and AUPRs of SAE+MOGCN are higher than that of SRC+MOGCN on all databases, and most evaluation metrics of SAE+GCN are higher than that of SRC+GCN on IC and GPCR. They show that using SAE to learn low level features is benefit for GCN and MOGCN.

Thirdly, MOGCN is better than GCN. It can be seen from Fig. 5 that most evaluation metrics of SRC+MOGCN and SAE+MOGCN are higher than that of SRC + GCN and SAE+GCN. It proves that using the multiple output graph convolutional network structure can improve the effectiveness of DTI prediction.

Fourthly, SAE+MOGCN is the best. It can be seen from Fig. 5 that most evaluation metrics of SAE+MOGCN are higher than that of the compared methods. Specially, AUCs of SAE+MOGCN are respectively 0.81%, 0.34%, 0.91%, 0.50% and 0.85% higher than that of the second best methods on datasets. AUPRs of SAE+MOGCN are respectively 1.16%, 1.49%, −0.29%, 0.62% and 1.55% higher than that of the second best methods on datasets. They prove that using SAE together with MOGCN is a good method for DTI prediction.

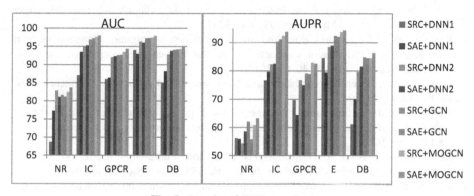

Fig. 5. Results of CVP experiments

4 Conclusion

This paper presents a MOGCN for DTI prediction. In MOGCN, SAE is used to learn low level features, a DNN and KNN based method is used to calculate the graph, and many auxiliary classifier layers are added to connect to the intermediate layers and the parameters are trained by multi loss functions. SAE makes that MOGCN can mainly focus on learning high-level features. The graph calculation method can makes that the graph contains both the label information and the manifold. The auxiliary classifier layers can increase discrimination in the lower stages in the classifier, enhance the gradient signal used for propagated back, and provides additional regularization. The conducted experiments validate that MOGCN is a competitive method compared to the previous ones.

As one of the further work, residual network family can used to increase the width and depth of the GCN. As another further work, a new GCN framework is used to calculate the graph, which can minimizing the distances among samples whose drugs and targets are with interactions and maximizing the distances among samples whose drugs and targets are without interactions.

Acknowledgments. The authors thank the members of Machine Learning and Artificial Intelligence Laboratory, School of Computer Science and Technology, Wuhan University of Science and

Technology, for their helpful discussion within seminars. This work was supported by, National Natural Science Foundation of China (No.61972299, 61502356), Zhejiang Provincial Natural Science Foundation (No.LQ18F020006, LQ18F020007), Hubei Province Natural Science Foundation of China (No. 2018CFB526).

References

1. Wang, H., Wang, J., Dong, C.: A novel approach for drug-target interactions prediction based on multimodal deep autoencoder. Front. Pharmacol. **10**, 1592 (2020)
2. Sturm, N., et al.: Industry-scale application and evaluation of deep learning for drug target prediction. J. Cheminform. **12**(1), 1–13 (2020). https://doi.org/10.1186/s13321-020-00428-5
3. Xie, L.W., et al.: Deep learning-based transcriptome data classification for drug-target interaction prediction. BMC Genom. **19**(667), 93–102 (2018)
4. Wang, L., et al.: Computational methods for the prediction of drug-target interactions from drug fingerprints and protein sequences by stacked auto-encoder deep neural network. Bioinform. Res. Appl. **10330**, 46–58 (2017)
5. Wen, M., et al.: Deep learning-based drug-target interaction prediction. J. Proteome Res. **16**(4), 1401–1409 (2017)
6. Wang, Y.B. et al. A deep learning-based method for drugtarget interaction prediction based on long short-term memory neural network, BMC Medical Informatics and Decision Making, **20**(49), 1–9 (2020)
7. Lee, I., Keum, J., Nam, H.: DeepConv-DTI: Prediction of drug-target interactions via deep learning with convolution on protein sequences, PLOS Comput. Biol. **15**(6) (2019)
8. Zhang, Y.F., et al.: SPVec: A Word2vec-inspired feature representation method for drug-target interaction prediction. Front. Chem. **7**, 1–11 (2020)
9. Rayhan, F. et al. FRnet-DTI: Deep convolutional neural network for drug-target interaction prediction, Heliyon. **6**(3), e03444 (2020)
10. Hu, S.S. et al. A convolutional neural network system to discriminate drug-target interactions, IEEE/ACM Trans. Comput. Biol. Bioinform. (2019), in press.
11. Monteiro, N.R.C., Ribeiro, B., Arrais, J.: Drug-target interaction prediction: end-to-end deep learning approach. IEEE/ACM Trans. Comput. Biol. Bioinform. (2020). https://doi.org/10.1109/TCBB.2020.2977335
12. Rifaioglu, A.S. et al. DEEPScreen: high performance drug–target interaction prediction with convolutional neural networks using 2-D structural compound representations, Chem. Sci. **9**, 1–68 (2020)
13. David, D. et al. Convolutional networks on graphs for learning molecular fingerprints. In: Proceedings of the 28th International Conference on Neural Information Processing Systems, pp. 2224–2232 (2015)
14. Feng, Q.Y. et al. PADME: A Deep Learning-based Framework for Drug-Target Interaction Prediction. Comput. Sci. arXiv:1807.09741 (2019)
15. Gao K.Y. et al. Interpretable drug target prediction using deep neural representation. In: International Joint Conference on Artificial Intelligence, pp. 3371–3377 (2018)
16. Torng, W., Altman, R.B.: Graph convolutional neural networks for predicting drug-target interactions. J. Chem. Inform. Model. **59**(10), 4131–4149 (2019). https://doi.org/10.1021/acs.jcim.9b00628
17. Sun, C., Xuan, P., Zhang, T., Ye, Y.: Graph convolutional autoencoder and generative adversarial network-based method for predicting drug-target interactions. IEEE/ACM Trans. Comput. Biol. Bioinform. (2020). https://doi.org/10.1109/TCBB.2020.2999084

18. Zhao, T.Y. et al. Identifying drug–target interactions based on graph convolutional network and deep neural network. Brief. Bioinform. **bbaa044**, 1–10 (2020)
19. .Yap, C.W.: PaDEL-descriptor: an open source software to calculate molecular descriptors and fingerprints. J. Comput. Chem. **32**(7), 1466–1474 (2011)
20. Sheng, D., Liang, Q.S., Zeng, Y.: Propy: a tool to generate various modes of Chou's PseAAC. Bioinformatics **29**(7), 960–962 (2013)
21. Li, G.H., Xiong, C.X., Thabet, A., Bernard Ghanem. DeeperGCN: All You Need to Train Deeper GCNs. arXiv:2006.07739 (2020)
22. Bengio, Y.: Learning deep architectures for AI, in Learning Deep Architectures for AI (2009)
23. Yamanishi, Y., Araki, M., Gutteridge, A., et al.: Prediction of drug–target interaction networks from the integration of chemical and genomic spaces. Bioinformatics **24**(13), 1232–1240 (2008)
24. DrugBank Release Version 5.1.7, https://go.drugbank.com/releases/latest
25. Kingma, D.P., Ba, L.J. Adam: A method for stochastic optimization. In: International Conference on Learning Representations (2015)

Inversion of k-Nearest Neighbours Algorithm for Extracting SNPs Discriminating Human Populations

Haihua Gu[1] and Xiaojun Ding[2(✉)]

[1] School of Artificial Intelligence, Nanjing Vocational College of Information Technology, Nanjing 210023, China
[2] School of Computer Science and Engineering, Yulin Normal University, Guangxi 537000, China

Abstract. With the development of new technologies, many multi-class and high dimension data have been accumulated in the biology field . The data contains much useful information. But how to mine the information is a hard problem. The international project (HapMap) has collected much SNP (Single-nucleotide polymorphism) data of individuals for different human races, however, which SNPs lead to the differences between human races is unknown. If these SNPs are extracted, it will be very useful for genetic studies. In the paper, a novel algorithm is proposed to extract the SNPs discriminating human races. The algorithm adopts an inversion of k-nearest neighbours algorithm (IKNN) which uses an iterative procedure to modify the weights of each SNP to make every individual belong to the same population as its k-nearest neighbours. When the weights convergences, most weights of the SNP site are zero which means that these SNPs are noises for classification. The rest SNPs are important for classification. We validate our method on HapMap data, IKNN has a better performance than neural network algorithm and KNN algorithm.

Keywords: KNN · Feature selection · HapMap · Human populations

1 Introduction

Humans are identical over most of their genomes. A relatively small number of genetic differences have resulted in many different aspects. SNPs (single nucleotide polymorphisms) are one kind of major differences between people [1]. A SNP is a DNA sequence variation occurring commonly within a population (e.g. 1%) in which a single nucleotide in the genome differs between members of a biological species or paired chromosomes [2]. The International HapMap Project is a collaboration among scientists and funding agencies from Japan, the United Kingdom, Canada, China, Nigeria, and the United States. Its goal is to identify and catalog genetic similarities and differences in human beings. There are many useful information contained in the SNP data achieved by the HapMap project [3]. Schwartz et al. [4] found the racial differences in the association between SNPs on chromosome 15q25.1 which contribute to risk of lung cancer in African

© Springer Nature Switzerland AG 2021
D.-S. Huang et al. (Eds.): ICIC 2021, LNAI 12838, pp. 100–108, 2021.
https://doi.org/10.1007/978-3-030-84532-2_10

Americans. Anno et al. [5] showed that SNP alleles at multiple loci can be considered the haplotype that contributes to significant differences between the two population groups and suggest a high probability of LD. Confirmation of these findings requires further study with other ethnic groups to analyze the associations between SNP alleles at multiple loci and skin color variation among races. Shi et al. [6], Mizuno et al. [7] and Wang et al. [8] all studied the informative SNP for discriminating East Asian populations. Narasimhan et al. [9] and Bulbul et al. [10] achieved some interesting results among the populations in South and Central populations.

Individual differences in DNA sequence are the genetic basis of human variability. The HapMap project [3] has accumulated much data. If SNPs discriminating human populations can be mined from the data. It will benefit the studies of human history and race-related diseases [11–13]. In the paper, we propose a simple method which can extract important SNPs resulting in population differences. The method can be used in many high dimension and multi-labeled data.

2 Method

The SNP data of different human populations is a high-dimension and multi-classes data. The technique of extracting the SNPs related to the differences between populations is a dimensionality reduction method or a feature selecting method. The usual dimensionality reduction technique in supervised learning is mainly based on linear discriminant analysis (LDA) [14], but it suffers from singularity or under-sampled problems. Support vector machine (SVM) is a typical and powerful machine learning algorithm to classify data [15]. The idea of SVM is to find a hyperplane with the maximum margin to separate two labeled data. It is usually thought that the hyperplane has a smaller generalization error than other decision hyperplane. Figure 1 shows an example of SVM.

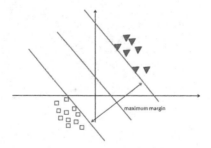

Fig. 1. An illustration of SVM

Zhang et al. [16] developed a recursive support vector machine algorithm to select important genes for the classification of noisy data and got a better performance in their experiments. Their method is suitable for two-labeled data. If we use linear kernel, $K(x, y) = <\phi(x), \phi(y)>$, $w = [w1, w2,... wn]$, $x = [x1, x2,...xn]$, $\phi(x) = [w1x1,$

w2x2,...wnxn], at here w is the weights of each features. The features with high absolute weight are selected as important features. The features with low absolute weight are regarded as noise. Thus the SVM algorithm can decide which features are good features for classification.

In practice, many data contain multiple labels. One SVM can only separate two-labeled data. For m-labeled data, we must use at least m-1 SVM to separate them. For example, in Fig. 2, at least two SVM can separate three-labeled data.

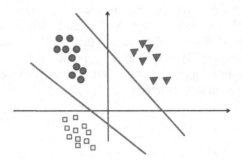

Fig. 2. Two SVM separate three-labeled data

In some times, the data is complex such as shown in Fig. 3. It is a little hard to find the suitable kernels. Even suitable kernels are found, they will be different for the two SVMs. From the two kernels, different features will be selected. While we want the common features which can distinguish the three-labeled data.

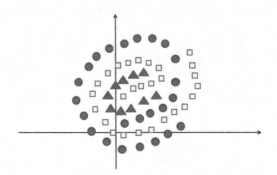

Fig. 3. The kernels of the two SVM will be different

As we know, if the features are known, k-nearest neighbours algorithm is simple and powerful method to classify data. In reverse, if the labels of data are obtained, the method should be able to extract the important features distinguishing the different labeled data. And k-nearest neighbours algorithm is also suitable for multi-label data.

In k-nearest neighbours algorithm, there is a concept of distance which determine the k-nearest neighbours. For two point $x = [x_1, x_2, ...x_n]$ and $y = [y_1, y_2, ...y_n]$, x_i and y_i is the value of the i-th feature. their distance is define as $d(x, y) = \sum_{i=1}^{n} (w_i x_i - w_i y_i)^2$, where $w = [w_1, w_2, ...w_n]$, w_i represents the importance of the i-th feature. If the absolute value of w_i is great, the corresponding feature is important. Otherwise, the feature is a noise. The good w should satisfy the following criteria as much as possibly.

Criteria: The k nearest neighbours of each point should take the same labels as that of the point.

In Fig. 1, Fig. 2 and Fig. 3, it is clearly shown that most points have the same label as their 2-nearest neighbours. When the distribution of data meet the criteria, we can think that some rules of the data have been reflected. So our aim is to find the w which makes the data meet the criteria. For the purpose, the measurements for the weights are defined as the formula (1) and (2).

$$Cost_1(w) = \sum_i I(label(i)! = label(neighbour(i))) \tag{1}$$

$$Cost_2(w) = \sum_j w_j \tag{2}$$

At here, neighbour(i) is one of the k nearest neighbour of point i in the linear kernel space based on the current weights. I(x) is a indicator function. When x equals to true, $I(x) = 1$, else $I(x) = 0$. The best weights should minimize the cost1 value and then minimize the cost2 value.

Next we will update each weight iteratively. Firstly, each weight is set to 0.5. We fix all other wk for k ! = i, then we change wi from two directions to see if it can improve the evaluation of the weights. If yes, the change is preserved. The procedure is repeated until a good weights is obtained. The idea of the algorithm is the inversion of k-nearest neighbours algorithm. We call it **IKNN**. The whole procedure is shown in **IKNN Algorithm**.

2.1 The Convergence of Algorithm

When all the weights are set to 0.5, the goal value can be computed. It is positive. In the iterative procedure, the goal value is descending and it is always non negative, the least step of changing weight is 0.25 which is not infinitesimal. So the descending steps are finite. The algorithm must convergence.

IKNN Algorithm

Input: SNP sequences of individuals for different human races

Output: the weights of each SNP site

Process:

Initialize: set all wk=0.5

Compute the cost with all wk=0.5

step=0.5

While (true)

  noChange=true

  For (j=0 to length of sequence)

      Seletct one SNP site randomly

      Change the weight of this site by +/- step

      Compute the new cost

      If new cost<old cost

        Accept the change

        Update the cost

      Else

        Accept the change according to simulated annealing rule

      EndIf

    EndFor

    If (noChange==true)

      step=step/2

      If (step< 0.25)

        Break the loop

      EndIf

    EndIf

  EndWhile

return the weights

3   Results

The Hapmap data is used to do the experiments. The data is obtained by sampling in 11 human races [3]. Abbreviations of the human populations are listed as Table 1.

Table 1. The information of 11 human populations in HapMap

Label	Population sample
ASW	African ancestry in Southwest USA
CEU	Utah residents with Northern and Western
CHB	European ancestry from the CEPH collection
CHD	Han Chinese in Beijing, China
GIH	Chinese in Metropolitan Denver, Colorado
JPT	Gujarati Indians in Houston, Texas
LWK	Japanese in Tokyo, Japan
MEX	Luhya in Webuye, Kenya
MKK	Mexican ancestry in Los Angeles, California
TSI	Maasai in Kinyawa, Kenya
YRI	Toscans in Italy
	Yoruba in Ibadan, Nigeria

The authors of the paper [17] observed difference in frequency distributions of haplotypes between the African and non-African populations was consistent with two high-frequency haplotypes PuRs in non-Africans populations from the West (CEU, MEX, TSI) to India (GIH), China (CHB and CHD), and the Japan (JPT) in the East and three major PuNR haplotypes in Africans (YRI, LWK, MKK, ASW) with very little haplotype sharing with non-Africans. The authors of the paper [9] thought that African = (ASW, LWK, MKK, YRI), East Asian = (CHB, CHD, JPT), European = (CEU, TSI), and GIH and MEX are two independent groups.

In our experiment, CEU, MEX and TSI are cataloged as the first class. CHB, CHD and JPT are cataloged as the second class. ASW, LWK, MKK and YRI are cataloged as the third class. GIH belongs to the forth class. MEX belongs to the fifth class. Their common SNPs are extract. For chromosome Y, there are 384 SNPs sequenced in 1397 individuals. We use 10 fold cross-validation to check the performance of our method.

Firstly, the data is splited into 90% training data and 10% test data. For briefness, IKNN3 is used to denote the IKNN algorithm with 3 nearest neighbours. The neural network algorithm is used as comparison. Their performances are listed in Table 2. From the Table 2, as can be seen that IKNN3 has better performance. The data is a high-dimension data, a small training data is not suitable for the neural network algorithm. However, IKNN algorithm is qualified for the work.

We set different number for the nearest neighbours and compare the IKNN algorithm to KNN algorithm. The results are shown in Table 3, Table 4 and Table 5.

For different number of nearest neighbours, the IKNN algorithm are always better than KNN algorithm. The reason is IKNN always use fewer SNPs to distinguish different populations, IKNN use a simply way to describe the data, so it has a greater generalization ability. For example, IKNN3 extract about 292.8 SNPs in average out of 384 SNPs on chromosome Y. On chromosome X, there are 26085 common SNPs, IKNN3 only extracts 270 SNPs and its generalization accuracy equals to 99%.

Table 2. The results of neural network and IKNN3 algorithms for 10-fold cross validation on chromosome Y

Order	Error (NN)	Accuracy (NN)	Error (IKNN$_3$)	Accuracy (IKNN$_3$)
1	86	0.39	10	0.93
2	80	0.43	17	0.88
3	82	0.41	8	0.94
4	95	0.32	7	0.95
5	85	0.39	9	0.94
6	87	0.38	6	0.96
7	46	0.67	9	0.94
8	90	0.36	7	0.95
9	75	0.46	11	0.92
10	76	0.46	7	0.95
Average	80.20	0.43	9.10	0.94

Table 3. The results KNN1 and IKNN1 algorithms for 10-fold cross validation on chromosome Y

Order	Error (KNN$_1$)	Accuracy (KNN$_1$)	Error (IKNN$_1$)	Accuracy (IKNN$_1$)
1	13	0.91	9	0.94
2	15	0.89	11	0.92
3	5	0.96	5	0.96
4	9	0.94	9	0.94
5	12	0.91	9	0.94
6	11	0.92	8	0.96
7	8	0.94	7	0.95
8	10	0.93	8	0.94
9	14	0.90	14	0.90
10	12	0.91	6	0.96
Average	10.90	0.92	8.60	0.94

Table 4. The results KNN3 and IKNN3 algorithms for 10-fold cross validation on chromosome Y

Order	Error (KNN$_3$)	Accuracy (KNN$_3$)	Error (IKNN$_3$)	Accuracy (IKNN$_3$)
1	14	0.90	10	0.93
2	18	0.87	17	0.88
3	7	0.95	8	0.94
4	7	0.95	7	0.95
5	13	0.91	9	0.94
6	9	0.94	6	0.96
7	9	0.94	9	0.94
8	12	0.91	7	0.95
9	12	0.91	11	0.92
10	7	0.95	7	0.95
Average	10.80	0.92	9.10	0.94

Table 5. The results KNN5 and IKNN5 algorithms for 10-fold cross validation on chromosome Y

Order	Error (KNN$_5$)	Accuracy (KNN$_5$)	Error (IKNN$_5$)	Accuracy (IKNN$_5$)
1	15	0.89	12	0.91
2	18	0.87	14	0.90
3	9	0.94	6	0.96
4	8	0.94	6	0.96
5	12	0.91	6	0.96
6	7	0.95	5	0.96
7	11	0.92	9	0.94
8	15	0.89	12	0.91
9	12	0.91	10	0.93
10	9	0.94	2	0.99
Average	11.60	0.92	8.20	0.94

4   Conclusion

In the paper, we propose a simple method to find the features related to their labels. The method is suitable for data with high-dimension and small samples. By comparing with neural network algorithm, we can see that the IKNN algorithm has a better performance of this kind of data. Compared with KNN algorithm, IKNN use fewer features to distinguish different classes, it has a better generalization ability. More importantly, the algorithm can extract the features related the labels for many distributions. The algorithm is a good feature-extracting algorithm and can be implemented parallelly.

References

1. Ding, X.J., Li, M., HaiHua, G., Peng, X.Q., Zhang, Z., Wu, F.X.: Detecting SNP combinations discriminating human populations from HapMap data. IEEE Trans. NanoBiosci. **14**(2), 220–228 (2015). https://doi.org/10.1109/TNB.2015.2391134
2. wikipedia_SNP. Single-nucleotide_polymorphism. http://en.wikipedia.org/wiki/Single-nucleotide_polymorphism
3. The HapMap Project Homepage. https://www.genome.gov/10001688/international-hapmap-project
4. Schwartz, A.G., Cote, M.L., Wenzlaff, A.S., Land, S., Amos, C.I.: Racial differences in the association between SNPs on 15q25.1, smoking behavior, and risk of non-small cell lung cancer. J. Thorac. Oncol. **4**(10), 1195–1201 (2009)
5. Anno, S., Abe, T., Yamamoto, T.: Interactions between SNP alleles at multiple loci contribute to skin color differences between caucasoid and mongoloid subjects. Int. J. Biol. Sci. **4**(2), 81–86 (2008)
6. Shi, C.M., et al.: Ancestry informative SNP panels for discriminating the major East Asian populations: Han Chinese, Japanese and Korean. Ann. Hum. Genet. **83**(5), 348–354 (2019)
7. Mizuno, F., et al.: The number of SNPs required for distinguishing Japanese from other East Asians. Legal Med. **49**, 101849 (2021)
8. Wang, C.-C., et al.: Genomic insights into the formation of human populations in East Asia. Nature **591**(7850), 413–419 (2021)
9. Narasimhan, V.M., et al. The formation of human populations in South and Central Asia. Science **365**(6457) (2019)
10. Bulbul, O., et al.: Improving ancestry distinctions among Southwest Asian populations. Forensic Sci. Int.: Genet. **35**, 14–20 (2018)
11. Li, L., et al.: Genome-wide screening for highly discriminative SNPs for personal identification and their assessment in world populations. Forensic Sci. Int.: Genet. **28**, 118–127 (2017)
12. Berisa, T., Pickrell, J.K.: Approximately independent linkage disequilibrium blocks in human populations. Bioinformatics **32**(2), 283 (2016)
13. Bergström, A., et al. Insights into human genetic variation and population history from 929 diverse genomes. Science **367**(6484) (2020)
14. Izenman, A.J.: Linear discriminant analysis, Modern Multivariate Statistical Techniques, pp. 237–280. Springer (2008)
15. Furey, T.S., Cristianini, N., Duffy, N., Bednarski, D.W., Schummer, M., Haussler, D.: Support vector machine classification and validation of cancer tissue samples using microarray expression data. Bioinformatics **16**(10), 906–914 (2000)
16. Zhang, X., et al.: Recursive SVM feature selection and sample classification for mass-spectrometry and microarray data. BMC Bioinform. **7**(1), 197 (2006)
17. Farheen, S., Basu, A., Majumder, P.P.: Haplotype variation in the ACE gene in global populations, with special reference to India, and an alternative model of evolution of haplotypes. HUGO J. **5**(1–4), 35–45 (2011)
18. Xue, C., et al.: Significantly fewer protein functional changing variants for lipid metabolism in Africans than in Europeans. J. Transl. Med. **11**(1), 67 (2013)

ComPAT: A Comprehensive Pathway Analysis Tools

Xiaojie Su[1], Chao Song[2,3], Chenchen Feng[2], Yu Gao[2], Ziyu Ning[2], Qiuyu Wang[2], Jiaxin Chen[2], Yuexin Zhang[2], Ling Wei[2], Xinyuan Zhou[2], and Chunquan Li[2(✉)]

[1] Department of Inspection, Harbin Medical University-Daqing, Daqing 163319, Heilongjiang, China
[2] Department of Medical Informatics, Harbin Medical University-Daqing, Daqing 163319, Heilongjiang, China
[3] Department of Pharmacology, Harbin Medical University-Daqing, Daqing 163319, Heilongjiang, China

Abstract. Pathway annotation or enrichment is often used as the efficient tool to uncover the molecular mechanism of interesting gene sets from genome-wide research. Up to now, numerous pathway databases or web servers that integrated fragmented pathway maps have been published, such as KEGG, Reactome, Net-Path, Pathway Commons, DAVID and PathwAX. However, all these data sources are not taking into account the pathway quantity or pathway topology information. Thus, to fill the gap, we developed ComPAT, which provides a web framework that enables users to perform pathway/subpathway enrichment analysis for interesting gene sets, browse and search detailed pathway annotation information. The current version of ComPAT contains a total of 2,881 pathways that were obtained from 10 pathway databases and extended gene interactions from 10 other gene interaction databases, including 10,760 genes and 1,136,971 interactive relationships. All pathways in ComPAT were converted into graphs. ComPAT provides comprehensive annotation for pathways, including network visualization and topology information, gene subcellular localization and gene–gene interaction strength. What's more, ComPAT integrated five types of subpathway algorithms to split pathways into 23,024 subpathways for small-scale gene sets enrichment. Users can input the interesting gene sets for pathway/subpathway annotation or enrichment analysis. Here, we performed the subpathway analysis for cardiac remodeling as a biological case. ComPAT also supports subpathway analysis pipeline for user-input networks. The server is freely available at http://bio.licpathway.net:8018/msg/ComPAT/index.do.

Keywords: Pathway integration · Pathway analysis · Subpathway analysis · Web tools

1 Introduction

Pathways capture knowledge of biological processes at the molecular level and can be used to decode the comprehensive molecular mechanism from genomic studies [1]. A

X. Su, C. Song and C. Feng—Contributed equally to this study.

© Springer Nature Switzerland AG 2021
D.-S. Huang et al. (Eds.): ICIC 2021, LNAI 12838, pp. 109–120, 2021.
https://doi.org/10.1007/978-3-030-84532-2_11

large amount studies also considered the pathways as the downstream effectors in pathology research and dysfunction of pathway signal transduction is the trigger of diseases. For example, biologists usually analyze biomolecular data such as gene expression to find which processes are activated in a given experiment. Focusing on pathway level to dissect biological problems has become a vital part in research fields of human complex diseases, such as cancer, diabetes and cardiovascular disease [2–5]. With the development of biological research, a growing number of biological pathway collections have accumulated rapidly [6]. The challenge no longer lies in identifying the over-represented pathways, but rather in improving the pathway annotation and coverage rates, which can help biologists to find more novel mechanism of interest.

Up to now, numerous popular pathway databases or web servers that integrated fragmented pathway maps have been published, such as KEGG [1], Reactome [7], NetPath [8], DAVID [9], Metascape [10] and Enrichr [11]. All these data sources accelerated the progression of biological and medical research. While these individual sources cover important information in certain areas of biological knowledge, integrated and reasonably comprehensive use of biological pathway datasets is severely hampered by the large number and fragmentation of available databases. For example, most of these data sources curate pathways in a scattered distribution, which is unfavorable for advanced pathway analysis. Pathway Commons is the first database that comprehensively collected pathways from multiple sources and provided integrated bulk sets of pathway information to enable users to perform pathway analysis [12]. GSEA also collected multi-source pathway gene sets in Msigdb for pathway enrichment analysis [13]. However, Pathway Commons and GSEA both ignored pathway topological information. As is known to all, biological pathways encompassed complex pathway structure information, including numerous gene targeting interactions and biochemical reaction [14, 15]. Graphic pathways that contained the entire molecule interactive relationships could help us understand the biological mechanism and provide a novel support to develop or improve bioinformatics analysis tools, such as network based pathway enrichment tools (SubpathwayMiner, PathwAX) or pathway associated algorithms [15–18]. Numerous studies have also demonstrated that gene crosstalks in pathway are crucial for identifying key disease genes. Meanwhile, perturbation of key regions (subpathways) of a network, rather than the entire pathway network, tends to affect the disease phenotype [16, 19, 20]. Therefore, a comprehensive pathway analysis tool that collects, integrates and graphically transforms publicly available biological pathways and embedded pathway/subpathway analysis function is required. Meanwhile, this tool should also provide the comprehensive annotation for pathway genes, such as subcellular localization and topology features information, which are critical for the pathway research and analysis.

Complemented with these absences, we developed ComPAT: A Web Tool for Comprehensive Pathway Analysis (http://bio.licpathway.net:8018/msg/ComPAT/index.do), which aims to provide a resource for efficient manipulation, browse and analysis of comprehensive information of pathways. The current version of ComPAT contains a total of 2,881 pathways that are obtained from 10 pathway databases (Fig. 1).

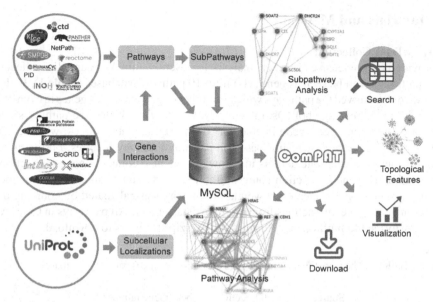

Fig. 1. The overview of ComPAT pipeline. ComPAT collects data from 20 gene interaction data sources. Functionally, ComPAT provides numerous functions for users, such as pathway/subpathway analysis, pathway browse, pathway search and pathway visualization.

Moreover, we extended gene interaction information from 10 other network interaction databases. These pathways are converted into graphs, including 10,760 protein-coding genes and 1,136,971 interactive relationships. ComPAT provides rapid and canonical pathway and subpathway analysis by inputting the gene sets of interest. Specifically, five types of subpathway identification algorithms were embedded in current version of ComPAT to divide subpathway and 23,024 subpathways were obtained for further analysis. ComPAT supports searching by either 'Pathway ID', 'Pathway Name' or 'Gene'. To better understand the content of pathways, ComPAT provides comprehensive annotations and interactive visualizations, including pathway gene subcellular location, subpathway/pathway visualization network diagram and pathway gene topology information in ComPAT background networks. Additionally, ComPAT also defines similarity scores between two pathways that identify pathways similar to the current pathways of interest. Our effort to establish this web server was prompted by the great need of researchers to understand the biology of pathway regulation. Moreover, graphic biological pathways are an indispensable basis for computer simulation of biological systems. The tools will help biologists locate the dysfunctional pathways or subpathways in a global pathway collection sets, and will also be a valuable resource in designing network-based pathway analysis solutions.

2   Materials and Methods

Pathway Data Collection

To provide comprehensive pathway analysis for users, ComPAT manually collected 2,881 pathways (can be seen as gene sets) from 10 pathway databases (Table 1). In this study, we only reserved the pathways with the number of genes > 5. All genes in ComPAT were indexed by gene symbol IDs. Importantly, ComPAT converted the pathways into graphs by integrating gene–gene interactions from original data sources, which could help users find more precise results based on pathway topology features. Furthermore, to complement the gene interactions in pathways, we also collected gene interactions from another 10 gene interaction sources (Table 2). Combining all gene interactions in pathways, gene–gene interaction weight of pathway was calculated by counting the number of gene–gene interactions from multiple data sources. All pathways in ComPAT were transformed to multiple data formats (gmt or zip) for users to download.

Table 1. The statistic of ComPAT data collection from 10 pathway databases.

Source	Interaction number	Gene number
HumanCyc	38,729	3677
Reactome	246,590	10,433
SMPDB	12,800	2070
KEGG	43,360	5767
INOH	36,430	2084
PANTHER	30,962	2240
pid	28,079	2627
NetPath	4698	1196
CTD	127,718	18,798
WikiPathways	602	1866

Gene Annotation Data Collection

ComPAT provided multi-dimension annotation information for genes in pathways. First, topological features (including Degree, Betweenness, Closeness and Transitivity) were calculated for genes in ComPAT via R packages "igraph". Here, we calculated three types of gene topological features in different background pathway network, including gene topological features in current pathways/subpathways, in whole ComPAT pathway net and in the original data source. Second, we supported gene subcellular information for pathway genes by collecting the source data from Uniprot database [21]. Third, ComPAT also supported different gene IDs, such as gene symbol, Ensembl ID and Entrez ID.

Pathway/Subpathway Enrichment Analysis

In this version of ComPAT, we supported pathway and subpathway enrichment analysis for users. To identify the statistically significant enriched pathways/subpathways,

Table 2. The statistic of ComPAT data collection from 10 gene interaction data sources.

Source	Interaction number	Gene number
IntAct	131,546	13,485
Recon X	58,173	2813
BioGRID	229,377	15,376
BIND	72,782	7038
HPRD	71,823	9970
DIP	16,201	3989
CORUM	37,590	2544
PhosphoSite	10,416	2284
TRANSFAC	101,343	13,304
DrugBank	9654	4606

hypergeometric test was used to calculate p-values as follows:

$$p-value = 1 - \sum_{i=0}^{r-1} \frac{\binom{t}{i}\binom{m-t}{n-i}}{\binom{m}{n}}$$

where, m represented the total number of genes in ComPAT, t represented the number of genes of interest, n represented the number of genes in a certain pathway, and r represented the number of genes occurs in this pathway.

Subpathway Division

Subpathway dysfunction has been considered as the key cause of disease pathogenesis. Thus, in ComPAT, we provided subpathway analysis for users to find the crucial subpathways. Five types of subpathway division algorithms were used to divide subpathways, including 'SubpathwayMiner' that our lab developed [16] and four other algorithms that are embedded in R package 'igraph' (edge betweenness [22], fast greedy [23], spin glass [24], and random walk [25]). Totally, 23,024 subpathways were divided for further analysis. Users have multiple options to find the key subpathways with different parameters.

Pathway Similarity Analysis

ComPAT provided pathway similarity analysis for users to find more relevant pathways of interest. To do this, we defined similarity scores between the two pathways as:

$$\text{Sim score} = \frac{|G_{p1} \cap G_{p2}|}{\min(|G_{p1}|,|G_{p2}|)}$$

where Gp represents the genes of pathway p, and |Gp| represents the number of genes in pathway p. The range of Sim score is 0 to 1. The higher the Sim score is, the more similar the two pathways are.

Database Implementation
ComPAT user interface was implemented using Hyper Text Markup Language (HTML), Cascading Style Sheet (CSS) and JavaScript. The backend is written in JAVA. The web services were developed using Spring, a Java web application framework, and Mybatis, which is a persistence framework that automates the mapping between MySQL databases and objects in Java, both of which help guarantee high performance and stability of web services. Google Chrome browser was recommended with 1440×900 resolution. ComPAT is freely available at http://www.licpathway.net/msg/ComPAT/index.jsp.

3 Results

Web Server Description
To build a comprehensive pathway analysis web server, the first step is to build a comprehensive background pathway datasets. Thus, we collected all pathways from 10 known pathway databases. Totally, 2881 pathways and 262,321 interactions were embedded in our web server (Table 1). Pathways were comprised by gene–gene interactions, to extend the capacity of our background pathways, all gene interactions from another 10 gene interaction databases were also collected. All these information can help user reveal the comprehensive biological mechanism in "one step search", which could improve the efficiency. On the other hand, an integrative pathway database could support the overall knowledge of system biology, reducing the bias among different pathway databases. As a result, 10,760 protein-coding genes and 1,136,971 gene interactions served as background datasets in ComPAT.

To help users understand pathway-based regulatory mechanism of interesting gene sets intuitively, all pathways were converted into graphs based on gene–gene interactions, which supplied topology information (up-stream and down-stream regulatory relationships) of genes in pathways. All these background datasets provided strong supports for pathway analysis. Furthermore, ComPAT also provided pathway enrichment analysis, sub-pathway enrichment analysis, subcellular localization information, pathway topology information and user-friendly visualization.

QuickStart
Users can perform the following pathway-associated analyses in the web-server: with the input of a geneset of interest (gene symbols) and set up options, ComPAT will respond quickly and identify significantly enriched subpathways/pathways. The detailed information of subpathways/pathways includes a subpathway/pathway visualization network diagram, gene subcellular location, topology information (including degree, betweenness, closeness and transitivity) of a gene under three conditions (pathway, network for source database of pathway and ComPAT network, respectively) and various corresponding statistical charts. Furthermore, users can also search, browse and download

all pathway information from ComPAT. To clear the puzzles in processing ComPAT, we provided the detailed guide for assisting users to use ComPAT on the 'Help' page.

Browse or Search Pathways

Users can use the "Browse" trigger to obtain the pathway overview sheets. Users can also use the "Search" trigger by selecting PathwayID, PathwayName or Pathway Gene to obtain the specific pathway/pathways overview information (Fig. 2).

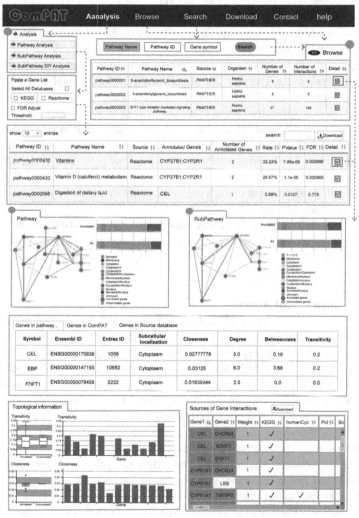

Fig. 2. The comprehensive workflow of ComPAT. Moreover, we also supported pathway annotation analysis. Briefly, if the user input the threshold as "1", ComPAT will retrieve the annotated pathway overview in a new webpage. This function partly remedied the defects of insufficient gene numbers in pathway enrichment analysis.

Furthermore, detailed pathway information such as pathway visualization, topology information, gene subcellular localization and gene–gene interaction strength will be retrieved in a new webpage by clicking the "Detail" trigger. Additionally, when users focused on detailed information of a specific pathway, ComPAT also provided the gene overlap-based similar pathways in ComPAT for users to comprehensively and thoroughly understand the biological problems.

Pathway Enrichment Analysis

Pathway enrichment analysis is the most important function of a pathway analysis tool. To enable users experience a convenient and rapid analysis process, we used hypergeometic test to implement this function. Especially, we extended the gene interactions for pathways in ComPAT from 10 gene interaction data sources to break the barrier of low pathway annotation rates. Thus, users can identify more functional pathways than existing pathway analysis tools. The protocol of pathway enrichment analysis in ComPAT is handy. Firstly, users can input the gene set of interest and select pathway data sources. We supported users to select the option of all pathway sources, the default option is two popular sources, "KEGG" and "Reactome". Secondly, users can input the threshold of pathway enrichment. Here, users can input the general thresholds, such as 0.05, 0.01. Users can also select FDR corrected P-value as the threshold. The enriched pathway overview sheets will be retrieved in a new webpage by clicking "Analysis". Users can browse the detailed information of each enriched pathway followed the protocol of the above "Browse or search pathways" section.

Moreover, we also supported pathway annotation analysis. Briefly, if the user input the threshold as "1", ComPAT will retrieve the annotated pathway overview in a new webpage. This function partly remedied the defects of insufficient gene numbers in pathway enrichment analysis.

Subpathway Enrichment Analysis

Subpathway analysis is a characteristic function in ComPAT. Regional gene dysfunction in pathways is usually ignored by the entire pathway enrichment, but we can identify these dysfunctional regions by subpathway analysis. Thus, in this version of ComPAT, we split 2,881 pathways into 23,024 subpathways for further analysis. Concretely, ComPAT used five algorithms to divide subpathways, including "SubpathwayMiner" and four igraph-embedded algorithms "Edge.betweenness.community", "Fastgreedy.community", "Spinglass.community" and "Walktrap.community". As a result, these algorithms split pathways into 5,209, 5,613, 3,207, 3,309 and 5,686 subpathways, respectively. Subpathway enrichment or annotation protocol is similar to the section of "Pathway enrichment analysis". The additional option is "Select Subpathway", users can select any one subpathway split algorithm for analysis.

ComPAT also supported third-party networks or user's own networks to perform subpathway analysis. Users can select "Subpathway DIY Analysis" in the "Analysis" option. After inputting the gene set and network interactions, selecting the subpathway split algorithm, ComPAT will retrieve the enrichment results as soon as possible.

Data Download in ComPAT

ComPAT is designed as a freely available database. In "Download" page, users can download data of multiple formats (such as GMT formats for GSEA analysis; xgmml formats for visualization in Cytoscape; RData formats for analysis in R; txt/csv formats for network analysis) and pathway detailed information, which could help users process data independently.

Case Study: Subpathway Analysis for Cardiac Remodeling

Subpathway analysis is an important strategy to decode the molecular mechanism of pathological phenotypes or complex diseases, as well as a representative feature in ComPAT. Here, to evaluate the ability of ComPAT in pathological processes, we used it to identify the risk subpathways for cardiac modeling based on the differentially expressed genes (DEGs). As known that, cardiac remodeling is the common irreversible pathological changes in multiple cardiovascular diseases, such as myocardiopathy and myocardial infarction, and is the major cause of heart failure. Firstly, we selected the myocardial infarction dataset that was published in Circulation journal (accession number: GSE132143) and calculated the DEGs between disease and healthy donors (threshold: |log2FC| > 2, P-value < 0.05). Secondly, we selected the high-expressed and up-regulated/down-regulated DEGs as the input gene sets to explore the biological function. Then, we selected the option of "All Databases", set the threshold with 0.01 and selected "SubPathwayMiner" algorithm to execute subpathway analysis. ComPAT will return the analysis results quickly.

As a result, for the up-regulated DEGs, 12 risk subpathways were identified and listed in the result panel, including two crucial biological processes, "Collagen biosynthesis and modifying enzymes" and "AP-1 transcription factor network". Normal and balanced collagen biosynthesis and degradation is critical for maintaining cardiac function. Cardiac injury induced abnormal collagen deposition will lead to the reduced cardiac contractility and cardiac remodeling. Intriguingly, ComPAT also excavated the subpathway from AP-1 regulatory network (Fig. 3A-C). AP-1 was a transcriptional factor complex and was composed of c-Jun and c-fos families. Numerous studies found that inhibition of AP-1 activity could attenuate the processes of cardiac remodeling. Especially, we found that four genes were annotated in this subpathway, including NPPA, FOSB, EGR1 and PENK. NPPA was the classical biomarker of heart failure, FOSB and EGR1 were also demonstrated as the risk transcriptional factors in cardiac remodeling. In this four genes-extracted subpathway, four genes were circled in red and subpathway structure was distributed by gene subcellular localization information (Fig. 3A). Thus, we could find the potential regulatory axes of DEGs and downstream targets directly. Additionally, ComPAT will display the multiple topological features of these genes in the result panel. These statistic graphs will help user quickly locate the crucial genes. For the down-regulated DEGs, ComPAT also identified the cardiac remodeling related subpathways, such as "Eicosanoids", "Endogenous TLR signaling" and "PPAR signaling pathway". In subpathway of "Endogenous TLR signaling", three DEGs were the skeletons, including "S100A8", "S100A9" and "TLR2" (Fig. 3D). These three genes were validated to participate in cardiac remodeling via inflammation response. Through above subpathway analysis, we believed that ComPAT would be more suitable for function enrichment or annotation research work.

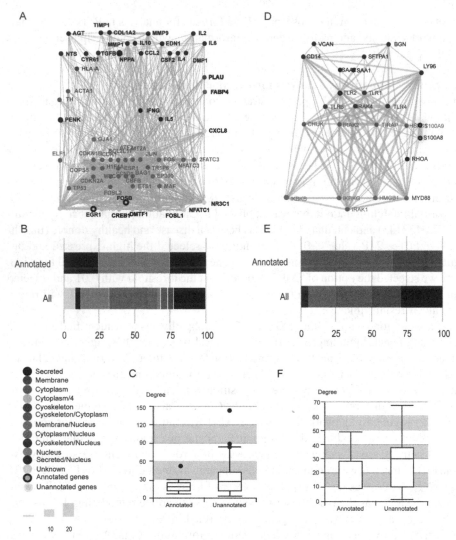

Fig. 3. Subpathway analysis results of cardiac remodeling. (A) Subpathway visualization of enrichment analysis for up-regulated genes. Node color represents the gene subcellular localization. (B) Gene subcellular localization distribution of annotated genes and all genes. (C) Comparison of node degree in pathway network between annotated genes and unannotated genes. (D) Subpathway visualization of enrichment analysis for down-regulated genes. (E) Gene subcellular localization distribution of annotated genes and all genes. (F) Comparison of node degree in pathway network between annotated genes and unannotated genes.

4   Discussion and Conclusion

With the development of biology, numerous pathway gene sets were summarized and released into the freely available data sources to enable researchers to reveal the dysfunctional biological processes [1, 12]. Thus, pathway analysis, such as pathway enrichment and upstream/downstream gene regulation extraction, has become the indispensable pattern to interpret the genome-wide data to gain insights into biological mechanisms [26]. Here, we developed ComPAT, a comprehensive pathway analysis tool, to help medical scientists and biologist to quickly and efficiently focus on dysfunctional pathways or subpathways. In the current version ComPAT, we integrated biological pathway from 10 known pathway databases, including 2,881 pathways and 262,321 interactions. Additionally, we also collected a large number of gene–gene interactions to extend the pathway topology from another 10 data sources. Totally, 10,760 protein-coding genes and 1,136,971 gene interactions were curated in ComPAT. All pathways in ComPAT were transformed into graphs, which supported researchers to find topology-based results.

ComPAT is the first integrative data source with pathway topology information. Importantly, ComPAT provides pathway and subpathway analysis for users to identify and visualize the high risk pathways. Comprehensive pathway annotation information is also provided in ComPAT, such as pathway gene subcellular location, subpathway/pathway visualization network diagram, pathway similarity analysis and pathway gene topology information in ComPAT background networks.

Previous studies had developed multiple platforms in pathway analysis fields, such as DAVID, Enrichr, Metascape and Pathway Commons [9–12]. Our previous works also focused on the subpathway enrichment analysis [16, 19, 27]. All these data sources particularly promoted the progress of the scientific research. ComPAT has some advantages over these similar data sources including (i) integrating 2,881 curated pathways from more than 20 pathway data sources, (ii) providing network-based graphic pathway storage and visualization, (iii) supporting large-scale subpathway annotation or enrichment analysis and (iv) providing comprehensive pathway gene annotation information. These characteristics of ComPAT will enable researchers to obtain a complete biological content from individual gene sets. Furthermore, the engineering and extensions of ComPAT will continue, network-based pathway enrichment analysis will be embedded in later updated release. The gene interaction data of some novel molecules, such as long noncoding RNAs, microRNAs and circular RNAs will also be extended in later updates. We believe that ComPAT will become an active and effective tool for pathway analysis.

References

1. Kanehisa, M., Goto, S.: KEGG: kyoto encyclopedia of genes and genomes. Nucl. Acids Res. **28**(1), 27–30 (2000)
2. Brumby, A.M., Richardson, H.E.: Using *Drosophila melanogaster* to map human cancer pathways. Nat Rev Cancer **5**(8), 626–639 (2005)
3. Evans, J.L., Goldfine, I.D., Maddux, B.A., Grodsky, G.M.: Oxidative stress and stress-activated signaling pathways: a unifying hypothesis of type 2 diabetes. Endocr. Rev. **23**(5), 599–622 (2002)
4. Hunter, J.J., Chien, K.R.: Signaling pathways for cardiac hypertrophy and failure. N. Engl. J. Med. **341**(17), 1276–1283 (1999)
5. Bracken, A.P., Pasini, D., Capra, M., Prosperini, E., Colli, E., Helin, K.: EZH2 is downstream of the pRB-E2F pathway, essential for proliferation and amplified in cancer. EMBO J. **22**(20), 5323–5335 (2003)
6. Bader, G.D., Cary, M.P., Sander, C.: Pathguide: a pathway resource list. Nucleic Acids Res **34**(Database issue) D504–506 (2006)

7. Joshi-Tope, G. et al.: Reactome: a knowledgebase of biological pathways. Nucleic Acids Res, **33**(Database issue) D428–432 (2005)
8. Kandasamy, K., et al.: NetPath: a public resource of curated signal transduction pathways. Genome Biol. **11**(1), R3 (2010)
9. Huang, D.W., Sherman, B.T., Lempicki, R.A.: Bioinformatics enrichment tools: paths toward the comprehensive functional analysis of large gene lists. Nucl. Acids Res. **37**(1), 1–13 (2009)
10. Zhou, Y., Zhou, B., Pache, L., Chang, M., Khodabakhshi, A.H., Tanaseichuk, O., Benner, C., Chanda, S.K.: Metascape provides a biologist-oriented resource for the analysis of systems-level datasets. Nat. Commun. **10**(1), 1523 (2019)
11. Kuleshov, M.V., et al.: Enrichr: a comprehensive gene set enrichment analysis web server 2016 update. Nucl. Acids Res. **44**(W1), W90-97 (2016)
12. Cerami, E.G. et al.: Pathway Commons, a web resource for biological pathway data. Nucleic Acids Res **39**(Database issue) D685–690 (2011)
13. Subramanian, A., et al.: Gene set enrichment analysis: a knowledge-based approach for interpreting genome-wide expression profiles. Proc. Natl. Acad. Sci. U. S. A. **102**(43), 15545–15550 (2005)
14. Antonov, A.V., Dietmann, S., Mewes, H.W.: KEGG spider: interpretation of genomics data in the context of the global gene metabolic network. Genome Biol. **9**(12), R179 (2008)
15. Sales, G., Calura, E., Cavalieri, D., Romualdi, C.: Graphite - a Bioconductor package to convert pathway topology to gene network. BMC Bioinform. **13**, 20 (2012)
16. Li, C. et al.: SubpathwayMiner: a software package for flexible identification of pathways. Nucleic Acids Res. **37**(19) e131 (2009)
17. Ogris, C., Helleday, T., Sonnhammer, E.L.: PathWAX: a web server for network crosstalk based pathway annotation. Nucl. Acids Res. **44**(W1), W105-109 (2016)
18. Ma, J., Shojaie, A., Michailidis, G.: Network-based pathway enrichment analysis with incomplete network information. Bioinformatics **32**(20), 3165–3174 (2016)
19. Li, C. et al.: Subpathway-GM: identification of metabolic subpathways via joint power of interesting genes and metabolites and their topologies within pathways. Nucleic Acids Res. **41**(9) e101 (2013)
20. Li, X., et al.: Dissection of human MiRNA regulatory influence to subpathway. Brief Bioinform. **13**(2), 175–186 (2012)
21. UniProt C: UniProt: a hub for protein information. Nucl. Acids Res. **43**(Database issue) D204–212 (2015)
22. Newman, M.E., Girvan, M.: Finding and evaluating community structure in networks. Phys. Rev. E Stat. Nonlin Soft Matter Phys. **69**(2 Pt 2) 026113 (2004)
23. Clauset, A., Newman, M.E., Moore, C.: Finding community structure in very large networks. Phys. Rev. E Stat Nonlin Soft Matter Phys. **70**(6 Pt 2) 066111 (2004)
24. Traag, V.A., Bruggeman, J.: Community detection in networks with positive and negative links. Phys. Rev. E. Stat. Nonlin. Soft Matter. Phys. **80**(3 Pt 2) 036115 (2009)
25. Pons, P., Latapy, M.: Computing communities in large networks using random walks. Jof Graph Alg Appbf **10**(2), 191–218 (2006)
26. Karp, P.D. et al.: Pathway Tools version 13.0: integrated software for pathway/genome informatics and systems biology. Brief Bioinform. **11**(1) 40–79 (2010)
27. Feng, C., et al.: ce-Subpathway: Identification of ceRNA-mediated subpathways via joint power of ceRNAs and pathway topologies. J. Cell Mol. Med. **23**(2), 967–984 (2019)

Incorporating Knowledge Base for Deep Classification of Fetal Heart Rate

Changping Ji[1] ⓘ, Min Fang[2](✉) ⓘ, Jie Chen[1] ⓘ, Muhammad Umair Raza[1], and Jianqiang Li[1] ⓘ

[1] College of Computer Science and Software Engineering, Shenzhen University, Shenzhen 518060, Guangdong, China
jichangping2018@email.szu.edu.cn, {chenjie,lijq}@szu.edu.cn
[2] Education Center of Experiments and Innovations, Harbin Institute of Technology (Shenzhen), Shenzhen 518055, China
fangmin@hit.edu.cn

Abstract. In recent years, remote fetal monitoring has become more and more popular, and it has also brought many challenges. Fetal heart rate records are generally recorded by pregnant women using a fetal monitor at home. Due to the improper operation of the pregnant woman and the surrounding noise, this makes it difficult for the doctor to give an accurate diagnosis. However, the existing methods are difficult to perform well in an environment with noisy data and unbalanced data. To solve the shortcomings of existing methods, we design a novel framework, classification fetal heart rate based on convolutional neural network incorporating knowledge base. In particular, we built a knowledge base for the task of fetal heart rate classification, which can solve the problem of noise and imbalance in the data. To verify the effectiveness of our proposed framework, we conduct extensive experiments on a real-world dataset. The experimental results show that the performance of our framework is better than other methods.

Keywords: Fetal heart rate · Knowledge base · Classification

1 Introduction

At present, fetal heart rate (FHR) [6, 10, 13] is an important feature for monitoring the health of the fetus. And electronic fetal monitoring (EFM) [2, 17] for recording FHR has also become an important technology for monitoring fetal health in utero. EFM can detect fetal distress and fetal hypoxia in time and has been widely used in clinical practice. In recent years, the main method of fetal monitoring is that pregnant women use a fetal monitor to record FHR at home [8], and then send it to the doctor for diagnosis through mobile devices, which can be found in Fig. 1. Due to the factors such as pregnant women's heartbeat, breathing and improper operation, the recorded FHR is not professional enough, which brings certain challenges to doctors in diagnosing FHR. Hence, improving the method of fetal monitoring has important clinical significance.

In recent years, due to the continuous development of computer science, EFM technology has been continuously improved, and many researchers have made different

© Springer Nature Switzerland AG 2021
D.-S. Huang et al. (Eds.): ICIC 2021, LNAI 12838, pp. 121–131, 2021.
https://doi.org/10.1007/978-3-030-84532-2_12

Fig. 1. Remote fetal monitoring system.

progress [4]. Georgoulas et al. [9] proposed to use hidden Markov models to classify FHR. Spilka et al. [15] proposed a combination of conventional and nonlinear features to analyze FHR, and later [16] proposed using a multi-scale feature representation method to quantify the variability of FHR, and then used a sparse support vector machine (SVM) to perform supervised classification of FHR. But the model is highly dependent on the accuracy of feature extraction. Yu et al. [18] proposed a FHR classification model that uses a non-parametric Bayesian model to distinguish between fetal hypoxia and normal FHR records. This model is mainly based on the hierarchical dirichlet model, which infers a mixed model from healthy FHR and unhealthy FHR, and finally uses the inferred mixed model to classify the new FHR. Dash et al. [7] proposed a FHR classification method based on Bayesian theory and generative models, this framework first extracts the features of fetal status from FHR records, then defines class-specific models for them and uses a set of training data to estimate the parameters of each model. Sbrollini et al. [14] proposed an automatic algorithm for recognition and classification of fetal deceleration, but the model completely relies on the feature of fetal movement records. Based on existing methods, Barnova et al. [3] proposed a hybrid model using multiple independent methods. Li et al. [11] proposed to use the convolutional neural network (CNN) to automatically classify FHR, and vote according to the class of each segment to get the final result, but they did not consider the data imbalance.

Although the above studies have made different progress, there are still problems and challenges, which can be summarized in two aspects: 1) Existing models are very dependent on the accuracy of data quality, and do not work well for noisy data; 2) Another prerequisite for the current methods to work well is data balance, but the data in the medical field is usually imbalance. To address the aforementioned challenges, we propose a framework, classification fetal heart rate based on convolutional neural network incorporating knowledge base (CNN-KB). First, we use the keywords in the pregnant women's question and doctor's answer to build a knowledge base (KB). In the training phase, the keywords in the pregnant woman's question and the doctor's answer are used as an auxiliary input. In the inference phase, because the doctor's answer is not provided, we need to use the keywords in question to query the KB, then use the queried information as an auxiliary input. For the FHR, the training phase and the inference phase are the same, we use CNN to extract its features. Finally, the features of FHR and auxiliary input are merged, and then used for classification. To verify the effectiveness of our framework, we conduct extensive experiments on a real-world dataset. The experimental results show that CNN-KB is much better than baseline methods.

2 Method

2.1 Knowledge Base

We will briefly introduce how the KB in the framework is constructed before introducing the proposed framework. The KB was constructed on data derived from the textual information of the pregnant woman's questions Q and the doctor's answers A. First, we use the word segmentation tool [5] to segment the texts of Q and A, we have also performed synonym substitution [1] processing on keywords because of the different expressions of each person, and then pick out the meaningful words under the guidance of the doctor. The keywords set of Q and A are represented by Q^w and A^w, respectively. Second, traverse the keywords of each question Q_i. If the keyword q of Q_i in the Q^w, then judge whether the keyword a of the corresponding answer A_i is in A^w, if so, create an entity-relationship triples $ert_{q,a}$ between q and a. After traversing, each keyword in Q_i may correspond to multiple keywords in A^w, or one, or even none. Finally, build the KB based on the relationship between keywords, the tool we use to build the KB is Protégé [12]. The construction details of KB are in Algorithm 1, ERT is the set of entity-relationship triples.

Algorithm 1: Construct Knowledge Base

Input: The questions Q and answers A.
Output: Knowledge Base.
1 perform word segmentation and pick out Q^w and A^w;
2 **foreach** $q \in Q_i$ **do**
3   **if** $q \in Q^w$ **then**
4   **foreach** $a \in A_i$ **do**
5   **if** $a \in A^w$ **then**
6   create an entity-relationship triple $ert_{q,a}$; $ERT \leftarrow ERT + ert_{q,a}$;
7   **else**
8   continue;
9   **else**
10   continue;
11 construct knowledge base based on ERT;

2.2 Classification with Knowledge Base

In order to solve the shortcomings of traditional methods, we propose a fetal heart rate classification framework based on convolutional neural network combined with KB. The model used in the experiment to extract FHR features is a one-dimensional CNN. The CNN-KB framework is shown in the Fig. 2.

In the training phase, because the doctor's answer is provided, the real relationship between the keywords in the question and the keywords in the answer is used as an auxiliary input. However, in the inference phase, the doctor's answer is not provided, we need to use the keywords in question to query the KB, then use the queried information as an auxiliary input. The KB can be defined as two parts, entity set $E = \{e_1, e_2, \cdots, e_n\}$ and relationship set $R = \{r_1, r_2, \cdots, r_m\}$. An entity-relationship triple in KB can be

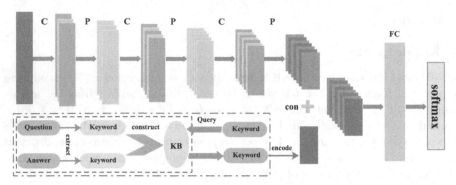

Fig. 2. The framework of CNN-KB.

defined as $S_{i,j} = \{e_i, r_k, e_j\}$, where e_i, e_j are the entities in E and r_k is the relationship in R. Assuming that an entity e_i in E is related to z entities, then the information set G_{e_i} queried from KB by e_i can be formally defined as follows:

$$G_{e_i} = S_{i,1} \cup S_{i,2} \cup \cdots \cup S_{i,z} \tag{1}$$

An example of querying information in KB through entity is shown in Fig. 3, "anemia" is a keyword entity used for query. The left side of the figure is the set of entities in the KB, and the right side of the figure is the relationship queried by the corresponding entity. Since there may be more than one keyword in each question, if there are multiple meaningful keywords, the queried information needs to be merged. Therefore, the general form of the KB information set K corresponding to a question can be defined as:

$$K = G_{e_i} \cup G_{e_{i+1}} \cup \cdots \cup G_{e_j} \tag{2}$$

Then embed and encode the information set K to obtain the feature vector representing T. The calculation formula for T is as follows:

$$T = f(Embedding(K)) \tag{3}$$

where f is LSTM in our framework. On the other hand, for the input FHR, the framework uses the CNN model to extract features. As shown in Figure, C represents the convolution operation, P represents the pooling operation, con represents the concatenation operation, and FC is the fully connected layer. The model contains three convolutional layers, and the output feature R of each convolutional layer is formally defined as follows:

$$R = P\left(\sigma\left(W_c * \hat{R} + b_c\right)\right) \tag{4}$$

where $\hat{R}$ is the input of the convolutional layer, the input of the first convolutional layer is FHR; W_c and b_c are the learnable parameters in the convolutional layer; σ is an activation function.

Finally, the features R and T are fused and input into the fully connected layer, then the activation function *softmax* is used for classification. The formula is defined as follows:

$$Z = softmax\big(W_{fc}(R \oplus T) + b_{fc}\big) \tag{5}$$

where Z is the classification result, W_{fc} and b_{fc} are the learnable parameters of the fully connected layer, $\oplus$ is the concatenation operation.

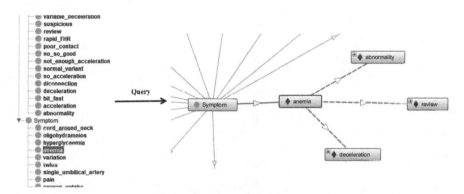

Fig. 3. Example of querying information from KB based on keywords.

3 Experiments Setup and Results

3.1 Dataset and Preprocessing

The experimental data for this work was provided by Shenzhen Sdyunban Health Technology Co., Lty. These data are recorded by pregnant women using electronic fetal monitoring at home and then submitted to doctors for diagnosis through the platform. The label of FHR and the answer to the question are all recorded by doctors. The sample of FHR recorded by electronic fetal monitoring is shown in the Fig. 4, which is a segment of data. The time of normal FHR data is at least 20 min.

We have performed four samples per second on the FHR data to generate sequence data according to the standard [11], that is, the length of a twenty-minute FHR data is 4800. We collected a total of 8,000 pieces of data, divided into three classes: normal, suspicious and abnormal. After deleting some data with missing information, the length distribution of FHR data is shown in the Fig. 5. According to the length distribution of the FHR data, FHR data with a length less than 4800 and a length greater than 8300 are deleted. Since the data was collected by pregnant women at home, some data was not collected due to the improper operation of pregnant women, that is, the value of the sequence data is 0. Therefore, during the data preprocessing, we counted the number of zero values in each data, and then deleted data with more than 500 zero values according to the doctor's opinion. The final number of experimental data is 6,392, of which 80% are used as training data, 10% are used as verification data, and 10% are used as test data.

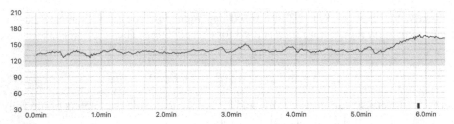

Fig. 4. A segment of FHR data, the ordinate is fetal heart rate, and the abscissa represents the time.

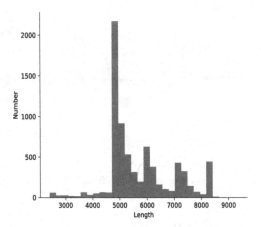

Fig. 5. The length distribution of FHR data.

It can be seen from Fig. 5 that if the length of the data is unified by directly using the padding or cropping method, the short data will be padded too much, and the useful information of the long data may be cropped. Therefore, we use FHR data with a length of 4800 as the standard to down-sample the data with a length of longer than 4800. The down-sampling algorithm is as follows:

$$index = \left\{ \left\lfloor \frac{L_X}{L_X - \hat{L}} \right\rfloor * i \right\}_{i=1}^{L_X - \hat{L}} \qquad (6)$$

Where *index* is the set of indexes (starting from 1) of the values to be discarded in data X, L_X is the length of the sequence data X, and $\hat{L}$ is the length of the standard sequence data. Even after using this down-sampling method for the longest sequence (8300) of data, the data sampling frequency is greater than two samples per second. In this case, sufficient feature information is still retained.

3.2 Implementation Details

The configuration and parameter settings of the experiment are mainly as follows: the deep learning framework used in the experiment is Keras whose bottom layer is Tensorflow, and the hardware configuration is two NVIDIA Quadro P5000 GPU. The CNN model includes three convolutional layers, and the number of convolution kernels in each layer is 32, 64, and 128, respectively, the corresponding convolution step size is 5, 5, and 3, respectively. After each convolutional layer, the *ReLU* activation function is used, as well as average pooling is used. When processing the information extracted from the KB, the Embedding layer is used first, and the output dimension is set to 128. Then use LSTM to encode the embedded features, and the output dimension is also set to 128. The learning rate is set to 0.0001, the optimizer uses *Adam*, the final activation function for multi-classification is *softmax*, the activation function for binary classification is *sigmoid*, batch-size is set to 32, and epoch is set to 200.

3.3 Evaluation Metrics

We use four evaluation metrics to evaluate the experimental results. The evaluation metrics are *Accuracy, Precision, Recall* and *F*1 − *score*. The calculation formula of *Accuracy* is as follows:

$$Accuracy = \frac{TP + TN}{TP + FP + TN + FN} \tag{7}$$

where *TP, TN, FP*, and *FN* are the number of true positive, true negative, false positive, and false negative, respectively. The difference between *Precision* and *Accuracy* is that *Precision* only pays attention to the number of positive samples predicted to be positive. The calculation formula of *Precision* is as follows:

$$Precision = \frac{TP}{TP + FP} \tag{8}$$

In the classification of medical diseases, data imbalance is a common phenomenon, so the *Recall* is necessary. The *Recall* is defined as follows:

$$Recall = \frac{TP}{TP + FN} \tag{9}$$

*F*1 − *score* can be regarded as the weighted average of *Accuracy* and *Precision*, the corresponding calculation formula is as follows:

$$F1 - score = 2 \cdot \frac{Precision \cdot Recall}{Precision + Recall} \tag{10}$$

3.4 Comparison Methods

In order to prove the effectiveness of the framework proposed in this paper, we compare with two methods, namely CNN and SVM. Li et al. [11] proposed to use one-dimensional CNN to classify FHR. This method first slices FHR data, then predicts the class of each segment, and finally uses voting to get the class of the entire FHR data. In this paper, we classify the entire FHR data. SVM is a feature extraction based on the basic statistical method.

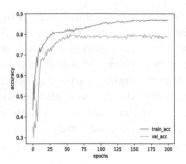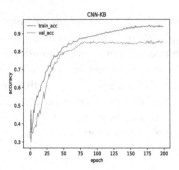

Fig. 6. The performance comparison of CNN (left) and CNN-KB (right) models in multi-classification.

3.5 Results Analysis

We first performed multi-classification (normal, suspicious, and abnormal) experiments on the three methods. The experimental results of the CNN and CNN-KB methods are shown in the Fig. 6. It can be seen from the figure that the fitting speed of the CNN model is faster than the CNN-KB model. This is because the CNN-KB model integrates KB information, which leads to slower model convergence. At the same time, it can also be seen that although the CNN-KB model has a slower fitting speed, the final performance of the model is higher than the CNN model, which also verifies the effectiveness of our proposed framework. It proves that the text information has a certain restraint ability on the classification results.

Table 1. Evaluation results of multi-class CNN and CNN-KB models on the test set.

	Accuracy	Precision	Recall	F1-score
SVM	0.7301	0.7413	0.7001	0.7301
CNN	0.7905	0.8172	0.7814	0.7989
CNN-KB	0.8218	0.8216	0.8131	0.8173

We evaluated the performance of the three models of SVM, CNN and CNN-KB on the test set, and the final evaluation results are shown in Table 1. It can be seen from the table that the SVM model has achieved the worst results on four metrics. This is because the experimental data has insufficient professionalism, which leads to poor quality of the features extracted for SVM. The performance of the CNN model and the CNN-KB model on the Precision metric is relatively close, while in the other three metrics, the performance of CNN-KB is higher than the CNN model. In general, although the proposed framework CNN-KB is slower in model fitting, its performance is higher than other methods.

In the FHR multi-classification task, the proportion of abnormal data is too small, about 3%, which will make the model perform poorly in abnormal classification. From the perspective of auxiliary diagnosis, we consider suspicious and abnormal as one

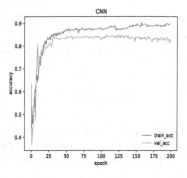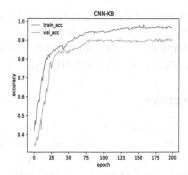

Fig. 7. Evaluation results of binary classification CNN (left) and CNN-KB (right) models on the test set.

class under the advice of doctors, and only need to distinguish whether it is a normal FHR. Therefore, we conducted binary classification experiments on three methods. The training results of the CNN model and the CNN-KB model are shown in Fig. 7. It can be seen from the figure that the performance of the binary classification task is better than the multi-class classification task, this is because the data imbalance becomes lower.

Table 2. Evaluation results of binary classification CNN and CNN-KB models on the test set.

	Accuracy	Precision	Recall	F1-score
SVM	0.7526	0.7612	0.7413	0.7511
CNN	0.8201	0.8331	0.8051	0.8189
CNN-KB	0.8454	0.8512	0.8269	0.8389

Finally, as with the multi-classification task, we also evaluated the performance of the three models of SVM, CNN and CNN-KB on the test set, and the final evaluation results are shown in Table 2. It can be seen from the results in the table that SVM still achieved the lowest score on the four metrics, and the reason is the same as in the multi-classification task. The performance of the CNN-KB model on the four metrics is still higher than the CNN model. The experimental results once again verify the effectiveness of the proposed framework.

4 Conclusion

In order to solve the problems of imbalance and lack of professionalism in FHR data. We propose a framework, classification fetal heart rate based on convolutional neural network incorporating knowledge base. We first use the keywords of the pregnant women's questions and the doctor's answers to build a KB. And then in the inference phase, we use the keywords in the pregnant women's questions to query the KB. Finally, the FHR features and the query information are merged and classified. To verify the effectiveness of our proposed framework, we conduct extensive experiments on a real-world dataset. The experimental results show that the performance of our framework is better than other methods. In the future, we will study how to automatically build a KB so that it can be applied to more scenarios.

References

1. Abrahamsson, E., Forni, T., Skeppstedt, M., Kvist, M.: Medical text simplification using synonym replacement: adapting assessment of word difficulty to a compounding language. In: Proceedings of the 3rd Workshop on Predicting and Improving Text Readability for Target Reader Populations, pp. 57–65 (2014)
2. Alfirevic, Z., Gyte, G.M., Cuthbert, A., Devane, D.: Continuous cardiotocography (CTG) as a form of electronic fetal monitoring (EFM) for fetal assessment during labour. Cochrane Database Syst. Rev. (2) (2017)
3. Barnova, K., Martinek, R., Jaros, R., Kahankova, R.: Hybrid methods based on empirical mode decomposition for non-invasive fetal heart rate monitoring. IEEE Access **8**, 51200–51218 (2020)
4. Cahill, A.G., Tuuli, M.G., Stout, M.J., López, J.D., Macones, G.A.: A prospective cohort study of fetal heart rate monitoring: deceleration area is predictive of fetal acidemia. Am. J. Obstet. Gynecol. **218**(5), 523-e1 (2018)
5. Chang, P.C., Galley, M., Manning, C.D.: Optimizing Chinese word segmentation for machine translation performance. In: Proceedings of the Third Workshop on Statistical Machine Translation, pp. 224–232 (2008)
6. Cömert, Z., Kocamaz, A.F.: Open-access software for analysis of fetal heart rate signals. Biomed. Signal Process. Control **45**, 98–108 (2018)
7. Dash, S., Quirk, J.G., Djurić, P.M.: Fetal heart rate classification using generative models. IEEE Trans. Biomed. Eng. **61**(11), 2796–2805 (2014)
8. Fanelli, A., et al.: Prototype of a wearable system for remote fetal monitoring during pregnancy. In: 2010 Annual International Conference of the IEEE Engineering in Medicine and Biology, pp. 5815–5818. IEEE (2010)
9. Georgoulas, G.G., Stylios, C.D., Nokas, G., Groumpos, P.P.: Classification of fetal heart rate during labour using hidden Markov models. In: 2004 IEEE International Joint Conference on Neural Networks (IEEE Cat. No. 04CH37541), vol. 3, pp. 2471–2475. IEEE (2004)
10. Ibrahimy, M.I., Ahmed, F., Ali, M.A.M., Zahedi, E.: Real-time signal processing for fetal heart rate monitoring. IEEE Trans. Biomed. Eng. **50**(2), 258–262 (2003). https://doi.org/10.1109/TBME.2002.807642
11. Li, J., et al.: Automatic classification of fetal heart rate based on convolutional neural network. IEEE Internet Things J. **6**(2), 1394–1401 (2018)
12. Musen, M.A.: The protégé project: a look back and a look forward. AI Matters **1**(4), 4–12 (2015)
13. Nageotte, M.P.: Fetal heart rate monitoring. Seminars in Fetal and Neonatal Medicine, vol. 20, pp. 144–148. Elsevier (2015)
14. Sbrollini, A., et al.: Automatic identification and classification of fetal heart-rate decelerations from cardiotocographic recordings. In: 2018 40th Annual International Conference of the IEEE Engineering in Medicine and Biology Society (EMBC), pp. 474–477. IEEE (2018)
15. Spilka, J., et al.: Using nonlinear features for fetal heart rate classification. Biomed. Signal Process. Control **7**(4), 350–357 (2012). https://doi.org/10.1016/j.bspc.2011.06.008
16. Spilka, J., Frecon, J., Leonarduzzi, R., Pustelnik, N., Abry, P., Doret, M.: Intrapartum Fetal Heart Rate Classification from Trajectory in Sparse SVM Feature Space, pp. 2335–2338 (2015)

17. Stout, M.J., Cahill, A.G.: Electronic fetal monitoring: past, present, and future. Clin. Perinatol. **38**(1), 127–142 (2011)
18. Yu, K., Quirk, J.G., Djurić, P.M.: Fetal heart rate classification by non-parametric bayesian methods. In: 2017 IEEE International Conference on Acoustics, Speech and Signal Processing (ICASSP), pp. 876–880. IEEE (2017)

Review of Methods for Data Collection Experiments with People with Dementia and the Impact of COVID-19

Matthew Harper[✉], Fawaz Ghali, Abir Hussain, and Dhiya Al-Jumeily

Liverpool John Moores University, Liverpool L3 3AF, UK
m.l.harper@2014.ljmu.ac.uk

Abstract. The development of a wearable-based system for detecting difficulties in the daily lives of people with dementia would be highly useful in the day-to-day management of the disease. To develop such a system, it would be necessary to identify physiological indicators of the difficulties, which can be identified by analyzing physiological datasets from people with dementia. However, there is no such data available to researchers. As such, it is vital that data is collected and made available in future. In this paper we perform a review of past physiological data collection experiments conducted with people with dementia and evaluate the methods used at each stage of the experiment. Consideration is also given to the impacts and limitations imposed by the COVID-19 pandemic and lockdowns both on the people with dementia- such people being one of the most at risk and affected groups- and on the efficacy and safety of each of the methods. It is concluded that the choice of method to be utilized in future data collection experiments is heavily dependent on the type and severity of the dementia the participants are experiencing, and that the choice of remote or COVID-secure methods should be used during the COVID-19 pandemic; many of the methods reviewed could allow for the spread of the virus if utilized during a pandemic.

Keywords: Dementia · Wearable · Data collection · COVID-19

1 Introduction

Dementia is a used to describe a range of symptoms which arise from several progressive neurodegenerative disorders which, through causing irreversible damage to neurons of the brain, cause the loss of cognitive functioning [1]. This neuronal damage eventually causes the patient to experience and exhibit symptoms which inhibit their ability to perform tasks in their daily life. In 2018, there were 448,300 people recorded as having dementia in England alone [2] with the global number of cases being estimated at approximately 50 million [3]. As of the writing of this paper, there is no curative treatment for dementia [4]. However, methods for the management of the disease are constantly improving with research and refinements in clinical practice, increasing the Quality of Life (QoL) and independence of people with dementia. However, caregiver burden and patient fears of loss of independence remain high despite progress made [5, 6]. The advent

© Springer Nature Switzerland AG 2021
D.-S. Huang et al. (Eds.): ICIC 2021, LNAI 12838, pp. 132–147, 2021.
https://doi.org/10.1007/978-3-030-84532-2_13

of personalised healthcare and wearable computing to track health could provide hope for overcoming these problems, with a system that could track and predict the difficulties of people with dementia and automatically intervene being feasible; personalised health systems already exist for other conditions [7–11].

In previous work, we identified that one of the main problems in the development of such a system was there being no publicly available physiological data from people with dementia with which to develop machine learning based systems for identifying dementia-related symptoms and difficulties [12]. As such, it is vital that such data is collected and made available to researchers. However, the conducting of such data experiments has been complicated by the emergence of COVID-19 and resulting lockdowns. Dementia is one of the most common co-morbidities with COVID 19 [13], meaning that it is vital that people with dementia are shielded and prevented from unnecessary contact. Therefore access to participants with dementia for data collection experiments is severely reduced [14]. However, this delay in research could lead to delays in finding better treatments and management techniques which could improve the quality of life for many dementia sufferers. As such, it is important the methods to be employed by future data collection experiments are carefully considered, with special consideration being given to the impact of COVID 19 on those methods.

In this paper, we review the methods used in past data collection experiments which aimed to collect physiological data which could be used to identify dementia related difficulties. We then discuss how the COVID-19 pandemic could potentially impact the tasks required to carry out such methods. This paper is novel as no existing literature could be found which reviewed the impact of COVID-19 on the conductance of physiological data collection experiments with subjects with dementia. The rest of the paper is structured as follows. Section II describes the search methodology used to find papers. Section III elaborates on the various stages or elements of past studies and the methods involved at each, evaluating their efficacy and effectiveness. This section will also describe the difficulties COVID 19 could cause regarding those methods and propose potential solutions to those problems. Finally, section IV provides a conclusion.

2 Methodology

The literature search was performed on the online resources IEEE Xplore, ACM Digital, PubMed, Scopus, Web Of Science and Google Scholar, using pre-specified keywords. Results were filtered to include journal and conference papers from January 2015 to December 2020. A total 1514 results were returned. The title review inclusion criteria were that the title includes: the words "dementia", "Alzheimer's", "cognitive impairment", or the name of a BPSD or dementia symptom; the words monitoring, smart device, assistive device, system, technology, or the name of a sensors or physiological feature. Excluded were studies whose title mention requirements elicitation, screening, diagnosis, smartphones, mobile applications, or social robots, and review papers. All duplicate results were also removed. For abstract review, the inclusion criteria were to include all studies which: are human studies; discuss the use of wearable devices as part of the system being tested. Excluded were studies which were: Purely smartphone-based; not focused on dementia and related difficulties, or behavioural and psychological symptoms of dementia (BPSD); not including data collection; using devices to locate missing persons; focusing on caregivers. In full paper screening, the inclusion criteria were to include studies which: include data collection experiments using people with dementia; provide sufficient details of methodology employed. Excluded were papers which: are inaccessible due to paywalls (due to financial constraints); containing data collection but with insufficient detail of methodology for meaningful critique. The methodology is illustrated in Fig. 1.

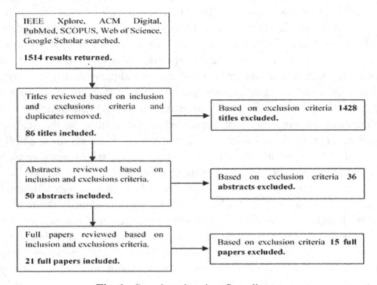

Fig. 1. Search and review flow diagram

3 Discussion

3.1 Recruitment

Recruitment is the process by which study participants are identified, approached, informed, and asked to participate [15]. Recruitment was discussed in 14 papers [16–29]. Different recruitment methods are employed depending on the setting of the experiment and stage of dementia studied. In 2 papers, hospitals are used for recruitment [20, 21]. In one, the subjects were recruited as outpatients of the hospital, as the study focused on tracking behaviours in subjects in a residential settings [21]. In another paper, the subjects were recruited as inpatients of the hospital, expected to remain in the hospital for 10 days [20]. One advantage of recruiting via hospitals is the high volume of patients admitted over any period of time, and thus, as in [20], it is easier to recruit large sample sizes over prolonged periods of time. Furthermore, the presence of trained healthcare professionals means that the patients can be medically and neuropsychological assessed with relative ease. Moreover, hospitals are often where the patient is diagnosed with dementia a, thus hospital recruitment could allow for recruitment of early stage dementia patients [30]. However, COVID 19 is likely to make this channel more difficult to use.

During the COVID-19 pandemic, hospitals have been in high demand. Several services have faced delays and cancellations to prevent hospitals becoming overwhelmed [31, 32]. The number of people being diagnosed with dementia experienced a 4% drop in England in 2020 [33]. This reduces the number of potential participants. Furthermore, staff are often busy with increased patients during the pandemic, so it may be difficult to obtain permissions and co-operation from hospitals.

Another channel for recruitment is dementia-specific care homes or residential institutions, as in 8 papers [22–29].One advantage of this is that the care home will contain many potential participants. However, people in care homes are often in the moderate to severe stage of dementia, so this channel may not be ideal for recruiting people in the early stages. Furthermore, COVID 19 has been prevalent in care homes, with care home residents experiencing one of the highest mortality risks of any group during the pandemic [34, 35]. As such, access to people in care homes may not be granted. Other methods of contacting and communicating with care home residents could be adopted to overcome this, such as video conferencing, however due to the age and impairment of many of the potential participants this solution will rely heavily on the aid of care home staff, who are experiencing increased workloads and stress during the pandemic.

One channel for the recruitment of community-based subjects with dementia is community support and advocacy groups, being used in the Behavioural and Environmental Sensing and Intervention (BESI) study [17–19]. A similar channel is a dementia day-care [16], where community-based dementia patients so that their caregivers can have a break. The support and advocacy groups are likely to be more useful for the recruitment of people in the earlier stages of dementia [16]. Overall, the recruitment channel used in an experiment likely depends heavily on the setting of the experiment and the stage of dementia focused on, with hospital outpatient facilities and community support and advocacy groups being good recruitment channels for community-based experiments and hospital inpatient facilities and nursing homes being good recruitment channels for hospital and care institution-based experiments. However, COVID 19 has caused a number of support groups to cease face-to-face meetings, and that could make it more difficult to contact potential participants and guardians about the study [32]. Therefore, remote communications are likely to provide the best methods for contacting potential participants during the pandemic, but the process may be much slower.

3.2 Consent and Assent Acquisition

The process for acquiring consent is specifically discussed in 9 papers [16, 20, 22–28]. Due to the subjects in all the studies in the 9 papers having some level of cognitive decline, the informed written consent is obtained from a proxy who is the subject's legal Power of Attorney (PoA) or guardian, usually a family member. In 8 papers, consent is primarily gained from the PoA, as the subjects are unable to consent [16, 22–28]. This is generally in the moderate to severe stages of dementia [15]. However, it is specified in 2 of those 8 papers that 1 subject is still able to consent, and as such their consent is obtained [25, 26]. In one paper, both the subject and PoA are asked for their consent for participation [20]. In 4 papers, it is specified that assent was gained from the subject, even if they were unable to give informed consent. For example, in [22–24] the participant's consent would be considered withdrawn if they refused to wear the device. In these cases, written consent was also acquired from a proxy, such as a PoA. To ensure that the consent was informed, before each experiment the PoA was given either written, verbal or written and verbal information about the experiment, including the procedures and ways in which they can end the subject's participation in the study should they later change their mind. The combination of written and verbal information is likely the best delivery method, as the written information can be referred back to, but the delivery of information verbally allows for the receiver to ask questions and seek clarification [15, 24]. In [24], written and verbal information was also given to the formal caregivers of the subject's, as they knew the subject well and thus would be able to provide input as to if the subject would be happy and safe to participate. Caregivers may also have to be asked for informed consent for their own participation, especially where the use of video cameras could lead to their own activities being recorded [15, 22, 23, 25, 26]. Overall, it is clearly vital to obtain informed, written consent from the subject's PoA, and assent of the subject to participate in the study should be taken into consideration. All stakeholders who are required to give consent should be given written and verbal information about the experiment. They should also be given the opportunity to withdraw consent at any stage. Moreover, contacting potential participants to inform them of the study and give adequate information to make the informed decision to participate may be difficult due to disruptions during to the pandemic [36].

3.3 Physiological Data Collection

Collection of physiological data is the central focus of the papers included [16–29, 37–43]. 4 aspects are highlighted: physiological data features monitored; device used; length of experiment; deployment methods and durations.

The selection of the device is heavily dependent upon the data features monitored, and the usability of the device for participants. The most used device is a smartwatch or wrist-worn medium, utilised as the lone wearable device in 12 of the included papers [17–24, 29, 40–42]. Accelerometers are the most common sensor deployed on wrists, with all but two of the papers with wrist-worn devices employing accelerometers to track movement and activity [17–20, 22, 23, 29, 40–42]. Wrist worn devices are usable with participant in all stages of dementia. An advantage of these devices is they can allow for the tracking of upper limb movement as well as full body movement, unlike chest or waist-based mediums. Wrist-worn mediums are also used in combination with other wearable devices too, with the most common combination being wrist and ankle devices, as in 3 papers [25, 26, 44]. Two papers use wrist and ankle accelerometer devices, allowing for the detection of upper body movement and leg movement [25, 26]. In 1 paper, an ankle sensor is the only to employ an accelerometer, as well as a GPS location monitor, while a wrist-worn device tracks EDA [43]. A smartwatch is also utilised in combination with a neck-worn microphone in 1 study to detect agitation [27]. In this study, an Android smartwatch is used to track the subjects' HR and limb movements. The data collected by the smartwatch correlated with the observed instance of agitation, indicating a high degree of accuracy. The combined use of 2 devices can increase the number of data features that can be collected, as in [27] and [43], or increase the number of locations one can acquire that feature from, as in [25] and [26]. A drawback is that the management of 2 devices will be more complicated. Furthermore, the more wearables in a system the more obtrusive and obstructive that system will be.

The placement of sensors on the subject's heel is used in 1 included paper, where the researchers are tracking the walking patterns of the participant to identify disorientation [37]. The participant wears an Inertial Measurement Unit (IMU) and is asked to walk a route in a laboratory setting. The researchers then used the data from the IMU to calculate the acceleration of the subject's foot, their movement duration and speed. Though deployment of a device on the heel is successful in this study, it has a limitation: a device deployed here is very limited as to the physiological data features it can track.

In 1 included paper, a chest-worn device- the Zephyr BioHarness 3.0- is utilised to track HR data in subjects exhibiting PV [28]. The placement of the device on the chest allows for very accurate measurement of ECG, and the device had been verified as useable for elderly people with dementia [28]. However, this deployment medium cannot measure things such as limb movement, and deployment of a device onto a chest is somewhat invasive. Deployment of waist or hip worn devices is less invasive than on the chest and is utilised in 3 of the included papers [16, 38, 39]. In two of the papers, the sensor deployed at the hip is an accelerometer and in 1 paper the device deployed is a Bluetooth sensor, used to track the location of the participant in relation to environmental Bluetooth sensors. In [16], the researchers experimented with placing the sensors on the ankle, wrist or waist, and waist was selected as that was most comfortable. Furthermore, in [38] the device can be attached by a strap, or simply worn in a pocket, the latter presenting the most convenient deployment method in the review. However, the limitation of not being able to track limb movement, EDA or HR from this location, without the addition of obtrusive and invasive wires and electrodes, makes the placement ideal only in situation where one is tracking full body movements and location. COVID 19 may also impact the choice of device for an experiment, as the need to reduce physical or face-to-face contact will mean that investigators may wish to choose a device which the participant or caregiver could simply and easily deploy themselves.

Deployment method and duration are also vital considerations. In the BESI study the Pebble smartwatch is utilised to track movements of the subjects to detect agitated behaviours. The physiological data collection period was 30 days, with subject-carer dyad numbers from 3 to 10 in each study iteration [17–19]. The Pebble is worn continuously, which means that the participant is tracked 24/7 [19]. However, continuous deployment is impractical for other multi-sensor devices. These devices include the Empatica E4 wristband, utilised in [42] to acquire accelerometry, EDA, HR and HR variability data relating to dementia-related crises, over a prolonged period of time. In this study, the device is deployed only during the day. Therefore, the researchers may miss crises the subjects experience of a night. A similar device deployment pattern is utilised also in the DAAD study, which also uses the Empatica E4 [22, 23]. In [23], the choice of deployment method is likely influenced by the collection experiment duration, with 481 days' of data being collected from 14 patients. Even a device with a low power-consumption is unlikely to last for such periods of time. Thus, for experiments with a long duration, the deployment for specific times is vital. Another deployment method is deploying the device for a short, specific period. This method is used in [28], where the Zephyr BioHarness 3.0 tracked HR in participants exhibiting PV. The belt is deployed for two 2-h deployments, one being on a day when the participant experienced PVs and another when they did not. A similarly short duration is used in [42], where an android smartwatch and smartphone tracked limb movement, HR, and voice. These short deployment periods and short overall experimental length is thanks to observation of the participants prior to the data collection, allowing researchers to identify the best times to deploy the device. Furthermore, the participants were in the later stages of dementia, so their difficulties occurred more frequently due to their increased cognitive impairment. As such, one could argue that the more advanced participants' stage of dementia the shorter experiment duration required, however this cannot be confirmed as many included papers do not specify participants' stages of dementia. COVID-19 lockdowns may limit the time that data collection can occur, with study visits being lessened to reduce contact [36] (Table 1).

Table 1. Summary of physiological data collection methods and impact of COVID-19

Consideration	Methods/options	Impacts of COVID-19
Device type & placement	Wrist-worn devices have good usability, sensing modalities can be less accurate Chest and waist devices less convenient but highly accurate sensors	Easy to deploy devices preferable as can be deployed by the participant or caregiver, reducing human contact
Features monitored	Limb-worn devices track limb movement and whole-body, chest and waist worn devices track whole-body HR & EDA reliably tracked from wrist, could be more accurate from chest/palm	The choice of features monitored not directly affected by pandemic, however features should be monitored using a pandemic-appropriate device
Experiment duration	Shorter durations required for severe dementia as difficulties more frequent Longer data collection periods used for people in community settings and with milder dementia	Study visits reduced due to need for less interaction or unwillingness of participants or researchers to travel and risk disease

3.4 Observational Data Collection

Observational data is a record of difficulties observed during experiments. Observational data collection methods are discussed in 16 papers. 4 different methods were identified: self-reporting; caregiver observation; cameras; and combined caregiver and camera observation.

Self-reporting is utilised in 2 studies [21, 43]. One of the studies focused on tracking and supporting situation awareness of dementia patients outdoors [43]. Each participant completed a mobility diary, in which they recorded details on journeys outside. The paper states that the information from the mobility diary had a low accuracy when comparing it to the activities demonstrated by the physiological data. This could suggest inaccuracy in self-reporting methods. Self-reporting of observations was also utilised in [21], with the subject similarly being asked to record on a printed weekly program notes about their activities, wake up times and more. No judgement is made on the accuracy of the self-reporting. One advantage of the use of self-reporting is that it is low cost [15]. Another advantage is that this method has the fewest ethical concerns of the 4 methods as the subject is not having their privacy compromised by other people [15, 45]. Moreover, this is the most COVID-secure of the methods as it requires no contact with the participant. However, one problem with self-reporting is that a disorientated or agitated participant may be incapable or unwilling to record the experienced difficulty [46]. Furthermore, people with mild dementia are often reluctant to admit that they have experienced problems beyond what is normal for an adult [47, 48], meaning self-reporting could be skewed to only include the most undeniable difficulties. The subject may also misplace the medium for self-reporting [49, 50].

Caregiver observation is utilised alone in 8 included papers [16–19, 24, 27, 41, 42]. There are two main categories: paper-based and app-based. Paper based observations are when the caregiver records observations on paper, in a journal [41, 42] or observation chart [24]. In [42], the caregiver recorded observed difficulties primarily with an event marker button on the wearable device, but were also given a journal in which to also record the difficulties. One reason for the journals use was that while the subject was experiencing difficulties, the button may be inaccessible. Also, the button could be accidently pressed, and the journal allowed distinction of accidental presses from genuine difficulties. Finally, the journal allowed the observer to give extra context about difficulties, which could be invaluable to properly understand the collected data. Paper-based recording is also used in [41], with a caregiver recording in a sleep diary the participant's sleep patterns. The diary was accurate as a strong correlation was found between the information in the diary and the physiological data. However, the information recorded in the diary is simple and easy to quantify and the accuracy could be reduced if the information recorded was more complicated. A printed observation chart is utilised for observation recording in [24], and this overcomes the difficulty of quantifying behaviours inherent in the use of free-form mediums. This is achieved by the observer, in a 24-h observation chart, marking specific colours for different difficulties. This means that the observations for all subjects are standardised, making it easy to compare one with another. However, a drawback of this method is that the observer may be able to record less context than if a journal or diary were used. This could make it more difficult to make full sense of the physiological data collected.

App-based recording of caregiver observations is utilised in 4 papers [17–19, 27]. In the BESI study, the caregiver is asked to record temporal, spatial and characteristic observations about agitation episodes that they observe, using a daily survey in an Android app. No information is given on the exact nature of the survey which makes evaluating it difficult [17–19]. An Android app is also used in [27], with the observer recording difficulties by selecting from a predetermined list. This is quick and easy for the observer, allowing them to record observations in a timely manner. Furthermore, predetermined options make the observations standardised and understandable.

Another consideration for use of caregivers is if the caregiver is informal or formal. Informal caregivers (ICs) are family or friends of the participant, who care for them in a non-professional role. Formal caregivers (FCs) care for the participant professionally. FCs, as utilised in [24, 27, 42], are trained professionals and so are more likely to understand and communicate their observations using accepted medical terms, meaning their observations have a higher likelihood of being standardised and understood [51]. Furthermore, FCs will likely better understand the difficulties and when they are occurring than an IC, as FCs tend to care for multiple patients over their professional life. Moreover, FCs are likely to be available for long periods in institutional settings, where subjects are more likely to have moderate to severe dementia [52, 53]. Alternatively, ICs –used in [17–19, 41]- are more likely to be caring for the participant dementia in a home setting, as in [41] where the caregiver is the subject's sister. This means ICs are likely available to observe participants for extended periods. However, ICs are highly susceptible to stress and burden resulting from caregiving responsibilities [54, 55]. Moreover, COVID-19 may restrict time ICs can spend with the participant. In institutional settings, PCs may be in contact with participants for long periods, but likely care for multiple residents [36]. ICs who reside with participants may be able to spend more time with them, and where they cohabitate, the method is relatively COVID-secure.

Cameras are utilised alone in 2 included papers [28, 39]. In [39], cameras are set up in a mock waiting room where participants complete tasks, with the recording being later analysed to identify the types and durations of behaviours exhibited by participants. The preliminary results of the study suggest a correlation between the observation and physiological data, supporting the use of cameras in such settings. Their use is further supported in [28], where the cameras were used to record subjects on a day when they experienced PVs and a day they did not. The video was then put into analysis software and matched with the physiological data, with great accuracy. One major advantage of cameras is that the videos can be re-watched and the observations refined, increasing accuracy [22]. Furthermore, as recording of video is passive this method does not increase burden on participants or caregivers. Moreover, cameras require no interaction with participants, thus are COVID-secure. However, cameras have privacy concerns. As such, the use of cameras should be limited to shared spaces and avoided in private areas [23]. Another disadvantage of cameras is the cost [15].

A combination of caregivers and cameras is utilised in 4 of the papers included in the review [22, 23, 25, 26]. Two of those papers are from the DAAD study [22, 23]. In these studies, the caregivers recorded the agitation episodes in observational charts, highlighting when agitation occurred and recording the location and context. Simultaneously, cameras recorded the behaviours of the person with dementia in shared spaces in the care facility, and the recorded clips were later used to check and refine the initial observations. A similar combination was utilised in [25], with the researchers videoing the subjects behaviours in the care facilities' shared spaces as a FC also recorded their observations on an observation chart. As the cameras were to be used in a shared space in the institution it was necessary for all who use that space to consent. One staff member in one home did not consent due to privacy concerns and thus cameras were not used there [25]. Similar privacy concerns are discussed in [26], in which the same combination is used. However, the authors mitigate the privacy concerns by limiting access to the recordings to 2 qualified, necessary individuals. This protects the privacy of the participant and informing them of it could allay concerns and increase the likelihood of them agreeing to participate. However, if consent is not given for the use of cameras despite this, caregivers can still gather valuable observational data (Table 2).

Table 2. Summary of observational data collection methods and impacts of COVID-19.

Consideration	Methods/options	Impacts of COVID-19
Observer	Self-reporting cheap and COVID-secure but can lack accuracy FCs accurate but lower availability while ICs less accurate but more availability Cameras are accurate however have expense and privacy concerns	FCs may not be able to attend or be with the participant due to increased risk of virus Cameras and self-reporting are COVID-secure. methods as they require no human interaction
Recording medium	Paper-based methods allow context, have low cost and are easy to use App-based methods can be more convenient for the observer	FCs likely to have less time with patient so app-based methods with predefined answers preferrable

3.5 Data Transfer and Storage

There are 2 methods identified for inclusion for the storage of physiological data. In 7 of the papers included in the review, the data is stored locally on the wearable's internal memory as it is collected and then transfer later. In 3 of these papers, the data is transferred from the device on to a computer. In 4 of the papers, the data is transferred on from the computer onto an online or cloud service. Both methods are potentially limited by COVID 19, as the devices would need to have a wired connection established to a computer. The investigators physically removing the smartwatch would require strict COVID-secure measures such as mask wearing and hand washing before and after handling the devices [56, 57]. Alternatively, participant or caregiver could upload the data, however this may require them to have certain computer competencies and be hampered by some devices requiring licenced software do so [58].

Another method for storing the data is to have it transfer automatically, via wireless connectivity, to an edge device or a computer or server. In the BESI study, the data is transferred via Bluetooth to room level nodes set up in the experimental environment, and these edge computing devices send the data on to a server where it is stored [17–19]. In [38], the data is temporarily stored on the Bluetooth anchors and then sent to a server via Wi-Fi, while in [40], the data is transferred to a base station which then sends the

Table 3. Summary of methods and COVID-19 considerations.

Experimental stage	Methods	COVID-19 Considerations
Recruitment	Hospitals and support groups best channels for people with mild to moderate dementia Care homes best recruitment channel for moderate to severe dementia	Reduced hospital services and fewer diagnoses of dementia Care homes and hospitals are busy and less likely to cooperate
Consent & assent acquisition	If participant has the capacity, the participant should give written informed consent If participant does not have capacity, assent should still be obtained but written, informed consent gained from legal guardian	Difficult to reach the participants and get consent May be more difficult for guardians or next of kin to discuss study with the participant
Physiological data collection	Position of one or multiple wearables can be on various body parts and depends heavily on the difficulty being tracked Longer duration of data collection required for participants in earlier stages; they may exhibit difficulties less frequently	Set-up or deployment of devices is more difficult to do in COVID-secure manner Participants may be less willing or unable to travel to study locations
Observation data collection	Self-reporting best for early stages of the disease. Can be unreliable Caregiver observation is more reliable than self-reporting but is impractical in data collection experiments of longer duration Cameras reliable but privacy concerns	Self-reporting and cameras COVID-secure as no increased contact required. Formal caregivers may have less time to observe due to increased safety and hygiene requirements
Data transfer & storage	Storing data locally on device has less infrastructure. Best for short experiments Data streaming has increased set-up. Best for use in long experiments	COVID-secure upload of data stored locally more difficult Data streaming most COVID-secure as least interaction

data onwards to cloud-based storage. The storage of the data locally on the device for later transfer to a computer needs little environmental infrastructure and can lead to extended battery life. However, it also means an increased workload for the researcher or caregiver who downloads the data. Wireless transfer of the data to edge computing devices or servers means reduced workloads for researchers and is useful where the data collection is to be continuous for prolonged periods. It is also the most COVID-secure method of data transfer, requiring little contact with the participants. However, this method requires the implementation of more infrastructure, which can increase the complexity and cost of the experiment [17–19]. Transfer of data to cloud-based services can allow for storage of large amounts of data [26]. However, online and cloud resources must be secured with access limited to authorised personnel (Table 3).

4 Conclusion

In conclusion, there are many considerations at each stage of the experimental process, with each being given extra weight and limitations thanks to the COVID-19 epidemic. It is important that accurate and reliable physiological and observational data are collected, however participant confidentiality and dignity must be always retained, especially where the participant is vulnerable. Furthermore, dementia sufferers are a group highly impacted by COVID-19, being some one of the most likely to contract the virus, be isolated from support, and have increased risk of mortality. All of this should mean any experiments during the pandemic have minimal contact and risk of transmission. Overall, though a data collection experiment is possible during the pandemic, there are extra considerations which may make it impractical for many researchers.

Future work could aim to understand the impact of COVID-19 on data collection experiments in other domains, especially domains in which the participants have heighten risk of mortality COVID-19. Work could also focus on the collection of a physiological dataset from people with dementia, which can be used to identify the occurrences of difficulties. Such a dataset could then be used to develop a system that could detect and predict the difficulties and automatically provide a digital intervention, reducing caregiver burden and increasing patient independence and QoL.

References

1. Koumakis, L., Chatzaki, C., Kazantzaki, E., Maniadi, E., Tsiknakis, M.: Dementia care frameworks and assistive technologies for their implementation: a review. IEEE Rev. Biomed. Eng. **12**, 4–18 (2019)
2. PHE: Statistical commentary: dementia profile, April 2019 update." Gov.uk. https://www.gov.uk/government/publications/dementia-profile-april-2019-data-update/statistical-commentary-dementia-profile-april-2019-update. Accessed 30 Jan 2020
3. WHO: "Dementia." World Health Organisation. https://www.who.int/news-room/fact-sheets/detail/dementia. Accessed 5 May 2020
4. Buckley, J.S., Salpeter, S.R.: A risk-benefit assessment of dementia medications: systematic review of the evidence. Drugs Aging **32**(6), 453–467 (2015)
5. P. Reed and S. Bluethmann, "Voices of Alzheimer's Disease: A summary report on the nationwide town hall meetings for people with early stage dementia. alzheimer's association (2008). https://www.alz.org/national/documents/report_townhall.pdf," ed (2017)

6. Connors, M.H., Seeher, K., Teixeira-Pinto, A., Woodward, M., Ames, D., Brodaty, H.: Dementia and caregiver burden: a three-year longitudinal study. Int. J. Geriatr. Psychiatry **35**(2), 250–258 (2020)

7. Aljaaf, A.J., Mallucci, C., Al-Jumeily, D., Hussain, A., Alloghani, M., Mustafina, J.: A study of data classification and selection techniques to diagnose headache patients. In: Applications of Big Data Analytics, pp. 121–134. Springer, Cham (2018). https://doi.org/10.1007/978-3-319-76472-6_6

8. Aljaaf, A.J., Al-Jumeily, D., Hussain, A.J., Baker, T., Alloghani, M., Mustafina, J.: H-diary: Mobile application for headache diary and remote patient monitoring. In: 2018 11th International Conference on Developments in eSystems Engineering (DeSE), pp. 18–22. IEEE (2018)

9. Alloghani, M., Aljaaf, A.J., Al-Jumeily, D., Hussain, A., Mallucci, C., Mustafina, J.: Data science to improve patient management system. In: 2018 11th International Conference on Developments in eSystems Engineering (DeSE), pp. 27–30. IEEE (2018)

10. Alloghani, M., Al-Jumeily, D., Hussain, A., Aljaaf, A.J., Mustafina, J., Petrov, E.: Healthcare services innovations based on the state of the art technology trend industry 4.0. In: 2018 11th International Conference on Developments in eSystems Engineering (DeSE), pp. 64–70. IEEE (2018)

11. Alloghani, M., Al-Jumeily, D., Aljaaf, A.J., Khalaf, M., Mustafina, J., Tan, S.Y.: The application of artificial intelligence technology in healthcare: a systematic review. In: Khalaf, M.I., Al-Jumeily, D., Lisitsa, A. (eds.) ACRIT 2019. CCIS, vol. 1174, pp. 248–261. Springer, Cham (2020). https://doi.org/10.1007/978-3-030-38752-5_20

12. Harper, M., Ghali, F.: A Systematic review of wearable devices for tracking physiological indicators of Dementia-related difficulties, presented at the Developments in E-Systems, Online (2020)

13. Bianchetti, A., et al.: Clinical presentation of COVID19 in dementia patients. J. Nutr. Health Aging **24**, 560–562 (2020)

14. Mok, V.C., et al.: Tackling challenges in care of Alzheimer's disease and other dementias amid the COVID-19 pandemic, now and in the future. Alzheimers Dement. **16**(11), 1571–1581 (2020)

15. Ye, B., et al.: Challenges in collecting big data in a clinical environment with vulnerable population: lessons learned from a study using a multi-modal sensors platform. Sci. Eng. Ethics **25**(5), 1447–1466 (2019)

16. Vuong, N., Chan, S., Lau, C.T., Chan, S., Yap, P.L.K., Chen, A.: Preliminary results of using inertial sensors to detect dementia-related wandering patterns. In: 2015 37th Annual International Conference of the IEEE Engineering in Medicine and Biology Society (EMBC), pp. 3703–3706. IEEE (2015)

17. Alam, R., et al.: Motion biomarkers for early detection of dementia-related agitation. In: Proceedings of the 1st Workshop on Digital Biomarkers, pp. 15–20 (2017)

18. Alam, R., Anderson, M., Bankole, A., Lach, J.: Inferring physical agitation in dementia using smartwatch and sequential behavior models. In: 2018 IEEE EMBS International Conference on Biomedical & Health Informatics (BHI), pp. 170–173. IEEE (2018)

19. Alam, R., Bankole, A., Anderson, M., Lach, J.: Multiple-instance learning for sparse behavior modeling from wearables: toward dementia-related agitation prediction. In: 2019 41st Annual International Conference of the IEEE Engineering in Medicine and Biology Society (EMBC), pp. 1330–1333. IEEE (2019)

20. Valembois, L., Oasi, C., Pariel, S., Jarzebowski, W., Lafuente-Lafuente, C., Belmin, J.: Wrist actigraphy: a simple way to record motor activity in elderly patients with dementia and apathy or aberrant motor behavior. J. Nutr. Health Aging **19**(7), 759–764 (2015)

21. Karakostas, A., Lazarou, I., Meditskos, G., Stavropoulos, T.G., Kompatsiaris, I., Tsolaki, M.: Sensor-based in-home monitoring of people with dementia using remote web technologies. In: 2015 International Conference on Interactive Mobile Communication Technologies and Learning (IMCL), pp. 353–357. IEEE (2015)

22. Khan, S.S., et al.: Agitation detection in people living with dementia using multimodal sensors. In: 2019 41st Annual International Conference of the IEEE Engineering in Medicine and Biology Society (EMBC), pp. 3588–3591. IEEE (2019)

23. Spasojevic, S., et al.: A pilot study to detect agitation in people living with dementia using multi-modal sensors

24. Melander, C., Martinsson, J., Gustafsson, S.: Measuring electrodermal activity to improve the identification of agitation in individuals with dementia. Dementia and geriatric cognitive disorders extra **7**(3), 430–439 (2017)

25. Goerss, D., et al.: Automated sensor-based detection of challenging behaviors in advanced stages of dementia in nursing homes. Alzheimer's & Dementia (2019)

26. Teipel, S., et al.: Multidimensional assessment of challenging behaviors in advanced stages of dementia in nursing homes—The insideDEM framework. Alzheimer's Dementia Diagnosis, Assessment Disease Monitoring **8**, 36–44 (2017)

27. Nesbitt, C., Gupta, A., Jain, S., Maly, K., Okhravi, H.R.: Reliability of wearable sensors to detect agitation in patients with dementia: a pilot study. In: Proceedings of the 2018 10th International Conference on Bioinformatics and Biomedical Technology, pp. 73–77 (2018)

28. Sefcik, J.S., Ersek, M., Libonati, J.R., Hartnett, S.C., Hodgson, N.A., Cacchione, P.Z.: Heart rate of nursing home residents with advanced dementia and persistent vocalizations. Health Technol. 1–5 (2019)

29. Kikhia, B., et al.: Utilizing ambient and wearable sensors to monitor sleep and stress for people with BPSD in nursing homes. J. Ambient. Intell. Humaniz. Comput. **9**(2), 261–273 (2015). https://doi.org/10.1007/s12652-015-0331-6

30. NHS. How to get a dementia diagnosis NHS.uk. https://www.nhs.uk/conditions/dementia/diagnosis/. Accessed 19 Apr 2020

31. MerseyCare: Important information about changes to our services. NHS. https://www.merseycare.nhs.uk/about-us/news/coronavirus-changes-to-mersey-cares-services/. Accessed 15 Mar 2021

32. Cuffaro, L., Di Lorenzo, F., Bonavita, S., Tedeschi, G., Leocani, L., Lavorgna, L.: Dementia care and COVID-19 pandemic: a necessary digital revolution. Neurol. Sci. **41**(8), 1977–1979 (2020). https://doi.org/10.1007/s10072-020-04512-4

33. Aveiro, M.: Rapid Response, Dementia patients: a vulnerable population during the COVID-19 Pandemic. BMJ. https://www.bmj.com/content/370/bmj.m3709/rr-6. Accessed 15 Mar 2021

34. ONS: Number of deaths in care homes notified to the Care Quality Commission, England. GOV.uk. https://www.ons.gov.uk/peoplepopulationandcommunity/birthsdeathsandmarriages/deaths/datasets/numberofdeathsincarehomesnotifiedtothecarequalitycommissionengland. Accessed 15 Mar 2021

35. A. Society: ONS figures show 50 per cent of all Covid-19 deaths in care homes also had dementia – Alzheimer's Society comment. https://www.alzheimers.org.uk/news/2020-07-03/ons-figures-show-50-cent-all-covid-19-deaths-care-homes-also-had-dementia. Accessed 15 Mar 2021

36. Canevelli, M., et al.: Facing dementia during the COVID-19 Outbreak. J. Am. Geriatrics Soc. (2020)

37. McCarthy, I., et al.: Infrastructureless pedestrian navigation to assess the response of Alzheimer's patients to visual cues (2015)

38. Kolakowski, M., Blachucki, B.: Monitoring wandering behavior of persons suffering from dementia using BLE based localization system. In: 2019 27th Telecommunications Forum (TELFOR), pp. 1–4. IEEE (2019)

39. Liu, Y., Batrancourt, B., Marin, F., Levy, R.: Evaluation of apathy by single 3D accelerometer in ecological condition: Case of patients with behavioral variant of fronto-temporal dementia. In: 2018 IEEE 20th International Conference on e-Health Networking, Applications and Services (Healthcom), pp. 1–4. IEEE (2018)

40. Gong, J., et al.: Home wireless sensing system for monitoring nighttime agitation and incontinence in patients with Alzheimer's disease. In: Proceedings of the conference on Wireless Health, pp. 1–8 (2015)

41. Radziszewski, R., Ngankam, H.K., Grégoire, V., Lorrain, D., Pigot, H., Giroux, S.: Designing calm and non-intrusive ambient assisted living system for monitoring nighttime wanderings. Int. J. Pervasive Comput. Commun. (2017)

42. Amato, F., et al.: CLONE: a promising system for the remote monitoring of Alzheimer's patients: an experimentation with a wearable device in a village for Alzheimer's care. In: Proceedings of the 4th EAI International Conference on Smart Objects and Technologies for Social Good, pp. 255–260 (2018)

43. Koldrack, P., Henkel, R., Krüger, F., Teipel, S., Kirste, T.: Supporting situation awareness of dementia patients in outdoor environments. In: 2015 9th International Conference on Pervasive Computing Technologies for Healthcare (PervasiveHealth), pp. 245–248. IEEE (2015)

44. Koldrack, P., Henkel, R., Krüger, F., Teipel, S., Kirste, T.: Supporting situation awareness of dementia patients in outdoor environments. In: presented at the Proceedings of the 9th International Conference on Pervasive Computing Technologies for Healthcare, Istanbul, Turkey (2015)

45. Khan, S.S., et al.: Daad: a framework for detecting agitation and aggression in people living with dementia using a novel multi-modal sensor network. In: 2017 IEEE International Conference on Data Mining Workshops (ICDMW), pp. 703–710. IEEE (2017)

46. Donaldson, M.: An assistive interface for people with dementia. In: Proceedings of the Australasian Computer Science Week Multiconference, pp. 1–5 (2018)

47. Kowalska, J., Mazurek, J., Rymaszewska, J.: Analysis of the degree of acceptance of illness among older adults living in a nursing home undergoing rehabilitation–an observational study. Clin. Interv. Aging **14**, 925 (2019)

48. Clare, L., Quinn, C., Jones, I.R., Woods, R.T.: "I Don't Think Of It As An Illness": Illness representations in mild to moderate dementia. J. Alzheimers Dis. **51**(1), 139–150 (2016)

49. Grober, E., Wakefield, D., Ehrlich, A.R., Mabie, P., Lipton, R.B.: Identifying memory impairment and early dementia in primary care. Alzheimer's Dementia: Diagnosis Assessment Disease Monitoring **6**, 188–195 (2017)

50. McGarrigle, L., Howlett, S.E., Wong, H., Stanley, J., Rockwood, K.: Characterizing the symptom of misplacing objects in people with dementia: findings from an online tracking tool. Int. Psychogeriatr. **31**(11), 1635–1641 (2019)

51. Bieber, A., Nguyen, N., Meyer, G., Stephan, A.: Influences on the access to and use of formal community care by people with dementia and their informal caregivers: a scoping review. BMC Health Serv. Res. **19**(1), 88 (2019)

52. Lord, K., Livingston, G., Robertson, S., Cooper, C.: How people with dementia and their families decide about moving to a care home and support their needs: development of a decision aid, a qualitative study. BMC Geriatr. **16**(1), 68 (2016)

53. Pierse, T., O'Shea, E., Carney, P.: Estimates of the prevalence, incidence and severity of dementia in Ireland. Irish J. Psychol. Med. **36**(2), 129–137 (2019)

54. Reed, C., et al.: Factors associated with long-term impact on informal caregivers during Alzheimer's disease dementia progression: 36-month results from GERAS. Int. Psychogeriatrics, 1–11 (2019)
55. Romero-Martínez, Á., Hidalgo-Moreno, G., Moya-Albiol, L.: Neuropsychological consequences of chronic stress: the case of informal caregivers. Aging Ment. Health **24**(2), 259–271 (2020)
56. Cheng, K.K., Lam, T.H., Leung, C.C., Wearing face masks in the community during the COVID-19 pandemic: altruism and solidarity. The Lancet (2020)
57. Cheng, V.C.-C., et al.: The role of community-wide wearing of face mask for control of coronavirus disease 2019 (COVID-19) epidemic due to SARS-CoV-2. J. Infect. **81**(1), 107–114 (2020)
58. Empatica: E4 Wristband. Empatica. https://www.empatica.com/en-gb/research/e4. Accessed 30 Jan 2020

KGRN: Knowledge Graph Relational Path Network for Target Prediction of TCM Prescriptions

Zhuo Gong, Naixin Zhang, and Jieyue He[✉]

School of Computer Science and Engineering, Key Lab of Computer Network and Information Integration, MOE, Southeast University, Nanjing 210018, China
jieyuehe@seu.edu.cn

Abstract. Accurately predicting the effect targets of Traditional Chinese Medicine (TCM) prescriptions is essential for exploring the molecular mechanism and clarifying the mechanism of TCM. Although some scholars have used network pharmacology to study the target prediction of TCM prescriptions, all of them are for the analysis of a specific prescription-disease association, and the universal method for predicting effect targets of TCM prescriptions has not discovered yet. Therefore, this paper proposes a Knowledge Graph Relational Path Network for Target Prediction of TCM Prescriptions (KGRN), which can integrate prescription's molecular and target information through the Knowledge Graph (KG). At the same time, the semantic information and high-level structure of the knowledge graph are extracted through Knowledge Graph Embedding and Graph Neural Networks, which can effectively capture the correlation between the prescriptions and the targets. Moreover, by emphasizing the KG relations when aggregating neighborhood information, the Relational Path Network of the KGRN model has the ability to capture the relationship dependence in the KG path, which enhances the ability to predict the relationship between the prescriptions and the targets. The experiments under multiple configurations demonstrate that KGRN outperforms the related competitive benchmarks.

Keywords: Target prediction of TCM prescriptions · Knowledge graph · Graph neural networks

1 Introduction

In practice, compared to a single herb, multi-herb formulas (TCM Prescriptions) are more commonly used to achieve optimal therapeutic efficacy [1]. Targets are specific biological macromolecules that have pharmacodynamic functions and can interact with drugs [2]. Correctly identifying and confirming the interactions between the drugs and targets is of great significance for exploring the molecular mechanism of the drugs. The interaction between the components of different herbs is believed to have a certain competitive and/or synergistic effect on multiple target proteins, thereby improving the pharmacological activity and/or reducing the adverse clinical reactions caused by some

© Springer Nature Switzerland AG 2021
D.-S. Huang et al. (Eds.): ICIC 2021, LNAI 12838, pp. 148–161, 2021.
https://doi.org/10.1007/978-3-030-84532-2_14

individual herbs [3]. Therefore, when the entire prescription is used as the research object, the identification of its effect targets should be exploring the targets that have a real relationship with the prescription in clinical treatment from a global perspective [4].

Most of the existing prescription-target prediction methods are based on network pharmacology [5–7]. This novel method challenges the traditional single-targeted drug discovery paradigm, and explores the multiple interactions between "genes, drugs, and diseases" from a global perspective [8]. However, most of the current prescription-targets predictions are only for a specific prescription-disease pair. At the same time, network pharmacology has the problems in the construction of a multi-level network of disease phenotype, target, component and drug for a prescription and its corresponding disease. This makes it more difficult to directly realize the target prediction of TCM prescriptions. A recent study [9] used knowledge graphs to predict drug targets of western medicine. It applied knowledge graphs to machine learning models for extracting drug and target features by using various embedding methods. However, this work directly learns the potential embedding of nodes for simply using the semantic representation information of drugs and targets in the knowledge graph; it's limited in obtaining rich neighborhood information of each entity in KG. Meanwhile, due to the characteristics of multiple components, multiple targets, low affinity and low selectivity of TCM prescriptions, this method cannot be directly applied to predict the effect targets of the prescriptions.

The essence of the target prediction problem of TCM prescriptions is to predict the effective prescription-target associations from the large-scale relevant data of prescriptions and targets. Therefore, this problem can be regarded as a target recommendation problem of TCM prescriptions. To this end, inspired by Graph Neural Networks [10–12], this paper proposed a model of Knowledge Graph Relational Path Network (KGRN) for predicting the effect targets of TCM prescription, which using the knowledge graph to integrate the molecular target information of the prescription, and automatically capture the high-level structure and semantic relationship in the KG. The KGRN model consists of three parts: the first part is to extract the prescription-target associations and construct the TCM knowledge graph from the dataset. The second part uses the graph neural networks to extract high-level structures and semantic relations, and learns prescriptions, targets and their topological neighborhood representations from the KG. The third part is to send the trained prescription and target samples to the collaborative filtering module to obtain a predictive function that can effectively predict the association between the prescriptions and targets. The contributions of this work are summarized as follows:

(1) Innovatively transforms the target prediction problem of TCM prescriptions into the problem of target recommendation in an end-to-end manner by using the knowledge graph embedding and graph neural networks to mine the semantic relationship and topological structure of prescription-target pair in the KG.

(2) Expands the contribution of the KG relation to the node representation through the aggregation process, and designs the relational message transfer mode to reveal the different meanings carried by the triples, which improves the potential prescription-target association prediction performance.

(3) Taking Recall and NDCG as evaluation indicators, the KGRN model has achieved the best performance compared with related competitive benchmarks.

2   Related Works

Traditional drug target identification methods based on biological experiments are usually difficult to develop because of their long cycle, high cost, and low output. Simultaneously, driven by intelligent computing technologies such as machine learning, pattern recognition and data mining, computer-aided drug-target prediction method has attracted more and more researchers' attention. Computer-aided drug-target prediction methods of western medicines can be generally classified into ligand-based methods, docking technology-based methods and network-based methods [13]. However, the objects of these methods are mostly single-molecule components of western medicine, they cannot be directly applied to the TCM prescriptions, which have the characteristics of multi-component multi-target, and multi-path regulation mechanisms, and must exert its efficacy through the active components of the herbs.

In view of the multi-components, multi-target, and multi-channel integrated regulation mode of TCM prescriptions, some researchers have explored the mechanism research of TCM prescriptions from the perspective of network pharmacology [14]. For example, Zhang et al. [4] constructed a binary network of Xuefu-Zhuyu Decoction and Gualou-Xiebai-Banxia Decoction based on the interactions between TCM components/western medicine drugs (drugs approved by the FDA for the treatment of coronary artery disease) and their related targets and obtained independent target networks by Matrix algebra. However, these integrated frameworks of TCM network pharmacology are only aimed at a specific prescription-disease pair, and the existing drug target prediction tools are used manually to search from chemical component to target. Based on the overall TCM targets and its network analysis process, they have insufficient generalization ability and fail to effectively utilize the relevant data of TCM prescription and target.

Unlike traditional graphs or networks that only have a single relationship, a knowledge graph usually consists of multiple entities (such as drugs, targets, and pathways) and different types of relations encoding heterogeneous information. Due to its advantages, the knowledge graph has been applied to drug target prediction [9]. This method uses the biomedical knowledge base to create a knowledge graph, and transforms the problem of drug target discovery into link prediction. This model uses knowledge graph embedding to extract the characteristics of drugs and targets, and directly learns the potential embedding representations of nodes. However, they only learn the semantic representations of nodes at the granularity of triples, while ignoring the rich neighborhood information of each entity in the knowledge graph and the interactions of the KG relations in the path.

3   Methods

Several relevant definitions are given to facilitate the interpretation of the KGRN model for target prediction of TCM prescriptions.

Definition 1 (Prescription-Target Associations). Define a set of prescriptions $\mathcal{P}$ and a set of targets $\mathcal{T}$ in a typical prescription-target prediction scenario. Here we represent the relational data as a prescription-target bipartite graph $\mathcal{G}_1$, and define it as

$\{(p, y_{pt}, t)|p \in \mathcal{P}, t \in \mathcal{T}\}$, where the link $y_{pt} = 1$ indicates that there is a functional relationship between target t and prescription p.

In addition to the interactive information of the prescription-target, we also consider the side information of the prescription and target (for example, the external knowledge of the target). These auxiliary data consist of real entities in the field of pharmacy and their configuration relationships. We organize these side information in the form of knowledge graph, which is a directed graph composed of subject-property-object triple facts [15].

Definition 2 (TCM Prescriptions Knowledge Graph). TCM Prescriptions Knowledge Graph is presented as $\{(h, r, t)|h, t \in \mathcal{E}, r \in \mathcal{R}\}$, where each triplet describes that there is a relation r from head entity h to tail entity t; $\mathcal{E}$ and $\mathcal{R}$ represent the entity set and relation set of the knowledge graph respectively.

Through the mapping between prescription and target in the prescription-target associations and knowledge graph entity $(\mathcal{P} \subset \mathcal{E}, \mathcal{T} \subset \mathcal{E})$ the knowledge graph can configure the prescription and target, and provide supplementary information of the interactive data. By expressing a prescription-target association as a triplet $((p, Associate, t)|p \in \mathcal{P}, t \in \mathcal{T})$, that is, $y_{pt} = 1$ is expressed as the additional relationship $Associate$ between prescription p and target t. The prescription-target association diagram and knowledge graph are coded into a unified relationship graph $\mathcal{G} = \{(h, r, t)|h, t \in \mathcal{E}, r \in \mathcal{R}'\}$, where $\mathcal{R}' = \mathcal{R} \cup \{Associate\}$.

Definition 3 (Target Prediction of TCM prescriptions). Given the prescription-target association diagram $\mathcal{G}_1$ and the knowledge graph $\mathcal{G}_2$, the task is to predict whether the target $t(t \in \mathcal{T})$ is a potential effect target of $p(p \in \mathcal{P})$, and this relationship has not been discovered before. In order to achieve this goal, a prediction function $\hat{y}_{pt} = \Gamma(p, t|\beta, \mathcal{G}_1, \mathcal{G}_2)$ is learned, where $\hat{y}_{pt}$ indicates the probability that the target t is the effect target of the prescription p, and β is the model parameter of the function Γ.

Figure 1 shows the overall framework of KGRN, which consists of three main parts: (1) The embedding layer, which parameterizes each node into a vector by retaining the structure of the prescription-target associations diagram and the knowledge graph; (2) The relational path-aware aggregation layer, which recursively propagates the embedding of node neighbors to update its representation, and uses a relation-oriented aggregation method to capture the interactions between the relations in the path; (3) The prediction layer, which aggregates the representations of the prescriptions and the targets from all the propagation layers, and outputs the predicted matching score.

3.1 Embedding Layer

Knowledge graph embedding is an effective way to parameterize entities and relations into vector representations, while maintaining the structure of the graph. Here we employ TransR [16], a widely used method on TCM Prescriptions Knowledge Graph. To be more specific, if a triplet $\{(h, r, t)|h, t \in \mathcal{E}, r \in \mathcal{R}\}$ exists in the graph, it learns to embed each entity and relation by optimizing the translation principle $e_h^r + e_r \approx e_t^r$. Herein, $e_h, e_t \in \mathbb{R}^d$ and $e_r \in \mathbb{R}^k$ are the embedding for h, t and r; e_h^r, e_t^r are the projected

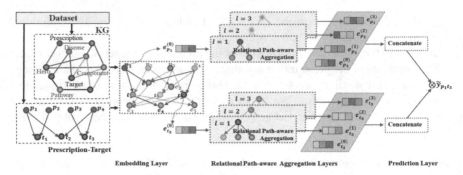

Fig. 1. Overall framework of KGRN

representations of e_h and e_t in the relation $r's$ space. Hence, for a given triplet (h, r, t), its plausibility score is formulated as follows:

$$g(h, r, t) = \|W_r e_h + e_r - W_r e_t\|_2^2 \tag{1}$$

where $W_r \in R^{k \times d}$ is the transformation matrix of relation r, which projects entities from the d-dimension entity space into the k-dimension relation space. A lower score of $g(h, r, t)$ suggests that the triplet is more likely to be true, and vice versa.

The training of TransR considers the relative order between valid triplets and broken ones, and encourages their discrimination through a pairwise ranking loss:

$$\mathcal{L}_{KG} = \sum_{(h,r,t,t')\in\mathcal{F}} -\ln\sigma(g(h, r, t') - g(h, r, t)) \tag{2}$$

where $\mathcal{F} = \{(h, r, t, t')|(h, r, t) \in \mathcal{G}, (h, r, t') \notin \mathcal{G}\}$, and (h, r, t') is a broken triplet constructed by replacing one entity in a valid triplet randomly; $\sigma(\cdot)$ is the sigmoid function. This layer models the entities and relations on the granularity of triples, working as a regularizer and injecting the direct connections into representations, and thus the representation ability of the model is improved.

3.2 Relational Path-Aware Aggregation Layer

After modeling entities and relations at the granularity of triples, this work uses graph neural networks to learn the local neighborhood information of entities to obtain the internal associations between the prescriptions and the targets. Previous GNN-based recommender models [17–19] have shown that the neighborhood aggregation scheme is a promising end-to-end way to integrate multi-hop neighbors into the representation.

However, Wang et al. [20] argue that current aggregation schemes are mostly node-based, which limit the benefit of the structural knowledge, due to two issues: (1) the aggregator focuses on combining the information of the neighborhood without distinguishing which path they come from. Therefore, they are not sufficient to store structural information in the presentation. Moreover, (2) current node-based aggregators usually model KG relations in the decay factors via attention networks [17, 19, 21] to control how much information is propagated from neighbors. This limits the contribution of KG relations to the representation of nodes. Therefore, we design a relational path-aware aggregation scheme to solve these two limitations. Here, we first discuss the aggregation logic of a single layer and then discuss how to generalize it to multiple layers.

An entity can participate in multiple triples, and it can take other connected entities as its attributes which makes the entity play a role as a bridge connecting two triples and disseminating information, and also reflects the content similarity between entities. Based on this, we perform information propagation between an entity and its neighbors. Considering an entity h, using $\mathcal{N}_h = \{(h, r, t)|(h, r, t) \in \mathcal{G}\}$ to denote the set of triplets with h is the head entity, and termed it neighborhood network. In order to characterize the first-order connectivity structure of entity h, the linear combination of $h's$ neighborhood network is defined as (3):

$$e_{\mathcal{N}_h} = f(\{(e_r, e_t)|(h, r, t) \in \mathcal{N}_h\}) \tag{3}$$

where $f(\cdot)$ is the aggregation function to extract and integrate information from each connection (h, r, t). Here we account for the relational context in the aggregator. Intuitively, each KG entity has different semantics and meanings in different relational contexts. We refer to the work of Wang et al. [20] and model the relational context in the aggregator as formula (4), which can expand the contribution of KG relations to nodes during the aggregation process, and capture the interactions between the relations in the path.

$$e_{\mathcal{N}_h} = \frac{1}{|\mathcal{N}_h|} \sum_{(h,r,t) \in \mathcal{N}_h} e_r \circ e_t \tag{4}$$

where e_t is the embedding representation of entity t in the knowledge graph. For each triplet (h, r, t), we devise a relational message $e_r \circ e_t$ by modeling the relation r as the projection or rotation operator [22]. As a result, the relational message is able to reveal different meanings carried by the triplets, even when they get the same entities.

The final phase is to aggregate the entity representation e_h and its neighborhood network representation $e_{\mathcal{N}_h}$ as the new representation of entity h, more formally, $e_h^{(1)} = f_{agg}(e_h, e_{\mathcal{N}_h})$. Here we use the Bi-Interaction Aggregator [19] to consider two feature-based interactions between e_h and $e_{\mathcal{N}_h}$:

$$f_{agg} = LeakyReLU\left(W_1(e_h + e_{\mathcal{N}_h})\right) + LeakyReLU\left(W_2(e_h \odot e_{\mathcal{N}_h})\right) \tag{5}$$

where $W_1, W_2 \in \mathbb{R}^{d' \times d}$ are the trainable weight matrices, $\odot$ denotes the element-wise product. Different from the general aggregation, Bi-Interaction aggregation encodes the feature interaction between e_h and $e_{\mathcal{N}_h}$. This term makes the information being propagated sensitive to the affinity between e_h and $e_{\mathcal{N}_h}$, e.g., passing more messages from similar entities.

Furthermore, we can stack more propagation layers to explore high-order connectivity information and collect information propagated from higher-hop neighbors. More formally, in the l-th steps, we recursively formulate the representation of an entity as:

$$e_h^{(l)} = f_{agg}(e_h^{(l-1)}, e_{\mathcal{N}_h}^{(l-1)}) \tag{6}$$

wherein the information propagated within l-neighborhood network for the entity h is defined as follows.

$$e_{\mathcal{N}_h}^{(l-1)} = f\left(\left\{\left(e_r, e_t^{(l-1)}\right) | (h, r, t) \in \mathcal{N}_h\right\}\right) \tag{7}$$

$e_t^{(l-1)}$ is the representation of the entity t generated from the previous information propagation step, and it saves information from its $(l-1)$-hop neighbors. $e_h^{(0)}$ is set as e_h at the initial information propagation iteration, and it further contributes to the representation of entity h at layer l. Obviously, high-order embedding propagation seamlessly injects the relationship dependency between pharmacological logic-based collaborative signals and the long paths into the representation learning process.

3.3 Prediction Layer

After performing L layers, we obtain multiple representations for prescription node p, namely $\left\{e_p^{(1)}, \ldots, e_p^{(L)}\right\}$; similarly, for the target node t, there are $\left\{e_t^{(1)}, \ldots, e_t^{(L)}\right\}$. As the output of the l-th layer is the message aggregation of the tree structure depth of l rooted at p(or t), the output of different layers emphasizes the connectivity information in different orders. Therefore, we use the layer aggregation mechanism [23] to connect the representation of each step into a vector, as shown below:

$$e_p^* = e_p^{(0)} \| \ldots \| e_p^{(L)}, e_t^* = e_t^{(0)} \| \ldots \| e_t^{(L)} \tag{8}$$

where $\|$ is the concatenation operation. In this way, we not only encode the KG relations dependency in the final representation by performing the embedding propagation operation, but also allow the intensity of propagation to be controlled by adjusting L. Finally, we conduct inner product of prescription and target representations, so as to predict the possibility of the target being acted by the prescription.

$$\hat{y}_{pt} = e_p^{*\top} e_t^* \tag{9}$$

3.4 Optimization

In order to optimize the KGRN model, we opt for the BPR loss [24]. Specifically, it assumes that the observed interactions, which indicate more pharmacological logic, should be assigned higher prediction values than unobserved ones:

$$\mathcal{L}_{BPR} = \sum_{(p,t,j) \in \mathcal{O}} -\ln \sigma\left(\hat{y}(p, t) - \hat{y}(p, j)\right) \tag{10}$$

where $\mathcal{O} = \left\{(p, t, j) | (p, t) \in \mathcal{R}^+, (p, j) \in \mathcal{R}^-\right\}$ represents the training set, $\mathcal{R}^+$ represents the verified (positive) interaction between the prescription p and the target t, $\mathcal{R}^-$ is the sampled and unverified (negative) interaction set, and $\sigma(\cdot)$ is the sigmoid function.

Finally, we obtain the joint objective function by learning Eqs. (2) and (10) together, as shown in (11).

$$\mathcal{L}_{KGRN} = \mathcal{L}_{KG} + \mathcal{L}_{BPR} + \lambda \|\Theta\|_2^2 \tag{11}$$

where $\Theta = \left\{ E, W_r, \forall r \in \mathcal{R}, W_1^{(l)}, W_2^{(l)}, \forall l \in \{1, \cdots, l\} \right\}$ is the model parameter set, and E is the embedding table for all entities and relations; L_2 regularization parameterized by λ on Θ is conducted to prevent overfitting.

4 Experiments

4.1 Dataset

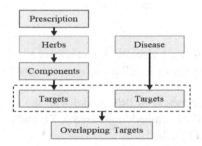

Fig. 2. The extraction process   **Fig. 3.** Pattern of knowledge graph

Since there is currently no publicly available dataset for prescription-target prediction problem, to evaluate the effectiveness of KGRN on the prescription-target prediction, we construct the dataset as follows:

Prescription-Target Relational Data Extraction: The extraction process of the prescription-target data is strictly implemented in accordance with the relevant literature [4–7] on target prediction of TCM prescription based on network pharmacology. The specific process is divided into four steps as shown in Fig. 2.

Construction of TCM Prescriptions Knowledge Graph: For the construction of the Knowledge Graph, we refer to the relevant literature on the construction of the knowledge graph in the field of TCM [25–27]. The pattern diagram of the TCM Prescriptions Knowledge Graph is shown in Fig. 3.

We named the constructed dataset as TCMDataset, and the basic statistics of the dataset are summarized in Table 1. For this dataset, we randomly select 80% of interactive data of each prescription to constitute the training set, and take the rest as the test set. In the training set, we randomly select 10% of interactions as validation set to tune hyper-parameters.

4.2 Experimental Settings

Evaluation Metrics: In the evaluation phase, we conduct the all-ranking strategy [28]. To be more specific, for each prescription, using the strategy mentioned in Sect. 4.1 for negative sampling, and the relevant targets in the testing set are treated as positive. All these targets are ranked based on the predictions of recommender model. To evaluate

Table 1. TCMDataset statistics

		TCMDataset
Prescription-target associations	#Prescription	100
	#Target	5160
	#Associations	10334
TCM prescriptions knowledge graph	#Entities	9881
	#Relations	6
	#Triplets	115425

top-K recommendation, we adopt the protocols [28]: Recall@K and ndcg@K, where K is set to 20 by default. We report the average metrics for all prescriptions in the testing set.

Alternative Baselines: We compare our proposed KGRN model with the state-of-the-art methods, including KG-free(FM and NFM), embedding-based (CKE and CFKG) and GNN-based (KGCN、KGNN and KGAT) methods:

- FM [29]: This is a factorization model that considers second-order feature interactions between inputs. Here, we treat the prescription, target and knowledge (ie, the entity connected to them) as input features.
- NFM [30]: This method is a state-of-the-art factorization model, which combines neural networks on the basis of FM. In particular, we use hidden layers as suggested to process the features of the input data.
- CKE [31]: This is a representative method based on regularization, which uses semantic embedding derived from TransR [16] to enhance matrix factorization.
- CFKG [32]: This model applies TransE [33] on the joint graph including prescription, target, entity and relationship, and converts the target prediction task into the authenticity judgment of (p, *associate*, t) triples.
- KGCN [18]: This method combines knowledge graph embedding and graph convolutional network GCN. The selected aggregator focuses on combining the information of the neighborhood to update the representation of the node and obtain high-level structural information.
- KGNN [34]: This method is similar to the KGCN method, but uses the sampling and aggregation method proposed by Hamilton et al. [35] when aggregating neighborhood information.
- KGAT [19]: This method clearly models the high-order connectivity in KG in an end-to-end manner, and models the KG relationship as a decay factor through the attention network, so as to achieve the effect of controlling how much information is transmitted from neighbors.

Parameter Settings: We implement our KGRN model in Tensorflow. Due to the high computational cost, the size of embedding dimension is fixed to 64 for all models. We optimize all models with Adam optimizer, where the batch size is fixed at 48. The default Xavier initializer is used to initialize the model parameters. We apply a grid search for hyper-parameters: the learning rate is tuned amongst {0.05, 0.01, 0.005, 0.001}, the coefficient of L2 normalization is searched in {10^{-5}, 10^{-4}, $\cdots$, 10^1, 10^2}, and the dropout ratio is tuned in {0.0, 0.1, $\cdots$, 0.8} for NFM, KGCN, KGNN, KGAT and KGRN. Besides, we employ the node dropout technique for KGCN, KGNN, KGAT and KGRN, where the ratio is searched in {0.0, 0.1, $\cdots$, 0.8}. Moreover, early stopping strategy is performed, i.e., premature stopping if Recall@20 on the validation set does not increase for 50 successive epochs. To model the third-order connectivity, we set the depth of KGRN L to 3 and the hidden dimensions to 64, 32 and 16.

4.3 Performance Comparison

We first report the performance of all the methods, Table 2 reports the average scores of Recall, Precision, F1, and ndcg for 10 runs on the TCMDataset dataset, the division of training set and test set is consistent with the dataset description in Sect. 4.1. From the Table 2, we have the following observations:

Table 2. Overall performance comparison

	Recall	Precision	F1	ndcg
FM	0.74404	0.80850	0.77493	0.85371
NFM	0.76196	0.82600	0.79268	0.86922
CKE	0.75937	0.82350	0.79013	0.86417
CFKG	0.72435	0.79607	0.75851	0.84140
KGCN	0.77660	0.83700	0.80567	0.87686
KGNN	0.77875	0.84400	0.81006	0.87963
KGAT	0.78660	0.85210	0.81804	0.88453
KGRN	**0.79306**	**0.85800**	**0.82425**	**0.89250**

(1) KGRN can produce the best performance on the TCMDataset. More specifically, the KGRN has a Recall value of 0.79306, while NFM, CKE and KGAT yield results of 0.76196, 0.75937, and 0.78660, respectively. At the same time, KGRN also achieved the best results 0.90195 on another evaluation index NDRG. By stacking multiple embedded propagation layers and considering the contribution of the KG relations, KGRN can explore high-order connectivity in an explicit way, and can effectively capture the relation dependence in the path. In addition, compared with KGAT modeling the KG relationship as a decay factor through the attention network, KGRN verifies the effectiveness of the relational path-aware aggregation, which better preserves the overall semantics of the path and collects more information.

(2) In most cases, the performance of FM and NFM is better than that of CFKG and CKE, while FM and NFM yield results of 0.74404 and 0.76196 in Recall, but

CFKG and CKE get the Recall results of 0.72435 and 0.75937. This indicates that embedding-based methods may not make full use of entities knowledge. It is worth pointing that in order to enrich the representation of the target, FM and NFM make full use of the embedded representation of their connected entities, while CFKG and CKE only use the embedded representation of their aligned entities. In addition, the crossover feature in FM and NFM is actually the second-level connection between the prescription and target, while CFKG and CKE model the connection on the granularity of triplets, without involving high-order connectivity.

(3) Compared with FM and NFM, the performance of GNN-based methods (KGCN, KGNN and KGAT) verifies that merging two-hop adjacent items is of great significance for enriching the expression of the prescription and target. More specifically, the KGCN, KGNN and KGAT have a Recall value of 0.77660, 0.77875 and 0.78660, respectively. Therefore, it reflects the positive effect of modeling high-order connectivity or neighborhood representation.

4.4 Hyper-parameters Study

In this section, we examine the influence of several key hyper-parameters on the performance of proposed KGRN model. We fixed other parameters when studying one of parameters.

Impact of Depth of Aggregation Layer. We change the depth L of KGRN to study the use efficiency of multiple relational path aggregation layers. Stacking more layers can integrate the information carried by longer-distance connections (longer paths) into the node representation. In particular, the number of layers is searched in the range of $\{1, 2, 3, 4\}$. We use KGRN-1 to represent the KGRN model with a depth of 1, and apply similar representations to other layers. We summarize the experimental results in Fig. 4, and have the following observations:

Increasing the depth of KGRN can greatly improve performance. Obviously, compared to KGRN-1, the KGRN-2 and KGRN-3 have achieved a certain improvement (nearly 0.84% average improvement) in all evaluation indicators. We attribute this improvement to the effective modeling of the high-level relationship between the prescription, target and entity. Stacking another layer on KGRN-3, we observe that KGRN-4 has almost no improvement, which shows that considering the third-order relationship between entities may be sufficient to capture the cooperative signal, and deeper layering may bring noise to the model.

Impact of Neighborhood Size. We change the neighborhood size k to explore its impact on model performance. In particular, the value of the neighborhood size is controlled in $\{8, 16, 32, 64, 128\}$, and the experimental results are shown in Fig. 5. The experimental results show that KGRN achieves the best performance when $k = 32$ (0.78899 in Recall) and $k = 64$ (0.78938 in Recall). This is because too small k makes the model unable to incorporate enough neighborhood information, and too large k makes the model easy to be noise misleading. Since $k = 32$ does not improve much on $k = 16$ and the time efficiency of the model needs to be considered, we refer the parameter settings in KGAT 19 and set the depths of the three-level relationship path aggregation layer to 64, 32, 16.

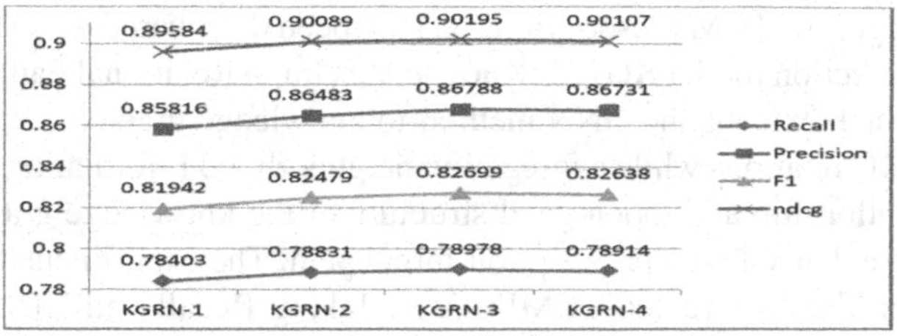

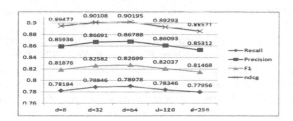

Fig. 4. Comparison of model performance at different depths

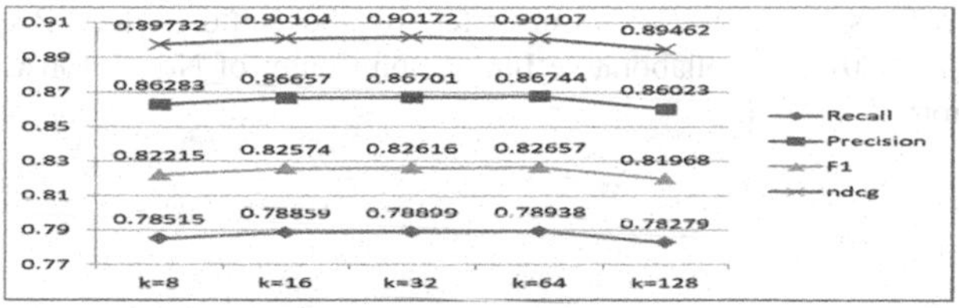

Fig. 5. Comparison of model performance under different sampling sizes

Impact of Dimension of Embedding. Lastly, we examine the influence of dimension of embedding d by varying from 8 to 256. The experimental results are shown in Fig. 6. The best results (0.78978 in Recall and 0.90195 in NDCG) appear when d is equal to 64, which shows that appropriately increasing the embedding dimension d can improve the performance of the model. Because high-dimensional embedding can effectively encode sufficient prescription, target, and entity information in the KG, while a too large dimension value adversely suffers from over-fitting.

Fig. 6. Comparison of model performance under different embedding dimensions

5 Conclusions

Drug target prediction is of great significance for exploring the molecular mechanism and clarifying the mechanism of drugs. As a fast and accurate method of drug target identification, computer-aided western medicine drug-target prediction method has attracted more and more researchers' attention. In view of the multi-component, multi-target, and multi-channel integrated regulation mode of TCM prescriptions, the universal method for predicting targets of TCM prescriptions has not been discovered yet. This paper proposes a target prediction model KGRN (Knowledge Graph Relational Path Network) for prescriptions, which extends the GNN method to knowledge graphs. It emphasizes the contribution of KG relations while aggregating neighborhood information, so as to learn the semantic relationship and topological structure of the knowledge graph, as well as the relations dependence in the prescription-target path. The experimental comparisons are conducted on the constructed TCMDataset. Taking Recall and NDCG as evaluation metrics, the KGRN achieved the best performance compared with state-of-the-art methods.

Acknowledgment. This work has been supported by the National Key R&D Program of China(2019YFC1711000) and Collaborative Innovation Center of Novel Software Technology and Industrialization.

References

1. Pan, S.Y., Chen, S.B., Dong, H.G., et al.: New perspectives on Chinese herbal medicine (Zhong-Yao) research and development. Evidence-based Complement. Alternative Med. **2011**(1), 403709 (2011)
2. Deans, R.M.: Parallel shRNA and CRISPR-Cas9 screens enable antiviral drug target identification. Nat. Chem. Biol. **12**(5), 361–366 (2016)
3. Yan-Tong, X.U.: Modern scientific connotation on formula compatibility in Chinese materia medica. Chinese Traditional Herbal Drugs **46**, 465–469 (2015)
4. Zhang, Q., Yu, H., Qi, J., et al.: Natural formulas and the nature of formulas: Exploring potential therapeutic targets based on traditional Chinese herbal formulas. PLoS ONE **12**(2), e0171628 (2017)
5. Zuo, H., Zhang, Q., Su, S., et al.: A network pharmacology-based approach to analyse potential targets of traditional herbal formulas: an example of Yu Ping Feng decoction. Sci. Rep. **8**(1), 11418–11423 (2018)
6. Wang, Z., Heng, H.: Novel compound-target interactions prediction for the herbal formula Hua-Yu-Qiang-Shen-Tong-Bi-Fang. Chem. Pharm. Bull. **67**(8), 778–785 (2019)
7. Zhang, D., Zhang, Y., Gao, Y., et al.: Translating traditional herbal formulas into modern drugs: a network-based analysis of Xiaoyao decoction. Chinese Med. **15** (2020)
8. Chandran, U., Mehendale, N., Patil, S., et al.: Network pharmacology. (2017)
9. Mohamed, S.K., Nováček, V., Nounu, A.: Discovering protein drug targets using knowledge graph embeddings. Bioinformatics **36**(2) (2019)
10. Hamilton, W.L., Ying, R., Leskovec, J.: Inductive representation learning on large graphs (2017)
11. Quan, Z., Guo, Y., Lin, X., et al.: GraphCPI: graph neural representation learning for compound-protein interaction. In: 2019 IEEE International Conference on Bioinformatics and Biomedicine (BIBM) (2020)
12. Wang, X., Huang, T., Wang, D., et al.: Learning Intents behind Interactions with knowledge graph for recommendation. In: WWW (2021)
13. Lilang, Z.: Research on predictive model and algorithm of drug potential target. National Defense University (2017)
14. Hopkins, A.L.: Network pharmacology: the next paradigm in drug discovery. Nat Chem Biol. **4**(11), 682–690 (2008)

15. Cao, Y., Xiang, W., He, X., et al.: Unifying knowledge graph learning and recommendation: towards a better understanding of user preferences. In: WWW (2019)
16. Lin, Y., Liu, Z., Sun, M., et al. Learning entity and relation embeddings for knowledge graph completion. In: AAAI, pp. 2181–2187 (2015)
17. Wang, H., Zhang, F., Zhang, M., et al.: Knowledge-aware graph neural networks with label smoothness regularization for recommender systems. In: The 25th ACM SIGKDD International Conference. ACM (2019)
18. Wang, H., Zhao, M., Xie, X., et al.: Knowledge graph convolutional networks for recommender systems. In: WWW, pp. 3307–3313 (2019)
19. Wang, X., He, X., Cao, Y., et al.: KGAT: knowledge graph attention network for recommendation. In: The 25th ACM SIGKDD International Conference (2019)
20. Wang, X., Huang, T., Wang, D., et al.: Learning intents behind interactions with knowledge graph for recommendation. In: Proceedings of the Web Conference 2021 (WWW 2021) (2021)
21. Wang, Z., Lin, G., Tan, H., et al.: CKAN: collaborative knowledge-aware attentive network for recommender systems. In: SIGIR 2020: The 43rd International ACM SIGIR conference on research and development in Information Retrieval. ACM, (2020)
22. Sun, Z., Deng, Z.H., Nie, J.Y., et al.: RotatE: Knowledge graph embedding by relational rotation in complex space. In: ICLR (2019)
23. Keyulu, X., Chengtao, L., Yonglong, T., et al.: Representation learning on graphs with jumping knowledge networks. In: ICML, pp. 5449–5458 (2018)
24. Rendle, S., Freudenthaler, C., Gantner, Z., et al.: BPR: Bayesian personalized ranking from implicit feedback. In: UAI 2009, Proceedings of the Twenty-Fifth Conference on Uncertainty in Artificial Intelligence, Montreal, QC, Canada, 18–21 June 2009
25. Tong, Y., Jing, L., Lirong, J., et al.: Research on the construction of large-scale traditional Chinese medicine knowledge graph. China Digital Med. **10**(3), 80–82 (2015)
26. Tong, R., Chenglln, S., Haofen, W., et al.: Construction and application of TCM Knowledge graph. J. Med. Inform. **37**(4), 8–13 (2016)
27. Dezheng, Z., Yonghong, X., Man, L., et al.: Construction of TCM knowledge graph based on ontology. Inf. Eng. **3**(1), 035–042 (2017)
28. Krichene, W., Rendle, S.: On sampled metrics for item recommendation. In: KDD 2020: The 26th ACM SIGKDD Conference on Knowledge Discovery and Data Mining, pp. 1748–1757. ACM (2020)
29. Rendle, S., Gantner, Z., Freudenthaler, C., et al.: Fast context-aware recommendations with factorization machines. In: International ACM SIGIR Conference on Research & Development in Information Retrieval, vol. 635. ACM (2011)
30. He, X., Chua, T.S.: Neural factorization machines for sparse predictive analytics. ACM Sigir Forum 51(cd), 355–364 (2017)
31. Zhang, F., Yuan, N.J., Lian, D., et al.: Collaborative knowledge base embedding for recommender systems. In: The 22nd ACM SIGKDD International Conference. ACM (2016)
32. Ai, Q., Azizi, V., Chen, X., et al.: Learning heterogeneous knowledge base embeddings for explainable recommendation. Algorithms 11(9) (2018)
33. Bordes, A., Usunier, N., Garcia-Duran, A., et al.: Translating embeddings for modeling multi-relational data. In: NeurIPS, pp. 2787–2795 (2013)
34. Lin, X., Quan, Z., Wang, Z.J., et al.: KGNN: knowledge graph neural network for drug-drug interaction prediction. In: Twenty-Ninth International Joint Conference on Artificial Intelligence and Seventeenth Pacific Rim International Conference on Artificial Intelligence (2020)
35. Hamilton, W.L., Ying, R., Leskovec, J.: Inductive representation learning on large graphs. In: NeurIPS, pp. 1024–1034 (2017)

Challenges in Data Capturing and Collection for Physiological Detection of Dementia-Related Difficulties and Proposed Solutions

Matthew Harper[✉], Fawaz Ghali, Abir Hussain, and Dhiya Al-Jumeily

Liverpool John Moores University, Liverpool L3 3AF, UK
m.harp@2014.ljmu.ac.uk

Abstract. Dementia is a neurodegenerative disease which leads to the individual experiencing difficulties in their daily lives. Often these difficulties cause a large amount of stress, frustration and upset in the individual, however identifying when the difficulties are occurring or beginning can be difficult for caregivers, until the difficulty has caused problematic behavior or undeniable difficulty to the person with dementia. Therefore, a system for identifying the onset of dementia-related difficulties would be helpful in the management of dementia. Previous work highlighted wearable computing-based systems for analyzing physiological data as particularly promising. In this paper, we outline the methodology used to perform a systematic search for a relevant dataset. However, no such dataset was found. As such, a methodology for collecting such a dataset and making it publicly available is proposed, as well as for using it to train classification models that can predict difficulties from the physiological data. Several solutions to overcome the lack of available data are identified and discussed: data collection experiments to collect novel datasets; anonymization and pseudonymization to remove all identifiable data from the dataset; and synthetic data generation to produce a larger, anonymous training dataset. In conclusion, a combination of all the identified methods should ideally be employed in future solutions. Future work should focus on the conductance of the proposed experiment and the sharing of the collected data in the manner proposed, with data ideally being collected from as many people as possible with as many different types of dementia as possible.

Keywords: Dementia · Data · Wearables · Physiological · Difficulties · BPSD

1 Introduction

Dementia is an umbrella term to describe several neurodegenerative diseases which cause the person with the disease to experience cognitive impairment and decline [1]. This impairment and decline then causes the person with dementia (PwD) to experience difficulties in their daily lives, such as misplacing items, forgetting appointments, temporal and spatial disorientation, and more [2]. Thus, a PwD will generally progressively become less independent and require more support and aid in living safely and meeting their needs. With the global number of people with dementia currently at 50 million and

© Springer Nature Switzerland AG 2021
D.-S. Huang et al. (Eds.): ICIC 2021, LNAI 12838, pp. 162–173, 2021.
https://doi.org/10.1007/978-3-030-84532-2_15

predicted to reach 130 million by 2050 [3], it is vital that effective methods to manage the disease and the resulting difficulties are found, so that more people with the disease can have greater independence and maintained quality of life for as long as possible [4].

Technology has been shown to be helpful in this regard, and over recent years much work has been done to develop support systems which can aid in the management of dementia and the related difficulties [5–11]. In previous work [12], we reviewed the use of wearable computing-based systems for identifying the occurrence of dementia-related difficulties from physiological data. Such systems were found to be able to provide accurate predictions and identifications of difficulties experienced by people with dementia from analysis of physiological data using machine learning. However, we found that no system exists that can predict and aid the management of a comprehensive range of dementia-related difficulties and current systems only predict or provide support for a small number of difficulties in a certain number of scenarios [12]. As such, further work is required to develop a system that can predict and identify a wide range of difficulties experienced by people with various types and stages of dementia. However, to create such a machine learning-based system data is vital, and no available physiological dataset could be found, containing the relevant physiological or behavioral data collected using wearable sensors, that could be used in the project to identify difficulties experienced by people with dementia.

This paper describes the methodology and results of a search for physiological data from people with dementia that was conducted, between June 2019 and December 2020. We also provide a methodology for collecting a physiological dataset from people experiencing dementia-related difficulties, which can be shared with other researchers while protecting the confidentiality of the participants, which would be a novelty as no physiological dataset is currently available in this domain. The rest of the paper is structured as follows. Section 2 provides an overview of the difficulties that a person with dementia may experience followed by a review of the methods used in previous literature to identify those difficulties from physiological data. Section 3 describes the search methodology used in the searches for physiological data that were conducted as part of the project, with the conclusion being that there are no publicly available datasets that meet the requirements of the project. Section 4 proposes a methodology for collecting a physiological dataset from people with dementia and making it available to other researchers. Finally, Sect. 5 provides a conclusion and overview of areas for future work.

2 Background

Much work has been conducted in recent years to develop systems which can identify dementia-related difficulties in a timely and accurate manner. Systems based on wearable computing can be used to collect physiological data to this end, in a passive, non-obstructive manner that is comfortable and convenient for the PwD. One such system for identifying dementia-related difficulties is the BESI system, in which a wrist-worn accelerometer, the Pebble smartwatch, is utilized to track movements of the subjects to detect agitated behaviors [5–7]. In the BESI study, the participant was asked to wear the smartwatch for 30 days, with subject and caregiver dyad numbers ranging from 3 to 10 in each paper and study iteration. Machine learning was then used on the data collected by the wearable to predict the occurrences of agitation. The researchers trained a number of models, such as support vector machines (SVM), adaptive boosting (AdaBoost), and an ensemble of decision trees by bagging (Tree-Bagging), with the latter providing the most robust prediction of agitated behaviors from unknown data [7]. Though the available literature from the study does not specify the stage of dementia experienced by the participants, it is likely from the community-based setting in which they were tracked that they still lived somewhat independently, or at least in their own home, implying mild to moderate dementia. A wrist-worn device was also used by Melander et al. to collect data from people with dementia in institutionalized settings [11]. The researchers asked several participants to wear an Empatica E4, which tracked the electrodermal activity (EDA) of the participant, while a nurse was asked to record observations of dementia-related agitation and difficulties on a provided chart. The EDA data was then labelled using the observations and the researchers found a high correlation not only with the data recorded at the time the difficulty was observed but also 1 to 2 h prior to the observation. Thus, EDA data could be used to predict the occurrence of a dementia-related difficulty up to 2 h before it is observed.

Sefcik et al. focused their research on the later stages of dementia, using a chest-worn ECG sensor to monitor the heart rate of people with advanced dementia who exhibit persistent vocalizations (PV) [13]. PV are described as uncontrolled or disruptive vocalizations with no specific communicative purpose. The participants are asked to wear the device for 2 h at a time, while caregivers recorded instances of PV. The participants heart rates where then compared on days that they exhibited PV and those they did not, and it was found that heart rate had a strong correlation with PV exhibition, supporting the use of physiological data from wearable computing devices to predict dementia-related difficulties in the moderate to severe stages of dementia. Heart rate was also tracked by Nesbitt et al. in their study to identify and predict dementia-related agitation, in which they used an android smartwatch to track limb movement and heart rate with an accelerometer and PPG sensor, respectively [14]. They also utilized an android smartphone's microphone, worn in a pouch around the neck of the participant. The data collected by the smartwatch was found to correlate with many of the observed instance of agitation, indicating a high degree of accuracy, whereas the data collected from the microphone does not correlate with the agitation, and the researchers posit this is due to background noise making the recordings too noisy to be valuable.

In all of the above cases, regardless of the severity of the dementia or the setting in which the data was collected, the analysis of physiological data was vital to the identification and prediction of dementia-related difficulties. Indeed, a useful, relevant, and complete dataset is the most important and fundamental building block or element of any research in computing related fields of study [15–17]. As such, it is vital that any researchers aiming to develop a machine learning model or method for identifying or predicting the occurrences of dementia-related difficulties, have access to a physiological dataset collected from people with dementia who are experiencing dementia-related difficulties.

3   Dataset Search Methodology

A search for physiological datasets from people with dementia was conducted between June 2019 and December 2020. The online resources and repositories searched include: UK.gov; data.europa.eu; GitHub Awesome Data; NHS Digital; European Health Information Gateway; reddit.com/r/datasets/; apps.who.int/gho/data/; UK Data Service; Google Search; alzpossible.org; CDC Data sets; Global Open Data Index; LJMU Open Data; biogps.org; niagads.org; nimhgenetics; ondri.ca; Ontario Brain Institute (OBI); alzheimersresearchuk.org. The predefined search terms and keywords include: Dementia, Alzheimer's, movement, activity, action, daily life, instrumental, basic, playing, games, dancing, wearable, sensor, BPSD, smart device, watch, heart rate, actigraph, GSR, EDA, galvanic skin response, electrodermal activity, cognitive impairment, and MCI. The criteria that a dataset had to meet to be useful to the project were: the dataset must contain physiological data, specifically at least one of heart rate, EDA, or limb movement; the dataset must be collected from people with dementia; the datasets must be legally and ethically available and useable for analysis and use in the project.

Another method employed was contacting authors of papers published on similar projects or in similar domains where physiological data was collected from people with dementia [6, 11, 14, 18, 19]. An email template was designed by the researchers on this project, with the structure being as follows. The first paragraph introduced the researchers, research institution and the current project. The second paragraph discussed the papers or other works that had been read by the researchers to make us aware of the research of the authors being contacted. Naturally, this second section was changed on each occasion and email was sent, with only a general outline being set out in the template. Finally, the third section of the template contained a request for access to the datasets which we wished to gain access to. This section was also changed for each paper, with the name of the datasets and the data features and types we wished to access being different for each of the authors contacted.

The search began in June 2019 and was continued in the following months until December 2020, with at least one of the repositories being searched every month, and four large-scale searches of all the repositories being undertaken in June 2019, December 2019 - January 2020, and March 2020-April 2020 and November-December 2020. Each large-scale search lasted around a month, giving researchers enough time to fully vet and evaluate every returned dataset for usefulness and applicability to the project's requirements. In January 2020, following the second large-scale search, authors were contacted using the strategy outlined in the previous paragraph to identify and access relevant datasets from researchers in a similar domain to the project, as it had become clear there was likely to be no available relevant dataset on the listed repositories. No more emails were sent to authors after May 2020, as it was clear that funding and/or privacy concerns were a common barrier for all researchers to sharing their data. Furthermore, and more importantly, a new plan of work had to be devised for the project in reaction to the Covid-19 pandemic, which delayed work on the data search. The search ended in December 2020, as it was clear no relevant datasets were available from the repositories or other researchers, and other avenues of work needed to be addressed.

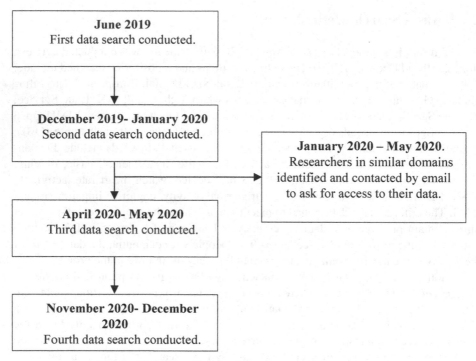

Fig. 1. Workflow diagram of the data search methodology.

4   Data Search Results

No datasets that met the requirement criteria of the project were found during the dataset search outlined in the methodology. The reasons for this are most likely related to the vulnerability of the individuals with dementia from whom the data was collected. People with dementia are classed as vulnerable adults due to their mental impairment [20], which can often make it more difficult to acquire ethical approval to conduct research which includes them as subjects [21]. Furthermore, physiological data collection from people with dementia using wearables can be difficult as the cognitive impairment can lead to problems in collecting the data, especially in the severe stages but also often in mild to moderate dementia [22]. This could be because the subject removes the device either due to discomfort or because the device is unfamiliar to them [8], or because the subject forgets to put a data collection device on [23, 24]. Moreover, caregivers of people with dementia are highly likely to experience stress and other adverse mental or physical burdens due to their caregiving responsibilities, especially in cases where the caregiver is informal i.e. a spouse, family member, or close friend [25–27]. This can also make data collection from people with dementia more difficult than with healthy or non-cognitively impaired subjects, as extra care must be taken to ensure that any caregivers do not experience any undue burden on top of the burden already commonly experienced. Also, even where data has been collected, it is often difficult to share that data, as the vulnerable status of people with dementia means that their personal data is subject to even greater legal protections than that of an adult not classified as vulnerable [28].

Furthermore, no dataset that met the requirements was found to be or made to be available to the researchers on this project from other authors and researchers in similar domains. Of the researchers who replied, none were willing to share their datasets. There were 2 reasons expressed for not sharing data with the researchers on this project. One of those reasons was privacy or confidentiality concerns, with some researchers stating that the sharing of data from their study would violate the privacy legislation in their respective country or legal jurisdiction or would violate the terms of the agreements signed with participants. Another reason stated for not sharing data was that the sharing of the data would violate the terms of funding agreements, that had clauses which prevented the sharing of the data.

In conclusion, it was concluded that there were no physiological datasets collected from people with dementia experiencing difficulties that were publicly available for use or analysis in the project.

5   Discussion of Solutions and Proposed Methodology

The search for datasets described in the methodology section yielded no useful datasets, and it was concluded that there was no physiological dataset matching the criteria for the project available to be used. In this section, we propose a methodology for developing a prototype support system, including collecting a dataset that does meet the criteria of the project, and is shareable with other researchers in future, so that future research in this domain can be done more easily and cheaply.

5.1   Data Collection Experiment

The first step in the methodology is performing a data collection experiment in which people physiological data is collected from people with dementia [8]. As the prototype to be developed is targeted to individuals with mild to moderate dementia, the best recruitment channel is likely to be hospital outpatient services or memory clinics [29, 30], or community support groups tailored to individuals with mild to moderate dementia [5–7]. As such, an agreement will be signed with the local memory clinic, and they will identify potential participants from their patient for us based on our inclusion criteria, and we shall request this co-operation in writing. The clinic shall, with the permission of the potential participant, give the details of the potential participant to a qualified medical doctor, who will act as a gatekeeper and approach the potential participant [31]. The gatekeeper will provide the participants with the Participant Information Sheet and go through the protocol and what the study entails with the potential participant and their caregiver(s) and answer any questions that they may have [32]. The inclusion criteria for eligible participants are: a diagnosis of mild to moderate dementia; living with a caregiver who can record instances of difficulties; have long-term access to a smartphone. The exclusion criterion is that the patient has other neurological disabilities or has significantly reduced ability to complete instrumental activities of daily living due to other non-dementia conditions. Informed and written consent shall be obtained from both the participant and their caregiver for both of their participations, however if the participant is incapable of consenting, their Next of Kin (NoK) or Power of Attorney (POA) will be asked to provide written and informed consent for them, with verbal assent being sought from the participant [11, 13, 14, 33–37]. All consenting and assenting parties will be informed they can withdraw from the study at any time without being required to give a reason or justification.

In previous work we identified the Empatica E4 as the most suitable device available for the proposed data collection experiment [12]. The devices and other items that are required to conduct the experiment are: Empatica E4; Empatica E4 Charger [8]; Smartphone and an Empatica E4 smartphone app; Observational Recording Sheets [11]; Instruction sheets for the participant and caregiver [38]. This instruction sheet will detail what each person should do, as well as providing contact details to the researchers so that they can ask any questions or issues. The participants will receive all the items required, bar the smartphone and app, by the gatekeeper. The gatekeeper will show the participant how the device is to be put on the dominant wrist and how to remove it and correctly charge it. The caregiver will also be shown how to fill in the observational recording sheets and be told when they will be required to do so. The app will be set-up on the smartphone and the phone, and the smartwatch shall be connected via Bluetooth [39].

The data collection will occur for between 2 and 4 weeks. The participant will be asked to wear the device 24 h a day, except for when it must be removed for charging. The participant will be asked to wear the device 24 h a day, except for when it must be removed for charging. While deployed on the participants wrist the device shall collect heart rate, electrodermal activity, movement, and skin temperature data from the participant [8]. The caregiver will be asked to record when the participant experiences difficulties, and to record what they were doing at the time and what the difficulty was. To help ensure that fewer potential difficulties are missed, the caregiver shall be sent an alert when the participants heart rate, electrodermal activity or movement is detected to be abnormal, for example if there is a rapid increase in the participants heart rate or is an abnormal amount of movement during the night-time. The caregiver will also be asked to record the activities that the participant has completed each day. This does not need to be 100% accurate and a rough estimation of times and overview of activities is acceptable. The physiological data shall be transferred to the smartphone and then on to the Empatica secure cloud storage service [8, 39]. The observational data recorded on paper shall be stored in the participants home and collected on each visit by the gatekeeper (which will happen once a week).

5.2 Anonymization and Pseudonymization

The next stage of the proposed methodology will be to protect the participants' confidentiality and privacy through anonymization & pseudonymization of the dataset. Anonymization in this instance refers to methods that make the data in the datasets anonymous, so that there is no way to identify the individual participants from which the data was collected [40]. Pseudonymization is slightly different in that it is the replacement of the participants identity with a pseudonym, for example referring to the participants as participant 1, participant 2, and so on [41]. Both methods attempt to protect the identity, privacy, and confidentiality of the individual participants, which is vital to ensuring that any data can be shared and used safely and in line with privacy policies and legislation.

However, once a dataset has been anonymized or pseudonymized and the participants confidentiality is ensured, the data may then be shareable with others [42]. This means that future researchers in this area would not have to conduct the time and resource consuming process of collecting their own dataset already outlined. However, it is important to remember that no secondary analysis of collected datasets should be conducted without the consent of the participants from whom the data is collected, especially if that data has any elements which could be in any way considered potentially identifiable of the participant [43]. Some of the datasets that were requested via email correspondence during the data search were anonymized or pseudonymized and yet as participant consent for sharing with or secondary analysis of the data by other researchers had not been acquired by the researchers, no data could be shared.

In the proposed methodology, the data will be pseudonymized, with each participant being allocated a number which will be associated with all their data. The only person who will be given access to personal information will be the gatekeeper, with the other members of the research team-who will have no face-to-face interaction with the participants-needing no such knowledge. As the already agreed gatekeeper is a doctor who already has access to the patient records of the potential participants, participant personal data will not be any less confidential than before the experiment.

The data shall also be pseudonymized in any future publications of the data or which discuss the data, with the participants being referred to as participant 1, participant 2, etc.

5.3 Synthetic Data

Synthetic datasets are datasets that are not collected from participants or situations in the relevant domain, instead being generated synthetically to resemble data from the relevant domain [44]. Synthetic datasets are produced by training a machine learning model, or using one already trained, to identify the statistical and mathematical properties of a dataset and then create a dataset of randomized data that shares the same statistical properties of the original dataset [45].

The use of synthetic data in the domain of dementia-related difficulty identification from physiological data has two major advantages. Firstly, the synthetic dataset will be entirely free from confidentiality or privacy concerns as the data was not collected form people with dementia and is merely computer generated to resemble such data [46]. Furthermore, collection of data from people with dementia is difficult and time consuming, and in many instances, it may be difficult to acquire the number of recruited participant or data collection devices to collect a large dataset. This could potentially lead to overfitting of the results of data analysis to a few small dataset, therefore low generalizability of those results or trained models. Generation of synthetic data with a few small differences to the original to represent different scenarios may help to prevent this overfitting problem and increase the generalizability of the results and trained models [45]. As such, this method shall also be employed in the proposed methodology to increase the volume of data available to train the required machine learning model.

5.4 Model Training and Data Sharing

Once all the data is collected and labelled, and a synthetic dataset has been generated, it shall be used to train several classification models with the MATLAB software [47]. This will allow for the identification of the best model for identifying and predicting the difficulties from the physiological dataset. This model will then be used in the development of a prototype which can identify the difficulties and provide an automatic digital intervention.

Furthermore, the collected and generated data will be completely anonymous and pseudonymized, and consent will have been sought from the participants for any collected data to undergo secondary analysis, after it has been entirely de-identified. This means that the data can be published on the host institution's secure data repository [48], meaning other researchers in this domain can access the data on request. This would be novel for the domain, as no other dataset of this nature is currently publicly available to researchers in this domain.

6 Conclusion

In conclusion, there is currently a lack of physiological datasets pertaining to dementia-related difficulties or from people with dementia, and this is impeding progress in the field of assistive technology for the management of dementia. Therefore, many people with dementia and their caregivers may miss out on the benefits of such a system due to increased time needed to research and develop them. It is thus vital that a relevant physiological dataset is collected, processed, and made available as soon as possible, so that further research can be done on this domain, and all the benefits of the proposed system can be realized by people with dementia and their caregivers-including increased QoL and independence, and reduced burden for caregivers-within the near future.

There are many methods which can be used, in combination, as solutions to overcome the problem of lack of data and make more data available to researchers for analysis and development. The most vital of these methods, that must be included in almost any solution to overcome the lack of data, is a data collection experiment to collect a dataset which contains the required physiological data features, which include heart rate, EDA, accelerometery and skin temperature. Such an experiment should be conducted in a way that provides the highest possible levels of privacy and confidentiality for the participant, while also getting their express permission to share a processed version of their data in a manner that does not compromise their privacy. One solution to ensure this is the use of anonymization and pseudonymization, both of which remove all personal data from the physiological data, and thus makes the resulting dataset non-personal data, thus more ethical to share. Finally, synthetic data generation can be used to further protect participant privacy and confidentiality, and to generate larger training datasets with which to train machine learning models. As such the proposed methodology shall include: a data collection experiment to collect an initial physiological dataset; anonymization or pseudonymization to protect the identity and confidentiality of participants; and synthetic dataset generation to provide a larger training dataset for machine learning. Once the data is labelled and completely de-identified it will be used to train a variety of machine learning models and it will be shared via a secure data repository, becoming a novel, publicly available dataset.

Future work in this area should include the conducting of the proposed data collection experiment, in which physiological data should be collected from people with dementia. It should be ensured that participants consent to the sharing and secondary analysis of the data collected from them, with that data sharing and secondary analysis being completing in a manner that protects participant confidentiality. Ideally, data should be collected from as many people with dementia, including people with different types and severity of dementia, as is possible, which will allow for greater generalizability of results from data analysis, as well as allowing research to be done on supporting individuals with every type and severity of dementia.

References

1. Koumakis, L., Chatzaki, C., Kazantzaki, E., Maniadi, E., Tsiknakis, M.: Dementia care frameworks and assistive technologies for their implementation: a review. IEEE Rev. Biomed. Eng. **12**, 4–18 (2019)
2. Okabe, K., et al.: Effects of neuropsychiatric symptoms of dementia on reductions in activities of daily living in patients with Alzheimer's disease. Geriatr. Gerontol. Int. **20**(6), 584–588 (2020)
3. WHO: Dementia. World Health Organisation. https://www.who.int/news-room/fact-sheets/detail/dementia. Accessed 5 May 2020
4. Howard, R., et al.: The effectiveness and cost-effectiveness of assistive technology and telecare for independent living in dementia: a randomised controlled trial. Age and Ageing (2021)
5. Alam, R., et al.: Motion biomarkers for early detection of dementia-related agitation. In: Proceedings of the 1st Workshop on Digital Biomarkers, pp. 15–20 (2017)
6. Alam, R., Anderson, M., Bankole, A., Lach, J.: Inferring physical agitation in dementia using smartwatch and sequential behavior models. In: 2018 IEEE EMBS International Conference on Biomedical & Health Informatics (BHI), pp. 170–173. IEEE (2018)
7. Alam, R., Bankole, A., Anderson, M., Lach, J.: Multiple-instance learning for sparse behavior modeling from wearables: toward dementia-related agitation prediction. In: 2019 41st Annual International Conference of the IEEE Engineering in Medicine and Biology Society (EMBC), pp. 1330–1333. IEEE (2019)
8. Amato, F., et al.: CLONE: a promising system for the remote monitoring of Alzheimer's patients: an experimentation with a wearable device in a village for Alzheimer's care. In: Proceedings of the 4th EAI International Conference on Smart Objects and Technologies for Social Good, pp. 255–260 (2018)
9. Kikhia, B., et al.: Utilizing a wristband sensor to measure the stress level for people with dementia. Sensors **16**(12), 1989 (2016)
10. Kikhia, B., et al.: Utilizing ambient and wearable sensors to monitor sleep and stress for people with BPSD in nursing homes. J. Ambient. Intell. Humaniz. Comput. **9**(2), 261–273 (2015). https://doi.org/10.1007/s12652-015-0331-6
11. Melander, C., Martinsson, J., Gustafsson, S.: Measuring electrodermal activity to improve the identification of agitation in individuals with dementia. Dementia Geriatric Cogn Disorders Extra **7**(3), 430–439 (2017)
12. Harper, V., Ghali, F.: A Systematic review of wearable devices for tracking physiological indicators of Dementia-related difficulties. In: presented at the Developments in E-Systems, Online (2020)

13. Sefcik, J.S., Ersek, M., Libonati, J.R., Hartnett, S.C., Hodgson, N.A., Cacchione, P.Z.: Heart rate of nursing home residents with advanced dementia and persistent vocalizations. Health Technol. 1–5 (2019)

14. Nesbitt, C., Gupta, A., Jain, S., Maly, K., Okhravi, H.R.: Reliability of wearable sensors to detect agitation in patients with dementia: a pilot study. In: Proceedings of the 2018 10th International Conference on Bioinformatics and Biomedical Technology, pp. 73–77 (2018)

15. Zhou, T., Song, Z., Sundmacher, K.: Big data creates new opportunities for materials research: a review on methods and applications of machine learning for materials design. Engineering **5**(6), 1017–1026 (2019)

16. Huck, N.: Large data sets and machine learning: applications to statistical arbitrage. Eur. J. Oper. Res. **278**(1), 330–342 (2019)

17. Lee, I., Shin, Y.J.: Machine learning for enterprises: applications, algorithm selection, and challenges. Bus. Horiz. **63**(2), 157–170 (2020)

18. Lai Kwan, C., Mahdid, Y., Motta Ochoa, R., Lee, K., Park, M., Blain-Moraes, S.: Wearable technology for detecting significant moments in individuals with dementia. BioMed Res. Int. **2019** (2019)

19. Valembois, L., Oasi, C., Pariel, S., Jarzebowski, W., Lafuente-Lafuente, C., Belmin, J.: Wrist actigraphy: a simple way to record motor activity in elderly patients with dementia and apathy or aberrant motor behavior. J. Nutr. Health Aging **19**(7), 759–764 (2015)

20. Thomas, K.S., Zhang, W., Cornell, P.Y., Smith, L., Kaskie, B., Carder, P.C.: State variability in the prevalence and healthcare utilization of assisted living residents with dementia. J. Am. Geriatr. Soc. **68**(7), 1504–1511 (2020)

21. Benson, C., Friz, A., Mullen, S., Block, L., Gilmore-Bykovskyi, A.: Ethical and methodological considerations for evaluating participant views on Alzheimer's and dementia research. J. Empirical Res. Hum. Res. Ethics **16**, 88–104 (2020). 1556264620974898

22. Kaenampornpan, M., Khai, N.D., Kawattikul, K.: Wearable computing for dementia patients. In: Meesad, P., Sodsee, S. (eds.) IC2IT 2020. AISC, vol. 1149, pp. 21–30. Springer, Cham (2020). https://doi.org/10.1007/978-3-030-44044-2_3

23. Grober, E., Wakefield, D., Ehrlich, A.R., Mabie, P., Lipton, R.B.: Identifying memory impairment and early dementia in primary care. Alzheimer's Dementia Diagnosis Assessment Disease Monitoring **6**, 188–195 (2017)

24. McGarrigle, L., Howlett, S.E., Wong, H., Stanley, J., Rockwood, K.: Characterizing the symptom of misplacing objects in people with dementia: findings from an online tracking tool. Int. Psychogeriatr. **31**(11), 1635–1641 (2019)

25. Connors, M.H., Seeher, K., Teixeira-Pinto, A., Woodward, M., Ames, D., Brodaty, H.: Dementia and caregiver burden: a three-year longitudinal study. Int. J. Geriatr. Psychiatry **35**(2), 250–258 (2020)

26. Allen, A.P., et al.: Informal caregiving for dementia patients: the contribution of patient characteristics and behaviours to caregiver burden. Age Ageing **49**(1), 52–56 (2020)

27. Su, J.-A., Chang, C.-C.: Association between family caregiver burden and affiliate stigma in the families of people with dementia. Int. J. Environ. Res. Public Health **17**(8), 2772 (2020)

28. Husebo, B.S., Heintz, H.L., Berge, L.I., Owoyemi, P., Rahman, A.T., Vahia, I.V.: Sensing technology to facilitate behavioral and psychological symptoms and to monitor treatment response in people with dementia. a systematic review. Front. Pharmacol. **10**, 1699 (2020)

29. Karakostas, A., Lazarou, I., Meditskos, G., Stavropoulos, T.G., Kompatsiaris, I., Tsolaki, M.: Sensor-based in-home monitoring of people with dementia using remote web technologies. In: 2015 International Conference on Interactive Mobile Communication Technologies and Learning (IMCL), pp. 353–357. IEEE (2015)

30. NHS: How to get a dementia diagnosis. NHS.uk. https://www.nhs.uk/conditions/dementia/diagnosis/. Accessed 19 Apr 2020

31. Bartlett, R., Milne, R., Croucher, R.: Strategies to improve recruitment of people with dementia to research studies. Dementia **18**(7–8), 2494–2504 (2019)
32. Waite, J., Poland, F., Charlesworth, G.: Facilitators and barriers to co-research by people with dementia and academic researchers: findings from a qualitative study. Health Expect. **22**(4), 761–771 (2019)
33. Khan, S.S., et al.: Agitation detection in people living with dementia using multimodal sensors. In: 2019 41st Annual International Conference of the IEEE Engineering in Medicine and Biology Society (EMBC), pp. 3588–3591. IEEE (2019)
34. Spasojevic, S., et al.: A pilot study to detect agitation in people living with dementia using multi-modal sensors
35. Goerss, D., et al.: Automated sensor-based detection of challenging behaviors in advanced stages of dementia in nursing homes. Alzheimer's Dementia (2019)
36. Teipel, S., et al.: Multidimensional assessment of challenging behaviors in advanced stages of dementia in nursing homes—the insideDEM framework. Alzheimer's Dementia Diagnosis, Assessment Disease Monitoring **8**, 36–44 (2017)
37. Vuong, N., Chan, S., Lau, C.T., Chan, S., Yap, P.L.K., Chen, A.: "Preliminary results of using inertial sensors to detect dementia-related wandering patterns. In: 2015 37th Annual International Conference of the IEEE Engineering in Medicine and Biology Society (EMBC), pp. 3703–3706. IEEE (2015)
38. Page, A., Potter, K., Clifford, R., McLachlan, A., Etherton-Beer, C.: Prescribing for Australians living with dementia: study protocol using the Delphi technique. BMJ open **5**(8), e008048 (2015)
39. Empatica: E4 Wristband. Empatica. https://www.empatica.com/research/e4/?utm_source=Google&utm_medium=cpc&utm_campaign=conversion&gclid=Cj0KCQiAvc_xBRCYAR IsAC5QT9l9EUAmaWXCRxEQ17aUYewwgoMkYIn-xFsuJld5R-Ib_6wGuhYqKToaA somEALw_wcB. Accessed 30 Jan 2020
40. Murthy, S., Bakar, A.A., Rahim, F.A., Ramli, R.: A comparative study of data anonymization techniques. In: 2019 IEEE 5th Intl Conference on Big Data Security on Cloud (BigDataSecurity), IEEE Intl Conference on High Performance and Smart Computing, (HPSC) and IEEE Intl Conference on Intelligent Data and Security (IDS), pp. 306–309. IEEE (2019)
41. Bolognini, L., Bistolfi, C.: Pseudonymization and impacts of Big (personal/anonymous) Data processing in the transition from the Directive 95/46/EC to the new EU General Data Protection Regulation. Comput. Law Secur. Rev. **33**(2), 171–181 (2017)
42. Deshpande, A.: Sypse: privacy-first data management through Pseudonymization and partitioning
43. Menner, J., Lewandowska, P., Zabel, F.: The impact of data privacy regulations on drug utilization data sharing for innovative pricing arrangements. In: Value in Health, vol. 21, pp. S211-S211. Elsevier Science Inc STE 800, 230 Park Ave, New York, NY 10169 USA (2018)
44. Nikolaidis, K., Kristiansen, S., Goebel, V., Plagemann, T., Liestøl, K., Kankanhalli, M.: Augmenting physiological time series data: a case study for sleep apnea detection. In: Joint European Conference on Machine Learning and Knowledge Discovery in Databases, pp. 376–399. Springer (2019)
45. Yale, A., Dash, S., Dutta, R., Guyon, I., Pavao, A., Bennett, K.P.: Generation and evaluation of privacy preserving synthetic health data. Neurocomputing **416**, 244–255 (2020)
46. Ping, H., Stoyanovich, J., Howe, B.: Datasynthesizer: privacy-preserving synthetic datasets. In: Proceedings of the 29th International Conference on Scientific and Statistical Database Management, pp. 1–5 (2017)
47. Manuel, A.L., et al.: Interactions between decision-making and emotion in behavioral-variant frontotemporal dementia and Alzheimer's disease. Social cognitive and affective neuroscience **15**(6), 681–694 (2020)
48. LJMU: Welcome to LJMU Data Repository. LJMU. http://opendata.ljmu.ac.uk/. Accessed 31 Mar 2021

Exploring Multi-scale Temporal and Spectral CSP Feature for Multi-class Motion Imagination Task Classification

Jian-Xun Mi[1,2(✉)], Rong-Feng Li[1,2], and Guo Chen[1,2]

[1] Chongqing Key Laboratory of Image Cognition, Chongqing University of Posts and Telecommunications, Chongqing 400065, China
[2] College of Computer Science and Technology, Chongqing University of Posts and Telecommunications, Chongqing 400065, China

Abstract. Effective features extracted from electroencephalogram (EEG) data greatly benefit the classification of motor imagery brain-computer interfaces (MI-BCI) systems. In this paper, we further investigate the factors affecting the performance of common spatial pattern (CSP). A novel method based on CSP is proposed to extract more discriminant features to improve the classification accuracy in training and testing for a support vector machine (SVM) classifier. We extend CSP feature extractor to multiscale temporal and spectral conditions. Experimental results show that compared with many improved CSP features and several deep learning methods of recent years, the multiscale temporal and spectral CSP features achieve superior classification accuracy.

Keywords: EEG · Motor imagery · Brain-computer interfaces · Multi-scale features · SVM

1 Introduction

A BCI is a system that uses information about brain activity to control or communicate with a device. Brain activity is commonly recorded by EEG due to the conveniences. BCI system needs to extract features from EEG signals and train a classifier to determine the class of brain activity. In a BCI system, the user receives stimuli (visual, auditory, or tactile) and/or performs mental tasks, and their brain signals are captured and processed at the same time. A series of phenomena or patterns extracted from EEG signals can be detected depending on the stimulus/task performed by the subject [1]. Motion imagery (MI) is a typical application of BCI, which identifies the brain's process that people only imagine specific movements but do not occur. For example, people imagine the movement of his/her left or right hand without its shift [2, 3]. Currently, the most widely used EEG patterns of the BCI system for control including sensorimotor rhythms (SMRs), event-related potentials (ERP) [4], and steady-state visual evoked potentials (SSVEP) [5–7]. In these patterns, SMR is characterized by changes in frequency band power that occur within a specific EEG frequency band in the sensorimotor region of the brain during motion-imaging [8]. Therefore, the BCI system can be designed to detect the

© Springer Nature Switzerland AG 2021
D.-S. Huang et al. (Eds.): ICIC 2021, LNAI 12838, pp. 174–184, 2021.
https://doi.org/10.1007/978-3-030-84532-2_16

EEG power change, which is assumed to be associated with the motor imagination task as control signals. However, as the EEG signal is so weak that it is likely to be contaminated by background noise, such as blinking or head movements, high accurate motion imagination classification is generally tricky [9]. Therefore, for BCI systems, how to extract robust and effective features from EEG data with noise is the crucial problem [10–12].

CSP has been widely used in various brain-computer interface applications, which is regarded as one of the most compelling feature extraction methods for MI applications. As a spatial filter, CSP extracts MI features for classification tasks by maximizing the discrimination of two classes [13, 14]. For applications of CSP, some of its limitations are discovered, including sensitivity to noises and severe over-fitting in small datasets [15, 16]. Besides, the performance of CSP is highly dependent on the choice of frequency bands. Once the crucial band range is not precisely selected, the classification performance of CSP features could significantly decrease. Therefore, to improve the CSP algorithm, many efforts are paid to select some specific frequency bands or select a wide frequency range for a specific object [17].

Several approaches have been proposed to solve the problem of artificial frequency range selection for the CSP algorithm. An influential approach is the Sub-band Common Spatial Pattern (SBCSP) [18]. It decomposes EEG data into sub-bands by Gabor filter Banks and then uses the spatial filter in the CSP algorithm to each sub-band EEG data for producing sub-band scores. After fusing these scores, classification is conducted to identify the category of a sample. Another well-known approach is the Filter Bank Common Spatial Pattern (FBCSP) [19]. In the FBCSP, a feature selection step is incorporated into SBCSP. An intensive investigation of various classification algorithms is conducted to discover the optimal one that can sufficiently exploit the selected features. In general, FBCSP outperforms SBCSP. Nevertheless, due to its use of many sub-bands, FBCSP involves extra computing costs. Discriminative filter bank CSP (DFBCSP) [20] is proposed to solve this problem. It uses the Fisher ratio (FR) of single-channel's (C3, C4, or Cz) band power to select the most discriminant sub-band from multiple overlapping sub-bands. Then, CSP features were extracted from each sub-band and classified by the linear SVM classifier (Because of the spatial physical significance of CSP algorithm, a spatial filter is found to make the features of different class have stronger separability. So we use the SVM with linear kernel function to deal with the separable problem). Compared with SBCSP and FBCSP, DFBCSP achieves higher classification accuracy and lower calculation cost. In summary, these three approaches typically split EEG data into several frequency bands and then using CSP to extract the features, respectively [10]. Although several later follow-up studies have been proposed, most of them only discuss the effect of dividing frequency bands on a fixed spectral band or scale, without further investigating the change of spectral band scale and the effect of combining multiple spectral band scales.

In addition to the optimization of selecting frequency bands, another particularly important but rarely studied issue is how to select optimal temporal windows for EEG data. For a MI-based BCI system, subjects are required to perform corresponding brain imagination tasks according to the cue. Although the starting time of a cue is known based on the timing scheme paradigm of a designed experiment, the trigger time of a subject's brain responding to a specific task is unknown. In the paradigm of a MI experiment, the time within the first one second after the subject is cued is usually considered as the motion imagination preparation stage. And the period from 3.5 s to 4 s is considered as the post-stage [21]. To extract effective features for different subjects, we should pay attention to select the appropriate EEG time window under the consideration that various detectable features could occur at different time points and have various durations that vary with each subject.

Therefore, it is necessary to select the appropriate EEG time window in advance to cover the EEG data segments that activate the motor imagination and remove the irrelevant data segments. Most previous studies [10, 22, 23] used a fixed time window to cover the entire time window (i.e., between 0.5 and 2.5 s after the cue) of MI activation and extract and classify the features of EEG data segments related to MI. However, because subjects' brain response delays vary from person to person, the perspective window for the optimal EEG data segment may vary from person to person [24]. It is difficult to capture the discriminative features of all subjects using fixed temporal windows or overlapping temporal windows using a fixed scale, thus affecting the accuracy of classification.

In this paper, we discuss the effect of CSP characteristics of different scales in temporal windows and spectral bands on the 4-class data set of the BCI competition IV-2a. We compared the performance of different temporal window scales and frequency band scales in different subjects to determine which scales had more motion-imaging information. We propose a framework to extract the CSP features of the combined multiscale spectral and temporal feature, which can increase the number of features effectively. This method achieves an average classification accuracy of 80.47% by an SVM classifier with a linear kernel for classification on the 4-classes data set of the BCI competition IV-2a.

This paper is organized as follows. Section 2 describes the characteristics of the BCI competition IV-2a dataset and the binary classification problem using the CSP feature extraction algorithm. Section 3 presents the method of extracting multiscale features in temporal windows and spectral bands, respectively, and the feature extraction method combining multiscale temporal and spectral features. In Sect. 4, we discuss and compare the experimental results with different multiscale feature fusion schemes and exiting studies. Section 4 draws the conclusions of proposed approach briefly.

2   Description of Dataset and CSP Feature Extraction

The BCI Competition IV 2a dataset [25] contains EEG of 9 different objects. All subjects were asked to complete four different MI tasks, imagining movements of the left hand, right hand, feet, and tongue. Two sessions were recorded on two different days for each subject. One session is used for training and the other for testing. The single test paradigm is shown in Fig. 1. The subjects perform the desired motor imagery task mainly occurred between the third and sixth seconds. Each session is comprised of 6 runs separated by short breaks. One run consists of 48 trials (12 for each of the four possible classes). Each subject consists of 72 trials per class, yielding a total of 288 trials per session. Twenty-two EEG electrodes were used to record the EEG. All signals were bandpass filtered between 0.5 Hz and 100 Hz and sampled with 250 Hz.

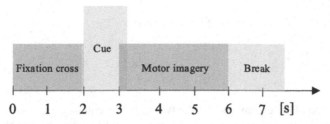

Fig. 1. A typical timing scheme of the motor imagery paradigm

The CSP is proposed to extract the discriminative features from EEG signals by means of maximizing the variance differences. We first compute the covariance of each class by:

$$C_d = \frac{E_d E_d^T}{tr\left(E_d E_d^T\right)} \tag{1}$$

where N_c represents the number of channels, and N_s represents the number of samples, E_d is the EEG signal belonging to the class d in all samples, where $d \in \{1, 2\}$. E_d^T is the transpose of E_d, and tr ($\bullet$) represents the trace of the matrix whose value is the sum of all the matrix eigenvalues. C_1 and C_2 are respectively used to represent the covariance matrix of two classes of EEG data.

The spatial covariance matrix CΩ consists of covariance matrices of all classes. Eigenvalue decomposition of the spatial covariance matrix CΩ is expressed as:

$$C_\Omega = C_1 + C_2 = Q\Sigma Q^T \tag{2}$$

where Q is a matrix consisting of the eigenvectors of the spatial covariance matrix CΩ, and Σ is the diagonal matrix of the eigenvalues of the spatial covariance matrix CΩ, where the eigenvalues are arranged in descending order. The whitening value matrix is:

$$P = \Sigma^{-1/2} Q^T. \tag{3}$$

Then, the C_1 and C_2 are transformed as follows:

$$S_1 = \left(\Sigma^{-1/2} Q^T\right) C_1 \left(\Sigma^{-1/2} Q^T\right)^T = PC_1 P^T, \tag{4}$$

$$S_2 = \left(\Sigma^{-1/2} Q^T\right) C_2 \left(\Sigma^{-1/2} Q^T\right)^T = PC_2 P^T. \tag{5}$$

Hence,

$$S_1 + S_2 = PC_1 P^T + PC_2 P^T = I \tag{6}$$

The principal component decomposition of S_1 and S_2 is performed, and the following results are obtained:

$$S_1 = B_1 \Sigma_1 B_1^T, \tag{7}$$

$$S_2 = B_2 \Sigma_2 B_2^T. \tag{8}$$

Hence, we have.

$$\Sigma_1 + \Sigma_2 = I \tag{9}$$

Since the sum of the eigenvalues of the two matrices equals a unit matrix, the eigenvector corresponding to the maximum eigenvalue of S_1 makes S_2 has the minimum eigenvalue, and vice versa.

We calculate the spatial filter matrix W by whitening matrix P and projection matrix B:

$$W = B^T P. \tag{10}$$

Then, the EEG data E_i of the single-task experiment is transformed by the spatial filter matrix W:

$$Z_i = W E_i \tag{11}$$

Finally, the feature vector f_i is extracted by comparing f_L and f_R as follows to determine whether the i-th imagination is left or right:

$$f_i = \frac{VAR(Z_i)}{\Sigma(VAR(Z_i))}. \tag{12}$$

Many approaches have been proposed to extend CSP to multi-class tasks. A common and effective method is to apply traditional CSP algorithms to pairwise combinations of all classes [26]. In the N class problem, there are $N(N-1)/2$ class pairs and need to be $N(N-1)$ spatial filters.

3 Multiscale Features Extracted by CSP

3.1 Multiscale Spectral CSP Features

EEG rhythms associated with motor imaging tasks include $\mu(8\text{--}13\text{ Hz})$ rhythm and $\beta(13\text{--}30\text{ Hz})$ rhythm [3]. During the motor imagination task, a reduction in the energy of μ band can be observed in the motor cortex. Simultaneously, when performing the motion imagination task, there would be an increase in the energy of β band. However, whether a frequency band is discriminative highly depends on the characteristics of the subjects. Therefore, we divide the signal into frequency band segments of different scales and then apply the CSP algorithm, respectively. As shown in Fig. 2, each trial was bandpass filtered in 4–36 Hz, which contains the μ rhythm and β rhythm and the bandwidth 32 Hz (36–32) is an integer power of 2. We use the bandwidth$_i = 2^{i-1}$ ($1 \le i \le 6$) bandwidths to divide the EEG signal into multiscale spectral components. Then we used CSP to extract the features of all the spectral bands.

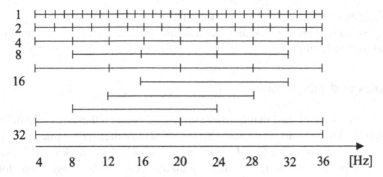

Fig. 2. The used overlapping spectral bands with bandwidths 1–32 Hz

3.2 Multiscale Temporal CSP Features

We extract the EEG signals in the temporal window from 2.5 s to 6 s. The reason is that not all the subjects start to have a motor imagination response at the same time point, and subjects maintain a different level of focused motor imagination between the third and sixth seconds of each run. We used temporal windows of different length scales to divide EEG data. As shown in Fig. 3, we use the following temporal window scales: 0.5 s, 1 s, 2 s, and 3.5 s. For each scale, we will divide 2.5–6 s into multiple temporal windows. For example, when the temporal window length is 2 s, we will divide the EEG data into the four temporal windows segments: 2.5–4.5 s, 3–5 s, 3.5–5.5 s, and 4–6 s. Then we apply CSP algorithm to extract the features of all the temporal windows.

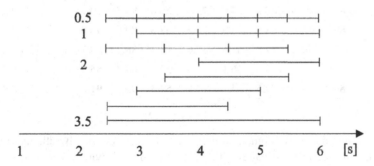

Fig. 3. The used overlapping temporal windows with length 0.5–3.5 s

3.3 Multiscale Temporal and Spectral CSP Features

So far, we have integrated temporal information and spectral information into the extraction method of CSP features separately. In order to acquire a more robust feature extractor, we combine the two kinds of information on the CSP feature extraction. Each temporal window is again segmented into different spectral bands using the filter. More feature information is obtained in the temporal window and spectral bands, which improves the robustness of the CSP feature extractor. Finally, we stack the CSP feature vectors that combine the temporal information and spectral information into one vector and then use a classifier to classify them.

4 Results and Discussions

All of the methods mentioned in this article were evaluated on the dataset 2a of the BCI competition IV. The features were classified by SVM classifier with a linear kernel. The regularization hyperparameter C is determined in tenfold cross-validation. Besides, the temporal windows and frequency bands were also selected in the cross-validation. The classification accuracy is defined as

$$Accuracy = \left(\frac{T_{correct}}{T_{total}} \right) \times 100\% \tag{13}$$

where T_{total} is the number of trials in the test set per subject and $T_{correct}$ is the number of correct classified trials.

Table 1. The classification accuracy (%) and standard deviation of different spectral band scales and multiscale spectral CSP features

Bandwidth	A01	A02	A03	A04	A05	A06	A07	A08	A09	AVE
1	88.6	57.8	**90.7**	59.6	70.6	42.4	90.8	87.4	72.1	73.4 ± 17.4
2	88.3	64.4	89.3	63.0	76.0	46.9	91.1	89.7	67.1	75.1 ± 15.7
4	87.9	63.3	87.4	64.5	73.3	56.0	**93.7**	90.9	66.2	75.9 ± 14.2
8	89.0	64.1	88.5	65.3	75.3	**57.0**	89.6	90.8	71.3	76.8 ± 13.1
16	87.2	**65.2**	87.8	**65.6**	57.6	55.2	88.2	89.7	69.2	74.0 ± 14.2
32 (Baseline)	72.6	58.2	85.6	56.1	35.5	53.4	69.7	85.5	63.7	64.5 ± 16.0
All	**89.4**	64.4	89.6	64.2	**77.9**	53.3	93.3	**91.6**	**72.2**	**77.3 ± 14.6**

As shown in Table 1, we compared the results of different bandwidth and all bandwidth combinations. For the bandwidth 32 Hz, compared with other bandwidths, it achieves the worst classification average accuracy. For four frequency bands including 16 Hz, 8 Hz, 4 Hz, and 1 Hz, they obtained the highest classification accuracy on different subjects. This indicates that the discriminable motor imaging EEG features of different subjects are distributed over different frequency bands. For the bandwidth 2 Hz, while it did not achieve the highest accuracy in any of the subjects, it achieved an average accuracy of 75.08%, 10.62% higher than baseline with bandwidth 32 Hz. All bandwidth combinations achieved the highest average accuracy of 77.32%, and it achieved the highest accuracy for subjects A01, A05, A08, and A09. This reveals that dividing the wide frequency band into smaller sub-bands can significantly improve the classification accuracy. In addition, better classification accuracy can be achieved by fusing different spectral bandwidths.

Table 2. The classification accuracy (%) and standard deviation of different temporal window scales and multi-scale temporal CSP features

Temporal windows	A01	A02	A03	A04	A05	A06	A07	A08	A09	AVE
0.5 s	70.7	55.6	83.3	49.6	40.9	47.4	62.7	80.6	84.3	63.9 ± 16.6
1 s	74.0	**65.2**	83.3	47.7	40.1	45.1	73.8	84.4	82.6	66.3 ± 17.6
2 s	**76.9**	60.7	85.2	55.7	35.1	47.0	**76.9**	**86.3**	81.4	**67.2 ± 18.3**
3.5 s (Baseline)	72.6	58.2	**85.6**	**56.1**	35.5	**53.4**	69.7	85.5	63.7	64.5 ± 16.0
All	74.7	57.0	81.1	48.8	**42.4**	53.3	70.1	82.5	**86.1**	66.2 ± 16.2

As shown in Table 2, we compare the results of different temporal scales and multi-scale temporal CSP features. Different temporal scales achieved the highest accuracy in different subjects. For the temporal window size 2 s, it achieved the highest average accuracy of 67.15% and performed best among the three subjects. When the temporal window size is 0.5 s, it achieved the worst average accuracy and performed worst on four subjects. Therefore, the effect of temporal window size on the classification effect is highly dependent on individual differences between subjects. A more robust model can be obtained by combining the feature information on different temporal window scales.

Table 3. The classification accuracy (%) and standard deviation of four schemes for multiscale temporal and spectral CSP features

Temporal windows	Bandwidth	A01	A02	A03	A04	A05	A06	A07	A08	A09	AVE
1, 2, 3.5 s	All	**86.8**	**70.7**	**91.5**	65.3	**85.1**	50.6	**93.7**	89.0	90.7	80.4 ± 14.8
1, 2, 3.5 s	2–16 Hz	86.4	70.4	90.4	64.2	84.3	**52.9**	93.4	**90.9**	**91.5**	**80.5 + 14.5**
All	2–16 Hz	84.6	68.5	89.6	**69.9**	79.4	50.2	92.2	89.4	89.4	79.3 ± 13.9
All	All	82.4	67.0	89.6	68.4	76.4	42.4	91.1	87.1	88.6	77.0 ± 15.8

According to the conclusion discussed above, we use the fusion of all temporal and spectral scales as a baseline, and we discussed the influence of abandoning some negative temporal and spectral scales on classification accuracy. As shown in Table 3, scheme 2 achieved the highest average classification accuracy of 80.47%. Scheme 1 achieved an average accuracy of 80.38% and the highest accuracy of 93.7% on subject A07. By comparing schemes, we found that the classification accuracy improved by 2.25% after removing spectral scales 1 and 32, and the classification accuracy improved by 3.38% after removing the temporal scale 0.5 s. The temporal scale 0.5 s and spectral scale 32 Hz are the scales with poor performance in the above experiment.

Table 4 shown the classification accuracy and standard deviation of existing methods and proposed method on the BCI competition IV-2a dataset. For subjects A02, A05, A07, the proposed method achieved the highest accuracy compared to existing methods of

Table 4. The classification accuracy (%) and standard deviation of the proposed method and other methods on the BCI competition IV-2a dataset

Methods	A01	A02	A03	A04	A05	A06	A07	A08	A09	AVE
WOLA-CSP	86.8	63.2	94.4	68.8	56.3	69.4	78.5	**97.9**	**93.8**	78.9 ± 15.1
SRCSP	88.9	63.2	**96.5**	66.7	63.2	63.9	78.5	95.8	92.4	78.8 ± 14.8
TLCSP1	**90.3**	54.2	93.8	64.6	57.6	65.3	62.5	91.0	85.4	73.8 ± 15.9
TLCSP2	**90.3**	57.6	95.1	66.0	61.1	65.3	61.1	91.7	86.1	74.9 ± 15.4
C2CM	87.5	65.3	90.3	66.7	62.5	45.5	89.6	83.3	79.5	74.5 ± 15.3
Modular network	84.9	66.4	84.7	**81.4**	79.2	**70.7**	86.1	83.8	83.0	80.0 ± 6.9
DFFN (F1)	83.2	65.7	90.3	69.4	61.7	60.7	85.2	84.2	85.5	76.4 ± 11.7
DFFN (F2)	85.4	69.3	90.3	71.1	65.4	69.5	88.2	86.5	93.5	79.9 ± 10.9
Proposed method	86.4	**70.4**	90.4	64.2	**84.4**	52.9	**93.4**	90.9	91.5	**80.5 ± 14.5**

the literature. For other subjects, our method did not achieve the best accuracy. This may be because the EEG pattern of these subjects exists at a particular scale. This gives us inspiration for further optimizing temporal and spectral scale. For other The proposed method improves the mean accuracy by 1.53%, 1.6%, 6.54%, and 5.46% in comparison with existing CSP improvement methods WOLA-CSP [27], SRCSP [10], TLCSP1[28], TLCSP2 [28], respectively. Compared with the deep learning model, the average accuracy of the proposed method are improved by 5.92%, 0.35%, 3.94%, and 0.48%, respectively compared with C2CM [29], Modular Network [30], DFFN (F1), and DFFN (F2) [31].

5   Conclusion

This paper discusses the effects of CSP features at different temporal and spectral scales on multi-class motion-imaging tasks. We propose a CSP feature extraction method based on combining multi-scale spectral bands and temporal windows. This method effectively improves the number of features and achieves an average classification accuracy of 80.47% on a public dataset from BCI competition. The proposed approach was validated to be better than many existing methods to extract CSP features and some deep learning methods. It confirms the importance of the fusion of multi-scale temporal and spectral features for multi-class motion imaging. However, a more detailed selection of temporal window scales and spectral band scales, as well as extraction of more discriminative feature information from noise data needs to be investigated in the future.

References

1. Kübler, A., Müller, K.: An Introduction to Brain-Computer Interfacing. MIT Press, Cambridge (2007)

2. Pfurtscheller, G., Müller-Putz, G., Scherer, R., Neuper, C.: Rehabilitation with brain-computer interface systems. Computer **41**(10), 58–65 (2008)
3. Pfurtscheller, G., Neuper, C.: Motor imagery and direct brain-computer communication. Proc. IEEE **89**, 1123–1134 (2001)
4. Silva, G.: Event-related EEG/MEG synchronization and desynchronization: basic principles. Clin. Neurophysiol. **110**, 1842–1857 (1999)
5. Pan, J., Li, Y., Zhang, R., Gu, Z., Li, F.: Discrimination between control and idle states in asynchronous SSVEP-based brain switches: a pseudo-key-based approach. IEEE Trans. Neural Syst. Rehabil. Eng. **21**(3), 435–443 (2013)
6. Jin, J., Sellers, E.W., Zhou, S., Zhang, Y., Wang, X., Cichocki, A.: A P300 brain-computer interface based on a modification of the mismatch negativity paradigm. Int. J. Neural Syst. **25**(03), 1550011 (2015)
7. Pfurtscheller, G., Brunner, C., Schlogl, A., Silva, F.: Mu rhythm (de)synchronization and EEG single-trial classification of different motor imagery tasks. Neuroimage **31**(1), 153–159 (2006)
8. Yuan, H., He, B.: Brain–computer interfaces using sensorimotor rhythms: current state and future perspectives. IEEE Trans. Biomed. Eng. **61**(5), 1425–1435 (2014)
9. Krusienski, D.J., et al.: Critical issues in state-of-the-art brain-computer interface signal processing. J. Neural Eng. **8**(2), 025002 (2011)
10. Lotte, F., Guan, C.: Regularizing common spatial patterns to improve BCI designs: unified theory and new algorithms. IEEE Trans. Biomed. Eng. **58**(2), 355–362 (2011)
11. Kai, K.A., Guan, C.: EEG-based strategies to detect motor imagery for control and rehabilitation. IEEE Trans. Neural Syst. Rehabil. Eng. **PP**(4), 1 (2017)
12. Lu, H., Eng, H.L., Guan, C., Plataniotis, K.N., Venetsanopoulos, A.N.: Regularized common spatial pattern with aggregation for EEG classification in small-sample setting. IEEE Trans. Biomed. Eng. **57**(12), 2936–2946 (2010)
13. Ramoser, H., Muller-Gerking, J.: Optimal spatial filtering of single trial EEG during imagined hand movement. IEEE Trans. Rehabil. Eng. **8**, 441–446 (2000)
14. Blankertz, B., Tomioka, R., Lemm, S., Kawanabe, M., Muller, K.R.: Optimizing spatial filters for robust EEG single-trial analysis. IEEE Signal Process. Mag. **25**(1), 41–56 (2007)
15. Reuderink, B., Poel, M.: Robustness of the Common Spatial Patterns algorithm in the BCI-pipeline. Centre for Telematics & Information Technology University of Twente (2008)
16. Grosse-Wentrup, M., Liefhold, C., Gramann, K., Buss, M.: Beamforming in noninvasive brain-computer interfaces. IEEE Trans. Biomed. Eng. **56**(4), 1209–1219 (2009)
17. Dornhege, G.: Combined optimization of spatial and temporal filters for improving brain-computer interfacing. IEEE Trans. Biomed. Eng. **53**(11), 2274 (2006)
18. Quadrianto, N., Cuntai, G., Dat, T.H., Xue, P.: Sub-band common spatial pattern (SBCSP) for brain-computer interface. In: International IEEE/EMBS Conference on Neural Engineering (2007)
19. Kai, K.A., Zhang, Y.C., Zhang, H., Guan, C.: Filter bank common spatial pattern (FBCSP) in brain-computer interface. In: IEEE International Joint Conference on Neural Networks (2008)
20. Higashi, H., Tanaka, T.: Simultaneous design of FIR filter banks and spatial patterns for EEG signal classification. IEEE Trans. Biomed. Eng. **60**(4), 1100–1110 (2013)
21. Song, L., Epps, J.: Classifying EEG for brain-computer interface: learning optimal filters for dynamical system features. Comput. Intell. Neurosci. **2007**, 57180 (2007)
22. Xie, X., Yu, Z.L., Lu, H., Gu, Z., Li, Y.: Motor imagery classification based on bilinear sub-manifold learning of symmetric positive-definite matrices. IEEE Trans. Neural Syst. Rehabil. Eng. **25**(6), 504–516 (2017)
23. Keng, A.K., Yang, C.Z., Wang, C., Guan, C., Zhang, H.: Filter bank common spatial pattern algorithm on BCI competition IV datasets 2a and 2b. Front. Neurosci. **6**, 39 (2012)

24. Higashi, H., Tanaka, T.: Common spatio-time-frequency patterns for motor imagery-based brain machine interfaces. Comput. Intell. Neurosci. **2013**(4), 537218 (2013)
25. Leeb, R., Brunner, C., Muller-Putz, G.R., Schlogl, A.: BCI Competition 2008---Graz data set B (2008)
26. Grosse-Wentrup, M., Buss, M.: Multiclass common spatial patterns and information theoretic feature extraction. IEEE Trans. Biomed. Eng. **55**(8), 1991–2000 (2008)
27. Belwafi, K., Romain, O., Gannouni, S., Ghaffari, F., Djemal, R., Ouni, B.: An embedded implementation based on adaptive filter bank for brain-computer interface systems. J. Neurosci. Methods **305**, 1–16 (2018)
28. Raza, H., Cecotti, H., Li, Y., Prasad, G.: Adaptive learning with covariate shift-detection for motor imagery-based brain–computer interface. Soft Comput. **20**(8), 3085–3096 (2016). https://doi.org/10.1007/s00500-015-1937-5
29. Bashivan, P., Rish, I., Yeasin, M., Codella, N.: Learning representations from EEG with deep recurrent-convolutional neural networks. Computer (2015)
30. Dose, H., Moller, J.S., Iversen, H.K., Puthusserypady, S.: An end-to-end deep learning approach to MI-EEG signal classification for BCIs. Expert Syst. Appl. **114**(Dec), 532–542 (2018)
31. Li, D., Wang, J., Xu, J., Fang, X.: Densely feature fusion based on convolutional neural networks for motor imagery EEG classification. IEEE Access **PP**(99), 1 (2019)

Gingivitis Detection by Wavelet Energy Entropy and Linear Regression Classifier

Yan Yan[1,2](✉)

[1] School of Informatics, The University of Leicester, University Road, Leicester LE1 7RH, UK
[2] Educational Information Center, Liming Vocational University, Quanzhou 362000, Fujian, China

Abstract. Gingivitis is a high-risk disease among middle-aged and elderly people, which greatly increases the difficulty of eating. People are increasingly concerned about the subhealth of gingivitis in order to solve the daily eating problems associated with gingivitis. In the field of medical image analysis, the process of studying gingivitis detection is more challenging because of the lack and difficulty of dental image analysis. The two key points of gingivitis image detection are the extraction of major features from gingival images and the accurate classification of different features. In this paper, a gingivitis detection method based on wavelet energy entropy is proposed. The energy of the wavelet spectrum of gingival image is calculated by using the information entropy, and a new wavelet energy entropy of image feature representation is obtained. The entropy is used to segment gingival image by linear regression classifier. The segmented gingival image sieves out redundant information, preserves key feature areas, and reduces the time required for classification. This improves diagnostic time consumption and helps dentists improve the efficiency of gingivitis diagnosis.

Keywords: Gingivitis diagnosis · Wavelet energy entropy · Image feature extraction · Pathological image classification · Linear regression classifier

1 Introduction

Gingivitis is a chronic inflammation of the gums. The common manifestations of gingivitis are redness, swelling, and pain in the gums. Gums bleed when brushed in the morning, and some patients have bad breath [1]. The danger of gingivitis is the progression of periodontitis with the atrophy of the alveolar bone. Gingivitis is a mild, reversible disease. However, if left untreated, it can develop into a serious infection that can lead to tooth loss [2]. Neglecting to remove dental plaque regularly may cause dental plaque to harden and form mineral deposits that form calculus, providing a place for bacteria to grow and irritate the gums. Accumulation of dental plaque and calculus that is difficult to clean increases the risk of gingivitis. Since the etiology of gingivitis is clear, dental plaque is the causative factor of gingivitis, and the lesion is limited to gingivitis, the obvious effect can be obtained by removing the etiology and eliminating plaque. Otherwise, gingivitis continues to invade deep periodontal tissue and develops into periodontitis.

© Springer Nature Switzerland AG 2021
D.-S. Huang et al. (Eds.): ICIC 2021, LNAI 12838, pp. 185–197, 2021.
https://doi.org/10.1007/978-3-030-84532-2_17

The timely treatment of gingivitis depends on the early and accurate diagnosis of inflammation. Risk factors for chronic gingivitis include bleeding gums due to blood diseases, necrotizing ulcerative gingivitis, and vitamin deficiency. Diagnosis of artificial gingivitis mainly depends on dental plaque detection of the patient's clinical manifestations and X-ray examination to confirm the diagnosis. Different symptoms have different treatment methods, and it is important to correctly identify the cause and predict the early stage of gingivitis. Recording a complete periodontal chart for a periodontal healthy patient at each visit can be time-consuming and laborious, and may even cause the patient to refuse to visit the dentist. Therefore, in patients with early features of periodontitis, gingival image assessment is essential to provide information on the pattern and extent of alveolar bone loss. Non-invasive image analysis is a key adjunct to monitoring patients' gingival status but is secondary to clinical examination results.

You, Hao, Li, Wang and Xia [3] used a classical neural network framework and trained with 886 intraoral photographs of deciduous teeth. To verify clinical feasibility, plaque areas labeled by experienced pediatric dentists were compared with the experimental results to determine the agreement between the AI model and the dentist's manual diagnosis. Rad, Rahim, Kolivand and Norouzi [4] proposed a segmentation method based on the level set. The initial contour was generated from the image morphological information, and the artificial neural network and motion filtering were used to segment the improved gingival X-ray images with an intelligent level set, to detect the caries area. Haghanifar, Amirkhani and Mosavi [5] discuss the development of a fuzzy cognitive map for classifying the severity of disease in patients. First, the relationship between the concept of disease and its weight is defined according to the expert dentists in the field. Finally, the Causal Weight was applied to the real code genetic algorithm to divide 86 samples into two categories: healthy and caries, and a higher correct classification rate was achieved. A Gingival Field of Interest (ROI) method based on SIFT and SURF and input neural networks was proposed by Yang, Xie, Liu, Xia, Cao and Guo [6] to train models for automated clinical quality assessment, achieving a method comparable to the diagnostic performance of professional dentists and radiologists. Lee, Kim, Jeong and Choi [7] divided a total of 3000 periodontal X-ray images into training and validation datasets and input the GoogleNet Inception V3 neural network for preprocessing and transfer learning. The accuracy, sensitivity, specificity, positive predictive value, negative predictive value, receiver operating characteristic curve and area under the curve of the neural network are calculated. The diagnostic performance of the proposed algorithm is obtained, which proves that the deep neural network algorithm is expected to be the most effective method for the diagnosis of dental caries.

The function improvement of medical equipment provides an opportunity for the research of computer diagnosis in the field of medicine. Early detection and treatment of gingivitis requires high-quality diagnostic results [8]. Our work is to develop a new neural network-based computer-aided diagnostic approach for gingivitis. Firstly, the tooth image is preprocessed uniformly, and the wavelet energy entropy is used to extract the eigenvalue of the periodontal image instead of the complete image. The linear regression method was used to classify and recognize the inputted periodontal image eigenvalues. The method can be used as an auxiliary tool to help dentists predict gingivitis and improve the time consumption of manual testing. The detection of this model brings superior recognition ability, which not only has a good application prospect also can bring reference value to the development of new gingival detection.

2 Dataset

The image data of the experiment were obtained from Nanjing Stomatological Hospital [9]. The two digital single lens reflex was used to collect 180 periodontal color photos, including 90 gingivitis gingival photos and 90 healthy gingival photos in the control group. All tooth photos were resized and manually cropped with a field of view ranging from 51 to 200 mm and a voxel resolution ranging from 0.1 mm to 0.39 mm to ensure that only one intact gingival tooth appeared in each image. The detectable neural network model learned plaque features from these photos. The Fig. 1 shows a legend of adjusted gingivitis and normal gingival.

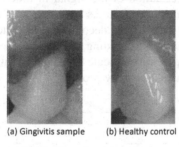

(a) Gingivitis sample   (b) Healthy control

Fig. 1. Samples of our dataset

3 Methodology

We divided manually adjusted 90 healthy gingival images and 90 gingivitis images into training and validation datasets with 180 color periodontal images in total. We performed discrete wavelet transform on the vibration signals collected from gingival images, and combined with information entropy, the wavelet transforms which calculated the maximum energy by wave coefficient was transformed into an effective energy entropy of the classification feature wavelet. Finally, the entropy signals were applied to the linear regression classifier to classify the health and pathology of gingival images.

3.1 Wavelet Energy Entropy

We use a novel method of gingivitis image feature extraction. We use discrete wavelet transform to calculate the maximum energy of gingivitis image signals, and then combine the information entropy to get the effective classification feature wavelet energy entropy.

Fourier analysis cannot describe the local characteristics of the signal in the time domain, is not effective for abrupt and unstable signals, and has no time–frequency analysis. In fact, in the representation of smooth and stationary signals, the Fourier basis has reached the approximate optimal representation [10]. However, the limitations of the

Fourier transform are increasingly obvious in a large number of applications. In practical applications, time–frequency localization is very necessary, and Fourier obviously lacks this ability [11]. The discrete Fourier transform is essentially the periodic continuation of the discrete signal and then the Fourier transform and then the interception of a period [12], and the inverse is the same thing. The discrete cosine transform derived from it has been the standard of image compression for a long time because of its good energy aggregation effect [13]. The emergence of wavelet transform solves the shortcomings of Fourier transform as the size of the window of the Fourier transform [14]. The wavelet transform directly changes the infinitesimally long trigonometric function basis into the infinitesimally long attenuated wavelet basis [15], which can not only obtain the frequency, but also locate the time. Wavelet packet decomposition is proposed to overcome the problem that the frequency resolution of wavelet decomposition in high frequency band is poor, while the time resolution of wavelet decomposition in low frequency band is poor. It is shown in Fig. 2 as a more sophisticated method of signal analysis and improves the resolution of the signal in time domain. The principle of extracting multi-scale spatial energy features based on wavelet packet decomposition is to solve the signal energy on different decomposition scales [16] and arrange these energy values into feature vectors according to the scale sequence for identification [17]. Selecting the best range of wavelet scale based on the ratio of maximum energy to information entropy can reduce the eigenvector.

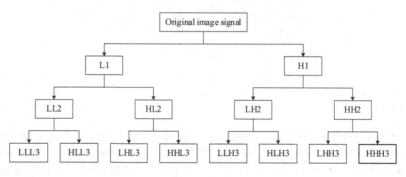

L: Approximate info of signals (Low Frequency Component)
H: Detail info of signals (High Frequency Component)

Fig. 2. Discrete wavelet decomposition of gingival image

The feature extraction process of gingival image is to select and retain important relevant information from the original signal. The original image signals are decomposed into frequency bands by wavelet transform, and then features are extracted from these decomposed energy signals by information entropy, wavelet energy entropy is obtained as the feature vector in final.

We transform the two-dimensional gingival image $I(a, c)$ into one-dimensional information. It is assumed that a discrete N as all of one-dimensional signals, and R is the number of rows that need to be averaged. The one-dimensional signals O_a that we convert are:

$$O_a = \frac{1}{R} \sum\nolimits_{c=1}^{R} I(a-1) * R + c \tag{1}$$

Where, $a = \{1, \ldots N\}$. After the one-dimensional signal of the gingival image is obtained, the energy entropy is calculated:

$$W_c = - \sum\nolimits_t P_{c,t} log(P_{c,t}) \tag{2}$$

Where W_c represents the energy entropy at the scale of c, and $P_{c,t}$ is the relative wavelet energy, which is the distribution probability at the time of t and the scale of c.

Each resolution level $c = \{1, \ldots N\}$, the energy $E_{c,t}$ is defined as:

$$E_{c,t} = |U_c(t)|^2 \tag{3}$$

U_c is the coefficient on time t, scale c. And finally, the total energy along the c scale is,

$$E_c = \sum\nolimits_{t=1}^{N} E_{c,t} \tag{4}$$

3.2 Linear Regression Classifier

Linear regression classification is a supervised machine learning algorithm [18] widely used in data analysis. There is a linear relationship between feature samples and classification results [19], so feature samples can be classified by linear subspace. Compared with nonlinear classification, linear classification does not have the advantage of multi-hyperplane combination due to unlimited, the programming complexity is reduced. Common Linear Classifier include Logistic Regression, Support Vector Machine and Perceptron. Linear regression classification model, refers to a probability distribution, can also be said to be a decision function [20]. Linear means that the model has a linear decision boundary, which can be regarded as a line in two-dimensional space and as a hyperplane in multidimensional space [21]. Regression represents problems that are used to solve classification types.

LRC is mainly composed of scoring function and loss function. The scoring function is a mapping function from the original image to the category score, and the loss function is used to quantify the consistency between the category label predicted score and the real label. Among them, the simplest dichotomy is to use a function to group the original data eigenvalues into a value set, so that the data features are mapped to [0, 1]. This means that the function maps the input to a decimal between 0 and 1, artificially interprets the decimal between 0 and 1 as a probability [22], and then classifies it according to a predefined threshold. The objective of the linear regression model is to find the relationship between the input variable and the target variable [23]. In this algorithm, we give the input x and obtain the predicted value y.

$$y = kx + b \tag{5}$$

Where, k is the slope of the line, x is the input value, and b is the y-intercept.

Because different models have different requirements for data, it is indispensable to process the data accordingly before modeling. The general linear regression model requires the data type of the attribute to be continuous value, so it is necessary to carry on the continuity of the discrete attribute. The error can vary by adjusting different values of k and b, and the minimum value of this formula will give the best k, b. This pair of (k, b) is the best model parameter that can describe the data relationship.

There is a linear relationship between the gingival image and the prognosis of gingivitis. By designing an assessment standard, a more accurate fitting scheme can be obtained from the quantified results. The performance of the model can be evaluated by measuring the error between the actual and predicted values. If the model can fit the data well, the error will be smaller; otherwise, the error will be larger. We set the error value C, and each C is equivalent to the difference between the real y and the predicted $\hat{y}$, so the total error L is set as:

$$L = c_{x1}^2 + c_{x2}^2 + c_{x3}^3 + \cdots + c_{xn}^2 \tag{6}$$

When we take the optimal solution, we have:

$$minimize : L = (kx + b - y)^2 \tag{7}$$

Suppose we define a dataset $G = \{(x_1, y_1), \ldots, (x_n, y_n)\}$, n is the total number of samples, so we get:

$$L = \sum_{i=1}^{n} (kx_i + b - y_i)^2 \tag{8}$$

We take the derivative of the parameters b and k, firstly:

$$\frac{\partial L}{\partial b} = \sum_{i=1}^{n} 2(kx_i + b - y_i) \cdot 1 = 0 \tag{9}$$

Then, we have:

$$k \sum_{i=1}^{n} x_i + \sum_{i=1}^{n} b - \sum_{i=1}^{n} y_i = 0 \tag{10}$$

And,

$$k \cdot n \cdot \bar{x} + b \cdot n - n \cdot \bar{y} = 0 \tag{11}$$

Where $\bar{x}, \bar{y}$ represents the mean of all x, y. Therefore, we have:

$$b = \bar{y} - k \cdot \bar{x} \tag{12}$$

And then we take the derivative with respect to k:

$$\frac{\partial L}{\partial k} = \sum_{i=1}^{n} 2(kx_i + b - y_i) \cdot x_i = 0 \tag{13}$$

Then, we have:

$$\sum_{i=1}^{n} 2(kx_i + \bar{y} - k \cdot \bar{x} - y_i) \cdot x_i = 0 \tag{14}$$

$$k \sum_{i=1}^{n} x_i^2 + \sum_{i=1}^{n} \bar{y} \cdot x_i - \sum_{i=1}^{n} k\bar{x} \cdot x_i - \sum_{i=1}^{n} x_i y_i = 0 \tag{15}$$

Finally, we get:

$$k = \frac{\overline{xy} - \overline{x}\overline{y}}{\overline{x^2} - \bar{x}^2} \tag{16}$$

Linear regression classifier has many advantages for most data analysis scenarios. Firstly, the model is simple and suitable for large quantities of data [24]. Combined with gradient descent method for training, model training with fast speed and less resource consumption can be obtained. In addition, the model itself has a very good interpretability. Through the training of the model, the effective and invalid characteristics can be learned. If there are problems in the model, the root of the problem can be quickly located. However, there are also over-fitting problems in linear regression, which can be solved by introducing regular terms or adding more data for training.

3.3 10-fold Cross Validation

Cross-validation is a practical method to cut data samples into smaller subsets for statistics. In the related experimental research of machine learning, the whole data set is usually divided into training set and test set [25]. The training set is used in the training of the model, and the test set is used to evaluate the errors of the model in the model after the training is completed [26]. Suppose an unknown model is consisting of one or more unknown parameters and there is a training set. This process is to adjust the parameters of the model so that the model can reflect the characteristics of the training set to the maximum. At the same time, the test set can verify that the model encounters over-fitting caused by undersize training set or inappropriate parameters. Therefore, cross validation is an effective method to predict model fitting performance.

The process of ten-fold cross-validation as show in Table 1. tenfold Cross-validation divides the data into ten training sets and validation sets. The division is to make full use

Table 1. The process of ten-fold cross-validation

The pseudo code of ten-fold cross-validation
Step1: Divide the learning sample space d into p parts of equal size
for i = 1 to p:
Take the i-th part as the test set
for j = 1 to p:
The j-th component is added to the training set as part of the training set
Step 3: for i in (p-1 training set):
The i-th training set is trained and a classification model is obtained
The model was tested on the q-th dataset to calculate and save the evaluation index of the model
Step 4: Calculate the average performance of the model
Step 5: The average classification accuracy of the p models in the final verification set is used as the performance index of this classifier

of the training data and make each part of the training data participate in the training. Randomly divide the training data into 10 equal parts: $D_1, D_2...D_{10}$. For each model M_i, the algorithm is executed 10 times, and one D_j is selected as the verification set each time [27], while the others are used as the training set to train model M_i. The trained model is tested on D_j, and an error is obtained each time. Finally, the generalization error of model M_i is obtained by averaging the errors obtained for 10 times [28]. After obtaining the optimal hyperparameters, the algorithm selects the model with the minimum generalization error as the final model, and retrains the model on the whole training set to get the final model [29]. The main purpose of tenfold cross validation is to select different model types, rather than to select specific parameters of specific models [30]. The ten-fold cross-validation feature is that each sample data is used as both training data and test data. Therefore, the occurrence of overlearning and underlearning can be avoided, and the results obtained are more convincing.

4 Experiment Results and Discussions

4.1 Wavelet Result

For wavelet transform, the signal of low frequency part for further decomposition, and the high frequency part of signal details will no longer continue to break down, so the wavelet transform can well characterize the groups with low frequency information as the main components of the signal, can't well decomposition and that contains a lot of detail information of the signal, and easy to have a great many of redundancy. During the wavelet packet decomposition of gingival image, on the basis of wavelet transform, the signal decomposition of gingival image at each level is carried out in addition to the further decomposition of low frequency subbands and the further decomposition of high frequency subbands, and then the low frequency approximate part is decomposed into only one point for each part. The wavelet decomposition of the gingival image is shown in Fig. 3. Finally, by minimizing a cost function, the optimal signal decomposition path is calculated, and the original signal is decomposed by this decomposition path. Moreover, the decomposition has neither redundancy nor omission, so the signal containing a good deal of medium and high frequency information can be better analyzed by time–frequency localization.

The essence of wavelet transform is the similarity between the original signal and the wavelet basis function. In numerical analysis, according to the similarity of two figures, if two figures are completely orthogonal, then the inner product is 0; if two figures are exactly the same with each other, then the coefficient is 1. Therefore, the wavelet coefficient is the coefficient in which the wavelet basis function is similar to the original signal. Wavelet decomposition can be used for data compression because the gingival image signal is decomposed by wavelet and the smaller wavelet coefficient is set to zero, which means that the information component with no obvious features is removed, and the effect of data simplification can be achieved. At the same time, the high-resolution information component is removed to achieve the effect of data smoothing.

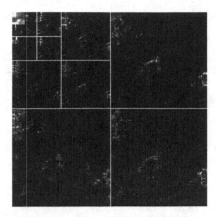

Fig. 3. Wavelet decompositions of gingival image

4.2 Statistical Analysis

We evaluated the performance of our proposed method through Matthews correlation coefficient (MCC), Fowlkes-Mallows coefficient (FMI), F1 score, precision, accuracy, sensitivity and specificity. MCC is essentially the correlation coefficient between the observed category and the predicted binary classification. It returns a value between −1 and +1, where 1, 0 and −1 represent perfect, average, and complete failure, respectively. Fowlkes-Mallows index is the geometric average of recall and precision obtained between the training set and the verification set, and its formula is as follows:

$$FMI = \frac{TP}{\sqrt{(TP + FP)(TP + FN)}} \tag{17}$$

Here, TP represents a true positive for correct judgment. FN represents the number of false judgements that are negative. FP represents the number of false positives. The best performance of the model is indicated when the average value of FMI is close to 1.

The results of our method representation are shown in the Table 2. We combined wavelet energy entropy with linear regression classifier for gingivitis detection to obtain MCC of $59.28 \pm 1.72\%$, FMI of $79.78 \pm 1.18\%$, F1 score of $79.76 \pm 1.18\%$, precision of $79.15 \pm 0.96\%$, accuracy of $79.61 \pm 0.87\%$, sensitivity of $80.44 \pm 2.68\%$, and specificity of $78.78 \pm 1.69\%$ after ten-fold cross-validation. In the future, some deep neural network [31, 32] models will be studied.

4.3 Comparison to State-of-the-art Approaches

We compared the existing image classification methods with our proposed classification methods for gingivitis. The sensitivity of $80.44 \pm 2.68\%$, specificity of $78.78 \pm 1.69\%$ and accuracy of $79.61 \pm 0.87\%$ were obtained by our method. Compared with the image detection method based on wavelet energy combined with biogeographic optimization algorithm [33], our sensitivity, specificity and accuracy are about 18% higher. Compared with other methods for gingivitis detection, the grey co-occurrence matrix [34], the

Table 2. Performance test results of gingivitis detection by ten-fold cross validation

Run	Sen	Spc	Prc	Acc	F1	MCC	FMI
1	82.22	80.00	80.43	81.11	81.32	62.24	81.32
2	74.44	82.22	80.72	78.33	77.46	56.84	77.52
3	81.11	78.89	79.35	80.00	80.22	60.01	80.22
4	82.22	78.89	79.57	80.56	80.87	61.15	80.89
5	78.89	78.89	78.89	78.89	78.89	57.78	78.89
6	83.33	75.56	77.32	79.44	80.21	59.07	80.27
7	82.22	77.78	78.72	80.00	80.43	60.06	80.45
8	78.89	78.89	78.89	78.89	78.89	57.78	78.89
9	78.89	78.89	78.89	78.89	78.89	57.78	78.89
10	82.22	77.78	78.72	80.00	80.43	60.06	80.45
MSD	80.44 ± 2.68	78.78 ± 1.69	79.15 ± 0.96	79.61 ± 0.87	79.76 ± 1.18	59.28 ± 1.72	79.78 ± 1.18

extreme learning machine, and the adaptive histogram equalization method with limited contrast [9] were all about 70% accurate, still about 5% lower than our method. Compared with the fractional Fourier entropy image extraction [35] method by standard genetic classification method, our method achieves about two percent higher scores. Overall results in Table 3 show that our method is more advanced than other existing methods and has a high rating. This shows that our method has superior performance over previous methods and can effectively help dentists reduce the time spent in diagnosis.

Table 3. Comparison of our method with state-of-the-art algorithms

Approach	Sen	Spc	Acc
WE-BBO [33]	62%	68%	65%
GLCM-ELM [34]	72%	70%	71%
CLAHE-GLCM-ELM [9]	75%	73%	74%
FRFE-SGA [35]	78.00 ± 2.71%	76.56 ± 3.00%	77.28 ± 1.90%
WEE-LRC (Our method)	80.44 ± 2.68%	78.78 ± 1.69%	79.61 ± 0.87%

5   Conclusions

We propose a new method for gingivitis detection by using a wavelet energy entropy feature extraction combined with a linear regression classifier. Wavelet energy entropy combines the key image signal decomposition and energy extraction of the wavelet packet calculated by information entropy, which reduces the massive memory footprint brought by high-definition color gingival image and removes the additional information of irrelevant detection, thus increasing the efficiency of image classification. Linear regression not merely has the advantage of fast modeling speed also does not need very complex calculation. It can ignore the size of the data and give the understanding and explanation of each variable according to the coefficient. At the same time, the linear relationship between variables can be considered to fit the data well. Compared with the existing similar methods, the proposed method has the advantages of accurate detection range, small space occupation, and low operating pressure.

Experimental results show that our method has a fast classification speed and strong robustness of the model. It not only provides a relaxed diagnostic environment for dentists, as well as provides a new research idea for the development of the automatic diagnosis of gingivitis.

References

1. Ebersole, J.L., Hamzeh, R., Nguyen, L., Al-Sabbagh, M., Dawson, D.: Variations in IgG antibody subclass responses to oral bacteria: effects of periodontal disease and modifying factors. J. Periodontal Res. 14 (2021)
2. Yarkac, F.U., Gokturk, O., Demir, O.: Interaction between stress, cytokines, and salivary cortisol in pregnant and non-pregnant women with gingivitis. Clin. Oral Investig. 25, 1677–1684 (2021). https://doi.org/10.1007/s00784-018-2569-9
3. You, W., Hao, A., Li, S., Wang, Y., Xia, B.: Deep learning-based dental plaque detection on primary teeth: a comparison with clinical assessments. BMC Oral Hesalth 20, 141 (2020)
4. Rad, A.E., Rahim, M.S.M., Kolivand, H., Norouzi, A.: Automatic computer-aided caries detection from dental x-ray images using intelligent level set. Multimedia Tools Appl. 77, 28843–28862 (2018). https://doi.org/10.1007/s11042-018-6035-0
5. Haghanifar, A., Amirkhani, A., Mosavi, M.R.: Dental caries degree detection based on fuzzy cognitive maps and genetic algorithm. In: Iranian Conference on Electrical Engineering (ICEE), pp. 976–981 (2018)
6. Yang, J., Xie, Y., Liu, L., Xia, B., Cao, Z., Guo, C.: Automated dental image analysis by deep learning on small dataset. In: 2018 IEEE 42nd Annual Computer Software and Applications Conference (COMPSAC), pp. 492–497 (2018)
7. Lee, J.H., Kim, D.H., Jeong, S.N., Choi, S.H.: Detection and diagnosis of dental caries using a deep learning-based convolutional neural network algorithm. J Dent. 77, 106–111 (2018)
8. Sangaiah, A.K.: Alcoholism identification via convolutional neural network based on parametric ReLU, dropout, and batch normalization. Neural Comput. Appl. 32, 665–680 (2020). https://doi.org/10.1007/s00521-018-3924-0
9. Li, W., et al.: A gingivitis identification method based on contrast-limited adaptive histogram equalization, gray-level co-occurrence matrix, and extreme learning machine. Int. J. Imaging Syst. Technol. 29, 77–82 (2019)
10. Wu, X.: Diagnosis of COVID-19 by Wavelet Renyi entropy and three-segment biogeography-based optimization. Int. J. Comput. Intell. Syst. 13, 1332–1344 (2020)
11. Akbari, H., Sadiq, M.T., Rehman, A.U.: Classification of normal and depressed EEG signals based on centered correntropy of rhythms in empirical wavelet transform domain. Health Inf. Sci. Syst. 9, 15 (2021). https://doi.org/10.1007/s13755-021-00139-7
12. Ramirez, J.: Unilateral sensorineural hearing loss identification based on double-density dual-tree complex wavelet transform and multinomial logistic regression. Integr. Comput.-Aided Eng. 26, 411–426 (2019)

13. Upadhyay, P., Upadhyay, S.K., Shukla, K.K.: Magnetic resonance images denoising using a wavelet solution to laplace equation associated with a new variational model. Appl. Math. Comput. **400**, 17 (2021)

14. Han, L.: Identification of alcoholism based on wavelet Renyi entropy and three-segment encoded Jaya algorithm. Complexity 2018 (2018)

15. Masoumi, M., Marcoux, M., Maignel, L., Pomar, C.: Weight prediction of pork cuts and tissue composition using spectral graph wavelet. J. Food Eng. **299**, 10 (2021)

16. Phillips, P.: Intelligent facial emotion recognition based on stationary wavelet entropy and Jaya algorithm. Neurocomputing **272**, 668–676 (2018)

17. Gungor, M.A.: A comparative study on wavelet denoising for high noisy CT images of COVID-19 disease. Optik **235**, 7 (2021)

18. Guttery, D.S.: Improved breast cancer classification through combining graph convolutional network and convolutional neural network. Inf. Process. Manag. **58**, 102439 (2021)

19. Koc, M.: A novel partition selection method for modular face recognition approaches on occlusion problem. Mach. Vis. Appl. **32**, 11 (2021). https://doi.org/10.1007/s00138-020-011 56-4

20. Zhang, Y.-D., Dong, Z.-C.: Advances in multimodal data fusion in neuroimaging: overview, challenges, and novel orientation. Inf. Fusion **64**, 149–187 (2020)

21. Haghighi, M.R.R., Sayari, M., Ghahramani, S., Lankarani, K.B.: Social, economic, and legislative factors and global road traffic fatalities. BMC Public Health **20**, 12 (2020). https://doi.org/10.1186/s12889-020-09491-x

22. Chen, Y.: A feature-free 30-disease pathological brain detection system by linear regression classifier. CNS Neurol. Disord.: Drug Targets **16**, 5–10 (2017)

23. Roshanzamir, A., Aghajan, H., Baghshah, M.S.: Transformer-based deep neural network language models for Alzheimer's disease risk assessment from targeted speech. BMC Med. Inform. Decis. Making **21**, 14 (2021). https://doi.org/10.1186/s12911-021-01456-3

24. Jorgensen, A.L., Kjelstrup-Hansen, J., Jensen, B., Petrunin, V., Fink, S.F., Jorgensen, B.: Acquisition and analysis of hyperspectral thermal images for sample segregation. Appl. Spectrosc. **75**, 317–324 (2021)

25. Wang, S.-H.: COVID-19 classification by CCSHNet with deep fusion using transfer learning and discriminant correlation analysis. Inf. Fusion **68**, 131–148 (2021)

26. Dyar, M.D., Ytsma, C.R.: Effect of data set size on geochemical quantification accuracy with laser-induced breakdown spectroscopy. Spectrochim. Acta Part B: At. Spectrosc. **177**, 15 (2021)

27. Wang, S.-H.: Covid-19 classification by FGCNet with deep feature fusion from graph convolutional network and convolutional neural network. Inf. Fusion **67**, 208–229 (2021)

28. Diale, R.G., Modiba, R., Ngoepe, P.E., Chauke, H.R.: Phase stability of TiPd1-xRux and Ti1-xPdRux shape memory alloys. Mater. Today: Proc. **38**, 1071–1076 (2021)

29. Wang, S.-H.: DenseNet-201-based deep neural network with composite learning factor and precomputation for multiple sclerosis classification. ACM Trans. Multimedia Comput. Commun. Appl. **16**, 1–19 (2020)

30. Fenu, G., Malloci, F.M.: Lands DSS: a decision support system for forecasting crop disease in Southern Sardinia. Int. J. Decis. Support Syst. Technol. **13**, 21–33 (2021)

31. Muhammad, K.: Image based fruit category classification by 13-layer deep convolutional neural network and data augmentation. Multimedia Tools Appl. **78**, 3613–3632 (2019)

32. Tang, C.: Cerebral micro-bleeding detection based on densely connected neural network. Front. Neurosci. **13**, 422 (2019)

33. Yang, G., et al.: Automated classification of brain images using wavelet-energy and biogeography-based optimization. Multimedia Tools Appl. **75**, 15601–15617 (2016). https://doi.org/10.1007/s11042-015-2649-7

34. Wen, L., Yiyang, C., Leiying, M., Mackenzie, B., Weibin, S., Xuan, Z.: Gingivitis identification via grey-level cooccurrence matrix and extreme learning machine. In: 8th International Conference on Education, Management, Information and Management Society (EMIM 2018), pp. 486–492. Atlantis Press (2018)
35. Yan, Y., Nguyen, E.: Gingivitis detection by fractional fourier entropy and standard genetic algorithm. In: Huang, D.S., Bevilacqua, V., Hussain, A. (eds.) Intelligent Computing Theories and Application, vol. 12463, pp. 585–596. Springer, Cham (2020). https://doi.org/10.1007/978-3-030-60799-9_53

Decomposition-and-Fusion Network for HE-Stained Pathological Image Classification

Rui Yan[1,2], Jintao Li[1], S. Kevin Zhou[1], Zhilong Lv[1], Xueyuan Zhang[1],
Xiaosong Rao[3], Chunhou Zheng[4(✉)], Fei Ren[1(✉)], and Fa Zhang[1(✉)]

[1] High Performance Computer Research Center, Institute of Computing Technology,
Chinese Academy of Sciences, Beijing, China
{renfei,zhangfa}@ict.ac.cn
[2] University of Chinese Academy of Sciences, Beijing, China
[3] Department of Pathology, Peking University International Hospital, Beijing, China
[4] College of Computer Science and Technology, Anhui University, Hefei, China

Abstract. Building upon the clinical evidence supporting that decomposing a pathological image into different components can improve diagnostic value, in this paper we propose a Decomposition-and-Fusion Network (DFNet) for HE-stained pathological image classification. The medical goal of using HE-stained pathological images is to distinguish between nucleus, cytoplasm and extracellular matrix, thereby displaying the overall layouts of cells and tissues. We embed this most basic medical knowledge into a deep learning framework that decomposes a pathological image into cell nuclei and the remaining structures (that is, cytoplasm and extracellular matrix). With such decomposed pathological images, DFNet first extracts independent features using three independent CNN branches, and then gradually merges these features together for final classification. In this way, DFNet is able to learn more representative features with respect to different structures and hence improve the classification performance. Experimental results on two different datasets with various cancer types show that the DFNet achieves competitive performance.

Keywords: Pathological image classification · Nuclei segmentation · Convolutional neural network · Knowledge modeling

1 Introduction

Hematoxylin and Eosin (HE) staining is the most widely used technique in histology and pathology. Pathologists perform microscopic examination of the HE-stained pathological sections to complete the pathological diagnosis, which is usually the gold standard. Hematoxylin is an alkaline dye, which mainly makes the chromatin in the nucleus and the nucleic acid in the cytoplasm colored purple-blue; In contrast to hematoxylin, eosin is an acidic dye, which mainly makes the components in the cytoplasm and extracellular matrix colored red. The staining shows the morphology of individual cells, the layout of

© Springer Nature Switzerland AG 2021
D.-S. Huang et al. (Eds.): ICIC 2021, LNAI 12838, pp. 198–207, 2021.
https://doi.org/10.1007/978-3-030-84532-2_18

cell populations, and the overall structure of the tissue, thereby providing an overview of the tissue sample. Therefore, the pathologist can easily distinguish the nuclear part from the non-nuclear part (that is, cytoplasm and extracellular matrix).

Pathological image classification is the cornerstone of the pathological image analysis [1]. On the basis of pathological image classification, mitosis detection, image retrieval and other methods can also be further studied. Although deep learning methods have greatly improved the accuracy of pathological image classification, they seldom exploit the inherent characteristics of pathological images, such as the irregularity of tumor cells and tissues, the inter- and intra-nuclear color variations, and object scale differences, which are different from natural images.

It is feasible to further improve the classification accuracy of algorithms with the help of medical knowledge [2]; but it's difficult that how to embed medical knowledge into the end-to-end learning of the algorithm framework or network model. Some current work has explored along this line, and one of the most effective methods is to leverage the medical anatomy knowledge embedded in medical images [3–5]. Li et al. [4] encoded medical anatomy knowledge embedded in CT into a deep network that decomposed a chest X-ray into lung, bone and the remaining structures. With augmented bone-suppressed images, classification performance was significantly improved. Gozes et al. [5] used fully convolutional neural networks based method for enhancing the contrast of soft lung structures in chest radiographs. Specifically, lung radiographs are enhanced by learning to extract lung structures from CT based simulated X-ray or Digitally Reconstructed Radiographs (DRR), and fusing with the original X-ray images. When the DenseNet-based architecture was trained to work directly on lung-enhanced X-ray images, very promising results were obtained. However, the medical anatomy knowledge cannot be well reflected in pathological images because pathological images observe phenotypes at the tissue level and cell level, which are too microscopic and not too many specific rules to follow. Especially cancer occurrence and development make it even more irregular.

In this paper, to leverage medical staining knowledge belonging to HE-stained pathological image, we propose a Decomposition-and-Fusion Network (DFNet) to further improve the accuracy of pathological image classification. The basic medical knowledge of HE staining is embedded into a deep learning framework that decomposes a pathological image into cell nuclei and the remaining structures (that is, cytoplasm and extracellular matrix). With such decomposed pathological images, the DFNet first extracts independent features using three independent CNN branches, and then gradually merges these features together for final classification. In this way, DFNet learns more representative features and hence further improves the classification performance. It is like decomposing a complex problem into sub-problems first with the help of prior knowledge and then fusing the answers to sub-questions in order to arrive at the final result. We conducted two experiments of breast cancer classification and colorectal cancer grading, and achieved average classification accuracy of 92.0% and 94.83%, respectively. The results show that the proposed method achieves competitive performance compared to the-state-of-art method and could play a fundamental role in HE-stained pathological images classification.

2 Method

In this section, we describe our proposed method in detail. In general, our framework is divided into two parts: the decomposition part and the fusion part. We will first describe the decomposition part (that is, the nuclei segmentation network) in Sect. 2.1. Using the well-trained nuclei segmentation network, we can get the nuclei segmentation mask of pathological image. Thus, a pathological image can decompose into the nuclear and non-nuclear parts. Then, we will describe the fusion part (that is, the architecture of DFNet) in Sect. 2.2. The DFNet first extracts independent features using three independent CNN branches from the decomposed image and the original image, and then gradually merges these features together to obtain more representative features with respect to different structures and hence improve the classification performance.

2.1 Nuclei Segmentation

The main purpose of HE staining is to distinguish the nuclear and non-nuclear parts (cytoplasm, extracellular matrix). By a simple color separation, it is impossible to realize the pathological image decomposition with medical significance because the inter- and intra-nuclear color variations are very big. However, if we complete the nuclei segmentation, the decomposition of HE-stained pathological images is realized.

Nuclei segmentation in pathological images is a very challenging task [6]. Traditional methods do not work effectively on challenging cases. In recent years, deep learning methods have made huge breakthroughs in the field of computer vision [7]. One of the important innovations of image segmentation algorithm is DeepLabV3+ [8], which has achieved excellent results on multiple datasets. The main innovations in DeepLabV3+ can be summarized in two aspects: firstly, DeepLabV3+ utilizes the Atrous Spatial Pyramid Pooling (ASPP) module to capture the contextual information at multiple scales. Secondly, encoder-decoder network structure is used for semantic segmentation. The encoder is able to encode multi-scale contextual information by using ASPP module, while the decoder can capture sharper object boundaries by gradually recovering the spatial information.

The two advantages of DeepLabV3+ are particularly helpful in solving the hurdle in nuclei segmentation task: some cells have large nuclei, while others are very small. Under different magnifications, the difference in nucleus size is even more significant. Therefore, this requires our network can not only use multi-scale features but also reconstruct small object information. Furthermore, nuclei stacking and adhering nuclei borders make nuclei segmentation more difficult, which requires our algorithm to have a strong ability to reconstruct border information. Both of these requirements have been addressed in DeepLabV3+. Therefore, after comparing with a variety of methods, we choose the DeepLabV3+ as our nuclei segmentation method. The network structure of DeepLabV3+ is shown in the Fig. 1. Given a pathological image I_{main}, the output of DeepLabV3+ is nuclei segmentation mask M.

2.2 DFNet Architecture

The proposed DFNet has three inputs $[I_{main}, I_{down}, I_{top}]$. The input to the main branch is the original pathological image I_{main}, and the inputs to the two auxiliary branches

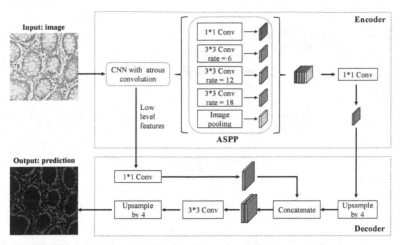

Fig. 1. The architecture of DeepLabV3+ we applied for nuclei segmentation.

are two images: one image I_{down} containing only the nucleus, and the other image I_{top} containing only the cytoplasm and extracellular matrix, respectively. The relationships between the three inputs are:

$$I_{down} = M * I_{main}; I_{main} = I_{down} + I_{top}.$$

In each branch of DFNet, the feature representation is extracted independently based on the CNN backbone network. Then through the mid and final fusion blocks for feature fusion and deriving the final classification output. The network structure is shown in Fig. 2.

In the main branch and two auxiliary branches, our network backbone uses the same network structure like Xception [9] for independent feature representation learning. Based on Inception-V3 [10], the Xception network further combines depth-wise convolution. This combination brings improved network efficiency: under the same number of parameters, the Xception performance is better than that of Inception-V3. Due to its lightweight design, the total parameter of Xception is about 23M, which gives rise to that the total parameter of our DFNet model is about 93M. Compared with a single VGG16 (139M), the parameter amount of our DFNet model is 33% lighter.

Our fusion is divided into two stages, namely the mid fusion stage and the final fusion stage. The detailed schematic diagram of fusion block is shown in Fig. 3. In the mid fusion stage, the output feature maps extracted from each auxiliary branch are concatenated with the output feature map extracted from the main branch, respectively. Next, the 1×1 and 3×3 convolutions follow. The purpose of the 1×1 convolution operation is to fuse information between channels and also to compress feature maps [11]. The purpose of 3×3 convolution operation is to perform feature representation learning again after fusion, so as to discover feature representations that could not be discovered by just single branch learning. In the final fusion stage, the output feature maps of the first stage are concatenated together and then processed using 1×1 and 3×3 convolutions. The formulas are defined as follows:

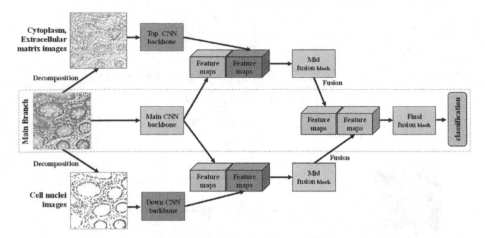

Fig. 2. The overall structure of our proposed DFNet.

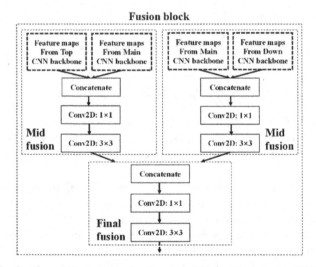

Fig. 3. The detailed schematic diagram of fusion block in the DFNet.

$$X_k = f_{Xcep}(I_k) \quad k \in \{main, down, top\},$$

$$X_{final} = f_{final}\left(f_{mid}\left(X_{main}, X_{down}\right), f_{mid}\left(X_{main}, X_{top}\right)\right),$$

where X represents the feature maps and I represents the input images. $f_{Xcep}(.)$ represent the extraction of last feature maps from Xception backbone. $f_{final}(.)$ and $f_{mid}(.)$ represent the final and mid fusion block, respectively. After two stages of fusion, the global average pooling (GAP) is used to compress the feature maps obtained after the fusion into one dimension. Finally, the one-dimensional vector is passed through the fully connected layer to obtain the final classification result.

$$Y = f_{FC}\left(f_{GAP}\left(X_{final}\right)\right),$$

where Y represents the class label, $f_{GAP}(.)$ is a global average pooling operation, and $f_{FC}(.)$ is the fully connected network. The loss function for DFNet is defined as multi-class cross entropy:

$$L = -\frac{1}{m}\sum\nolimits_{i=1}^{m}\sum\nolimits_{k=1}^{k} q_k^m \log\left(p_k^m\right),$$

where q_k^m and p_k^m indicates the ground truth and prediction probability of mth image for k^{th} class.

Two-stage fusion strategy is more effective than the one-stage fusion strategy. Because the fusion of the main branch and auxiliary branches is a process of strengthening the nuclear-related features or the cytoplasm-related and extracellular matrix-related features. Therefore, separating the fusion process can enable them to perform feature fusion without interfering with each other first, then perform the final feature fusion after each sub-feature is well extracted. Meanwhile, this is also similar to the attention mechanism. DFNet first focuses on learning feature representations in different interesting parts, and then merges them together to obtain the final feature representation. Thus, custom areas can be emphasized, this is different from the conventional attention mechanism that can only adaptively find the area of attention through model learning.

It should be pointed out that our DFNet framework is general. DFNet can also be extended to any other stain-based image analysis problems. We integrate image semantic segmentation into the framework of classification algorithms. The results of segmentation are used to decompose the interesting part (through medical prior knowledge) of the original image. Through end-to-end learning, the general CNN is strengthened with the help of medical prior knowledge to further improve the classification performance. This provides a new end-to-end modeling method for embedding medical knowledge into the network structure.

3   Experiments

3.1   Datasets and Preprocessing

Breast Cancer Classification Dataset. The publicly available dataset of breast cancer (BC) classification proposed by Yan et al. [12] contains 3,771 high-resolution (2,048 × 1,536 pixels) images. Among them, the number of pathological images of normal, benign, in situ carcinoma and invasive carcinoma is 299, 1,106, 1,066, and 1,300, respectively. All images are divided into non-overlapping 512 × 512 image patches. Some image patches contain large blank areas, and we delete these image patches. Also, because the amount of data in the normal category is too small, which leads to data imbalance, we have separately enhanced the normal category. After preprocessing, our final BC dataset includes 45,660 image patches, which consists of 10,000 normal, 10,672 benign, 11,630 in situ, and 13,358 invasive image patches.

Colorectal Cancer Grading Dataset. For the task of colorectal cancer (CRC) grading, Awan et al. [13] P proposed a dataset consisting of 139 high resolution (4,548 × 7,548 pixels) pathological images, comprising 71 normal, 33 low grade, and 35 high grade. After the same preprocessing steps of the above BC dataset, our final CRC dataset includes 45,660 image patches: 6,716 normal, 4,348 low grade, and 4,239 high grade.

Nuclei Segmentation Dataset. Neeraj Kumar et al. [14] published a well-labeled nucleus segmentation dataset. This dataset of HE-stained pathological images including 21,623 annotated nuclear boundaries. Because this released dataset is collected from different hospitals and includes a diversity of nuclear appearances from several cancers, disease states, and organs, the model trained based on it is likely to generalize well on other HE-stained pathological images.

3.2 Classification Results

We have compared not only with the state-of-the-art methods, but also with the classic CNN: ResNet50 and Xception. After the classic CNN gets the classification results of small image patches, the majority voting (MV) is used as the decision fusion method for whole image classification. To focus on verifying the classification effect of the DFNet on general pathological images, we control the variables to reduce the influence of the decision fusion method. Therefore, we use the simplest majority voting (MV) method to fuse the results of image patches to obtain the final result of the whole pathological image. For the 4-class BC classification, based on the dataset published by Yan et al. [12], our framework achieved average accuracy of 92.0%. For the 3-class CRC grading, based on the dataset published by Awan et al. [13], our framework achieved average accuracy of 94.83%. Our proposed framework refers to: patch-wise method (DFNet with Xception backbone) + image-wise method (MV). The performance of our proposed framework is shown in Table 1.

For the 4-class BC classification, even with such a simple decision fusion method, we still achieved higher classification accuracy (92.0%) than the state-of-the-art method proposed by Yan et al. [12]. Yan's method integrated the advantages of convolutional and recurrent neural networks to preserve the short-distance and long-distance spatial relationship between patches and achieved an image-wise classification accuracy of 91.3%. In order to control variables, our proposed framework uses the simplest MV method in the image-wise decision fusion part. Although the MV method is not as effective as Yan's method in processing high-resolution pathological images, our overall classification accuracy is still higher than Yan's method.

For the 3-class CRC grading, the state-of-the-art method is proposed by Shaban et al. [15], which incorporates large contextual regions and aggregates information via patch-based feature-cubes. It achieved average accuracy of 95.70%. Since the image resolution is too high (4,608 × 7,680), the contextual information of the image will be very important. However, only using the simplest MV as the image-wise method, our proposed framework still achieved a classification accuracy (94.83%) almost close to that of Shaban et al. [15]. This further illustrates that our DFNet has a stronger learning ability of feature representation.

Finally, the overall patch-wise classification performance of DFNet is demonstrated by the confusion matrix and ROC curve. The confusion matrix of the predictions is presented in Fig. 4a and b on test set. And Fig. 4c and d show the AUC based on ROC analysis. Both BC and CRC datasets are randomly split into training, validation and testing sets with an 8:1:1 ratio.

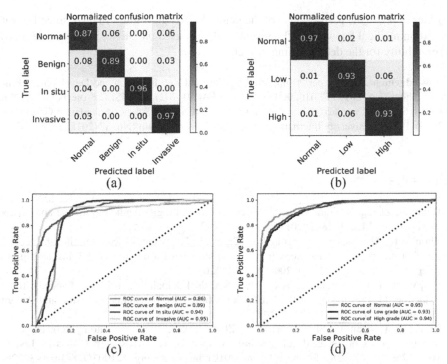

Fig. 4. Visualization of normalized confusion matrix and ROC curve. Figure 4a and 4c are the test results on the breast cancer dataset; Fig. 4b and 4d are the test results on the colorectal cancer grading dataset.

Table 1. Comparison of accuracy with previous methods and the classic CNN.

Methods (BC)	Accuracy (%)	Methods (CRC)	Accuracy (%)
Vang et al. [16]	87.5	Awan et al. [13]	90.66
Golatkar et al. [17]	85.0	Korsuk et al. [18]	89.96
Yan et al. [12]	*91.3*	Shaban et al. [15]	**95.70**
ResNet50 [19] + MV	84.9	ResNet50 [19] + MV	92.08
Xception [9] + MV	85.7	Xception [9] + MV	92.09
Our proposed	**92.0**	Our proposed	*94.83*

4 Conclusions

In this paper, to leverage medical staining knowledge, we proposed a decomposition-and-fusion network for HE stained pathological image classification. Through extensive assessments and comparisons on different pathological image dataset, it was shown that our framework achieved competitive classification results. In general, the DFNet provides a new way of exploiting the embedding of medical knowledge into the algorithm to further improve the performance of the general CNN algorithm. In turn, since DFNet is based on medical knowledge, the visual analysis based on DFNet may provide more interpretability for the deep learning model.

Acknowledgement. This paper is supported by National Key Research and Development Program of China (No. 2017YFE0103900 and 2017YFA0504702), the NSFC projects Grant (No. 61932018, 62072441 and 62072280), Beijing Municipal Natural Science Foundation Grant (No. L182053), Peking University International Hospital Research Grant (No. YN2018ZD05).

References

1. Deng, S., Zhang, X., Yan, W., et al.: Deep learning in digital pathology image analysis: a survey. Front. Med. 1–18 (2020)
2. Zhou, S.K., Greenspan, H., Davatzikos, C., et al.: A review of deep learning in medical imaging: image traits, technology trends, case studies with progress highlights, and future promises. arXiv preprint arXiv:2008.09104 (2020)
3. Lin, W.-A., Liao, H., Peng, C., et al.: DudoNet: dual domain network for CT metal artifact reduction. In: Proceedings of the IEEE/CVF Conference on Computer Vision and Pattern Recognition, pp. 10512–10521 (2019)
4. Li, Z., Li, H., Han, H., Shi, G., Wang, J., Zhou, S.: Encoding CT anatomy knowledge for unpaired chest x-ray image decomposition. In: Shen, D., et al. (eds.) MICCAI 2019. LNCS, vol. 11769, pp. 275–283. Springer, Cham (2019). https://doi.org/10.1007/978-3-030-32226-7_31
5. Gozes, O., Greenspan, H.: Lung structures enhancement in chest radiographs via CT based FCNN training. In: Stoyanov, D., et al. (eds.) RAMBO/BIA/TIA -2018. LNCS, vol. 11040, pp. 147–158. Springer, Cham (2018). https://doi.org/10.1007/978-3-030-00946-5_16
6. Hayakawa, T., Prasath, V.S., Kawanaka, H., et al.: Computational nuclei segmentation methods in digital pathology: a survey. Arch. Comput. Methods Eng. 1–13 (2019)
7. Litjens, G., Kooi, T., Bejnordi, B.E., et al.: A survey on deep learning in medical image analysis. Med. Image Anal. **42**(9), 60–88 (2017)
8. Chen, L.-C., Zhu, Y., Papandreou, G., Schroff, F., Adam, H.: Encoder-decoder with atrous separable convolution for semantic image segmentation. In: Ferrari, V., Hebert, M., Sminchisescu, C., Weiss, Y. (eds.) ECCV 2018. LNCS, vol. 11211, pp. 833–851. Springer, Cham (2018). https://doi.org/10.1007/978-3-030-01234-2_49
9. Chollet, F.: Xception: deep learning with depthwise separable convolutions. In: Proceedings of the IEEE Conference on Computer Vision and Pattern Recognition, pp. 1251–1258 (2017)
10. Szegedy, C., Vanhoucke, V., Ioffe, S., et al.: Rethinking the inception architecture for computer vision, 2818–2826 (2015)
11. Lin, M., Chen, Q., Yan, S.: Network in network. arXiv preprint arXiv:1312.4400 (2013)
12. Yan, R., Ren, F., Wang, Z., et al.: Breast cancer histopathological image classification using a hybrid deep neural network. Methods **173**, 52–60 (2020)
13. Awan, R., Sirinukunwattana, K., Epstein, D., et al.: Glandular morphometrics for objective grading of colorectal adenocarcinoma histology images. Sci. Rep. **7**(1), 1–12 (2017)
14. Kumar, N., Verma, R., Sharma, S., et al.: A dataset and a technique for generalized nuclear segmentation for computational pathology. IEEE Trans. Med. Imaging **36**(7), 1550–1560 (2017)
15. Shaban, M., Awan, R., Fraz, M.M., et al.: Context-aware convolutional neural network for grading of colorectal cancer histology images. IEEE Trans. Med. Imaging 2395–2405 (2020)

16. Vang, Y.S., Chen, Z., Xie, X.: Deep learning framework for multi-class breast cancer histology image classification. In: International Conference Image Analysis and Recognition, pp. 914–922 (2018)
17. Golatkar, A., Anand, D., Sethi, A.: Classification of breast cancer histology using deep learning. In: Campilho, A., Karray, F., ter Haar Romeny, B. (eds.) ICIAR 2018. LNCS, vol. 10882, pp. 837–844. Springer, Cham (2018). https://doi.org/10.1007/978-3-319-93000-8_95
18. Sirinukunwattana, K., Alham, N.K., Verrill, C., Rittscher, J.: Improving whole slide segmentation through visual context - a systematic study. In: Frangi, A.F., Schnabel, J.A., Davatzikos, C., Alberola-López, C., Fichtinger, G. (eds.) MICCAI 2018. LNCS, vol. 11071, pp. 192–200. Springer, Cham (2018). https://doi.org/10.1007/978-3-030-00934-2_22
19. He, K., Zhang, X., Ren, S., et al.: Deep residual learning for image recognition. In: Proceedings of the IEEE Conference on Computer Vision and Pattern Recognition, pp. 770–778 (2016)

Complex Diseases Informatics

A Novel Approach for Predicting Microbe-Disease Associations by Structural Perturbation Method

Yue Liu and Shu-Lin Wang[✉]

College of Computer Science and Electronics Engineering, Hunan University,
Changsha 410082, Hunan, China

Abstract. Recently, the development of sequencing technology has enabled researchers to explore the pathogenesis of human diseases from the perspective of microbes. Facts proved that microbes have important implications for disease prevention and diagnosis. Clinical trials consume a lot of manpower to explore a large number of microbe-disease associations. And, this knowledge in this field is very limited. Therefore, there is an urgent need for effective calculation methods to predict the associations between microbes and diseases. Here, we proposed a new approach for prediction of human microbe-disease associations. In this work, we constructed a bi-layer network by integrating the microbe-disease network, the microbial similarity network and the disease similarity network. Based on the bi-layer network, a derivative algorithm, called structural perturbation method (SPM), was applied to predict potential associations between microbes and diseases. In addition, 5-fold cross-validation was used to measure the performance of our model. Our method achieved reliable results with AUC (area under receiver operating characteristic curve) of 0.9203 ± 0.0034, significantly higher than the existing state-of-the-art methods. At last, for the case studies of asthma, all of predicted microbes in the top 10 have been confirmed by previously published literature, respectively. In short, our method can be considered as an effective model for predicting the relationship between microbes and diseases.

Keywords: Microbe · Disease · Microbe-disease similarity · Bi-layer network · Structural perturbation

1 Introduction

Microbe is a small individual such as bacteria, viruses, and some small primitive organisms, closely related to humans [1]. Microbes are everywhere, and they can be parasitized in many places including the human body. Such as, skin [2], digestive tract [3] and oral [4]. On the one hand, these microbes are beneficial to the human body. For example, the gut microbiome promotes nutrition and energy harvest by fermenting food components that cannot be digested by the host [5]. In addition, microbes can help develop the immune system [6], maintain homeostasis [7], and prevent pathogens [8]. On the other hand, some microbes also do harm to the human body. The researchers found that

© Springer Nature Switzerland AG 2021
D.-S. Huang et al. (Eds.): ICIC 2021, LNAI 12838, pp. 211–221, 2021.
https://doi.org/10.1007/978-3-030-84532-2_19

the distribution density of microbes is related to several human diseases. For example, low microbial diversity can lead to obesity [9] and enteritis [10], while high microbial diversity is associated with bacterial vaginosis [2, 11]. Therefore, researchers need to fully understand the relationship between microbes and diseases, which is not only conducive to the prevention and diagnosis of human diseases, but also helps to further understand the pathogenesis of the disease. Therefore, there is an urgent need for effective calculation methods to predict the relationship between microbes and diseases [12, 13].

Taking into account the medical value of microbes, some large-scale sequencing projects are trying to explore the relationship between microbes and human diseases, such as the Human Microbiome Group (HMP) [14] and the Earth Microbiome Group Project (EMP) [15]. Similarly, based on existing literature collections, the Human Microbe Disease Association Database called HMDAD [16] is considered as the basic tool for predicting microbe-disease associations. It integrates 483 microbe-disease relationship items. Based on this database, Chen et al. proposed that KATZHMDA (KATZ measure for Human Microbe–Disease Association) infers potential disease-associated microbes by integrating walks of different lengths in the heterogeneous network [17]. Huang et al. introduced PBHMDA (Path-Based Human Microbe–Disease Association) to obtain the predictive scores of each candidate microbe-disease pair by evaluating all paths between microbes and diseases [18]. Wen et al. developed the Human Microbe-Disease Association Predictive Network Consensus Projection Model (NCPHMDA) to predict potential microbial-disease associations [19]. In addition, some efficient prediction methods are proposed [20, 21].

In this article, our new method SPMMDA (Structural Perturbation Method Microbe-Disease Associations) was based on known microbe-disease associations, using a Gaussian interaction profile kernel similarity measure to calculate microbial similarity and disease similarity, and constructing a bi-layer network. Based on the known relationship between disease and microbe, a structural perturbation model was utilized to simultaneously identify potential microbe-disease associations. Then, 5-fold cross validation was used to evaluate the performance of our model. It reached the reliable AUC(area under receiver operating characteristic curve) of 0.9203 ± 0.0034, which is higher than KATZHMDA, NCPHMDA and PBHMDA. In addition, asthma disease was considered as independent case studies. All of predicted microbes were confirmed by recent experiments, respectively. In conclusion, SPMMDA can be considered as an effective tool for predicting potential microbe-disease associations.

2   Material and Methods

2.1   Datasets

The database explored in this work was downloaded from the human microbe–disease association database (HMDAD, http://www.cuilab.cn/hmdad) [16]. It integrated 483 high-quality microbe-disease entries, mainly from the 16S RNA sequencing of the microbial literature collection. After removing the duplicate association records, 450 distinct microbe-disease associations were finally obtained, including 292 microbes and 39 diseases. We used these data to construct microbe-disease adjacency matrix

$Y \in R^{292 \times 39}$ (where $Y_{ij} = 1$ if microbe m_i has a known association with disease d_j, otherwise $Y_{ij} = 0$). Two variables n_m and n_d denoted the numbers of microbe and disease in this study, respectively.

2.2 Methods Overview

The SPMMDA method will be introduced in details which mainly consists of the following three steps shown in Fig. 1. Firstly, calculating disease semantic similarity and microbe Cosine similarity. Secondly, constructing a bi-layer network of microbe and diseases. Finally, we use the structural perturbation method to find the perturbation matrix of the bi-layer network.

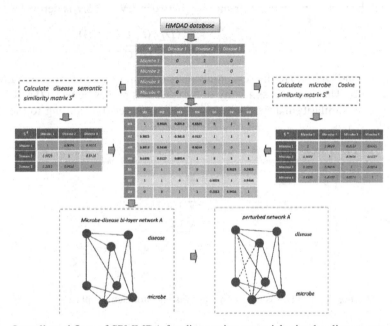

Fig. 1. Overall workflow of SPMMDA for discovering potential microbe-disease associations.

to diseases,

2.3 Disease Similarity Measure

There are many existing methods to calculate the similarity, and the accuracy will be improved based on the existing dataset and the calculation of semantic similarity [22]. Directed acyclic graph (DAG) is a typical structure that represents the characteristics of diseases, and its nodes represent the related annotations of diseases. Figure 2 shows the DAGs of two diseases "Stomach Neoplasms (SN)" and "Liver Neoplasms (LN)". The DAG of LN is denoted as $DAG(LN) = (T_{LN}, E_{LN})$, where T_{LN} is a set that includes all the ancestor nodes of LN and LN node itself, and E_{LN} is a set of edges connecting these nodes. Each node t $(t \in T_{LN})$ has its semantic contribution score, which is defined by

$$D_{LN}(t) = \begin{cases} 1 & if\ t = LN \\ max\{\beta * D_{LN}(t')|t' \in children\ of\ t\} & otherwise \end{cases} \quad (1)$$

Here, β is an semantic contribution adjustment factor for the edges linking node t with its child t'. β is set to 0.5. The overall semantic value of disease LN, $DV(LN)$, is defined as

$$DV(LN) = \sum_{t \in T_{LN}} D_{LN}(t) \quad (2)$$

If the two diseases have more common nodes in DAG, the similarity between the two diseases will be higher, the semantic similarity between LN and SN is defined as

$$DS(LN, SN) = \frac{\sum_{t \in T_{LN} \cap T_{SN}} (D_{LN}(t) + D_{SN}(t))}{DV(LN) + DV(SN)} \quad (3)$$

where $D_{LN}(t)$ and $D_{SN}(t)$ are the semantic values of term t related to diseases LN and SN, respectively. The semantic similarity of two diseases ranges between 0 and 1.

The disease similarity matrix $S^d \in R^{39 \times 39}$ is constructed according to the above formula (3).

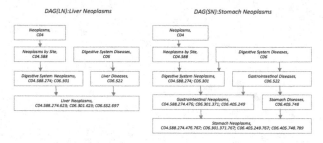

Fig. 2. The DAGs of liver neoplasms and stomach neoplasms.

2.4 Microbe Similarity Measure

In the microbe-microbe similarity network, there are 292 nodes representing the microbes. The value of the edge between two nodes is the similarity of the two microbes. We utilized the Cosine similarity measurement to calculate microbe similarity with the known microbe-disease associations.

The similarity of two microbes m_i and m_j was calculated by Cosine similarity as

$$MS(m_i, m_j) = \cos(\overline{DS(m_i)}, \overline{DS(m_j)}) \quad (4)$$

It can be tanslated to

$$MS(m_i, m_j) = \frac{\overline{DS(m_i)} \cdot \overline{DS(m_j)}}{|\overline{DS(m_i)}||\overline{DS(m_j)}|} \quad (5)$$

Where

$$DS(m_i) = [D_1(m_i), \ldots, D_j(m_i), \ldots, D_{N_d}(m_i)] \tag{6}$$

N_d is the number of disease. $DS(m_i)$ denoted the associations of microbe i with all the diseases.

The microbial similarity matrix $S^m \in R^{292 \times 292}$ is constructed according to the above formula (5).

2.5 Construction of Bi-layer Network

The original microbe-disease association matrix $Y \in R^{292 \times 39}$ (where $Y_{ij} = 1$ if microbe m_i has a observed association with disease d_j, otherwise $Y_{ij} = 0$) represent the microbe-disease network. The matrix $S^m \in R^{292 \times 292}$ represent the microbial similarity network and $S^d \in R^{39 \times 39}$ represent the disease similarity network. By integrating these three networks, we can get a bi-layer network G as shown in Fig. 3. A bi-layer microbe-disease associations network can be represented as an adjacency matrix $A_{N \times N}$.

$$A = \begin{bmatrix} S^m & Y \\ Y^T & S^d \end{bmatrix} \tag{7}$$

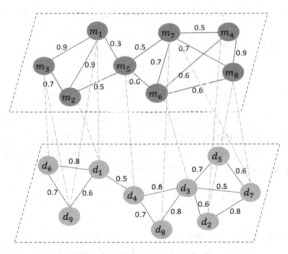

Fig. 3. Bi-layer network G.

2.6 Structural Perturbation Model

The microbe disease association network is represented by $G(N, E, W)$, where N is a set containing all nodes, E is an edge set, and W is a weight set. We randomly select a fraction of the links and the nodes to constitute the perturbation set ΔE, while the rest of the links is $E^R (E^R = E - \Delta E)$. ΔA and A^R represent their corresponding adjacency matrices; obviously, $A = A^R + \Delta A$.

A^R is a real symmetric matrix and it is diagonalizable. A^R can be represented as:

$$P^{-1} A^R P = \Lambda. \tag{8}$$

The columns of the P are the eigenvectors of the A^R, and the values on the main diagonal of Λ are the eigenvalues of the A^R. Then, Eq. (8) can be transformed into:

$$A^R = \sum_{k=1}^{N} \lambda_k x_k x_k^T \tag{9}$$

where λ_k and x_k are the eigenvalue and the corresponding orthogonal and normalized eigenvector for A^R, respectively.

We consider the set ΔE as a perturbation to the network A^R and construct the perturbed matrix by first-order approximation. First-order approximation allows the eigenvalue to change but keep the eigenvector constant. After perturbation, the eigenvalue λ_k is corrected to be $\lambda_k + \Delta \lambda_k$ and its corresponding eigenvector is corrected to be $x_k + \Delta x_k$. Left-multiplying the eigenfunction:

$$(A^R + \Delta A)(x_k + \Delta x_k) = (\lambda_k + \Delta \lambda_k)(x_k + \Delta x_k) \tag{10}$$

By x_k^T and neglecting second-order terms $x_k^T \Delta A \Delta x_k$ and $\Delta \lambda_k x_k^T \Delta x_k$, we obtain:

$$x_k^T A^R (x_k + \Delta x_k) + x_k^T \Delta A x_k = \lambda_k x_k^T (x_k + \Delta x_k) + \Delta \lambda_k x_k^T x_k \tag{11}$$

Since $x_k^T A^R = \lambda_k x_k^T$, we obtain:

$$\Delta \lambda_k \approx \frac{x_k^T \Delta A x_k}{x_k^T x_k} \tag{12}$$

This formula reminds us of the expected value of the first-order perturbation Hamiltonian in quantum mechanics. Perturbation theory includes mathematical methods for finding approximate solutions to problems. In the case of keeping the eigenvector unchanged, the perturbation matrix can be obtained by using the perturbation eigenvalues:

$$A' = \sum_{k=1}^{N} (\lambda_k + \Delta \lambda_k) x_k x_k^T \tag{13}$$

A is the input matrix of SPM model, and A' is the final result matrix. We average the set of t independent perturbations to get a. A' where the elements represent the score of association between microbes and diseases represented by the row and column [23].

3   Results

3.1   Model Design

Lu used structural perturbation on undirected networks. Different from his experiments, we use structural perturbation on a weighted bi-layer network. The association in HMDAD is first processed into a matrix. Using this matrix as input, Gaussian kernel similarity is calculated for disease and microbes, and expressed as a matrix. A bi-layer weighted network is constructed according to the formula (7). Based on this bi-layer network, SPMMDA was developed to calculate the predicted score for each candidate disease-microbe pair. Finally, the prediction results of each disease are sorted in descending order, and the higher ranking microbe is more related to this disease. In addition, the experiment shows that the number of perturbations is $t = 5$, which provides the best performance. Figure 4 shows the change in AUC values as t increase.

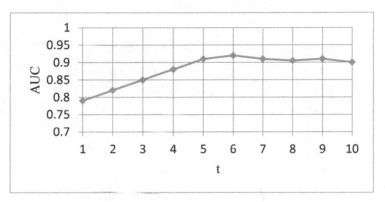

Fig. 4. AUC values versus parameter t

3.2 Performance Evaluation

To evaluate the performance of our model, we used leave-one-out cross validation (LOOCV) and 5-fold cross validation (5-fold CV). In the framework of 5-fold CV, 450 known relational samples were randomly divided into five groups. For each trial, one group was used as the test set and the other four groups were used as the training set [24]. LOOCV was implemented on the known verified microbe-disease association pairs, each of which was left out in turns to be a test sample when others were used for training model. Moreover, to reduce the chance of data partitioning, we conducted 100 trials. Our result was the average of these 100 trials.

The ROC curve was plotted by setting different thresholds. The abscissa of the ROC curve is 1-specificity (FPR), and the ordinate is sensitivity (TPR). Sensitivity represents the percentage of test samples ranked above a given threshold, while specificity indicates the opposite. The ROC curve is obtained, and the AUC value can be calculated accordingly. If AUC = 1 indicates perfect performance, AUC = 0.5 indicates random performance [25]. As a result, our model obtained the high AUCs of 0.9203 ± 0.0034 and 0.9163 ± 0.0029 in the frameworks of 5-fold CV and LOOCV.

3.3 Compared with Other the-State-of-Art Methods

It is known that KATZHMDA [17], NCPHMDA [19] and PBHMDA [18] are the state-of-the-art methods for predicting the similarity of microbes and diseases. These methods also used HMDAD to calculate the microbe similarity and disease similarity. Then build a two-layer similarity network. We put the code of these methods into the same folder, call them with a main function, and draw the ROC curve of each method in the same coordinate system. Figure 5 shows the ROC curves for these methods. Their AUC are 0.8301, 0.8918 and 0.9082 respectively. The results show that our SPMMDA is better than other methods.

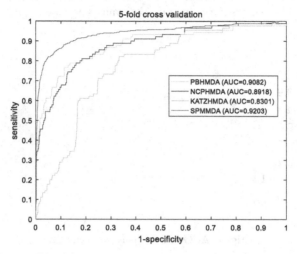

Fig. 5. The ROC curves for the four methods.

3.4 Case Studies

In order to further test the ability of the model to detect disease-related microbes, we conducted case studies on asthma. The specific process is to use our model to predict the original relationship matrix, then remove all the known correlations from the results of three diseases, and finally rank the prediction scores of each disease. According to ranking, the top ten microbes were listed separately. Finally, we searched the literature to find out whether the ten microbes were related to the disease.

Asthma is a relatively common allergic disease. As an indicator of early asthma, Bacteroides (1th in the prediction list) colonization can determine whether children may have asthma in the future [26]. It has been reported that Pseudomonas (2nd in the prediction list) can induce asthma. In addition, in mice, Lactobacillus (3th in the prediction list) can induce asthma attack by inhibiting ovalbumin. Although it is not a human trial, this finding may provide a perspective for understanding the potential preventive effect of asthma [27]. The top 10 candidate microbes of asthma obtained by our method are also listed in Table 1, all of them have been confirmed by the existing literature.

Table. 1. Effect in the case study of asthma, all of top-10 predicted microbes have been supported by literature evidences.

Rank	Microbes	Evidence
1	*Bacteroides*	PMID:18822123
2	*Pseudomonas*	PMID:13268970
3	*Lactobacillus*	PMID:20592920
4	*Fusobacterium*	[28]
5	*Veillonella*	PMID: 25329665
6	*Lachnospiraceae*	PMID:20592920
7	*Propionibacterium*	PMID:27433177
8	*Propionibacterium acnes*	PMID: 27433177
9	*Streptococcus*	PMID:17950502
10	*Bacteroidaceae*	PMID:28968779

4 Conclusion

A large number of studies have shown that microbes have a particularly important relationship with human health and disease. The exploration of the relationship between diseases and microbes is not only conducive to the prevention and diagnosis of human diseases, but also helps to further understand the pathogenesis of the disease. However, few people are committed to this work. Therefore, we proposed a new method called SPMDMA based on HMDAD database to predict the relationship between them. SPMDMA uses the Gaussian interaction profile nuclear similarity to measure the disease-disease similarity and microbe-microbe similarity. And, a structural perturbation method was utilized to simultaneously identify potential microbe-disease associations. In addition, 5-fold cross validation was used to measure the performance of our method. SPMDMA achieved a 0.9203 AUC in five-fold cross validation, which fully demonstrated the feasibility of our approach. Finally, we conducted separate study on asthma. Among the top ten predicted microbes of the asthma disease, all of species were confirmed by previously published literature. We hope our method can be a good method for further clinical research.

The key factors that make our method feasible are summarized below. First, the HMDAD database provides a reliable microbe-disease association as a basic information resource. Secondly, the use of Gaussian interaction profile nuclear similarity to accurately measure microbial similarity and disease similarity. Last but not least, the use of structural perturbation model makes prediction results are satisfactory.

Of course, there are some limitations inhibiting the performance of SPMMDA. First, microbe-disease associations collected from the database is very sparse. However, we believe that with the in-depth research in this area, the database will be further improved to support more exploration. Second, the Gaussian interaction profile nuclear similarity is extremely dependent on the known microbe-disease associations. The solution to this problem is to integrate databases from different sources. Finally, our methods cannot work well for the new microbes without known associated diseases and new diseases without known associated microbes.

Acknowledgement. This work was supported by the grants of the National Science Foundation of China (Grant Nos. 61672011 and 61472467) and the National Key R&D Program of China (2017YFC1311003).

References

1. Methé, B.A., et al.: A framework for human microbiome research. Nature **486**(7402), 215–221 (2012). https://doi.org/10.1038/nature11209
2. Fredricks, D.N.: Microbial ecology of human skin in health and disease. J. Investig. Dermatol. Symp. Proc. **6**(3), 167–169 (2001). https://doi.org/10.1046/j.0022-202x.2001.00039.x
3. Grenham, S., Clarke, G., Cryan, J.F., Dinan, T.G.: Brain-gut-microbe communication in health and disease. Front. Physiol. (2011). https://doi.org/10.3389/fphys.2011.00094
4. Handfield, M., Baker, H.V., Lamont, R.J.: Beyond good and evil in the oral cavity: insights into host-microbe relationships derived from transcriptional profiling of gingival cells. J. Dent. Res. **87**(3), 203–223 (2008). https://doi.org/10.1177/154405910808700302
5. Kau, A.L., Ahern, P.P., Griffin, N.W., Goodman, A.L., Gordon, J.I.: Human nutrition, the gut microbiome and the immune system. Nature (2011). https://doi.org/10.1038/nature10213
6. Gollwitzer, E.S., et al.: Lung microbiota promotes tolerance to allergens in neonates via PD-L1. Nat. Med. **20**(6), 642–647 (2014). https://doi.org/10.1038/nm.3568
7. Bouskra, D., et al.: Lymphoid tissue genesis induced by commensals through NOD1 regulates intestinal homeostasis. Nature **456**(7221), 507–510 (2008). https://doi.org/10.1038/nature07450
8. Kreth, J., Zhang, Y., Herzberg, M.C.: Streptococcal antagonism in oral biofilms: streptococcus sanguinis and streptococcus gordonii interference with streptococcus mutans. J. Bacteriol. **190**(13), 4632–4640 (2008). https://doi.org/10.1128/JB.00276-08
9. Turnbaugh, P.J., et al.: A core gut microbiome in obese and lean twins. Nature **457**(7228), 480–484 (2009). https://doi.org/10.1038/nature07540
10. Qin, J., et al.: A human gut microbial gene catalogue established by metagenomic sequencing. Nature **464**(7285), 59–65 (2010). https://doi.org/10.1038/nature08821
11. Fredricks, D.N., Fiedler, T.L., Marrazzo, J.M.: Molecular identification of bacteria associated with bacterial vaginosis. N. Engl. J. Med. (2005). https://doi.org/10.1056/nejmoa043802
12. Zhao, Y., Wang, C.-C., Chen, X.: Microbes and complex diseases: from experimental results to computational models. Brief. Bioinform. (2020). https://doi.org/10.1093/bib/bbaa158
13. Chen, X., Liu, H., Zhao, Q.: Editorial: bioinformatics in microbiota. Front. Microbiol. **11** (2020). https://doi.org/10.3389/fmicb.2020.00100
14. Althani, A.A., et al.: Human Microbiome and its association with health and diseases. J. Cell. Physiol. **231**(8), 1688–1694 (2016). https://doi.org/10.1002/jcp.25284
15. Gilbert, J.A., Jansson, J.K., Knight, R.: The earth microbiome project: successes and aspirations. BMC Biol. **12**(1), 69 (2014). https://doi.org/10.1186/s12915-014-0069-1
16. Ma, W., et al.: An analysis of human microbe–disease associations. Brief. Bioinform. **18**(1), 85–97 (2017). https://doi.org/10.1093/bib/bbw005
17. Chen, X., Huang, Y.-A., You, Z.-H., Yan, G.-Y., Wang, X.-S.: A novel approach based on KATZ measure to predict associations of human microbiota with non-infectious diseases. Bioinformatics **33**(5), 733–739 (2017). https://doi.org/10.1093/bioinformatics/btw715

18. Huang, Z.-A., et al.: PBHMDA: path-based human microbe-disease association prediction. Front. Microbiol. **8** (2017). https://doi.org/10.3389/fmicb.2017.00233
19. Bao, W., Jiang, Z., Huang, D.S.: Novel human microbe-disease association prediction using network consistency projection. BMC Bioinf. (2017). https://doi.org/10.1186/s12859-017-1968-2
20. Huang, Y.-A., You, Z.-H., Chen, X., Huang, Z.-A., Zhang, S., Yan, G.-Y.: Prediction of microbe–disease association from the integration of neighbor and graph with collaborative recommendation model. J. Transl. Med. **15**(1), 209 (2017). https://doi.org/10.1186/s12967-017-1304-7
21. Wang, F., et al.: LRLSHMDA: laplacian regularized least squares for human microbe-disease association prediction. Sci. Rep. **7**(1), 7601 (2017). https://doi.org/10.1038/s41598-017-08127-2
22. Wang, D., Wang, J., Lu, M., Song, F., Cui, Q.: Inferring the human microRNA functional similarity and functional network based on microRNA-associated diseases. Bioinformatics **26**(13), 1644–1650 (2010). https://doi.org/10.1093/bioinformatics/btq241
23. Lü, L., Pan, L., Zhou, T., Zhang, Y.-C., Stanley, H.E.: Toward link predictability of complex networks. Proc. Natl. Acad. Sci. **112**(8), 2325–2330 (2015). https://doi.org/10.1073/pnas.1424644112
24. Zou, Q., Li, J., Wang, C., Zeng, X.: Approaches for recognizing disease genes based on network. Biomed Res. Int. **2014**, 1 (2014). https://doi.org/10.1155/2014/416323
25. Sun, D., Li, A., Feng, H., Wang, M.: NTSMDA: Prediction of miRNA-disease associations by integrating network topological similarity. Mol. Biosyst. (2016). https://doi.org/10.1039/c6mb00049e
26. Vael, C., Nelen, V., Verhulst, S.L., Goossens, H., Desager, K.N.: Early intestinal Bacteroides fragilis colonisation and development of asthma. BMC Pulm. Med. **8**(1), 19 (2008). https://doi.org/10.1186/1471-2466-8-19
27. Yu, J., et al.: "The effects of Lactobacillus rhamnosus on the prevention of asthma in a murine model", allergy. Asthma Immunol. Res. **2**(3), 199 (2010). https://doi.org/10.4168/aair.2010.2.3.199
28. Dang, H.T., ah Kim, S., Park, H.K., Shin, J.W., Park, S.-G., Kim, W.: Analysis of oropharyngeal microbiota between the patients with bronchial asthma and the non-asthmatic persons. J. Bacteriol. Virol. **43**(4), 270 (2013). https://doi.org/10.4167/jbv.2013.43.4.270
29. Xiao, Q., Luo, J., Liang, C., Cai, J., Ding, P.: A graph regularized non-negative matrix factorization method for identifying microRNA-disease associations. Bioinformatics **34**(2), 239–248 (2018). https://doi.org/10.1093/bioinformatics/btx545

A Reinforcement Learning-Based Model for Human MicroRNA-Disease Association Prediction

Linqian Cui, You Lu$^{(\boxtimes)}$, Qiming Fu$^{(\boxtimes)}$, Jiacheng Sun, Xiao Xu, Yijie Ding, and Hongjie Wu

School of Electronic and Information Engineering, Suzhou University of Science and Technology, Suzhou 215009, China
luyou@usts.edu.cn

Abstract. MicroRNA (miRNA) is involved in many life processes and is closely associate with complex diseases such as cancer. Therefore, predicting the association between miRNA and disease has become a research hotspot. The bioinformatics method has great advantages, it is efficient, fast and less expensive. We have developed a reinforcement learning-Based model for Human microRNA-disease association prediction. This model puts three sub-method models CMF, NRLMF and LapRLS into the Q-learning model of reinforcement learning. We can get an optimal weight value. On the benchmark data set, the results of our method are comparable and even better than existing models.

Keywords: Human microRNA-disease association · Q-learning · Collaborative matrix factorization · Neighborhood regularized logistic matrix factorization · Laplacian regularized least squares

1 Introduction

A lot of evidence shows that microRNA is involved in many life processes of organisms and it is closely associated to human complex diseases such as cancer. The bioinformatics method predicts the association between miRNA and disease by using a certain algorithm. Predecessors have proposed some calculation methods to predict the miRNA-disease association. For example, Jiang et al. [1, 3] used microRNA-target data and phenotypic similarity data to extract features, it achieved good prediction results. Xuan et al. [2] developed a prediction method HMDP based on weighted K most similar neighbors to predict potential miRNA-disease association. Subsequently, Chen et al. [3] proposed the RWRMDA calculation model. They used a random walk algorithm to spread miRNA on the network.

We developed a miRNA-disease association prediction model based on reinforcement learning. We put the three sub-method models CMF [4], NRLMF [5], and LapRLS [6] into Q-learning for learning, Comparing our model with other models.

© Springer Nature Switzerland AG 2021
D.-S. Huang et al. (Eds.): ICIC 2021, LNAI 12838, pp. 222–230, 2021.
https://doi.org/10.1007/978-3-030-84532-2_20

2 Materials and Methods

2.1 Human miRNA-Disease Associations

The HMDD database (http://www.cuilab.cn/hmdd) contains important data for the studying human microRNAs and diseases. The HMDD database collected 5430 miRNA-disease associations, involving 383 diseases and 495 miRNAs.

2.2 miRNA Functional Similarity

Under the assumption that miRNAs with similar functions are more likely to be associated with similar diseases, Wang et al. [7] calculated miRNA functional similarity score (http://www.cuilab.cn/files/images/cuilab/misim.zip).

2.3 Disease Semantic Similarity

The data for calculating the semantic similarity of diseases is obtained through the Mesh database (http://www.ncbi.nlm.nih.gov/). Based on disease DAG, the semantic value contribution of the required disease term t to the disease $d(i)$ and the semantic value of the disease $d(i)$ itself can be calculated [19–22]. The formula used is as follows:

$$D_{d(i)}(t) = \begin{cases} 1 & if\ t = d(i) \\ max\{\Delta * D_{d(i)}(t')|t' \in chidren\ of\ t\} & if\ t \neq d(i) \end{cases} \quad (1)$$

$$DV(d(i)) = \sum_{t \in T_{d(i)}} D_{d(i)}(t) \quad (2)$$

The semantic similarity of diseases is calculated by the following equation:

$$K_{d,sem}(d(i), d(j)) = \frac{\sum_{t \in T_{d(i)} \cap T_{d(j)}}(D_{d(i)}(t) + D_{d(j)}(t))}{DV(d(i)) + DV(d(j))} \quad (3)$$

For details, please refer to the references Ding et al. [8].

2.4 Method Models

Collaborative Matrix Factorization
Collaborative matrix factorization (CMF) model [4] is easy to understand, using other data to improve prediction performance when doing relational learning tasks. These data are related to the data to be predicted. The formula of the CMF model is as follows:

$$Y \approx AB^T \quad (4)$$

$$arg\min_{A,B} \|Y - AB^T\|_F^2,$$

$$S_m \approx AA^T, S_d \approx BB^T \quad (5)$$

where $\|.\|_F$ is Frobenius norm. Finally, the matrix of predicted miRNA-disease interactions F is given as follows:

$$F = AB^T \tag{6}$$

Neighborhood Regularized Logistic Matrix Factorization

Neighborhood Regularized Logistic Matrix Factorization (NRLMF) [5], the method combines Logical Matrix Factorization (LMF) with domain regularization to predict miRNA-disease associations. The formula of the NRLMF model is as follows:

$$\min_{U,V} \sum_{i=1}^{m} \sum_{j=1}^{n} (1 + cy_{ij} - y_{ij}) ln\left[1 + exp\left(u_i v_j^T\right)\right] - cy_{ij} u_i v_j^T + \frac{1}{2} tr\left[U^T\left(\lambda_d I + \alpha L^d\right)U\right]$$
$$+ \frac{1}{2} tr\left[V^T\left(\lambda_t I + \beta L^t\right)V\right] \tag{7}$$

Where $P \in R^{m \times n}$ in which the (i, j) element is p_{ij}, using L to represent the objective function of formula (7), and the partial gradients relative to U and V are as follows:

$$\frac{\partial L}{\partial U} = PV + (c-1)(Y \odot P)V - cYV + \left(\lambda_d I + \alpha L^d\right)U \tag{8}$$

$$\frac{\partial L}{\partial V} = P^T U + (c-1)\left(Y^T \odot P^T\right)U - cY^T U + \left(\lambda_t I + \beta L^t\right)V \tag{9}$$

Laplacian Regularized Least Squares

Laplacian Regularized Least Squares (LapRLS) [6] is a semi-supervised learning method, it builds a manifold model by constructing a nearest neighbor graph, and introduces the Laplacian graph as a regularization in the least square loss function factor. Some of the formulas we will use are as follows:

$$F_d^* = \min_{F_d} J(F_d) = \|Y - F_d\|_F^2 + \beta_d Trace\left(F_d^T L_d F_d\right) \tag{10}$$

where $\|.\|_F$ is Frobenius norm and *Trace* is the trace of a matrix.

$$F_d^* = W_d \alpha_d^* \tag{11}$$

$$\alpha_d^* = (W_d + \beta_d L_d W_d)^{-1} Y,$$

$$-W_d(Y - W_d \alpha_d) + \beta_d \alpha_d^T W_d L_d W_d \alpha_d = 0 \tag{12}$$

In the end, we can get:

$$F_d^* = W_d(W_d + \beta_d L_d W_d)^{-1} Y,$$

$$F_m^* = W_m(W_m + \beta_m L_m W_m)^{-1} Y^T$$

$$F^* = \frac{F_d^* + F_m^{*T}}{2} \tag{13}$$

Reinforcement Learning

Reinforcement learning is an important branch of machine learning. It mainly contains four elements, agent, environmental state, action, and reward. The agent tries to take actions to manipulate the environment and transition from one state to the next. When it completes the task, it gives a positive reward. Otherwise, give a negative reward [9–12]. The goal of reinforcement learning is to obtain the most accumulated reward.

Q-learning is a value-based algorithm in the reinforcement learning algorithm. It uses the time difference method for off-policy learning, and uses the Bellman equation to solve the optimal strategy for the Markov process. Q is $Q(s, a)$, that is, in the state at a certain moment, taking action a can get a timely reward r, and the environment will feedback the corresponding reward according to the action of the agent. Therefore, the main idea of the algorithm is to construct state and action into a Q-table to store the Q value, and then select the action that can obtain the greatest benefit based on the Q value.

In this study, the miRNA-disease association prediction based on reinforcement learning, we divide the data set according to the ratio of 8:1:1 through five-fold cross-validation, and divide it into training set, validation set and test set. After training the three sub-models CMF, NRLMF and LapRLS on the training set, Q-learning is used to weight the model. The principle of reinforcement learning is to perform an action and get a new state and reward. In the study, the weight of each sub-model is set to the state space S, the weight change value of each sub-model is set to the action space A, and the AUC change obtained by F^* on the verification set is used as reward. If the AUC value of the new state is greater than that of the previous state, we will give a positive reward. Otherwise, a negative reward will be given. Under continuous iterative training, the three weight parameters will approach the optimal solution. The closer to the optimal solution, the greater Q value, until the Q value converges, we get the optimal weight value. Finally, we tested on the test set and we got better results. Obtained an AUC of 0.9416, The weight value is $S(0.1735, 0.2913, 0.5352)$.

The overview of our proposed method is list in Algorithm 1.

Algorithm 1.   Algorithm of proposed method

Require: Sub-method models CMF, NRLMF and LapRLS, state space S, action space A, reward value R.

Ensure :   The prediction of F^*;

1: Training three sub-method models CMF, NRLMF and LapRLS, respectively;

2: Calculating the weights of models F_1 , F_2 and F_3 by Algorithm 2, respectively;

3: Combining F_1 , F_2 , F_3 and $S(a, b, c)$ by $F^* = a * F_1 + b * F_2 + c * F_3$.

Algorithm 2.   Algorithm of Q-learning

Require: State space $S(a,b,c)$, action space $A(m,n,-m-n)$, reward value R,
discount rate γ, learn rate α.

Ensure: Prediction of $S(a,b,c)$ and $Q(s,a)$;

1.   Initialize $Q(s,a)$ arbitrarily

2.   repeat (for each episode):

3. | Initialize s

4. | repeat (for each step of episode):

5. | | choose a from s using policy derived from Q(e.g. , ε-greedy)

6. | | calculating the AUC by $F^* = a * F_1 + b * F_2 + c * F_3$

7. | | take action a, observe R, s'

8. | | $Q(s,a) \leftarrow Q(s,a) + \alpha[r + \gamma maxa'Q(s',a') - Q(s,a)]$

9. | | $s \leftarrow s'$

10. | until s is terminal

11.   until $Q(s,a)$ convergence

The flow chart of our proposed method is shown in Fig. 1.

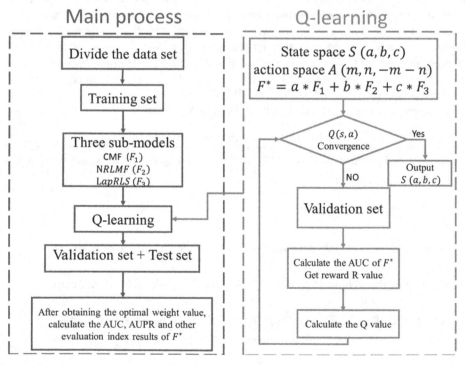

Fig. 1. Algorithm flow chart

3   Results

3.1   Evaluation Measurements

AUC (Area Under Curve) is a commonly used evaluation index for classifiers in machine learning. It is the area under the ROC curve.

AUPR is the area under the PR curve, and PR is the graph composed of the recall rate and the correct rate.

The results of our method are listed in Table 1, Fig. 2 and Fig. 3.

Table 1. The performance (AUC and AUPR) of different models under 5-CV.

Model	AUPR	AUC
Q-learning	**0.5408**	**0.9416**
Mean weighted	0.5335	0.9383
CMF	0.4923	0.9091
NRLMF	0.4834	0.9315
LapRLS	0.5307	0.9367

The best results in each column are in bold faces.

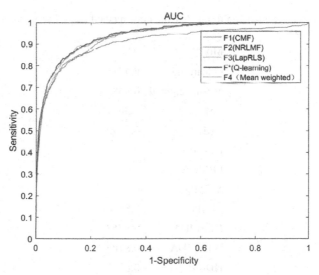

Fig. 2. The AUC of different models under 5-CV

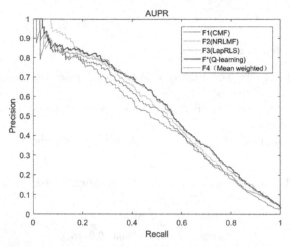

Fig. 3. The AUPR of different models under 5-CV

3.2 Comparison with Other Methods

In order to further evaluate the prediction model based on reinforcement learning, we compared our method with the existing methods [19–27]. The comparison results are listed in Table 2. The prediction model based on reinforcement learning can be cut to obtain the best prediction performance under 5-CV.

Table 2. The comparison results between our method and other eight models.

Model	AUC
Q-learning	**0.9416**
Mean weighted	0.9383
CMF	0.9091
NRLMF	0.9315
LapRLS	0.9367
PBMDA	0.9172
MCMDA	0.8767
MaxFlow	0.8579
NCPMDA	0.8763
WBSMDA	0.8185
HDMP	0.8342
RLSMDA	0.8569
LRSSLMDA	0.9181

The best results in each column are in bold faces.

4 Conclusion and Discussion

In this study, we proposed a miRNA-disease association prediction model, it based on reinforcement learning to predict miRNA-disease association. Which is trained the three sub-method models by Q-learning model of reinforcement learning, and finally obtain an optimal weight value.

In the existing calculation methods for predicting the miRNA-disease association, the combination of reinforcement learning methods has not been considered for prediction, and we have compared with the existing models on the benchmark data set. Our method is in 5-CV Has the highest predictive performance.

Acknowledgement. This paper is supported by the National Natural Science Foundation of China (62073231, 61772357, 61902272, 61876217, 61902271), National Research Project (2020YFC2006602) and Anhui Province Key Laboratory Research Project (IBBE2018KX09).

References

1. Jiang, Q., et al.: Prioritization of disease microRNAs through a human phenome-microRNAome network. BMC Syst. Biol. **4**(1), 1–9 (2010)
2. Xuan, P., et al.: Prediction of microRNAs associated with human diseases based on weighted k most similar neighbors. PLoS ONE **8**(8), e70204 (2013)
3. Chen, X., Liu, M.-X., Yan, G.-Y.: RWRMDA: predicting novel human microRNA–disease associations. Mol. BioSyst. **8**(10), 2792–2798 (2012)
4. Zheng, X., et al.: Collaborative matrix factorization with multiple similarities for predicting drug-target interactions. In: Proceedings of the 19th ACM SIGKDD International Conference on Knowledge Discovery and Data Mining (2013)
5. Liu, Y., et al.: Neighborhood regularized logistic matrix factorization for drug-target interaction prediction. PLoS Comput. Biol. **12**(2), e1004760 (2016)
6. Xia, Z., et al.: Semi-supervised drug-protein interaction prediction from heterogeneous biological spaces. BMC Syst. Biol. **4**(2) (2010). BioMed Central
7. Wang, D., et al.: Inferring the human microRNA functional similarity and functional network based on microRNA-associated diseases. Bioinformatics **26**(13), 1644–1650 (2010)
8. Ding, Y., et al.: Identification of human microRNA-disease association via hypergraph embedded bipartite local model. Comput. Biol. Chem. **89**, 107369 (2020)
9. Peng, L.-H., et al.: A computational study of potential miRNA-disease association inference based on ensemble learning and kernel ridge regression. Front. Bioeng. Biotechnol. **8** (2020)
10. Qu, Y., et al.: KATZMDA: prediction of miRNA-disease associations based on KATZ model. IEEE Access **6**, 3943–3950 (2017)
11. Zhao, Y., Chen, X., Yin, J.: Adaptive boosting-based computational model for predicting potential miRNA-disease associations. Bioinformatics **35**(22), 4730–4738 (2019)
12. Zhao, Q., et al.: Integrating bipartite network projection and KATZ measure to identify novel CircRNA-disease associations. IEEE Trans. Nanobiosci. **18**(4), 578–584 (2019)
13. Chen, X., et al.: Deep-belief network for predicting potential miRNA-disease associations. Brief. Bioinform. (2020)
14. Chen, X., Sun, L.-G., Zhao, Y.: NCMCMDA: miRNA–disease association prediction through neighborhood constraint matrix completion. Brief. Bioinform. **22**(1), 485–496 (2021)
15. Chen, X., et al.: Potential miRNA-disease association prediction based on kernelized Bayesian matrix factorization. Genomics **112**(1), 809–819 (2020)

16. Qu, J., et al.: Prediction of potential miRNA-disease associations using matrix decomposition and label propagation. Knowl. Syst. **186**, 104963 (2019)

17. Ding, Y., Tang, J., Guo, F.: Identification of drug-side effect association via multiple information integration with centered kernel alignment. Neurocomputing **325**, 211–224 (2019)

18. Ding, Y., Tang, J., Guo, F.: Identification of Drug–Target interactions via dual Laplacian regularized least squares with multiple kernel fusion. Knowl. Syst. **204**, 106254 (2020)

19. Chen, X., et al.: HGIMDA: heterogeneous graph inference for miRNA-disease association prediction. Oncotarget **7**(40), 65257 (2016)

20. Chen, X., et al.: MDHGI: matrix decomposition and heterogeneous graph Inference for miRNA-disease association prediction. PLoS Comput. Biol. **14**(8), e1006418 (2018)

21. You, Z.-H., et al.: PRMDA: personalized recommendation-based MiRNA-disease association prediction. Oncotarget **8**(49), 85568 (2017)

22. Chen, X., Wu, Q.-F., Yan, G.-Y.: RKNNMDA: ranking-based KNN for MiRNA-disease association prediction. RNA Biol. **14**(7), 952–962 (2017)

23. You, Z.-H., et al.: PBMDA: a novel and effective path-based computational model for miRNA-disease association prediction. PLoS Comput. Biol. **13**(3), e1005455 (2017)

24. Gu, C., et al.: Network consistency projection for human miRNA-disease associations inference. Sci. Rep. **6**(1), 1–10 (2016)

25. Li, J.-Q., et al.: MCMDA: matrix completion for MiRNA-disease association prediction. Oncotarget **8**(13), 21187 (2017)

26. Chen, X., Huang, L.: LRSSLMDA: Laplacian regularized sparse subspace learning for MiRNA-disease association prediction. PLoS Comput. Biol. **13**(12), e1005912 (2017)

27. Chen, X., et al.: WBSMDA: within and between score for MiRNA-disease association prediction. Sci. Rep. **6**(1), 1–9 (2016)

Delineating QSAR Descriptors to Explore the Inherent Properties of Naturally Occurring Polyphenols, Responsible for Alpha-Synuclein Amyloid Disaggregation Scheming Towards Effective Therapeutics Against Parkinson's Disorder

Chandrasekhar Gopalakrishnan[2], Caixia Xu[1], Pengyong Han[1], Rajasekaran Ramalingam[2(✉)], and Zhengwei Li[3(✉)]

[1] Changzhi Medical College, Changzhi 046000, China
[2] Bioinformatics Lab, Department of Biotechnology, School of Bio Sciences and Technology, Vellore Institute of Technology (Deemed to be University), Vellore 632014, Tamil Nadu, India
rrajasekaran@vit.ac.in
[3] School of Computer Science and Technology, China University of Mining and Technology, Xuzhou 221116, China
zwli@cumt.edu.cn

Abstract. Parkinson's is a debilitating neurodegenerative disorder, that greatly affects motor functions. It is characterized by the deposition of pathogenic amyloid form of alpha-synuclein protein, in tissues of brain, to cause its neurodegeneration. Effective therapeutics against this ruinous malady, is yet be formulated. Although, naturally occurring polyphenolic compounds have been known to exhibit disaggregation potency against alpha-synuclein aggregates, its mechanism behind disaggregation remains elusive yet. In the present study, through a robust feature selection pipeline we have elucidated the biochemical features of naturally occurring polyphenols that can be mathematically associated with its experimentally observed disaggregation effect against alpha-synuclein amyloid aggregates. Accordingly, 308 descriptors were computed for the polyphenols, out of which an iteratively increasing subset of various descriptors in various distinct combinations were taken in tandem to build and fit Multiple linear regression (MLR) models against their IC50 values. Approximately, 15000000 MLR models were contrived and evaluated for the feature selection process. Applying stringent criterion, an MLR model with six features: Largest Moment of Inertia of Mass, HOMO Energy, Sum Nucleophilic Reactivity Index of All C Atoms, Average Bond Length for an O Atom, Minimum Bond Length for a C-C Bond, and Average Bond Order for a C Atom, fitted against IC50 was elucidated with statistically significant $R2 = 0.89$, F stat $= 38.29$. The mathematical association postulated in this feature selection study between polyphenols' aforementioned descriptors and its disaggregation potency can help researcher better perceive the sanative anti-aggregation nature of polyphenols and enable them develop effective therapeutics against Parkinson's.

C. Gopalakrishnan and C. Xu—Contributed to the work equally.

© Springer Nature Switzerland AG 2021
D.-S. Huang et al. (Eds.): ICIC 2021, LNAI 12838, pp. 231–241, 2021.
https://doi.org/10.1007/978-3-030-84532-2_21

Keywords: Feature selection · Machine learning · Multiple linear regression

1   Introduction

Parkinson's is a systemic progressive neurological disorder which has debilitating impact on the nervous system. It is descried by body stiffness, shaking, lack of balance and coordination, and difficulty in walking. As the disease worsens, people tend to be afflicted with difficulty in talking, slurred speeches and walking. Prolonged immobility can also lead to blood clots. Patients with Parkinson's pose high risk of falling, which can deem fatal, and they contrive high risk for aspiration pneumonia, which can also be life threatening. Besides, in certain cases people with Parkinson's, are known to have dementia [1–5].

This nocuous affliction is caused due to the aggregation and deposition of pathogenically malformed alpha-synuclein protein in pertinent brain tissues. Alpha-synuclein, a pre-synaptic neuroprotein with obscure function is transcribed by the SCNA gene. It gets misfolded into its pathogenic amyloid form, due to genetic mutations and other elusive circumstances. The amyloid, rich in beta-sheet, aggregates and gets accumulated in brain's neuronal tissues, to engender neurodegeneration [6, 7].

Sadly, the therapeutics for this ruinous detrimental disorder is limited to mitigating the symptoms [8]. Although, naturally occurring polyphenols have been discerned to exhibit anti aggregation effects on the amyloid fibrils. They have been known to destabilize the distinct amyloid architecture and to distort and disaggregate the existing preformed amyloid aggregates in neuronal tissues of brains [9]. However, the biochemical mechanism by which the polyphenols act on amyloids to disrupt aggregated fibrils remains elusive. And, to formulate effective therapeutics fashioned out of polyphenolic lead compounds, it is pertinent to elucidate and comprehend its inherent features that drives polyphenols to interact with amyloids and actuate disaggregation.

Propitiously, recent computational advancements in advanced statistical models and machine learning, have helped better comprehending crucial characteristics of biomolecules, debilitating disorders, protein-protein interactions and ascertaining biomolecular features of chemical compounds against a target protein [10–16]. Hence in the present analysis, with the help of proficient and robust feature selection and model building pipelines, we have delineated the prominent biochemical descriptors/features among polyphenols that could potentially be the basis for their disaggregation effect against alpha-synuclein amyloid aggregates.

2   Methodology

2.1   Dataset

The dataset for present feature selection study was procured from prior work of Masuda et al. [17]. Wherein, he and his coworkers, have elucidated experimentally, the list of polyphenols that have shown potency against alpha synuclein amyloid aggregates. Besides, Masuda et al. have quantified the naturally occurring polyphenols' inhibitory effect against amyloid aggregates in terms of their IC50 values (μM), the micromolar concentration required to produce 50% of intended sanative inhibitory effect [18]. 26 polyphenols have experimentally exhibited curative effects against alpha synuclein amyloid aggregates, which were availed in the present study for feature selection process, along with their amyloid IC50 values.

2.2 Polyphenols' Structural Information

The 3D coordinates of aforementioned polyphenols were retrieved from PubChem database, a comprehensive repository of small molecules and drugs [19]. The polyphenols' 3D conformations were modelled with the help of parameters specified by MMFF94s force filed. Further, the polyphenols' structures were refined availing Austin Model 1 (AM1), a semi-empirical computational quantum estimation of molecular electron structure [20]. AM1 was implemented though the AMPAC quantum semiempirical computational chemistry program [21].

2.3 Computing Descriptors/Features of Polyphenols

Subsequently, Comprehensive Descriptors for Structural and Statistical Analysis (CODESSA) (SemichemInc., ShawneeMission, KS) was used to calculate structurally refined polyphenols' biochemical and biomolecular features. It is a robust program to expeditiously compute extensive descriptors based on chemical compound's structure. And also, an efficacious quantitative structure-activity/property (QSA/PR) relationship modelling software [22, 23]. The descriptors are computed and ascribed in terms of these broad category: topological, geometrical, constitutional, electrostatic, thermodynamic, and quantum-chemical. In the present study, 308 descriptors were calculated for structurally refined polyphenols, within reasonable amount of time.

2.4 Feature Selection

Once the descriptors have been computed for the polyphenols, next step is to search among them, the set of descriptors which directly affects the compounds' IC50 value, mathematically with the help of CODESSA. This process is called as feature selection, wherein a set of n descriptors are permutatively taken at tandem and a Multiple linear regression (MLR) learning algorithm is effectuated to fit and model the selected n descriptors with compounds' IC50 as the observed empirical value, based on the following equation:

$$Y = b0 + b1 \times 1 + b2 \times 2 \ldots \ldots bn \times n$$

Here, Y depicts the observed empirical value, in this case is the IC50 values of polyphenol compounds, while n is the number of descriptors taken in tandem for the MLR, x1...xn is the computed descriptor values of polyphenols, and b0...bn is the parameters that are optimized in due course of the MLR learning algorithm to best fit the values and minimize the error. Concretely, if the resulting R2 value and p-value is significant enough, then the modelled n set of descriptors can be construed to have potential influence on polyphenols' IC50.

The entire procedure can be delineated by the following algorithm:

Here n is the number of variables used in tandem for MLR model fitting, and its limited to a maximum of 20, by the software. In other words, at a given instance, the tool can select up to combinations of 20 descriptors in tandem for feature selection.

For n in 1…20:
    D = NCn (get total combinations of n set descriptors from total number of N descriptors computed and store it in D)
For each combination in D:
    Fit the MLR model as per equation:
        $Y = b0 + b1x1 + b2x2 ……..bnxn$
    If (model is statically significant):
        Retain the model and the set of n descriptors
    Else:
        Reject the model and its descriptors

---

3 Results and Discussion

Over the past decade there has been an increased surge in the use of advanced statistical QSA/PR modelling to better comprehend the protein-drug interactivity dynamics [24]. To this effect, in the present study, the basis for naturally occurring polyphenols' interaction and disaggregation potency against alpha synuclein amyloid aggregates, was probed through a robust QSAR feature selection computational pipeline.

Accordingly, the naturally occurring polyphenols and their inhibitory activities were procured from prior experimental study [17]. And, the structures were quantum semi-empirically refined (Fig. 1). Further, the polyphenols' descriptors were quantified. A total of 308 descriptors were delineated. With **n** values ranging from 1 to 20, iteratively, various combinations of **n** descriptors in tandem, from total list of computed descriptors, were availed to compute MLR models. In the due process, approximately 15000000 mathematical models were contrived based on iteratively fitting '**n**' tandem descriptors against experimentally observed empirical IC50 values. Then, the mathematical models were evaluated based on R2 value and p-value. Applying stringent criteria, a statistical model with six descriptors was ascertained, and formulated by the following equation:

$$Y_{IC50} = b_0 + b_1x_1^{\text{Moment of Inertia of Mass, Largest}} + b_2x_2^{\text{HOMO Energy}} + b_3x_3^{\text{Sum Nucleophilic Reactivity Index of All C Atoms}} + b_4x_4^{\text{Average Bond Length for an O Atom}} + b_5x_5^{\text{Minimum Bond Length for a C–C Bond}} + b_6x_6^{\text{Average Bond Order for a C Atom}}.$$

Herein, $b_0…b_6$ is the parameter constant that was adjusted during the MLR learning program to best fit the models. The values elucidated are as follows: $b_0 = -1064.4$ (p-value = 1.3347e-09), $b_1 = -0.0186688$ (p-value = 3.6408e-10), $b_2 = -8.3629$ (p-value = 8.4570e-11), $b_3 = 204.114$ (p-value = 6.9187e-11), $b_4 = 326.262$ (p-value = 1.3851e-08), $b_5 = 257.115$ (p-value = 6.7966e-07), and $b_6 = 97.3962$ (p-value = 1.8505e-05). And, $x_1…x_6$, are the set of descriptors (listed in the equation) feature selected by the program, best fitted against the observed IC50 value that is depicted by Y.

Further, R2 of the fitted model is found to be 0.89, with F stat = 38.29 and the overall p-value 1.2817e-09. Statistical analyses have indicated that a R2 value > 0.7 is generally construed to have strong effect size, meaning it's a considerably fitted model [25]. Hence, the model fitted in the present study with feature selected six descriptors: Moment of Inertia of Mass Largest, HOMO Energy, Sum Nucleophilic Reactivity Index of All C Atoms, Average Bond Length for an O Atom, Minimum Bond Length for a C-C Bond, and Average Bond Order for a C Atom fitted against polyphenols' inhibitory IC50 values (Fig. 2), provides plausible insights into polyphenols' biochemical features that can be associated with their disaggregation potential. Besides, the fitted model with descriptors and parameters evinced a minimal overall error of **4.3155** (Table 1). The predicted IC50 values from aforementioned model, was almost on par with the experimentally observed IC50 values (Fig. 3). Therefore, it is sufficed to say that the polyphenols' biochemical descriptors elucidated by the feature selection program, contrives considerable associativity with the polyphenols' amyloid disaggregation potency, mathematically.

Moreover, from a bio-organic-chemical reaction kinetics standpoint, the feature selected descriptors could be quite crucial for compounds' interactivity. Accordingly, studies have indicated that highest occupied molecular orbital (HOMO) energy is closely associated with chemical reactivity through electrophilic attack, owing to the presence of highest energy orbital containing electrons [26], and also, the descriptor HOMO energy is well complimented by the elucidation of another descriptor Sum Nucleophilic Reactivity Index of All C Atoms, since both of them allude to the electron availability of the compound which in turn affects its reactivity. Besides, nucleophilic reactions are observed frequently among various biomolecules [27, 28], might also hint on polyphenol's interaction with Amyloid fibril. Next, the polar nature of hydroxyl group in phenols can be directly attributed with its reactivity characteristics [29]. Likewise, in 'poly'phenols (meaning: multi phenols), with a vast majority of oxygen atoms placed in hydroxyl groups, Average Bond Length for an O Atom, could very well influence reactive polar nature of hydroxyl groups which in turn affects polyphenols reactivity. Similarly, Average Bond Order for a C Atom in polyphenol, which illustrates the association of C-atom with other C-atoms and other atoms such H, O and N, is important, since it ascertains the conformational orientation of functional groups (required for compounds' reaction) and general orientation of overall polyphenols' conformation. To this effect, Minimum Bond Length for a C-C Bond also factors into polyphenols reactivity, as C-C bonds are pertinent for the structural framework of any biochemical compound [30] and together with Bond order, is crucial for maintaining the structural integrity of the compound. Since a compound's structure is directly associated with its function [31], both Minimum Bond Length for a C-C Bond and Average Bond Order for a C Atom could play substantial role in polyphenols reactivity with amyloid fibrils. On the same note, Moment of Inertia of Mass Largest, could also greatly influence the structural conformational dynamics of a compound.

Additionally, since these descriptors are elucidated by fitting mathematical models against experimentally quantified values, along with the use of quantum-semi empirical structural refinement procedures, it makes the presented methodology a bit more robust and efficacious, when compared to traditional protein-drug interaction analysis procedures.

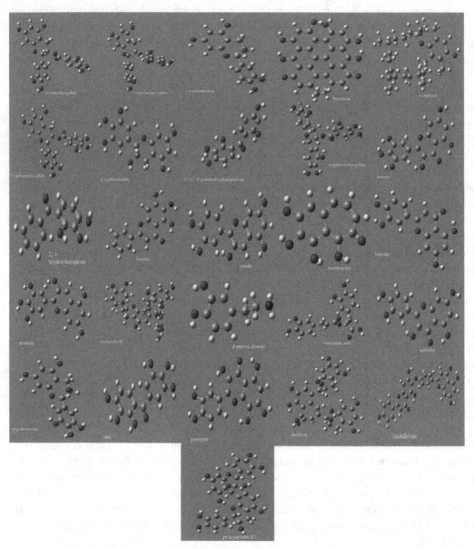

Fig. 1. 3D structure of quantum semi empirically optimized polyphenolic compounds availed in this study. Carbon atoms are depicted in grey bread, oxygen in red, hydrogen in white and nitrogen in blue. (Color figure online)

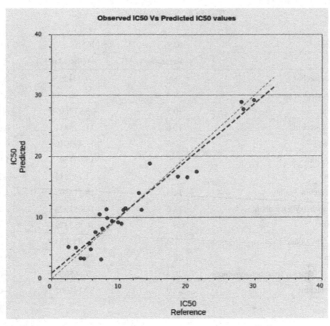

Fig. 2. Line graph depicting the descriptor-based model (predicted) fitted against the experimentally observed IC50 (Reference).

Table 1. Quantification of deviation/error between the descriptor-based model (predicted) fitted against the experimentally observed IC50 (Reference) for each polyphenol.

S.no	Structure	IC50	IC50	Error
	Name	Reference (μM)	Predicted (μM)	
1	Exifone	2.5	5.1895778	2.6895778
2	(-)-gallocatechin gallate	3.6	5.0600352	1.4600352
3	procyanidin B2	4.3	3.3238084	−0.9761916
4	rosmarinic acid	4.8	3.2633039	−1.5366961
5	Gossypetin	5.6	5.7594331	0.1594331
6	Theaflavin	5.8	4.7991897	−1.0008103
7	Delphinidin	6.5	7.6138213	1.1138213
8	dopamine chloride	7.1	10.517399	3.417399
9	procyanidin B1	7.3	3.1397387	−4.1602613
10	Hypericin	7.5	8.1582023	0.6582023
11	Hinokiflavone	8.1	11.339364	3.2393641
12	Baicalein	8.2	9.9055751	1.7055751

(continued)

Table 1. (*continued*)

S.no	Structure	IC50	IC50	Error
	Name	Reference (μM)	Predicted (μM)	
13	(-)-gallocatechin	8.9	9.4042559	0.5042559
14	epigallocatechin gallate	9.8	9.1991506	−0.6008494
15	Cyanidin	10.3	8.9776079	−1.3223921
16	Epigallocatechin	10.6	11.226411	0.6264114
17	Tocopherol	10.9	11.493016	0.5930162
18	Purpurogallin	12.9	13.98159	1.0815901
19	Myricetin	13.3	11.245813	−2.0541872
20	(-)-epicatechin 3gallate	14.5	18.815593	4.3155934
21	2,3,4-trihydroxybenzophenone	18.6	16.651923	−1.9480775
22	Quercetin	20	16.532372	−3.4676283
23	(-)-catechin gallate	21.4	17.450854	−3.9491464
24	Luteolin	28	28.841899	0.8418986
25	2,3,4,2',4'-pentahydroxybenzophenone	28.3	27.665005	−0.6349953
26	(-)-epicatechin	29.9	29.145062	−0.754938

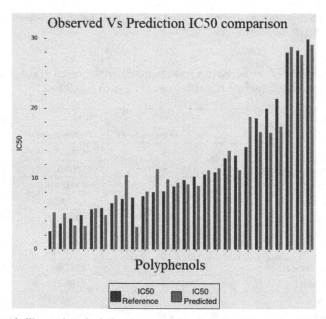

Fig. 3. Bar graph illustrating deviation between the descriptor-based model (predicted) fitted against the experimentally observed IC50 (Reference) for each polyphenol.

4   Conclusion

Therefore, in the present study, through a robust feature selection pipeline we have mathematically formulated an association between naturally occurring polyphenols' six pertinent descriptors and its IC50 value against alpha-synuclein amyloid aggregates. We have also probed the significance of these descriptors from a biochemical reactivity standpoint. Mathematically delineating these descriptors could help chemist and pharmacist to better comprehend the inherent properties of naturally occurring polyphenols, that are responsible for amyloid disaggregation. Which will in turn enable them the contrive effective therapeutics against inimical Parkinson's disorder.

Acknowledgment. This study was supported by Science and technology innovation project of Shanxi province universities (2019L0683), Changzhi Medical College Startup Fund for PhD faculty (BS201922), Provincial university innovation and entrepreneurship training programs (2019403). And also, the authors would like to thank Vellore Institute of Technology (Deemed to be University) for providing "VIT SEED GRANT (VIT/SG/2020–21/43)" for carrying out this research work.

Conflict of Interest. The authors declare that they have no conflict of interest.

References

1. Sveinbjornsdottir, S.: The clinical symptoms of Parkinson's disease. J. Neurochem. **139**(Suppl1), 318–324 (2016). https://doi.org/10.1111/jnc.13691
2. Kalia, L.V., Lang, A.E.: Parkinson's disease. Lancet **386**, 896–912 (2015). https://doi.org/10.1016/S0140-6736(14)61393-3
3. Savica, R., et al.: Survival and causes of death among people with clinically diagnosed synucleinopathies with parkinsonism: a population-based study. JAMA Neurol. **74**, 839 (2017). https://doi.org/10.1001/jamaneurol.2017.0603
4. Lisak, R.P., Truong, D., Carroll, W.M., Bhidayasiri, R. (eds.): International Neurology. Wiley, Chichester, Hoboken (2016)
5. Adams, B., et al.: Parkinson's disease: a systemic inflammatory disease accompanied by bacterial inflammagens. Front Aging Neurosci. **11**, 210 (2019). https://doi.org/10.3389/fnagi.2019.00210
6. Stefanis, L.: α-synuclein in Parkinson's disease. Cold Spring Harb. Perspect. Med. **2**, a009399 (2012). https://doi.org/10.1101/cshperspect.a009399
7. Filippini, A., Gennarelli, M., Russo, I.: α-synuclein and Glia in Parkinson's disease: a beneficial or a detrimental duet for the endo-lysosomal system? Cell. Mol. Neurobiol. **39**(2), 161–168 (2019). https://doi.org/10.1007/s10571-019-00649-9
8. Zahoor, I., Shafi, A. (eds.): Parkinson's Disease: Pathogenesis and Clinical Aspects. Bioinformatics Centre, University of Kashmir, Srinagar, J&K, India, Department of Biotechnology, University of Cambridge, UK, pp. 129–144. Codon Publications (2018). https://doi.org/10.15586/codonpublications.parkinsonsdisease.2018.ch7
9. Freyssin, A., Page, G., Fauconneau, B., RiouxBilan, A.: Natural polyphenols effects on protein aggregates in Alzheimer's and Parkinson's prion-like diseases. Neural Regen Res. **13**, 955–961 (2018). https://doi.org/10.4103/1673-5374.233432

10. Bao, W., et al.: Mutli-features prediction of protein translational modification sites. IEEE/ACM Trans. Comput. Biol. Bioinf. **15**, 1453–1460 (2018). https://doi.org/10.1109/TCBB.2017.2752703

11. Taha, M.O., et al.: Pharmacophore modeling, quantitative structure-activity relationship analysis, and in silico screening reveal potent glycogen synthase Kinase-3β inhibitory activities for cimetidine, hydroxychloroquine, and gemifloxacin. J. Med. Chem. **51**, 2062–2077 (2008). https://doi.org/10.1021/jm7009765

12. Li, Z.-W., et al.: Accurate prediction of protein-protein interactions by integrating potential evolutionary information embedded in PSSM profile and discriminative vector machine classifier. Oncotarget **8**, 23638–23649 (2017). https://doi.org/10.18632/oncotarget.15564

13. Deng, S.-P., Zhu, L., Huang, D.-S.: Mining the bladder cancer-associated genes by an integrated strategy for the construction and analysis of differential co-expression networks. BMC Genomics **16**(Suppl 3), S4 (2015). https://doi.org/10.1186/1471-2164-16-S3-S4

14. Lei, Y.-K., You, Z.-H., Ji, Z., Zhu, L., Huang, D.-S.: Assessing and predicting protein interactions by combining manifold embedding with multiple information integration. BMC Bioinformatics **13**, S3 (2012). https://doi.org/10.1186/1471-2105-13-S7-S3

15. Yuan, L., et al.: Integration of multi-omics data for gene regulatory network inference and application to breast cancer. IEEE/ACM Trans. Comput. Biol. Bioinf. **16**, 782–791 (2019). https://doi.org/10.1109/TCBB.2018.2866836

16. Xu, W., Zhu, L., Huang, D.-S.: DCDE: an efficient deep convolutional divergence encoding method for human promoter recognition. IEEE Trans Nanobiosci. **18**, 136–145 (2019). https://doi.org/10.1109/TNB.2019.2891239

17. Masuda, M., et al.: Small Molecule Inhibitors of α-synuclein filament assembly. Biochemistry **45**, 6085–6094 (2006). https://doi.org/10.1021/bi0600749

18. Stewart, M.J., Watson, I.D.: Standard units for expressing drug concentrations in biological fluids. Br. J. Clin. Pharmacol. **16**, 3–7 (1983). https://doi.org/10.1111/j.1365-2125.1983.tb02136.x

19. Kim, S., et al.: PubChem in 2021: new data content and improved web interfaces. Nucleic Acids Res. **49**, D1388–D1395 (2021). https://doi.org/10.1093/nar/gkaa971

20. Dewar, M.J.S., Zoebisch, E.G., Healy, E.F., Stewart, J.J.P.: Development and use of quantum mechanical molecular models. 76. AM1: a new general purpose quantum mechanical molecular model. J. Am. Chem. Soc. **107**, 3902–3909 (1985). https://doi.org/10.1021/ja00299a024

21. Young, D.C.: Computational Chemistry: A Practical Guide for Applying Techniques to Real World Problems. Wiley, New York (2001)

22. Liu, Y., Holder, A.J.: A quantum mechanical quantitative structure–property relationship study of the melting point of a variety of organosilicons. J. Mol. Graph. Model. **31**, 57–64 (2011). https://doi.org/10.1016/j.jmgm.2011.08.003

23. Katritzky, A.R., et al.: Antimalarial activity: a QSAR modeling using CODESSA PRO software. Bioorg. Med. Chem. **14**, 2333–2357 (2006). https://doi.org/10.1016/j.bmc.2005.11.015

24. Muratov, E.N., et al.: QSAR without borders. Chem. Soc. Rev. **49**, 3525–3564 (2020). https://doi.org/10.1039/D0CS00098A

25. Moore, D.S., Notz, W.I., Fligner, M.A.: The Basic Practice of Statistics. W.H. Freeman and Company, New York (2018)

26. Talmaciu, M.M., Bodoki, E., Oprean, R.: Global chemical reactivity parameters for several chiral beta-blockers from the density functional theory viewpoint. Clujul Med. **89**, 513–518 (2016). https://doi.org/10.15386/cjmed-610

27. Vale, N.: Biomedical Chemistry: current trends and developments. De Gruyter Open Poland (2015).https://doi.org/10.1515/9783110468755

28. Skipper, P.L.: Influence of tertiary structure on nucleophilic substitution reactions of proteins. Chem. Res. Toxicol. **9**, 918–923 (1996). https://doi.org/10.1021/tx960028h
29. Speight, J.G.: Organic Chemistry. In: Environmental Organic Chemistry for Engineers, pp. 43–86. Elsevier (2017). https://doi.org/10.1016/B978-0-12-804492-6.00002-2
30. Effert, S., MeyerErkelenz, J.D. (eds.): Biochemistry. TCC, vol. 83. Springer, Heidelberg (1979). https://doi.org/10.1007/BFb0019660
31. Petrucci, R.H.: General Chemistry: Principles and Modern Applications. Pearson/Prentice Hall, Upper Saddle River (2007)

Study on the Mechanism of Cistanche in the Treatment of Colorectal Cancer Based on Network Pharmacology

Yuan Dong[1], Caixia Xu[3], Chenxia Ren[2], Pengyong Han[2], Fei Ren[2], Zhengwei Li[4(✉)], and Zibai Wei[1(✉)]

[1] Affiliated Heping Hospital, Changzhi Medical College, Changzhi, Shanxi, China
weizhibai@czmc.edu.cn
[2] Central Lab, Changzhi Medical College, Changzhi 046000, China
[3] Department of Pharmacy, Changzhi Medical College, Changzhi 046000, China
[4] School of Computer Science and Technology, China University of Mining and Technology, Xuzhou 221116, China

Abstract. To study the mechanism of Cistanche deserticola in the treatment of colorectal cancer by network pharmacology. Methods: The chemical constituents of Cistanche deserticola and the related targets were screened by TCMSP. Gene Cards, OMIM, PharmGkb, GrugBank, and TTD databases were used to screen colorectal cancer-related targets. The network of "active components-targets" was constructed and the common targets were chosen as potentially therapeutic. The GO function enrichment analysis and KEGG pathway analysis were carried out for the target screening by the R package cluster profiler. Finally, Auto dock Vina was used to realize the molecular docking of core components and key targets. Results: There were 6 active compounds and 154 potential targets for Cistanche deserticola; 12877 targets for Colorectal cancer were obtained. There were 149 intersecting targets, which were enriched in multiple malignancies including colorectal cancer pathways. Conclusion: This study provides a scientific basis for explicating the potential of Cistanche deserticola in the treatment of colorectal cancer and establishing a foundation for further investigation of the role of its active components in cancer drug design.

Keywords: Network pharmacology · Cistanche deserticola · Colorectal cancer · Mechanism of action

1 Introduction

Colorectal cancer (CRC) is one of the most common cancers in the world. The incidence and mortality of colorectal cancer in China ranked third and fifth among all malignant tumors in the 2018 China Cancer Statistics Report respectively. The incidence of colon cancer has increased significantly, and most patients are already in the middle and

Y. Dong, C. Xu and C. Ren—Contributed to the work equally.

© Springer Nature Switzerland AG 2021
D.-S. Huang et al. (Eds.): ICIC 2021, LNAI 12838, pp. 242–252, 2021.
https://doi.org/10.1007/978-3-030-84532-2_22

advanced stages at the time of diagnosis [1]. A large number of clinical studies have shown that although chemical drugs improve the cure rate of malignant tumors, they have strong side effects and drug resistance defects. Traditional Chinese medicine has a long history of treating tumors. The effective ingredients of traditional Chinese medicine mainly destroy the micro-environment of cancer cells, promote apoptosis, enhance the body's immunity, and eliminate pathogens through the body's immune system to exert anti-cancer effects.

Cistanche deserticola (Latin name: Cistanche deserticola Ma) is known as the "desert ginseng and has extremely high medicinal value. It has been used to treat male Yang deficiency, male impotence, female infertility, waist and knee weakness, Alzheimer's disease, Parkinson's disease, Intestinal dryness, constipation, and other diseases, and can be used as functional foods to improve immune function, anti-fatigue, anti-oxidation, improve memory, prevent and treat Alzheimer's, anti-aging, etc. Cistanche cistanche polysaccharides can regulate the diversity of intestinal flora and increase the beneficial flora. it can enhance or activate the host's reaction to tumor cells by promoting the proliferation of lymphocytes, regulating the immune response, and increasing the content of interferon γ (IFN-γ) in the peripheral blood. Immune response [3–5]. Studies have found that the aqueous extract of Cistanche has a significant inhibitory effect on intestinal hyperplasia in colon cancer-prone mice, activates macrophages, and reduces the number of intestinal Helicobacter pylori infections [6, 7]. The above shows that Cistanche has the potential to prevent and treat colorectal cancer, and can provide an effective strategy for the prevention and treatment of colorectal cancer. Its anti-colorectal cancer mechanism is worthy of further study.

Network pharmacology is the method to study Traditional Chinese medicine from a holistic perspective. It has become a new strategy to scientifically explain the effectiveness and scientificity of Chinese medicine. It has had successful application experience in many aspects of Chinese medicine research [8]. This study uses network pharmacological methods to predict the pharmacologically active components, targets, and cell signal transduction pathways that may be involved in the regulation of Cistanche in the prevention and treatment of colorectal cancer, and improve the basis for revealing the modern pharmacological mechanism of Cistanche against colorectal cancer.

2   Materials and Methods

2.1   The Effective Ingredients and Targets of Cistanche

In the Traditional Chinese Medicine Systems Pharmacology Database and Platform (TCMSP), active ingredients and targets of Cistanche were screened with the parameters like the bioavailability (OB) is greater than or equal to 30, and the drug-likeness (DL) is greater than or equal to 0.18. The human gene name corresponding to the target protein was obtained via the UniProt database (https://www.uniprot.org/) while the protein species is set to "homo sapiens (human)", matching and sorting out drug targets.Related targets for colorectal cancer.

Use "colorectal cancer" as the keyword, respectively retrieved colorectal cancer-related targets in five databases such as GeenCards, OMIM, PharmGkb, GrugBank, TTD, integrate and delete the duplicated target genes. The disease-related targets and the Cistanche targets are intersected to obtain the common targets of Cistanche and colorectal cancer through the R software. The intersected gene is the potential target of Cistanche in the treatment of colorectal cancer.

2.2 Drug-Disease Target Network Construction

"Cistanche components-colorectal cancer targets" network was constructed through Cytoscape software (version 3.8.0) (see Fig. 3). The nodes in the network diagram are chemical components and targets respectively. The relationship between the components and the target is represented by an edge. The node on the right of the network represents the potential targets of Cistanche for colorectal cancer after the screening, the node on the left of the network represents the active ingredients of Cistanche, and the side represents the relationship between the active ingredients of Cistanche and the potential targets.

2.3 Construction of Target Interaction Network and Screening of Core Genes

Input the intersection genes obtained in 1.2 into the String (https://string-db.org) database, select homo sapiens for the species, with the confidence of 0.900, and obtain the protein-protein interactions (PPI) network (See Fig. 4), save the result into tsv file. Import the resulting files into Cytoscape, and use the Cyto NCA plug-in to analyze the core targets of the network. The analysis content includes betweenness centrality (BC), closeness centrality (CC), and degree centrality (DC), eigenvector centrality (EC), local average connectivity-based method (LAC), etc. The selected node is the key node i.e., the core genes.

2.4 GO and KEGG Signal Pathway Enrichment Analysis

Install and run the Bioconductor software package "org.Hs.eg.db" in the R software which will convert the drug-disease common target into entrezID. Use the "clusterProfiler" package to perform GO and KEGG enrichment analysis on the intersection target obtained by "part 1.2", and the screening conditions are $P < 0.05$, $Q < 0.05$. Select the top 30 functional annotation catalogs and signal pathway catalogs for analysis, and display the results in the form of bar graphs and bubble graphs, respectively.

2.5 The Simulation of Drug Active Ingredient and Target Protein via Molecular Docking

Download the 2D structure of the main active ingredients of Cistanche in Pubchem (https://pubchem.ncbi.nlm.nih.gov/), transform it into a three-dimensional structure with ChemBio3D Ultra (version 14.0), and optimize it with the MM2 force field. The corresponding protein name of the core target screened will be retrieved from the UniProt database, and the three-dimensional structure of the target protein is downloaded from the RCSB Protein Data Bank,Pymol (version 2.4.0)) was used to extract the target protein ligand and delete the water molecule. Both the target protein and the active ingredient of the drug are converted into PDBQT format using AutodockTools (version 1.5.6), and then AutoDock Vina (version 1.5.6) is used for molecular docking, and the conformation with the lowest Vina score is selected for mapping analysis with Pymol (Fig. 1).

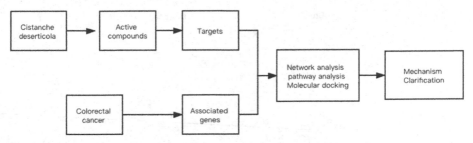

Fig. 1. Chart illustrating the workflow employed in the analysis

3 Results

3.1 Screening of Active Ingredients and Prediction of the Target of Cistanche

Search the keyword "Cistanche" in the TCMSP database, select "Ingredients" to obtain the active ingredients, set the threshold OB $\geq$ 30% and DL $\geq$ 0.18, and screen out 6 active ingredients (see Table 1). Select "Related Targets" to obtain 658 target proteins corresponding to all active ingredients, screen and eliminate ingredients without corresponding targets, and convert the target protein names into gene names in the Uniprot database, delete duplicates and non-human targets, In the end, 154 potential targets were obtained.

Table 1. Active ingredients of Cistanche after screening

ID	Active ingredients	OB/%	DL
MOL000358	Beta-sitosterol	414.79	8.08
MOL005320	Arachidonate	304.52	6.41
MOL005384	Suchilactone	368.41	3.73
MOL007563	YANGAMBIN	446.54	2.6
MOL000098	Quercetin	302.25	1.5
MOL008871	MARCKINE	475.69	5.3

3.2 Potential Targets of Cistanche in the Treatment of Colorectal Cancer

Search the Gene Cards, OMIM, TTD, DrugBank, and PharmGkb databases with "colorectal cancer" as a keyword. After all target genes are integrated, duplicate values are eliminated, and 12,877 colorectal cancer targets are screened (see Table 1). Use R software to intersect disease-related targets and drug targets, and finally obtain 149 potential targets of Cistanche for the treatment of colorectal cancer (see Fig. 2).

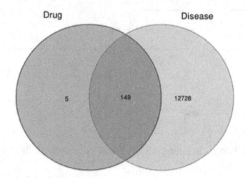

Fig. 2. Venn diagrams of potential targets in drug related genes and diseases relate genes

3.3 Construction of Active Pharmaceutical Ingredient-Disease Target Network

The "active drug-disease targets" network of Cistanche for the treatment of colorectal cancer will be drawn by importing the active ingredients of the drug, potential targets, and their attributes into Cytoscape software (see Fig. 3). The figure directly indicates the action mechanism of Cistanche's multi-component and multi-target treatment of colorectal cancer. The nodes with different colors respectively represent the active ingredient of the drug and the disease target, and the edges represent the interaction relationship between the active ingredient and the target.

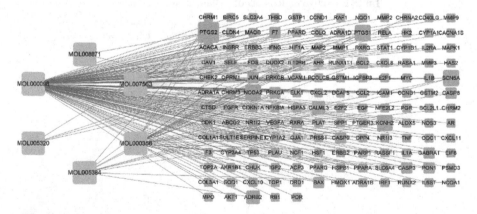

Fig. 3. Cytoscape visualization of active pharmaceutical ingredient-disease target network

3.4 Construction and Analysis of Target Protein PPI Network

The intersection genes obtained by Venn analysis were imported into the String database, the species was limited to humans, the confidence level was set to 0.900, and free targets were eliminated, and 126 nodes and 449 interaction relationships were obtained (Fig. 4). Use Cytoscape software cytoNCA plug-in to analyze the network topology characteristics, calculate the median of the 5 parameters BC, CC, DC, EC, LAC (BC > 53.458730155, CC > 0.146028037, DC > 5, EC > 0.040624168, LAC > 2.267857143), perform the first screening and select 38 key nodes. The second screening set thresholds for DC > 9, CC > 0.528571429, BC > 19.031172835, LAC > 4, EC > 0.1312125255, and finally, 11 core targets were obtained, including *CCND1, MAPK1, AKT1, AKT1, TNF, MYC, RELA, RXRA, JUN, TP53, PPARA, FOS*, these may be the main material basis for Cistanche in the treatment of colorectal cancer.

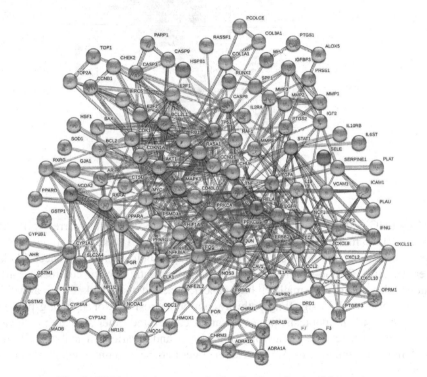

Fig. 4. PPI interaction network visualization of potential targets

3.5 GO and KEGG Signal Pathway Enrichment Analysis

The GO results show that 2430 biological processes and functions are enriched according to the corrected P-value. Biological Process (BP) and Cellular Component (CC) and molecular function (Molecular Function, MF) each part of the top 10 bar graph display (see Fig. 5). A large number of enriched genes is mainly related to the biofeedback regulation process of drugs, bacteria-derived molecules, lipopolysaccharides, oxidative stress, chemical stress, metal ions, toxic substances, etc. cell localization includes membrane regions, membrane microregions, and plasma membranes Raft, transcription regulation complex, RNA polymerase II ranscription regulation complex, inherent components of presynaptic membrane, components of postsynaptic membrane, etc. Molecular functions mainly involve: DNA binding transcription factor binding, transcription coactivator binding, drugs Binding, cytokine receptor binding, ubiquitin protein ligase binding, nuclear receptor active ligand activation, inhibition of transcription factor binding, etc.

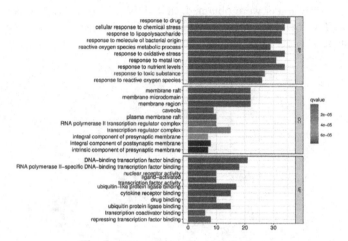

Fig. 5. GO analysis of potential targets

164 KEGG pathways were enriched after sorted according to the corrected P-value and selected the first 30 for bar graph display (see Fig. 6). The key target genes of the research are enriched in a variety of tumor pathways: such as prostate cancer, bladder cancer, hepatitis B, non-small cell lung cancer, pancreatic cancer, colorectal cancer, hepatocellular carcinoma, small cell lung cancer, etc., and also regulate such as MAPK signaling pathway, P53 signaling pathway, tumor necrosis factor signaling pathway, cell senescence, cell apoptosis, proteoglycan in cancer and other signaling pathways. It shows that Cistanche can treat colorectal cancer and a variety of malignant tumors through multiple signaling pathways, and its target may be a common target of multiple malignant tumors.

3.6   Molecular Docking

AutoDock Vina (version 1.1.2) was used to molecularly dock the 11 core protein targets screened with the corresponding active pharmaceutical ingredients. The docking result only retains the predicted binding affinity (kcal·mol-1) of each pair of molecules with the highest absolute value. Vina score is the score of the complex obtained by molecular docking of the receptor and the ligand using the Vina program with the corresponding pocket parameters. The lower the score, the higher the affinity between the receptor and

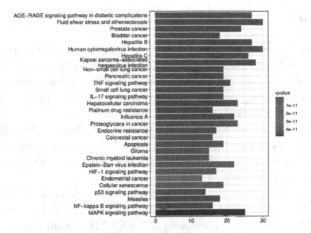

Fig. 6. KEGG analysis of potential targets

the ligand. The docking results suggest that the top four in the order of affinity between the drug components and the target protein from high to low (Vina score from low to high) are *FOS* and quercetin (Vina score -10.0kcal·mol^{-1}), *AKT1* and quercetin (Vina score -9.8kcal·mol^{-1}), TNF and quercetin (Vina score -8.7kcal·mol^{-1}), *RXRA* and quercetin (Vina score −8.4kcal·mol^{-1}), and the scores are relatively close. The molecular docking model is shown in Fig. 6. This indicates that *FOS, AKT1, TNF*, and *RXRA* are likely to be potential targets for Cistanche in the treatment of colorectal cancer, quercetin is an effective ingredient, and the Vina score (i.e., binding energy) of the interaction between quercetin and *FOS* is the best, which is −10.0kcal/mol (Fig. 7).

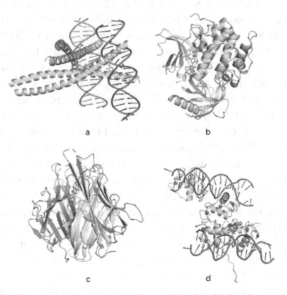

Fig. 7. Molecular docking of potential chemical and targets

4 Discussion

Traditional Chinese medicine occupies an important position in the treatment of colorectal cancer. The clinical use of integrated Chinese and Western medicine has obvious advantages in improving symptoms and physical conditions, increasing efficiency and reducing toxicity, reversing or delaying multidrug resistance, preventing recurrence, extending the survival period of patients, and improving their quality of life. Traditional Chinese medicine has a long history in the treatment of tumors. Traditional Chinese medicine formulations involve multiple targets and multiple signal pathways, regulating the activity or expression of a series of proteins, to achieve a synergistic therapeutic effect that cannot be achieved by a single chemical drug [9].

This study shows that the main active ingredients of Cistanche are β-sitosterol, Arachidonate, Suchilactone, Yangambin, Quercetin, Alkaloid (1R)-1-[[(2S,3R,11bS)-3-ethyl-9,10-dimethoxy-2,3,4,6,7,11b-hexahydro-1H-Pyrido[2,1-a] isoquinolin-2-yl]methyl]-2,3,4,9-tetrahydro-1H-pyrido[3,4-b]indol-6-ol (Marckine). Previous studies have found that quercetin promotes tumor cell apoptosis by regulating mitochondrial cytochrome C, inhibits the production of cancer stem cells, and stabilizes the structure of telomere DNA to produce anti-tumor proliferation [10]. Quercetin is also used for anti-tumor drug precursors as it has a good anti-tumor activity after modification [11]. In in vitro model experiments, β-sitosterol has a protective effect on colon cancer. It can increase the immunity of the body by inducing the proliferation of lymphocytes [12] and can inhibit the proliferation of cancer cells by influencing the expression of *TP53* [13]. In this study, 154 targets are corresponding to the 6 main components of Cistanche, of which 149 are related to colorectal cancer.

Through network analysis, the results show that the core genes of Cistanche in the treatment of colorectal mainly include *CCND1, MAPK1, AKT1, TNF, MYC, RELA, RXRA, JUN, TP53, PPARA, FOS*, etc. These genes are involved in cell proliferation, differentiation, and apoptosis, and it is related to the occurrence and development of a variety of tumors. Studies have shown that down-regulation of *CCND1* expression can inhibit tumor cell proliferation, while overexpression can cause tumor cell proliferation [14]. Abnormally activated *AKT* can promote colorectal cancer cells to escape apoptosis by inhibiting the activity of the proteolytic enzyme Caspase9, and at the same time activate the downstream key kinase mTOR, thereby triggering a series of responses to regulate tumor cell proliferation, invasion, angiogenesis, etc. [15]. *TP53* (ie p53) is one of the tumor suppressor genes. The protein encoded by it is a transcription factor with a molecular weight of 53kDa, which can regulate the cell cycle, repair damaged DNA, and induce apoptosis of abnormally dividing cells. The mutation status of p53 is associated with colorectal cancer. Progress and prognosis are closely related [16]. Analyzing the network diagram, it can be found that the same active ingredient in Cistanche can act on multiple targets at the same time, and the same target corresponds to multiple active ingredients, which proves that Cistanche can play a therapeutic role with multiple components and multiple targets. The active ingredients of Cistanche mainly exert anti-tumor effects through the regulation of transcription factors and activation of nuclear receptor active ligands; target proteins are enriched in a variety of malignant tumors including colorectal cancer pathways, indicating that Cistanche has a greater correlation with cancer. The results of molecular docking indicated that the active ingredient quercetin has good binding to many key targets such as *FOS, AKT1, TN*F, and *RXRA*, among which the Vina score with *FOS* is the lowest.

Network pharmacology is a branch of pharmacology that uses network methods to analyze the "multi-component, multi-target, multi-pathway" synergistic relationship between drugs and diseases and targets. It is holistic, systemic, and focuses on the interaction between drugs. The characteristics of the function are consistent with the basic characteristics of Chinese medicine and build a bridge for the study of the relationship between traditional Chinese medicine and modern pharmacology [17, 18]. Network pharmacology broadens the channels for discovering new signaling pathways, regulating highly enriched genes and signaling pathways to treat diseases, and fully understanding the relationship between traditional Chinese medicine and diseases. This study analyzed the relationship between Cistanche and colorectal cancer as a whole, and explored the mechanism of Cistanche in the treatment of colorectal cancer. It can also provide a certain theoretical basis for future molecular biology experiments and deeper pharmacological exploration. Although network pharmacology research has a certain guiding effect, this method still has certain limitations. There may be omissions in the process of recruiting targets. Therefore, it is still necessary to combine prediction and verification to better explain the multi-prescriptions of traditional Chinese medicine. The biological characteristics of ingredients-multiple targets-multiple pathways and their mechanism of action.

References

1. 中国结直肠癌诊疗规范（2020年版）[J].中国实用外科杂**40**, 601–625 (2020)
2. Song, Z.H., Lei, L., Tup, F.: Advances in research of pharmacological activity in plants of Cistanche Hoffing.et Link. Chin. Tradit. Herb. Drugs **34**, 16–18 (2003)
3. Fu, Z., Han, L., Peng, Z., et al.: Cistanche polysaccharides enhance echinacoside absorption in vivo and affect the gut microbiota. Int. J. Biol. Macromol. **149**, 732–740 (2020)
4. Wu, X.M., Gao, X.M., Tsim, K.W., et al.: An arabinogalactan isolated from the stems of Cistanche deserticola induces the proliferation of cultured lymphocytes. Int. J. Biol. Macromol. **37**, 278–282 (2005)
5. Zhang, A., Yang, X., Li, Q., et al.: Immunostimulatory activity of water-extractable polysaccharides from Cistanche deserticola as a plant adjuvant in vitro and in vivo. PLOS One **13**, e0191356 (2018)
6. Luo, H., Cao, R., Wang, L., Zhu, L.: Protective effect of Cistanchis A on ethanol-induced damage in primary cultured mouse hepatocytes. Biomed Pharmacother. **83**, 1071–1079 (2016)
7. Jia, Y., Guan, Q., Guo, Y., et al.: Reduction of inflammatory hyperplasia in the intestine in colon cancer-prone mice by water-extract of cistanche deserticola. **26**, 812–819 (2012)
8. 李泮霖, 苏薇薇. 网络药理学在中药研究中的最新应用进展[J]. 中草药**47**, 2938–2942 (2016)
9. Fan, Y., Ma, Z., Zhao, L.L., et al.: Anti-tumor activities and mechanisms of Traditional Chinese medicines formulas: a review. **132** (2020)
10. Ezzati, M., Yousefi, B., Velaei, K., et al.: A review on anti-cancer properties of quercetin in breast cancer. Life Sci. **248**, 117463 (2020)
11. 李珂, 张方瑞, 李书平. 以槲皮素为先导化合物的抗癌剂研究进展[J]. 中草药**49**, 4678 (2018)
12. Backhouse, N., Rosales, L., Apablaza, C., et al.: Analgesic, anti-inflammatory and antioxidant properties of Buddleja globose, Buddlejaceae. J. Ethnopharmacol. **116**, 263 (2008)

13. 肖志彬, 贾韩学, 刘小雷.β-谷甾醇药理活性的研究现状[J].世界最新医学信息文摘 **15**, 66 (2015)
14. Morisaki, T., Uchiyama, A., Yuzuki, D., et al.: Interleukin 4 regulates G1 cell cycle progression in gastric carcinoma cells. Cancer Res. **54**, 1113–1118 (1994)
15. 张雪群,高卫,潘盼, et al.: PI3K/AKT及其相关因子在结肠癌中的表达[J].山东大学学报 **1**, 52–57.12 (2016)
16. Li, X., Zhou, J., Chen, Z., et al.: p53 mutations in colorectal cancer-molecular pathogenesis and pharmacological reactivation. World J. Gastroenterol. **21**, 84–93 (2015)
17. Hopkins, A.: Network pharmacology. Nat Biotechnol. **25**(10), 1110–1111 (2007)
18. Liu, Z.H., Sun, X., et al.: Network pharmacology: new opportunity for the modernization of traditional Chinese medicine. Acta Pharm. Sin. **47**, 696–703 (2012)

A Novel Hybrid Machine Learning Approach Using Deep Learning for the Prediction of Alzheimer Disease Using Genome Data

A. Alatrany[1,2(✉)], A. Hussain[1], J. Mustafina[3], and D. Al-Jumeily[1]

[1] School of Computer Science and Mathematics,
Liverpool John Moores University, Liverpool, UK
A.S.Alatrany@2020.ljmu.ac.uk, {A.Hussain,D.Aljumeily}@ljmu.ac.uk
[2] University of Information Technology and Communications, Baghdad, Iraq
[3] Kazan Federal University, Kazan, Russia
DNMustafina@kpfu.ru

Abstract. Genome-wide association studies are aimed at identifying associations between commonly occurring variations in a group of individuals and a phonotype, in which the Deoxyribonucleic acid is genotyped in the form of single nucleotide polymorphisms. Despite the exsistence of various research studies for the prediction of chronic diseases using human genome data, more investigations are still required. Machine learning algorithms are widely used for prediction and genome-wide association studies. In this research, Random Forest was utilised for selecting most significant single nucleotide polymorphisms associated to Alzheimer's Disease. Deep learning model for the prediction of the disease was then developed. Our extesnive similation results indicated that this hybrid model is promising in predicting individuals that suffer from Alzheimer's disease, achieving area under the curve of 0.9 and 0.93 using Convolutional Neural Network and Multilayer perceptron respectively.

Keywords: GWAS · Machine learning · Random forest · CNN · ANN

1 Introduction

Alzheimer disease (AD) is a neurodegenerative disease and a leading cause of dementia. According to World Alzheimer Report (2018) [1] around 50 million patients are diagnosed with dementia. People who suffer from AD account between 60% and 80% of dementia patients. Typically, Alzheimer's symptoms mature after the age of sixty, affecting both the mental and physical condition of the patient. A person diagnosed with Alzheimer's could suffer from various syndromes including memory efficiency decreases, speaking difficulties, lack of attention, decline in the quality of lifestyle. More critically, the disease could develop to cause serious damage, and this could lead patients to start forgetting their family and friends [2].

Based on the age of the onset, there are two subtypes to the disease, they are: Eary-onset AD (EOAD) and late-onset AD (LOAD). Approximately 5% of AD cases [3]

© Springer Nature Switzerland AG 2021
D.-S. Huang et al. (Eds.): ICIC 2021, LNAI 12838, pp. 253–266, 2021.
https://doi.org/10.1007/978-3-030-84532-2_23

show EOAD, the age-onset ranges from the 30's to early 60's. EOAD gene association includes 3 types, amyloid precursor, Presenilin 1 and Presenilin 2 [4]. In comparison with EOAD, LOAD is shown to occur later in life, showing from late 60's onwards. The incidence of LOAD has a rate of 90%–95% [3]. Apolipoprotein is a risk factor gene, associated with LOAD, which has been confirmed as the most common [5]. Genetic and environmental factors are both part of the LOAD which seems showing more complex disorder. Several genetic variants could influence the complex disease AD. Due to the difficulty of accessing pathological information, generally it is a challenge to predict neurodegenerative disorders [6].

The manner of development of AD continues to be difficult to grasp therefore, the course of AD also remains irreversible. Currently, there are no available medication to fight and cure AD, hence the progression of this disease cannot be reversed. Thus, by achieving an early diagnosis of AD, it can provide the patient with medication to slow the disease.

Machine learning algorithms have shown promising results when used for the prediction of diseases using genome wide dataset. Kim and his team [7] used The Nurses' Health Study (NHS) and the Health Professionals Follow-up Study (HPFS) datasets to build a deep learning classifier for Type 2 Diabetes (T2D) from genome wide data and clinical factors. The dataset was randomly split into 75% and 25% for training and testing, respectively. Deep neural network was trained as a classifier for T2D using various number of genetic variants and tested on males and females. To evaluate the performance of the classifier, the Area Under the Curve (AUC) is used as a performance measurement. Their simulation results indicated that using high number of Single Nucleotide Polymorphisms (SNPs) during training can improve the performance of their proposed network. Their model outperformed logistic regression. Furthermore, the model accuracy improved when clinical data such as age, weight and hypertension were utilized. In another study [8], the authors tried to build a Deep Learning (DL) classifier to predict T2D from genotype - phenotype data as in the previous study. They used logistic regression to detect the most influencing SNPs associated with the disease, then constructed a multi-layer feedforward Artificial Neural Network (ANN) for the classification task. The authors claim that their proposed model achieved AUC of 0.52, when trained on SNPs with p-value of 5×10^{-8}, and achieved an AUC of 0.96 using larger set of SNPs by setting the p-value to 5×10^{-2}, their results indicated a performance outperformed Random Forest (RF) network.

Ghanem and colleagues [9] used supercomputer to apply parallel deep learning based on Map/Reduce framework to process data by multi-nodes to find SNP-SNP interactions. The proposed method consists of 2 stages: first stage, is the pre-processing of data, and filter SNPs pairs. In the second stage, a super-computer is used to apply the Deep Learning model. The computer clusters is controlled by H2O program accessed by R interface allowing the user to connect and organize the H2O server. Each node is responsible for training a subset of the DL network. The authors used GAMETES tool [10] to generate 12 simulated datasets by presenting different values of minor allele frequency, each dataset contains 1600 samples: 800 cases and 800 controls with 100 SNPs and 2 functional SNPs to simulate the pair-wise interaction. The model showed high accuracy between (83–98) for each of the simulated datasets.

Sun et al. [11] developed a multilayer deep neural network as a prediction tool of age-related macular degeneration (AMD) which is an eye disease using genetic data. Various simulation experiments were conducted to benchmark the performance of their proposed method with other machine learning algorithms. GWAS data of AMD from the age-related eye disease studies (AREDS and AREDSs) contains 7800 samples used for development and evaluation of the model. Deep Neural Network model achieved the best results train on 666 variables of the genetic variant reaching AUC of 81.8% which outperformed all other models.

Ghafouri-Fard et al. [12] constructed an ANN to predict individuals with Autism Spectrum Disorder (ASD) from genetics variants of 487 cases and 455 control of Iranian population. The authors selected only 15 SNPs associated with ASD reported in the literature as a feature set to the model. The model reached an AUC, accuracy, sensitivity, and specificity of 80.59%, 73.67%, 82.75% and 63.95%, respectively.

Different to previous researches, in this work we are proposing a hybrid machine learning model based on random forest and deep learning for the early detection of Alzheimer disease using genetic data.

Genome Wide Association Studies (GWAS) are associated with detecting associations between commonly occurring variations in a group of individuals and a phonotype [13]. Normally, GWAS requires a large number of participants, in which the Deoxyribonucleic Acid (DNA) is genotyped in the form of single nucleotide polymorphisms. Statistical tests are usually conducted to evaluate how each SNP asso-ciated with a human trait being studied [14]. There are two existing approaches of GWAS: family-based studies and population-based studies. Most GWA studies employ a case-control form [15].

GWAS shows a unique way of analysing genetic material, which involve some advantages and disadvantages. Previously, GWAS has been criticised due to the high expense cost. This limitation has been reduced significantly due to technological advancements. GWAS also shows some disadvantages which could prove to be critical in discovering new and existing biomarkers. These include the overlooking of some rare alleles along with an elevated rate of false discoveries [16].

Therefore, the most significant feature of GWA studies are the requirements of using a sample size larger enough to achieve the desired reliability of the results.

Machine Learning (ML) algorithms are computational methods developed to extract information from a raw data and turn it into useful resources [17]. Various studies have looked at individuals who are diagnosed with a specific disease and healthy people, by genotyping their DNA sequence, with the use of machine learnings to predict the susceptibility of individuals to the disease through their sequencing data [8, 9, 18, 19]. Machine learning algorithms, can be trained using supervised and unsupervised learning. In the former, the algorithm is trained on labelled data i.e. each observation includes its output class, a good model should make an accurate prediction when presented with new example. Whereas in the latter, the task is to identify and understand structures of data without prior knowledge of the output [20]. A supervised learning model would be used in the genetics context to aid in the identification of individuals who suffer from a disease vs healthy individual based on their sequence data [8, 12]. Machine learning can be utilised when the output of individuals diagnosis is unknown, therefore, an unsupervised learning model can be used to from separate groups of these individuals, based on similar characteristics of their blood sequence [21].

Supervised learning algorithms have been extensively used by researchers in the genetics fields. Vivian-Griffiths et al. [22] used support vector machines to build predictive model of schizophrenia from genomic data. Laksshman and his colleagues [23] used decision trees, random forest and neural network to point out genomic mutations for bipolar disorder using exomes data. Yang et al. [24] applied a liner regression model on genetics data after passing quality control procedures in the aim to explain missing heritability of human height. The authors show that considering all 294,831 SNPs can explain 45% of the heritability. Whereas in [25, 26], the authors illustrated the applicability of CNN to DNA sequence data.

For unsupervised learning, Scholz and his team [27] applied non-liner principal component analysis to impute data. While in [28] used class purity maximization clustering to solve the problem of genetic data imbalance.

The reminder of this paper is organised as follows. Section 2 will provide details about our proposed methodology. Results will be presented in Sect. 3 alongside the discussions. Finally, conclusion and future directions are summarized in Sect. 4.

2 Methodology

This section provides the details about the analysis of genetic data and the proposed methodology for the early prediction of Alzheimer Disease.

Our methodology consists from various phases as will be explained in the following subsections.

2.1 Dataset

The GWAS case-control dataset obtained from [29]. The inclusion criteria for participates are those who reported themselves to be from European ethnicity, board-certified neuropathologists confirmed late-onset Alzheimer disease (LOAD) for cases or no neuropathology present for controls according to the National Alzheimer's Coordinating Centre protocols. Death age of participants greater than 65 years. Plaque and tangle assessment (unique structures that effect cells in the brain which could contribute to the pathophysiology of the disease) conducted on all cases and controls. Samples that suffered previously from stroke, Lewy bodies, or any other neurological disease were excluded. The dataset consists of 191 males and 173 females divided into 176 cases and 188 controls with genotype information across 502,627 SNPs. The DNA of participants were genotyped via Affymetrix GeneChip Human Mapping 500K Array Set. Detailed information regarding the dataset can be found in [29].

2.2 Quality Control

Plink [30] is an open-source software utilized to efficiently conduct basic analyses for genotype/phenotype data. Plink v1.9 is used in this study to perform all quality control procedures and pre-liminary analysis. Quality control procedures conducted as follows on genetic markers filtering. SNPs were removed due to genotype missing rate larger than 5%, Hardly-Weinberg test with p-value less than 0.001, minor allele frequency less than 0.05. In addition, quality control procedures performed on each sample, including missing genotype data rate of 0.05, related individuals, and sex-homozygosity. After completing all the aforementioned steps, a total of 356499 SNPs in the samples were retained for the subsequent analysis.

2.3 Association Test - Logistic Regression

GWAS utilizes highly dimensional data thus making it extremely difficult to process the data directly in which most of the SNPs are irrelevant and uninformative. Therefore, selecting the most important SNPs is essential.

Logistic regression is one of the simplest machine learning algorithms and is the first algorithm to be used for classification problems. Logistic regression explains and assess the relations between the SNPs and the dependent variable.

The association test model is based on a logistic function that is described as:

$$f(x) = \frac{1}{1 + e^{-x}} \tag{1}$$

Association test used in the current work to rank each SNP with a significant value. Due to computational need, only the first 5000 SNPs with lowest p-value are extracted, to meet the machine learning classifier requirements.

2.4 Feature Selection

Random forest [31] is constructed by combining multiple decision trees to reach a more powerful model than using single model. Random forest algorithm is able to process noisy data. Additionally, random forest can efficiently deal with unbalance data set.

Feature selection techniques is required since many bioinformatics datasets have a high dimensional nature. There are two aims within feature selection, firstly is to gain and understand a more in-depth reasoning and insight to the process of selecting the given data and to enhance the model performance along with trying to avoid any/all overfitting. Machine learning interpretation into how a decision was made through its specific process, is as important as the accuracy of the output results of the model. Specially, in safety critical and medical applications, where some decisions could lead to fatal outcome. Feature selection can be performed using random forest along with the construction of classification rules.

Within the current study, the Gini measure which is one of the most popular and used methods to measure feature importance within RF is utilized as a feature selector based on the traning dataset. The attribute overall importance is calculated by averaging the importance value of all the trees within random forest. Due to the nature of the GWAS data, many SNPs are irrelevant and have an extremely low importance value. Therefore, all SNPs reached a Gini value of 0.0009 or above are selected within the feature set for the classification. The importance threshold of 0.0009 was selected by trial as it can capture the appropriate SNPs which reflect positive results in the classification task.

2.5 Classification

GWA studies use linear models to associate SNPs to a phenotype [32], liner models showed outstanding performance in their ability to make accurate decisions of various problems in different applications. However, GWASs consist of big, complex, and highly interacted data [33], all together making it a flavorful recipe to deep learning models. In recent years DL has been used by scientists as a knowledge discovery tool. Major work presented an understanding to the genetic background of a disease. Previous research [9, 12, 34, 35] showed that by taking advantage of the high computation power of DL, dense relationships from genetic data can be detected. However, the application of DL techniques to GWAS data still requires further investigation.

In this study, we have utilised both multilayer percepton (MLP) and Convolution Neurla network (CNN) for our experrimets.

Multilayer perceptron is a feedforward Neural Networks, in which the connections of layers are in one direction. The input layer passes the input signal to the next layer and the process continued until it reaches the output layer, in which an output is produced.

Figure 1A shows basic structure of MLP network consisting of two hidden layers and a single output node. There is no limit or constraints on the number of inputs, outputs, layers, or nodes per layers [36]. The output of such neural networks depends totally on the current input therefore nodes are memoryless. The output of a single layer network is computed by:

$$y = \sigma(wx + b) \tag{2}$$

Where w is the weight of the network, x is the inputs to the network, b is the bias value, and σ represents the activation function. MLP netwrok used in our work consists of 60 inputs, 4 hidden layers with 32,12,6,3 nodes respectivly with using rectified liner activation function at the hidden layers and sigmoid function at the output layer. Learning rate of 0.001 used during the training phase with binary cross entropy loss function.

Convolutional Neural Network reduces the size of the connections from the input layer to the hidden layer by applying a filter over the input matrix. Therefore, neurons in the hidden layer are connected to local regions of the input. For efficient results, it is preferable to add several hidden layers. The layers are not limited to specific filter, but rather each layer can be associated with a different filter. Consequently, different patterns can be extracted from the input data [37].

To reduce the input complexity for the next layer, pooling layer is usually added after the conventional layer. Max-pooling is used in the current work. It divides the input into sub-regions and return the max value of each region. The output of pooling layer then flatten to be fully connected with the next layer.

Figure 1B shows a typical CNN architecture with convolution layers, pooling layers and one fully connected layer. Details of the architecture of CNN used in this paper are presented in Table 1. Learning rate of 0.001 used during the training phase with categorical cross entropy loss function.

The classifier is a constructed model to solve a specific problem. The model requires an input data consist of attributes of each observation, usually known as a feature set. Besides the given attributes, a set of hyper-parameters are also needed to train the model.

To obtain a high accuracy classifier, usually extensive hyper-parameter is required. In the current work a grid search is conducted on user defined hyper-parameters values.

Table 1. CNN architecture

Layer type	Description	Output shape
Input		(60,1)
1D Convolution	16 kernel (1X5) relu	(56,16)
1D Convolution	32 Kernel (1X5) tanh	(54,32)
1D Pooling	Max Pooling (1X2)	(27,32)
Dropout	Dropout_rate = 0.1	(27,32)
1D Convolution	64 Kernel (1 × 4) tanh	(25,64)
1D Pooling	Max Pooling (1 × 2)	(12,64)
Dropout	Dropout_rate = 0.1	(12,64)
Reshape	64 nodes, sigmoid	768
Dese	Flatten	64
Dropout	Dropout_rate = 0.1	64
Output	2 nodes, softmax	2

2.6 The Proposed Model

The proposed system presented in the current work aims to diagnose and early classify individuals with Alzheimer's disease as shown in Fig. 1C. The main intentions of the model are (1) reduce the number of features of the GWAS SNPs to allow fast and computational efficiently processing of data and (2) improve the classification accuracy of Alzheimer's' vs healthy individuals. The hybrid system consists of two stages specifically a feature selection stage and classification stage. Random forest was conducted as feature selector to find the ideal set of SNPs. For the second stage, ANN and CNN models are used as classifier. Algorithm 1 shows the proposed process.

Algorithm 1: Alzahimer Disease Classification using SNPs data
Let A to be the set of Alzehimer GWAS SNPs data
Let B to be the set of pre-prossed data set where B ∈ A
Let C to be the feature seletced set
∀ b ∈ B, b ∈ C if b is selected by LR and RF
Let ML to be a set of ML
ML = { ANN, CNN}
A_z = ML (C) where A_z = { 0, 1}

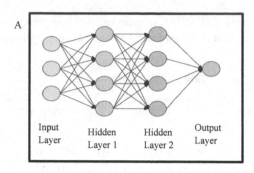

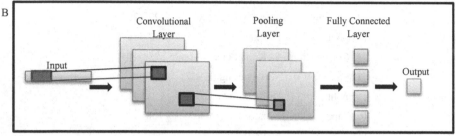

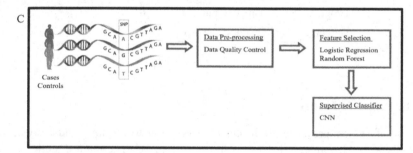

Fig. 1. Proposed model (A) Typical ANN architecture, (B) Typical CNN architecture, (C) Proposed model stages

3 Results and Discussion

This section presents the results of the stages explained in the methods section. After applying logistic regression for the association test, the top 5000 SNPs with the lowest p-value were selected for further analysis (Fig. 2).

Producing the most informative SNPs for the classification task is a challenging problem, in which random forest algorithm was used for SNPs selection in this work. The reason is because the tree-based strategies used by random forests naturally ranks attributes by how well they improve the purity of the node.

Table 2 shows the SNPs associated to AD according to RF Gini metric. The first two SNPs (rs429358 and rs4420638) are proven to be associated with the disease as illustrated in the Manhattan plot which reached the genome-wide significance level (P $< 1.2 \times 10^{-8}$). This suggests that the model is accurate in selecting good features for the

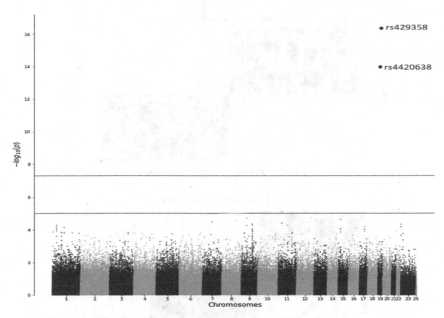

Fig. 2. Manhattan plot of associated SNPs with AD

classification task. However, more investigation is required to examine the associations of the rest of SNPs.

Table 2. Top 10 SNPs

SNP
rs429358
rs4420638
rs867198
rs3011823
rs5939190
rs8030415
rs1522940
rs2383559
rs7677027
rs862245

SNPs selected during the previous stage, are used as a feature set for two deep machine learning models (ANN and CNN) for the classification task of AD and Non-AD. The dataset is split into 80% and 20%, training and testing sets, respectively.

Table 3 shows the performance of the two models on testing set (Fig. 3).

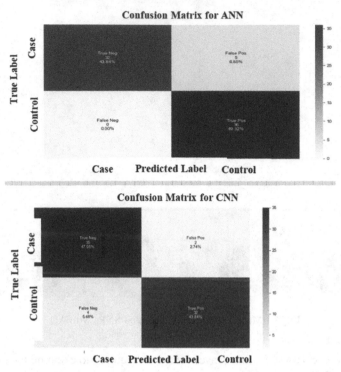

Fig. 3. Confusion matrix for ANN and CN

Table 3. Performance metrics for ANN and CNN testing set

Model	Accuracy	Precision	Recall	F1 score	Cohens kappa
ANN	0.93	0.88	1.00	0.94	0.86
CNN	0.92	0.94	0.89	0.91	0.84

Figure 4 presents the area under the carve for ANN and CNN, the performance of both models is approximately similar. This demonstrates the capability of these models to deal with complex genetic data.

The genetics of complex phenotype such as Alzheimer disease is challenging [38]. Multiple genetic markers contribute into the development of complex human disease. Although GWA studies were successful in revealing SNPs associated to complex traits, this method lacks the identification markers that together have influence on the disease. In our study, we aimed to explore DL models in classification of AD based solely on GWAS. DL offers a well renowned analytical models used in classification applications of diseases.

Few studies reported the use of Deep Learning in diagnostics of complex diseases using SNPs as fea-ture set. Some studies used SNPs that are proven to be associated with

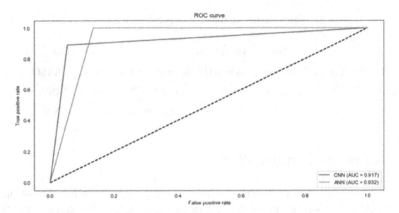

Fig. 4. Performance ROC curve for ANN and CNN

a phonotype. In [12] authors have applied ANN in the diagnosis of Autism Spectrum Disorder using genotyping data of 15 SNPs within four genes. While other studies demonstrated that the use of higher number of SNPs can increase the accuracy of the model [8]. In [39] the authors applied CNN in the diagnosis of amyotrophic lateral scle-rosis using the promoter regions within four genes of the human genome.

This study demonstrates a novel approach for application of genetic markers in the area of Alzheimer disease. Formed of two stages: a feature selection stage and classification stage.

ANN showed a slightly better results than CNN. This could be due to the nature and size of the input data, as CNN are more effective when analysing images data [40]. For data problem solving, ANN is an ideal candidate to do so. Feedforward NN are used to process text data, tabular data and image data with ease. To achieve the desired elevated accuracy, CNN needs a higher number of data inputs. The detection of complex relations, such as nonlinear relations in regard to independent and dependent variables, is achievable by ANN.

The proposed method has few advantages over its competitive. By reducing the feature set size using RF a simpler model can be built. Therefore, it can work on low-performance computing. Feature selection will also reduce the variance of the model, and therefore overfitting and we can reduce the computational cost of training a model.

The results of the proposed model in the current study outperform other models in the area of LOAD GWAS data classification as illustrated in Table 4. However, our study utilized smaller database and future works will involve the use of larger dataset to provide reliable benchmark.

Our work demonstrates the capability of deep learning for classification of AD using correct genetic markers. Romero-Rosales, et al. [41] applied regression analysis method to classify cases from controls by involve the addition of incorrectly classified samples to increase model accuracy.

Table 4. Comparison with previous work

Paper	Year	Dataset size	Classifier	AUC
Romero-Rosales et al. [41]	2020	1,856 AD cases and 2,000 controls	LASSO	0.80
Jansen et al. [42]	2019	71,880 cases and 383,378 controls	PRS	0.827
Proposed model	2021	176 cases and 188 controls	ANN	0.93

4 Conclusion and Future Work

The paper presents the use of hybrid machine learning algorithms for classification of late-onset Alzheimer's disease. To the best of our knowledge, this work is the first of applying these models for Alzheimer's disease. Both models showed promising results, generally ANN showed slightly improved accuracy than CNN. Contrast to various work within the field, our model used two stages for feature selection. First, logistic regression is applied to select the most significant SNPs associated with the disease. Second, Random Forest is applied to further reduces the number of SNPs. Thus, making the classification task computationally efficient.

Future works will invlove the use of larger dataset, helping improve the model, as well as expending our experimnets to other diseases.

References

1. World Alzheimer Report 2018. https://www.alzint.org/u/WorldAlzheimerReport2018.pdf, Accessed 15 Jan 2021
2. Ford, A.: Alzheimer disease. Mol. Chem. Neuropathol. **28**(1–3), 121–124 (1996). https://doi.org/10.1007/BF02815213
3. Isik, A.T.: Late onset alzheimer's disease in older people. Clin. Interv. Aging **5**, 307 (2010)
4. Williamson, J., Goldman, J., Marder, K.S.: Genetic aspects of alzheimer disease. Neurologist **15**(2), 80–86 (2009). https://doi.org/10.1097/NRL.0b013e318187e76b
5. Bekris, L.M., Yu, C.-E., Bird, T.D., Tsuang, D.W.: Review article: genetics of alzheimer disease. J. Geriatr. Psychiatry Neurol. **23**(4), 213–227 (2010). https://doi.org/10.1177/0891988710383571
6. Hofmann-Apitius, M., et al.: Bioinformatics mining and modeling methods for the identification of disease mechanisms in neurodegenerative disorders. Int. J. Molec. Sci. **16**(12), 29179–29206 (2015). https://www.mdpi.com/1422-0067/16/12/26148
7. Kim, J., Kim, J., Kwak, M.J., Bajaj, M.: Genetic prediction of type 2 diabetes using deep neural network. Clin. Genet. **93**(4), 822–829 (2018). https://doi.org/10.1111/cge.13175
8. Abdulaimma, B., Fergus, P., Chalmers, C., Montanez, C.C.: Deep learning and genome-wide association studies for the classification of type 2 diabetes, pp. 1-8. IEEE (2020)
9. Ghanem, S.I., Ghoneim, A.A., Ghanem, N.M., Ismail, M.A.: High performance computing for detecting complex diseases using deep learning. In: 2019 International Conference on Advances in the Emerging Computing Technologies, AECT 2019 (2020). https://doi.org/10.1109/AECT47998.2020.9194158, https://www.scopus.com/inward/record.uri?eid=2-s2.0-85092376858&doi=10.1109%2fAECT47998.2020.9194158&partnerID=40&md5=0252fbd3c9bf9226aaa8482e30f8aaec, https://ieeexplore.ieee.org/document/9194158/

10. Urbanowicz, R., Kiralis, J., Sinnott-Armstrong, N., Heberling, T., Fisher, J., Moore, J.: GAMETES: a fast, direct algorithm for generating pure, strict, epistatic models with random architectures. BioData Mining **5**(1) (2012). https://doi.org/10.1186/1756-0381-5-16

11. Sun, T., Wei, Y., Chen, W., Ding, Y.: Genome-wide association study-based deep learning for survival prediction. Stat. Med. Article (2020). https://doi.org/10.1002/sim.8743

12. Ghafouri-Fard, S., Taheri, M., Omrani, M.D., Daaee, A., Mohammad-Rahimi, H., Kazazi, H.: Application of single-nucleotide polymorphisms in the diagnosis of autism spectrum disorders: a preliminary study with artificial neural networks. J. Mol. Neurosci. **68**(4), 515–521 (2019). https://doi.org/10.1007/s12031-019-01311-1

13. Guo, X., Yu, N., Gu, F., Ding, X., Wang, J., Pan, Y.: Genome-wide interaction-based association of human diseases-a survey. Tsinghua Sci. Technol. **19**(6), 596–616 (2014)

14. Bush, W.S.: Genome-wide association studies. In: Ranganathan, S., Gribskov, M., Nakai, K., Schönbach, C. (eds.) Encyclopedia of Bioinformatics and Computational Biology, pp. 235–241. Academic Press, Oxford (2019)

15. Clarke, G., Anderson, C., Pettersson, F., Cardon, L., Morris, A., Zondervan, K.: Basic statistical analysis in genetic case-control studies. Nat. Protocols **6**(2), 121–133 (2011). https://doi.org/10.1038/nprot.2010.182

16. Pearson, T.A., Manolio, T.A.: How to interpret a genome-wide association study. JAMA **299**(11), 1335–1344 (2008)

17. Witten, I.H., Frank, E., Hall, M.A.: Chapter 1 - what's it all about? In: Witten, I.H., Frank, E., Hall, M.A. (eds.) Data Mining: Practical Machine Learning Tools and Techniques (Third Edition), pp. 3–38. Morgan Kaufmann, Boston (2011)

18. Lin, E., et al.: A deep learning approach for predicting antidepressant response in major depression using clinical and genetic biomarkers. Front Psychiatry **9** (2018). https://doi.org/10.3389/fpsyt.2018.00290, (in eng)

19. Okser, S., Pahikkala, T., Airola, A., Salakoski, T., Ripatti, S., Aittokallio, T.: Regularized machine learning in the genetic prediction of complex traits. PLoS Genet. **10**(11), e1004754 (2014)

20. Emre Celebi, M., Aydin, K. (eds.): Unsupervised learning algorithms. Springer, Cham (2016). https://doi.org/10.1007/978-3-319-24211-8

21. Lopez, C., Tucker, S., Salameh, T., Tucker, C.: An unsupervised machine learning method for discovering patient clusters based on genetic signatures. J. Biomed. Inf. **85**, 30–39 (2018). https://doi.org/10.1016/j.jbi.2018.07.004

22. Vivian-Griffiths, T., et al.: Predictive modeling of schizophrenia from genomic data: Comparison of polygenic risk score with kernel support vector machines approach. Am. J. Med. Genet. B Neuropsychiatr. Genet. **180**(1), 80–85 (2019)

23. Laksshman, S., Bhat, R.R., Viswanath, V., Li, X.: DeepBipolar: Identifying genomic mutations for bipolar disorder via deep learning. Hum. Mutat. **38**(9), 1217–1224 (2017)

24. Yang, J., et al.: Common SNPs explain a large proportion of the heritability for human height. Nat. Genet. **42**(7), 565–569 (2010)

25. Alipanahi, B., Delong, A., Weirauch, M.T., Frey, B.J.: Predicting the sequence specificities of DNA-and RNA-binding proteins by deep learning. Nat. Biotechnol. **33**(8), 831–838 (2015)

26. Zhou, J., Troyanskaya, O.G.: Predicting effects of noncoding variants with deep learning–based sequence model. Nat. Methods **12**(10), 931–934 (2015)

27. Scholz, M., Kaplan, F., Guy, C.L., Kopka, J., Selbig, J.: Non-linear PCA: a missing data approach. Bioinformatics **21**(20), 3887–3895 (2005)

28. Yoon, K., Kwek, S.: An unsupervised learning approach to resolving the data imbalanced issue in supervised learning problems in functional genomics. In: Fifth International Conference on Hybrid Intelligent Systems (HIS 2005), p. 6. IEEE (2005)

29. Webster, J.A., et al.: Genetic control of human brain transcript expression in Alzheimer disease (in eng). Am. J. Hum. Genet. **84**(4), 445–458 (2009). https://doi.org/10.1016/j.ajhg.2009.03.011

30. Purcell, S., et al.: PLINK: a tool set for whole-genome association and population-based linkage analyses. Am. J. Hum. Gen. **81**(3), 559–575 (2007). https://doi.org/10.1086/519795

31. Breiman, L.: Random forests. Mach. Learn. **45**(1), 5–32 (2001)

32. Cook, J., Mahajan, A., Morris, A.: Guidance for the utility of linear models in meta-analysis of genetic association studies of binary phenotypes. Eur. J. Hum. Gen. **25**(2), 240–245 (2016). https://doi.org/10.1038/ejhg.2016.150

33. Chang, M., He, L., Cai, L.: An overview of genome-wide association studies. In: Huang, Tao (ed.) Computational Systems Biology. MMB, vol. 1754, pp. 97–108. Springer, New York (2018). https://doi.org/10.1007/978-1-4939-7717-8_6

34. Curbelo, C., et al.: SAERMA: stacked autoencoder rule mining algorithm for the interpretation of epistatic interactions in GWAS for extreme obesity. IEEE Access **8**, 112379–112392 (2020). https://doi.org/10.1109/ACCESS.2020.3002923

35. Fergus, P., Montanez, C.C., Abdulaimma, B., Lisboa, P., Chalmers, C., Pineles, B.: Utilizing deep learning and genome wide association studies for epistatic-driven preterm birth classification in African-American women. IEEE/ACM Trans. Comput. Biol. Bioinf. **17**(2), 668–678 (2020). Art no. 8454302, https://doi.org/10.1109/TCBB.2018.2868667

36. Aggarwal, C.C.: Neural networks and deep learning. Springer **10**, 978–983 (2018)

37. Yamashita, R., Nishio, M., Do, R.K.G., Togashi, K.: Convolutional neural networks: an overview and application in radiology. Insights Imag. **9**(4), 611–629 (2018). https://doi.org/10.1007/s13244-018-0639-9

38. Bush, W., Moore, J.: Chapter 11: genome-wide association studies. PLoS Comput. Biol. **8**(12), e1002822 (2012). https://doi.org/10.1371/journal.pcbi.1002822

39. Yin, B., et al.: Using the structure of genome data in the design of deep neural networks for predicting amyotrophic lateral sclerosis from genotype (in eng). Bioinformatics **35**(14), i538–i547 (2019). https://doi.org/10.1093/bioinformatics/btz369

40. Sharma, P., Singh, A.: Era of deep neural networks: a review. In: 2017 8th International Conference on Computing, Communication and Networking Technologies (ICCCNT), 3–5 July 2017, pp. 1–5 (2017). https://doi.org/10.1109/ICCCNT.2017.8203938.

41. Romero-Rosales, B.-L., Tamez-Pena, J.-G., Nicolini, H., Moreno-Treviño, M.-G., Trevino, V.: Improving predictive models for Alzheimer's disease using GWAS data by incorporating misclassified samples modeling. PloS One **15**(4), e0232103 (2020). https://www.ncbi.nlm.nih.gov/pmc/articles/PMC7179850/pdf/pone.0232103.pdf

42. Jansen, I.E., et al.: Genome-wide meta-analysis identifies new loci and functional pathways influencing Alzheimer's disease risk. Nat. Gen. **51**(3), 404–413 (2019). https://www.ncbi.nlm.nih.gov/pmc/articles/PMC6836675/pdf/nihms-1031924.pdf

Prediction of Heart Disease Probability Based on Various Body Function

Wentian Yin, Yanwen Yao, Yujian Gu, Wenzheng Bao[✉], and Honglin Cheng

School of Information Engineering (School of Big Data), Xuzhou University of Technology,
Xuzhou 221018, China
baowz55555@126.com

Abstract. Heart disease is a kind of common circulatory system disease. It is a common disease in internal medicine, which can significantly affect the labor force of patients. The various indicators of the human body can respond to our physical condition in real time. Through these data, we can effectively adjust and treat our bodies ahead of time. Currently, many prediction methods based on machine learning have been proposed to predict heart attack. In this essay, we construct a decision tree, which can effectively predict the risk of heart disease. In this model, the indicators of human body are mapped into digital features to construct the initial data set. A new data set is formed by randomly selecting data blocks to form a decision tree, and then a decision tree forest is formed by different decision trees generated many times. Then we take out 25% of the remaining data sets to verify the prediction performance of our method. Finally, the prediction accuracy of the method for the current data set is 0.857143. The results show that the method is a stable and reliable prediction model.

Keywords: Heart attack · Random forest · Prediction

1 Introduction

Heart disease is the number one killer of human health. One third of the world's deaths are caused by heart disease. In China, hundreds of thousands of people die of heart disease every year. Therefore, if we can analyze the influence of different features on heart disease through [1–3] data mining, it will play a vital role in the prediction and prevention of heart disease. The goal of the project is to build a model that can predict the probability of heart disease according to the combination of characteristics describing the disease. To achieve this, we used the dataset collected by Rashik Rahman on kaggle. The data set used in this project contains 14 characteristics for heart disease. We have 303 pedestrian data, 13 consecutive observations of different symptoms. This project [4–6] studies different classical machine learning models and their discovery in disease risk.

In this article, we use the random forest to build a classifier to predict [7, 8]. Through the directional classification and adjustment of the data, we constantly optimize the accuracy of our model, and finally achieve a relatively high accuracy [9–13].

© Springer Nature Switzerland AG 2021
D.-S. Huang et al. (Eds.): ICIC 2021, LNAI 12838, pp. 267–275, 2021.
https://doi.org/10.1007/978-3-030-84532-2_24

2   Methods and Materials

2.1   Data

This data is a data set in the medical field, there are many professional feature terms, in order to follow-up data cleaning process of feature extraction, feature selection and other engineering, we must first understand the meaning of each feature [14–16].

About this data:

- Age: Age of the patient
- Sex: Sex of the patient
- exang: exercise induced angina (1 = yes; 0 = no)
- ca: number of major vessels (0–3)
- cp: Chest Pain type chest pain type

o Value 1: typical angina
o Value 2: atypical angina
o Value 3: non-anginal pain
o Value 4: asymptomatic

- trtbps: resting blood pressure (in mm Hg)
- chol: cholestoral in mg/dl fetched via BMI sensor
- fbs: (fasting blood sugar >120 mg/dl) (1 = true; 0 = false)
- rest_ecg: resting electrocardiographic results

o Value 0: normal
o Value 1: having ST-T wave abnormality (T wave inversions and/or ST elevation or depression of >0.05 mV)
o Value 2: showing probable or definite left ventricular hypertrophy by Estes' criteria

- thalach: maximum heart rate achieved
- target: 0 = less chance of heart attack 1 = more chance of heart attack

We can see that a lot of data are described by words. In the process of data preprocessing, we need to convert the character type into numerical value according to the meaning of each field.

1) Binary data
   Binary class is relatively easy to convert. For example, the sex field has two forms: female and male. We can express female as 0 and male as 1.
2) Data of multivalued class

For example, the CP field represents the chest pain [17–21]. We can map the pain from light to heavy to a value of 0–3 (Fig. 1).

63.0	male	ang...	145.0	233.0	true	hyp	150.0	fal	2.3	down	0.0	fix	buff	H
67.0	male	asy...	160.0	286.0	fal	hyp	108.0	true	1.5	flat	3.0	norm	sick	S2
67.0	male	asy...	120.0	229.0	fal	hyp	129.0	true	2.6	flat	2.0	rev	sick	S1
37.0	male	not...	130.0	250.0	fal	norm	187.0	fal	3.5	down	0.0	norm	buff	H
41.0	fem	abn...	130.0	204.0	fal	hyp	172.0	fal	1.4	up	0.0	norm	buff	H
56.0	male	abn...	120.0	236.0	fal	norm	178.0	fal	0.8	up	0.0	norm	buff	H
62.0	fem	asy...	140.0	268.0	fal	hyp	160.0	fal	3.6	down	2.0	norm	sick	S3
57.0	fem	asy...	120.0	354.0	fal	norm	163.0	true	0.6	up	0.0	norm	buff	H

Fig. 1. The feature of this work

3   Results and Discussion

We analyze the correlation of features first.
As the follow picture shows.
As the results:

1. There was a strong correlation between heart disease and CP, thalach, Exang and oldpeak, with correlation coefficient over 0.4
2. Heart disease is related to age, sex, slope, Ca and thalassemia a little
3. The correlation between heart disease and Chol (cholesterol), FBS (fasting blood glucose) is weak (Figs. 2 and 3)

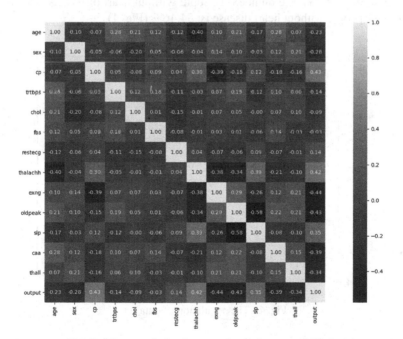

Fig. 2. The correlation between heart disease and Chol

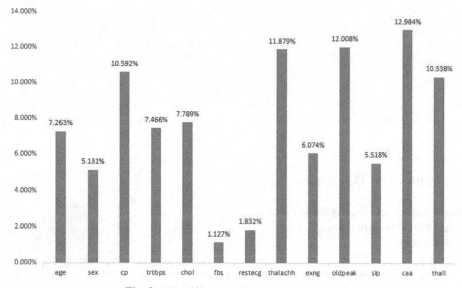

Fig. 3. The different performance of features

We can start by looking at the sample data as a whole.

The number of people without heart disease is: 138, and the proportion of people without heart disease is: 45.54%. The number of people without heart disease is: 165, and the proportion of people without heart disease is: 54.46% (Fig. 4).

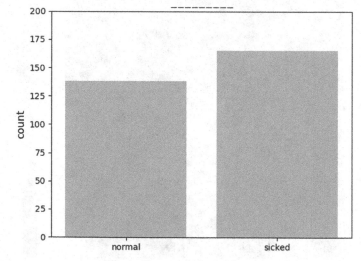

Fig. 4. The population of data set

And then, we analyze each feature one by one. The population of this data set is concentrated in the middle age, and the middle-aged people are more sicked.

According to our information collected, general heart disease includes congenital and acquired. The first stage of congenital heart disease is 5–10 years old, the second stage is about 20 years old, and the third stage is middle age. At the same time, the middle age of the third stage is also the time period of acquired heart disease because of various factors such as work pressure. This side 1 shows the universality of the data set (Figs. 5 and 6).

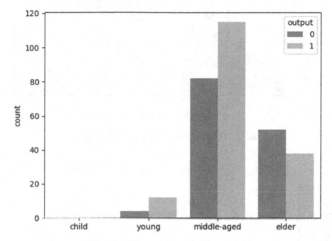

Fig. 5. The output of this model

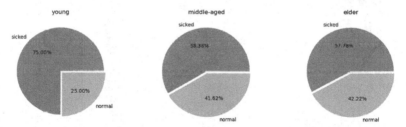

Fig. 6. The percentages of different levels

As the plot show the proportion of women suffering from heart disease was significantly higher than that of men (Fig. 7).

The probability of heart disease in patients with typical angina pectoris is relatively low. It is just pure angina rather than heart disease. The rate of heart disease in patients with other types 1 to 3 angina pectoris is higher, indicating that there is a certain relationship between heart disease and angina pectoris. The relationship with angina pectoris should be a negative correlation (Fig. 8).

We can see that as the age increases, the maximum heart rate gradually decreases. At the same time, in the same age group, the heart rate of people with heart disease is generally higher than that of normal people. In the elderly stage, heart disease is usually caused as a comorbidity. Such data seems to be less in the elderly. Good judgment, not very general (Fig. 9).

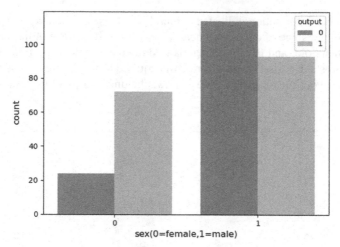

Fig. 7. The output of with different sex

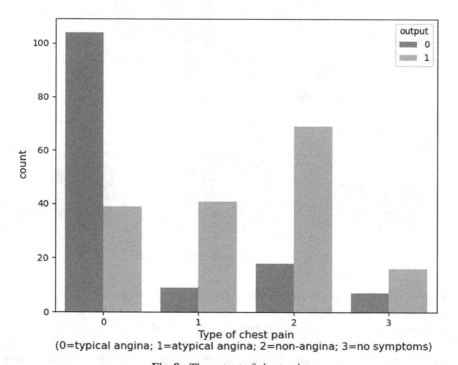

Fig. 8. The output of chest pain

Angina pectoris caused by exercise is less likely to be diagnosed as heart disease. So only exercise is the phenomenon of angina, first consider other diseases, but if you have heart disease, you must follow the doctor's instructions to rest, high-intensity exercise can still cause angina (Fig. 10).

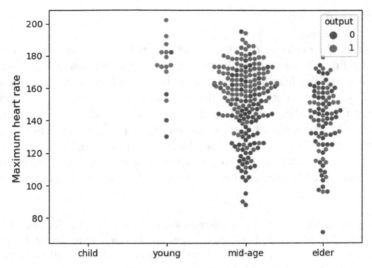

Fig. 9. The results of different age levels

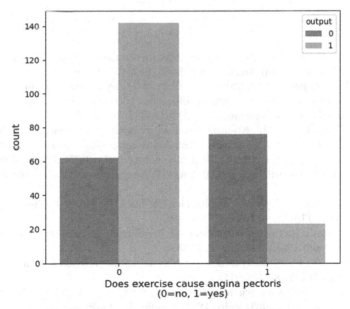

Fig. 10. The output of exercise cause angina pectoris

The resting blood pressure of normal people is slightly higher than that of heart patients. The author did not have a special research on medicine, so he didn't do much analysis to get a specific reason. But this is contrary to normal common sense, maybe it can be used as a research point to cut into research.

4 Conclusion

In recent years, the exploration of heart disease has become deeper and deeper, and our understanding of it has become broader. Some people are determined to solve this problem. Now machine learning methods have been widely used in model predictions. We analyze the collected data, extract effective data to make relevant adjustments to the model, and build a predictor that can make high-quality predictions. Through various experiments, we can conclude that our model has better performance in most cases. The prediction accuracy of our method for heart disease data reaches 0.857143. Experimental results show that our model can effectively predict heart disease. It has good performance on current data sets and can be used as a research tool to support biomedicine and other fields.

Acknowledgement. This work was supported by the Natural Science Foundation of China (No. 61902337), Natural Science Fund for Colleges and Universities in Jiangsu Province (No. 19KJB520016), Jiangsu Provincial Natural Science Foundation (No. SBK2019040953), Young talents of science and technology in Jiangsu.

References

1. Molinie, B., Giallourakis, C.C.: Genome-wide location analyses of N6-Methyladenosine modifications (m(6)A-Seq). Methods Mol. Biol. **1562**, 45–53 (2017)
2. Nye, T.M., van Gijtenbeek, L.A., Stevens, A.G., et al.: Methyltransferase DnmA is responsible for genome-wide N6-methyladenosine modifications at non-palindromic recognition sites in Bacillus subtilis. Nucleic Acids Res. **48**, 5332–5348 (2020)
3. O'Brown, Z.K., Greer, E.L.: N6-methyladenine: a conserved and dynamic DNA mark. In: Jeltsch, A., Jurkowska, R.Z. (eds.) DNA Methyltransferases - Role and Function. AEMB, vol. 945, pp. 213–246. Springer, Cham (2016). https://doi.org/10.1007/978-3-319-43624-1_10
4. Zhang, G., et al.: N6-methyladenine DNA modification in drosophila. Cell **161**(4), 893–906 (2015)
5. Janulaitis, A., et al.: Cytosine modification in DNA by BCNI methylase yields N4-methylcytosine. FEBS Lett. **161**, 131–134 (1983)
6. Unger, G., Venner, H.: Remarks on minor bases in spermatic desoxyribonucleic acid. Hoppe-Seylers Z. Physiol. Chem. **344**, 280–283 (1966)
7. Fu, Y., et al.: N6-methyldeoxyadenosine marks active transcription start sites in Chlamydomonas. Cell **161**, 879–892 (2015)
8. Greer, E.L., et al.: DNA methylation on N6-adenine in C. elegans. Cell **161**, 868–878 (2015)
9. Zhang, G., et al.: N6-methyladenine DNA modification in drosophila. Cell **161**, 893–906 (2015)
10. Wu, T.P., et al.: DNA methylation on N6-adenine in mammalian embryonic stem cells. Nature **532**, 329–333 (2016)
11. Xiao, C.L., et al.: N-methyladenine DNA modification in the human genome. Mol. Cell **71**, 306–318 (2018)
12. Zhou, C., et al.: Identification and analysis of adenine N6-methylation sites in the rice genome. Nat. Plants **4**, 554–563 (2018)
13. Chen, W., et al.: i6mA-Pred: identifying DNA N6-methyladenine sites in the rice genome. Bioinformatics **35**, 2796–2800 (2019)

14. Almagor, H.A.: A Markov analysis of DNA sequences. J. Theor. Biol. **104**, 633–645 (1983)
15. Borodovsky, M., et al.: Detection of new genes in a bacterial genome using Markov models for three gene classes. Nucleic Acids Res. **17**, 3554–3562 (1995)
16. Durbin, R., et al.: Biological Sequence Analysis Probabilistic Models of Proteins and Nucleic Acids. Cambridge University Press, Cambridge (1998)
17. Ohler, U., et al.: Interpolated Markov chains for Eukaryotic promoter recognition. Bioinformatics **15**, 362–369 (1999)
18. Reese, M., et al.: Improved splice site detection in genie. J. Comput. Biol. **4**, 311–323 (1997)
19. Wren, J.D., et al.: Markov model recognition and classification of DNA/protein sequences within large text databases. Bioinformatics **21**, 4046–4053 (2005)
20. Yakhnenko, O., et al.: Discriminatively trained Markov model for sequence classification. In: IEEE International Conference on Data Mining (2005)
21. Matthews, B.W.: Comparison of the predicted and observed secondary structure of t4 phage lysozyme. Biochim. Biophys. Acta **405**(2), 442–451 (1975)

Classification of Pulmonary Diseases from X-ray Images Using a Convolutional Neural Network

Adrian Trueba Espinosa, Jessica Sánchez-Arrazola$^{(\boxtimes)}$, Jair Cervantes, and Farid García-Lamont

Posgrado E Investigación, UAEMEX (Autonomous University of Mexico State), 56259 Texcoco, México

{atruebae,jcervantesc,fgarcial}@uaemex.mx,
jsancheza560@alumno.uaemex.mx

Abstract. In this work, the classification of current diseases in population that can be detected from X-ray radiographs is proposed; the diseases are COVID-19 that threaten life and health, also tuberculosis, which continues to be a global health problem, and viral and bacterial cases of pneumonia that present initial symptoms similar to COVID-19 and Tuberculosis. For the classification, a convolutional neural network (CNN) of its own and the ResNet-50 were proposed, which has had good results in other investigations. The results obtained regarding the Accuracy metric for ResNet-50 is 0.72%, while for the proposed model, it is 0.87%. Therefore, this proposal has better correct predictions. However, it is noted that there is a lot of confusion between viral pneumonia and bacterial pneumonia, as they have very similar symptoms and characteristics. The radiographs without diseases are also not classified adequately since, although they do not present any disease of those classified, that does not guarantee that they do not have a problem of another type. These two problems were evident in both models.

Keywords: Tuberculosis · Chest X-rays · Convolutional neural networks

1 Introduction

Respiratory diseases have similar symptoms in their early stages, affecting the lungs. A disease that has not been eradicated in the world is tuberculosis (TB). It is a contagious bacterial infection caused by the bacterium Mycobacterium or "Koch's bacillus" [1]. It is a disease that can be cured and can be prevented. It is transmitted from one person to another through the air. When a person with pulmonary tuberculosis coughs, sneezes, or spits, he expels tubercle bacilli into the air. It is enough for a person to inhale a few bacilli for them to become infected [2].

The World Health Organization (WHO) estimates that a third of the world's population has latent tuberculosis; that is, people are infected with the bacillus, but they have not gotten sick (yet) and cannot transmit the infection. People infected with the TB bacillus have a 10% chance of getting sick throughout their life. Since 2015, the WHO has been implementing a protocol to lower the infection rate by this disease. However, they

© Springer Nature Switzerland AG 2021
D.-S. Huang et al. (Eds.): ICIC 2021, LNAI 12838, pp. 276–289, 2021.
https://doi.org/10.1007/978-3-030-84532-2_25

need the diagnoses given by doctors to be quick and without errors so that patients start treatment as soon as possible. WHO has also recognized the disease of global impact COVID-19, caused by the infection of a new coronavirus (SARS-CoV-2) which has affected much of the world. According to official WHO figures, there are more than 126 million infected people, causing a large number of deaths worldwide [3]. However, there is also a prevalent condition that attacks the lungs, "Pneumonia" is a general term that encompasses lung infections, which can be caused by various microorganisms, such as viruses, bacteria, fungi and parasites and are generally not as aggressive as tuberculosis and COVID-19.

Studies [4] show that the uses of chest radiographs (X-rays) have helped diagnose and detect COVID-19, tuberculosis, and pneumonia. In this sense, experts interpret and differentiate the attack of each disease in chest images to issue an accurate diagnosis and provide proper treatment. However, it is also known that in many places, these experts lack to have a quick and effective diagnosis.

This work proposes a deep artificial neural network to classify from chest images tuberculosis, COVID-19 and Pneumonia diseases, which helps the inexperienced doctor make decisions for a final diagnosis and recommend the appropriate treatment.

2   State of the Art

In order to detect tuberculosis (TB) patterns in chest radiographs, researchers from the University of Ukraine used two data sets; the first was with an image segmentation technique, the second set without segmenting the image. To classify the images, they used deep convolutional neural networks (DCNN). The results obtained show that the technique is acceptable; the classification precision did not exceed 90% [5].

In another work to diagnose tuberculosis from chest radiographs, classifiers were used; multi-layer neural networks (MLNN) with two different structures, a general regression neural network (GRNN). For training, Levenberg-Marquardt algorithms were run in multi-layer neural networks. The results refer that the coincidence between algorithm results and the expert physician is 60.72%, with a precision of 57.14% [6]. The results suggest promising but with a low level of acceptance for an adequate diagnosis.

On the other hand, three convolutional neural networks (CNN) were evaluated at the University of Chulalongkorn Thailand: AlexNet, VGG-16 and CapsNet; These were used to classify tuberculosis in chest images (X-rays) (CXR), they used a sample of 1390 images, using random sampling to increase the images to 1986 images; later a third set with 3310 images was created; for each set of images, 80% were used for training and 20% for testing. They did three trainings for each data set and compared them. The classifier with the best performance was VGG-16 for the set of (3310), achieving maximum sensitivity of 92.83% and specificity of 96.06% [7].

Stefan Jaeger [8] designed a CAD (Computer-Aided Diagnosis) system where he used chest radiographs to perform lung segmentation based on graphical slices for disease classification. They used Support Vector Machines (SVM) to detect abnormal patterns caused by tuberculosis on radiographs. The area under the curve (AUC) that they obtained was 87%–90%, with a precision of 78.3%–84%. With support vector machines, the results are more encouraging. Similarly, in Korea, they designed a CAD system based on convolutional networks, achieving an accuracy of 0.674%–0.83% [9].

In Brazil, they designed three proposals for the application of pre-training for convolutional neural networks to extract characteristics to train an SVM classifier. The results are shown in Table 1, and at the same time, they compare with other works and their results. P1 and P2 (refer to their deductions), EP1 and EP2 (refer to data sets created using other authors' GoogLeNet and ResNet classifiers). As can be seen, proposal P2 and EP2 outperform the other two authors [10].

Table 1. Comparison between literature and results obtained. Source [10]

Datasets	Literature approaches		Approach [10]			
	[8]	[9]	P1	P2	EP1	EP2
Montgomery	0.783	0.674	0.782	0.826	0.760	0.826
Shenzhen	0.840	0.837	0.834	**0.847**	0.846	**0.846**

The results suggest that using support vector machines contribute to better results.

In paper [11], they worked with pneumonia and tuberculosis, performing preprocessing to the data set of chest radiographs (X-rays), they created an architecture of CNN's own. They considered three models to learn specific characteristics; They used three data sets; in the first model, they only used data sets with pneumonia (RSNA), pediatric pneumonia, and the Indiana hospital set to learn the specifics of chest X-rays and classify them into normal and abnormal. In the second model, data sets with tuberculosis were used to classify them into regular and infected classes, and in the third model, the first previously trained model was used and fitted with the second model.

Each model was trained by six classifiers (custom CNN, VGG-16, Inception-V3, InceptionResNet-V2, Xception and DenseNet-211), values of; precision, AUC, sensitivity, specificity, F score, and MCC. Table 2 shows the comparison of the results with the personalized CNN and other authors.

Table 2. Comparison of results. Source [11]

Parameters	Jaeger [12]	Hwang [9]	Lopes [10]	Proposed method
Accuracy	0.840	0.837	0.847	0.941 [0.899,0.985]
AUC	0.900	0.926	0.926	0.990 [0.945,1.00]
Sensitivity	–	–	–	0.926 [0.850,1.00]
Specificity	–	–	–	0.957 [0.883,1.00]
F-score	–	–	–	0.941 [0.898,0.985]
MCC	–	–	–	0.884 [0.802,0.967]

Although they do not show specific results by disease, it can be seen that the results presented substantially improve those proposed by other authors already mentioned and those considered by the author.

In [13], three databases (Montgomery, Shenzhen, Belarus TB) with 1007 images were used. Same that was systematized in a 256 × 256 matrix and used two deep neural networks (AlexNet and GoogLeNet); obtained an AUC of 0.99 and a sensitivity of 97.3%. It is noteworthy that the authors mention three patterns of tuberculosis (pleural, miliary and cavitation), but in the conclusions of the work, they only comment on the classification of the categories normal and with tuberculosis.

In [14], the authors divided the chest radiograph with tuberculosis into three parts: upper lobe, middle lobe and lower region. They classify tuberculosis images into four categories: cavity lesions, fibrotic lesions, acute lesions, and miliary lesions. The digitized image was 512 * 512 pixels and was in jpg format. Later the original image was compressed to 50 * 50 pixels. The optimal neural network they obtained contains the following parameters: hidden layers 1, hidden neurons 5, learning rate 0.2 and error rate 0.05.

In another work, they proposed a method to detect; tuberculosis, pneumonia and lung cancer with the help of an artificial neural network, [15] extracted two classes: normal and abnormal. Geometric and contrast characteristics are considered for certification. The proposed method involves pre-processing the images, eliminating irrelevant data, retrieving helpful information, and strengthening the area of interest. They considered filtering the image to remove noise and high-pass filtering to improve image sharpness. For image segmentation, they used the edge detection method; this method works on individual pixels and converts the image to binary grayscale. For the extraction of characteristics, the previous phase of image segmentation is required, and the characteristics that are considered are the geometric areas, perimeters, diameters and standard deviations. The area of the lung region is calculated by the pixels with the value "1" in a digital image. The binary image obtained from the threshold is used to calculate the area. The perimeter is the distance between a pair of pixels around the edge of the lung region. The chest radiography database was for 80 patients, and an accuracy of 92% was obtained.

In another investigation [16], chest radiographs are used to detect tuberculosis using radiological patterns with convolutional neural networks (Faster RCNN, FPN -Feature Pyramid Network- and a proprietary neural network) considering the patterns; free pleural, miliary, encapsulated pleural, nodules, calcification and exudation. The results are shown in Table 3, where the precisions obtained by the pattern are observed, considering three classification methods; How can you see the highest precision obtained in the miliary pattern with the FPN method.

Table 3. Precision. Source [16]

Method	Mean average precision	Exudation	Calcification	Nodule	Miliary TB	Free pleural effusion	Encapsulated pleural effusion
Faster RCNN	22.66	41.49	5.52	0.37	40.57	45.65	2.36
FPN	50.96	52.89	42.84	17.50	87.72	52.67	52.13
Method	53.74	55.54	41.82	22.72	84.62	64.92	52.79

It is noteworthy that in this work, a segmentation method is used to reduce data processing costs with good results. The authors used the Montgomery data set. It is noteworthy that this work has the virtue of considering tuberculosis patterns; this is important since the detection of tuberculosis patterns allows to dictate a specific treatment to treat the disease effectively.

In [17], it is mentioned that the issue of tuberculosis continues to be urgent, especially in low-resource countries. That is why they propose to develop a convolutional neural network that will give a reliable diagnosis, but they optimized it so that using a cell phone, they can capture the X-ray, and in it, the diagnosis can be shown, this to make a faster pre-diagnosis.

COVID-19 is a new disease that has affected the whole world; it requires a quick medical diagnosis, and, like tuberculosis, it is considered a significant disease to diagnose; both can be diagnosed by chest X-ray. In [3], the author proposed a faster diagnosis, where 14 pre-trained deep neural networks were used. The features vectors were extracted, five categories of chest X-ray images were classified, which are: Covid-19, Tuberculosis, Bacterial pneumonia and Viral pneumonia and Healthy. The number of images per category was balanced, giving a total of 2,186 images. The precision obtained through the 14 trainings was classified with three methods: quadratic SVM, mean Gaussian SVM, and subspace discriminant assembly. The training that gave the best precision was the ResNet -50 with a precision of 95%. The performance of the classification is shown in Table 4.

Table 4. CNN ResNet-50 training assessment source [3]

Class	Precision	Recall	Specificity	F-score	AUC
COVID-19	99	98.6	99.8	98.8	1
Healthy	94	97.2	98.5	95.6	0.99
Bacterial pneumonia	81	88.4	95	83.1	0.97
Viral pneumonia	86.3	77.2	97	81.5	0.97
Tuberculosis	97.3	99.3	99.3	98.3	1

In this same work, the ResNet-50 network was used to classify only three classes: Covid-19, normal and tuberculosis, obtaining a general precision of 98%; Table 5 shows the results.

In another similar work [4], they comment that X-ray images have much potential when making diagnoses. They used five CNN models already trained: VGG16, VGG19, ResNet-18, ResNet-50 and ResNet-101. Later, they used the SVM method for classification with four kernel functions, namely Linear, Quadratic, Cubic, and Gaussian. They set epsilon value with the linear and quadratic kernel functions at 0.04 and 0.02, respectively, and for the cubic kernel and the Gaussian function was set at 0.01. The

Table 5. ResNet-50 training with 3 categories. Source [3]

Class	Precision	Recall	Specificity	F-score	AUC
COVID-19	98.39	98.39	99.20	98.39	1
Healthy	100	98.86	100	99.43	1
Tuberculosis	97.49	98.62	98.74	98.3	1

characteristics extracted from the ResNet-50 model and the SVM classifier with the linear kernel function obtained an accuracy of 94.7%. And the adjusted ResNet-50 model of 92.6% (Table 6).

Table 6. Precision results. Source [4]

	ResNet-18	ResNet-50	ResNe-t101	VGG16	VGG19	Average
Linear Kernel	86.3	94.7	88.4	89.5	88.4	89.5
Quadratic Kernel	87.4	91.6	89.5	89.5	87.4	89.1
Cubic Kernel	89.5	90.5	91.6	90.5	89.5	90.3
Gaussian Kernel	86.3	93.7	88.4	89.5	87.4	89.1
Average	87.4	92.6	89.5	89.8	88.1	

3   Proposed Method

3.1   Convolutional Neural Network (CNN)

Several CNN architectures were designed for classifying diseases; The one that yielded the best results is shown in Fig. 1. In each layer, the Dropout function was used to help the network not memorize since it disconnects neurons randomly; in the same way, the MaxPooling function was used to decrease the output characteristics.

Input layer: Input layer [18] x^l in the form of a 3rd order tensor, where $x^l \in \mathbb{R}^{M_l \times N_l \times K_d}$ where M is the height and N is the width and there are 3 channels; red, green, and blue, in this case M = 256, N = 256. Each element is designated by the index (i;j;d), where $0 \leq i < M$, $0 \leq j < N$ and $0 \leq d < 3$.

Convolutional Layer. In this layer w^l multiple kernels and convolutions are used.

The kernel is assumed as K and each M x N kernel used is denoted as f, where f is a fourth order tensor $\mathbb{R}^{M \times N \times k^l \times k}$ and the index variable $0 \leq i < M$, $0 \leq j < N$, $0 \leq d^l < K^1 y 0 \leq d < K$ are used to indicate the element of the nucleus.

Stride is the kernel step that the image will go through, where its value $s = 1$. The convolution process is expressed:

$$y_{i^{l+1},j^{l+1},d} = \sum_{i=0}^{M} \sum_{j=0}^{N} \sum_{d^l=0}^{d^l} f_{i,j,d^l,d} \times x^l_{i^{l+1}+i,j^{l+1}+j,d^l} + b_k \tag{1}$$

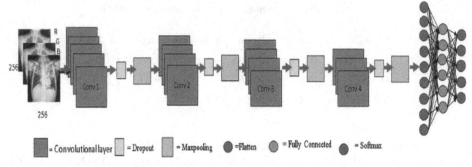

= Convolutional layer = Dropout = Maxpooling =Flatten = Fully Connected = Softmax

Fig. 1. Network architecture used

Where the bias constant b_k is added to the equation with the value of 1.

ReLU Layer. It is the activation function, it is denoted by:

$$y_{i,j,d} = \max\left(0, x_{i,j,d}^l\right) \tag{2}$$

Where $0 \leq i < H^l = M^{l+1}, 0 \leq j < W^l = W^{l+1}$, and $0 \leq d < K^l = K^{l+1}$.

Pooling Layer. Provides a reduction operation; reduces the dimensionality in the plane of feature maps. This generates another output vector, the function is denoted:

$$max : y_{i^{l+1}, j^{l+1}, d} = \max x_{i^{l+1} \times M + i, j^{l+1} \times N + j, d}^l,$$

$$0 \leq i < M, 0 \leq j < N \tag{3}$$

Where $0 \leq i^{l+1} < M^{l+1}, 0 \leq J^{l+1} < W^{l+1}$, and $0 \leq d < K^{l+1} = K^l$.
Usually the square size filter is established with size $f = 2$.

Fully Connected Layer. It is a layer that lies between the convolutional layer and the output layer, each element in the input layer x^l with each element in the output layer $x^{l+1} oy$.

Output Layer. Once you have this new layer, the function called Softmax is applied to it, which connects to the output layer, it contains the number of neurons that are being classified. The logical function of r-dimensioning (z) with value between [0; 1]. It is shown:

$$\sigma : \mathbb{R}^r \rightarrow [0, 1]^r$$

$$\sigma(z) = \frac{e^{zj}}{\sum_{r=1}^{r} e^{zr}} \, for \, j = 1, \dots, r \tag{4}$$

Where z is the input to the output layer and r is the dimension of the vector z *and* j are the indices of the output unit [19].

Table 7. Proposed network configuration

Layer	Output shape	Kernel	Param #
1	(256,256,64)	3	1792
1	(256,256,55)	5	88055
1	(256,256,32)	5	44032
Dropout	(256,256,32)		0
Maxpooling	(128,128,32)		0
2	(128,128,32)	5	25632
2	(128,128,32)	3	9248
2	(128,128,32)	3	9248
Dropout	(128,128,32)		0
Maxpooling	(64,64,32)		0
3	(64,64,32)	5	25632
3	(62,62,32)	3	9248
Dropout	(62,62,32)		0
Maxpooling	(31,31,32)		0
4	(31,31,32)	5	25632
4	(29,29,64)	3	18496
Dropout	(29,29,64)		0
Maxpooling	(14,14,64)		0
Dropout	(14,14,64)		0
Flatten	(12544)		0
Fully Connected	(100)		1254500
Dropout	(100)		0
Fully Connected	(190)		19190
Dropout	(190)		0
Softmax	(5)		955

For the network's training, the dimension of the model is 256×256, the size of the batch size is 10, and the value of the learning rate is 0.0001, for the loss function, the Adam optimizer was used [20].

Table 7 shows the proposed network configuration, considering the layers, image dimension, number of convolutions, kernel size, and resulting parameters. And the arrangement of the Dropout, Maxpooling functions. Fully connected and Softmax, the flatten was also performed. This architecture was designed through tests, different architectures were made with different numbers of layers and convolutions and as the training showed better results, that architecture was adapted to improve it until there were no improvements.

3.2 Data Set

X-ray radiographs of the chest were obtained from various databases; the first was from Montgomery. This set contains 138 radiographs, of which 80 are healthy radiographs and 56 radiographs with manifestations of tuberculosis; the second set was collected from the Shenzhen China hospital, it has 326 healthy radiographs and 336 tuberculosis radiographs; the third set of the tuberculosis category was obtained from Kaggle, it was created by a team of researchers from the Universities: Qatar, Doha, Tatar and from Dhaka, Bangladesh together with support from the doctors of Hamad Medical Corporation in which already the Montgomery and Shenzhen databases were integrated [21].

Similarly, four sets of images were obtained from the Kaggle page corresponding to COVID-19 [22], Viral pneumonia and bacterial pneumonia, and healthy images [23]. The tuberculosis images that were extracted from Kaggle web; the repeated images were eliminated. The preprocessing consisted of changing the tonality of the radiographs to have more images. In this research work, no image is repeated.

4 Experimental Results

4.1 Network Training

The images were stored in 5 folders according to each class (tuberculosis, COVID-19, viral pneumonia, bacterial pneumonia and healthy).

For the balancing of the images, the number of COVID-19 images was considered. A total of 1870 images were placed in each category. Considering that the images have different resolutions, the images were reduced to a scale of 256×256, so that they were homogenized.

The image sets were divided into 3 folders; the first training session with 1456 images; in the second, 364 were used for validation and in the third, 50 for the tests (the selection of images was carried out at random). To avoid bias in the classification, the pixel values of $[0,\ldots, 255]$ were normalized; It consisted of dividing the value of the pixels into 255, so that there are values between $[0,\ldots, 1]$.

The 5 classes were labeled; considering the selection of each one of them at random, in each class (0 = Normal; 1 = Tuberculosis; 2 = COVID-19; 3 = Viral pneumonia; 4 = Bacterial pneumonia). As shown in Fig. 2.

The training was carried out on an Inspiron 15 500 series laptop with a CORE i7, 7th processor. Generation, with 6 GB RAM and 1 TB hard drive.

The network was programmed with Python, with the machine learning libraries: TensorFlow, Sklearn, NumPy and pandas.

In Fig. 3, the performances of the training of both networks can be observed.

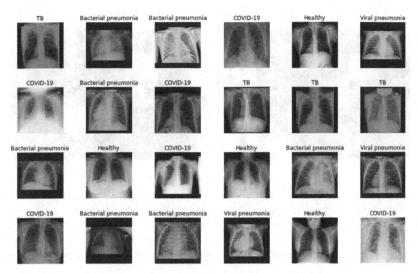

Fig. 2. Selection and labeling of radiographs by class

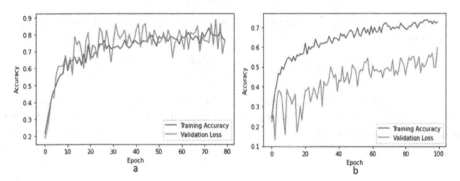

Fig. 3. Training behavior a) our proposal, b) ResNet-50

4.2   Test

In the experiments, 50 images of each class were used for the test. To measure the performance, we use the Confusion Matrix. In Fig. 4, the results of the confusion matrix (a) our proposal and (b) the ResNet-50 are presented.

With these parameters the Accuracy, Precision, Recall, f1-score were calculated. [23].

Accuracy. It is equal to the proportion of predictions that the model correctly classified.

$$Accuracy = \frac{TP + TN}{TP + TN + FP + FN} \tag{5}$$

Precision. It is the positive predictive value.

$$Precision = \frac{TP}{TP + FP} \tag{6}$$

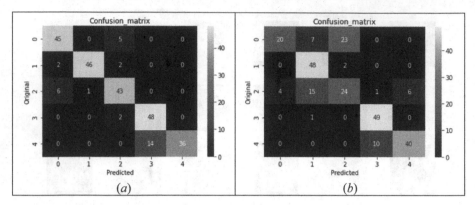

Fig. 4. Confusion matrix

Recall. Rate of positive hits that were correctly identified by the something-rhythm.

$$Recall = \frac{TP}{TP + FN} \tag{7}$$

f1-score. It is a measure of precision and recovery; it can have a maximum score of 1 or a minimum of 0.

$$f1 - score = \frac{2TP}{2TP + FP + FN} \tag{8}$$

Table 8 and 9 show the results obtained from the confusion matrix of our proposal and that of ResNet-50, respectively. It can be seen that the Accuracy that the ResNet-50 has of 0.72%, being better in our proposal of 0.87%. Therefore, this proposal has better correct predictions.

Table 8. Evaluation of the model of our proposal

	Precision	Recall	F1-score	Support
0 = Healthy	0.85	0.90	0.87	50
1 = Tuberculosis	0.98	0.92	0.95	50
2 = COVID-19	0.83	0.86	0.84	50
3 = Viral pneumonia	0.77	0.96	0.86	50
4 = Bacterial pneumonia	1.00	0.72	0.84	50
Accuracy			0.87	250
Macro avg	0.89	0.87	0.87	250
Weighted avg	0.89	0.87	0.87	250

The average precision in ResNet-50 was 0.74%, in contrast to the proposed model, which was 0.89%. In this experiment, repeated images were not used, but the authors of

Table 9. ResNet50 model evaluation

	Precision	Recall	F1-score	Support
0 = Healthy	0.83	0.40	0.54	50
1 = Tuberculosis	0.68	0.96	0.79	50
2 = COVID-19	0.49	0.48	0.48	50
3 = Viral pneumonia	0.82	0.98	0.89	50
4 = Bacterial pneumonia	0.87	0.80	0.83	50
Accuracy			0.72	250
Macro avg	0.74	0.72	0.71	250
Weighted avg	0.74	0.72	0.71	250

the investigation [3], who had a 91.52% average precision, mention that if they repeated images to balance the data sets (we know that this can cause noise and bias in the results). The results obtained in this work suggest that CNNs can be very sensitive when using the over-sampling technique and can be reflected in the precisions.

Since the Recall metric is a classification of diseases, it should be considered with greater interest since it identifies the positive cases of each disease. For Recall, the average performance for ResNet-50 is 0.72%, and for our proposal, it is 0.87%.

It is noteworthy that viral pneumonia is detected satisfactorily with 96% with our proposal and 98% with ResNet-50; however, to detect bacterial pneumonia with ResNet-50, it is 80%, for our proposal has a low performance for our proposal 72%.

ResNet-50 has a better performance with 96% correct answers to detection of tuberculosis, and in our proposal, it has 92%.

ResNet-50 has low performance in detecting the healthy class of only 0.40%, and it is also low in detecting COVID-19, only detecting 48%. Our proposal improves the detection in the healthy class with 90% and for COVID-19 86%.

With these results, it can be affirmed that the network model proposed in this research is better than ResNet-50.

The data set can play an essential role in training the network to obtain good Accuracy.

In both models, the confusion of pneumonia is relevant. The same happens in both models in the case of the healthy class (without diseases).

Regarding Score f1, it is recognized that it can be considered acceptable if it is greater than 80%; our model is 87%, and the ResNet-50 only reached 71%, which is not acceptable.

5   Conclusions

Our proposal was better than the ResNet-50, although accuracy will be better needed in future work.

The results obtained in this research suggest that it is better to work with balanced data without applying over-sampling techniques since they can cause noise in the training of NNC, although this should be further investigated to reach a solid conclusion.

It is noteworthy that there is much confusion between viral pneumonia and bacterial pneumonia, which is not strange since it has very similar symptoms and characteristics. Some techniques will have to be found to improve network performance. It can be said that it is another problem to solve in future work.

For the healthy class, it is understandable that classifiers do not work well. The reason can be the following: Although they do not have any diseases of the classes that the system was trained with, that does not guarantee that they do not have other diseases, such as damage from smoking or another disease.

It is advisable to continue investigating to increase the degree of classification but considering elements that allow better results.

For future work, new CNN's will be considered to have a better comparison, techniques will also be used to increase the data, and Transfer Learning will be applied to extract characteristics.

Acknowledgments. I want to thank Kaggle for making the radiography databases available to the public.

References

1. López, E., Amador, Y.: Tuberculosis. Revista Cubana de Estomatología **38**, 33–51 (2001)
2. Garza-Velasco, R., A-d, J.J., Perea-Mejía, L.M.: Tuberculosis pulmonar: la epidemia mundial continúa y la enseñanza de este tema resulta crucial y compleja. Educación Química **28**(1), 38–43 (2017). https://doi.org/10.1016/j.eq.2016.09.009
3. Al-Timemy, A., Khushaba, R., Musa, Z., Escudero, J.: An Efficient Mixture of Deep and Machine Learning Models for COVID-19 and Tuberculosis Detection Using X-Ray Images in Resource Limited Settings (2020)
4. Ismael, A.M., Sengür, A.: Deep learning approaches for COVID-19 detection based on chest X-ray images. Expert Syst. Appl. **164**, 114054 (2021) https://doi.org/10.1016/j.eswa.2020.114054
5. Stirenko, S., et al.: Chest x-ray analysis of tuberculosis by deep learning with segmentation and augmentation. In: 2018 IEEE 38th International Conference on Electronics and Nanotechnology (ELNANO), IEEE (2018) https://doi.org/10.1109/elnano.2018.8477564
6. Omisore, M.O., Samuel, O.W., Atajeromavwo, E.J.: A genetic-neuro-fuzzy inferential model for diagnosis of tuberculosis. Appl. Comput. Inf. **13**(1), 27–37 (2017). https://doi.org/10.1016/j.aci.2015.06.001
7. Karnkawinpong, T., Limpiyakorn, Y.: Classification of pulmonary tuberculosis lesion with convolutional neural networks. J. Phys. Conf. Ser. **1195**, 012007 (2019). https://doi.org/10.1088/1742-6596/1195/1/012007
8. Jaeger, S., et al.: Automatic tuberculosis screening using chest radiographs. IEEE Trans. Med. Imaging **33**(2), 233–245 (2014). https://doi.org/10.1109/tmi.2013.2284099
9. Hwang, S., Kim, H.-E., Jeong, J., Kim, H.-J.: A novel approach for tuberculosis screening based on deep convolutional neural networks. In: Georgia, D.T., Samuel, G.A., (ed.) Medical Imaging 2016: Computer-Aided Diagnosis SPIE (2016) https://doi.org/10.1117/12.2216198
10. Lopes, U.K., Valiati, J.F.: Pre-trained convolutional neural networks as feature extractors for tuberculosis detection. Comput. Biol. Med. **89**, 135–143 (2017). https://doi.org/10.1016/j.compbiomed.2017.08.001

11. Rajaraman, S., Antani, S.K.: Modality-specific deep learning model ensembles toward improving TB detection in chest radiographs. IEEE Access **8**, 27318–27326 (2020). https://doi.org/10.1109/access.2020.2971257

12. Jaeger, S., Candemir, S., Antani, S., Wáng, Y.-X.J., Lu, P.-X., Thoma, G.: Two public chest X-ray datasets for computer-aided screening of pulmonary diseases. Quant. Imaging Med. Surg. **4**(6) (2014) https://doi.org/10.3978/j.issn.2223-4292.2014.11.20

13. Lakhani, P., Sundaram, B.: Deep learning at chest radiography: automated classification of pulmonary tuberculosis by using convolutional neural networks. Radiology **284**(2), 574–582 (2017). https://doi.org/10.1148/radiol.2017162326

14. Ramana, K.V., Basha, S.K.: Neural image recognition system with application to tuberculosis detection. In: Proceedings of International Conference on Information Technology: Coding and Computing 2004, ITCC 2004, IEEE (2004). https://doi.org/10.1109/itcc.2004.1286735

15. Khobragade, S., Tiwari, A., Patil, C.Y., Narke, V.: Automatic detection of major lung diseases using chest radiographs and classification by feed-forward artificial neural network. In: 2016 IEEE 1st International Conference on Power Electronics, Intelligent Control and Energy Systems (ICPEICES), IEEE (2016). https://doi.org/10.1109/icpeices.2016.7853683

16. Xie, Y., et al.: Computer-aided system for the detection of multicategory pulmonary tuberculosis in radiographs. J. Healthc. Eng. **2020**, 1–12 (2020). https://doi.org/10.1155/2020/9205082

17. Curioso, W.H., Brunette, M.J.: Inteligencia artificial e innovación para optimizar el proceso de diagnóstico la tuberculosis. Revista Peruana de Medicina Experimental y Salud Publica **37**, 554–558 (2020). https://doi.org/10.17843/rpmesp.2020.373.5585

18. Wang, L., et al: CORD-19: The Covid-19 Open Research Dataset, ArXiv (2020)

19. Kermany, D.S., et al.: Identifying medical diagnoses and treatable diseases by image-based deep learning. Cell **172**(5), 1122–1131.e9 (2018). https://doi.org/10.1016/j.cell.2018.02.010

20. Triwijoyo, B., Sabarguna, B., Budiharto, W., Abdurachman, E.: ICIC express letters ICIC international c 2020 ISSN. ICIC Exp. Lett. **14**, 635–641 (2020). https://doi.org/10.24507/icicel.14.07.635

21. Rahman, T., et al.: Reliable tuberculosis detection using chest x-ray with deep learning, segmentation and visualization. IEEE Access **8**, 191586–191601 (2020) https://doi.org/10.1109/access.2020.3031384

22. Kingma, D.P., Ba, J.: Adam: A Method for Stochastic Optimization (2017)

23. Visa, S., Ramsay, B., Ralescu, A., Knaap, E.: Confusion matrix-based feature selection. In: MAICS, pp. 120–127 (2011)

Predicting LncRNA-Disease Associations Based on Tensor Decomposition Method

Xinguo Lu[✉], Yue Yuan, Guanyuan Chen, Jinxin Li, and Kaibao Jiang

College of Computer Science and Electronic Engineering, Hunan University, Changsha, China

Abstract. Long non-coding RNA (lncRNA) plays an important role in many biological processes. A large number of studies have shown that predicting the associations between lncRNAs and diseases may uncover the causation of various diseases. However, experimental determination of the lncRNA-disease associations is expensive and time-consuming. Many methods are emerging, but it is still a challenge to predict the associations between lncRNAs and diseases more accurate. More and more evidences suggest that lncRNA has interaction with miRNA, which is highly related to the occurrence of cancer, gene regulation, and cell metabolism. Therefore, in this paper, we design a new method based on the interactions of lncR-NAs, diseases and miRNAs. We represent the lncRNA-disease-miRNA triplet as a tensor, innovatively, and predict the potential associations between lncRNAs and diseases via tensor decomposition. First, we build lncRNAs similarity matrix by integrating semantic information and functional interactions. Second, we collect the pairwise associations between lncRNAs, diseases, and miRNAs, respectively, and integrate them into a three-dimensional association tensor. Third, we utilize the lncRNAs similarity matrix and diseases similarity matrix as auxiliary information to perform tensor decomposition with the association tensor to obtain factor matrices of lncRNAs, diseases and miRNAs, respectively. Finally, we use the factor matrices to reconstruct the association tensor for new prediction of triplet associations. To evaluate the performance of TDLDA, we compare our method with other methods and find it more superior.

Keywords: Tensor decomposition · Disease similarity · LncRNA similarity · LncRNA-MiRNA-disease association · LncRNA-disease association

1 Introduction

LncRNA (long noncoding RNAs, lncRNA) is a non-coding RNA molecule with a length greater than 200 nucleotides [1]. LncRNA participates in the regulation of cell differentiation, cell proliferation, apoptosis and other different physiological cycles of cells in the organism. And it also controls the transfer process, transcription process, and post-transcriptional regulation and epigenetic regulation in the cell [2, 3]. A large number of studies have shown that the dysfunction of lncRNA is related to many human cancers or diseases, so it is very crucial to explore the potential relationship between lncRNAs and various diseases. Nevertheless, expensiveness and high failure rate of the biological verification experiment make disease-related lncRNA screening is still challenging.

© Springer Nature Switzerland AG 2021
D.-S. Huang et al. (Eds.): ICIC 2021, LNAI 12838, pp. 290–300, 2021.
https://doi.org/10.1007/978-3-030-84532-2_26

Recently, with the rapid development of high-throughput technologies, many algorithms and tools are proposed to predict the potential associations between lncRNAs and diseases, mainly consisting of four categories: (i) biological information-based models, (ii) network-based models, (iii) machine learning-based models, (iiii) matrix factorization-based models.

Biological information-based models use biological information, such as lncRNA gene location and tissue specificity to predict the potential lncRNA-disease associations. For example, based on the neighbor relationship between lncRNAs and genes, Chen et al. [4] utilized known gene-disease associations to predict the lncRNA-disease associations. Using the sequence information of lncRNAs and miRNAs, Wang et al. [5] predicted the lncRNA-disease associations and developed the lncRNA-disease database named LncRNADisease. Liu et al. [6] predicted potential human lncRNA-disease associations by integrating known gene-disease associations, gene expression profiles and lncRNA expression profiles. However, this kind of methods is not effective for disease-related lncRNAs without relevant gene records.

By constructing an association network between lncRNAs and diseases, network-based methods were proposed to identify potential lncRNA-disease associations. For example, Zhang et al. [7] proposed the LincRDNetFlow algorithm, which integrated multiple similarity networks, including lncRNA similarity networks, protein interaction networks, disease similarity networks, and lncRNA-disease association networks. It carried out label propagation on heterogeneous networks to predict the lncRNAs related to diseases. With the in-depth study of the mechanism for lncRNA showed, the regulation of lncRNAs largely depended on the co-expressed miRNAs [8]. Zhou et al. [9] proposed the RWRHLD method to predict lncRNA-disease associations, integrating miRNA-related lncRNA-lncRNA interaction networks, disease-disease similarity networks and known lncRNA-disease association networks into a heterogeneous network. And it predicted lncRNA-disease associations utilizing random walks in heterogeneous networks. However, random walk-based method was very sensitive to the cutoff value of lncRNA and disease similarity. Therefore, when the cutoff value changed, the performance would fluctuate greatly.

Machine learning-based methods utilized known lncRNA-disease associations to train learning models, and then applied the learned models to predict new associations. For example, Hu et al. [10] proposed a deep learning framework NNLDA to predict potential lncRNA-disease associations. NNLDA was the first algorithm using deep neural networks to predict the lncRNA-disease associations. Based on the assumption that similar diseases were usually associated with similar lncRNAs, Chen et al. [11] developed the Laplacian Regularized Least Squares Method (LRLSLDA) in a semi-supervised learning framework to identify the lncRNA-disease associations by integrating known lncRNA-disease associations and expression profiles. By integrating genomic and transcriptome data, Zhao et al. [12] proposed a computational model based on the Naive Bayes Classifier method to predict cancer-related lncRNAs. Machine learning-based methods require a large number of negative samples to avoid unbalanced training. Randomly selecting the unknown correlations between lncRNAs and diseases as negative sample data hided the true lncRNA-disease associations, which greatly affected the prediction Algorithm performance.

Up to now, many matrix factorization-based methods were applied for the prediction of lncRNA-disease associations. For example, to achieve clustering of multiple types of related data sources, Wang et al. [13] proposed a symmetric non-negative matrix collaborative decomposition method (S-NMTF). Zitnik et al. [14] proposed a data integration framework (DFMF), which utilized a three-factor collaborative matrix factorization technique to integrate multiple heterogeneous data sources, and obtained a low-rank representation of each biomolecule after decomposition and optimization, and then reconstructed lncRNA-disease associations. However, when the label space of DFMF was large, the time consumption for calculating the semantic similarity was relatively large. Lu et al. [15] inferred and extracted the associations for the feature vectors applying inductive matrix completion. Most of matrix factorization-based methods could not integrate multiple types of association information to improve performance.

Although existing studies have achieved effective performance in some applications, the prediction of lncRNA-disease associations is still full of challenges due to sparse data and a large number of unknown associations. Here, from the point of interactions between lncRNAs, diseases and miRNAs, we propose tensor decomposition-based method to predict the lncRNA-disease associations. First, by integrating semantic information and functional interaction, we construct lncRNAs similarity matrix. Second, collecting the pairwise associations between lncRNAs, diseases and miRNAs, we integrate them into a three-dimensional association tensor. Third, utilizing the lncRNA similarity matrix and disease similarity matrix as auxiliary information, we perform tensor decomposition together with the association tensor and auxiliary information to obtain factor matrices for lncRNAs, diseases and miRNAs, respectively. Finally, applying three factor matrices, we reconstruct the association tensor to predict the potential associations between lncRNAs and diseases. We test TDLDA, DBNLDA [16] and two existing tensor decomposition methods (CP [17], TFAI [18]) in five-fold cross validation. The experimental results show that our method can effectively predict the lncRNA-disease associations in the 5-fold cross-validation and obtain better performance than other methods.

2   Method and Materials

In our paper, we proposed a new method to predict the lncRNA-disease association information by studying the associations of lncRNAs, diseases and miRNAs. First, we integrate the pairwise associations between lncRNAs, diseases, and miRNAs into a three-dimensional association tensor. Then, to improve performance, we combine the three-dimensional tensor with lncRNA similarity and disease similarity to perform tensor decomposition to infer potential factors and predict new associations. Therefore, the input data are known pair-wise associations between lncRNAs, diseases and miRNAs, together with some auxiliary information about them. The output is the predicted lncRNA-disease-miRNA three-dimensional new tensor.

2.1   Datasets

We used the dataset provided by [16] to evaluate our algorithm. In their dataset, they collected the miRNA-lncRNA interactions and miRNA-disease interactions in the miRNet

[19] and Starbase [20] databases, respectively. And they downloaded LncRNA-disease associations from the LncRNADisease database [4] and the lnc2cancer database [21]. Then, they applied the dataset in the previous study to obtain lncRNA-Disease correlations, lncRNA-miRNA interactions, lncRNA functional similarity, and disease semantic similarity. The dataset contained 240 lncRNAs, 412 diseases and 2697 known lncRNA-disease interaction pairs. We recalculated the similarity of lncRNAs. Table 1 shows the statistics of the dataset.

Table 1. Summary of dataset in this study.

Samples	Count	Percentage
LncRNAs	290	24.23%
Diseases	412	34.42%
MiRNAs	495	41.35%
LncRNA-Disease associations	2697	2.73%
LncRNA-MiRNA associations	1002	6.65%
MiRNA-Disease associations	13562	0.84%
L-D-M associations	15299	0.03%

2.2 Tensor Integration

Let $L = \{l_1, l_2, \cdots, l_l\}$ is the set of lncRNAs, $D = \{d_1, d_2, \cdots, d_d\}$ is the set of diseases, and $M = \{m_1, m_2, \cdots, m_m\}$ is the set of miRNAs.

To simulate the triple association for lncRNAs, diseases and miRNAs, we used the third-order tensor χ, where χ_{ijk} represented the triple association of lncRNA i, disease j, and miRNA k. When $\chi_{ijk} = 1$, it means that there was a triple association among lncRNA i, disease j and miRNA k; otherwise, the triple association did not exist or remained unobserved.

Collecting the pairwise associations for lncRNAs, diseases and miRNAs, we constructed a three-dimensional association tensor by integrating these associations [22]. We defined that if and only if all three conditions were satisfied, $\chi_{ijk} = 1$: (1) lncRNA i interacted with disease j, (2) disease j interacted with miRNA k, (3) lncRNA i interacted with miRNA k, Otherwise, $\chi_{ijk} = 0$. We can deduce a total of 15299 three-dimensional associations from this.

2.3 Construct Disease Matrix and LncRNA Matrix

Through the downloaded disease-disease correlation data, we build a disease similarity matrix. The disease similarity function to the disease pair (d_i, d_j) is defined as follows:

$$S_{ij}^d = S_{dis}(d_i, d_j) \tag{1}$$

Then, to construct the lncRNA matrix, we utilize the contribution of relative diseases to a single lncRNA to measure the functional similarity of lncRNAs [23].

Here, we define the functional similarity of lncRNA l_i and lncRNA l_j as follows:

$$S_{ij}^l = S_{lnc}(l_i, l_j) \tag{2}$$

$$S_{lnc}(l_i, l_j) = \frac{\sum_{d \in D(l_i)} \underset{d_j \in D(l_j)}{\text{argmax}} S_{dis}(d, d_j) + \sum_{d \in D(l_j)} \underset{d_i \in D(l_i)}{\text{argmax}} S_{dis}(d, d_i)}{|D(l_i)| + |D(l_j)|} \tag{3}$$

Where $D(l_i)$ is the disease set associated with lncRNA l_i which at least one miRNA relative to, $D(l_j)$ is the disease set associated with lncRNA l_j to which at least one miRNA related. $|D(l_i)|$ and $|D(l_j)|$ are the number of elements in $D(l_i)$ and $D(l_j)$, respectively. And $\underset{d_j \in D(l_j)}{\text{argmax}} S_{dis}(d, d_j)$ represents the maximum value of the correlations between disease d and each disease in $D(l_j)$.

2.4 Reconstruct Association Tensor

CP Decomposition. We usually assume that the tensor representing the data is low-rank, but the definition of low-rank tensor is not unique [18]. We use one of the most common tensor decomposition method, CP decomposition, which is natural extension of the matrix rank. We define the CP decomposition model of χ as the following optimization problem:

$$\min_{U,V,W} \|\chi - [\![U, V, W]\!]\|^2 \tag{4}$$

Where $\|\cdot\|^2$ is the F norm of the tensor. χ represents the three-dimensional tensor of lncRNAs, diseases and miRNAs. $[\![U, V, W]\!]$ denotes the reconstructed tensor. And $U \in R^{l \times r}$, $V \in R^{d \times r}$, and $W \in R^{m \times r}$ are the factor matrix for lncRNAs, diseases, miRNAs as latent representation of the corresponding pattern in the tensor. r is the rank of reconstruction tensor $[\![U, V, W]\!]$, generally set to r << min(l, d, m).

LncRNA-Disease Association Prediction. The CP model only uses associated information, therefore, the tensor χ is very sparse. So, we apply lncRNA similarity and disease similarity as auxiliary information to robust the model. We model the lncRNA-disease-miRNA triple association prediction problem as a tensor decomposition with auxiliary information:

$$\min_{U,V,W,L} \frac{1}{2} \|\chi - [\![U, V, W]\!]\|^2 + \frac{\alpha}{2} \left\| S_l - UL_lU^T \right\|_F^2 + \frac{\beta}{2} \left\| S_d - VL_dV^T \right\|_F^2$$
$$+ \frac{\lambda}{2} \left(\|L_l\|_F^2 + \|L_d\|_F^2 \right) \tag{5}$$

Where λ is the l_2 regularization coefficient. α and β represent the control of the influence of lncRNA similarity and disease similarity, respectively. L_l and L_d capture the scale difference between auxiliary information. S_l and S_d are the matrix form of lncRNA similarity S_{ij}^l and disease similarity S_{ij}^d, respectively.

2.5 Optimization

Regarding the optimization problem, we use the Alternating Least Squares (ALS) method [17] to solve, that is, we update one parameter by fixing the other two parameters.

Update the Factor Matrix U. The CP model only uses associated information, therefore, the tensor χ is very sparse. So, we apply lncRNA similarity and disease similarity as auxiliary information to robust the model. We model the lncRNA-disease-miRNA triple association prediction problem as a tensor decomposition with auxiliary information:

We update the factor matrix U by solving the following objective function:

$$\min_{U} \frac{1}{2}\left\|\chi_{(1)} - U(V \circledast W)^T\right\|_F^2 + \frac{\alpha}{2}\left\|S_l - U L_l U^T\right\|_F^2 \tag{6}$$

Where $\chi_{(1)}$ represents the mode-1 matrixzation of the tensor χ,s $\circledast$ is the Khatri-Rao product. Equation (6) is the fourth-order function of U [24], which makes the solution more troublesome, so we introduce an auxiliary variable $J_1 = U$ to convert it into an equivalent problem [25]:

$$\min_{U J_1} \frac{1}{2}\left\|\chi_{(1)} - U(V \circledast W)^T\right\|_F^2 + \frac{\alpha}{2}\left\|S_l - U L_l J_1^T\right\|_F^2 \tag{7}$$

Refer to [26], we utilize the alternating direction method of multipliers (ADMM) to solve Eq. (7). First, we define the augmented Lagrangian function of Eq. (7).

$$L(U, J_1, Y_1) = \frac{1}{2}\left\|\chi_{(1)} - U(V \circledast W)^T\right\|_F^2 + \frac{\alpha}{2}\left\|S_l - U L_l J_1^T\right\|_F^2 + tr\left(Y_1^T(U - J_1)\right)$$
$$+ \frac{\rho_1}{2}\|U - J_1\|_F^2 \tag{8}$$

Where $\rho_1 > 0$ is the penalty factor and Y_1 denotes the Lagrange multiplier.

Second, we solve for the first derivative for J_1 and U and make it 0, and the result as follows:

$$J_1 = (\alpha S_l U L_l + \rho_1 U + Y_1)\left(\alpha(U L_l)^T(U L_l) + \rho_1 I\right)^{-1} \tag{9}$$

$$U = \left(\chi_{(1)}(V \circledast W) + \alpha S_l\left(L_l J_1^T\right)^T + \rho_1 J_1 - Y_1\right)$$
$$\left((V \circledast W)^T(V \circledast W) + \alpha\left(L_l J_1^T\right)\left(L_l J_1^T\right)^T + \rho_1 I\right)^{-1} \tag{10}$$

Where I is the identity matrix of $r \times r$.

Third, we update the Lagrange multiplier and the penalty factor as follows:

$$Y_1 = Y_1 + \rho_1(U - J_1) \tag{11}$$

$$\rho_1 = \mu \rho_1 \tag{12}$$

Where $\mu > 1$ is the given parameter.

Update the Factor Matrix V. We define the update of the factor matrix V is the same as the U as follows:

$$J_2 = (\beta S_d VL_d + \rho_2 V + Y_2)\Big(\beta(VL_d)^T(VL_d) + \rho_2 I\Big)^{-1} \tag{13}$$

$$P = \Big(\chi_{(2)}(U \circledast W) + \beta S_d\big(L_d J_2^T\big)^T + \rho_2 J_2 - Y_2\Big)$$
$$\Big((U \circledast W)^T(U \circledast W) + \beta\big(L_d J_2^T\big)\big(L_d J_2^T\big)^T + \rho_2 I\Big)^{-1} \tag{14}$$

$$Y_2 = Y_2 + \rho_2(V - J_2) \tag{15}$$

$$\rho_2 = \mu\rho_2 \tag{16}$$

Where $\chi_{(2)}$ represents the mode-2 matrixzation of the tensor χ.

Update the Factor Matrix W. We update the factor matrix w through the following function:

$$\min_W \frac{1}{2}\Big\|\chi_{(3)} - W(U \circledast V)^T\Big\|_F^2 \tag{17}$$

Where $\chi_{(3)}$ represents the mode-2 matrixzation of the tensor χ. And the closed-form solution of F is obtained by:

$$W = X_{(3)}(U \circledast V)\Big((U \circledast V)^T(U \circledast V)\Big)^{-1} \tag{18}$$

Update L_l and L_d. We optimize L_l and L_d by solving the objective function as follows:

$$\min_X \frac{v}{2}\Big\|O - MXN^T\Big\|_F^2 + \frac{\lambda}{2}\|X\|_F^2 \tag{19}$$

We apply the conjugate gradient (CG) algorithm [27] to efficiently solve Eq. (19). We show the kth iteration process of CG as follows:

$$\alpha^{(k)} = \frac{\big\|R^{(k)}\big\|_F^2}{v\big\|MB^{(k)}N^T\big\|_F^2 + \lambda\big\|B^{(k)}\big\|_F^2} \tag{20}$$

$$X^{(k+1)} = X^{(k)} + \alpha^{(k)}B^{(k)} \tag{21}$$

$$R^{(k+1)} = R^{(k)} - \alpha^{(k)}\Big(vM^TMB^{(k)}N^TN + \lambda B^{(k)}\Big) \tag{22}$$

$$\beta^{(k)} = \frac{\big\|R^{(k+1)}\big\|_F^2}{\big\|R^{(k)}\big\|_F^2} \tag{23}$$

$$B^{(k+1)} = R^{(k+1)} + \beta^{(k)}B^{(k)} \tag{24}$$

Where $X^{(0)} = 0$, $R^{(0)} = vM^T ON - vM^T MX^{(0)} N^T N - \lambda X^{(0)}$ and $B^{(0)} = R^{(0)}$. We can obtain the approximate solution of Eq. (14) by continuing to iterate until $R^{(k)2}_F$ is small enough. We denote the approximate solution as $CG(O, M, N, v, \lambda)$.

Then we can update L_l and L_d as follows:

$$L_l = CG(S_l, U, U, \alpha, \lambda) \qquad (25)$$

$$L_d = CG(S_d, V, V, \beta, \lambda) \qquad (26)$$

3   Result

3.1   Experimental Setting and Evaluation Metrics

We use 5-fold cross validation (5-CV) to measure and evaluate the performance of the model. The dataset includes 15299 lncRNA-disease-miRNA positive associations. We randomly divide the positive samples into 5 subsets of equal size. In each fold, we use one of the subsets as the test set, and the remaining 4 subsets as the training set. Then we obtain a new tensor that our model will train. We randomly select some unknown triples as negative samples in each fold, which are the same size as the training set. To avoid biased data segmentation, we run our cross-validation process for 5 times, independently, and take the average of the results for 5 times as the final prediction result.

Here, in each cross-validation process, we sort the predictions of all lncRNA-disease-miRNA triple associations in the test set for each model. Then we obtain the highest precision, recall, the area under the ROC curve (AUC) and the area under the precision-recall curve (AUPR). Since the lncRNA-disease-miRNA triple association data is sparse and AUPR integrates recall and precision, we utilize AUPR as the main evaluation metric.

3.2   Parameter Analysis

Our method TDLDA has four hyperparameters: r, α, β and λ. r is the rank of the reconstruction tensor. α and β control the contribution of lncRNA functional similarity and disease semantic similarity, respectively. And λ denotes the regularization coefficient. First, we set $\lambda = 0.001$ according to experience [24]. Then, we apply grid search to traverse r in the range [2, 4, 6, 8, 10] and α and β are both in $\left[2^{-3}, 2^{-2}, 2^{-1}, 2^0, 2^1\right]$ for the evaluation of TDLDA. Finally, we found that TDLDA has the best performance (in terms of accuracy) when $r = 8$, $\alpha = 2.0$, and $\beta = 0.25$.

3.3   Comparison with Other Existing Methods

We select a method DBNLDA [16] that also uses miRNA-disease association information to predict lncRNA-disease associations and two tensor decomposition methods, CP and TFAI, to compare with TDLDA. The result is shown in Fig. (1). Figure 1 shows the overall results of the AUC value, AUPR value and accuracy value of all comparison methods. We can obtain that TDLDA, AUC, AUPR and accuracy are better than

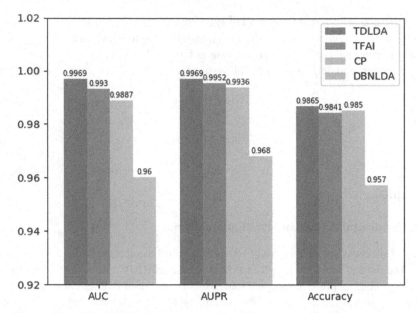

Fig. 1. The AUCs, AUPRs, Accuracy averaged over 10 runs by different methods.

other algorithms under the five-fold cross validation. Compared with the network-based method DBNLDA, tensor decomposition-based method has a significant improvement. We believe that tensor decomposition analyzes data from high-dimensional perspective and can capture more complex three-dimensional related information.

Table 2 shows the Precision and Recall of different tensor decomposition methods. The precision and recall of TDLDA are 0.9901 and 0.9851, which is 0.36% and 0.21% higher than the method TFAI, 0.69% and 0.05% higher than the method CP, respectively. Therefore, our method has better performance.

Table 2. The Precision and Recall of different tensor decomposition methods.

Method	Precision	Recall
CP	0.9832	0.9846
TFAI	0.9865	0.9830
TDLDA	0.9901	0.9851

4   Conclusions

In our paper, we propose to use tensor decomposition to predict the lncRNA-disease association information from the interaction of lncRNAs, diseases and miRNAs. Based on the pairwise correlation between lncRNAs, diseases, and miRNAs, our method constructs a three-dimensional correlation tensor. Then, we use the lncRNA similarity matrix and disease similarity matrix as auxiliary information to decompose together with the association tensor to obtain factor matrices for lncRNAs, diseases and miRNAs, respectively. Finally, we use three factor matrices to reconstruct the association tensor to predict the potential associations between lncRNAs and diseases. We compare TDLDA with DBNLDA, CP, and TFAI. The results show that the performance of TDLDA algorithm is better than other methods on sparse and unbalanced data, and it can predict new lncRNA-disease associations. In the future, we will consider incorporating more auxiliary information and predict the potential associations between more entities.

Acknowledgements. This work was supported by Natural Science Foundation of China (Grant. No. 61972141).

References

1. Wapinski, O., Chang, H.Y.: Long noncoding RNAs and human disease. Trends Cell Biol. **21**(6), 354–361 (2011)
2. Ping, X., Ke, H., Guo, M., et al.: Prediction of micrornas associated with human diseases based on weighted k most similar neighbors. PLoS ONE **8**(8), e70204 (2013)
3. Xuan, P., Han, K., Guo, Y., et al.: Prediction of potential disease-associated microRNAs based on random walk. Bioinformatics **31**(11), 1805 (2015)
4. Chen, G., Wang, Z., Wang, D., et al.: LncRNADisease: a database for long-non-coding RNA-associated diseases. Nucleic Acids Res. **41**(D1), D983–D986 (2012)
5. Cheng Q.X., Thomson D.W., Maag Jesper, L.V., et al.: lncRNAdb v2.0: expanding the reference database for functional long noncoding RNAs. Nucleic Acids Res. **43**(D1), 168–173 (2015)
6. Liu, M.X., Chen, X., Chen, G., et al.: A computational framework to infer human disease-associated long noncoding RNAs. PLoS ONE **9**(1), e84408 (2014)
7. Zhang, J., Zhang, Z., Chen, Z., et al.: Integrating multiple heterogeneous networks for novel LncRNA-disease association inference. IEEE/ACM Trans. Comput. Biol. Bioinf. 1 (2017)
8. Paraskevopoulou, M.D., Hatzigeorgiou, A.G.: Analyzing MiRNA–LncRNA Interactions. Methods Mol Biol. **1402**(1), 271–286 (2016)
9. Zhou, M., Wang, X., et al.: Prioritizing candidate disease-related long non-coding RNAs by walking on the heterogeneous lncRNA and disease network. Mol. Biosyst. Electron. Ed. **11**(3), 760–769 (2015)
10. Hu, J., Gao, Y., Li, J., et al.: Deep learning enables accurate prediction of interplay between lncRNA and disease. Front. Genet. **10**, 937 (2013)
11. Chen, X., Yan, G.Y., et al.: Novel human lncRNA–disease association inference based on lncRNA expression profiles. Bioinformatics **29**, 2617–2624 (2013)
12. Zhao, T., Xu, J., Liu, L., et al.: Identification of cancer-related lncRNAs through integrating genome, regulome and transcriptome features. Mol. BioSyst. **11**(1), 126–136 (2015)
13. Hua, W., Huang, H., Ding, C.: Simultaneous clustering of multi-type relational data via symmetric nonnegative matrix tri-factorization. In: Proceedings of the 20th ACM Conference on Information and Knowledge Management, CIKM, Glasgow, United Kingdom, 24–28 October. ACM (2011)
14. Zitnik, M., Zupan, B.: Data fusion by matrix factorization. IEEE Trans. Pattern Anal. Mach. Intell. **37**(1), 41–53 (2015). https://doi.org/10.1109/TPAMI.2014.2343973
15. Lu, C., Yang, M., Luo, F., et al.: Prediction of lncRNA-disease associations based on inductive matrix completion. Bioinformatics **34**(19), 3357–3364 (2018)

16. Madhavan, M., Gopakumar, G.: Deep Belief Network based representation learning for lncRNA-disease association prediction (2020)
17. Kolda, T.G., Ba Der, B.W.: Tensor decompositions and applications. Siam Rev. **51**(3), 455–500 (2009)
18. Narita, A., Hayashi, K., Tomioka, R., Kashima, H.: Tensor factorization using auxiliary information. Data Min. Knowl. Disc. **25**, 298–324 (2012) https://doi.org/10.1007/s10618-012-0280-z
19. Fan, Y., Keith, S., Arora, S.K., et al.: miRNet - dissecting miRNA-target interactions and functional associations through network-based visual analysis. Nucleic Acids Res. **W1**, W135–W141 (2016)
20. Li, J.H., Liu, S., Hui, Z., et al.: starBase v2.0: decoding miRNA-ceRNA, miRNA-ncRNA and protein–RNA interaction networks from large-scale CLIP-Seq data. Nucleic Acids Res. **42**(D1), D92–D97 (2014)
21. Ning, S., Zhang, J., Peng, W., et al.: Lnc2Cancer: a manually curated database of experimentally supported lncRNAs associated with various human cancers. Nucleic Acids Res. **D1**, D980–D985 (2016)
22. Ran, W., Shuai, L., Man, H.W., et al.: Drug-protein-disease association prediction and drug repositioning based on tensor decomposition. In: IEEE International Conference on Bioinformatics and Biomedicine (BIBM). IEEE (2018)
23. Xiao, Q., Luo, J., Liang, C., Cai, J., Ding, P.: A graph regularized non-negative matrix factorization method for identifying microRNA-disease associations. Bioinformatics **34**(2), 239–248 (2017)
24. Huang, F., Yue, X., Xiong, Z., et al.: Tensor decomposition with relational constraints for predicting multiple types of MicroRNA-disease associations (2019)
25. Kang, Z., Yiwei, L., Yuanzhang, S., Li, C., Zenglin, X.: Similarity learning via kernel preserving embedding. Proc. AAAI Conf. Artif. Intell. **33**, 4057–4064 (2019)
26. Boyd, S., Parikh, N., Hu, E.C., et al.: Distributed optimization and statistical learning via the alternating direction method of multipliers. Found. Trends Mach. Learn. **3**(1), 1–122 (2010)
27. Hestenes, M.R., Stiefel, E.L.: Methods of conjugate gradients for solving linear systems. J. Res. Nat. Bur. Standards Sect. **5**, 409–436 (1952)

AI in Skin Cancer Detection

Haya Al-Askar[1], Rasul Almurshedi[2], Jamila Mustafina[3]([⊠]), Dhiya Al-Jumeily[2], and Abir Hussain[2]

[1] Prince Sattam Bin Abdulaziz University, KSA, Al-Kharj, Saudi Arabia
[2] Liverpool John Moores University, Liverpool, UK
[3] Kazan Federal University, Kazan, Russia
DNMustafina@kpfu.ru

Abstract. Skin cancer is classified as one of the most dangerous cancer. Malignant melanoma is one of the deadliest types of skin cancer. Early detection of malignant melanoma is essential for treatment, hence saving lives and can significantly help to achieve full recovery. Current method heavily relies on clinical examination along with supportive methods to reach the correct clinical diagnosis. This paper considers the use of Machine Learning tools in early detection of skin cancer. It also presents the results of the data analysis of Skin Lesions Distribution according to age and gender and localization.

Keywords: Skin cancer · Early detection · Machine learning · Deep learning · Intelligent systems

1 Introduction

Skin cancer is one of the most dangerous and the deadliest type cancer. Because of its danger it requires early detection. Some cases of skin cancer cannot be treated if diagnosed lately. The current approach of detecting skin lesions are performed manually by doctors. The ways that currently are used are either a naked eye or by using dermoscopy. Dermoscope is like a handheld light used as part of clinical examination (Codella et al. 2017, Mishra and Celebi 2016, Waheed et al. 2017). The use of dermoscopy in diagnosis produces more accuracy than the naked eye. However, for both ways the patients need to take an appointment and wait for their turn and the result. All that takes time and delay the treatment (Eltayef 2017, Albahar 2019). Moreover, it is challenging as skin lesions can vary considerably in colour and size (Albahar 2019, Lopez et al. 2017). In addition, there sometimes can be a very low-contrast between lesion area and healthy area, especially in early stages (Eltayef 2017). Current trends are moving towards the use of computers and electronics in detecting skin lesion. The essential of using computers in healthcare was start by built Electronic health records (EHR) (Hripcsak et al. 2013). EHR are used to collect data from patients for Personalized Healthcare (PH). One of the most important new trends currently is the using for detecting skin cancer (Albahar 2019, Mishra and Celebi 2016, Waheed et al. 2017). For this reason, both machine learning (ML) and deep learning (DL) algorithms are used in image processing in detecting skin

© Springer Nature Switzerland AG 2021
D.-S. Huang et al. (Eds.): ICIC 2021, LNAI 12838, pp. 301–311, 2021.
https://doi.org/10.1007/978-3-030-84532-2_27

lesion. The using of ML and DL help to reduce patients' anxiety by checking the lesion from home so the patient does not need to make an appointment. Also, the using of machine learning and deep learning can provide a higher accuracy over the traditional approach of using dermoscopy.

Skin cancer occurs when the multiplication of cells is abnormal which give color to the skin, malignant tumors occur when DNA damage triggers mutations of cells that cause them to rapidly multiply. Basically, there are two forms of skin tumors - malignant and benign, each of both types begins with different cell of skin. There are two types of skin cancer which are: the melanoma and non-melanoma skin cancer. Melanoma skin cancer is the most difficult and deadly type. Squamous cell carcinoma (SCC), Basal cell carcinoma (BCC), Seborrheic keratosis, actinic keratosis and the most common type of skin cancer which is Melanoma. The other skin cancer which form less than 1% is non-melanoma skin cancer. Advanced melanoma is still incurable specially if it is a late case. So, the early detection of melanoma is able to reduce the mortality rate. Dermatologists and researchers say that the disease needs early detection to help start treatment and cure. The use of non-invasive ways to detect the cancer is costly and needs intensive training for dermatologists taking time and effort. While the detection by naked eye is not reliable as the dermatologists need to have experience in all skin lesions which is unlikely possible because it is different in shape, position and size from one patient to another. Also, naked eye has led previously to wrong diagnosing which cause delay in start of the treatment or unnecessary surgery. For these reasons, scholars encourage doctors to use automated detection systems since it is reliable and helpful in prevention or early detection of skin cancer.

2 Skin Cancer

Skin cancer occurs as a result of abnormal multiplication of pigment producing cells that give color to the skin or occurs when the DNA damage of the skin cells triggers mutations that cause the skin cells to rapidly multiply and form malignant tumors (Nasr-Esfahani et al. 2016). Skin cancers are divided into two types: melanoma and non-melanoma skin cancer. Melanoma is the most dangerous and deadly form of skin cancer. The most common types of skin cancer are:

- Squamous cell carcinoma (SCC): It is the second most common type of skin cancer which happen as a result of rushing abnormal growth of squamous cells; the early detecting of this type is curable (Ekimci et al. 2019).
- Basal cell carcinoma (BCC): one of the most common type of skin cancer that occurs as a result of uncontrolled and abnormal growth of basal cell; this type of skin cancer is widely identified - about 4 million detected cases in the USA every year. However, this type is curable when early detected because the cell grows slowly (Beetner et al. 2003).
- Seborrheic keratosis which is a common non-cancerous skin growth, and does not need treatment (Wang et al. 2019).
- Actinic keratosis: scaly spots on the top layer of skin. It occurs because of exposure of the skin to the sun for years (Darvin et al. 2016).

- Melanoma which is usually developing of a mole and can be malignant or benign. All other skin cancers which are classified as non-melanoma skin cancer form less than 1% of diagnoses. Currently, 132,000 of skin cancer are melanoma skin cancers and from two to three million are non-melanoma skin cancer occur worldwide each year.

Malignant melanoma is one of the most highly spread tumors. Its malignancy and its death-rates have been rapidly increasing - more than any other cancer in recent years. It is usually happening in or near existing mole, changing in shape, size, or color. Also, if the mole starts to be painful or itch the patient should be aware (Chatterjee et al. 2015). Sun exposure is one of the risk factors for melanoma patients, especially the sun's ultraviolet rays (De Gruijl 1999). Studies have shown that melanoma cancer of the head and neck is more common in people often exposed to sunlight. Exposure to sunlight at an early age and tanning are the most likely to develop melanoma. Also, people with white skin, fair or red hair, and blue eyes are more likely to develop skin cancer than others, and so are people with freckles. The most common site for melanoma is in trunk in males and in legs and hips in females. People with these factors have a higher probability of developing melanoma (Nayman 2017):

- have 50 or more moles especially unusual or irregular-looking or big size.;
- fair or red hear, green or blue eyes;
- blood relatives with melanoma or other skin cancer;
- weak immune system due to disease;
- age 50 or older.

The Clark Scale has 5 levels:

- ells are in the out layer of the skin (epidermis);
- cells are in the layer directly under the epidermis (pupillary dermis);
- cells are touching the next layer known as the deep dermis;
- cells have spread to the reticular dermis;
- cells have grown in the fat layer.

According to the National Cancer Institute Surveillance, Epidemiology and End Results (SEER) database (Mahendraraj et al. 2017), over the last 10 years rates for melanoma of the skin cases have been rising on average 1.5% each year. Advanced melanoma remains practically incurable. So, the early detection is an important step to reduce the mortality. Researchers agree that the skin cancer requires early mediation to be able to identify symptoms to make it easy for the dermatologists to prevent it. Various methods are used in detecting skin cancer, one of these methods is ABCD rule (Kasmi and Mokrani 2016). ABCD is used in identification of superficial spreading melanomas and it is referring to:

- Asymmetry: the shape of one half of lesion does not match the other half.
- Border irregularity: usually the edge is blurred, ragged, notched, or irregular, the color of the lesion sometimes spread to the area surrounding skin.

- Color patterns: color is different from lesion to another. It may be brown, black, or even tan, sometimes pink, white, blue, grey or red.
- Diameter: the size of the lesion is changing and increasing. The diameter of melanoma is usually at least 6 mm (like the diameter of pencil).

ABCD rule is used by dermatologists to depend these factors to detect melanomas. Researchers have suggested that the use of the naked eye in the diagnosis of melanoma is cheaper than non-invasive methods which require extensive training. This means that dermatologists have to do extensive training to be able to analyse and explain features derived from dermoscopic images. Dermatologists are often frustrated to use the naked eye as it has previously caused wrong diagnoses of melanoma. Because of these reasons, scientist encourage dermatologists to start using automated detection systems along with the traditional ways, since they are considered to be very effective in preventing and early detecting of melanoma.

3   Skin Lesions Distribution: Age and Gender

This section highlights the skin lesions distribution according to the age and gender based on the ISIC data-set. According to Fig. 1 most of the patients are aged between 30 to 80. The gender distribution is not equal as the percentage of the male patients is 51.7% of the total patients, while the percentage of females is 48.3% as per Fig. 2. Moreover, the statistics shows that the males to female ratio of infection is higher for male patients as per Fig. 3, hence males are more in risk concerning the skin cancer.

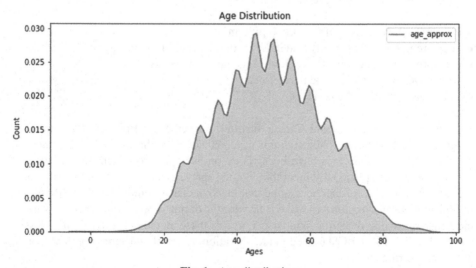

Fig. 1. Age distribution

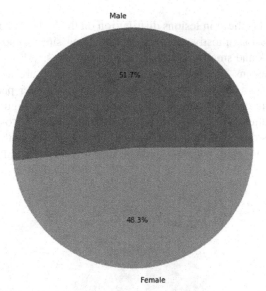

Fig. 2. Gender distribution for all patients

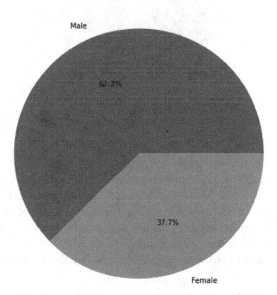

Fig. 3. Gender distribution for malignant patients

4 Skin Lesions Sites

This section highlights the skin lesions distribution on the body. According the data-set statistics the skin lesions mostly occur in the following sites: torso, upper and lower extremity, head/neck and small percentage for oral and soles.

Although the lesions sites vary across all genders, they are not necessary to be diagnosed as malignant. Moreover, some site can have a higher percentage of being malignant depending on other factors such as age and gender. Figures 4 and 5 shows the percentage of patients for each lesions site. Figures 4 shows the overall for all cases, while Figs. 5 shows only the malignant cases. It is clear that lesions on body parts are more likely to be malignant, head/neck comes first followed by oral/genital and upper extremity.

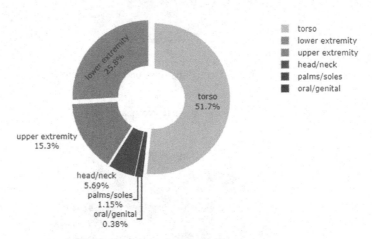

Fig. 4. Anatomy site for all cases

Moreover, it is clear that malignant image scan locations differ based on the patient's gender. For example, the torso is most common location in males (almost half of the scans), while in females it is around 39%. However, the lower extremity is more common with female scans than males, with the percentage male's scans of around 18%, while females around 26%. Again, upper extremity malignant scans are more common with females than males, with the percentage ranges 23% and 17% respectively. Scanned body part locations are similar in order between males and females with small differences on distribution.

Site of Focus - Malignant Cases

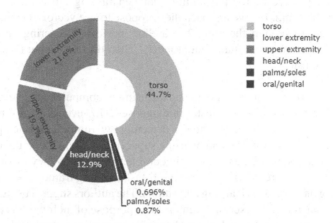

Fig. 5. Anatomy site for only malignant cases

5 Applied Deep Learning for Detecting the Skin Cancer: Related Research

Albahar et al. (Albahar 2019) proposed a new model by using CNNs to detect skin lesion whether benign or malignant. The data-set they are using for testing and evaluation is from ISIC archives which is a set of data used by Pomponiu and Harangi and consists of images of skin lesion to benign and malignant. The data-set consists of 23906 of different classes images. The authors divided it into three parts of about 8000 images of benign and malignant cases of 600 × 600 resolutions. They trained the model on each part and computed accuracy according to that. According to authors they got high accuracy, the proposed model outperformed other detection methods. The model is testing different cases and showing better AUC-ROC result than other methods (Albahar 2019).

The electronic health records (EHRs) cannot be used directly to take information because the similarity is not accurate. Therefore, the authors in (Suo et al. 2018) have adopted the using of a convolutional neural network (CNN) to collect information from patients and learn about them to produce the electronic health record so that it can be relied upon later in the future diagnosis. The dataset used in this study consists of 100000 patients was collected over two years and classify the data according to diseases and their history.

The authors of (Hussein et al. 2019) considered that the use of computer-aided diagnosis (CAD) tools is more accurate and faster than radiology images. So, they depend on using two ways:

- The first approach: they use supervised learning and deep learning algorithms and they found a gain specially with the use of 3D convolutional neural network. The task of this approach is to incorporate feature representations with computer-aided diagnosis (CAD) through multi-task learning framework.

- The second approach: to solve a common problem in medical imaging applications which is the restricted availability of labeled training data using an unsupervised learning algorithm. In this approach they propose to use vector machine for characterizing tumors to support the ratio. The authors perform clustering on the features gained from the images to make initial labels. Then they are using these labels to compare each cluster.

Sarfaraz Hussein et al. claim that the using of computer-aided diagnosis (CAD) tools will be more accurate and faster in diagnoses. However, they use both supervised and unsupervised learning algorithms in detecting two tumors: lung and pancreas. In the first approach, the authors depend on using supervised learning with the use of deep learning algorithms using 3D convolutional neural network. Then they incorporate the data into CAD via graph-regularized sparse multi-task learning framework. The second approach is using unsupervised learning algorithms. The authors suggest using proportion-support vector machine for describing tumors. The purpose of their work is to get the benefits of deep learning and the evaluation of supervised and unsupervised learning algorithms in two tumor diagnoses: lung and pancreas. The authors use LIDC-IDRI dataset which is one of the largest datasets available. This dataset includes 1018 CT scans with thickness 0.45 mm to 5.0 mm. According to authors, this is the largest evaluation of using CAD however they do not mention the accuracy they get from this work (Hussein et al. 2019).

Gola Isasi et al. produced automated tool that can be used to determine melanomas. This tool is based on the ABCD rule and the pattern of the skin. The use three algorithms for images processing and show that the system is reliable for diagnosis and possess 85% accuracy. They used data-set consisting of 20 images per pattern (which is cataloged by dermatologists) and the images are 160 500 × 500 pixel RGB. According to the authors beside the main aim of this study which is to produce a new tool to simplify skin lesion detection, there is another objective of this study - to create a database that is categorized by doctors, clear and reliable to use. Also, they are developing algorithms used in image processing. The database that was used for development algorithm was created within the collaboration of dermatologists from Ana Sanchez Basurto hospital in Spain (taking images with Molemax II digital dermatoscope) (Isasi et al. 2011). Martin et al. have developed an approach based also on image processing, ABCDE classification (E refer to Evaluation) and neural networks to evaluate lesions, they got 76% sensibility and 87% specificity (Marín et al. 2015).

Chang et al. did a study to develop CAD (computer aided diagnosis) to detect melanocytic and non-melanocytic skin lesions by using conventional digital micrographs. The method they used is to include conventional and new color feature using SVM (support vector machine). The work got 90% accuracy (Chou et al. 2013).

Researchers in (Kanimozhi and Murthi 2016) used Neural Network (Back Propagation Algorithm.) to implement emergency support system which is cost-effective to use in medical image processing. They used MATLAB to analyse melanoma parameters like Asymmetry, Border, Color, Diameter (ABCD). After that they used Neural Network to classify the stage of tumors, the initial training of the system was done on a known target value. According to the authors the system has accuracy of about 96.9%.

The authors in (Alasadi and AL-Safy 2016) use digital image processing in diagnosing skin cancer at early stage to be treated. The system contains two phases: the first phase is to determine whether the skin lesion is malignant or benign, the second phase is to detect the malignant skin cancer type. After input, the next stage before the processing starts is to reduce the noise by Median Filtering and object removal by Dull Razor filter. Then they use Neural Network classification to classify the benign from malignant melanoma by using Tamura method. If the lesion is malignant melanoma it is taken to the next stage to distinguish between skin cancer types by using feature extraction techniques. According to the authors the experimental results are 98% for recognition of melanoma skin cancer and 93% for recognition of malignant melanoma types.

Esteva et al. have designed an application to detect skin cancer by using Deep convolutional neural networks (CNNs). They use single CNN to demonstrate classification of skin lesions trained directly from images. The CNN uses pixels and disease labels as inputs. They compare the performance of the system with 21 board-certified dermatologists on detection of biopsy proven. The CNN achieves performance on par with the experts. that shows the artificial intelligence is able to detect and classify skin cancer at a level comparable to dermatologists (Esteva et al. 2017).

As shown above, there are many applications that are used in the detection of skin cancer and they differ in the algorithms used. Some of them are used on smart devices, and some are using computers. However, there are some improvements that can be adopted to improve the accuracy of these programs.

6   Conclusion

In this paper we presented the overview of skin cancer. Then background of using Machine Learning (ML) and Deep Learning in detecting skin cancer was presented as well as neural networks (NNs) and convolutional neural networks (CNNs) and some other machine learning algorithms and technique. We also referred to the related work including some application using machine learning in healthcare in general. We believe that AI has a huge perspective in detecting all types of cancer and especially skin cancer as image processing of skin conditions offers more opportunities than image processing of other types of cancer. In our future work we are planning to develop a system - deep learning model for skin lesion classification.

References

Alasadi, A.H.H., AL-Safy, B.M.R.: Early Detection and Classification of Melanoma Skin Cancer. LAP LAMBERT Academic Publishing, Sunnyvale (2016)

Albahar, M.A.: Skin lesion classification using convolutional neural network with novel regularizer. IEEE Access **7**, 38306–38313 (2019)

Beetner, D.G., Kapoor, S., Manjunath, S., Zhou, X., Stoecker, W.V.: Differentiation among basal cell carcinoma, benign lesions, and normal skin using electric impedance. IEEE Trans. Biomed. Eng. **50**(8), 1020–1025 (2003)

Chatterjee S., Dey D., Munshi, S.: Mathematical morphology aided shape, texture and colour feature extraction from skin lesion for identification of malignant melanoma. In: International Conference on Condition Assessment Techniques in Electrical Systems (CATCON), pp. 200–203 (2015)

Chou, S.-T., Chang, W.-L., Chang, C.-T., Hsu, S.-L., Lin, Y.-C., Shih, Y.: Cinnamomum cassia essential oil inhibits α-msh-induced melanin production and oxidative stress in murine b16 melanoma cells. Int. J. Mol. Sci. **14**(9), 19186–19201 (2013)

Codella, N.C., et al.: Deep learning ensembles for melanoma recognition in dermoscopy images. IBM J. Res. Dev. **61**(4/5), 5–1 (2017)

Darvin M., Klemp M., Weinigel M., Meinke M., König K., Lademann, J.: In vivo imaging for detection and discrimination of actinic keratosis and squamous cell carcinoma from healthy human skin using two-photon tomography. In: International Conference Laser Optics (LO), pp. S2–20 (2016)

De Gruijl, F.: Skin cancer and solar uv radiation. Eur. J. Cancer **35**(14), 2003–2009 (1999)

Ekimci, G.D., Onak, G., Karaman, O., Ercan, U.K.: Assessment of direct and fluid-mediated cold atmospheric plasma treatment eficacy on squamous cell carcinoma. In: Medical Technologies Congress (TIPTEKNO), pp. 1–4 (2019)

Eltayef, K.A.A.: Segmentation and lesion detection in dermoscopic images. PhD thesis, Brunel University London (2017)

Esteva, A., et al.: Dermatologist-level classification of skin cancer with deep neural networks. Nature **542**(7639), 115–118 (2017)

Hripcsak, G., Albers, D.J.: Next-generation phenotyping of electronic health records. J. Am. Med. Inform. Assoc. **20**(1), 117–121 (2013)

Hussein, S., Kandel, P., Bolan, C.W., Wallace, M.B., Bagci, U.: Lung and pancreatic tumor characterization in the deep learning era: novel supervised and unsupervised learning approaches. IEEE Trans. Med. Imaging **38**(8), 1777–1787 (2019)

Isasi, A.G., Zapirain, B.G., Zorrilla, A.M.: Melanomas non-invasive diagnosis application based on the abcd rule and pattern recognition image processing algorithms. Comput. Biol. Med. **41**(9), 742–755 (2011)

Kanimozhi T., Murthi, A.: Computer aided melanoma skin cancer detection using artificial neural network classifier. Singaporean J. Sci. Res. (SJSR), J. Sel. Areas Microelectron. (JSAM) **8**(2), 35–42 (2016)

Kasmi, R., Mokrani, K.: Classification of malignant melanoma and benign skin lesions: implementation of automatic abcd rule. IET Image Process.**10**(6), 448–455 (2016)

Lopez, A.R., Giro-i Nieto, X., Burdick, J., Marques, O.: Skin lesion classification from dermoscopic images using deep learning techniques. In: 13th IASTED International Conference on Biomedical Engineering (BioMed), pp. 49–54 (2017)

Mahendraraj, K., Sidhu, K., Lau, C.S.M., McRoy, G.J., Chamberlain, R.S., Smith, F.O.: Malignant melanoma in African–Americans: a population-based clinical outcomes study involving 1106 African–American patients from the surveillance, epidemiology, and end result (SEER) database (1988–2011). Medicine **96**(15), e6258 (2017)

Marín, C., Alférez, G.H., Córdova, J., González, V.: Detection of melanoma through image recognition and artificial neural networks. In: Jaffray, D.A. (ed.) World Congress on Medical Physics and Biomedical Engineering, June 7–12, 2015, Toronto, Canada. IP, vol. 51, pp. 832–835. Springer, Cham (2015). https://doi.org/10.1007/978-3-319-19387-8_204

Mishra, N.K., Celebi, M.E.: An overview of melanoma detection in dermoscopy images using image processing and machine learning. arXiv preprint arXiv:1601.07843 (2016)

Nasr-Esfahani, E., et al.: Melanoma detection by analysis of clinical images using convolutional neural network. In: 38th Annual International Conference of the IEEE Engineering in Medicine and Biology Society (EMBC), pp. 1373–1376 (2016)

Nayman, T., Bostan, C., Logan, P., Burnier, M.N., Jr.: Uveal melanoma risk factors: a systematic review of meta-analyses. Curr. Eye Res. **42**(8), 1085–1093 (2017)

Suo, Q., et al.: Deep patient similarity learning for personalized healthcare. IEEE Trans. Nanobiosci. **17**(3), 219–227 (2018)

Waheed, Z., Waheed, A., Zafar, M., Riaz, F.: An efficient machine learning approach for the detection of melanoma using dermoscopic images. In: International Conference on Communication, Computing and Digital Systems (C-CODE), pp. 316–319 (2017)

Wang, Y., Cai, J., Louie, D.C., Lui, H., Lee, T.K., Wang, Z.J.: Classifying melanoma and seborrheic keratosis automatically with polarization speckle imaging. In: IEEE Global Conference on Signal and Information Processing (GlobalSIP), pp. 1–4 (2019)

miRNA-Disease Associations Prediction Based on Neural Tensor Decomposition

Yi Liu, Jiawei Luo[✉], and Hao Wu

College of Computer Science and Electronic Engineering, Hunan University,
Changsha 410082, China
luojiawei@hnu.edu.cn

Abstract. As a kind of regulatory factor in the human body, miRNAs function by targeting mRNAs. Dysfunction of miRNAs has an important relationship with diseases. miRNA-disease associations prediction algorithm aims to find potential pathogenic miRNAs based on known miRNA-related and disease-related data. With the development of miRNA-disease prediction algorithm research and the accumulation of biological data, integrating gene information in the prediction of pathogenic miRNAs is not only helpful to improve the accuracy of prediction but also helpful to further explore the pathogenesis of diseases. Therefore, in this paper, we propose a miRNA-disease association prediction algorithm, which is based on neural tensor decomposition, named NTDMDA, integrating the idea of weighted K nearest neighbors (WKNN) and a neural tensor decomposition model to identify pathogenic miRNAs. The experimental results show that the performance of NTDMDA is better than other comparison methods (improving up to at least 1.4% in AUC) in the prediction of miRNA-disease associations. At the same time, NTDMDA can realize the prediction of miRNA-gene-disease associations and provide richer information for the understanding of the complex biological mechanism between miRNAs and diseases.

Keywords: MiRNA-disease associations · Neural tensor decomposition · Data integration

1 Introduction

As a kind of non-coding RNA that widely exists in organisms, miRNAs are produced from genome transcription. miRNAs regulate gene expression by targeting mRNAs and participate in many biological processes such as cell growth and development [1]. In human bodies, the dysfunction of miRNAs becomes a factor that affect diseases by directly or indirectly changing the function of the genes that they regulate. In recent years, many studies show that miRNAs are involved in the pathogenesis of many human diseases [2]. Therefore, making miRNA a biomarker of disease has a positive effect and significance on understanding the molecular mechanism of disease.

With the emergence of various biological data, integrating miRNA-related and/or disease-related gene information becomes a popular way for miRNA-disease association research [3]. Shi et al. [4] proposed a random walk method to search for reliable

© Springer Nature Switzerland AG 2021
D.-S. Huang et al. (Eds.): ICIC 2021, LNAI 12838, pp. 312–323, 2021.
https://doi.org/10.1007/978-3-030-84532-2_28

pathogenic miRNAs from miRNA-gene and gene-disease networks. Li et al. [5] identified pathogenic miRNAs by using the functional classes of miRNA-related and disease-related genes. Xiao et al. [6] used miRNA-related gene information and gene function interaction network to evaluate miRNA similarity and applied the miRNA similarity information as a constraint in the graph regularized non-negative matrix decomposition framework to predict the miRNA associated with diseases. Guo et al. [7] updated miRNA-disease association matrix by using miRNA similarity information which is computed by miRNA-related gene information. Peng et al. [8] constructed a disease network by using disease-related gene information and applied an unbalanced random walk algorithm to extract information from the network to predict pathogenic miRNAs. Integrating gene information can provide great help for pathogenic miRNA studies. In recent studies, miRNA-related gene information and disease-related gene information have been used as independent parts, and this way ignores the biological links among miRNAs, genes, and diseases partly, it is more necessary to express the complex relationship among miRNAs, genes and diseases as a whole and fully consider their internal connections.

As a tool for representing data, a tensor can be represented as a N-dimensional array and called N-order tensor. One dimension of a tensor can represent one kind data. Tensor decomposition is an effective way to explore potential structures in tensors. As an effective method to study multi-type data, tensors and different tensor decomposition methods have been applied in bioinformatics, such as drug repositioning [9], miRNA synergy [10], and protein function research [11]. Classical tensor decomposition methods assume that potential structures in tensors are multi-linear, and thus insufficient to capture complex associations in data since most associations are non-linear in the real world [12]. Therefore, the neural tensor decomposition methods have been proposed to explore complex associations represented by tensors [13–15].

In this paper, we propose a neural tensor decomposition-based method, named NTD-MDA, for the prediction of miRNA-disease associations. First, we construct a miRNA-gene-disease association tensor by known miRNA-disease, miRNA-gene, gene-disease association information to model associations among miRNAs, diseases, and genes as a whole. Three dimensions of the association tensor represent miRNA, gene, and disease, respectively. We use a data preprocessing step, which is based on weighted K nearest neighbors, to update the association tensor by biological similarity information for getting a weighted association tensor. Finally, we apply a neural tensor decomposition model to learn features of elements in association tensor and get the prediction scores of unknown miRNA-disease associations. The experimental results of experiments show that compared with other advanced prediction methods, NTDMDA can achieve competitive performance.

2 Method

2.1 MiRNA-Gene-Disease Association Tensor

MiRNA-gene-disease association tensor $\mathcal{X}$ is constructed by known miRNA-disease, miRNA-gene, and gene-disease association information. If miRNA m_i related to disease

d_l, miRNA m_i is related to gene t_j and gene t_j is related to disease d_l, we set $\mathcal{X}_{i,j,l}$ to 1, which indicates that the element $\mathcal{X}_{i,j,l}$ is observed, otherwise set $\mathcal{X}_{i,j,l}$ to 0.

2.2 Task Description

In this paper, we finish the miRNA-disease association prediction task by complementing the miRNA-gene-disease association tensor. We get miRNA-gene-disease association prediction scores by applying a neural tensor decomposition model and obtain miRNA-disease association prediction scores by employing the concept of tensor fibers. A fiber in miRNA-gene-disease association tensor $\mathcal{X}$ can be thought of as a vector that denotes associations between a miRNA-disease pair and all genes. For miRNA m_i-disease d_l pair, we can obtain a vector $\mathcal{X}$ to denote prediction scores of this pair and all genes, then we get the prediction score of miRNA m_i. -disease d_l pair by calculating the average of the vector $\hat{\mathcal{X}}_{i,:,l}$ since we assume that a miRNA-disease pair has the same probabilities related to all genes:

$$PScore(m_i, d_l) - avg\left(\sum_{j=1}^{J} \hat{\mathcal{X}}_{i,j,l}\right) \tag{1}$$

where J is the number of genes and $PScore(m_i, d_l)$ is the prediction score of miRNA m_i-disease d_l pair.

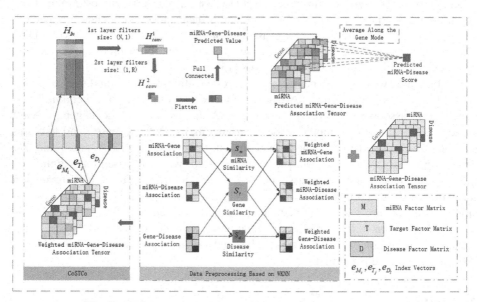

Fig. 1. The overall workflow of the proposed method NTDMDA

2.3 NTDMDA Method

In this section, we introduce NTDMDA, which is a miRNA-disease prediction method based on neural tensor decomposition. The NTDMDA algorithm consists of two components. The first one is the data preprocessing step based on WKNN, it is used to alleviate the problem of tensor sparsity. The second one is the CoSTCo model [13], which is a neural decomposition model, for obtaining miRNA-gene-disease association prediction scores. The framework of NTDMDA is shown in (see Fig. 1).

Data Preprocessing Based on WKNN. The miRNA-disease association matrix $Y_{md} \in \mathbb{R}^{I \times L}$, miRNA-gene association matrix $Y_{mt} \in \mathbb{R}^{I \times J}$ and gene-disease association matrix $Y_{td} \in \mathbb{R}^{J \times L}$ are constructed by binary association information that is used to construct the miRNA-gene-disease association tensor. The similarity score in the miRNA similarity matrix S_m, gene similarity matrix S_t, disease similarity matrix S_d are used as metrics to find the K nearest neighbors related miRNA, gene, disease, respectively. The information of K nearest neighbors related to different objects in an association matrix is used to update this association matrix.

Since the ways of updating association matrices Y_{md}, Y_{mt} and Y_{td} are same, we use a generalized matrix $Y \in \mathbb{R}^{G \times H}$ to unify matrices Y_{md}, Y_{mt} and Y_{td}. We use a set $U = \{u_1, u_2, ..., u_G\}$ to denote the objects represented by the rows of matrix Y and use a set $V = \{v_1, v_2, ..., v_H\}$ to denote the objects represented by the columns of matrix Y. The way to update the association matrix Y is as follows:

Firstly, weighted association matrix Y_u related to set U is obtained:

$$Y_{u\,i,:} = \frac{1}{\sum_{k=1}^{K} S_{u\,i,x_k}} \sum_{k=1}^{K} \omega^{k-1} S_{u\,i,x_k} Y_{x_k,:} \tag{2}$$

where $S_u \in \mathbb{R}^{G \times G}$ is similarity matrix related to set U. K is the number of nearest neighbors. The neighbors of u_i are sorted in descending order according to the similarity scores in the matrix S_u. x is the index vector related to rows of matrix Y. x_k is the index to find the location of k-th neighbor related to u_i in set U. $\omega \in (0, 1]$ is the weight coefficient.

Secondly, weighted association matrix Y_v related to set V is obtained:

$$Y_{v\,:,j} = \frac{1}{\sum_{k=1}^{K} S_{v\,j,y_k}} \sum_{k=1}^{K} \omega^{k-1} S_{v\,j,y_k} Y_{:,y_k} \tag{2}$$

where $S_v \in \mathbb{R}^{H \times H}$ is similarity matrix related to set V. The neighbors of v_j are sorted in descending order according to the similarity scores in the matrix S_v. y is the index vector related to columns of matrix Y. y_k is the index to find the location of k-th neighbor related to v_j in set V.

Then matrix Y can be updated by weighted matrix Y_u and weighted matrix Y_v, and we can obtain weighted association matrix $Y_w \in \mathbb{R}^{G \times H}$:

$$Y_w = max\left(Y, \frac{\alpha_1 Y_u + \alpha_2 Y_v}{\sum_{i=1}^{2} \alpha_i}\right) \tag{3}$$

When matrix Y denotes miRNA-disease association matrix Y_{md}, S_u denotes miRNA similarity matrix S_m, S_v denotes disease similarity matrix S_d, and we can obtain weighted miRNA-disease association matrix $Y_{wmd} \in \mathbb{R}^{I \times L}$. When matrix Y denotes miRNA-gene association matrix Y_{mt}, S_u denotes miRNA similarity matrix S_m, S_v denotes gene similarity matrix S_t, and we can obtain weighted miRNA-gene association matrix $Y_{wmt} \in \mathbb{R}^{I \times J}$. When matrix Y denotes gene-disease association matrix Y_{td}, S_u denotes gene similarity matrix S_t, S_v denotes disease similarity matrix S_d, and we can obtain weighted gene-disease association matrix $Y_{wtd} \in \mathbb{R}^{J \times L}$. α_1, α_2 are weight coefficient and set to 1 in this study.

Finally, we use the weighted association matrix Y_{wmd}, Y_{wmt}, Y_{wtd} to update association tensor $\mathcal{X}$ for getting weighted miRNA-gene-disease association tensor χ_w:

$$\chi_{w\ i,j,l} = \begin{cases} \chi_{w\ i,j,l} & \chi_{w\ i,j,l} > \chi_{temp\ i,j,l} \\ \chi_{temp\ i,j,l} & otherwise \end{cases} \tag{4}$$

where $\chi_{temp\ i,j,l} = \frac{\beta_1 Y_{wmd\ i,l} + \beta_2 Y_{wmt\ i,j} + \beta_3 Y_{wtd\ j,l}}{\sum_{i=1}^{3} \beta_i}$, β_1, β_2, β_3 are weight coefficient and set to 1 in this study.

CoSTCo Model. CoSTCo model [13] is a tensor decomposition model based on a convolutional neural network. The input of this model is the index vectors and the values of the observed elements in the tensor. Through the index vector, we can find the corresponding factor vector of the observed element in miRNA factor matrix $M \in \mathbb{R}^{I \times R}$, gene factor matrix $T \in \mathbb{R}^{J \times R}$ and disease factor matrix $D \in \mathbb{R}^{L \times R}$. The convolution operation in the convolutional neural network and the full connection operation are applied to calculate the prediction score of the unknown miRNA-gene-disease association according to the three factor vectors. The specific calculation process is as follows:

Firstly, the element index vector $e_{MTD\ i,j,l}$ is used to obtain factor vectors corresponding to element from miRNA factor matrix M, gene factor matrix T, and disease factor matrix D.

The element index vector is calculated as follows:

$$e_{MTD\ i,j,l} = \begin{bmatrix} e_{M\ i} \\ e_{T\ j} \\ e_{D\ l} \end{bmatrix} \in \mathbb{R}^{I+J+L} \tag{5}$$

where $e_{Mi} \in \mathbb{R}^I$ is the index vector of the miRNA factor matrix, represented by a one-hot vector, used to extract the i-th factor vector $M_{i,:}$ from miRNA factor matrix M. When I = 6 and i = 1, $e_{M1} = [1, 0, 0, 0, 0, 0]^T$. $e_{T\ j} \in \mathbb{R}^J$ is the index vector of the gene factor matrix, $e_{D\ l} \in \mathbb{R}^L$ is the index vector of the disease factor matrix.

The factor vectors $M_{i,:}$, $T_{j,:}$, $D_{k,:}$ in miRNA, gene, disease factor matrix M, T, D are adopted by the element index vector $e_{MTD\ i,j,l}$. These three vectors are remolded into an N (N = 3)-order tensor as the input convolution layer for learning the feature representation of the element $\mathcal{X}_{i,j,l}$:

$$\mathcal{H}_{In} = reshape\left(\begin{bmatrix} M^T & & \\ & T^T & \\ & & D^T \end{bmatrix}\begin{bmatrix} e_{M\ i} \\ e_{T\ j} \\ e_{D\ l} \end{bmatrix} = \begin{bmatrix} M_{i,:}^T \\ T_{j,:}^T \\ D_{k,:}^T \end{bmatrix} \in \mathbb{R}^{1 \times (R \times N)}\right) \in \mathbb{R}^{1 \times R \times N} \tag{6}$$

Then, through a two-layer convolution operation, the feature representation of the element $\mathcal{X}_{i,j,l}$ is learned from the three factor vectors, where each convolution layer contains C filters with a channel number of 1. Therefore, C feature representations can be extracted from each convolution layer.

In the first convolution layer, the size of the convolution kernel is set as (N, 1), and the feature tensor, which is learned by the n-th filter in the first convolution layer, can be expressed as:

$$\mathcal{H}_{conv}^{1,n} = ReLU\left(Conv\left(\mathcal{H}_{In}; W_1^n; b_1\right)\right) \in \mathbb{R}^{1 \times R} \tag{7}$$

where, $W_1^n \in \mathbb{R}^{N \times 1}$ is weight matrix, b_1 is bias term, $ReLU()$ is the activation function.

In the second convolution layer, the size of the convolution kernel is set as (1, R), and the feature tensor, which is learned by the n-th filter in the second convolution layer, can be expressed as:

$$\mathcal{H}_{conv}^{2,n} = ReLU\left(Conv\left(\mathcal{H}_{conv}^{1,n}; W_2^n; b_2\right)\right) \in \mathbb{R}^{1 \times 1} \tag{8}$$

where, $W_2^n \in \mathbb{R}^{1 \times R}$ is weight matrix, b_2 is a bias term.

Finally, we can obtain a prediction score $\hat{\chi}_{i,j,l}$ of element $\chi_{i,j,l}$ by full connection operation:

$$\hat{\chi}_{i,j,l} = FC\left(Flatten\left(\mathcal{H}_{conv}^{2,n}\right) \in \mathbb{R}^{1 \times c}; W_a; b_a\right) \tag{9}$$

where $W_a \in \mathbb{R}^{1 \times C}$ is weight matrix, n is the n-th filter and $n \in [1, 2, ..., C]$, C is set to 16 in our work. $Flatten()$ denotes full connection operation, b_a is a bias term.

We use cross-entropy to be the loss function of NTDMDA:

$$Loss = \frac{1}{Q} \sum_{q=1}^{Q} -\left[y_q \log(p(\hat{y}_q)) + (1 - y_q) \log(1 - p(\hat{y}_q))\right] \tag{10}$$

where Q is the number of observed elements in association tensor $\mathcal{X}$, y_q is the real value of the q-th element in tensor $\mathcal{X}$, $\hat{y}_q$ is predicted value of y_q. $p(.)$ represents the probability that the observed element is predicted to be positive.

3 Experiments

3.1 Data Collection

We collect miRNA-disease association information, microRNA-gene association information, gene-disease association information from HMDDv3.0 database [16], miRTar-Base database [17], DisGeNET database [18], respectively. To construct association tensor $\mathcal{X}$ and link biological similarity information, we only focused on miRNAs and microRNA with identifiers in miRbase [19], diseases with identifiers in Mesh (https://www.ncbi.nlm.nih.gov/mesh), and genes with identifiers in Entrez Gene [20]. We use miRNA-microRNA association information and microRNA-gene association information to build miRNA-gene association information. To get denser associations, we only selected miRNA-gene associations, called "Functional MTI" in the "Support Type" item, and the genes which interact with less than three miRNAs. Then, the miRNA-gene-disease association tensor contains 15167 triple associations, and the other information is shown in Table 1.

Table 1. Data statistics.

miRNA	Gene	Disease	miRNA-disease	miRNA-gene	Gene-disease
369	486	238	5113	4040	2405

Biological similarity information in our work contains miRNA sequence similarity information, gene functional interaction information, and symptom-based disease similarity information. The biological similarity information is applied to build a miRNA similarity matrix S_m, gene similarity matrix S_t, disease similarity matrix S_d.

We collected miRNA sequence information from miRbase. Then the sequence similarity score between miRNA m_i and miRNA m_j, $MSscore(m_i, m_j)$, was calculated by pairwise2 function in a set of tools for biological computation, named Biopython. We set the match and mismatch scores to 5 and -4 and set gap penalties to -1 and -0.5 when opening a gap and extending the gap. Then, we calculated the average of all sequence similarity scores and set the scores below the average to zeros. The gene functional interaction score between gene t_i and gene t_j, $TFscore(t_i, t_j)$, was obtained from HumanNet [21]. The symptom-based similarity score between disease d_i and d_j, $DSscore(d_i, d_j)$, was collected from symptom-based similarity [22]. The elements in matrix S_d are symptom-based similarity scores, $DSscore$. The elements in matrix S_m and elements in matrix S_t can be obtained by min-max normalization of $MSscore$ and $TFscore$:

$$S_{M\ i,j} = \frac{MSscore(m_i, m_j) - S_{mmin}}{S_{mmax} - S_{mmin}} \tag{11}$$

$$S_{t\ i,j} = \frac{TFscore(t_i, t_j) - S_{tmin}}{S_{tmax} - S_{tmin}} \tag{12}$$

where S_{mmax} and S_{mmin} are the maximum and minimum sequence similarity scores. S_{tmax} and S_{tmin} the maximum and minimum gene functional interaction scores.

3.2 Performance Evaluation

NTDMDA mainly contains four parameters, K, ω, R, lr. K is the number of nearest neighbors selected in data preprocessing; ω is the weight coefficient in data preprocessing; R is the rank of the tensor and lr is the learning rate. K = 6, $\omega = 0.8$, R = 4, $lr = 1e^{-5}$ were set to evaluate the performance of NTDMDA. Two types of 5-fold cross-validation were designed and carried out. For each method, we repeated all cross-validations ten times independently and reported average results.

Type 1: Performance for Predicting MiRNA-Disease Associations. All known miRNA-disease pairs were used as positive samples and randomly divided into 5 subsets. In each-fold validation, one subset was used to test, and the rest subsets were used to train. We selected some unknown associations as negative samples and make the positive and negative sample ratio equal to 1:1. We use AUC value and AUPR value as metrics to evaluate the performance of NTDMDA for predicting miRNA-disease associations.

Under Type 1 setting, we compared our method with CP [23], TDRC [24], two methods based on tensor decomposition, and IMCMDA [25], NIMCGCN [26], and MDA-CNN [27], methods for the prediction of miRNA-disease associations. In the experiment, the rank of the CP decomposition was set to 4, and the remaining parameters of the contrast algorithm were set to the optimal parameters (TDRC: $R = 4$, $\alpha = 0.125$, $\beta = 0.125$; IMCMDA: $R = 50$; NIMCGCN: $l = 0.01$, $t = 2$, $\alpha = 0.4$; MDA-CNN: hidden layer: $l = 0.01$, number of neurons $= 256$, batch_size $= 128$, convolution layer: $l = 0.01$, batch_size $= 64$). The average AUC values of NTDMDA, CP, TDRC, IMCMDA, NIMCGCN, and MDA-CNN are 0.940, 0.893, 0.927, 0.806, 0.926, 0.817 respectively, and the average AUPR values of NTDMDA, CP, TDRC, IMCMDA, NIM-CGCN, and MDA-CNN are 0.938, 0.905, 0.927, 0.795, 0.930, 0.813, respectively (see Fig. 2). NTDMDA achieves better performance than other methods. The performance under the two metrics indicates that tensor decomposition-based methods can be an effective way for miRNA-disease association prediction.

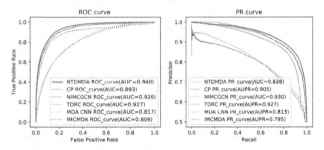

Fig. 2. The ROC and PR curves of different methods under the Type 1 setting.

Type 2: Performance for Predicting MiRNA-Gene-Disease Associations. All known miRNA-gene-disease associations were randomly used as positive samples and divided into 5 parts. In each-fold validation, one part was treated as testing set in turn. We randomly selected unknown triple associations as negative samples with size as same as the positive ones. We use AUC value and MSE value, as metrics to evaluate the performance of our method for predicting miRNA-gene-disease associations.

Under the Type 2 setting, we compared our method with CP, TDRC. Table 2 shows the prediction performance of different methods. The average AUC values of NTDMDA, CP, and TDRC are 0.971 0.937, and 0.969 respectively, the average MSE values of NTDMDA, CP, and TDRC are 0.081, 0.437, and 0.168. The performance of NTDMDA is better than others.

Table 2. The AUC and MSE values of different methods under Type 2 setting.

Method	AUC	MSE
CP	0.937	0.437
TDRC	0.969	0.168
NTDMDA	**0.971**	**0.081**

3.3 Case Study

We further evaluate the performance of NTDMDA in a case study. We used all known miRNA-disease associations to predict and considered all unknown associations as candidates. Gastric Neoplasms, Breast Neoplasms, and Lung Neoplasms were selected as representative objects to show the results of the prediction. For each object, we ranked the candidate miRNAs by prediction scores, listed the top 10 candidates, and verified them by one of dbDEMC 2.0 database [28], miRCancer database [29], literature at least. The results are shown in Table 3. For gastric neoplasms, breast neoplasms, and lung neoplasms respectively, 7, 7, and 7 of 10 candidate miRNAs were supported by at least one of dbDEMC 2.0, miRCancer, and literature.

Table 3. Top-10 candidate miRNAs for gastric neoplasms, breast neoplasms, and lung neoplasms.

Disease	Rank	miRNAs	Support	Rank	miRNAs	Support
Gastric Neoplasms	1	mir-625	dbDEMC, miCancer	6	mir-26a-2	dbDEMC
	2	mir-29b-2	dbDEMC	7	mir-29b-1	dbDEMC
	3	mir-454	dbDEMC, miCancer	8	mir-4775	-
	4	mir-1296	dbDEMC, miCancer	9	mir-181a-1	[30]
	5	mir-320b-1	-	10	mir-138–1	-
Breast Neoplasms	1	mir-454	dbDEMC	6	mir-181a-1	-
	2	mir-625	dbDEMC, miCancer	7	mir-138–1	dbDEMC
	3	mir-320b-1	-	8	mir-138–2	-
	4	mir-1296	dbDEMC, miCancer	9	mir-524	dbDEMC
	5	mir-4775	dbDEMC	10	mir-19b-2	dbDEMC
Lung Neoplasms	1	mir-125b-2	dbDEMC	6	mir-1296	dbDEMC
	2	mir-320b-1	-	7	mir-16–2	dbDEMC
	3	mir-454	dbDEMC, miCancer	8	mir-16–1	dbDEMC
	4	mir-625	dbDEMC, miRCancr	9	mir-4775	[31]
	5	mir-199a-2	-	10	mir-181a-1	-

3.4 The Impact of Parameters

Impact of R. We explored the impact of R on the performance of NTDMDA by parameter δ. We set $R = \delta \times minI, J, L$, the I, J, L are the number of miRNAs, genes, and diseases. We fixed $K = 6$, $\omega = 0.8$, $lr = 1e^{-4}$. We set the range of δ to be [0.01, 0.02, 0.03, 0.04, 0.05, 0.06, 0.07, 0.08, 0.09] and traversed each of them. NTDMDA achieved optimal performance when $\delta = 0.02$. We selected $\delta = 0.02$ to obtain the optimal rank (see Fig. 3 (a) and 3(b)).

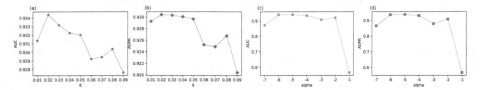

Fig. 3. Impact of R,*lr*

Impact of K, ω. We fixed $\delta = 0.02$ and $lr = 1e^{-4}$ and set the range of K to be [2, 4, 6, 8, 10] and the range of ω to be [0.2, 0.4, 0.6, 0.8, 1.0]. We found when $K = 8$ and $\omega = 0.6$, the performance of NTDMDA is stable, therefore, we choose 8 and 0.6 to be the best values of K and ω (see Fig. 4).

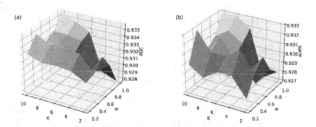

Fig. 4. Impact of K, ω.

Impact of *lr*. We explored the impact of *lr* on the performance of NTDMDA by parameter α. We fixed $\delta = 0.02$, $K = 6$, $\omega = 0.8$ and set the range of *lr* to be [$1e^{-7}$, $1e^{-6}$, $1e^{-5}$, $1e^{-4}$, $1e^{-3}$, $1e^{-2}$, $1e^{-1}$], it equals that we set the range of α to be [$-7, -6, -5, -4, -3, -2, -1$]. Traversing each value of α, NTDMDA achieved optimal performance when $\alpha = -5$, therefore, we made *lr* equal to $1e^{-5}$ to achieve the optimal performance of NTDMDA (see Fig. 3(c) and 3(d)).

4   Conclusion

MiRNA is one of the important biomolecules that influence the occurrence and development of disease. The miRNA-disease association prediction algorithm identifies valuable pathogenic miRNAs and provides credible candidates for subsequent biological experiments. In this study, we construct a miRNA-gene-disease association tensor and propose a neural tensor decomposition method, named NTDMDA to predict miRNA-disease associations. The prediction performance of NTDMDA is verified by 5-fold cross-validation under two settings and a case study. The results of experiments inspire us that the neural tensor decomposition methods can be an effective strategy for predicting miRNA-disease association and encourage us to integrate more types of biological data and associations for miRNA-disease association research in the future.

Funding. This work has been supported by the Natural Science Foundation of China (Grant no.61873089) and (Grant no. 62032007).

References

1. Bartel, D.P.: MicroRNAs: Genomics, Biogenesis, Mechanism, and Function. Cell (2004)
2. Luo, J., Shen, C., Lai, Z., et al.: Incorporating clinical, chemical and biological information for predicting small molecule-microRNA associations based on non-negative matrix factorization. IEEE/ACM Trans. Comput. Biol. Bioinform. **PP**(99), 1–1 (2020)
3. Ding, P., Luo, J., Liang, C., Xiao, Q., Cao, B., et al.: Human disease MiRNA inference by combining target information based on heterogeneous manifolds. J. Biomed. Inform. **80**, 26–36 (2018)
4. Shi, H., Xu, J., Zhang, G., et al.: Walking the interactome to identify human miRNA-disease associations through the functional link between miRNA targets and disease genes. BMC Syst. Biol. **7**(1), 101 (2013)
5. Li, X., Wang, Q., Zheng, Y., et al.: Prioritizing human cancer microRNAs based on genes' functional consistency between microRNA and cancer. Nucleic Acids Res. **39**(22), e153 (2011)
6. Xiao, Q., Luo, J., Liang, C., et al.: A graph regularized non-negative matrix factorization method for identifying microRNA-disease associations. Bioinformatics (2017)
7. Guo, L., Shi, K., Wang, L.: MLPMDA: multi-layer linear projection for predicting miRNA-disease association - ScienceDirect. Knowledge-Based Systems (2020)
8. Wei, P., Wei, L., et al.: A framework for integrating multiple biological networks to predict MicroRNA-Disease associations. IEEE Trans. Nanobiosci. **16**, 100–107 (2017)
9. Ran, W., Shuai, L., Man, H.W., et al.: Drug-protein-disease association prediction and drug repositioning based on tensor decomposition. In: Proceedings of 2018 IEEE International Conference on Bioinformatics and Biomedicine(2018)
10. Liu, P., Luo, J., Chen, X.: miRCom: tensor completion integrating multi-view information to deduce the potential disease-related miRNA-miRNA pairs. In: IEEE/ACM Trans. Comput. Biology Bioinform. **PP**(99), 1 (2020)
11. Mohamed, S.K.: Predicting tissue-specific protein functions using multi-part tensor decomposition - ScienceDirect. Inf. Sci. **508**(C), 343–357(2020)
12. Liu, B., He, L., Li, Y., Zhe, S., Xu, Z.: NeuralCP: bayesian multiway data analysis with neural tensor decomposition. Cogn. Comput. **10**(6), 1051–1061 (2018). https://doi.org/10.1007/s12 559-018-9587-4
13. Liu, H., Li, Y., Tsang, M., et al.: CoSTCo: a neural tensor completion model for sparse tensors. In: Proceedings of the 25th ACM SIGKDD International Conference on Knowledge Discovery & Data Mining, Anchorage, AK, USA, pp. 324–334 (2019)
14. Wu, X., Shi, B., Dong, Y., et al.: neural tensor factorization for temporal interaction learning. In: Proceedings of the Twelfth ACM International Conference on Web Search and Data Mining, Melbourne VIC, Australia, pp. 537–545 (2019)

15. Chen, H., Li, J.: Neural tensor model for learning multi-aspect factors in recommender systems. In: Proceedings of (2020)

16. Zhou, H., Shi, J., et al.: HMDD v3.0: a database for experimentally supported human microRNA-disease associations. Nucleic Acids Research (2018)

17. Chou, C.H., Shrestha, S., Yang, C.D., et al.: MiRTarBase update 2018: A resource for experimentally validated microRNA-target interactions. Nucleic Acids Research, 46(Database issue) (2017)

18. Piero, J., Bravo, L., Queralt-Rosinach, N., et al.: DisGeNET: a comprehensive platform integrating information on human disease-associated genes and variants. Nucleic Acids Res. **45**(Database issue) (2016)

19. Kozomara, A., Birgaoanu, M., et al.: miRBase: from microRNA sequences to function. Nucleic Acids Research (2018)

20. Donna, M., Jim, O., Pruitt, K.D., et al.: Entrez Gene: gene-centered information at NCBI. Nucleic Acids Res. **33**(Database issue), D54–D58 (2005)

21. Sohyun, H., Yeong, K.C., Yang, S., et al.: HumanNet v2: human gene networks for disease research. Nuclc Acids Res. 2018(D1), D1 (2018)

22. Zhou, X.Z., Menche, J., Barabási, A., et al.: Human symptoms–disease network. Nature Communications (2014)

23. Harshman, R.A.: Foundations of the PARAFAC procedure: Model and conditions for an "explanatory" multi-mode factor analysis. Ucla Working Papers in Phonetics(1970).

24. Huang, F., Yue, X., Xiong, Z., et al.: Tensor Decomposition with Relational Constraints for Predicting Multiple Types of MicroRNA-disease Associations (2019)

25. Chen, X., Wang, L., Jia, Q., et al.: Predicting miRNA-disease association based on inductive matrix completion. Bioinformatics **2018**(24), 4256–4265 (2018)

26. Li, J., Zhang, S., Liu, T., et al.: Neural Inductive Matrix Completion with Graph Convolutional Networks for miRNA-disease Association Prediction. Bioinformatics (2020)

27. Jiajie, P., Hui, W., et al.: A learning-based framework for miRNA-disease association identification using neural networks. Bioinformatics (Oxford, England) (2019)

28. Yang, Z., Wu, L., Wang, A., et al.: dbDEMC 2.0: updated database of differentially expressed miRNAs in human cancers. Nuclc. Acids Res. **2017**(D1), D812–D818 (2017)

29. Xie, B., Ding, Q., Han, H., et al.: miRCancer: a microRNA-cancer association database constructed by text mining on literature. Bioinformatics **2013**(5), 638–644 (2013)

30. Silin, C., Zhu, J., et al.: Combination of miRNA and RNA functions as potential biomarkers for gastric cancer. Tumour biology: the journal of the International Society for Once developmental Biology and Medicine (2015)

31. Liu, Y., Fan, X., Zhao, Z., et al.: LncRNA SLC7A11-AS1 contributes to lung cancer progression through facilitating TRAIP expression by inhibiting miR-4775. Onco. Targets. Ther. **13**, 6295–6302 (2020)

Gene Regulation Modeling and Analysis

SHDC: A Method of Similarity Measurement Using Heat Kernel Based on Denoising for Clustering scRNA-seq Data

Jian-ping Zhao[1](✉), Hai-yun Wang[1], and Chun-Hou Zheng[1,2](✉)

[1] College of Mathematics and System Sciences, Xinjiang University, Urumqi, China
[2] School of Computer Science and Technology, Anhui University, Hefei, China

Abstract. Identifying cell types is one of the most important goals in single cell sequencing data analysis. The similarity between cells is the principal basis for dividing cell subpopulations. However, it usually brings higher computational complexity when using multi kernel learning. In this paper, a new method SHDC was proposed for single cell clustering. SHDC denoised scRNA-seq datasets to obtain a more stable data structure and only a heat kernel was used to measure the similarity between cells. We used several real scRNA-seq datasets to test the performance of SHDC and compared with previous single cell clustering methods. The results show that our method is effective.

Keywords: Clustering · scRNA-seq · Heat kernel · Deep count autoencoder network · Uniform Manifold Approximation and Projection

1 Introduction

In recent years, single cell sequencing technology has developed rapidly.It helps researchers explore the nature and laws of life activities [1]. Identifying cell types is main goal of scRNA-seq study. It is necessary to use unsupervised learning method clustering to identify cell types [2].

High dimension and high noise are two characteristics of single cell RNA sequencing data. So far, many single cell clustering methods and tools taking them into account have been proposed. Such as SC3 [2], SIMLR [3], SSCC [4], PARC [5], CIDR [6], TSCAN [7], Scater [8] and so on.

SC3 has good performance in processing scRNA-seq data with a high dropout rate, but it takes a long time and SIMLR is the same. SSCC is a new single cell clustering framework based on subsampling-clustering-classifying (SCC) [4, 13]. It should be pointed out that the proportion of sub datasets used for classification should not be too high, otherwise the accuracy of classification will be affected. CIDR considers the influence of dropouts on clustering. The biggest advantage of PARC is that it can process large-scale data in less time, but the dropout event in the dataset will seriously affect the construction of the graph in PARC.

In this paper, we proposed a new method combining denoising and kernel method. Deep count autoencoder network (DCA) [9] was used to denoise data. Only a heat

© Springer Nature Switzerland AG 2021
D.-S. Huang et al. (Eds.): ICIC 2021, LNAI 12838, pp. 327–335, 2021.
https://doi.org/10.1007/978-3-030-84532-2_29

kernel [10] that has less computational complexity compare to a gaussian kernel [3] was used to measure the similarity between cells. We extensively evaluated our approach with competing methods using several real scRNA-seq datasets. Experimental results showed that our method has better performance.

2 Method

2.1 Framework Overview

SHDC pipelines consists of following steps (Fig. 1).

Firstly, the DCA is used to denoise and reconstruct data. The output data of DCA model need to be log-transformed and standardized.

Secondly, the similarity matrix S is obtained by using heat kernel to measure the similarity between cells.

Thirdly, extract k-nearest neighbors (k-NN) graph from similarity matrix S to obtain adjacency matrix W.

Next, project adjacency matrix W to a lower dimensional space using the Uniform Manifold Approximation and Projection (UMAP) [11] algorithm.

Finally, the k-means was used to obtain the final clustering result in this low dimensional space.

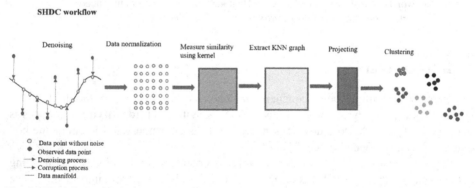

Fig. 1. Workflow of SHDC. In step projecting, UMAP was used to project adjacency matrix W into a three-dimensional space that was used for clustering.

2.2 Denoising Using DCA

Noise has always been a major challenge for single-cell clustering. We all know that the lower the ratio of dropouts in single cell RNA sequencing data, the better for single cell clustering. Therefore, data denoising is also an effective means to improve the accuracy of clustering.

Deep count autoencoder network (DCA) has been widely used in scRNA-seq data for denoising. DCA uses the framework of autoencoder to denoise single cell RNA data by learning the manifold of noisy data. DCA uses zero-inflation- negative-binomial (ZINB) distribution to fit the real manifold of noisy scRNA-seq data. In additional, raw scRAN-seq read count datasets used in DCA are preprocessed by the Python package SCANPY, genes with no count in any cell are filtered out.

2.3 Using Single Kernel Instead of Multi-Kernel

A conclusion can be drawn from SIMLR [3]. It is that multiple Gaussian kernels are an effective method to measure cell similarity for high-noise single-cell RNA data with an unstable data structure. But it takes 2000 to 3000 s for SIMLR to process a dataset of more than 2000 cells. In this paper, we found that the performance of using a single Gaussian kernel for denoised data is similar to that of using multiple Gaussian kernels for original data. The detailed results were listed in Table 1.

Table 1. Comparison results of single gaussian kernel and multi gaussian kernel on raw data for clustering

Dataset	NMI		Running time (s)	
	Single gaussian kernel	Multi gaussian kernel (SIMLR)	Single gaussian kernel	Multi gaussian kernel (SIMLR)
10X_PBMC_DCA	0.793	0.775	419.58	2877.47
mouse_bladder_DCA	0.722	0.696	175.64	2898.50
mouse_ES_DCA	0.966	0.829	172.37	1892.61
worm_neuron_DCA	0.697	0.684	401.29	1728.67

2.4 Selecting Heat Kernel Instead of Gaussian Kernel

Single kernel function can save computation time to some extent, but the computation of gaussian kernel is still complex. In order to speed up the calculation, the heat kernel was used to replace the gaussian kernel. It can be seen from (1–3) and (4) that the computational complexity of heat kernel is smaller than that of gaussian kernel.

$$S_{ij} = K(x_i, x_j) = \frac{1}{\varepsilon_{ij}\sqrt{2\pi}} \exp(\frac{||x_i - x_j||_2^2}{2\varepsilon_{ij}^2}). \tag{1}$$

$$\mu_i = \frac{\sum_{j \in KNN(x_i)} ||x_i - x_j||_2}{k}. \tag{2}$$

$$\varepsilon_{ij} = \frac{\sigma(\mu_i + \mu_j)}{2}. \tag{3}$$

$$S_{ij} = k(x_i, x_j) = \exp(\frac{||x_i - x_j||^2}{2t^2}). \tag{4}$$

Where the (1) represents gaussian kernel. Where (4) represents heat kernel. We found that the heat kernel not only greatly reduces the calculation time, but also improved the clustering accuracy (Fig. 2).

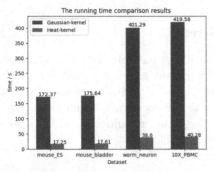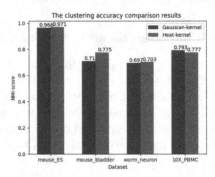

Fig. 2. The differences between gaussian kernel and heat kernel in running time and clustering accuracy are shown here.

3 Results

3.1 scRNA-seq Datasets

In the part of numerical experiments, we selected six scRNA-seq datasets from different sequencing platforms to demonstrate the performance of SHDC. The detailed information about these real scRNA-seq datasets was listed in Table 2.

Table 2. Basic information about scRNA-seq datasets

Dataset	Cell number	Gene number	Cluster number
Zheng	500	32738	3
mouse_ES_cell	2717	24046	4
mouse_bladder_cell	2746	19079	16
Zeisel	3005	19972	9
worm_neuron_cell	4186	11955	10
10X_PBMC	4271	16499	8

3.2 Clustering Accuracy

In the part of numerical experiments, five popular single-cell clustering methods with default parameters are used to compare with our method. These five methods include SC3, SSCC, PARC, Seurat and "DCA + kmeans".

We compared our method with these five methods on all datasets in Table 2. We used Normalized mutual information (NMI) [5] and Adjusted Rand Index (ARI) [3] to evaluate the model performance and details were listed in Table 3 and Table 4.

Table 3. NMI score under different datasets

Methods	SC3	SSCC	PARC	Seurat	DCA + Kmeans	SHDC
Zheng	**0.989**	0.961	0.843	0.980	0.978	**0.989**
10X_PBMC	0.744	0.642	0.653	0.735	0.735	**0.777**
mouse_bladder_cell	0.731	0.580	0.701	0.751	0.648	**0.775**
mouse_ES_cell	0.858	0.741	0.560	0.771	0.856	**0.971**
worm_neuron_cell	0.655	0.486	0.621	0.684	0.467	**0.703**
Zeisel	0.759	0.545	0.708	0.646	0.452	**0.764**

Table 4. ARI score under different datasets

Methods	SC3	SSCC	PARC	Seurat	DCA + Kmeans	SHDC
Zheng	**0.994**	0.977	0.846	0.988	0.988	**0.994**
10X_PBMC	0.746	0.485	0.481	0.632	0.723	**0.762**
mouse_bladder_cell	0.558	0.344	0.565	0.521	0.529	**0.669**
mouse_ES_cell	0.803	0.705	0.433	0.597	0.852	**0.983**
worm_neuron_cell	0.404	0.312	0.451	0.476	0.280	**0.505**
Zeisel	**0.820**	0.441	0.481	0.469	0.313	0.732

3.3 Parameter Sensitivity Analysis

The t in heat kernel (4) and k in in KNN graph are two important parameters in SHDC. To study the influence of them on the performance of SHDC, in this section, six scRNA-seq datasets are employed. By observing the change of clustering accuracy when the two parameters take different values, we can get that their different values have little effect on SHDC (Fig. 3).

Based on this, we set the default parameter t as 100 and k as 50 during other experiments.

3.4 Evaluation of Denoising

In this paper, we use DCA to denoise the data. Since we use all the genes in the cells rather than a few differentially expressed genes in tAs can be seen from the Fighe whole

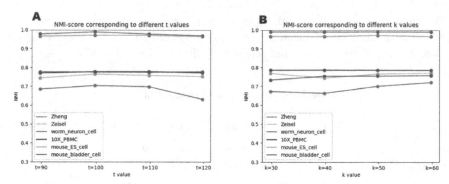

Fig. 3. A refers to the influence of parameter *t* on clustering effect for all datasets, B refers to the influence of parameter *k*. Whether it's A or B, six different color curves represent six different scRNA-seq datasets.

calculation process, we need to assume that the single cell data approximately follows a distribution, otherwise the noise denoising using all genes will have a large deviation. DCA is based on the premise that the single cell data approximately obey the Zero Inflation Negative Binomial distribution (ZINB).

To study the impact of denoising for clustering results, the datasets used in last section were employed again. In this section, the most commonly used clustering method k-means was used to cluster scRNA-seq datasets with denoising or without. NMI score was used to evaluate the accuracy of clustering. From Fig. 4A, we can see that denoising has a significant impact on the clustering results.

3.5 The Scalability of SHDC

The progress of sequencing technology also makes the scale of scRNA-seq data increasing, which requires the single-cell clustering method to be scalable. The computational complexity determines the scalability of the method.

Gökcenraslan et al. [9] showed that under a certain number of genes, the computational complexity of DCA was linear with the number of cells. We needed to find relevance between the computational complexity of constructing similarity matrix using heat kernel and the number of cells. The datasets used previously with cell numbers ranging from 500 to 4271 were selected, and we used 50 highly variable genes to construct similarity matrixes using heat kernel for every dataset. We can see from Fig. 4B that the running time of constructing similarity matrix between cells using heat kernel is approximately linear with the number of cells in scRNA-seq dataset.

For a scRNA-seq dataset with n cells and m genes, we discuss the time complexity of constructing similarity matrix using heat kernel. For any cell, it is necessary to calculate the similarity between it and each cell in the dataset. So, the time complexity of constructing similarity matrix is $O(mn)$. When extracting k-NN graph, it is necessary to sort the n similarities. The time complexity of quick sort is $O(nlogn)$, so the time complexity of the second part of the SHDC is $O(nm + nlogn)$.

Therefore, the computational complexity of SHDC is approximately linear with the number of cells in the dataset, which means that SHDC has good scalability.

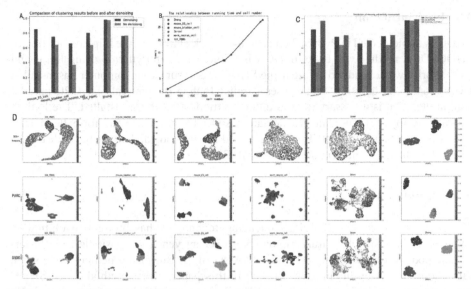

Fig. 4. A shows the influence of denoising on clustering results. B describes time complexity of constructing similarity matrix. C includes contributions of denoising and similarity measurement to SHDC. D refers to cell visualization results for all scRNA-seq datasets. The six graphs in each row are the cell visualization results of six datasets by a certain method.

3.6 Cell Visualization

In this study, we did cell visualization for all scRNA-seq datasets using UMAP. From the results of cell visualization, we can see that SHDC can well divide different types of cells into different clusters.

As can be seen from the Fig. 4D, for dataset Zheng, except PARC, other methods can get better visualization results. For other scRNA-seq datasets, the visualization results of SHDC show better intra cluster consistency and inter cluster separability. The visualization results of method "DCA + kmeans" seem to show good data manifold, but the effect of intra cluster consistency and inter cluster separability is not so good.

3.7 Contributions of Denoising and Similarity Measure to SHDC

In this paper, the contribution of denoising and similarity measure to SHDC is the biggest. Denoising using DCA can improve the quality of the data, which lays the foundation for the subsequent similarity measurement. In addition, using heat kernel can measure the similarity between cells more quickly and accurately.

Denoising and similarity measurement are two inseparable parts, the lack of any one will affect the performance of SHDC. In order to illustrate the synergy of these two parts, we have done the following experiments. For six different datasets, we did three different experiments, "Denoising with heat kernel", "No denoising" and "Denoising without heat kernel", respectively. By comparing the final clustering effect, we show the synergy between noise reduction and similarity measurement (Fig. 4C).

3.8 Implementation

SHDC is implemented in Python 3 on HP Z840 work-station. In the implementa-tion of SHDC, DCA module will be used. DCA is implemented in Python 3 using Keras and its TensorFlow backend. So before using SHDC, make sure your computer has installed DCA module. In addition, SHDC uses Parallel Python (pp) module for CPU parallel computing, so it is necessary to ensure that pp module has been installed. The Python package scanpy [12] is used in the calculation, so SHDC supports h5ad-formatted HDF5 files and anndata data format. The datasets used in this study and all source code can be available at https://github.com/WHY-17/SHDC.

4 Conclusion

The progress of single cell RNA sequencing technology has brought revolutionary changes to the research of transcriptomics. In recent years, many single-cell cluster-ing methods have been proposed for scRNA-seq data. But many methods have some limitations in solving the impact of noise. In this paper, a new method called SHDC was proposed for single cell clustering. SHDC denoised scRNA-seq datasets to obtain a more stable data structure and only a heat kernel was used to measure the similarity between cells. Experimental results show that SHDC has good performance.

The progress of sequencing technology also makes the scale of scRNA-seq data increasing. For large-scale scRNA-seq datasets, there is still room for further improvement of clustering accuracy. These problems are the direction of our future efforts.

Acknowledgements. This work was supported by grants from the Xinjiang Autonomous Region University Research Program (No. XJEDU2019Y002) and the National Natural Science Foundation of China (No. U19A2064, 61873001).

References

1. Cheng, N., et al.: Comparison and integration of computational methods for deleterious synonymous mutation prediction. Brief. Bioinform. **21**(3), 970–981 (2020)
2. Kiselev, V., Kirschner, K., Schaub, M., et al.: SC3: consensus clustering of single-cell RNA-seq data. Nat. Methods **14**, 483–486 (2017)
3. Wang, B., Zhu, J., Pierson, E., et al.: Visualization and analysis of single-cell RNA-seq data by kernel-based similarity learning. Nat. Methods **14**, 414–416 (2017)
4. Ren, X., Zheng, L., Zhang, Z.: SSCC: a novel computational framework for rapid and accurate clustering large-scale single cell RNA-seq data. Genomics Proteomics Bioinform. **17**(2), 201–210 (2019)
5. Shobana, V., Dickson, M., Kelvin, C., Joshua, W., Hayden, K., Kevin, K.: PARC: ultrafast and accurate clustering of phenotypic data of millions of single cells. Bioinformatics **36**(9), 2778–2786 (2020)
6. Lin, P., Troup, M., Ho, J.W: CIDR: ultrafast and accurate clustering through imputation for single-cell RNA-seq data. Genome Biol 18, 59 (2017). https://doi.org/10.1186/s13059-017-1188-0

7. Zhicheng, J., Hongkai, J.: TSCAN: pseudo-time reconstruction and evaluation in single-cell RNA-seq analysis. Nucleic Acids Res. **14**(13), 117 (2016)
8. Davis, J., Kieran, R.C., Aaron, T.L., Quin, F.W.: Scater: pre-processing, quality control, normalization and visualization of single-cell RNA-seq data in R. Bioinformatics **33**(8), 1179–1186 (2017)
9. Eraslan, G., Simon, L.M., Mircea, M., et al.: Single-cell RNA-seq denoising using a deep count autoencoder. Nat. Commun. **10**, 390 (2019)
10. Hao, D., Michael, S., Chao, W., Kun, H., Raghu, M.: Integrative cancer patient stratification via subspace merging. Bioinformatics **35**(10), 1653–1659 (2019)
11. McInnes, L, Healy, J., Melville, J.: Umap: Uniform manifold approximation and projection for dimension reduction. arXiv preprint arXiv 1802.03426(2018)
12. Wolf, F.A., Angerer, P., Theis, F.J.: SCANPY: large-scale single-cell gene expression data analysis. Genome Biol. **19**(1), 1–5 (2018)
13. Wang, H.Y., Zhao, J.P., Zheng, C.H.: SUSCC: secondary construction of feature space based on UMAP for rapid and accurate clustering large-scale single cell RNA-seq dat. Interdiscip. Sci. Comput. Life Sci. **13**, 83–90 (2021)

Research on RNA Secondary Structure Prediction Based on MLP

Weizhong Lu, Xiaoyi Chen, Yu Zhang, Hongjie Wu$^{(\boxtimes)}$, Jiawei Shen, Nan Zhou, and Yijie Ding

School of Electronic and Information Engineering, Suzhou University of Science and Technology, Suzhou 215009, China

Abstract. RNA has important structure, function and regulation in cells. It is closely related to biological functions. Pseudoknot is an important secondary structure in RNA. It is the most difficult part to predict. In order to solve this problem, this article attempts to use Multi-Layer Perceptron (MLP) neural network to predict and study RNA secondary structure. And compared with support vector machine (SVM), random forest (Random Forests), decision tree (Decision Tree) and other algorithms on the authoritative data set RNA STRAND. Experiments show that the classification accuracy and model score of MLP are more advantageous, which verifies the feasibility and effectiveness of the MLP method.

Keywords: RNA secondary structure · Pseudoknot · MLP neural network

1 Introduction

RNA is ribonucleic acid. It is a biological macromolecule that exists in cells and viruses. It has a variety of biological functions and is essential in living organisms. RNA not only participates in the expression of biological genetic information, but also plays an irreplaceable role in biological processes such as protein translation and gene regulation [1]. Therefore, understanding its secondary structure is of great significance for life research and application. Although traditional methods such as X-ray and nuclear magnetic resonance can play a predictive role, they are too expensive, inefficient, and unable to identify and predict all RNA structures. Therefore, the use of computers to predict RNA secondary structure is an important field of computational molecular biology. Pseudoknot is the most difficult to predict secondary structure of RNA, and some early algorithms do not consider it at all. In 1960, Fresco [2] et al. proposed the first RNA secondary structure prediction algorithm. In the 1970s, Zuker [3–5] proposed a minimum free energy model with a prediction accuracy of 73%, but both algorithms can not predict the pseudoknots. RNAfold is a dynamic programming algorithm proposed by Hofacker et al. [6] in 1994, but the existence of pseudoknots is usually not considered. In 1999, Rivas and Eddy [7, 8] proposed the PKnotsRE algorithm, which is an improvement on the minimum free energy model algorithm proposed by Zuker. It can predict pseudoknots and is another dynamic programming algorithm. Although the pseudoknots can be predicted, its time complexity reaches $O(n^6)$ and space complexity reaches $O(n^4)$.

© Springer Nature Switzerland AG 2021
D.-S. Huang et al. (Eds.): ICIC 2021, LNAI 12838, pp. 336–344, 2021.
https://doi.org/10.1007/978-3-030-84532-2_30

In 1999 and 2003, Knudsen [9] and Hein [10] respectively proposed and improved the PFOLD algorithm. This algorithm is a typical multiple sequence alignment algorithm, using a covariation model and a random context-free model [11]. Compared with the minimum free energy model, this method has better results, but has higher requirements for the homologous sequence of the sequence. In 2007, Reeder, Jens, Giegerich, Robert and others [12] improved the PKnotsRE algorithm and proposed the PKnotsRG algorithm, which is an improved prediction algorithm based on dynamic programming. Compared with the PKnotsRE algorithm, its time complexity is reduced to $O(n^4)$, the space complexity drops to $O(n^2)$. Later, Ren Jihong and Baharak Rastegari based on the idea of iteratively forming stable stems, proposed a new HotKnots [13] algorithm to predict RNA secondary structure including pseudoknots. In 2008, Wiese, KC, Deschenes, A and others [14] proposed the RnaPredict algorithm. The algorithm is based on the evolution of the evolutionary algorithm, which can predict RNA structures containing pseudoknots. The average base pair prediction accuracy rate of the algorithm reaches 70.4%, and the overall structure prediction rate reaches 52.5%. In 2009, SatOK [15] and others proposed a free CentroidFold web server for predicting the secondary structure of RNA. In 2011, Hamada M [16] and others improved the CentroidFold method and obtained results that were better than other algorithms. However, these algorithms are still not accurate enough to predict RNA secondary structure with pseudoknots.

According to the basic characteristics of RNA planar pseudo-structure, this method vectorizes the primary sequence of RNA, and then uses the form of window as the input of the model, combined with MLP neural network for modeling. Experiments show that MLP neural network can better solve the problem. The prediction problem of plane pseudoknots improves the prediction accuracy of the secondary structure of RNA molecules containing pseudoknots.

2   RNA Pseudoknot Structure and Label Introduction

2.1   RNA Pseudoknot Structure

The single-stranded RNA molecule folds back on itself, making the base complementary pairing between A and U, C and G [17], forming a double-stranded helical structure, which is called the secondary structure of RNA. Pseudoknot is a special structure of RNA, which plays an important role in the secondary research of RNA. As shown in Fig. 1, the RNA secondary structure turns back to form a hairpin loop, which forms a stem after base pairing. The one near the 5'end is the positive stem, and the one near the 3'end is the negative stem. The part where the bases are not paired and protruding is called the inner loop. The bases inside the ring and the bases outside the ring pair with each other to form a false knot. As shown in Fig. 2, it is very intuitive to show the existence of pseudoknots in the RNA secondary structure.

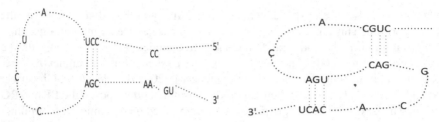

Fig. 1. RNA secondary structure diagram   **Fig. 2.** Pseudoknot diagram

2.2 RNA Pseudoknot Label

In RNA secondary structure, the definition of pseudoknot is as follows: In a certain RNA sequence, if there are four bases at A, B, C and D (A < B < C < D), in which A is paired with C and B is paired with D. Then there are pseudoknots structure in the RNA sequence. Therefore, in response to this feature, this article uses the E-NSSEL label [18] to express the RNA secondary structure with pseudoknots. As shown in Table 1: The E-NSSEL label divides RNA secondary structure into 5 categories, which are represented by numbers 1–5: 1 represents the base subsequence in the positive stem (+Stem); 2 represents the pseudoknot base subsequence (+pseudoknots) near the 5'end; 3 represents the base subsequence in the negative stem (−Stem); 4 represents the close Subsequence of pseudoknots at the 3'end (−pseudoknots); 5 means all bases that are not matched (Loop). The dot diagram in Fig. 3 can very intuitively show the E-NSSEL labels corresponding to different bases:

Table 1. E-NSSEL label

SSE	E-NSSEL label
+Stem	1
+Pseudoknots	2
−Stem	3
−Pseudoknots	4
Loop	5

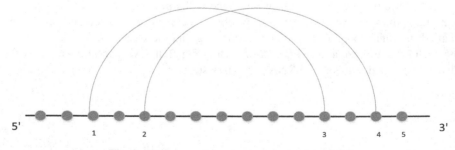

Fig. 3. RNA secondary structure pseudoknot label

3   MLP Neural Network Prediction Model

MLP neural network is a multi-layer fully connected neural network model. It is an artificial neural network that uses a back propagation algorithm and has a feed-forward network structure. MLP neural network can solve nonlinear inseparable problems. It is composed of an input layer, an output layer, and one or more hidden layers. Its network is simple and malleable. This article applies it to the prediction of RNA secondary structure. In the RNA secondary structure prediction model proposed in this study, a sliding window is used in combination with MLP neural network to model the prediction of RNA secondary structure. Base as a model feature. Each base uses 0–1 encoding to indicate the type of base (ACGU). The corresponding coding of each base is: A-1000; C-0100; G-0010; U-0001; Other -0000. The label of each window is one of the E-NSSEL label in the middle position of the base.

In order to obtain better experimental results and reduce the number of unpredictable bases at the beginning and end, the window with the best index should be selected as the experimental input window size in the case of the smallest number of windows. According to many experiments, the prediction effect is better when the window length is 15. The experimental results are shown in Table 2.Therefore, when predicting, select the 7 adjacent bases in front of a base and the 7 adjacent bases in the back, a total of 15 bases as the input of the MLP neural network. The input form of the MLP neural network model is as follows:

[000101001000001000011000010010000000000010100001010000100010].

Table 2. Comparison of experimental results in different windows

Size	sen	ppv	mcc	acc
3	0.457	0.416	−0.017	0.497
7	0.785	0.651	0.402	0.695
11	0.871	0.753	0.574	0.785
15	0.888	0.806	0.644	0.823
19	0.883	0.81	0.646	0.824
23	0.891	0.812	0.655	0.828

Then, the hidden layer and the output layer find the optimal solution by training the weight w and bias b. Finally, output layer output label categories. Its structure is shown in Fig. 4. Among them, x_i is the input of the input layer. $i = 1, 2,..., 9$; w_{ij} is the weight between the i-th node in the hidden layer and the j-th node in the input layer; f is a nonlinear activation function; y_i is the output of the i-th node in the output layer.

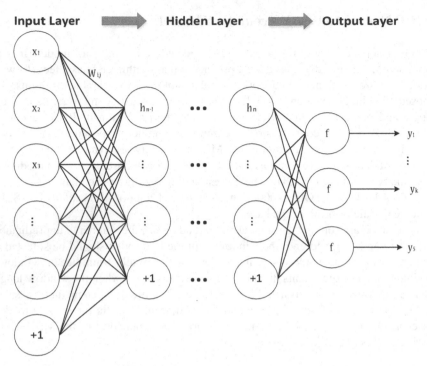

Fig. 4. MLP neural network structure

4 Experiments and Analysis

4.1 Data Set

This study uses the authoritative data set of RNA STRAND [19] and selects 5 sub-data sets among them. They are ASE (RNase P Database), TMR (The tmRNA website), SRP (Signal recognition particle database), RFA (The RNA family database) and SPR (SprinzltRNA Database). There are a total of 2493 RNA sequences in the five data sets, of which 1158 sequences contain pseudoknots. The total number of pseudoknots is 3116, and the average length is 267.37, the longest sequence has 553 bases. Specific information is shown in Table 3:

Table 3. Data set

Datasets	TMR	SPR	SRP	RFA	ASE
Total number	721	622	383	313	454
Pseudoknots	713	0	0	29	416
Average length	361.1	77.3	224.7	118.9	332.6
Max length	463	93	533	553	486
Min length	102	54	66	40	189

4.2 Evaluation Indicators

Generally speaking, we most commonly use 4 evaluation indicators: sensitivity (sen), specificity (ppv) [20], Matthews correlation coefficient (mcc) [21], and accuracy (acc) to evaluate the performance of the model. Their calculation formula is as follows:

$$sen = \frac{TP}{TP + FN} \tag{1}$$

$$ppv = \frac{TP}{TP + FP} \tag{2}$$

$$mcc = \frac{TP \times TN - FP \times FN}{\sqrt{(TP + FP)(TP + FN)(TN + FP)(TN + FN)}} \tag{3}$$

$$acc = \frac{TP + TN}{TP + TN + FP + FN} \tag{4}$$

Among them, TP represents the number of correctly predicted base pairings.TN represents the number of bases that are correctly predicted to be unpaired. FP represents the number of bases that are actually not matched but are incorrectly predicted as matched bases. FN represents the number of bases that actually matched but are incorrectly predicted as unpaired bases.

4.3 Analysis of Results

This paper uses Support vector machines, Random Forests, Decision Tees and MLP [22, 23] neural networks to model and predict on five data sets, SPR, TMR, SRP, RFA, and ASE. Comparative experiments are carried out. The experimental results are shown in the Table 4 shows:

Table 4. Comparison of experimental results

Dataset	Method	sen	ppv	mcc	acc
SPR	SVM	0.786	0.839	0.657	0.829
	RF	0.589	0.851	0.529	0.758
	DT	0.832	0.776	0.628	0.814
	MLP	0.915	0.887	0.808	0.904
TMR	SVM	0.502	0.689	0.348	0.683
	RF	0.268	0.747	0.253	0.618
	DT	0.656	0.672	0.425	0.720
	MLP	0.857	0.783	0.661	0.830
SRP	SVM	0.682	0.566	0.167	0.581
	RF	0.662	0.598	0.193	0.597
	DT	0.775	0.633	0.301	0.650
	MLP	0.838	0.769	0.523	0.767
RFA	SVM	0.151	0.748	0.182	0.581
	RF	0.329	0.847	0.360	0.660
	DT	0.812	0.759	0.604	0.803
	MLP	0.902	0.821	0.742	0.873
ASE	SVM	0.707	0.657	0.355	0.677
	RF	0.633	0.634	0.290	0.645
	DT	0.804	0.693	0.457	0.725
	MLP	0.888	0.806	0.644	0.823

It can be seen from Table 4 that in the MLP neural network model, the sensitivity (sen), specificity (ppv), Matthews interaction (mcc) and accuracy rate (acc) are much higher than Support vector machines (SVM), Random Forests and Decision Trees prediction results, this is because the MLP neural network has better self-learning and fault tolerance, and is better at handling nonlinear relationships. Among these prediction methods, MLP neural network has the highest prediction accuracy. Therefore, in the prediction of RNA secondary structure, the prediction effect of MLP neural network is better in each evaluation index. On the 5 sub-data sets of SPR, TMR, SRP, RFA, and ASE, the accuracy rates are increased by 9%, 11%, 11.7%, 7%, and 9.8% respectively.

5   Conclusion

Using MLP neural network to predict RNA secondary structure is a new attempt. In this way, combined with the E-NSSEL labels, the prediction of the secondary structure of RNA molecules with plane pseudoknots has been successfully achieved. Experiments show that the model can get ideal prediction results. However, the connection between the hidden layers of the MLP neural network is "fully connected", which causes (1) too many training parameters; (2) Due to the reason (1), it is impossible to have too many layers. This limits its ability and cannot solve more complex problems. Therefore, the author will continue to study in depth to further improve the accuracy of the data.

Acknowledgement. This paper is supported by the National Natural Science Foundation of China (62073231, 61772357, 61902272, 61876217, 61902271), National Research Project (2020YFC2006602) and Anhui Province Key Laboratory Research Project (IBBE2018KX09).

References

1. Chan, J.J., Tay, Y.: Noncoding RNA: RNA regulatory networks in cancer. Int. J. Mol. Sci. **19**(5), 1310 (2018)
2. Zuker, M.: Mfold web server for nucleic acid folding and hybridization prediction. Nucleic Acids Res. **31**(13), 3406–3415 (2003)
3. Sakakibara, Y., Brown, M., Hughey, R., et al.: Stochastic context-free grammars for tRNA modeling. Nucleic Acids Res. **22**(23), 5112 (1994)
4. Rivas, E., Eddy, S.R.: A dynamic programming algorithm for RNA structure prediction including pseudoknots. J. Mol. Biol. **285**(5), 2053–2068 (1999)
5. Horesh, Y., Doniger, T., Michaeli, S., et al.: RNAspa: a shortest path approach for comparative prediction of the secondary structure of ncRNA molecules. BMC Bioinform. **8**(1), 366 (2007)
6. Hofacker, I.L., Fontana, W., Stadler, P.F., et al.: Fast folding and comparison of RNA secondary structures. Monatshefte fir Chemie/Chem. Mon. **125**(2), 167–188 (1994)
7. Rivas, E., Eddy, S.R.: A dynamic programming algorithm for RNA structure prediction including pseudoknots. J. Mol. Biol. **285**(5), 2053–2068 (1998)
8. Eddy, S.R.: How do RNA folding algorithms work? Nat. Biotechnol. **22**(11), 1457 (2004)
9. Knudsen, B., Heinm, J.: RNA secondary structure prediction using stochastic context-free grammars and evolutionary history. Bioinformatics **15**(6), 446–454 (1999). (Oxford,England)
10. Knudsen, B., Hein, J.: Pfold: RNA secondary structure prediction using stochastic context-free grammars. Nucleic Acids Res. **31**(13), 3423–3428 (2003)
11. Andrews, M.W.: Stochastic Context-Free Grammars (2004)
12. Reeder, J., Steffen, P., Giegerich, R.: pknotsRG: RNA pseudoknot folding including near optimal structures and sliding windows. Nucleic Acids Res. **35**(Web Server), W320–W324 (2007)
13. Ren, J., Rastegari, B., Condon, A., et al.: HotKnots: heuristic prediction of RNA secondary structures including pseudoknots. RNA **11**(10), 1494–1504 (2005)
14. Wiese, K.C., Deschenes, A.A., Hendriks, A.G.: RNA Predict–an evolutionary algorithm for RNA secondary structure prediction. IEEE/ACM Trans. Comput. Biol. Bioinform. **5**(1), 25–41 (2008)
15. Sato, K., Hamada, M., Asai, K., et al.: CENTROIDFOLD: a web server for RNA secondary structure prediction. Nucleic Acids Res. **37**(suppl_2), W277–W280 (2009)
16. Hamada, M., Sato, K., Asai, K.: Improving the accuracy of predicting secondary structure for aligned RNA sequences. Nucleic Acids Res. **39**(2), 393–402 (2010)
17. PENALVALOF. RNA secondary structure. Encyclopedia of Systems Biology, New York, pp. 1864–1864 (2013)
18. Jing yuan, H., Zhong, H., Dongsheng, Z.: SVM model for RNA secondary structure prediction. Computer science **35**(4), 181–183 (2008)

19. Hongjie, W., Qiang, L., Jinzhen, W., et al.: A parallel ant colony method to predict protein skeleton and its application in CASP8/9. ScientiaA Sinica Informationis **42**(8), 1034–1048 (2012)
20. Gardner, P.P., Giegerich, R.: A comprehensive comparison of comparative RNA structure prediction approaches. BMC Bioinform. **5**(1), 1–32 (2004)
21. Mathews, D.H.: How to benchmark RNA secondary structure prediction accuracy. Methods **162–163**, 60–67 (2019)
22. Lili, J., Tingting, S.: RNA secondary structure prediction based on long-range interaction and support vector machine. Acad. J. Comput. Inform. Sci. **3**, 43–52 (2020) (ISSN: 2616-5775, vol. 3)
23. Huan, L., Meng ying, X., Bin, N., et al.: Randomized forest study of fusion factor analysis. Comput. Eng. Appl. 1808–0266 (2019)

Inference of Gene Regulatory Network from Time Series Expression Data by Combining Local Geometric Similarity and Multivariate Regression

Guangyi Chen and Zhi-Ping Liu[✉]

School of Control Science and Engineering, Shandong University, Jinan 50061, Shandong, China
zpliu@sdu.edu.cn

Abstract. Gene regulatory network (GRN) plays a pivotal role in cells. Existing high-throughput experiments facilitate abundant time-series expression data to reconstruct GRN to gain insight into the mechanisms of diverse biological procedure when organisms response to external changing conditions. However, many proposed approaches do not effectively elucidate local dynamic temporal information and time delay based on time-series expression data. In this paper, we introduce local geometric similarity and multivariate regression (LESME) to infer gene regulatory networks from time-course gene expression data. We simultaneously consider the local shape of time series and global multivariate regression to effectively detect the gene regulation. Moreover, LESME combines adaptive sliding window technique and grey relational analysis to track and capture local geometric similarity for improving the quality of global network inference. We incorporate the local and global contributions to reconstruct the GRN. LESME outperforms eight state-of-the-art methods on DREAM3 and DREAM4 in-silico challenges and achieves a meaningful result on hepatocellular carcinoma gene expression data.

Keywords: Gene regulatory networks inferences · Adaptive sliding window · Grey relational analysis · Local geometric shape · Global multivariate regression

1 Introduction

Illustrating the mechanism of the dynamic interplays of genes is crucial to disclose the operations and functions in organisms. Gene regulatory network (GRN) is an abstract casting of gene regulations that can help to demonstrate pathology, predict clinical outcome, and identify drug targets [1, 2].

Reconstructing GRN from time-series gene expression accurately and efficiently is still a tremendous challenge. Numerous methods have been proposed to infer GRNs from time-series gene expression data. Mutual Information (MI) [3] is widely used to infer GRNs based on information theory. However, the network inferred by MI is naturally without regulatory direction. Although the extension of MI [4] is proposed to

© Springer Nature Switzerland AG 2021
D.-S. Huang et al. (Eds.): ICIC 2021, LNAI 12838, pp. 345–355, 2021.
https://doi.org/10.1007/978-3-030-84532-2_31

infer the directed network, MI still cannot efficiently infer large-scale networks. Ordinary Differential Equation (ODE) [5] describes the kinetics of gene expression by time derivative. Nonetheless, ODE is extremely computationally intensive to infer GRN via a high dimension dataset. Bayesian networks (BN) [6] represent conditional dependencies between random variables with a directed acyclic graph (DAG). The Bayesian model needs to learn the conditional dependencies between two genes in the structure of a network. If the network is on a large scale, it will be plagued with a computational hurdle.

Regression is also a common network inference method. TIGRESS [7] combines least angle regression (LARS) with stability selection to GRN inference. TIGRESS redesigns a novel score for stability selection to improve feature selection with LARS. In recent years, the emergence and rise of tree-based regression methods have dated back to GENIE3 [8], winning the DERAM4 (Dialogue on Reverse Engineering Assessment and Methods) in-silico multi-factorial challenge. Large scale tree-based methods decompose the inference of p genes of GRNs into p different regression subproblems. In every subproblem, one gene is regarded as the target and the other p-1 genes are the inputs. Therefore, tree-based methods are potentially able to detect multivariate interacting effects and variables with higher dimension. However, GENIE3 could only be efficient on steady-state expression data, not specifically applied to time-series expression data. Then, Jump3 [9] exploited time-series of gene expression data based on a formal on/off the dynamic model. Jump3 utilized a stochastic differential equation (SDE) to model the expression of a target gene. The basic procedure of Jump3 is to learn the promoter state of the target gene from candidate regulators based on tree methods. SWING [10] employed a fixed length sliding window to address heterogeneous time delays in biological systems. Different from the above bagging methods, BTNET [11] and BiXGBoost [12] introduced a boosting algorithm to reconstruct GRNs, which can significantly reduce the bias to improve accuracy.

In this paper, we propose a hybrid method called LESME, i.e., local geometric similarity and multivariate regression, to reconstruct gene regulatory networks based on time-series gene expression data. We simultaneously consider the local geometric structure and global feature ranking to improve the quality of the network inference. We design an adaptive sliding window technique and apply grey relational analysis to evaluate local structure to address time delays and track local instant regulations. Then, the boosting tree method is utilized to reconstruct the global regulatory network. We assimilate local and global contributions to the final inferred network. To further validate the effectiveness of LESME, we apply it to the benchmarked DREAM challenges and real hepatocellular carcinoma time-course expression data, which shows good performances on DREAM3 and DREAM4 in-silico challenges and achieves a meaningful GRN result for hepatocellular carcinoma.

2   Methods

In this section, we describe LESME to reconstruct the directed graph of GRN from time-series expression data. For datasets $D\{G|G \in R^{m \times n}\}$, v represents nodes or vertexes and

e_{ij} represents the link between pairwise nodes that gene j is under the regulation of gene i. The arrangement of whole time series expression is as follows:

$$G(i,j) = \begin{bmatrix} g_1^1 & g_2^1 & \cdots & g_{m-1}^1 & g_m^1 \\ g_1^2 & g_2^2 & \cdots & g_{m-1}^2 & g_m^2 \\ \vdots & \vdots & \ddots & \vdots & \vdots \\ g_1^{n-1} & g_2^{n-1} & \cdots & g_{m-1}^{n-1} & g_m^{n-1} \\ g_1^n & g_2^n & \cdots & g_{m-1}^n & g_m^n \end{bmatrix} \tag{1}$$

where each column represents an instance and each row represents the expression value of the selected instance at a specific timestamp. The overall framework of LESME is shown in Fig. 1. We will introduce the major steps in the following.

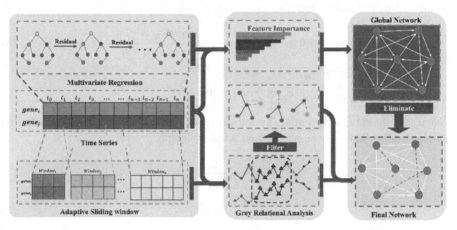

Fig. 1. The overview of LESME. The input of LESME is time-series expression data. For the input, we simultaneously apply global multivariate regression and adaptive sliding window technique. The multivariate regression will reconstruct a global network. The data in the window will be evaluated by local shape to filter the low significance links of the target. Ultimately, we will eliminate the low significance links from the global network to get the final network.

2.1 Local Geometric Similarity

Adaptive Sliding Window. The similarity and association of two components is variational evolving with the time in the biological systems. It is less useful to assign a single static score fraction to two variables over an entire time series. In this case, it is necessary to capture the changing relationships from individual local regions from time series [13]. On account of this, we introduce an adaptive sliding window technique to effectively track local temporal information as shown in Fig. 1. Compared with fixed windows [10, 13], the adaptive sliding window is more flexible and scalable. We evaluate the information content of the partial time series based on the time derivative. Time derivative can efficiently indicate the fluctuation and tendency of time series. Then, we transform the time derivative into a probability to achieve information entropy (IE). IE can quantify the information in each window individually which can be a guideline to modify the length of the window automatically. To design the adaptive sliding window, we firstly give the default window length L_0, which is also the minimum window length. Then, we differentiate the points in the window, i.e.,

$$d_0 = \{g_0, g_1, ..., g_{L_0}\} \tag{2}$$

$$\nabla d = \{\nabla g_1, \nabla g_2, ..., \nabla g_{L_0}\} \tag{3}$$

$$\nabla g_i = g_i - g_{i-1} \tag{4}$$

Then, we use the softmax function to transform the time derivative into the probability to quantify the information entropy.

$$p_i = soft \max(|\nabla d|) = \frac{\exp(|\nabla g_i|)}{\sum_{\nabla g_i \in \nabla d} \exp(|\nabla g_i|)} \tag{5}$$

$$E_i = \sum p_i \times \log_2(p_i) \tag{6}$$

Next, we divide the current IE by the previous window IE to obtain the window coefficient. After that, we can get the next window length.

$$coff = \frac{E_n}{E_{n-1}} \tag{7}$$

$$L_i = L_{i-1} \times coff \tag{8}$$

Considering the stability of the model, we preset the max length of the window $L_{\max}$.

Grey Relational Analysis. Grey relational analysis (GRA) [14] is an important accomplishment in the uncertainty research domain. Compared with traditional statistic methods, it is widely applied to analyze multivariate time series data. GRA defines the Grey Relational Grade (GRG) on the geometric similarity of the time series of two variables without any assumption [15]. GRA can be used to describe the relationships between the node attributes and to identify the dominant factors that have a significant impact on the certain target gene [16].

In this paper, we combine adaptive sliding window with grey relational analysis to infer local variation between the target gene and its peripheral ones. We recursively choose one gene as the target gene and assume that others are peripheral nodes of the target in the inferring GRN. The target vector is given by $y = \{g^1, g^2, ..., g^n\}$, and the peripheral nodes are given by $x_k = \{g_1^1, ..., g_{k-1}^n, g_k^1, ..., g_m^n\}$. Every peripheral node subtracts the target gene's corresponding element in the window, and then we attain the first-order norm of the residual as:

$$\nabla = |y(i) - x_k(i)| \tag{9}$$

From maximum and minimum of the residual ∇, the association coefficient is given by:

$$\xi_k(i) = \frac{\min_k \min_i \nabla + \rho * \max_k \max_i \nabla}{\nabla + \rho * \max_k \max_i \nabla} \tag{10}$$

$$r_i = \frac{1}{L} \sum_{i=1}^{L} \xi_k(i) \tag{11}$$

where L is the length of the adaptive sliding window. ρ is the distinguishing coefficient which is positively related to distinguish the difference. For all the windows of the target gene, we average the local grey relational grade (LGRG) as shown:

$$LGRG = \frac{1}{n} \sum_{i=1}^{n} r_i \tag{12}$$

LGRG determines the dominant factors between the multivariable and target gene based on shape. The higher value of LGRG, the higher association of two variables.

2.2 Multivariate Regression

Multivariate regression is to reconstruct the GRN directly from the entire time series. In this paper, we introduce a feature selection method based on boosting tree methods to detect the global network. We apply a powerful and scalable model to evaluate the feature importance, Xgboost [17]. The gradient boosting method is to ensemble numerous weak estimators to comprise a strong estimator [18].

$$F_t(x) = F_{t-1}(x) + lr \times f_t \tag{13}$$

where lr is a learning rate; f_t is a newly added estimator. The objective function is given by:

$$obj^{(t)} = \sum_{i=1}^{n} l(y_i, (\hat{y}^{(t-1)} + f_t(x_i))) + \Omega(f_t) \tag{14}$$

where Ω penalizes the complexity of the model to overcome overfitting. The criteria of splitting is modified by:

$$L_{split} = \frac{1}{2} \left[\frac{(\sum_{i \in I_L} g_i)^2}{\sum_{i \in I_L} h_i + \lambda} + \frac{(\sum_{i \in I_R} g_i)^2}{\sum_{i \in I_R} h_i + \lambda} - \frac{(\sum_{i \in I} g_i)^2}{\sum_{i \in I} h_i + \lambda} \right] - \gamma \tag{15}$$

where g_i and h_i are the first and second-order gradient statistics respectively. Both λ and γ are complexity parameters. $I = I_R \cup I_L$, I_L and I_R are the left and right samples after splitting. The goal of attaining the best split is to maximize L_{split}. In every splitting task during the global regression task, the number of a specific node expression we selected across all trees split is utilized to be the global score (GS), which ranks the regulatory links globally.

2.3   Combining Local and Global Contributions

GRN depicts the directed relationships among multivariable. We cannot simply and directly reconstruct the network globally by ignoring the local instantly consistent and inconsistent changes. Besides, it is difficult to distinguish relevant from irrelevant variables from feature ranking only [19]. The association and interaction relationships between two genes may change over time in the real biological systems. In this case, it is necessary to find the local coordinated variation between the target gene and peripheral genes in the global network to capture dynamic intricate relationships. In this paper, LGRG captures similar curves from the local region, which can be considered as a filter to evaluate the global significance of an edge [20, 21]. In consideration of the unweighted network and filter, we binarize LGRG over a user-defined threshold to get bLGRG. Ultimately, we apply a modified final score (FS) to rank the regulatory links:

$$FS = bLGRG * GS \qquad (16)$$

3   Results

3.1   In DREAM In-Silico Datasets

In DREAM3 in-silico dataset, the results of AUROC and AUPR are listed in Table 1. There are three sub-challenges in DREAM3, i.e., in-silico size10, in-silico size50, and in-silico size100. Each sub-challenge has five networks with multi-samples. Each sample has 21 timepoints with the same interval [22]. From Table 1, we can see that LESME achieves the best AUROC in size50 network. LESME also gets the highest AUPR in DREAM3 in-silico size10 and size50. The highest AUROC and AUPR are shown in bold.

Table 1. The network inference performance in DREAM3 datasets

DREAM3 in-silico						
Methods	Size10		Size50		Size100	
	AUROC	AUPR	AUROC	AUPR	AUROC	AUPR
LESME	0.682	**0.311**	**0.645**	**0.121**	0.612	0.083
BTNET(GB)	0.546	0.217	0.614	0.100	0.586	0.074
BTNET(AB)	0.584	0.207	0.596	0.097	0.582	0.051
SWING-RF	0.584	0.233	0.607	0.104	**0.620**	**0.093**
SWING-Dionesus	0.550	0.222	0.583	0.084	0.537	0.043
BiXGBoost	**0.684**	0.269	0.591	0.074	0.600	0.049
GENIE3-lag	0.597	0.236	0.621	0.104	0.612	0.081
Jump3	0.600	0.237	0.595	0.091	0.596	0.053
TIGRESS	0.618	0.236	0.582	0.064	0.571	0.043

In DREAM4 in-silico dataset, the results of AUROC and AUPR are shown in Table 2. There are two sub-challenges in DREAM4, i.e., in-silico size10 and in-silico size100. Both sub-challenges have five networks with multi-samples. Each sample has 21 timepoints with the same interval [23]. From Table 2, we can see that LESME achieves the highest AUROC and AUPR in both two different size of network.

Table 2. The inference performance of LESME in DREAM4 datasets

DREAM4 in-silico				
Methods	Size10		Size100	
	AUROC	AUPR	AUROC	AUPR
LESME	**0.854**	**0.622**	**0.768**	**0.222**
BTNET(GB)	0.794	0.537	0.742	0.168
BTNET(AB)	0.801	0.519	0.753	0.175
SWING-RF	0.816	0.555	0.758	0.175
SWING-Dionesus	0.779	0.508	0.736	0.149
BiXGBoost	0.809	0.529	0.714	0.106
GENIE3-lag	0.798	0.520	0.759	0.157
Jump3	0.748	0.451	0.680	0.076
TIGRESS	0.709	0.306	0.544	0.030

3.2 In HCC Datasets

LESME is effective to infer large-scale GRN from real time series gene expression data. We implement it to reconstruct the HCC GRN via 8 timepoints with 162 HCC-related genes. The time-course HCC gene expression data is downloaded from NCBI GEO (GSE6764) [24]. We select the top 500 regulatory relationships as our inferred HCC GRN. The network topology is shown in Fig. 2. We analyze and enrich the network by NOA [25]. The result of the enriched Gene Ontology (GO) biological process and documented pathways in KEGG are shown in Table 3. From Table 3, we can see that the deregulations of the multiple signal pathways in HCC affect cell proliferation, angiogenesis, invasion, and metastasis [26], which are the recognized cancer hallmarks.

In HCC, the insulin-like growth factor (IGF) signal pathway regulates growth and development. The IGF system consists of IGF-1, IGF-2, bonding to IGF-1R, IGF-2R, and the insulin receptor (IR). Activated phosphoinositide 3-kinase (PI3K) increases phosphatidylinositol 3,4,5-triphosphate (PIP3), which activates protein AKT/PKB and then results in promoting glucose metabolism and preventing cell death [27]. Preclinical research suggested that selective blockade of IGF signaling had antitumoral effects in experimental models of HCC [28]. Transforming growth factor-β (TGF-β) participates in proliferation, migration, adhesion, differentiation, and modification of the cellular microenvironment. In the early stage of tumor development, TGF-β inhibits proliferation

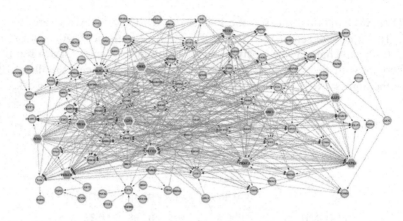

Fig. 2. Top 500 regulatory links in hepatocellular carcinoma network reconstructed by LESME. In the network, the larger orange hexagon nodes represent high in-degree or out-degree nodes. (Color figure online)

and induces apoptosis. While TGF-β contributes to tumor procession in carcinogenesis [29]. Ras cascade plays an important role in HCC since it is one of the main targets of sorafenib, the systematic therapy effective for advanced HCC [30]. Also, the GTPase Ras is one of the key molecular signal regulators within the RAF/MEK/ERK pathway, which could be a promising therapeutic target in HCC [31]. In the Wnt/β-catenin signal pathway, the cascade inhibits the glycogen synthase kinase 3 (GSK3). GSK3 regulates transcriptional co-activator β-catenin which is inactivated by GSK3-mediated phosphorylation and targeted for proteasomal degradation in unstimulated cells. Upon the activation of Wnt, cytoplasmic β-catenin enters the nucleus, interacting with TCF (T cell factor) and LEF (lymphoid enhancer-binding factor). This leads to cell proliferation, angiogenesis and anti-apoptosis [31–33]. The enriched functions are consistent with the prior knowledge of HCC oncogenesis that provide more evidence for the effectiveness of LESME in inferring GRN.

Table 3. The enrichment of GO biological process and KEGG pathway in inferred HCC GRN

GO: term	Term name	Representative genes	P-value
GO:0007264	Small GTPase mediated signal transduction	MAPK1, SHC2, RAF1, NRAS, HRAS, GRB2, MAP2K1, SHC1, MAP2K2, SOS1, MAPK3, BRAF, RB1, KRAS, SOS2, SHC3, CDKN1A, TP53	4.60E-17
GO:0007169	Transmembrane receptor protein tyrosine kinase signaling pathway	PTEN, GRB2, SHC1, SOS1, SHC3, IGF2, IGF1R, EGFR, PIK3R3, AKT2, AKT1, PIK3R1, TGFB1	1.20E-12

(continued)

Table 3. (*continued*)

GO: term	Term name	Representative genes	P-value
GO:0043491	Protein kinase B signaling cascade	PIK3CA; RPS6KB1; RPS6KB2; AKT2; AKT1	3.80E-10
GO:0045935	Positive regulation of nucleobase, nucleoside, nucleotide and nucleic acid metabolic process	MAPK1, HRAS, MAP2K1, PRKCG, SHC1, RB1, ELK1, IGF1R, WNT7A, SMAD4, AKT2, MYC, WNT10B, WNT1, SMARCB1, TGFB1, TP53	4.50E-10
GO:0007173	Epidermal growth factor receptor signaling pathway	GRB2, SHC1, SHC3, EGFR, TGFB1	6.40E-08
GO:0048009	Insulin-like growth factor receptor signaling pathway	IGF1R, AKT1, PIK3R1	4.90E-06
GO:0046324	Regulation of glucose import	PRKCA, AKT2, AKT1, PIK3R1	6.60E-06
GO:0016055	Wnt receptor signaling pathway	WNT7A, WNT8B, WNT10B, WNT1, WNT6, FZD4	1.10E-05
GO:0051090	Regulation of transcription factor activity	MAPK3, RB1, KRAS, SMARCB1, TGFB1	1.10E-04
GO:0046578	Regulation of Ras protein signal transduction	NRAS, HRAS, SOS1, KRAS, SOS2	1.30E-04
GO:0000187	Activation of MAPK activity	PIK3CB, TGFA, MAP2K1, SHC1	2.40E-04
GO:0008283	Cell proliferation	PTEN, RAF1, TGFA, BAD, EGFR, MYC, TGFB1, TP53	2.60E-04
GO:0045792	Negative regulation of cell size	MTOR, AKT1	3.20E-04
GO:0014065	Phosphoinositide 3-kinase cascade	IGF1R, PIK3R1	4.30E-04
GO:0007183	SMAD protein complex assembly	SMAD4, TGFB1	4.30E-04
GO:0006916	Anti-apoptosis	PIK3CA, BRAF, IGF1R, AKT1, BCL2L1	0.0012
GO:0033198	Response to ATP	PTEN, PLCG2	0.0013
GO:0007179	Transforming growth factor beta receptor signaling pathway	SMAD4, TGFBR2, TGFB1	0.0013
GO:0006338	Chromatin remodeling	RB1, SMARCB1	0.0224
GO:0071634	Regulation of transforming growth factor-beta production	SMAD4	0.043

4   Conclusion

In this study, we proposed an ensemble framework, LESME, to infer GRN from the time series of gene expression data. We simultaneously considered local and global contributions to the final network inference. We combined the local shape of the time series and global feature rank to improve the quality of the inferring network. LESME performs competitively on DREAM3 and DREAM4 challenge datasets with other state-of-the-art methods. LESME has also demonstrated its effectiveness to infer large-scale GRN from real datasets. Also, in case of low rate of signal-to-noise, fusing prior knowledge could be an anticipated solution to reconstruct a more real and accurate topology of gene regulatory network [34–36].

Acknowledgements. This work was partially supported by National Key Research and Development Program of China (No. 2020YFA0712402); National Natural Science Foundation of China (NSFC) (61973190); Natural Science Foundation of Shandong Province of China (ZR2020ZD25) and Shandong Provincial Key Research and Development Program (Major Scientific and Technological Innovation Project, 2019JZZY010423); the Program of Qilu Young Scholars of Shandong University.

References

1. Saint-Antoine, M.M., Singh, A.: Network inference in systems biology: recent developments, challenges, and applications. Curr. Opin. Biotechnol. **63**, 89–98 (2020)
2. Rubiolo, M., Milone, D.H., Stegmayer, G.: Mining gene regulatory networks by neural modeling of expression time-series. IEEE/ACM Trans. Comput. Biol. Bioinf. **12**(6), 1365–1373 (2015)
3. Wang, J.X., et al.: Reconstructing regulatory networks from the dynamic plasticity of gene expression by mutual information. Nucleic Acids Res. **41**(8), e97 (2013)
4. Yang, B., Yaohui, X., Maxwell, A., Koh, W., Gong, P., Zhang, C.: MICRAT: a novel algorithm for inferring gene regulatory networks using time series gene expression data. BMC Syst. Biol. **12**(7), 115 (2018)
5. Bonneau, R., et al.: The Inferelator: an algorithm for learning parsimonious regulatory networks from systems-biology data sets de novo. Geno. Biol. **7**(5), R36 (2006)
6. Barker, N.A., Myers, C.J., Kuwahara, H.: Learning genetic regulatory network connectivity from time series data. IEEE/ACM Trans. Comput. Biol. Bioinf. **8**(1), 152–165 (2011)
7. Haury, A.C., Mordelet, F., Vera-Licona, P., Vert, J.P.: TIGRESS: trustful inference of gene REgulation using stability selection. BMC Syst. Biol. **6**, 145 (2012)
8. Huynh-Thu, V., Irrthum, A., Wehenkel, L., Geurts, P.: Inferring regulatory networks from expression data using tree-based methods. PLoS ONE **5**(9), e12776 (2010)
9. Huynh-Thu, V., Sanguinetti, G.: Combining tree-based and dynamical systems for the inference of gene regulatory networks. Bioinformatics **31**(10), 1614–1622 (2015)
10. Finkle, J., Wu, J., Bagheri, N.: Windowed Granger causal inference strategy improves discovery of gene regulatory networks. Proc. Natl. Acad. Sci. **115**(9), 2252–2257 (2018)
11. Park, S., et al.: BTNET: boosted tree based gene regulatory network inference algorithm using time-course measurement data. BMC Syst. Biol. **12**, 20 (2018)
12. Zheng, R., Li, M., Chen, X., Fang-Xiang, W., Pan, Y., Wang, J.: BiXGBoost: a scalable, flexible boosting-based method for reconstructing gene regulatory networks. Bioinformatics **35**(11), 1893–1900 (2019)

13. Papadimitriou, S., Sun, J.M., Yu, P.S.: Local correlation tracking in time series. In: ICDM 2006: Sixth International Conference on Data Mining, Proceedings, pp. 456–465. IEEE, Hong Kong (2006)
14. Deng, J.L.: Introduction to grey system theory. J. Grey Syst. **1**, 1–24 (1989)
15. Huang, Y., Shen, L., Liu, H.: Grey relational analysis, principal component analysis and forecasting of carbon emissions based on long short-term memory in China. J. Cleaner Prod. **209**, 415–423 (2019)
16. Sallehuddin, R., Shamsuddin, S.M.H., Hashim, S.Z.M.: Application of grey relational analysis for multivariate time series. In: Isda 2008: Eighth International Conference on Intelligent Systems Design and Applications 2, Proceedings, pp. 432–437. IEEE, Taiwan (2008)
17. Chen, T.Q., Guestrin, C.: XGBoost: a scalable tree boosting system. In: Kdd'16: Proceedings of the 22nd ACM SIGKDD International Conference on Knowledge Discovery Data Mining, pp. 785–794. ACM, San Francisco (2016)
18. Friedman, J.: Greedy function approximation: a gradient boosting machine. Ann. Stat. **29**(5), 1189–1232 (2001)
19. Degenhardt, F., Seifert, S., Szymczak, S.: Evaluation of variable selection methods for random forests and omics data sets. Brief. Bioinf. **20**(2), 492–503 (2019)
20. Geng, Z., Liu, Y., Liu, C., Miao, W.: Evaluation of causal effects and local structure learning of causal networks. Ann. Rev. Stat. Appl. **6**(1), 103–124 (2019)
21. Feizi, S., Marbach, D., Medard, M., Kellis, M.: Network deconvolution as a general method to distinguish direct dependencies in networks. Nat. Biotechnol. **31**(8), 7 (2013)
22. Marbach, D., Schaffter, T., Mattiussi, C., Floreano, D.: Generating realistic in silico gene networks for performance assessment of reverse engineering methods. J Comput Biol **16**(2), 229–239 (2009)
23. Marbach, D.: Wisdom of crowds for robust gene network inference. Nat. Methods **9**, 796–804 (2012)
24. Wurmbach, E., et al.: Genome-wide molecular profiles of HCV-induced dysplasia and hepatocellular carcinoma. Hepatology **45**(4), 938–947 (2007)
25. Wang, J., et al.: NOA: a novel Network Ontology Analysis method. Nucleic Acids Res. **39**(13), e87–e87 (2011)
26. Farazi, P., DePinho, R.: Hepatocellular carcinoma pathogenesis: from genes to environment. Nat. Rev. Cancer **6**(9), 674–687 (2006)
27. Denduluri, S.K., et al.: Insulin-like growth factor (IGF) signaling in tumorigenesis the development of cancer drug resistance. Genes Dis. **2**(1), 13–25 (2015)
28. Yang, J., Nakamura, I., Roberts, L.: The tumor microenvironment in hepatocellular carcinoma: Current status and therapeutic targets. Semin. Cancer Biol. **21**(1), 35–43 (2011)
29. Sia, D., Villanueva, A.: signaling pathways in hepatocellular carcinoma. Oncology **81**, 18-23 (2011)
30. Moeini, A., Cornellà, H., Villanueva, A.: Emerging signaling pathways in hepatocellular carcinoma. Liver Cancer **1**(2), 83–93 (2012)
31. Dimri, M., Satyanarayana, A.: Molecular signaling pathways and therapeutic targets in hepatocellular carcinoma. Cancers **12**(2), 491 (2020)
32. Niehrs, C.: The complex world of WNT receptor signalling. Nat. Rev. Molec. Cell Biol. **13**(12), 767–779 (2012)
33. Waisberg, J.: Wnt-/-β-catenin pathway signaling in human hepatocellular carcinoma. World J. Hepatol. **7**(26), 2631–2635 (2015)
34. Ideker, T., Dutkowski, J., Hood, L.: Boosting signal-to-noise in complex biology: prior knowledge is power. Cell **144**(6), 860–863 (2011)
35. Liu, Zhi-Ping., Hulin, W., Zhu, J., Miao, H.: Systematic identification of transcriptional and post-transcriptional regulations in human respiratory epithelial cells during influenza a virus infection. BMC Bioinf. **15**(1), 336 (2014)
36. Che, D.D., Guo, S., Jiang, Q.S., Chen, L.F.: PFBNet: a priori-fused boosting method for gene regulatory network inference. BMC Bioinf. **21**(1), 308 (2020)

Deep Convolution Recurrent Neural Network for Predicting RNA-Protein Binding Preference in mRNA UTR Region

Zhen Shen[1](✉), YanLing Shao[1], and Lin Yuan[2]

[1] School of Computer and Software, Nanyang Institute of Technology, Changjiang Road 80, Nanyang 473004, Henan, China
{3161111,shaoyl}@nyist.edu.cn
[2] School of Computer Science and Technology, Qilu University of Technology (Shandong Academy of Sciences), Daxue Road 3501, Jinan 250353, Shandong, China
yuanl@qlu.edu.cn

Abstract. mRNA translated region contains the genetic information needed to encode the protein, and the function of mRNA untranslated region is to regulate the process of protein translation. The binding of translation factors to specific sequences in the untranslated region can regulate the translation process. Predicting the binding between translation factor and mRNA sequences can help understand the mechanism of mRNA translation regulation. In this paper, We use CNN to extract local features, and LSTM to extract correlation features between different potential binding sites. By adjusting model structure, we tested the impact of CNN and LSTM on model performance. The results show that our model is better than the existing model.

Keywords: CNN · LSTM · mRNA · Untranslated region · RNA-Protein binding

1 Introduction

mRNA is one of the products transcribed from DNA [1–3], which stores important genetic information needed to encode proteins [4–6]. Similar to the transcribed and non-transcribed regions in DNA, mRNA also contains translated and untranslated regions [7]. Proteins are very important for the normal progress of life activities in organisms. The translation regions can encode proteins needed for life activities, while the non-translation regions have the ability to regulate the translation process [8]. The translation factor realizes the regulation of the mRNA translation process by binding to the untranslated region of the mRNA, which is very important for the normal progress of the mRNA translation activity [9, 10]. Loss of control of the translation process may lead to a variety of complex diseases [11–13]. Therefore, accurate prediction of the binding of translation factors and proteins can deepen the understanding of translation regulation mechanisms and help find the treatments of complex malignant diseases.

It takes a lot of time and resources to identify the binding site by technical means in the laboratory, and the recognition accuracy is not high [14]. On the other hand, the continuous development of high-throughput sequencing technology provides researchers with a large amount of experimental data [15–17]. Researchers try to use machine learning models to analyze the experimental data to identify binding sites [18]. For example, Oli [19], GraphProt [20], etc. These methods can speed up the identification of binding sites and improve the accuracy of identification. However, when faced with a large amount of sequence data, there are still defects such as noise sensitivity and high time complexity. With the continuous advancement of computer software and hardware, deep learning is widely used in computer vision [21], natural language processing [22], speech recognition [23] and other fields [24]. In view of the similarities between genome sequence and text data, researchers tried to use deep learning models for genome sequence analysis and achieved good results [25–28].

Given that CNN and LSTM are also used in binding site prediction, CNN can extract local features, and LSTM can extract correlation features between different sites. In this paper, we use CNN and LSTM to extract features from input data, and then use these features to predict RNA-Protein binding preference. We also tested model performance when the model only uses CNN or LSTM. Experimental results show that the prediction performance of our proposed model is better than other methods.

The rest of this article is arranged as follows. In the next section, we introduced the composition of the model and the functions of the different parts. Section 3 records and analyzes the experimental results of our proposed model. Finally, Sect. 4 concludes this paper and look forward to future research.

2 Methods

In this paper, FastText [29–31] is used to encode input data. CNN and Bidirectional LSTM are used to extract features from input RNA sequence. Our proposed model consists of the following parts: Encoding Layer, Convolution Layer, LSTM Layer, and Output layer. The workflow of our proposed model is shown in Fig. 1.

2.1 Encoding Layer

This layer consists of two stages: sequence split and k-mer encoding. The details are as follows.

1) Sequence split: the purpose is to convert RNA sequence to k-mer sequence KS:

$$N_k = \left\lfloor \frac{(Len - l_k)}{s_k} \right\rfloor + 1 \tag{1}$$

where, Len represents RNA sequence length, N_k represents the number of k-mer in k-mer sequence KS. l_k represents k-mer length, s_k represents k-mer stride window.

2) k-mer encoding: FastText is used to encode k-mer sequence. In this stage, input data will be converted into a matrix.

2.2 Convolution Layer

In this section, convolution is used to extract features from the output of encoding layer ks_{EM}. Formula (2) shows how the convolution calculation is implemented.

$$c_i = ReLU\left(\sum (ks_{EM}[i, i + l] \otimes Ker) + b\right) \tag{2}$$

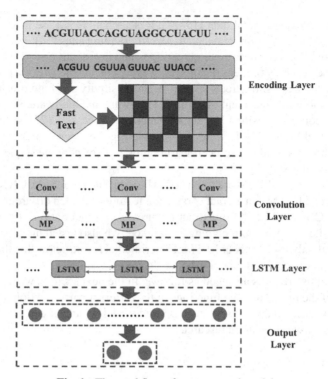

Fig. 1. The workflow of our proposed model

where, *Ker* denotes convolution kernel. $ks_{EM}[i, i + l]$ denotes the current calculation window k-mer sequence. $b \in \mathbb{R}$ represents a bias term.$\otimes$ represents the multiplication of the corresponding elements of matrix ks_{EM} and *Ker*.

By applying convolution kernel *Ker* to each possible window in kmer sequence, we will obtain the convolution feature set $c = [c_1, c_2, \ldots, c_s]$. What's more, max pooling is used to select important information from convolution feature set c.

2.3 LSTM

The internal architecture of LSTM unit is shown in Fig. 2.

$$f_t = sigmoid\left(W_f \cdot \left[h_{t-1}, x_t\right] + b_f\right)$$
$$i_t = sigmoid\left(W_i \cdot \left[h_{t-1}, x_t\right] + b_i\right)$$
$$C_t^N = \tanh\left(W_C \cdot \left[h_{t-1}, x_t\right] + b_C\right)$$
$$C_t = f_t * C_{t-1} + i_t * C_t^N$$
$$o_t = sigmoid\left(W_o \cdot \left[h_{t-1}, x_t\right] + b_o\right)$$
$$h_t = o_t * \tanh(C_t) \tag{3}$$

where, i_t represents input gate,o_t represents output gate, f_t represents forget gate.

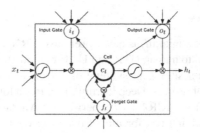

Fig. 2. LSTM unit.

$t \in [1, 2, 3, \ldots, T]$. C_t^N represents the candidate cell state. C_t represents the cell state. h_t represents the hidden state. h_{t-1} denotes the hidden state of the previous LSTM unit. x_t represents the input data of current unit. W and b represents the weight metrics and biases, respectively.

In this layer, we use bidirectional LSTM to learn correlation features from input matrix. After the merger of fwo_t and bwo_t, we will get the output of this layer blo_t.

$$fwo_t = LSTM_f(mat), t \in [1, 2, \ldots, T]$$

$$bwo_t = LSTM_b(mat), t \in [T, \ldots, 2, 1] \tag{4}$$

where, fwo_t represents the output of the forward LSTM, bwo_t represents the output of the backward LSTM. mat represents the input matrix. blo_t is obtained by merge fwo_t and bwo_t.

2.4 Output Layer

The task of this layer is to use Eq. 5 to convert v_{att} into a probability value p:

$$h = max(0, w^T v_{att} + b)$$

$$p = \frac{1}{1 + e^{-h}} \tag{5}$$

where, h is the output of the first full connection layer.

3 Experiments

Several experiments are executed to verify the performance of our proposed model on 42 datasets. Our model is used to compare with Oli, GraphProt and DeepBind. By adjusting model structure, we also tested the impact of CNN, LSTM and attention on model performance.

3.1 Datasets and Metrics

AURA2 (http://aura.science.unitn.it/) is a comprehensive RNA data source. It contains a lot of information related to human UTR and UTR regulatory, such as RNA sequence data, regulatory and variation sites, gene synteny, and so on. For different function sites, it contain different number of records. Deep learning requires a lot of data to learn feature, so we choose 42 datasets from AURA2 for experiments. All data in this study is divided into three parts train, valid and test for model training, verification and testing. Area under the receiver operating characteristic curve (AUC) and average precision (AP) are used to evaluate model performance.

3.2 Results and Analysis

We use the mean and median of AUC and AP as indicators to measure the performance of the three models Oli, GraphProt, DeepBind, and our proposed model. Figure 4 shows the distribution of AUC and AP of four methods. Figure 5 shows the performance comparison of AUC and AP of four methods: Oli, GraphProt, DeepBind, and our model. Table 1 shows the performance of our proposed model and other three baseline methods. It can be seen from Fig. 3 that the distribution of prediction results of our model is better than other models. From Fig. 3 and Fig. 4, we can see that the performance of our proposed model outperforms other three methods. This is mainly because our model uses CNN to extract local feature information and LSTM to extract correlation features between potential functional sites.

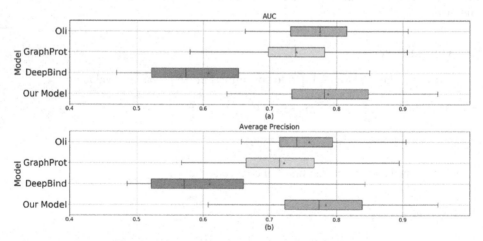

Fig. 3. Distribution of AUC and AP of four methods

3.3 The Effects of Model Structure Changes on Model Performance

As we all known, CNN is good at extracting local features, LSTM can extract correlation features between different data. Previous studies have shown that CNN and LSTM can

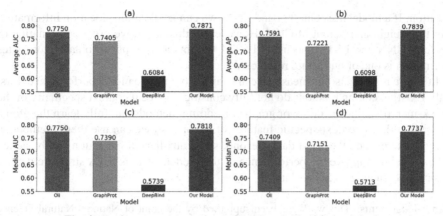

Fig. 4. Performance comparison of AUC and AP of four methods

be used for genome sequence analysis and have good model performance. In this section, in order to test the impact of different structures on the performance of our model, the model uses LSTM and Attention. Table 1 shows the experiment results. From table 1, we can see that the performance of our model is better than model uses LSTM + Attention or uses only Attention. CNN and LSTM have made a great contribution to the improvement of model performance. In this section, three models use FastText to encode the input data, because compared with onehot, FastText can learn the distribution characteristics of kmer. CNN and LSTM can learn the local features of the sequence and the correlation features between function sites. If only LSTM or attention are used, this task cannot be completed.

Table 1. Performance comparison of model with LSTM, and attention.

Metrics	AUC		AP	
Model	Average	Median	Average	Median
FastText + LSTM + Attention	0.7649	0.7717	0.7468	0.7494
FastText + Attention	0.7624	0.7635	0.7464	0.7378
Our model	0.7871	0.7818	0.7839	0.7737

4   Conclusions

In this study, we first split the RNA sequence into k-mer sequences, then use FastText to encode the input data, and then use CNN and SLTM to extract features from input data and make predictions. The experimental results show that the performance of our proposed model is better than other models. In addition, we also modified the model structure to test the performance of the model using LSTM + Attention and only using

Attention. If a model uses One-hot and CNN, we can get the motif location information from the weight and output of CNN. However, in this paper, we use a combination of FastText, CNN and LSTM, so using LSTM weights and output to obtain motif sites information is one of our future research directions.

In future research, some measures can be used to improve model performance. First of all, Existing coding methods do not fully consider the local context specificity of the same k-mer, dynamic encoding or graph embedding methods can fully learn the global features and local context-specific features of the site, so we can use these methods in the model to encode the input data. Second, some auxiliary information can be added to the model to improve the performance of the model, such as RNA structure data or physical and chemical feature data.

Acknowledgements. This work has been supported by the grant of National Natural Science Foundation of China (No. 62002189), supported by the grant of Natural Science Foundation of Shandong Province, China (No. ZR2020QF038).

References

1. de Klerk, E., AC't, P.: Alternative mRNA transcription, processing, and translation: insights from RNA sequencing. Trends Genet. **31**(3), 128–139 (2015)
2. Inukai, S., Kock, K.H., Bulyk, M.L.: Transcription factor–DNA binding: beyond binding site motifs. Curr. Opin. Genet. Dev. **43**, 110–119 (2017)
3. Zaccara, S., Ries, R.J., Jaffrey, S.R.: Reading, writing and erasing mRNA methylation. Nat. Rev. Mol. Cell Biol. **20**(10), 608–624 (2019)
4. Roux, P.P., Topisirovic, I.: Signaling pathways involved in the regulation of mRNA translation. Mol. Cell. Biol. **38**(12), e00070-18 (2018)
5. Thelen, M.P., Kye, M.J.: The role of RNA binding proteins for local mRNA translation: implications in neurological disorders. Front. Mol. Biosci. **6**, 161 (2020)
6. Cioni, J.-M., et al.: Late endosomes act as mRNA translation platforms and sustain mitochondria in axons. Cell 176(1–2), 56–72, e15, (2019)
7. Leppek, K., Das, R., Barna, M.: Functional 5′ UTR mRNA structures in eukaryotic translation regulation and how to find them. Nat. Rev. Mol. Cell Biol. **19**(3), 158 (2018)
8. Slobodin, B.: Transcription impacts the efficiency of mRNA translation via co-transcriptional N6-adenosine methylation. Cell **169**(2), 326–337, e12 (2017)
9. Genuth, N.R., Barna, M.: Heterogeneity and specialized functions of translation machinery: from genes to organisms. Nat. Rev. Genet. **19**(7), 431–452 (2018)
10. Donlin-Asp, P.G., Polisseni, C., Klimek, R., Heckel, A., Schuman, E.M.: Differential regulation of local mRNA dynamics and translation following long-term potentiation and depression. In: Proceedings of the National Academy of Sciences, vol. 118, issue number 13 (2021)
11. Feigerlová, E., Battaglia-Hsu, S.F.: Role of post-transcriptional regulation of mRNA stability in renal pathophysiology: focus on chronic kidney disease. FASEB J. **31**(2), 457–468 (2017)
12. Romo, L., Ashar, A., Pfister, E., Aronin, N.: Alterations in mRNA 3′ UTR isoform abundance accompany gene expression changes in human Huntington's disease brains. Cell Rep. **20**(13), 3057–3070 (2017)
13. Singh, P., Saha, U., Paira, S., Das, B.: Nuclear mRNA surveillance mechanisms: function and links to human disease. J. Mol. Biol. **430**(14), 1993–2013 (2018)

14. Garzia, A., Meyer, C., Morozov, P., Sajek, M., Tuschl, T.: Optimization of PAR-CLIP for transcriptome-wide identification of binding sites of RNA-binding proteins. Methods **118**, 24–40 (2017)

15. Uhl, M., Houwaart, T., Corrado, G., Wright, P.R., Backofen, R.: Computational analysis of CLIP-seq data. Methods **118**, 60–72 (2017)

16. Pfeiffer, F., Tolle, F., Rosenthal, M., Brändle, G.M., Ewers, J., Mayer, G.: Identification and characterization of nucleobase-modified aptamers by click-SELEX. Nat. Protoc. **13**(5), 1153 (2018)

17. Zhuo, Z., et al.: Recent advances in SELEX technology and aptamer applications in biomedicine. Int. J. Mol. Sci. **18**(10), 2142 (2017)

18. Kazan, H., Ray, D., Chan, E.T., Hughes, T.R., Morris, Q.: RNAcontext: a new method for learning the sequence and structure binding preferences of RNA-binding proteins. PLoS Comput Biol. **6**(7),(2010)

19. Livi, C.M., Blanzieri, E.: Protein-specific prediction of mRNA binding using RNA sequences, binding motifs and predicted secondary structures. BMC Bioinform. **15**(1), 1–11 (2014)

20. Maticzka, D., Lange, S.J., Costa, F., Backofen, R.: GraphProt: modeling binding preferences of RNA-binding proteins. Genome Biol. **15**(1), 1–18 (2014)

21. Tian, C., Fei, L., Zheng, W., Xu, Y., Zuo, W., Lin, C.-W.: Deep learning on image denoising: an overview. Neural Netw. **131**, 251–275 (2020)

22. Sorin, V., Barash, Y., Konen, E., Klang, E.: Deep learning for natural language processing in radiology—fundamentals and a systematic review. J. Am. Coll. Radiol. **17**(5), 639–648 (2020)

23. Zhang, Z., Geiger, J., Pohjalainen, J., Mousa, A.E.-D., Jin, W., Schuller, B.: Deep learning for environmentally robust speech recognition: an overview of recent developments. ACM Trans. Intell. Syst. Technol. (TIST) **9**(5), 1–28 (2018)

24. Grigorescu, S., Trasnea, B., Cocias, T., Macesanu, G.: A survey of deep learning techniques for autonomous driving. J. Field Robot. **37**(3), 362–386 (2020)

25. Alipanahi, B., Delong, A., Weirauch, M.T., Frey, B.J.: Predicting the sequence specificities of DNA-and RNA-binding proteins by deep learning. Nat. Biotechnol. **33**(8), 831–838 (2015)

26. Quang, D., Xie, X.: DanQ: a hybrid convolutional and recurrent deep neural network for quantifying the function of DNA sequences. Nucleic Acids Res. **44**(no. 11, pp. e107-e107, 2016.

27. Shen, Z., Deng, S.-P., Huang, D.-S.: RNA-protein binding sites prediction via multi scale convolutional gated recurrent unit networks. IEEE/ACM Trans. Comput. Biol. Bioinf. **17**(5), 1741–1750 (2019)

28. Zhou, J., Troyanskaya, O.G.: Predicting effects of noncoding variants with deep learning–based sequence model. Nat. Methods **12**(10), 931–934 (2015)

29. Joulin, A., Grave, E., Bojanowski, P., Douze, M., Jégou, H., Mikolov, T.: Fasttext. zip: Compressing text classification models, arXiv preprint arXiv:1612.03651, (2016)

30. Bojanowski, P., Grave, E., Joulin, A., Mikolov, T.: Enriching word vectors with subword information. Trans. Assoc. Comput Linguist. **5**, 135–146 (2017)

31. Joulin, A., Grave, E., Bojanowski, P., Mikolov, T.: Bag of tricks for efficient text classification, arXiv preprint arXiv:1607.01759 (2016)

Joint Association Analysis Method to Predict Genes Related to Liver Cancer

Lin Yuan[1] and Zhen Shen[2(✉)]

[1] School of Computer Science and Technology, Qilu University of Technology (Shandong Academy of Sciences), Jinan 250353, Shandong, China
[2] School of Computer and Software, Nanyang Institute of Technology, Changjiang Road 80, Nanyang 473004, Henan, China
3161111@nyist.edu.cn

Abstract. Genes are closely related to the occurrence of cancer. Many complex diseases and cancers have been discovered. Liver cancer is a malignant tumor of the liver, which can be divided into primary and secondary categories. Primary malignant tumors of the liver originate from the epithelial or mesenchymal tissues of the liver. Many methods have been proposed to predict genes related to liver cancer. In this article, in order to predict genes related to the occurrence and development of liver cancer, we use multi-omics data combined with a variety of analysis methods to predict genes that are differentially expressed in liver cancer. Firstly, we used different data sources to build a data set. Then, we performed GO (Gene Ontology) analysis, KEGG (Kyoto Encyclopedia of Genes and Genomes) analysis, PPI (Protein Protein Interaction) analysis and DO (Disease Ontology) analysis methods on the potential liver cancer-related genes contained in the data. GO analysis is used to describe the role of genes and proteins in cells, so as to fully describe the properties of genes and gene products in organisms. KEGG is a database that systematically analyzes the metabolic pathways of gene products in cells, and is the most commonly used metabolic pathway analysis. PPI network analysis is helpful for studying molecular mechanisms of diseases and discovering new drug targets from a systematic perspective. DO analysis helps to analyze the relationship with the occurrence and development of the disease.

Keywords: Gene expression · Multi-omics data · Liver cancer · KEGG analysis · GO analysis

1 Introduction

Genes are closely related to the occurrence of cancer [1, 2]. Many complex diseases and cancers have been discovered [3, 4]. Liver cancer is a malignant tumor of the liver, which can be divided into primary and secondary categories. Primary malignant tumors of the liver originate from the epithelial or mesenchymal tissues of the liver [5]. The former is called primary liver cancer, which is a high-incidence and extremely harmful malignant tumor in my country, the latter is called sarcoma, which is compared with primary liver cancer [6, 7]. Secondary or metastatic liver cancer refers to malignant tumors originating

© Springer Nature Switzerland AG 2021
D.-S. Huang et al. (Eds.): ICIC 2021, LNAI 12838, pp. 364–373, 2021.
https://doi.org/10.1007/978-3-030-84532-2_33

from multiple organs throughout the body that invade the liver [8, 9]. Liver metastasis of malignant tumors in stomach, biliary tract, pancreas, colorectal, ovary, uterus, lung, breast, etc.

Many methods have been proposed to predict genes related to liver cancer. Yuan proposed a multi-omics network analysis method to predict gene-disease pathways [10, 11]. Zheng proposed a method based on multi-subnet and double-weighted median correlation to infer genes related to liver cancer [12, 13]. However, due to the complex relationship between genes and diseases, the accuracy of current disease-related gene prediction methods needs to be further improved. With the rapid growth of sequencing data, this provides more opportunities for people to study new methods [14].

In this article, in order to predict genes related to the occurrence and development of liver cancer, we use multi-omics data combined with a variety of analysis methods to predict genes that are differentially expressed in liver cancer (Comprehensive Multi-Analysis Method for Predicting Disease-related Genes, CMAMPDG). Firstly, we used different data sources to build a data set. Then, we performed GO (Gene Ontology) analysis, KEGG (Kyoto Encyclopedia of Genes and Genomes) analysis, PPI (Protein Protein Interaction) analysis and DO (Disease Ontology) analysis methods on the potential liver cancer-related genes contained in the data. GO analysis is used to describe the role of genes and proteins in cells. KEGG is a database that systematically analyzes the metabolic pathways of gene products in cells. PPI network analysis is helpful for studying molecular mechanisms of diseases and discovering new drug targets from a systematic perspective. DO analysis helps to analyze the relationship with the occurrence and development of the disease. These methods are also widely used analysis methods [15, 16].

Our contributions could be summarized as follows:

- We proposed a new multi-omics joint analysis framework for gene-liver cancer association by combining GO analysis, KEGG analysis, PPI analysis and DO analysis.
- We used a variety of new bioinformatics data.

2   Methods and Materials

We extract gene and disease information from multi-omics datasets including, construct characteristic matrix for lncRNA and disease We downloaded data from LncRNADisease v2.0 and constructed characteristic matrix through Gaussian interaction profile. We used GO, KEGG, PPI and DO analysis to improve the accuracy of the model, and predict unknown gene-disease associations. These methods can effectively discover the differential expression of genes and genes that are potentially associated with diseases. We downloaded data from DisGeNet database and build dataset.

2.1   GO Analysis

First, we perform GO analysis on multi-omics data. GO analysis is used to describe the role of genes and proteins in cells, so as to fully describe the properties of genes and gene products in organisms (Figs. 1, 2 and Table 1).

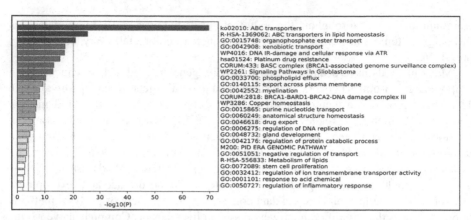

Fig. 1. Bar graph of enriched terms across input gene lists, colored by p-values.

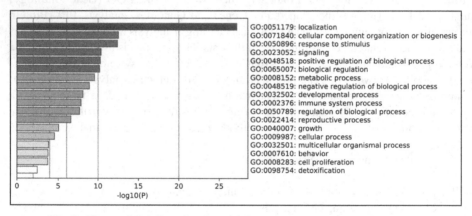

Fig. 2. The top-level Gene Ontology biological processes can be viewed here.

Table 1. Top 20 clusters with their representative enriched terms (one per cluster). "Count" is the number of genes in the user-provided lists with membership in the given ontology term. "%" is the percentage of all of the user-provided genes that are found in the given ontology term (only input genes with at least one ontology term annotation are included in the calculation). "Log10(P)" is the p-value in log base 10. "Log10(q)" is the multi-test adjusted p-value in log base 10.

GO	Category	Description	Count	%	Log10(P)	Log10(q)
ko02010	KEGG Pathway	ABC transporters	29	48.33	−69.66	−65.30
R-HSA-1369062	Reactome Gene Sets	ABC transporters in lipid homeostasis	11	18.33	−25.31	−21.79

(continued)

Table 1. (*continued*)

GO	Category	Description	Count	%	Log10(P)	Log10(q)
GO:0015748	GO Biological Processes	Organophosphate ester transport	14	23.33	−20.74	−17.38
GO:0042908	GO Biological Processes	Xenobiotic transport	9	15.00	−17.02	−13.74
WP4016	WikiPathways	DNA IR-damage and cellular response via ATR	11	18.33	−16.83	−13.59
hsa01524	KEGG Pathway	Platinum drug resistance	10	16.67	−15.31	−12.19
CORUM:433	CORUM	BASC complex (BRCA1-associated genome surveillance complex)	6	10.00	−13.18	−10.31
WP2261	WikiPathways	Signaling Pathways in Glioblastoma	9	15.00	−12.85	−10.05
GO:0033700	GO Biological Processes	Phospholipid efflux	5	8.33	−10.33	−7.74
GO:0140115	GO Biological Processes	Export across plasma membrane	6	10.00	−9.32	−6.83
GO:0042552	GO Biological Processes	Myelination	7	11.67	−8.06	−5.70
CORUM:2818	CORUM	BRCA1-BARD1-BRCA2-DNA damage complex III	3	5.00	−8.04	−5.69
WP3286	WikiPathways	Copper homeostasis	5	8.33	−6.96	−4.77
GO:0015865	GO Biological Processes	Purine nucleotide transport	4	6.67	−6.72	−4.54
GO:0060249	GO Biological Processes	Anatomical structure homeostasis	9	15.00	−6.44	−4.29
GO:0046618	GO Biological Processes	Drug export	3	5.00	−5.48	−3.46
GO:0006275	GO Biological Processes	Regulation of DNA replication	5	8.33	−5.44	−3.43
GO:0048732	GO Biological Processes	Gland development	7	11.67	−4.55	−2.66
GO:0042176	GO Biological Processes	Regulation of protein catabolic process	6	10.00	−3.71	−1.94
M200	Canonical Pathways	PID ERA GENOMIC PATHWAY	3	5.00	−3.48	−1.75

2.2 KEGG Analysis

Second, we perform KEGG analysis on multi-omics data. KEGG is a database that systematically analyzes the metabolic pathways of gene products in cells, and is the most commonly used metabolic pathway analysis (Fig. 3).

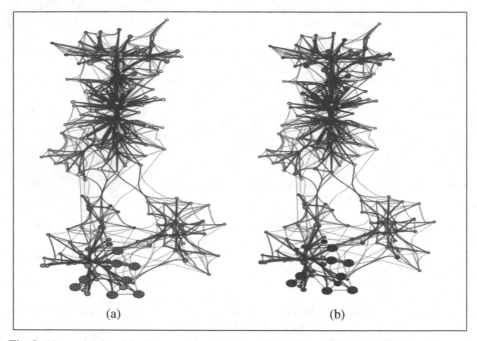

(a)   (b)

Fig. 3. Network of enriched terms: (a) colored by cluster ID, where nodes that share the same cluster ID are typically close to each other; (b) colored by p-value, where terms containing more genes tend to have a more significant p-value. The top-level Gene Ontology biological processes can be viewed here.

2.3 PPI Analysis

Third, we perform PPI analysis on multi-omics data. PPI network analysis is helpful for studying molecular mechanisms of diseases and discovering new drug targets from a systematic perspective (Figs. 4, 5, 6 and Tables 2, 3).

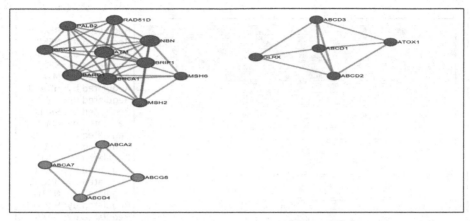

Fig. 4. Protein-protein interaction network and MCODE components identified in the gene lists.

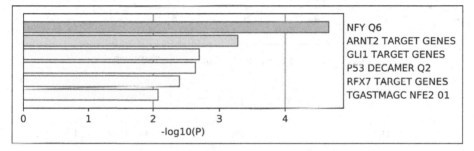

Fig. 5. Summary of enrichment analysis in Transcription_Factor_Targets.

Table 2. Top 6 GO.

GO	Description	Count	%	Log10(P)	Log10(q)
M9868	NFY Q6	6	10.00	−4.70	−3.10
M29890	ARNT2 TARGET GENES	7	12.00	−3.30	−1.90
M29978	GLI1 TARGET GENES	6	10.00	−2.70	−1.40
M16079	P53 DECAMER Q2	4	6.70	−2.60	−1.30
M30142	RFX7 TARGET GENES	5	8.30	−2.40	−1.10
M8004	TGASTMAGC NFE2 01	3	5.00	−2.10	−0.77

2.4 DO Analysis

Fourth, we perform DO analysis on multi-omics data. DO analysis helps to analyze the relationship with the occurrence and development of the disease. DO (Disease Ontology) analysis provides an effective method for exploring the biological information related to human diseases (Fig. 7).

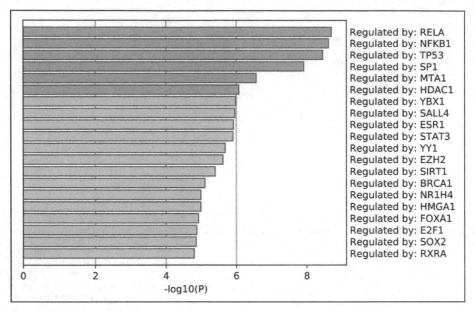

Fig. 6. Summary of enrichment analysis in TRRUST.

Table 3. Top 9 GO.

GO	Description	Count	%	Log10(P)	Log10(q)
TRR01158	Regulated by: RELA	10	17.00	−8.70	−6.60
TRR00875	Regulated by: NFKB1	10	17.00	−8.60	−6.60
TRR01419	Regulated by: TP53	8	13.00	−8.50	−6.40
TRR01256	Regulated by: SP1	11	18.00	−7.90	−6.00
TRR00769	Regulated by: MTA1	4	6.70	−6.60	−4.80
TRR00466	Regulated by: HDAC1	5	8.30	−6.10	−4.40
TRR01546	Regulated by: YBX1	4	6.70	−6.00	−4.30
TRR01211	Regulated by: SALL4	3	5.00	−6.00	−4.30
TRR00275	Regulated by: ESR1	5	8.30	−5.90	−4.20

2.5   Comparison with Other Methods

OPM [15] and kNNA-based [17] methods are two classic methods of using KEGG and GO analysis to analyze and predict oncogenes. The comparison results of these three methods are shown in the Table 4 below (Fig. 8).

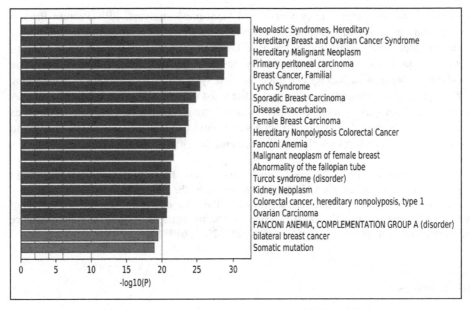

Fig. 7. Summary of enrichment analysis in DisGeNET.

Table 4. Comparison results of three methods

	Method	AUC
Data	OPM	0.8465
	kNNA-based	0.7928
	CMAMPDG	**0.9015**

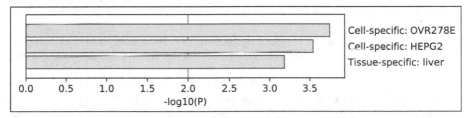

Fig. 8. Summary of enrichment analysis in PaGenBase.

3 Conclusion

In this work, in order to predict genes related to the occurrence and development of liver cancer, we use multi-omics data combined with a variety of analysis methods to predict genes that are differentially expressed in liver cancer. Firstly, we used different data sources to build a data set. Then, we performed GO (Gene Ontology) analysis,

KEGG (Kyoto Encyclopedia of Genes and Genomes) analysis, PPI (Protein Protein Interaction) analysis and DO (Disease Ontology) analysis methods on the potential liver cancer-related genes contained in the data. GO analysis is used to describe the role of genes and proteins in cells, so as to fully describe the properties of genes and gene products in organisms. KEGG is a database that systematically analyzes the metabolic pathways of gene products in cells, and is the most commonly used metabolic pathway analysis. PPI network analysis is helpful for studying molecular mechanisms of diseases and discovering new drug targets from a systematic perspective. DO analysis helps to analyze the relationship with the occurrence and development of the disease.

Acknowledgement. This work was supported by the National Key R&D Program of China (Grant nos. 2019YFB1404700, 2018AAA0100100), supported by the grant of National Natural Science Foundation of China (No. 62002189), supported by the grant of Natural Science Foundation of Shandong Province, China (No. ZR2020QF038), and partly supported by National Natural Science Foundation of China (Grant nos. 61861146002, 61732012, 61932008).

References

1. Sia, D., Villanueva, A., Friedman, S.L., Llovet, J.M.: Liver cancer cell of origin, molecular class, and effects on patient prognosis. Gastroenterology **152**(4), 745–761 (2017)
2. Zheng, C.-H., Yuan, L., Sha, W., Sun, Z.-L.: Gene differential coexpression analysis based on biweight correlation and maximum clique. BMC Bioinformatics **15**(15), 1–7 (2014)
3. Yuan, L., Zheng, C.-H., Xia, J.-F., Huang, D.-S.: Module based differential coexpression analysis method for type 2 diabetes. BioMed Res. Int. **2015**, 836929 (2015)
4. Wesselhoeft, R.A., Kowalski, P.S., Anderson, D.G.: Engineering circular RNA for potent and stable translation in eukaryotic cells. Nat. Commun. **9**(1), 1–10 (2018)
5. Ge, S.-G., Xia, J., Sha, W., Zheng, C.-H.: Cancer subtype discovery based on integrative model of multigenomic data. IEEE/ACM Trans. Comput. Biol. Bioinf. **14**(5), 1115–1121 (2016)
6. Wei, P.-J., Zhang, D., Xia, J., Zheng, C.-H.: LNDriver: identifying driver genes by integrating mutation and expression data based on gene-gene interaction network. BMC Bioinformatics **17**(17), 467 (2016)
7. Stagsted, L.V., Nielsen, K.M., Daugaard, I., Hansen, T.B.: Noncoding AUG circRNAs constitute an abundant and conserved subclass of circles. Life Sci. Alliance **2**(3), e201900398 (2019)
8. Yuan, L., et al.: Nonconvex penalty based low-rank representation and sparse regression for eQTL mapping. IEEE/ACM Trans. Comput. Biol. Bioinf. **14**(5), 1154–1164 (2016)
9. Velasco, M.X., Kosti, A., Penalva, L.O.F., Hernández, G.: The diverse roles of RNA-binding proteins in glioma development. In: Romão, L. (ed.) The mRNA Metabolism in Human Disease. AEMB, vol. 1157, pp. 29–39. Springer, Cham (2019). https://doi.org/10.1007/978-3-030-19966-1_2
10. Yuan, L., Yuan, C.-A., Huang, D.-S.: FAACOSE: a fast adaptive ant colony optimization algorithm for detecting SNP epistasis. Complexity **2017**, 1–10 (2017)
11. Freeman, J.L., et al.: Copy number variation: new insights in genome diversity. Genome Res. **16**(8), 949–961 (2006)
12. Yuan, L., et al.: Integration of multi-omics data for gene regulatory network inference and application to breast cancer. IEEE/ACM Trans. Comput. Biol. Bioinf. **16**(3), 782–791 (2018)

13. Lauer, S., Gresham, D.: An evolving view of copy number variants. Curr. Genet. **65**(6), 1287–1295 (2019). https://doi.org/10.1007/s00294-019-00980-0
14. Gentile, G., La Cognata, V., Cavallaro, S.: The contribution of CNVs to the most common aging-related neurodegenerative diseases. Aging Clin. Exp. Res. **33**(5), 1187–1195 (2020). https://doi.org/10.1007/s40520-020-01485-4
15. Xing, Z., Chu, C., Chen, L., Kong, X.: The use of gene ontology terms and KEGG pathways for analysis and prediction of oncogenes. Biochimica et Biophysica Acta (BBA)-General Subjects **1860**(11), 2725–2734 (2016)
16. Mo, S., et al.: KEGG-expressed genes and pathways in intervertebral disc degeneration: Protocol for a systematic review and data mining. Medicine **98**(21), e15796 (2019)
17. Zhang, T., Jiang, M., Chen, L., Niu, B., Cai, Y.: Prediction of gene phenotypes based on GO and KEGG pathway enrichment scores. BioMed Res. Int. **2013**, 1–7 (2013)

A Hybrid Deep Neural Network for the Prediction of In-Vivo Protein-DNA Binding by Combining Multiple-Instance Learning

Yue Zhang[1], Yuehui Chen[2], Wenzheng Bao[3(✉)], and Yi Cao[4]

[1] School of Information Science and Engineering, University of Jinan, Jinan, China
[2] School of Artificial Intelligence Institute and Information Science and Engineering, University of Jinan, Jinan, China
[3] School of Information Engineering (School of Big Data), Xuzhou University of Technology, Xuzhou, China
baowz55555@126.com
[4] Shandong Provincial Key Laboratory of Network Based Intelligent Computing (School of Information Science and Engineering), University of Jinan, Jinan, China

Abstract. Not only is modeling in-vivo protein-DNA binding basic to a deeper comprehension of regulatory mechanisms, but a complicated job in computational biology. Although current deep-learning based methods have achieved some success in-vivo protein-DNA binding, on the one hand, they tend to ignore the weakly supervised information genome sequences, that is, the bound DNA sequence has a high probability of containing more than one TFBS. On the other hand, One-hot encoding requires each category to be independent of each other, and the dependence between nucleotides is ignored when it is used to encode DNA sequences. In order to solve this problem, we developed a framework based on weakly-supervised. The structure proposed in this paper combines multi-instance learning with hybrid deep neural networks and uses K-mer encoding instead of one-hot encoding to process DNA sequences, this operation simulates in-vivo protein-DNA binding. First of all, we use the concepts of MIL to segments the input sequence into many overlapping instances, and then use K-mer encoding to convert these instances into high-order dependent inputs of the image-like. Then hybrid deep neural network that integrates convolutional and recurrent neural networks is used to calculate the score of all the instances contained in the same bag. Finally, it uses the "Noisy-and" method to integrate the predicted values for all instances into the final predicted values for the bag. This paper discusses the effect of K-mer encoding on the function of the framework and verifies the function of "Noisy-and" compared with other fusion methods.

Keywords: Motif finding · Protein-DNA binding · Multiple-instance learning

1 Introduction

Transcription Factors (TFs) refer to protein molecules that can be specifically combined with a gene with a specific sequence to ensure that the target gene is expressed at a

© Springer Nature Switzerland AG 2021
D.-S. Huang et al. (Eds.): ICIC 2021, LNAI 12838, pp. 374–384, 2021.
https://doi.org/10.1007/978-3-030-84532-2_34

specific time and space with a specific strength. When transcription factors regulate gene expression, the regions that bind to the gene template chain are called transcription factor binding sites (TFBs). A necessary but challenging step in decoding transcriptional regulatory networks is modeling in-vivo TF-DNA binding, also known as motif discovery [1, 2].

Over the past few decades, the introduction of high-throughput sequencing technologies, especially ChIP-seq [3], has substantial enlarged the quantity and spatial resolution of available data, which contributes to the deeply researched of in-vivo protein-DNA binding. Nevertheless, in that the outputs of the DNA sequence extracted directly from ChIP-seq contains a mass of noisy [4], it cannot accurately predict the representative TFBS. Therefore, many methods including traditional algorithms [5–9] and deep-learning based methods [10–12] have been developed to accurately predict protein-DNA binding sites. There is no doubt that traditional algorithms are inferior to deep-learning based methods in modeling protein-DNA binding. DeepBind [10] and DeepSea [11] were two prominent deep-learning based methods that took advantage of convolutional neural network (CNN) to model binding preferences for DNA proteins and perform better than traditional methods. DanQ [12] developed a hybrid deep neural network to quantify the function of DNA sequences, the network first used a convolutional layer to detect motif features that regulate DNA sequences, and then used a bi-directional recurrent layer to capture long-term dependencies between motif features [13–17].

Although deep-learning based methods have attained prominent function on modeling in-vivo protein-DNA binding, the weakly supervised information of genomic sequences is often neglected that a bound DNA sequence may have manifold TFBS(s). With this information in mind, Gao et al. [18] developed a multiple-instance learning (MIL) based algorithm that combines MIL with TeamD [19] to model protein-DNA binding. Zhang et al. [20] also lately developed a weakly supervised convolutional neural network (WSCNN) that combines MIL with CNN for modeling protein-DNA binding. In addition, they prefer to encode DNA sequences using one-hot encoding method, which means that ignoring the dependence between nucleotides. Nevertheless, recent studies have shown that considering higher-order dependencies between nucleotides can improve the function of modeling protein-DNA binding [21–23]. Based on this information, Zhou et al. [24] evaluated the specificity of DNA binding based on the identity of mononucleotide (1-mer), dinucleotide (2-mer), and trinucleotide (3-mer), and concluded that the implicit DNA shape information may exist in 2-mer and 3-mer, and some degree captured impact on the DNA shape variation on binding. Zhang et al. [25] developed a high-order convolutional neural network, the network first converts DNA sequences into high-order dependent image-like inputs through K-mer encoding, and then extracts the motif features from the inputs by using CNN.

Based on the above observations, this article expands the preliminary work of WSCNN in three aspects. On the first hand, WSCNN mainly used CNN to learn its motif features from DNA sequences, ignored the long-term dependence between motif features. Therefore, in order to capture the forward and backward long-term dependencies between motif features, we added a bi-directional recurrent layer after the convolution layer in the weakly supervision framework. On the other hand, WSCNN tried to fuse the predicted values of all instances in four fusion ways in a bag, and then chose the best one as the final prediction. However, the disadvantage is that the four fusion methods need to be tried one by one, so it is inconvenient to choose which one is better. Therefore, we proposed a better way of Noisy-and [26] fusion to replace it. On the third hand, the same as other deep-learning based methods, WSCNN used one-hot encoding to convert DNA sequences into image-like inputs. However, the relationship between nucleotides does not exist independently in reality. So we converted the DNA sequence into a high-order dependent image-like inputs using K-mer encoding, and studied the performance of the frame when dinucleotide (2-mer) and trinucleotide (3-mer) were used as inputs to the weakly supervised framework. In a world, the proposed framework firstly divides the DNA sequence into several instances by MIL concept, then converts the sequence into high-order dependence into image-like inputs using K-mer encoding, and finally Noisy-and is used to fuse the predicted values of all instances into the final predicted value of the bag. To verify the performance of our proposed framework over other competing approaches, we conducted a large number of comparative experiments on in-vivo datasets. In addition, we also show the function advantage of K-mer encoding in proposing the framework, and make a comparison among other fusion methods with Noisy-and method to prove the effectiveness of adding recurrent layers.

2   Materials and Methods

2.1   Benchmark Dataset

We collected 50 public ChIP-seq datasets from the HaibTfbs group, which stems from three different cell lines (Gm12878, H1hesc, and K562). For every public datasets, we take the average number of top ~16000 as positive data, each sequence is composed of 200 basis points, the corresponding negative data set is generated by matching the repeat part, the length of the positive data and GC content changes according to the work9, the number of negative data is 1–3 times of positive data. During the training process, 1/8 of the training data were randomly selected as the verification data.

2.2   Methods

2.2.1   Data Processing

Data Segmentation
The concept of MIL takes into account the weakly supervised information of DNA sequences, so it is logical to use it to process DNA sequences. We divide it into multiple overlapping instances according to the work, which ensures that weakly supervised information can be retained and a mass number of instances containing TFBS can be generated. The MIL method divides DNA sequences of length l into several overlapping instances through a sliding window of length c, with a stride s. All possible instances in the identical sequence constitute a bag with the number of instances $\lceil (l - c)/s \rceil + 1$, and the two hyper-parameters s and c need to be adjusted by cross-validation. If $(l - c)/s$ is not an integer, a "0" is padded at the end of the DNA sequences.

When k = 1, the data processing stage is shown in Fig. 1, where l = 7, c = 5, s = 1, and the red box indicates the sliding window with length c = 5. After data processing,

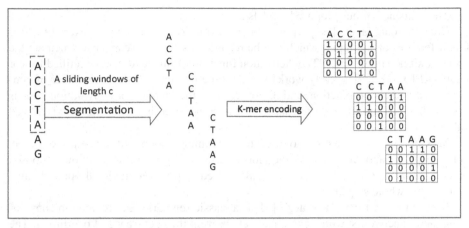

Fig. 1. A graphical illustration of data processing when k = 1. (Color figure online)

the input DNA sequence is encoded into into image-like inputs, so that CNN can better process it.

K-mer Encoding
The data segmentation process converts all instances into image-like inputs that can be processed by CNN. Then, under the premise of considering the high-order dependence of nucleotides, we use K-mer encoding to encode the input instances, and convert all the instances into image-like matrices with high-order dependence. K-mer method is realized according to (1):

$$X_{i,j} = \begin{cases} 1 & \text{if } x_i \dots x_{i+k-1} = j^{th}\text{base in } \{4^k \text{ k - mer}\} \\ 0 & \text{otherwise} \end{cases} \tag{1}$$

where $i \in [1, \text{ c} - k + 1]$, c represents the length of instances, and $X_{i,j}$ represents a possible character from {A, C, G, T}, $X_{i,j}$ represents a matrix generated using K-mer encoding. According to the formula, we find that the K-mer encoding is one-hot encoding when the value of k is 1.

2.2.2 Model Designing

We design a hybrid deep neural network to solve the spatial and sequential characteristics of DNA sequences, which is a combination of convolutional neural network and recurrent neural network. A peculiar version of article neural network (ANN) [27–29], convolutional neural network (CNN), is a forward neural network that uses a weight-sharing strategy to capture local patterns in data (such as DNA sequences). Recurrent neural network (RNN) is another type of article neural network in witch connections between neurons form a directed graph. Differ from CNN, RNN has the property of time sequence, and when RNN displaying behavior in dynamic time or space can use its internal state or memory in dynamic time or space. We plan to capture motif features in the convolution layer, and in the recurrent layer, we plan to capture long-term dependencies among the motif features.

The sequence of our proposed models is shown below:

Convolutional layer. The purpose of the convolution operation is to extract the different features of the input, which can be regarded as a motif scanner to calculate the score of all potential topics. The Activation function of this layer uses Rectified Linear Units (RELU) [30]. The early work13 studied the impact of different number of convolutional kernels on function, and discovered that the increase of convolution kernels has an effective impact on performance, so the kernel used in this framework is a fixed value 16.

Max-pooling layer. In order to select the maximum response of the entire sequence, both DeepBind and DeepSea use the global max-pooling layer, while in our proposed model, the max-pooling layer of size (1,8) is used to preserve the local optimal value order of the whole sequence.

Dropout layer. Dropout strategy [31] is a classic regularization method in convolutional neural networks, which can effectively prevent the occurrence of overfitting. The dropout-based convolutional neural network deletes some nodes in a completely random manner during training, and the resulting local network lacks the distinction of different samples. Dropout ratio is a hyper-parameter, which was studied in cross-validation in this study.

Recurrent layer. We use a bi-directional recurrent layer to capture long-term forward and backward dependencies among pattern features, it consists of long short-term memory (LSTM) units [32]. Long Short Term Memory Networks solve the problem of short-term dependence, and they are deliberately designed to avoid long-term dependence. A LSTM units generally contain four parts: a cell, an input gate, a forget gate, and an output gate, in which the cell memorizes the values at any time interval, and the three gates control the flow of information into and out of the cell. In this layer, the quantity of neurons is set to 32, so the output size of this layer is 64.

Softmax layer. Softmax layer is composed of two neurons. Each neuron is closely connected to the previous layer and calculates the probability. The purpose is to obtain a probability distribution on two labels representing bound or non-bound sequences.

Noisy-and. WSCNN made use of three additional fusions methods (Linear Regression, Average, and Top-Bottom Instances [33]) to take advantage of all instances that might include useful information. Nevertheless, not only average regression but also linear regression use all the information, which must contain useless information. The number of instances with the highest and lowest scores of the Top-Bottom instances needs to be manually determined. Besides, it is also a key question to valid utilize the rich positive instances. To solve these problems, we proposed a method called Noisy-and [26], which is based on the diverse assumption that if the positive instances in the bag greater than a threshold, the bag is marked as positive. The definition of this method is shown below:

$$P_i = \frac{\sigma(a(\overline{p_i} - b_i)) - \sigma(-ab_i)}{\sigma(a(1 - b_i)) - \sigma(-ab_i)}, \overline{p_i} = \frac{1}{n_i} \sum_j p_{i,j} \tag{2}$$

where $P_{i,j}$ represents the score of the j-th instance at the i-th bag, and n_i refers to the quantity of instances in the i-th bag, and $\overline{P_i}$ represents the average score of n instances in the i-th bag. The setting of Noisy-and is that if the average value of the probability

P_i of the bag level is higher than a certain set threshold, the bag level probability P_i is activated. a represents the slope of the Noisy-and is a fixed hyper-parameter. b_i refers to the adaptive soft threshold of each class i, which requires to be learned in the course of training. For $a > 0$ and b_i in $[0, 1]$, $\sigma(a(1 - b_i))$ and $\sigma(-ab_i)$ are included to normalized P_i to $[0, 1]$. The developed framework is shown in Fig. 2.

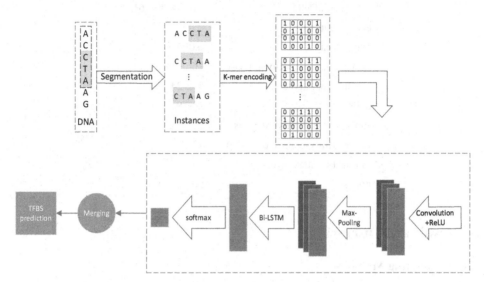

Fig. 2. A graphical illustration of the developed framework.

2.3 Evaluation Metrics

We used three methods, area under receiver operating characteristic curve (ROC AUC), area under precision-recall curve (PR AUC), and F1-score to evaluate the performance of WSCNNLSTM. PR AUC is often used in the case of data imbalance, such as too many negative samples. Because PR AUC does not need to contemplate the number of true negative samples, it is less likely to be affected by category imbalance than ROC AUC metric value is [12, 34–35]. F1 score (F1-score) is a measure of the classification problem, while considering the precision and the recall of the classification model [36].

2.4 Hyper-parameter Settings

In the deep-learning based methods, we use the glorot unfied initilizer [37] by AdaDelta algorithms [38] as the optimizer, and the minimun batch size is 300. Set the training epoch to 60 and use early stopping to prevent over fitting. After each epoch of training, we evaluate and monitor the accuracy of the verification set.,and then save the best efficiency model. The instance length c and segmentation stride s are set to 120 and 10, the hyper-parameter a in Noisy-and is setting to 7.5 after working [26]. The hyper-parameter settings used in this paper are shown in Table 1.

Table 1. Hyper-parameter settings

Hyper-parameters	Search space
Dropout ratio	{0.2, 0.5}
Momentum in AdaDelta	{0.9, 0.99, 0.999}
Delta in AdaDelta	{1e−4, 1e−6}
Learning rate	0.001
Weight decay	0.005
Numbers of convolutional neurons	16
Convolutional kernel size	1×24
Pooling size	1×8
Numbers of bi-LSTM neurons	32
Neurons (fully-connected layer)	32
Neurons (softmax layer)	2
Epochs	60

3 Result and Discussion

3.1 Competing Methods

We built three deep-learning based models to compare and evaluate the function of WSC-NNLSTM, they closely resembled DeepBind [10], DanQ [12] and WSCNN [20]. We can find that WSCNNLSTM is obviously superior to others methods in three indicators.

The average values of ROC AUC, PR AUC and F1 score are recorded in Fig. 3, we can find that WSCNNLSTM is obviously superior to others methods in three indicators. Because WSCNNLSTM connect.s the weakly supervised information of MIL learning sequence with RNN to capture the long-term dependence between the forward and backward of motif features, its performance is much better than DeepBind. WSCNNLSTM is significantly better than DanQ, which shows the advantage of allowing sequence weakly supervised information. The performance of WSCNNLSTM is significantly better than WSCNN, which shows the advantage of combined input, which is more conducive to extracting motif features.

3.2 Comparison K-mer

We conducted some comparative experiments on ChIP-seq datasets of Gm12878 cell line to test the performance of K-mer encoding in the weakly supervised framework. The average ROC AUC, PR AUC and F1-scores are recorded in Fig. 4, which indicates that K-mer encoding is better than one-hot encoding. With the increase of k, the performance of WSCNNLSTM increases. The reason for the performance improvement may be that the high-order dependence between nucleotides is explicitly considered.

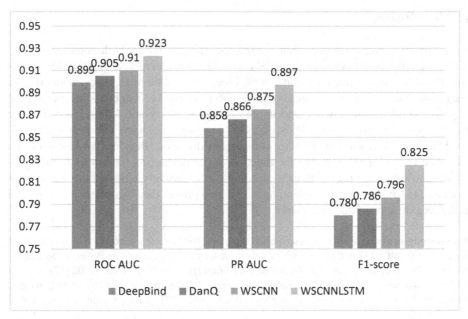

Fig. 3. A comparison of WSCNNLSTM and the competing methods on in-vivo data under the ROC AUC, PR AUC and F1-score metrics.

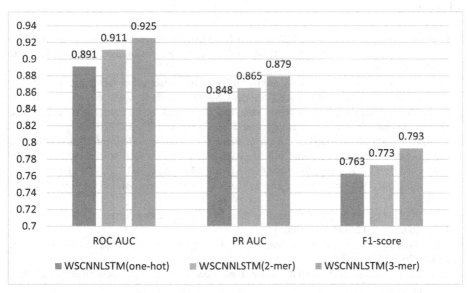

Fig. 4. A comparison of WSCNNLSTM when using one-hot, 2-mer, and 3-mer encoding under the ROC AUC, PR AUC and F1-score metrics

4 Conclusion

In this paper, a weakly supervision framework was proposed, which combines multi-instance learning with hybrid deep neural networks, to model in-vivo protein-DNA binding. The developed framework consists of three stages: data processing, model design and results merging. The first stage is data segmentation and K-mer encoding, the second stage is hybrid neural network, and the third stage is Noisy-and fusion method. After experiments on the in-vivo ChIP-seq datasets, the results obtained show that our developed framework is superior to other comparison methods. Besides, we discussed the influence of K-mer encoding on the function of the developed framework, and experiments show that the use of K-mer encoding can effectively enhance the function of modeling in-vivo protein-DNA binding, and it also proves the advantages of Noisy-and in the weakly supervision framework.

Acknowledgments. This work was supported in part by the University Innovation Team Project of Jinan (2019GXRC015), and in part by Key Science &Technology Innovation Project of Shandong Province (2019JZZY010324), the Natural Science Foundation of China (No. 61902337), Natural Science Fund for Colleges and Universities in Jiangsu Prov-ince (No. 19KJB520016), Jiangsu Provincial Natural Science Foundation (No. SBK2019040953), Young talents of science and technology in Jiangsu.

References

1. Elnitski, L., Jin, V.X., Farnham, P.J., Jones, S.J.M.: Locating mammalian transcription factor binding sites: a survey of computational and experimental techniques. Genome Res. **16**, 1455–1464 (2006)
2. Orenstein, Y., Shamir, R.: A comparative analysis of transcription factor binding models learned from PBM, HT-SELEX and ChIP data. Nucleic Acids Res. **42**, e63–e63 (2014)
3. Furey, T.S.: ChIP–seq and beyond: new and improved methodologies to detect and characterize protein–DNA interactions. Nat. Rev. Genet. **13**, 840–852 (2012)
4. Jothi, R., Cuddapah, S., Barski, A., Cui, K., Zhao, K.: Genome-wide identification of in vivo protein–DNA binding sites from ChIP-Seq data. Nucleic Acids Res. **36**, 5221–5231 (2008)
5. Stormo, G.D.: Consensus patterns in DNA. Methods Enzymol. **183**, 211–221 (1990)
6. Stormo, G.D.: DNA binding sites: representation and discovery. Bioinformatics **16**, 16–23 (2000)
7. Zhao, X., Huang, H., Speed, T.P.: Finding short DNA motifs using permuted Markov models. J. Comput. Biol. **12**, 894–906 (2005)
8. Badis, G., et al.: Diversity and complexity in DNA recognition by transcription factors. Science **324**, 1720–1723 (2009)
9. Ghandi, M., et al.: gkmSVM: an R package for gapped-kmer SVM. Bioinformatics **32**, 2205–2207 (2016)
10. Alipanahi, B., Delong, A., Weirauch, M.T., Frey, B.J.: Predicting the sequence specificities of DNA-and RNA-binding proteins by deep learning. Nat. Biotechnol. **33**, 831–838 (2015)
11. Zhou, J., Troyanskaya, O.G.: Predicting effects of noncoding variants with deep learning-based sequence model. Nat. Methods **12**, 931–934 (2015)
12. Quang, D., Xie, X.: DanQ: a hybrid convolutional and recurrent deep neural network for quantifying the function of DNA sequences. Nucleic Acids Res. **44**, e107–e107 (2016)

13. Zeng, H., Edwards, M.D., Liu, G., Gifford, D.K.: Convolutional neural network architectures for predicting DNA–protein binding. Bioinformatics **32**, i121–i127 (2016)
14. Kelley, D.R., Snoek, J., Rinn, J.L.: Basset: learning the regulatory code of the accessible genome with deep convolutional neural networks. Genome Res. **26**, 990–999 (2016)
15. Hassanzadeh, H.R., Wang, M.D.: DeeperBind: enhancing prediction of sequence specificities of DNA binding proteins. In: IEEE International Conference on Bioinformatics and Biomedicine, pp. 178–183 (2017)
16. Shrikumar, A., Greenside, P., Kundaje, A.: Reverse-complement parameter sharing improves deep learning models for genomics. bioRxiv, 103663 (2017)
17. Lo Bosco, G., Di Gangi, M.: Deep learning architectures for DNA sequence classification. In: Petrosino, A., Loia, V., Pedrycz, W. (eds.) WILF 2016. LNCS (LNAI), vol. 10147, pp. 162–171. Springer, Cham (2017). https://doi.org/10.1007/978-3-319-52962-2_14
18. Gao, Z., Ruan, J.: Computational modeling of in vivo and in vitro protein-DNA interactions by multiple instance learning. Bioinformatics **33**(14), 2097–2105 (2017)
19. Annala, M., Laurila, K., Lähdesmäki, H., Nykter, M.: A linear model for transcription factor binding affinity prediction in protein binding microarrays. PloS One **6**, e20059 (2011)
20. Zhang, Q., Zhu, L., Bao, W., Huang, D.S.: Weakly supervised convolutional neural network architecture for predicting protein-DNA binding. IEEE/ACM Trans. Comput. Biol. Bioinform. **17**, 679–689 (2018)
21. Keilwagen, J., Grau, J.: Varying levels of complexity in transcription factor binding motifs. Nucleic Acids Res. **43**, e119 (2015)
22. Siebert, M., Söding, J.: Bayesian Markov models consistently outperform PWMs at predicting motifs in nucleotide sequences. Nucleic Acids Res. **44**, 6055–6069 (2016)
23. Eggeling, R., Roos, T., Myllymäki, P., Grosse, I.: Inferring intra-motif dependencies of DNA binding sites from ChIP-seq data. BMC Bioinformatics **16**, 1–15 (2015)
24. Zhou, T., et al.: Quantitative modeling of transcription factor binding specificities using DNA shape. Proc. Natl. Acad. Sci. **112**(15), 4654–4659 (2015)
25. Zhang, Q., Zhu, L., Huang, D.S.: High-order convolutional neural network architecture for predicting DNA-protein binding sites. IEEE/ACM Trans. Comput. Biol. Bioinf. **1**, 1–1 (2018)
26. Kraus, O.Z., Ba, J.L., Frey, B.J.: Classifying and segmenting microscopy images with deep multiple instance learning. Bioinformatics **32**, i52–i59 (2016)
27. Huang, D.S.: Systematic Theory of Neural Networks for Pattern Recognition, vol. 201. Publishing House of Electronic Industry of China, Beijing (1996)
28. Huang, D.S.: Radial basis probabilistic neural networks: model and application. Int. J. Pattern Recogn. Artif. Intell. **13**, 1083–1101 (1999)
29. Huang, D.S., Du, J.X.: A constructive hybrid structure optimization methodology for radial basis probabilistic neural networks. IEEE Trans. Neural Netw. **19**, 2099–2115 (2008)
30. Glorot, X., Bordes, A., Bengio, Y.: Deep sparse rectifier neural networks. In: Proceedings of the Fourteenth International Conference on Artificial Intelligence and Statistics, pp. 315–323 (2011)
31. Srivastava, N., Hinton, G.E., Krizhevsky, A., Sutskever, I., Salakhutdinov, R.: Dropout: a simple way to prevent neural networks from overfitting. J. Mach. Learn. Res. **15**, 1929–1958 (2014)
32. Hochreiter, S., Schmidhuber, J.: Long short-term memory. Neural Comput. **9**, 1735–1780 (1997)
33. Durand, T., Thome, N., Cord, M.: WELDON: weakly supervised learning of deep convolutional neural networks. In: Proceedings of the IEEE Conference on Computer Vision and Pattern Recognition, pp. 4743–4752 (2016)
34. Fawcett, T.: An introduction to ROC analysis. Pattern Recogn. Lett. **27**, 861–874 (2006)

35. Davis, J., Goadrich, M.: The relationship between precision-recall and ROC curves. In: ICML 2006: Proceedings of the International Conference on Machine Learning, New York, NY, USA, pp. 233–240 (2006)
36. Sasaki, Y.: The truth of the F-measure. Teach. Tutor. Mater. 1(5), 1–5 (2007)
37. Glorot, X., Bengio, Y.: Understanding the difficulty of training deep feedforward neural networks. J. Mach. Learn. Res. 9, 249–256 (2010)
38. Zeiler, M.D.: ADADELTA: an adaptive learning rate method. Computer Science (2012)

Using Deep Learning to Predict Transcription Factor Binding Sites Combining Raw DNA Sequence, Evolutionary Information and Epigenomic Data

Youhong Xu[1,2,3](✉), Qinghu Zhang[1,2,3], Zhanheng Chen[1,2,3], Changan Yuan[1],
Xiao Qin[2], and Hongjie Wu[3]

[1] Guangxi Academy of Science, Nanning 530007, China
[2] School of Computer and Information Engineering,
Nanning Normal University, Nanning 530299, China
[3] School of Electronic and Information Engineering,
Suzhou University of Science and Technology, Suzhou 215009, China

Abstract. DNA-binding proteins (DBPs) have an important role in various regulatory tasks. In recent years, with developing of deep learning, many fields like natural language processing, computer vision and so on have achieve great success. Some great model, for example DeepBind, brought deep learning to motif discovery and also achieve great success in predicting DNA-transcription factor binding, aka motif discovery. But these methods required integrating multiple features with raw DNA sequences such as secondary structure and their performances could be further improved. In this paper, we propose an efficient and simple neural network-based architecture, DBPCNN, integrating conservation scores and epigenomic data to raw DNA sequences for predicting in-vitro DNA protein binding sequence. We show that conservation scores and epigenomic data for raw DNA sequences can significantly improve the overall performance of the proposed model. Moreover, the automatic extraction of the DBA-binding proteins can enhance our understanding of the binding specificities of DBPs. We verify the effectiveness of our model on 20 motif datasets from in-vitro protein binding microarray data. More specifically, the average area under the receiver operator curve (AUC) was improved by 0.58% for conservation scores, 1.29% for MeDIP-seq, 1.20% for histone modifications respectively, and 2.19% for conservation scores, MeDIP-seq and histone modifications together. And the mean average precision (AP) was increased by 0.62% for conservation scores, 1.46% for MeDIP-seq, 1.27% for histone modifications respectively, and 2.29% for conservation scores, MeDIP-seq and histone modifications together.

Keywords: Convolution neural network · Deep learning · Conversation scores · Epigenomic data · One-hot representation · Motif discovery · DNA-binding protein · Transcription factor

© Springer Nature Switzerland AG 2021
D.-S. Huang et al. (Eds.): ICIC 2021, LNAI 12838, pp. 385–395, 2021.
https://doi.org/10.1007/978-3-030-84532-2_35

1 Introduction

DNA-binding proteins (DBPs), or transcription factors [1], play an important role in cell biological processes including transcription, translation, repair, and replication machinery [2–4]. In addition, it has also been reported that some genomic variants in TFBSs are related to serious diseases [5]. Therefore, discovering transcription factor binding site (TFBS), a subsequence of DNA where the binding between the DBPs and its DNA subsequence targets take place, is crucial for further understanding of the transcriptional regulation mechanism in gene expression. A better understanding of protein-DNA binding preferences helps to annotate and study the function of cis-regulatory elements, and identifying in-vitro protein-DNA binding sites is the first step in understanding protein-DNA binding preferences [6].

With the development of high-throughput sequencing technologies, especially protein binding microarrays (PBMs [7]), it provides a large amount of in-vitro binding data to help us study in-vitro protein-DNA binding preferences. The elements in PBMs represent a probability distribution over DNA alphabet {A, C, G, and T} for each position in motif sequence. There are many detection technologies to study protein-DNA binding preferences from raw DNA sequences based on PBMs [8]. However, these methods assume that the nucleotides in the binding site are independently contributed to the calculation of the binding preference and have nothing to do with the nucleotides in other positions. Dependencies between nucleotides can be explicitly encoded by kmers [9, 10], and the result shows that using kmers as encoding rule is better than PBMs. But these methods have some weak points, like having difficulty in handling large-scale data, poor generalization performance and so on. With the rapid development of deep learning in recent years, new computational methods such as convolutional neural networks (CNNs) and recurrent neural networks (RNNs) have shown their superior ability in predicting protein-DNA binding sites [11–20]. Also, there are some research works by data processing [21–25]. DeepBind is the earliest attempts to apply deep learning to the motif discovery task and has proved to be an effective model. But them only use raw DNA sequences as input data, Various studies showed that transcription factor binding sites are conserved among species [26–30]. Conservation scores [31] and epigenomic data [32] could be a nice data supplement to raw DNA sequences. In other words, integrating conservation scores and epigenomic data to raw DNA sequences can help us study in-vitro protein-DNA binding preferences.

In this paper, we first focus on in-depth exploitation of deep convolution neural network with application on in-vitro motif discovery task in Sect. 2. We call our model DBPCNN, which uses CNNs extract features from input data, i.e. raw DNA sequences, conservation scores and epigenomic data, and then train model to predict DNA-protein binding sites. Then we will show some experiment results in Sect. 3 and discuss the promotion of conservation scores and epigenomic data. At last, we have a concise summary and future outlook for further research.

2 Materials and Methods

In this section, we first introduce the relevant in-vitro DNA protein binding dataset, evolutionary information, epigenomic data and its data preprocessing procedure. Second, architecture of our deep convolution network namely eDeepCNN is presented in detail. Third, we give a briefing of evaluation metric and training hyper-parameters in our experiment.

2.1 Dataset and Preprocessing

2.1.1 DNA Sequence

We downloaded 20 universal protein binding microarrays (uPBMs) datasets from the DREAM5 project [20], which comes from a variety of protein families. Each TF dataset, consisting of ~40,000 unaligned 35-mer probe sequences, comprises a complete set of PBM probe intensities from two distinct microarray designs named HK and ME. These datasets have been normalized according to the total signal intensity.

2.1.2 Evolutionary Information and Epigenomic Data

The evolutionary information was obtained from (http://hgdownload.cse.ucsc.edu/gol denpath/hg19/phyloP100way/) where we used the conservation scores of multiple alignments of 99 vertebrate genomes to the human genome.These scores were obtained from the PHAST package (http://compgen.bscb.cornell.edu/phast/). The values of these scores were scaled to 0–1. In this paper, we use two kinds of data, i.e. MeDIP-seq and histone modifications. The information was obtained from ENCODE Epigenetics database (http://hgdownload.cse.ucsc.edu/goldenpath/hg19/encodeDCC/wgEnco deRegMarkH3k27ac/).

2.1.3 Data Preprocessing

To accurately evaluate the performance of our proposed method, five-fold cross-validation strategy was adopted in this paper. Five-fold cross-validation strategy repeated five times in total. Within each time, TF dataset was randomly divided into 5 folds of roughly equal size, and four of them were used as the training data while the rest was used as the test data. During training, we randomly sampled 1/8 of the training set as the validation set.

Each input RNA sequence $S = (s1, s2,..., sn)$ was one-hot encoded. Thus, A, C, G, T, and N were encoded as (1000), (0100), (0010), (0001), and (0000) respectively. The length of the input sequence is $n = 101$nt. In addition to one-hot encoding, we added conservation (evolutionary) information (Convs), MeDIP-seq (MDS) and histone modifications (HMS) of each nucleotide of the input sequence. Thus, each input sequence S with n nucleotides is encoded as $n \times 7$ such as four channels for one-hot encoding and the other three channels for conservation scores, MeDIP-seq and histone modifications respectively.

2.2 Network Architecture

DeepBind [20] introduced a single layer convolution neural network followed by a max global pooling layer to extract sequence features in motif discovery, which was proved to be a great success.

The length of the transcription factor binding sites in eukaryotes ranges from 5nt to 30nt as reported by Stewart et al. [33]. Therefore, the input length of the proposed models is set to 101nt. Each sequence is centered on the transcription factor binding site and the additional nucleotides were used for providing contextual information.

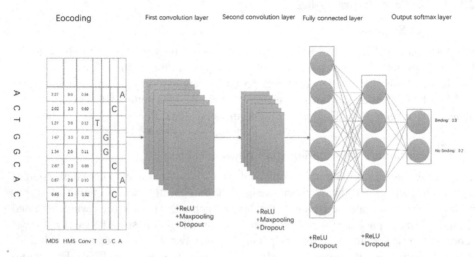

Fig. 1. An overview of the DBPCNN model. A raw DNA sequence is first encoded into a one-hot matrix and MDS, HMS, Convs. The first convolutional layer computes a score for all potential local motif. The second convolution layer discovers the interactions between the learned motifs of the first convolution layer. The learned features from the convolution layers go through fully connected layers with a softmax layer at the output for prediction.

Therefore, we proposed a deeper neural network model composed of two convolution layers accompanied by dropout and local pooling strategies, namely DBPCNN. The first convolutional layer computes a score for all potential local motif, which is the same as DeepBind. And we design the second convolutional layers, in the hope that it can capture the interaction pattern in neighboring sequence. The second convolution layer takes the motif score sequence computed by the first convolution layer as input and recognizes the distribution pattern of the motif score sequence, which, in other words, takes the interaction of the local motifs into consideration. Combining multiply convolution layer improves the receptive field of DBPCNN model and allows an overall pattern recognition of the candidate sequence. Each convolution layer is followed by a local max pooling layer and a dropout layer. It should be noticed that dropout strategy plays an important role in our model, in the light of the overfitting risk accompanied by the expanding parameter size and model complexity. A global max pooling layer is used to capture the global context information of DNA sequences and feeds it into a two layer fully connected neural network to obtain final prediction.

The convolution layer is a one-dimensional convolution expressed in Eq. (1). I is the input, o and k are the indices of the output position and the kernels, respectively, and W^k is the weight matrix of $S \times N$ shape with S filters and N input channels.

$$X_o^k = \sum_{m=0}^{S-1} \sum_{n=0}^{N-1} I_{o+m,n} W_{m,n}^k \tag{1}$$

The fully connected layer is expressed in Eq. (2).

$$z_m = w_{d+1} + \sum_{i=1}^{d} w_{i,m} * y_i \tag{2}$$

The dropout layer is added to switch off certain neurons at training time in order to reduce overfitting. Adding dropout after fully connected layer results in Eq. (3) where m_i is sampled form Bernoulli distribution.

$$z_m = w_{d+1} + \sum_{i=1}^{d} m_i * w_{i,m} * y_i \tag{3}$$

The rectified linear unit activation function was used in this design and it is given in Eq. (4). ReLU function introduces non-linear features to DBPCNN model.

$$ReLU(x) = \begin{cases} 0, x < 0 \\ x, others \end{cases} = \max(0, x) \tag{4}$$

The final layer is the softmax layer that normalizes its input vector z into a probability distribution having M probabilities proportional to the exponential of the input numbers, expressed by Eq. (5).

$$softmax(z_i) = \frac{\exp(z_i)}{\sum_{m=1}^{M} \exp(z_m)} \tag{5}$$

Figure 1 plots a graphical illustration of DBPCNN and the detailed parameter settings including convolution kernel size and number of filters in each layer are listed in Table 1. Input data is (B, 101, 7). It should be mentioned that part of our hyper-parameter settings inherent from classic deep learning methods in motif discovery like DeepBind, which have proved to be optimal choices, while some other parts were chosen from hyper-parameter grid search in training procedure.

2.3 Evaluation Metric

We select positive and negative samples with the ratio 1:1. Our DBPCNN model uses AUC (Area under the Curve of ROC) as metric evaluation. In the binary classification problem, it is generally said that the category which is predicted positive is positive, while the category which is predicted negative is negative. If the prediction is correct, the result is true, and if the prediction is wrong, the result is false (True). For a two-category prediction problem, combining the above four cases, you can get the confusion matrix shown in Table 2. We can draw ROC curve according to confusion matrix.

Table 1. Parameter setting of DBPCNN model in detail.

Architectures	Settings	Output shape
Input data	–	(B, 101, 7)
1st convolution layer	Kernel number = 64, kernel size = 15, stride = 1, padding = 0	(B, 87, 64)
ReLU layer	–	(B, 87, 64)
Max-pooling layer	Kernel size = 4, stride = 4, padding = 0	(B, 21, 64)
Dropout layer	ratio = 0.2	(B, 21, 64)
2nd convolution layer	Kernel number = 64, kernel size = 5, stride = 1, padding = 0	(B, 16, 64)
ReLU layer	–	(B, 16, 64)
Max-pooling layer	Kernel size = 4, stride = 4, padding = 0	(B, 4, 64)
Dropout layer	ratio = 0.2	(B, 4, 64)
1st fully connected layer	Dim = 64, kernel regularizer = 'l2'	(B, 64)
ReLU layer	–	(B, 64)
Dropout layer	Ratio = 0.2	(B, 64)
2nd fully connected layer	Dim = 1	(B, 1)
Softmax layer	–	(B, 1)

Table 2. Confusion matrix.

		Real category	
		True (1)	False (0)
Predicted category	Positive (1)	True positive sample (TP)	False positive sample (FP)
	Negative (0)	False negative sample (FN)	True negative sample (TN)

2.4 Experiment Setting

The learnable parameters (e.g. weights and bias) in neural network were initialized by Glorot uniform initializer [34], and optimized by Adam [35] algorithm with a mini-batch-size of 100. We implemented grid search strategy over some sensitive hyper-parameters, i.e. dropout ratio, L2 weight decay, and momentum in SGD optimizer. An early stopping strategy was also adopted to fight against overfitting problem in our model. Detailed hyper-parameter setting is listed in Table 3.

Table 3. A list of sensitive hyper-parameters and grid search space in experiment.

Hyper-parameters	Settings
Dropout ratio	0.2, 0.5
Learning rate	0.001
Momentum in AdaDelta	0.999, 0.99, 0.9
Weight decay	5E-4, 1E-3, 5E-3
Early stopping tolerance	20
Mini-batch size	100
Loss function	L2 loss

3 Results and Analysis

3.1 Results Display

In order to verify the effectiveness of conservation scores (Convs), MeDIP-seq (MDS) and histone modifications (HMS), we conduct series of experiments. We use different data as model input, i.e. raw DNA sequences, raw DNA sequences + Convs, raw DNA sequences + MDS, raw DNA sequences + HMS, raw DNA sequences + Convs + MDS + HMS respectively. The result of comparison is illustrated in Fig. 2, and Fig. 3.

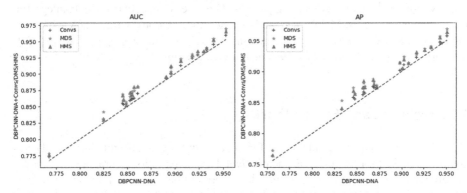

Fig. 2. A scatter plot comparing the achieved AUC (left) and AP (right) of the proposed model DBPCNN using raw DNA sequences only and by integrating Convs, MDS, HMS respectively to raw DNA sequences.

3.2 Effect of Conservation Scores (Convs), MeDIP-seq (MDS), Histone Modifications (HMS)

In order to study the importance of adding evolutionary information, we trained the DBPCNN model using raw DNA sequences only. For a fair comparison, we have

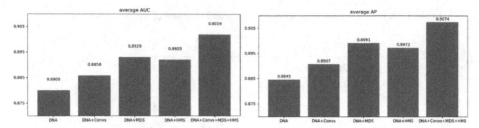

Fig. 3. The comparison of the performance of DBPCNN with different input data in term of average AUC and average AP.

searched the best hyper-parameters again in the case of using raw DNA sequences only using similar grid search parameters as shown in Table 3. The average AUC of using raw DNA sequence only was 88.00% while it was 88.58% integrating the conservation scores, 89.29% integrating the MeDIP-seq, and 89.20% integrating the histone modifications to raw DNA sequences respectively. On the other hand, the mean AP of using raw DNA sequences only was 88.45% while it was 89.07% integrating the conservation scores to raw DNA sequences, 89.91% integrating the MeDIP-seq, and 89.72% integrating the histone modifications to raw DNA sequences respectively. Thus, adding conservation scores to the raw DNA sequences improved the performance by 0.58% and 0.62% in terms of AUC and AP respectively, MeDIP-seq by 1.29% and 1.46%, and histone modifications by 1.20% and 1.27%. The Figs. 3 show that AUC and AP scores of all 20 in-vitro uPBM datasets experiments were improved by integrating the conservation scores with raw DNA sequences. Then we conduct experiments integrating the conservation scores, MeDIP-seq, and histone modifications to raw DNA sequences, and the average AUC was 90.19% comparing 88.00% and the average AP was 90.74% comparing 88.45%. There was 2.19% increase to average AUC and 2.29% to average AP.

4   Conclusion and Future Work

Motif discovery is an important process for a better studying of different biological tasks. In this paper, we propose a simple and efficient deep convolution neural network model, namely DBPCNN for predicting in-vitro DNA-protein binding site, integrating the conservation scores, MeDIP-seq, and histone modifications with raw DNA sequences. Integrating three data to DNA sequences respectively can achieve the average AUC and AP, and while including the conservation scores, MeDIP-seq, and histone modifications together to raw DNA sequences, we can get better result comparing only any data.

Although we get outstanding result by integrating the conservation scores, MeDIP-seq, and histone modifications to raw DNA sequences to predict in-vitro DNA-protein binding site, there are many evidences show that shape in local DNA sequence plays an important role in DNA-protein binding process [36–38]. And different encoding rules also can influence results [39–43]. As we know, encoding input to embedding vector is a commonly used data-preprocessing way, which can convert sparse vector to dense vector to reduce dimension. Therefore, incorporating the DNA shape information into deep convolution neural network and using embedding method as data-preprocessing way would be a promising method to improve DNA binding site prediction, which would be our future work direction.

Acknowledgements. This work was supported by the grant of National Key R&D Program of China (No. 2018AAA0100100 & 2018YFA0902600) and partly supported by National Natural Science Foundation of China (Grant nos. 61861146002, 61732012, 61772370, 62002266, 61932008, 61772357, and 62073231) and supported by "BAGUI Scholar" Program and the Scientific & Technological Base and Talent Special Program, GuiKe AD18126015 of the Guangxi Zhuang Autonomous Region of China.

References

1. Lambert, S.A., et al.: The human transcription factors. Cell **172**, 650–665 (2018)
2. Vaquerizas, J.M., Kummerfeld, S.K., Teichmann, S.A., Luscombe, N.M.: A census of human transcription factors: function, expression and evolution. Nat. Rev. Genet. **10**, 252 (2009)
3. Stormo, G.D.J.B.: DNA binding sites: representation and discovery. Bioinformatics **16**, 16–23 (2000)
4. Lee, T.I., Young, R.A.: Transcriptional regulation and its misregulation in disease. Cell **152**, 1237–1251 (2013)
5. Zhu, L., Zhang, H.-B., Huang, D.-S.: Direct AUC optimization of regulatory motifs. Bioinformatics **33**, i243–i251 (2017)
6. Tianyin, Z., Ning, et al.: Quantitative modeling of transcription factor binding specificities using DNA shape. Proc. Natl. Acad. Sci. 112–115 (2015)
7. Berger, M.F., Philippakis, A.A., Qureshi, A.M., et al.: Compact, universal DNA microarrays to comprehensively determine transcription-factor binding site specificities. Nat. Biotechnol. **24**(11), 1429–1435 (2006)
8. Stormo, G.D., Zhao, Y.: Determining the specificity of protein-DNA interactions. NAT Rev. Genet. **11**(11), 751–760 (2010)
9. Gordân, R., et al.: Genomic regions flanking c-box binding sites influence DNA binding specificity of bHLH transcription factors through DNA shape. Cell Rep. **3**, 1093–1104 (2013)
10. Fletezbrant, C., Lee, D., Mccallion, A.S., Beer, M.: kmer-SVM: a web server for identifying predictive regulatory sequence features in genomic data sets. Nucleic Acids Res. **41**, 544–556 (2013)
11. Shen, Z., Bao, W., Huang, D.: Recurrent neural network for predicting transcription factor binding sites. Sci. Rep. **8**, 15270 (2018)
12. Zhang, Q., Zhu, L., Bao, W., Huang, D.S.: Weakly-supervised convolutional neural network architecture for predicting protein-DNA binding. IEEE/ACM Trans. Comput. Biol. Bioinform. **17**(2), 679–689 (2020)
13. Zhang, Q., Zhu, L., Huang, D.S.: High-order convolutional neural network architecture for predicting DNA-protein binding sites. IEEE/ACM Trans. Comput. Biol. Bioinform. **16**(4), 1184–1192 (2019)
14. Zhang, Q., Shen, Z., Huang, D.-S.: Modeling in-vivo protein-DNA binding by combining multiple-instance learning with a hybrid deep neural network. Sci. Rep. **9**, 8484 (2019)
15. Xu, W., Zhu, L., Huang, D.S.: DCDE: an efficient deep convolutional divergence encoding method for human promoter recognition. IEEE Trans. NanoBioscience **18**(2), 136–145 (2019)
16. Zhang, H., Zhu, L., Huang, D.S.: DiscMLA: an efficient discriminative motif learning algorithm over high-throughput datasets. IEEE/ACM Trans. Comput. Biol. Bioinform. **15**(6), 1810–1820 (2018)

17. Zhang, H., Zhu, L., Huang, D.S.: WSMD: weakly-supervised motif discovery in transcription factor ChIP-seq data. Sci. Rep. **7** (2017). https://doi.org/10.1038/s41598-017-03554-7
18. Yu, W., Yuan, C.-A., Qin, X., Huang, Z.-K., Shang, L.: Hierarchical attention network for predicting DNA-protein binding sites. In: Huang, D.-S., Jo, K.-H., Huang, Z.-K. (eds.) ICIC 2019. LNCS, vol. 11644, pp. 366–373. Springer, Cham (2019). https://doi.org/10.1007/978-3-030-26969-2_35
19. Weirauch, M.T., et al.: Evaluation of methods for modeling transcription factor sequence specificity. Nat. Biotechnol. **31**, 126–134 (2013)
20. Alipanahi, B., Delong, A., Weirauch, M.T., Frey, B.J.: Predicting the sequence specificities of DNA-and RNA-binding proteins by deep learning. Nat. Biotechnol. **33**, 831–838 (2015)
21. Zhu, L., Bao, W.Z., Huang, D.S.: Learning TF binding motifs by optimizing fisher exact test score. IEEE/ACM Trans. Comput. Biol. Bioinform. (2017)
22. Zhu, L., Zhang, H.-B., Huang, D.S.: LMMO: a large margin approach for optimizing regulatory motifs. IEEE/ACM Trans. Comput. Biol. Bioinform. **15**(3), 913–925 (2018)
23. Zhu, L., Zhang, H.-B., Huang, D.-S.: Direct AUC optimization of regulatory motifs. Bioinformatics **33**(14), i243–i251 (2017). https://doi.org/10.1093/bioinformatics/btx255
24. Zhu, L., Guo, W., Deng, S.-P., Huang, D.S.: ChIP-PIT: Enhancing the analysis of ChIP-Seq data using convex-relaxed pair-wise interaction tensor decomposition. IEEE/ACM Trans. Comput. Biol. Bioinform. **13**(1), 55–63 (2016)
25. Guo, W.L., Huang, D.S.: An efficient method to transcription factor binding sites imputation via simultaneous completion of multiple matrices with positional consistency. Mol. Biosyst. **13**, 1827–1837 (2017)
26. Boffelli, D., et al.: Phylogenetic shadowing of primate sequences to find functional regions of the human genome. Science **299**(5611), 1391–1394 (2003)
27. Bpffelli, D., Nobrega, M.A., Rubin, E.M.: Comparative genomics at the vertebrate extremes. Nat. Rev. Genet. **5**(6), 456–465 (2004)
28. McGuire, A.M., Hughes, J.D., Church, G.M.: Conservation of dna regulatory motifs and discovery of new motifs in microbial genomes. Genome Res. **10**(6), 744–757 (2000)
29. Li, H., Rhodius, V., Gross, C., Siggia, E.D.: Identification of the binding sites of regulatory proteins in bacterial genomes. Proc. Natl. Acad. Sci. **99**(18), 11772–11777 (2002)
30. Woolfe, A., et al.: Highly conserved non-coding sequences are associated with vertebrate development. PLoS Biol. **3**(1), e7 (2004)
31. Tayara, H., Chong, K.: Improved predicting of the sequence specificities of RNA binding proteins by deep learning. IEEE/ACM Trans. Comput. Biol. Bioinform. (2020)
32. Jing, F., Zhang, S.-W., Cao, Z., Zhang, S.: Combining sequence and epigenomic data to predict transcription factor binding sites using deep learning. In: Zhang, F., Cai, Z., Skums, P., Zhang, S. (eds.) ISBRA 2018. LNCS, vol. 10847, pp. 241–252. Springer, Cham (2018). https://doi.org/10.1007/978-3-319-94968-0_23
33. Stewart, A.J., Hannenhalli, S., Plotkin, J.B.: Why transcription factor binding sites are ten nucleotides long. Genetics **192**(3), 973–985 (2012)
34. Glorot, X., Bengio, Y.: Understanding the difficulty of training deep feedforward neural networks. In: International Conference on Artificial Intelligence and Statistics, pp. 249–256 (2010)
35. Zeiler, M.D.: ADADELTA: an adaptive learning rate method. arXiv abs/1212.5701 (2012)
36. Rohs, R., West, S.M., Sosinsky, A., Liu, P., Mann, R.S., Honig, B.: The role of DNA shape in protein–DNA recognition. Nature **461**, 1248–1253 (2009)
37. Zhou, T., et al.: Quantitative modeling of transcription factor binding specificities using DNA shape. Proc. Natl. Acad. Sci. U.S.A. **112**, 4654–4659 (2015)
38. Zhang, Q., Shen, Z., Huang, D.: Predicting in-vitro transcription factor binding sites using DNA sequence + shape. IEEE/ACM Trans. Comput. Biol. Bioinform. 1 (2019)

39. Tsatsaronis, G., Panagiotopoulou, V.: A generalized vector space model for text retrieval based on semantic relatedness. In: Conference of the European Chapter of the Association for Computational Linguistics, pp. 70–78 (2009)

40. Wang, J., Huang, P., Zhao, H., Zhang, Z., Zhao, B., Lee, D.L.: Billion-scale commodity embedding for E-commerce recommendation in Alibaba. In: Knowledge Discovery and Data Mining, pp. 839–848 (2018)

41. Wang, D., Zhang, Q., Yuan, C.-A., Qin, X., Huang, Z.-K., Shang, L.: Motif discovery via convolutional networks with K-mer embedding. In: Huang, D.-S., Jo, K.-H., Huang, Z.-K. (eds.) ICIC 2019. LNCS, vol. 11644, pp. 374–382. Springer, Cham (2019). https://doi.org/10.1007/978-3-030-26969-2_36

42. Zhu, L., Guo, W.-L., Huang, D.S., Lu, C.-Y.: Imputation of ChIP-seq datasets via low rank convex co-embedding. In: 2015 IEEE International Conference on Bioinformatics and Biomedicine (BIBM), pp. 141–144 (2015)

43. Chen, Z.-H., et al.: Prediction of drug-target interactions from multi-molecular network based on deep walk embedding model. Front. Bioeng. Biotechnol. 8, 338 (2020)

An Abnormal Gene Detection Method Based on Selene

Qiang Zhang[(✉)] and Yizhang Jiang

School of Artificial Intelligence and Computer Science, Jiangnan University, 1800 Lihu Avenue, Wuxi 214122, Jiangsu, People's Republic of China

Abstract. When screening abnormal genes [7] (such as cancer genes), it is very difficult to only rely on the experience of bioinformatics scientists, so we usually use deep learning methods for calculation and processing. But for bioinformatics scientists with relatively weak programming experience, it is unrealistic for them to independently develop abnormal gene recognition models. A Selene-based abnormal gene detection system developed in this paper completely solves this problem. It can detect abnormal genes without writing a lot of code. This article uses DeepSea and DeepSea-AlexNet convolutional neural network models to realize the function of gene detection. DeepSea-AlexNet is a model constructed by combining the characteristics of the DeepSea network and the AlexNet network. It is very useful for improving the accuracy of identifying abnormal genes.

Keywords: Deep learning · Selene · Gene dection · Pytorch

1 Introduction

Entering the 21st century, people's life pace has gradually picked up and life pressure has also followed with it. Poor work and rest, unhealthy eating habits and serious environmental pollution have gradually increased the incidence of cancer. According to statistics from Chinese Health Organization, the number of cancer patients diagnosed by doctors every day is as high as 10,000 in China [1]. As we all know, with the current medical level, not only the cure rate of cancer is very low, but also the treatment methods and methods will bring great pain to the patients. What makes people happy is according to the latest research by bioinformatics scientists, the incidence of cancer is closely related to certain abnormal genes in the human body. From another perspective, early detection and prevention of cancer can be inferred and intervened from the genetic map [2]. However, the amount of genetic data is very large and extremely complex and has been in a state of exponential growth [3]. It is obviously impossible to make a diagnosis by comparing the difference between abnormal genes and normal genes through the clinical experience of doctors. Therefore, we need to use some speculative analysis tools to help doctors complete this huge task. Many algorithms and tools now require users to have a strong ability to write codes and analyze data and their operations are also very complicated.

D.-S. Huang et al. (Eds.): ICIC 2021, LNAI 12838, pp. 396–406, 2021.
https://doi.org/10.1007/978-3-030-84532-2_36

The Selene-based abnormal gene recognition system introduced in this article is used to solve these problems and help doctors judge and label abnormal genes [4]. The machine learning algorithm [15] is different from other conventional algorithms [5]. It is an algorithm that automatically detects and recognizes the data provided and performs recognition and judgment. It is a data-driven algorithm. However, genetic science is a data-driven science, so machine learning algorithms and gene-driven science can be well combined to finally solve the problem of abnormal gene identification and labeling. Although there is a suitable algorithm, it is very difficult for a doctor with no programming experience to develop a system for identifying and classifying abnormal genes [7].

In order to solve the problem of doctors' lack of programming experience and difficulty in developing classification model, we applied the Selene framework to this method. We can use this tool to develop a deep learning model. This framework provides model training, model evaluation and model testing for doctors who have no programming experience. The Selene framework [4] contains not only the collected data and training modules used to develop the model, but also a module that visualizes the final training results. The doctor community can use Selene to develop a new model and use a trained model more easily.

It is not enough to have a framework related to biological information [19] such as genes. The model with strong gene classification capabilities is also needed. What model is good at classifying abnormal genes? This requires a lot of experiments to obtain step by step and continuously improve the classification ability of the model. In this article, we use the DeepSea model and a model that refers to the Alexnet framework and the DeepSea framework, which is called the DeepSea_Alexnet model in this article. The values of ROC_AUC of these two models in this experiment are all above 0.93 and the classification accuracy is above 60%.

2 Related Work

2.1 Introduction to the Selene Framework

Deep learning [21] is a science that utilizes neural network methods to extract the internal expression law of data from complex and high-dimensional data [1]. The deep learning method is a data-driven method and the essence of genes is also a series of linear data which is also quite difficult to process manually. Therefore, it has a great possibility that using deep learning methods to process genetic data becomes a trend in future. But the implementation of deep learning in genetics is currently facing many problems. Whether developing new models or training old models on new data, both lack a deep learning library which is comprehensive, easy-to-use and designed specifically for bioinformatics such as genetics.

Selene is a framework developed to solve this problem. This is a deep learning framework specially designed for genetics and other bioinformatics [4]. You can use this Pytorch-based deep learning library to develop and train models. The structure and work process diagram of the Selene framework is shown in Fig. 1. According to our investigation and research, Python already has development kits related to biological information, such as pysster and DragoNN. However, both methods have shortcomings and limitations. Pysster can only use a specific architecture and DragoNN can only be applied to specific tasks.However,the Selene framework is not restricted by specific frameworks and specific tasks. Users can use this framework to apply existing models, use new data to retrain existing models and develop new models [22].

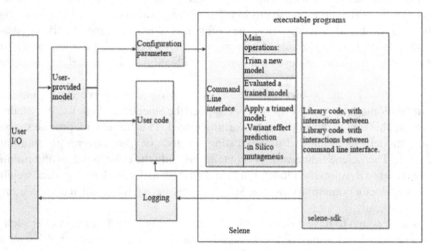

Fig. 1. The Selene framework consists of a command line interface and an application programming interface. The user provides the data set the model architecture and configuration parameters required for training in the user interface. Selene provides training, evaluation and prediction for user-written sequence-based models.

This paragraph will give a detailed description of how to run the framework to conduct experiments. First, prepare the model and data set we use to train in the experimental software. Then configure the corresponding yml file of the model. In the yml file, these attributes are needed: the path address, the class name and data required by the model. After the yml file configuration is over, start the Selene framework and wait for the visualization results given by the Selene framework. The specific schematic diagram is shown in Fig. 2.

2.2   Acquisition and Processing of Data Sets

The data sets needed for the experimental study in this paper were all from the Cistrome DB [8], a gene database. Developed by researchers at Tongji University, Cistrome DB [8] provides the most comprehensive data resource for the study of gene transcription and epigenetic regulation in humans and mice. The data includes information from NCBI, encode and some epigenomics project samples. Genetics researchers around the world can freely access data in the database, which is a great convenience for the study of genes. However, Selene [5] has strict requirements for the format of the data. The data downloaded from the database cannot be directly experimented, so it is through a series of processing. However, genetic data has a special format, mostly SAM and VCM format, which requires special software to process. In this paper, we used the software tool Samtools17 and we processed the data according to the process in Fig. 3.

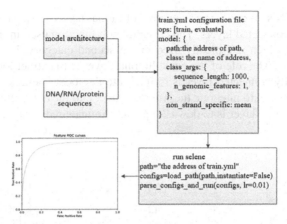

Fig. 2. This figure shows the steps to run Selene. You can also see from this picture that Selene is easy to use. With Selene, users only need to write a small amount of code to train and evaluate a new model, enter the required parameters in a given yml file and then run the Selene framework to view the final result visually. Finally display it in a visual form.

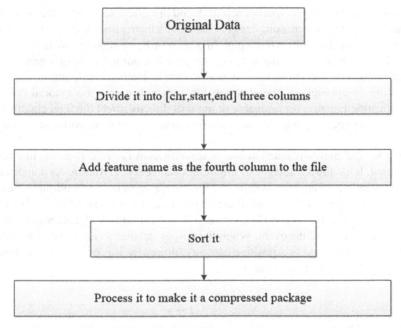

Fig. 3. The process of data processing

2.3 Introduction to Models

Before introducing the model used in the experiments in this article, I will briefly introduce a convolutional neural network. Deep learning methods are often used to process some complex data and CNN is one of the particularly classic algorithms [9]. Figure 4 shows a simple CNN. It consists of two convolutional layers [13], two pooling layers and several fully connected layers. The classification function used in this model is the Sigmod function, which is typically used in the second category. Each layer plays a very important role. The role of the convolutional layer is to extract local features and the role of the fully connected layer is to integrate the local features extracted by the convolutional layer and to integrate the weight matrix into the complete data. The main function of the pooling layer is to downsample to eliminate redundant information.

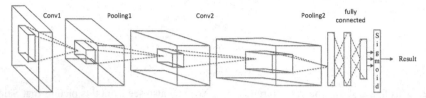

Fig. 4. This picture shows a simple CNN, which consists of two convolutional layers, two pooling layers and several convolutional layers. The function implemented is to classify something. Each layer in this network has its role.

The main function of the experiment introduced in this article is to find the abnormally copied genes among the more complex genes and mark them visually, in order to judge the patient's prognosis clinically in the future. In other words, we need to realize the function of gene classification, identifying whether the gene is a normal gene or a gene with an abnormal copy. For a convolutional neural network, feature extraction is important, but selecting an appropriate classification function also cannot be ignored. Whether the classification function is reasonable or not will directly affect the final classification result. Generally speaking, the classification functions of neural networks are as follows:

(1) Sigmod: The Sigmoid function is a commonly used Logistic function in machine learning. It has the advantages of smoothness and easy derivation. As it approaches positive infinity or negative infinity, the function approaches a smooth state. Because the output range of the Sigmoid function is (0,1), this function is often used to implement the two-class function. In the binary classification task, the output of Sigmoid is the probability of the event. When the output satisfies a certain probability condition, it is classified as a positive category, otherwise it is classified as a negative category. His formula is as follows:

$$f(x) = \frac{1}{1 + e^x} \tag{1}$$

(2) Softmax: The function of Softmax is similar to Sigmod and it has the advantage of convenient calculation. The output range of the Sigmoid function is also (0,1). It can also be regarded as the probability of classification [10].

$$f(x1) = \frac{1}{1 + e^{-(x1-x2)}} \tag{2}$$

The main function of the experiment in this article is to divide genes into positive and negative types. From the formulas (1) and (2), there is no difference between the two functions, but the method and effect of these two funtions are different. Because the Sigmoid function is only divided into goals and not goals. There is actually only one target class and the other is a background class. However, the Softmax function classifies the target into two categories. This is the main reason for the difference between the two functions. In other words, the Sigmoid function, we can regard it as a "modeling" of a category. After modeling the category, the other relative category is directly obtained by subtracting 1 from it. The softmax function models two categories. Similarly, the sum of the probabilities of the two categories is 1. For dividing genes into two categories, Sigmod's results are better than Softmax.

2.3.1 DeepSea

The DeapSea [11] model has a wide range of applications in genomics [16]. It only uses DNA sequence [14] as a basis. By directly inputting fasta sequence, vcf [23] or bed files, it can predict binding sites, Dnase I super sensitive sites and histone targets. The principle of its algorithm is to learn a large number of known chromatin modification data.Through continuous training and fitting to learn many kinds of sequence patterns or sequence features [6] in non-coding regions. Then it can predict how single-base mutations in the sequence will affect the modification function of chromatin. The basic structure of the DeepSea model is show on Fig. 5.

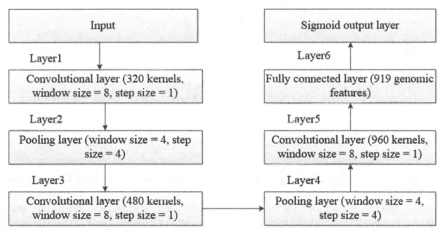

Fig. 5. This is the network structure diagram of DeepSea. Its structure is composed of three convolutional layers, two pooling layers and a fully connected layer. The dropout proportion of Layer2 is 20% and the dropout proportion of Layer4 is also 20%.The dropout proportion of Layer5 is 50% and the dropout proportion of the other layers without special instructions are all 0%.

2.3.2 Alexnet-DeepSea

Alexnet is a very classic convolutional neural network designed in 2012 by Hinton and Alex Krizhevsky [12]. It is a milestone in the development of convolutional neural networks. Approches such as Relu, Dropout and LRN have been successfully applied to convolutional neural networks, resulting in significant network performance improvements. In addition, Alexnet uses the GPU [17] to speed up its calculations. Alexnet has the following innovations:

(1) The activation function did not choose Sigmod, tanh and so on, but relu.
(2) Use Dropout to randomly ignore some neurons, which can prevent overfitting.
(3) Use overlapped maximum pooling. Before the emergence of Alexnet, most convolutional neural networks used average pooling. Average pooling has a drawback, which may make the effect obscure. Alexnet all uses max pooling, which avoids its drawbacks.
(4) Use the LRN layer to create an activity mechanism in the activity of local neurons. This mechanism is like this:continue to make the larger responding neurons respond greater and the neurons that have not been excited.
(5) Use GPU and CUDA to accelerate calculations (Fig. 6).

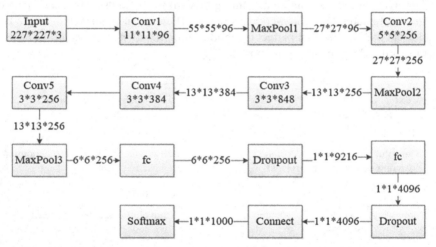

Fig. 6. The Alexnet model has eight layers: five convolutional layers and three fully connected layers. Each convolutional layer contains Relu and LRN and downsampling. Alexnet uses Relu as the activation function to increase the nonlinear relationship between networks and the use of Droupout is to prevent the network from overfitting. This allows the function of the neural network to be greatly increased and has a better effect when processing complex data.

DeepSea has very good results in processing genetic data sets. Alexnet is very good at processing complex data. We combined the characteristics of these two models and improved them. Based on the DeepSea and AlexNet model, we designed a new model named DeepSea-Alexnet. We increased the depth of the network. Three more convolutional layers [20] are added. Dropout and Batch normalization are added between the fixed layers (please see Fig. 7). We refer to the AlexNet classifier. Before using the Sigmod function for the final processing, We process the features extracted from the fully connected layer. The the specific modifications to the classifier are shown in Fig. 8.

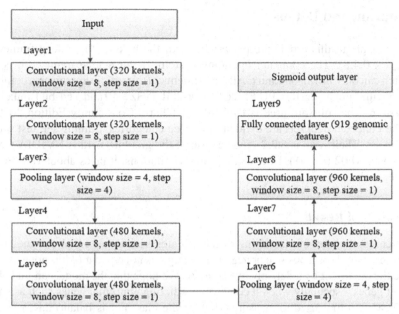

Fig. 7. The network structure shown in this figure is designed by combining the DeepSea model and the Alexnet model. After Layer5, dropout was added and the proportion of dropout proportion was 20%; after Layer8, dropout was also added and the proportion of dropout proportion was 50%. In addition, after Layer2, Layer5 and Layer8, we added Batch normalization before dropout. The function is to normalize the data and make the network easier to calculate.

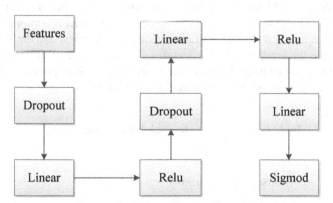

Fig. 8. This picture describes the classifier of DeepSea-Alexnet. After obtaining the features extracted by the fully connected layer, perform Droupout twice, Linear Three times and Relu twice to use Sigmod to classify the data.

3 Experimental Details

All experiments in this article are performed with the help of the Selene framework (selene_sdk 0.4.8). The computer operating system of the Selene framework is limited,which can only be run on Linux. All experiments in this article are run on a computer equipped with Intel Xeon(R) CPU E5-2640 v4@2.40 GHz * 40 and a 64-bit Linux operating system. The software used is Pycharm (PyCharm Community Edition 2020.2.2 x64). The collected data sets are divided into three categories: training set, test set and validation set. Their ratio is 6:2:2. The version of the graphics card is NVIDIA Corporation Device 1b02 (rev a1). Due to equipment limitations, it takes about 18 h to train the model each time.

3.1 Analysis of Results

In most cases, the cost of classifying different categories is not equal and the cost of classifying a sample as a positive or negative example is not equal too. It is not enough to measure the quality of a model only by accuracy. We hope that the model can find all the abnormal genes, especially when it comes to predicting abnormal genes such as cancer genes. ROC is a tool used to measure whether the classifier is balanced.ROC curves and AUC are often used to evaluate ROC curve and AUC are often used to evaluate the effect of a binary classifier. Both DeepSea and DeepSea-Alexnet use the same dataset for training and testing, as shown in Table 1 and Fig. 9. The AUC value of them are both above 0.93, indicating that both are excellent classifiers. The correct answer rates of them for the test are 62.02% and 64.18%, respectively.

Whether from ROC AUC or test performance,the DeepSea-Alexnet model is better than the DeepSea model.I think the DeepSea_Alexnet model is better than the DeepSea model for the following reasons: (1) The structure of the model is complicated, but the Dropout function is added so that the gradient does not disappear and the Relu function is added to make the gradient. (2) The features extracted by the fully connected layer are not directly classified using Sigmod. After three times Linear, twice Relu and three times Droupout, the Sigmod function is used for the final classification.

Table 1. The result of DeepSea and DeepSea-Alexnet

Model	ROC_AUC	Test_Performance
DeepSea	0.9348	0.6202
DeepSea-Alexnet	0.9385	0.6418

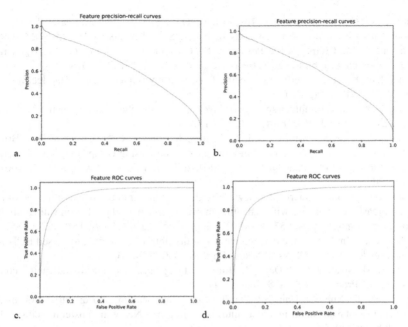

Fig. 9. a is the features precision-recall curve of the test result of the model DeepSea-Alexnet; b is is the features precison-recall curve curve of the test result of the model DeepSea.; c is the feature ROC curve of the model DeepSea-Alexnet; d is the feature ROC curve of the model DeepSea. Their ROC curves are very similar and the ROC values are both around 0.93.

4   Conclusion

This paper introduces a Selene-based method for abnormal gene detection, which aims to solve the problem that bioinformatics scientists lack programming experience and cannot independently develop deep learning models.With the help of it, people who conduct an experiment don't need to be fully capable of coding, they just need to configure the parameters of the model in the yml file.The two models introduced in this paper have achieved good results and the accuracy of the experiment is above 60%. However, the performance of the model is still not very good and there are many aspects that can be improved. We will consider combining various methods, not just sticking to CNN.

References

1. Shen, Y., et al.: Global profile of tRNA-derived small RNAs in gastric cancer patient plasma and identification of tRF-33-P4R8YP9LON4VDP as a new tumor suppressor. Int. J. Med. Sci. **18**(7), 1570–1579 (2021)
2. Jabbar, M.A., Abraham, A., Dogan, O., Madureira, A.M., Tiwari, S.: Deep Learning in Biomedical and Health Informatics: Current Applications and Possibilities. CRC Press, Boca Raton (2021)
3. Eid, S.A., et al.: Gene expression profiles of diabetic kidney disease and neuropathy in eNOS knockout mice: predictors of pathology and RAS blockade effects. FASEB J. Official Publ. Fed. Am. Soc. Exp. Biol. **35**(5), e21467 (2021)

4. Chen, K.M., Cofer, E.M., Zhou, J., Troyanskaya, O.G.: Selene: a PyTorch-based deep learning library for sequence data. Nat. Methods Tech. Life Sci. Chemists **16**(4), 315–318 (2019)
5. Camacho, D.M., Collins, K.M., Powers, R.K., Costello, J.C., Collins, J.J.: Next-generation machine learning for biological networks. Cell **173**(7), 1581–1592 (2018)
6. Jaganathan, K., et al.: Predicting splicing from primary sequence with deep learning. Cell **176**(3), 535–548.e24 (2019)
7. Xiong, H.Y., et al.: The human splicing code reveals new insights into the genetic determinants of disease. Science **347**(6218), 1254806 (2015)
8. Zheng, R., Dong, X., Wan, C., Shi, X., Zhang, X., Meyer, C.A.: Cistrome Data Browser and Toolkit: analyzing human and mouse genomic data using compendia of ChIP-seq and chromatin accessibility data. Quant. Biol. **8**(3), 267–276 (2020). https://doi.org/10.1007/s40 484-020-0204-7
9. Sivanandan, R., Jayakumari, J.: A new CNN architecture for efficient classification of ultrasound breast tumor images with activation map clustering based prediction validation. Med. Biol. Eng. Comput. **59**(4), 957–968 (2021). https://doi.org/10.1007/s11517-021-02357-3
10. Luo, J., et al.: Improving the performance of multisubject motor imagery-based BCIs using twin cascaded softmax CNNs. J. Neural Eng. **18**(3), 036024 (2021)
11. Kamjam, M., Sivalingam, P., Deng, Z., Hong, K.: Deep sea actinomycetes and their secondary metabolites. Front. Microbiol. **8**, 760 (2017)
12. Lu, T., Yu, F., Xue, C., Han, B.: Identification, classification, and quantification of three physical mechanisms in oil-in-water emulsions using AlexNet with transfer learning. J. Food Eng. **288**, 110220 (2021)
13. Dzhezyan, G., Cecotti, H.: Symmetrical filters in convolutional neural networks. Int. J. Mach. Learn. Cybern. **12**(7), 2027–2039 (2021). https://doi.org/10.1007/s13042-021-01290-z
14. Haque, H.M.F., Rafsanjani, M., Arifin, F., Adilina, S., Shatabda, S.: SubFeat: feature subspacing ensemble classifier for function prediction of DNA, RNA and protein sequences. Comput. Biol. Chem. **92**, 107489 (2021). (prepublish)
15. Infante, T., et al.: Machine learning and network medicine: a novel approach for precision medicine and personalized therapy in cardiomyopathies. J. Cardiovasc. Med. **22**(6), 429–440 (2021)
16. Tang, G., Teotia, S., Tang, X., Singh, D. (eds.): RNA-Based Technologies for Functional Genomics in Plants. CSPS, Springer, Cham (2021). https://doi.org/10.1007/978-3-030-649 94-4
17. Krupa, J., et al.: GPU coprocessors as a service for deep learning inference in high energy physics. Mach. Learn. Sci. Technol. **2**(3), 035005 (2021)
18. Rosa, D., MacDermid, J., Klubowicz, D.: A comparative performance analysis of the International classification of functioning, disability and health and the item-perspective classification framework for classifying the content of patient reported outcome measures. Health Qual. Life Outcomes **19**(1), 132 (2021)
19. Liu, Q., Piao, H., Wang, Y., Zheng, D., Wang, W.: Circulating exosomes in cardiovascular disease: novel carriers of biological information. Biomed. Pharmacother. = Biomedecine Pharmacotherapie **135**, 111148 (2021)
20. Rahim, T., Hassan, S.A., Shin, S.Y.: A deep convolutional neural network for the detection of polyps in colonoscopy images. Biomed. Sig. Process. Control **68**, 102654 (2021)
21. Nikhil, K., Jojo, M.: Deep Learning with Python (2021)
22. Li, J., Wilkinson, J.L., Boxall, A.B.A.: Use of a large dataset to develop new models for estimating the sorption of active pharmaceutical ingredients in soils and sediments. J. Hazard. Mater. **415**, 125688 (2021)
23. Deorowicz, S., Danek, A., Kokot, M.: VCFShark: how to squeeze a VCF file. Bioinformatics (Oxford England) (2021)

A Method for Constructing an Integrative Network of Competing Endogenous RNAs

Seokwoo Lee, Wook Lee, Shulei Ren, and Kyungsook Han[(⊠)]

Department of Computer Engineering, Inha University, Incheon, South Korea
{22211270,renshulei}@inha.edu, {wooklee,khan}@inha.ac.kr

Abstract. Since the new gene regulation involving competing endogenous RNA (ceRNA) interactions targeted by common microRNAs (miRNAs) was found, several computational methods have been proposed to derive ceRNA networks. However, most of the ceRNA networks are restricted to represent either miRNA-target RNA interactions or lncRNA-miRNA-mRNA interactions. From the extensive data analysis, we found that competition for miRNA-binding occurs not only between lncRNAs and mRNAs but also between lncRNAs or between mRNAs. Furthermore, a large number of pseudogenes also act as ceRNAs, thereby regulate other genes. In this study, we considered all lncRNAs, mRNAs and pseudogenes as potential ceRNAs and developed a method for constructing an integrative ceRNA network which includes all possible interactions of ceRNAs mediated by miRNAs: lncRNA-miRNA-mRNA, lncRNA-miRNA-lncRNA, lncRNA-miRNA-pseudogene, mRNA-miRNA-mRNA, mRNA-miRNA-pseudogene, and pseudogene-miRNA-pseudogene. We constructed integrative ceRNA networks for breast cancer, liver cancer and lung cancer, and derived several triplets of ceRNAs which can be used as potential prognostic biomarkers. The potential prognostic triplets could not be found when only lncRNA-miRNA-mRNA interactions were considered. Although preliminary, our approach to constructing integrative ceRNA networks is applicable to multiple types of cancer and will help us find potential prognostic biomarkers in cancer.

Keywords: Competing endogenous RNA · ceRNA network · Cancer · Prognosis

1 Introduction

Only 2% of the RNA transcripts in the human genome are translated into proteins. The remaining 98% of the RNA transcripts do not code for proteins and these are collectively called non-coding RNAs (ncRNAs). Due to advances in sequencing technologies and genomic analysis, a large number of ncRNAs have been discovered for the past decade. ncRNAs can be classified into two groups based on their size. One group includes long ncRNAs (lncRNAs) of 200 nucleotides or more in length [1]. The other group of ncRNAs includes short RNAs, such as microRNAs (miRNAs) which typically contain 22 nucleotides or less. miRNAs are responsible for the post-transcriptional regulation of gene expression and are involved in the RNA silencing pathway which is known as RNA interference [2].

© Springer Nature Switzerland AG 2021
D.-S. Huang et al. (Eds.): ICIC 2021, LNAI 12838, pp. 407–420, 2021.
https://doi.org/10.1007/978-3-030-84532-2_37

Many lncRNAs and miRNAs are known to be functionally associated with human diseases, in particular cancer. For instance, lncRNA BC032469 is known to upregulate the expression of hTERT by binding to miR-1207-5p, which promotes proliferation of cancer cells in gastric cancer [3]. Recently a new gene regulation mechanism called the competing endogenous RNA (ceRNA) hypothesis has been proposed by Salmena et al. [4]. The ceRNA hypothesis suggests that RNAs with similar miRNA response elements compete to bind to the same miRNA, thereby regulate each other indirectly. Since the hypothesis was proposed, evidence supporting the hypothesis has been accumulated and several computational methods have been developed to derive a network of ceRNAs. For example, Jiang et al. [5] generated a ceRNA network after calculating correlation coefficients of miRNA-mRNA and miRNA-lncRNA pairs. Zhu et al. [6] constructed a network of lncRNA-miRNA-mRNA triplets from miRNA-lncRNA associations and miRNA-mRNA associations.

However, most ceRNA networks constructed by these methods are restricted to represent either miRNA-lncRNA interactions, miRNA-mRNA interactions or lncRNA-miRNA-mRNA interactions. From the extensive data analysis, we found that competition for miRNA-binding occurs not only between lncRNAs and mRNAs but also between lncRNAs or between mRNAs. Furthermore, pseudogenes, another important group of ceRNAs, are missing in most ceRNA networks. A large number of pseudogenes regulate the expression of functional genes by competitive binding with miRNA to inhibit or promote the occurrence of cancer [7].

In this study, we considered all lncRNAs, mRNAs and pseudogenes as potential ceRNAs and constructed an integrative ceRNA network of the RNAs. Our ceRNA network includes all possible interactions of ceRNAs mediated by miRNAs: lncRNA-miRNA-mRNA, lncRNA-miRNA-lncRNA, lncRNA-miRNA-pseudogene, mRNA-miRNA-mRNA, mRNA-miRNA-pseudogene, and pseudogene-miRNA-pseudogene. We constructed ceRNA networks for three types of cancer and identified several triplets of ceRNAs which might be used as potential prognostic biomarkers in cancer. The rest of this paper presents our approach and its results.

2   Materials and Methods

2.1   Data Collection and Filtering

For primary tumor samples of three types, breast cancer (BRCA), lung cancer (LUAD), and liver cancer (LIHC), we collected RNA-seq gene expression data of lncRNAs, mRNAs, pseudogenes and miRNAs and clinical data from the Cancer Genome Atlas (TCGA) data portal (https://tcga-data.nci.nih.gov/). The gene expression data collected from TCGA are raw read counts without normalization. Normal samples of each type of cancer were also extracted from the TCGA data portal (refer to Table 1 for the number of tumor and normal samples for the three types of cancer).

The gene names of TCGA are represented by Ensembl ID, so we obtained annotation files from Ensembl (http://www.ensembl.org) to classify them into mRNAs, lncRNAs, and pseudogenes. To identify differentially expressed genes between normal and tumor samples, we ran the R package EdgeR based on the read counts. edgeR uses the Trimmed

Means of M values (TMM), in which highly expressed genes and those with a large variation of expression are excluded, whereupon a weighted average of the subset of genes is used to calculate a normalization factor [8]. We selected those mRNAs, lncRNAs, and pseudogenes for which |log2 fold change| >1 with an adjusted p-value <0.001, and removed the others. Due to a smaller number of miRNAs than other types of RNAs, we lowered the criteria for selecting differentially expressed miRNAs between normal and tumor samples to those with |log2 fold change| >0.6 with an adjusted p-value <0.001.

From the differential gene expression analysis, we identified 4,867 differentially expressed mRNAs, 1,791 lncRNAs, 649 pseudogenes, and 243 miRNAs for breast cancer. Using the same criteria, we identified differentially expressed genes for liver cancer and lung cancer as well. Table 1 shows the number of the genes for three types of cancer. Details of the genes are available in Additional file 1.

Table 1. The number of samples, ceRNA-miRNA-ceRNA triplets, and ceRNAs of each type in the triplets.

Cancer	#tumor samples	#normal samples	#triplets	#lncRNAs	#miRNAs	#mRNAs	#pseudogenes
BRCA	1,079	104	2,472,785	1,791	243	4,867	649
LIHC	369	50	1,249,638	1,279	222	3,867	393
LUAD	509	20	1,226,772	1,602	199	4,166	524

2.2 Deriving ceRNA-miRNA-ceRNA Interactions

As mentioned earlier, most ceRNA networks proposed by other studies are restricted to represent either miRNA-target RNA interactions or lncRNA-miRNA-mRNA interactions [5, 6]. Competition for binding to miRNAs occurs not only between lncRNAs and mRNAs but also between lncRNAs or between mRNAs. In addition to lncRNAs and mRNAs, pseudogenes also compete for binding to miRNAs.

All lncRNAs, mRNAs, and pseudogenes with common miRNA response elements (MREs) can act as ceRNAs, thereby indirectly regulate each other [4]. For an integrative ceRNA network, we considered all lncRNAs, mRNAs, and pseudogenes as potential ceRNAs and their competitive relation. Therefore, there are six possible types of ceRNA-miRNA-ceRNA interactions: lncRNA-miRNA-lncRNA, lncRNA-miRNA-mRNA, lncRNA-miRNA-pseudogene, mRNA-miRNA-mRNA, mRNA-miRNA-pseudogene, and pseudogene-miRNA-pseudogene. Note that the order of two ceRNAs in the ceRNA-miRNA-ceRNA interactions does not matter. For example, the lncRNA-miRNA-mRNA triplet represents the same type of interaction as the mRNA-miRNA-lncRNA triplet. Throughout the paper, two notations, X-miRNA-Y and (X, miRNA, Y), will be used interchangeably to denote the ceRNA-miRNA-ceRNA interactions.

There is no publicly available resource that provides a large amount of data on ceRNA-miRNA-ceRNA interactions. Thus, we derived initial ceRNA-miRNA-ceRNA relations by merging miRNA-target interactions with a common miRNA. From miRTar-Base for breast cancer [9], we obtained 15,389 miRNA-mRNA interactions, 76 miRNA-lncRNA interactions, and 31 miRNA-pseudogene interactions. Due to an insufficient number of experimentally validated miRNA-target interactions, we additionally obtained computationally predicted miRNA-lncRNA interactions and miRNA-pseudogene interactions from miRcode [10] and TargetScan [11]. By combining miRNA-target pairs with a same miRNA, we obtained non-overlapping 2,472,785 initial ceRNA-miRNA-ceRNA triplets for breast cancer. In a similar way, we obtained 1,249,638 initial triplets for liver cancer and 1,226,772 initial triplets for lung cancer (Table 1). The initial triplets are listed in Additional file 2.

2.3 Constructing an Integrative CeRNA Network

For every pair of target genes X and Y in the X-miRNA-Y triplet, we computed the Pearson correlation coefficient (PCC) between their expression levels by Eq. 1. In the equation, N is the number of samples, X_i is the expression level of X, and $\overline{X}$ is the average expression level of X in all samples.

$$PCC(X, Y) = \frac{\sum_{i=1}^{N}(X_i - \overline{X})(Y_i - \overline{Y})}{\sqrt{\sum_{i=1}^{N}(X_i - \overline{X})^2 \sum_{i=1}^{N}(Y_i - \overline{Y})^2}} \qquad (1)$$

From the initial triplets, we selected those triplets with |PCC| > 0.6 and removed the remaining triplets. We generated a ceRNA network with the selected triplets and visualized the network using Cytoscape v3.8.2. Several studies reported that a node with a high value of centrality in a ceRNA network tends to be a prognostic gene [12, 13]. Hence, we calculated the betweenness centrality, closeness centrality, and degree centrality for every pair of nodes in the ceRNA network.

Betweenness centrality (BC) [14] determines whether a node is important based on how many shortest paths have passed through the node. BC is defined by Eq. 2, in which n is the set of nodes in the network, $d_{s,t}$ is the number of shortest paths between nodes s and t and $d_{s,t}(v)$ is the number of shortest paths between s and t which pass through node v.

$$BC(v) = \sum_{s,t \in n} \frac{d_{s,t}(v)}{d_{s,t}} \qquad (2)$$

Closeness centrality (CC) [14] assumes that important nodes will be closer to other nodes, and the evaluation criterion is based on the average of the minimum distances from the node to all other nodes.

$$CC(v) = \frac{p(v)}{|n| - 1} \cdot \frac{p(v)}{\sum_{u \in p(v)} d(v, u)} \qquad (3)$$

where $p(v)$ the number of nodes that node v can connect to, n is the set of nodes in the network and $d(v, u)$ is length of the shortest path from v to u.

Degree centrality (DC) [14] refers to the number of connections of the node, and defined by Eq. 4. In the equation, n is the set of nodes in the network and d_v is the degree of node v.

$$DC(v) = \frac{d_v}{|n| - 1}$$ (4)

Every node in the network was scored with the sum of its BC, CC and DC values (Eq. 5), and those nodes with high scores were selected to find potential prognostic triplets and for further analysis.

$$Score(v) = BC(v) + CC(v) + DC(v)$$ (5)

2.4 Finding Potential Prognostic Triplets

For each X-miRNA-Y triplet in the ceRNA network, we clustered tumor samples into two groups with respect to the expression levels (high or low) of genes X and Y. The criteria for "high" and "low" expression levels are the average expression levels of the gene in all tumor samples of the same type.

Group 1: Samples with opposite expression patterns of X and Y (one gene shows a high expression level and the other shows a low expression level).

Group 2: Samples with similar expression patterns of X and Y (both genes show either high expression levels or low expression levels).

The criteria for clustering samples can be represented by Eq. 6. In the following equation, X_i is the expression level of X in sample i, $\overline{X}$ is the average expression level of X in all tumor samples.

$$\begin{cases} (X_i - \overline{X})(Y_i - \overline{Y}) < 0, & i \in Group\ 1 \\ (X_i - \overline{X})(Y_i - \overline{Y}) > 0, & i \in Group\ 2 \end{cases}$$ (6)

We then selected X-miRNA-Y triplets for which both |PCC(X, miRNA)| and |PCC(Y, miRNA)| are greater than 0.3 in at least one group. This filtering was done to reflect the ceRNA hypothesis because two target genes must be co-regulated by a common miRNA.

With the selected X-miRNA-Y triplets we performed the log-rank test and compared the survival rate of two groups. The triplets with p-values <0.05 were obtained as potential prognostic triplets for each type of cancer.

2.5 Constructing a Subnetwork of Potential Prognostic Triplets

In addition to an integrative ceRNA network, we constructed a subnetwork with potential prognostic triplets and performed enrichment analysis using Enrichr [15]. Enrichr is an integrative web-based software application that includes a lot of gene-set libraries and various interactive visualization tools [15]. We used gene ontology (GO) and the Kyoto Encyclopedia of Genes and Genomes (KEGG) libraries.

3 Results and Discussion

3.1 Integrative ceRNA Network

For lung cancer, we obtained a total of 1,226,772 ceRNA-miRNA-ceRNA triplets by merging ceRNA-miRNA associations with a common miRNA. After computing PCC between two ceRNAs in each of the ceRNA-miRNA-ceRNA triplets, we selected 13,965 ceRNA-miRNA-ceRNA triplets with |PCC| >0.6. With the 13,965 triplets, we constructed a ceRNA network for lung cancer (Fig. 1). The ceRNA network for lung cancer includes 3,268 interactions among 976 RNAs (28 lncRNAs, 152 miRNAs, 730 mRNA, and 66 pseudogenes). In a similar method, we constructed ceRNA networks for breast cancer and liver cancer, which are available in Additional file 3.

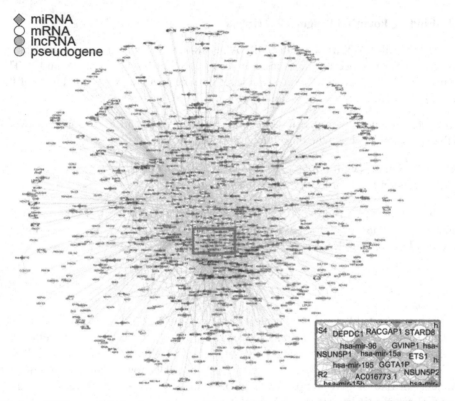

Fig. 1. ceRNA network for lung cancer. The network was constructed with 13,965 ceRNA-miRNA-ceRNA triplets, which include 3,268 interactions among 976 RNAs (28 lncRNAs, 152 miRNAs, 730 mRNA, and 66 pseudogenes). The network enclosed in a red box is a blowup of the marked subnetwork. (Color figure online)

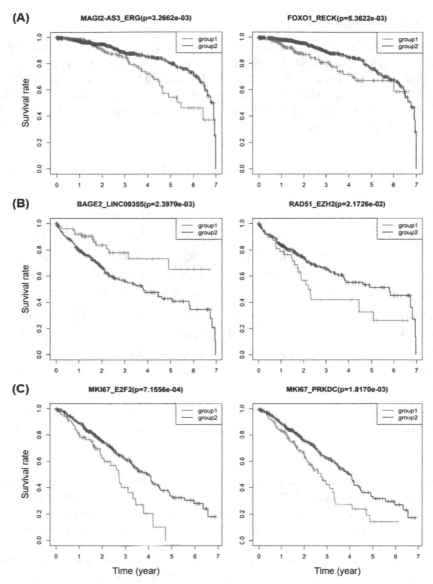

Fig. 2. The Kaplan-Meier (KM) plots from the log-rank test with ceRNA pairs in the X-miRNA-Y triplet. Group 1: patients with opposite expression patterns of X and Y. Group 2: patients with similar expression patterns of X and Y. (A) KM plots comparing the overall survival rates of two groups of breast cancer patients with respect to two triplets. MAGI2-AS3 is a lncRNA, and ERG, FOXO1 and RECK are mRNAs. (B) KM plots comparing the overall survival rates of two groups of liver cancer patients. BAGE2 is a pseudogene, LINC00355 is a lncRNA, and RAD51 and EZH2 are mRNAs. (C) KM plots comparing the overall survival rates of two groups of lung cancer patients. MKI67, E2F2, and PRKDC are all mRNAs.

3.2 Potential Prognostic Triplets

From the ceRNA network, we identified target genes with high scores of sum of BC, CC and DC values (see Eq. 5 for the definition of the score). Table 2 shows top 10 target genes for each type of cancer. The triplets which contain at least one of the top 10 target genes are listed in Additional file 4. As mediators, miRNAs have much higher scores than other types of RNAs, and this table shows high-scored genes targeted by miRNAs rather than high-scored miRNAs.

Table 2. Top 10 target genes with high scores of BC, CC and DC for each cancer type. The RNA types are also shown.

BRCA		LIHC		LUAD	
Gene	Type	Gene	Type	Gene	Type
MEG3	lncRNA	RACGAP1	mRNA	GVINP1	pseudo
AP000695.1	lncRNA	KPNA2	mRNA	LMNB2	mRNA
ADAMTS9-AS2	lncRNA	RAD51	mRNA	GGTA1P	pseudo
TGFBR2	mRNA	LINC00221	lncRNA	ANKRD36BP2	pseudo
MAGI2-AS3	lncRNA	AC006305.1	lncRNA	NSUN5P1	pseudo
FOXO1	mRNA	BAGE2	pseudo	MKI67	mRNA
NFAT5	mRNA	PRIM1	mRNA	RACGAP1	mRNA
BIRC5	mRNA	PKM	mRNA	MIAT	lncRNA
WHAMMP2	pseudo	CDC25A	mRNA	RAD51	mRNA
GGTA1P	pseudo	E2F1	mRNA	HMGA1	mRNA

GGTA1P, RACGAP1, and RAD51 were commonly selected as high-scored genes in the three types of cancer. GGTA1P is known to be associated with patient prognosis in cancer [16]. RACGAP1 is an important marker in various carcinomas such as liver cancer, gastric cancer, and colorectal cancer [17–19]. RAD51 is also considered as a potential prognostic biomarker in several cancers [20, 21].

From the log-rank test with respect to ceRNA pairs in the high-scored ceRNA genes, we derived 17, 9, and 49 ceRNA-miRNA-ceRNA triplets as potential prognostic biomarkers for breast cancer, liver cancer, and lung cancer, respectively (Additional file 5).

Figure 2 shows a few Kaplan-Meier plots, which compare the overall survival rates of two groups with respect to (X, Y) in the X-miRNA-Y triplet. It is interesting to note that BAGE2-LINC00355, as a pseudogene-lncRNA pair, is a potentially good prognostic marker for liver cancer (Fig. 2B). This ceRNA pair could not be found if we did not consider pseudogenes as ceRNAs.

The Kaplan-Meier plots in Fig. 2A show a relatively smaller difference between two groups than those in Figs. 2B and C. The reason for the smaller difference between two groups of breast cancer patients is mainly due to a low death rate from breast. The number of tumor samples in the TCGA breast cancer dataset (BRCA) is more than twice that of liver cancer (LIHC) and lung cancer (LUAD) (see Table 1). But, BRCA has a much smaller number of dead patients than LIHC and LUAD. Since BRCA has a much lower death rate than LIHC and LUAD, differences in patient survival rates are smaller than those in the other types of cancer.

For the ceRNA pairs shown in Fig. 2, Table 3 lists ceRNA-miRNA-ceRNA triplets along with PCC for every RNA pair in the triplet. As expected, two ceRNAs involved in a same ceRNA-miRNA-ceRNA triplet exhibit opposite correlations in two groups. What is interesting is that the two groups show different correlations between miRNAs and their target genes.

Table 3. Potential prognostic X-miRNA-Y triplets with the lowest p-value of the log-rank test. The PCCs between RNAs in the triplets are also shown.

Cancer	X-miRNA-Y triplet	Group	PCC of the RNA pair		
			X-Y	X-miRNA	miRNA-Y
BRCA	MAGI2-AS3_hsa-mir-145_ERG	1	−0.582	−0.092	0.214
		2	0.855	0.475	0.488
	FOXO1_hsa-mir-15a_RECK	1	−0.515	0.041	−0.149
		2	0.809	−0.324	−0.360
	FOXO1_hsa-mir-15b_RECK	1	−0.515	−0.117	−0.104
		2	0.809	−0.395	−0.383
	FOXO1_hsa-mir-96_RECK	1	−0.515	0.079	−0.088
		2	0.809	−0.447	0.383
LIHC	BAGE2_hsa-mir-214_LINC00355	1	−0.655	0.092	−0.178
		2	0.900	−0.306	−0.310
	RAD51_hsa-mir-25_EZH2	1	−0.499	−0.301	0.263
		2	0.825	0.333	0.407
LUAD	MKI67_hsa-mir-218_E2F2	1	−0.601	−0.164	0.072
		2	0.855	−0.386	−0.407
	MKI67_hsa-mir-218_PRKDC	1	−0.605	−0.284	0.124
		2	0.795	−0.367	−0.322

3.3 Subnetwork of Potential Prognostic Triplets

We constructed a subnetwork with the 17 potential prognostic triplets for breast cancer, which includes 31 edges among 27 nodes (Fig. 3A). The subnetwork includes only those correlations between genes, which show significantly different survival rates between two groups of breast cancer patients. MAGI2-AS3 (enclosed in a red box) is a lncRNA and has the most interactions with other RNAs in the network. MAGI2-AS3 is known to function as an important tumor suppressor in breast cancer [22]. Among the miRNAs in the network, hsa-mir-200c mediates many interactions. hsa-mir-200c is considered as prognostic factor in several cancers [23, 24].

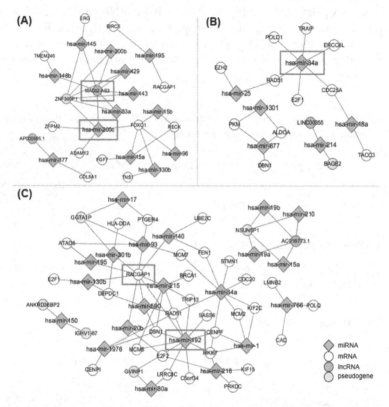

Fig. 3. Subnetwork of prognostic ceRNA triplets for three types of cancer. miRNAs are represented by light green diamonds. The lncRNAs, mRNAs, and pseudogenes are represented by white, green, and pink circles, respectively. (A) Subnetwork of prognostic ceRNA triplets for breast cancer. MAGI2-AS3 (enclosed in a red box), which is a lncRNA, has the most interactions with other RNAs in the network. Among the miRNAs, hsa-mir-200c mediates the most interactions. (B) Subnetwork of prognostic ceRNA triplets for liver cancer. hsa-mir-34a has the most interactions in the network. (C) Subnetwork of prognostic ceRNA triplets for lung cancer. RACGAP1, which is an mRNA, has the most interactions, and hsa-mir-192 is a miRNA with many interactions in the network. (Color figure online)

The subnetwork of potential prognostic triplets for liver cancer consists of 17 interactions among 19 RNAs (Fig. 3B). hsa-mir-34a is a miRNA with the highest degree. hsa-mir-34a is well known as a tumor suppressor, and dysregulation of hsa-mir-34a implicates tumor genesis [25, 26].

The subnetwork of potential prognostic triplets for lung cancer includes 76 interactions among 57 RNAs (Fig. 3C). hsa-mir-192 is a miRNA with the highest degree in the network. The hsa-mir-192 family has been suggested as a potential prognostic in a recent study [27]. RACGAP1 is the RNA with the second highest degree in the network. RACGAP1 plays an important role in various types of cancer [17–19].

For all genes involved in the subnetworks of potential prognostic triplets, we performed a functional enrichment analysis. Figure 4 shows the result of running Enrichr with two gene-set libraries, GO and KEGG. Most of the top 10 GO terms are related with cell cycle, DNA metabolism, DNA replication, and DNA repair. It is well known fact that cancer is highly related with aberrant cell cycle regulation and DNA metabolism [28] (Fig. 4A). The result of analysis with the KEGG library (Fig. 4B) also shows that the RNAs included in the potential prognostic triplets are highly related to the cell cycle and DNA replication.

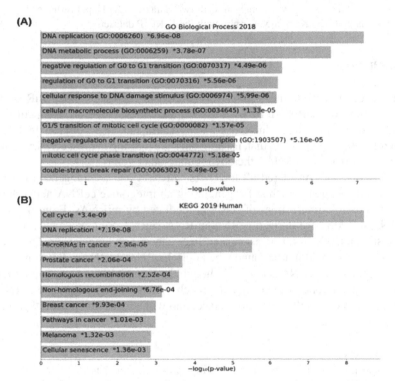

Fig. 4. Functional enrichment analysis using two gene-set libraries (GO and KEGG) for the genes involved in the potential prognostic triplets identified in our study. The p-values were computed using Fisher's exact test. Most genes in the triplets are related with cell cycle, DNA metabolism, DNA replication, DNA repair, and cancer. (A) Functional enrichment analysis with the GO biological process library. (B) Functional enrichment analysis with the KEGG library.

For the validation of our method, we tested it on an independent dataset from Liver Cancer-RIKEN, Japan (LIRI-JP) obtained from the ICGC data portal (https://dcc. icgc.org). Most potential prognostic gene pairs found in the TCGA LIHC dataset were also found in the LIRI-JP dataset and showed similar predictive power of the survival rates in the LIRI-JP dataset as well (Fig. 5).

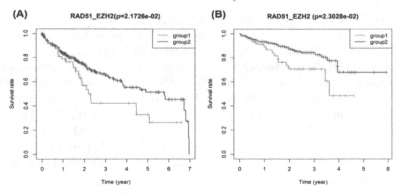

Fig. 5. Comparison of the survival analysis with two datasets. (A) Kaplan-Meier plot with the TCGA-LIHC dataset. (B) Kaplan-Meier plot with the LIRI-JP dataset.

4 Conclusion

So far most of the ceRNA networks are restricted to represent either miRNA-target RNA interactions or lncRNA-miRNA-mRNA interactions. However, competitive relation exists not only between lncRNAs and mRNAs but also between lncRNAs or between mRNAs. In addition to that, pseudogenes are missing in most ceRNA networks. Pseudogenes also act as ceRNAs, thereby regulate other genes.

In this study, we considered all lncRNAs, mRNAs and pseudogenes as potential ceRNAs and developed a method for generating an integrative ceRNA network which includes all possible interactions of ceRNAs mediated by miRNAs. From the integrative ceRNA network, we derived ceRNA-miRNA-ceRNA triplets which can be used as prognostic biomarkers for breast cancer, liver cancer and lung cancer. The potential prognostic triplets could not be found when only lncRNA-miRNA-mRNA interactions were considered for a ceRNA network. Although the potential prognostic triplets require further investigation for clinical use, our approach to constructing integrative ceRNA networks is applicable to multiple types of cancer and will help us find potential prognostic biomarkers in cancer.

Additional Files
All additional files are available at http://bclab.inha.ac.kr/icic2021.

Additional file 1: Differentially expressed RNAs and their types.

Additional file 2: Initial ceRNA-miRNA-ceRNA triplets.

Additional file 3: ceRNA networks for breast cancer and liver cancer.

Additional file 4: Triplets that contain at least one of the top 10 target genes.

Additional file 5: Potential prognostic ceRNA-miRNA-ceRNA triplets for three types of cancer.

Acknowledgements. This work was supported by the National Research Foundation of Korea (NRF) grant funded by the Ministry of Science and ICT (NRF-2020R1A2B5B01096299, NRF-2018K2A9A2A11080914).

References

1. Wilusz, J.E., Sunwoo, H., Spector, D.L.: Long noncoding RNAs: functional surprises from the RNA world. Genes Dev. **23**, 1494–1504 (2009)
2. Bartel, D.P.: Metazoan microRNAs. Cell **173**, 20–51 (2018)
3. Lü, M.H., et al.: Long noncoding RNA BC032469, a novel competing endogenous RNA, upregulates hTERT expression by sponging miR-1207-5p and promotes proliferation in gastric cancer. Oncogene **35**, 3524–3534 (2016)
4. Salmena, L., Poliseno, L., Tay, Y., Kats, L., Pandolfi, P.P.: A ceRNA hypothesis: the Rosetta Stone of a hidden RNA language? Cell **146**, 353–358 (2011)
5. Jiang, R., Zhao, C., Gao, B., Xu, J., Song, W., Shi, P.: Mixomics analysis of breast cancer: long non-coding RNA linc01561 acts as ceRNA involved in the progression of breast cancer. Int. J. Biochem. Cell Biol. **102**, 1–9 (2018)
6. Zhu, Y., Bian, Y., Zhang, Q., et al.: Construction and analysis of dysregulated lncRNA-associated ceRNA network in colorectal cancer. J. Cell Biochem. **120**, 9250–9263 (2019)
7. Poliseno, L., Salmena, L., Zhang, J., Carver, B., Haveman, W.J., Pandolfi, P.P.: A coding-independent function of gene and pseudogene mRNAs regulates tumour biology. Nature **465**, 1033–1038 (2010)
8. Robinson, M.D., McCarthy, D.J., Smyth, G.K.: edgeR: a bioconductor package for differential expression analysis of digital gene expression data. Bioinformatics **26**, 139–140 (2010)
9. Huang, H.Y., et al.: miRTarBase 2020: updates to the experimentally validated microRNA-target interaction database. Nucleic Acids Res. **48**, D148–D154 (2020)
10. Jeggari, A., Marks, D.S., Larsson, E.: miRcode: a map of putative microRNA target sites in the long non-coding transcriptome. Bioinformatics **28**, 2062–2063 (2012)
11. Agarwal, V., Bell, G.W., Nam, J.-W., Bartel, D.P.: Predicting effective microRNA target sites in mammalian mRNAs. Elife **4**, e05005 (2015)
12. Zhou, M., et al.: Characterization of long non-coding RNA-associated ceRNA network to reveal potential prognostic lncRNA biomarkers in human ovarian cancer. Oncotarget **7**, 12598–12611 (2016)
13. Liu, H., et al.: Integrative analysis of dysregulated lncRNA-associated ceRNA network reveals functional lncRNAs in gastric cancer. Genes **9**, 303 (2018)
14. Wasserman, S., Faust, K., Iacobucci, D., Granovetter, M.: Social Network Analysis: Methods and Applications. Cambridge University Press (1994)
15. Chen, E.Y., et al.: Enrichr: interactive and collaborative HTML5 gene list enrichment analysis tool. BMC Bioinf. **14**, 128 (2013)
16. Zhou, W., Liu, T., Saren, G., Liao, L., Fang, W., Zhao, H.: Comprehensive analysis of differentially expressed long non-coding RNAs in non-small cell lung cancer. Oncol. Lett. **18**, 1145–1156 (2019)
17. Wang, S.M., Ooi, L.L., Hui, K.M.: Upregulation of Rac GTPase-activating protein 1 is significantly associated with the early recurrence of human hepatocellular carcinoma. Clin. Cancer Res. **17**, 6040–6051 (2011)
18. Saigusa, S., et al.: Clinical significance of RacGAP1 expression at the invasive front of gastric cancer. Gastric Cancer **18**, 84–92 (2015)
19. Imaoka, H., et al.: RacGAP1 expression, increasing tumor malignant potential, as a predictive biomarker for lymph node metastasis and poor prognosis in colorectal cancer. Carcinogenesis **36**, 346–354 (2015)
20. Zhang, X., Ma, N., Yao, W., Li, S., Ren, Z.: RAD51 is a potential marker for prognosis and regulates cell proliferation in pancreatic cancer. Cancer Cell Int. **19**, 356 (2019)
21. Nowacka-Zawisza, M., et al.: RAD51 and XRCC3 polymorphisms are associated with increased risk of prostate cancer. J. Oncol. **2019**, 2976373 (2019)

22. Du, S., et al.: Long non-coding RNA MAGI2-AS3 inhibits breast cancer cell migration and invasion via sponging microRNA-374a. Cancer Biomarkers Sect. A Dis. markers **24**, 269–277 (2019)

23. Tang, H., et al.: miR-200b and miR-200c as prognostic factors and mediators of gastric cancer cell progression. Clin. Cancer Res. Official J. Am. Assoc. Cancer Res. **19**, 5602–5612 (2013)

24. Liu, X.G., et al.: High expression of serum miR-21 and tumor miR-200c associated with poor prognosis in patients with lung cancer. Med. Oncol. (Northwood, London, England) **29**, 618–626 (2012)

25. Liu, C., et al.: The microRNA miR-34a inhibits prostate cancer stem cells and metastasis by directly repressing CD44. Nat. Med. **17**, 211–215 (2011)

26. Li, N., et al.: miR-34a inhibits migration and invasion by down-regulation of c-Met expression in human hepatocellular carcinoma cells. Cancer Lett. **275**, 44–53 (2009)

27. Mishan, M.A., Tabari, M.A.K., Parnian, J., Fallahi, J., Mahrooz, A., Bagheri, A.: Functional mechanisms of miR-192 family in cancer. Genes Chromosom. Cancer **59**(12), 722–735 (2020)

28. Hoeijmakers, J.H.: DNA damage, aging, and cancer. N. Engl. J. Med. **361**, 1475–1485 (2009)

Intelligent Computing in Computational Biology

Detection of Drug-Drug Interactions Through Knowledge Graph Integrating Multi-attention with Capsule Network

Xiao-Rui Su[1,2,3], Zhu-Hong You[1,2,3(✉)], Hai-Cheng Yi[1,2,3], and Bo-Wei Zhao[1,2,3]

[1] The Xinjiang Technical Institute of Physics and Chemistry, Chinese Academy of Sciences,
Urumqi 830011, China
[2] University of Chinese Academy of Sciences, Beijing 100049, China
[3] Xinjiang Laboratory of Minority Speech and Language Information Processing,
Urumqi 830011, China

Abstract. Drug-drug interaction (DDI) prediction is a challenging problem in drug development and disease treatment. Current computational studies mainly solve this problem by designing features and extracting features from multi-sources. They have limitations in accuracy, knowledge and universality. In this paper, a universal computational method for DDI prediction is proposed. The model is made up of several identical layers. Each layer is composed by a multi-attention unit and a capsule unit. Multi-attention is responsibility for extracting neighborhood features and capturing representation under various semantic relation. Capsule unit is responsibility for features aggregating. Each layer can be viewed as first-order representation. High-order representation is obtained by increasing layers. The structure of whole method is easily understood and implemented. Experiment results show that proposed method can achieve a promising predicting performance and stands out when compared with several popular network embedding methods. Proposed method is a reliable model for DDI prediction and is suitable for other interaction predictions.

Keywords: Drug-drug interaction · Feature aggregation · Capsule network · Multi-attention · Knowledge graph representation learning

1 Introduction

Drug-drug interactions (DDIs) constitute an important concern in drug development and disease treatment [1]. Taking two or more drugs at the same time can affect efficacy and safety of drug profiles. Drug interactions are considered as the cause of adverse drug effects [2, 3], preventing disease treatment or threatening to patient life. As a result, detecting drug interactions has been widely exploited to accelerate drug discovery process and decrease public health costs.

In order to solve this issue, various DDI prediction methods and models have been proposed to date. Early prediction methods [4–11] relied on pharmacogenomics and pharmacology. This type of method concentrates on similarity calculating through drug

© Springer Nature Switzerland AG 2021
D.-S. Huang et al. (Eds.): ICIC 2021, LNAI 12838, pp. 423–432, 2021.
https://doi.org/10.1007/978-3-030-84532-2_38

basic information, such as drug molecular 2D/3D structures, fingerprints, pharmacology and indications, etc. However, these approaches can only deal with a limited range of DDI cases because of clinical and laboratory data lacking. With the development of scientific fields such as bioinformatics, systems biology and pharmacogenomics [12], big data sources of drug information are accessible, which accelerates the development of multi-source computational methods [13–20] for drug feature extraction. However, these multi-source computational methods cannot deal with unknown drugs and deep links because of local perspective, solving DDI prediction problem only from drug perspective and ignoring the integrity of whole molecular system. It is for this reason that knowledge graph-based computational prediction methods [21–24] which rely on data rich graph structure have received ever increasing attention due to their capability of enabling automatic, fast assessments and accurate prediction of possible DDIs.

Knowledge graph-based computational prediction methods are benefited from network representation learning development. At this stage, graph structure as an important data carrier is considered as the most suitable structure to present entities and their corresponding relationships. In addition, graph structure is suitable for most of application scenarios, such as communication network, citation network and even biomedical interaction network. For this reason, current studies concentrate on network representation learning, which aims to learn a low-dimension global representation for each of nodes. Compared with previous studies, network representation learning is able to handle complex and deep information. According to the learning strategy, there are three groups, which are Matrix Factorization-based model [25, 26], Random Walk-based model [27, 28], and Neural Network-based model [29, 30]. Meanwhile, a number of works are proposed based on representation learning for drug interaction prediction [22, 31–35].

Knowledge graph as a special case of graph structure is constructed by entities and relationships and is widely researched. Knowledge graph representation learning is harder than network representation learning since knowledge graph representation learning has to spend time to process semantic relationship, which exists as numerical in network representation learning. It is important to balance accuracy and efficiency in knowledge graph-based computational prediction model.

In this paper, we proposed a new computational method for DDI prediction based on knowledge graph representation learning. Multi-attention and capsule network are adopted and integrated into proposed method. The whole method is stacked by the same layer. The layer contains two units, one is multi-attention unit and the other is capsule network. Multi-attention is used to capture various semantic relation and capsule network is used to aggregate feature from different neighbors. Each layer in proposed method is able to capture first-order information. Proposed method is able to capture high-dimension structural information by stacking layers. We argue that proposed method is a better option for the DDI prediction task because of its promising results and universality.

2   Related Work

The development of computational methods for DDI prediction have experienced three periods. The first stage mainly focuses on similarity calculation. These methods utilized kinds of drug basic information to calculate similarity of drug pairs. Then, selecting drug pairs with high confidence as final results. For example, Vilar *et al.* [36] calculated drug fingerprints similarity to predict DDIs. Drug pair score was calculated by two drugs similarity multiply. In addition, they also used 2D and 3D to further detect drug target and side effect. The work of Guo *et al.* [11] extracted drug features by calculating drug SMILES (Simplified Molecular Input Line Entry Specification) similarity. They counted the number of times different substructures appeared and then recorded them in corresponding position. Finally, a vector whose length was equal to the number of substructures. Increasing information promotes the second stage. The approaches in this stage are good at using multi-sources information to predict DDIs. For example, Peng *et al.* [37] proposed an approach integrating six kinds of similarities of drugs by Bayesian neural network.

In recent, embedding methods are widely used in a widely range of applications. The third stage will follow. In this period, the computational methods attempt to learn graph structure and obtain a global representation for each of nodes. A large number of representation methods occur and are applied in biomedical interaction research. For instance, Su *et al.* [31] applied SDNE to extract drug node representation from a molecular association network. In addition, they integrated drug fingerprint feature with representation to construct a combined drug feature, which could be used in further link prediction task. Different from the previous one, Chen *et al.* [32] detected drug interactions using Node2Vec embedding methods. Knowledge graph embedding methods or models are also used in biomedical field. For example, KGNN [23] is based on both knowledge graph and neural network.

3   Materials and Methods

3.1   Dataset

In order to valid the predictive performance of proposed model, we test our model on OGB-biokg dataset [38], which is constructed by Stanford University. It is a biomedical knowledge graph containing five types of entities, comprising diseases, proteins, drugs, side effects and protein functions. There are 51 types of directed relations connecting two types of entities, including 39 kinds of drug-drug interactions, 8 kinds of protein-protein interaction, as well as drug-protein, drug-side effect, drug-protein, function-function relations. There are 10,533 approved drugs and 1,195,972 approved drug-drug interactions and 5,088,434 interactions, respectively. The statistics of the used datasets are summarized in Table 1.

3.2   Multi-attention Learning Strategy

Different from traditional graph structure, the relationship in knowledge graph is clearly exist and it is important for potential DDI prediction. Multi-attention learning strategy is adopted in proposed method in order to capture neighborhoods feature under various semantic relation.

More specifically, proposed method learns representation for each node layer by layer. We start by describing a single multi-attention learning layer, as the sole unit

Table 1. The statistic of OGB-biokg dataset.

OGB-biokg dataset properties	Number
#Drugs	10,533
#DDIs	1,195,972
#Entity	93,773
#Relation	51
#Triples	5,088,434

utilized throughout all of the proposed method used in our experiments. Each triple in OGB-biokg can be represented by $T = (h, r, t) \in \mathbb{N}$.

The input to multi-attention learning layer is a set of triples that head entities are drugs, $T = \{(h_1, r_1, t_1), (h_2, r_2, t_2), \ldots, (h_N, r_N, t_N)\}$. After original random embedding, triples can be represented as $\mathbf{h} = \{\vec{h}_1, \vec{h}_2, \vec{h}_3, \ldots, \vec{h}_N\}$, $\vec{h}_i \in \mathbb{R}^F$, $\mathbf{r} = \{\vec{r}_1, \vec{r}_2, \vec{r}_3, \ldots, \vec{r}_N\}$, $\mathbf{t} = \{\vec{t}_1, \vec{t}_2, \vec{t}_3, \ldots, \vec{t}_N\}$, $\vec{h}_i, \vec{r}_i, \vec{t}_i \in \mathbb{R}^F$. The output of this layer is a new set of node features, $\mathbf{O} = \{\vec{O}_1, \vec{O}_2, \vec{O}_3, \ldots, \vec{O}_N\}$, $\vec{O}_i \in \mathbb{R}^F$. In order to utilize sufficient triple information and specialize semantic relation, completing the mapping: $m : \vec{h} \times \vec{r} \rightarrow \vec{h'}$, $\vec{t} \times \vec{r} \rightarrow \vec{t'}$ for each node. Then perform self-attention on the nodes $a : \mathbb{R}^F \times \mathbb{R}^F \rightarrow \mathbb{R}$ computes attention coefficients. Considering the graph structural information, only neighborhood nodes are computed, named first-order neighbors of drug node. Then the attention weight after normalization can be represented by:

$$e_{ij} = a\left(m\left(\vec{h}_i\right), m\left(\vec{t}_j\right)\right), \ j \in S(i) \tag{1}$$

$$\alpha_{ij} = \frac{\exp\left(e_{ij}\right)}{\sum_{k \in S(i)} \exp(e_{ik})} \tag{2}$$

Where $S(i)$ represents the neighborhood set of node i, which can be obtained by interaction matrix. For node i, the output $\mathbf{O}$ is $\{\alpha_{i1}\vec{t}_1, \alpha_{i2}\vec{t}_2, \alpha_{i3}\vec{t}_3, \ldots, \alpha_{iN}\vec{t}_N\} \in \mathbb{R}^{N \times F}$. If node i and node j has no directly relation, then set α_{ij} as 0.

The multi-attention mechanism can increase the adaptability of the model to various relationships and improve the robustness of the model. In fact, the embedding of relation can be viewed as a trainable attention weight matrix.

3.3 Capsule Network

After obtaining attention weights, it is important to aggregate features. Different from previous aggregation strategy, capsule network is adopted in proposed method. Capsule network aggregate output features dimension by dimension. Each of dimension is called a capsule and setting a serious trainable weight matrix $\mathcal{W} \in \mathbb{R}^{C \times N}$, where C is number of weight matrices and N represents node number to scan whole capsules. The aggregation feature is obtained after routing process. The whole process can be formulated by:

$$\mathbf{O'} = routing\,(\mathcal{W}\mathbf{O}) \tag{3}$$

Where $\mathbf{O'}$ is the output of capsule unit and the learning layer, which can be viewed as the drug node first-order representation.

3.4 Knowledge Graph Representation Learning

The whole model is stacked by multi-attention unit and capsule unit (see Fig. 1). Each layer is constructed by a multi-attention unit and capsule unit. As a result, the layer number is a hyperparameter. In addition, in order to capture high-order structural information. Tail nodes of next layer directly interacts with tail nodes of current layer. The entire representation learning strategy can be formulated by:

$$e_{ij}^k = ||_{k=1}^K a\left(m\left(\overrightarrow{h_i}\right), m(\overrightarrow{t_j})\right), \; j \in S(i) \tag{4}$$

$$\alpha_{ij}^k = ||_{k=1}^K \frac{\exp\left(e_{ij}^k\right)}{\sum_{m \in S(i)} \exp(e_{im})} \tag{5}$$

$$O = ||_{k=1}^K \alpha_{ij}^k \, \mathbf{t} \tag{6}$$

$$\mathbf{O'} = ||_{k=1}^K routing\left(\mathcal{W}^k O^k\right) \tag{7}$$

$$Tail^{next} = S\left(Tail^{current}\right) \tag{8}$$

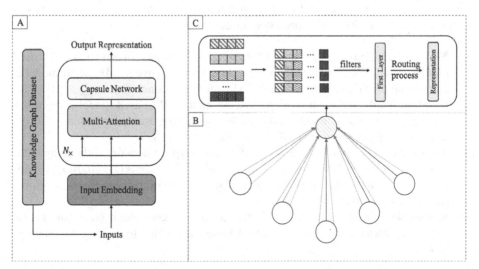

Fig. 1. A) An illustration of proposed method. B) An illustration of multi-attention (K = 3). The black nodes represent neighborhood nodes of colorful node. Colorful node is targeted node. Different arrow colors denote independent attention computations. C) An illustration of capsule network unit, aiming to aggregate features from first-order neighbors.

3.5 Performance Evaluation Indicators

Proposed method is tested by five-fold cross validation. The entire dataset is randomly divided into 5 parts. In each turn, one part as test dataset and the other four parts as training dataset. The whole process has 5 turns. As a result, each part can be tested. Five metrics are used to evaluate the method performance, comprising Accuracy, Precision, Recall, F1 Score and Area Under Curve (AUC).

$$Accuracy = \frac{TN + TP}{FP + TP + FN + TN} \tag{9}$$

$$Precision = \frac{TP}{TP + FP} \tag{10}$$

$$Recall = \frac{TP}{TP + FN} \tag{11}$$

$$F1\ Score = \frac{2 * Precision * Recall}{Precision + Recall} \tag{12}$$

4 Experiments

4.1 Baseline

As mentioned above, there are four kinds of representation learning methods in total. In this section, we introduce and implement a few baseline models from four types to demonstrate the effectiveness of proposed model.

(1) **Matrix Factorization:** Laplacian [25] as one of the most representative MF-based models, is selected as MF baseline. The learning objective of MF-based model is factorizing the matrix of input data into lower dimensional matrices.

(2) **Random Walk:** Different from MF-based model, RW-based model generates a sequence of nodes randomly and then learns the representation from sequence. DeepWalk [27] is selected as DW-based baseline model.

(3) **Neural Network:** In this section, we choose the typical network embedding algorithms LINE [29] as NN-based baseline model. LINE designs two kinds of proximity to learn graph representation, which is good for learning both local and global structures of networks.

(4) **Knowledge Graph:** KGNN [23] is based on both knowledge graph and neural network, which can capture structure of knowledge graph by mining the relations in KG.

4.2 Prediction Performance of Proposed Method

During the training process, five-fold cross validation is adopted to test proposed method. Table 2 reports the performance of proposed method across five-fold cross validation on OGB-biokg dataset.

Table 2. Performance of proposed method on OGB-biokg dataset.

Fold	Accuracy	Precision	Recall	F1 Score	AUC
0	0.8632	0.8584	0.8705	0.8644	0.9315
1	0.8637	0.8591	0.8705	0.8648	0.9319
2	0.8630	0.8660	0.8733	0.8646	0.9309
3	0.8636	0.8564	0.8735	0.8648	0.9311
4	0.8635	0.8594	0.8708	0.8651	0.9316
Average	**0.8634 ± 0.0003**	**0.8599 ± 0.0032**	**0.8717 ± 0.0014**	**0.8647 ± 0.0002**	**0.9314 ± 0.0004**

According to the results shown in Table 2. Proposed method achieved an average accuracy of 0.8634, an average precision of 0.8599, an average recall of 0.8717, an average F1 score of 0.8647 and an average AUC value of 0.9314, which demonstrated that proposed model had a strong predictive ability. In addition, the standard deviations of five metrics were 0.0003, 0.0032, 0.0014, 0.0002 and 0.0004, respectively. Small standard deviations indicated that applying proposed method to learn representation for node in network was stability.

4.3 Comparison of Several Types of Representation Learning Method

To further valid the effectiveness of proposed method, several baseline models are used in the same task. Meanwhile, it is necessary to illustrate parameters used in baseline models and proposed model. For DeepWalk, the settings are that walk length is 80 and number of walks is 10. For LINE, we adapt first order proximity and second order proximity together. Moreover, the final dimension of embedding is set as 32. The results are shown in Table 3.

Table 3. Performance of proposed methods and baseline models.

Methods	Accuracy	Precision	Recall	F1 Score	AUC
Laplacian	0.7955 ± 0.0050	0.7994 ± 0.0045	0.8135 ± 0.0051	0.8008 ± 0.0049	0.8634 ± 0.0047
DeepWalk	0.7516 ± 0.0041	0.7443 ± 0.0033	0.7675 ± 0.0049	0.7556 ± 0.0044	0.8148 ± 0.0049
LINE	0.7504 ± 0.0076	0.7468 ± 0.0058	0.7721 ± 0.0065	0.7541 ± 0.0073	0.8155 ± 0.0068
KGNN	0.8355 ± 0.0013	0.8365 ± 0.0031	0.8335 ± 0.0028	0.8340 ± 0.0023	0.8868 ± 0.0044
Ours	**0.8634 ± 0.0003**	**0.8599 ± 0.0032**	**0.8717 ± 0.0014**	**0.8647 ± 0.0002**	**0.9314 ± 0.0004**

On the one hand, it can be observed that proposed method performs better than any of baseline models among five metrics, which mainly because proposed methods took knowledge and semantic relation into consideration. In addition, proposed model concentrated on more important graph part by multi-attention mechanism. Compared with proposed method, Laplacian, DeepWalk and LINE model paid more attention on network structure, ignoring the relationship. Though KGNN could capture semantic relation, our method was more adaptable since attention mechanism adopting.

On the other hand, proposed method had the least standard deviations among five metrics. As a result, it could be obtained that proposed method is more stable than other models, which was suitable for large-scale knowledge graph applications and interaction prediction. Consequently, proposed method was not only an accurate but stable prediction model.

5 Conclusion

In conclusion, an end-to-end prediction model was proposed for drug-drug interaction prediction based on multi-attention and capsule network. In order to capture node representation under various sematic space, multi-attention is adopted to learn neighbor nodes and targeted nodes. In order to aggregate neighbor feature and targeted feature reasonably, capsule network is adopted to aggregate representations. The whole model is easily understood and stacked by attention unit and capsule unit. The easily structure decides that proposed method is easy to be applied to other fields. Experiment results prove that proposed method is suitable for DDI prediction and is a promising model.

Funding. This work was supported in part by Awardee of the NSFC Excellent Young Scholars Program, under Grant 61722212, in part by the National Natural Science Foundation of China, under Grants 61702444, in part by the Chinese Postdoctoral Science Foundation, under Grant 2019M653804, in part by the West Light Foundation of The Chinese Academy of Sciences, under Grant 2018-XBQNXZ-B-008.

References

1. Evans, W.E., McLeod, H.L.: Pharmacogenomics—drug disposition, drug targets, and side effects. N. Engl. J. Med. **348**, 538–549 (2003)
2. Edwards, I.R., Aronson, J.K.: Adverse drug reactions: definitions, diagnosis, and management. Lancet **356**, 1255–1259 (2000)
3. Meyer, U.A.: Pharmacogenetics and adverse drug reactions. Lancet **356**, 1667–1671 (2000)
4. Jia, J., Zhu, F., Ma, X., Cao, Z.W., Li, Y.X., Chen, Y.Z.: Mechanisms of drug combinations: interaction and network perspectives. Nat. Rev. Drug Discov. **8**, 111–128 (2009)
5. Palleria, C., Paolo, A.D., Giofrè, C., Caglioti, C., Gallelli, L.: Pharmacokinetic drug-drug interaction and their implication in clinical management. J. Res. Med. Sci. **18**, 601–610 (2013)
6. Vilar, S., et al.: Similarity-based modeling in large-scale prediction of drug-drug interactions. Nat. Protoc. **9**, 2147–2163 (2014)
7. Rohani, N., Eslahchi, C.: Drug-drug interaction predicting by neural network using integrated Similarity. Sci. Rep. **9**, 1–11 (2019)
8. Sridhar, D., Fakhraei, S., Getoor, L.: A probabilistic approach for collective similarity-based drug–drug interaction prediction. Bioinformatics **32**, 3175–3182 (2016)
9. Guo, Z.-H., You, Z.-H., Li, L.-P., Chen, Z.-H., Yi, H.-C., Wang, Y.-B.: Inferring drug-miRNA associations by integrating drug SMILES and MiRNA sequence information. In: Huang, D.-S., Jo, K.-H. (eds.) Intelligent Computing Theories and Application. LNCS, vol. 12464, pp. 279–289. Springer, Cham (2020). https://doi.org/10.1007/978-3-030-60802-6_25

10. Wang, T., et al.: A gated recurrent unit model for drug repositioning by combining comprehensive similarity measures and Gaussian interaction profile kernel. In: Huang, D.-S., Jo, K.-H., Huang, Z.-K. (eds.) Intelligent Computing Theories and Application. LNCS, vol. 11644, pp. 344–353. Springer, Cham (2019). https://doi.org/10.1007/978-3-030-26969-2_33
11. Guo, Z.-H., Yi, H.-C., You, Z.-H.: Construction and comprehensive analysis of a molecular association network via lncRNA–miRNA –disease–drug–protein graph. Cells **8**(8), 866 (2019)
12. Vilar, S., Hripcsak, G.: The role of drug profiles as similarity metrics: Applications to repurposing, adverse effects detection and drug-drug interactions. Briefings Bioinf. **18**, bbw048 (2016)
13. Ji, Z., Su, J., Liu, C., Wang, H., Huang, D., Zhou, X.: Integrating genomics and proteomics data to predict drug effects using binary linear programming. PLoS ONE **9**, e102798 (2014)
14. Wang, Y.-B., You, Z.-H., Yang, S., Yi, H.-C., Chen, Z.-H., Zheng, K.: A deep learning-based method for drug-target interaction prediction based on long short-term memory neural network. BMC Med. Inform. Decis. Mak. **20**, 1–9 (2020)
15. Wang, L., You, Z.-H., Li, L.-P., Yan, X.: RFDTI: using rotation forest with feature weighted for drug-target interaction prediction from drug molecular structure and protein sequence. bioRxiv (2020)
16. Li, Y., Liu, X.-Z., You, Z.-H., Li, L.-P., Guo, J.-X., Wang, Z.: A computational approach for predicting drug–target interactions from protein sequence and drug substructure fingerprint information. Int. J. Intell. Syst. **36**(1), 593–609 (2021)
17. Zhan, X., et al.: Prediction of drug-target interactions by ensemble learning method from protein sequence and drug fingerprint. IEEE Access **8**, 185465–185476 (2020)
18. Huang, Y.-A., Hu, P., Chan, K.C., You, Z.-H.: Graph convolution for predicting associations between miRNA and drug resistance. Bioinformatics **36**, 851–858 (2020)
19. Huang, Y.-A., You, Z.-H., Chen, X.: A systematic prediction of drug-target interactions using molecular fingerprints and protein sequences. Curr. Protein Pept. Sci. **19**(5), 468–478 (2018)
20. Wang, L., et al.: A computational-based method for predicting drug–target interactions by using stacked autoencoder deep neural network. J. Comput. Biol. **25**, 361–373 (2018)
21. Dai, Y., Guo, C., Guo, W., Eickhoff, C.: Drug–drug interaction prediction with Wasserstein adversarial autoencoder-based knowledge graph embeddings. Brief. Bioinf. (2020)
22. Karim, M.R., Cochez, M., Jares, J.B., Uddin, M., Beyan, O., Decker, S.: Drug-drug interaction prediction based on knowledge graph embeddings and convolutional-LSTM network (2019)
23. Lin, X., Quan, Z., Wang, Z.J., Ma, T., Zeng, X.: KGNN: knowledge graph neural network for drug-drug interaction prediction. In: 29th International Joint Conference on Artificial Intelligence and 17th Pacific Rim International Conference on Artificial Intelligence, IJCAI-PRICAI-20 (2020)
24. Wang, Z., Zhang, J., Feng, J., Chen, Z.: Knowledge graph embedding by translating on hyperplanes. In: AAAI, pp. 1112–1119. Citeseer (2014)
25. Belkin, M., Niyogi, P.: Laplacian eigenmaps for dimensionality reduction and data representation. Neural Comput. **15**(6), 1373–1396 (2003)
26. Cao, S., Lu, W., Xu, Q.: GraRep: learning graph representations with global structural information. In: Proceedings of the 24th ACM International on Conference on Information and Knowledge Management, Melbourne, Australia, pp. 891–900. Association for Computing Machinery (2015)
27. Perozzi, B., Al-Rfou, R., Skiena, S.: DeepWalk: online learning of social representations. In: Proceedings of the 20th ACM SIGKDD International Conference on Knowledge Discovery and Data Mining, New York, New York, USA, pp. 701–710. Association for Computing Machinery (2014)
28. Grover, A., Leskovec, J.: node2vec: scalable feature learning for networks. In: ACM SIGKDD International Conference on Knowledge Discovery & Data Mining (2016)

29. Tang, J., Qu, M., Wang, M., Zhang, M., Yan, J., Mei, Q.: Line: large-scale information network embedding. In: Proceedings of the 24th International Conference on World Wide Web, pp. 1067–1077. International World Wide Web Conferences Steering Committee (2015)

30. Zhang, Q.C., et al.: Structure-based prediction of protein–protein interactions on a genome-wide scale. Nature **490**, 556 (2012)

31. Su, X.-R., You, Z.-H., Zhou, J.-R., Yi, H.-C., Li, X.: A novel computational approach for predicting drug-target interactions via network representation learning. In: Huang, D.-S., Jo, K.-H. (eds.) Intelligent Computing Theories and Application. LNCS, vol. 12464, pp. 481–492. Springer, Cham (2020). https://doi.org/10.1007/978-3-030-60802-6_42

32. Chen, Z.-H., You, Z.-H., Guo, Z.-H., Yi, H.-C., Luo, G.-X., Wang, Y.-B.: Predicting drug-target interactions by Node2vec node embedding in molecular associations network. In: Huang, D.-S., Jo, K.-H. (eds.) Intelligent Computing Theories and Application. LNCS, vol. 12464, pp. 348–358. Springer, Cham (2020). https://doi.org/10.1007/978-3-030-60802-6_31

33. Hu, P., et al.: Learning from deep representations of multiple networks for predicting drug-target interactions. In: Huang, D.-S., Jo, K.-H., Huang, Z.-K. (eds.) Intelligent Computing Theories and Application. LNCS, vol. 11644, pp. 151–161. Springer, Cham (2019). https://doi.org/10.1007/978-3-030-26969-2_14

34. Yi, H.-C., You, Z.-H., Huang, D.-S., Guo, Z.-H., Chan, K.C., Li, Y.: Learning representations to predict intermolecular interactions on large-scale heterogeneous molecular association network. iScience **23**, 101261 (2020)

35. Chen, Z.-H., Yi, H.-C., Guo, Z.-H., Luo, G.-X., Wang, Y.-B.: Prediction of drug-target interactions from multi-molecular network based on deep walk embedding model. Front. Bioeng. Biotechnol. **8**, 338 (2020)

36. Vilar, S., Uriarte, E., Santana, L., Tatonetti, N.P., Friedman, C.: Detection of drug-drug interactions by modeling interaction profile fingerprints. PLOS ONE **8**, e58321 (2013)

37. Peng, L., et al.: Large-scale exploration and analysis of drug combinations. Bioinformatics **31**, 2007–2016 (2015)

38. Hu, W., et al.: Open graph benchmark: datasets for machine learning on graphs (2020)

SCEC: A Novel Single-Cell Classification Method Based on Cell-Pair Ensemble Learning

Wei Fan, Haonan Peng, Siyin Luo, Chujie Fang, and Yuanyuan Li$^{(\boxtimes)}$

Wuhan Institute of Technology, Wuhan 430205, China

Abstract. With the development of single-cell sequencing technology, the increasing amount of single-cell transcription data enables a deeper understanding of cellular heterogeneity and mechanisms at the cell level. Single-cell type identification is a crucial step of single-cell RNA sequencing (scRNA-seq) data analysis. The classification of single-cells and the discovery of new cell types are of great significance for oncology, immunology, and developmental biology research. Various data preprocessing approaches and classification algorithms have been applied to scRNA-seq data analysis. However, single-cell type identification methods that integrate multiple dimensionality reduction methods and unsupervised classification are still rare. Here, we proposed SCEC (Single Cell Ensemble Classify), an ensemble learning based approach, to integrate the clustering results of different clustering methods and SCEC significantly improves type identification on several representative datasets. Furthermore, the consensus result given by SCEC also shows obvious advantages in the process of data visualization. The advantages in classification and visualization performance make SCEC a promising method for large-scale scRNA-seq data.

Keywords: Single-cell classification · Ensemble learning · scRNA-seq · Cell type identification

1 Introduction

It is well known that the analysis of gene and protein expression sequence or time sequence is involved in many bioinformatics problems. Each cell has its unique phenotype and biological functions, which are reflected in different expression levels of RNA. Bulk RNA-sequencing is based on the study of a large number of cells, and its expression level is the relative level of a group of cells. Therefore, bulk RNA-sequencing cannot analyze the key differences of single cells. The emergence of single-cell RNA-sequencing (scRNA-seq) technology solves the above problems. It uses optimized next-generation sequencing technology to provide gene expression information of single cells, so it can better reflect the internal molecular biology process of specific cells [1]. With the continuous development of high-throughput sequencing technology, single-cell RNA sequencing has become a powerful method that can simultaneously measure gene expression differences among thousands of cells at the single-cell level, thereby revealing cell identity and function or discovering novel cell types [2].

© Springer Nature Switzerland AG 2021
D.-S. Huang et al. (Eds.): ICIC 2021, LNAI 12838, pp. 433–444, 2021.
https://doi.org/10.1007/978-3-030-84532-2_39

Clustering cell population based on gene expression profile of cells is a key step to define the cell type during single cell analysis [3]. The main process of single-cell clustering includes the preprocessing of single-cell RNA sequencing raw data, feature selection, dimensionality reduction, data visualization, clustering analysis, and evaluation [4]. Many clustering methods have been used to detect cell types from single-cell RNA sequencing data. These methods can be roughly divided into four categories: k-means clustering, hierarchical clustering, community detection based clustering, and density-based clustering. SAIC [5] uses iterative k-means clustering to determine the best subset of characteristic genes that divide single-cell into different categories. SC3 [6] integrates the k-means clustering results with different initial conditions as the consensus clustering result. RaceID2 [7] replaced k-means clustering with k-medoids clustering and used Pearson correlation coefficient instead of Euclidean Distance as a cluster distance metric. RaceID3 [8], as the advanced version of RaceID2, adds feature selection and uses the random forest to reclassify the k-means clustering results. CIDR [9] integrates dimensionality reduction and hierarchical clustering-based algorithms into single-cell RNA sequencing data analysis and uses implicit interpolation to achieve the dropout effect, providing a stable estimate of the distance between pairs of cells. BackSPIN [10] provides a bi-clustering method based on divisive hierarchical clustering and classifying points into neighborhoods to simultaneously cluster genes and cells. SINCERA [11], as a simple analysis process, uses hierarchical clustering with central Pearson correlation and average link method to identify cell types. Louvain [12] is the most popular community detection algorithm, which is widely used in single-cell RNA sequencing data processing. The most popular density-based clustering algorithm is DBSCAN [13], which does not require a preset number of clusters, but two additional parameters need to be set, including *eps* and the minimum number of points *minPts* to form dense regions, these parameters will affect the final clustering results. Besides, algorithms such as SIMLR [14] and SinNLRR [15] based on spectral clustering algorithms can also be used for single-cell clustering, but they require a preset number of clusters.

In recent years, comprehensive classification methods such as neural networks and ensemble learning have also been gradually applied to single-cell clustering. The classification methods using neural networks usually combine autoencoders to reduce the dimensionality of the gene expression matrix, such as DESC [16] and VASC [17]. ScClassify [18], which adopts ensemble learning, integrates a variety of gene selection methods and k-NN algorithm to obtain better consistent clustering results. However, the current research on single-cell clustering algorithms that integrate the results of multiple clustering methods for ensemble learning is still relatively scarce.

In this paper, we intend to cluster scRNA-seq data based on a combination of multiple dimensionality reduction methods and multiple unsupervised learning algorithms. We proposed an ensemble classify approach named Single Cell Ensemble Classify (SCEC) based on evaluating the cell-pair relationship. This method uses supervised learning methods to integrate the results of various combinations to get more reliable results. The main process is shown in Fig. 1. Firstly, we use 7 methods to reduce the dimensionality of the data. Secondly, we use four unsupervised clustering algorithms to obtain clustering results. Then we utilize the clustering results to construct an indicator vector for each pair of cells, perform neural network training and prediction, and get the consensus result.

Finally, we tested the performance of this method on several datasets, and demonstrate that SCEC brings significant accuracy improvement over competing basic clustering methods.

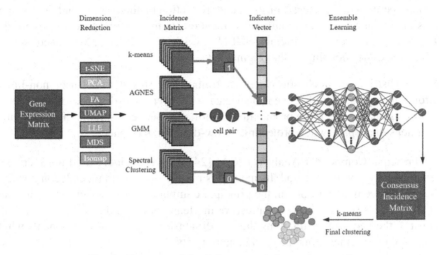

Fig. 1. Structure of the fully connected neural network

2 Materials and Method

2.1 Datasets

SCEC accepts scRNA-seq data in the form of an $n \times g$ expression matrix denoted as $X_{n \times g}$ where n is the number of cells and g is the number of genes. In this article, we collected several datasets including the PBMCs dataset [19], Chu cell type dataset [20], Klein dataset [21], and Zeisel dataset [22] from works of literature. These datasets can be download from Gene Expression Omnibus (GEO) by GEO accession number. The attributes and sources of each dataset are shown in Table 1.

Table 1. Datasets used for validation of SCEC

Datasets	Numbers of cells	Numbers of cell types	Numbers of genes used	Data sources
PBMCs	3694	6	6713	GSE92495
Chu cell type	1018	7	19097	GSE75748
Klein	2717	4	24175	GSE65525
Zeisel	3005	9	19972	GSE60361

2.2 Dimension Reduction Methods

Due to the high-dimensionality and high noise characteristics of single-cell RNA sequencing data, many single-cell clustering methods combine classic dimensionality reduction operations. Effective dimensionality reduction methods can avoid the curse of dimensionality and are critical to the subsequent clustering performance. In this article, we applied seven methods including t-SNE, PCA, FA, UMAP, LLE, MDS, and Isomap to reduce the dimensionality of the original data.

t-SNE. T-Distributed Stochastic Neighbor Embedding (t-SNE) [23] uses non-linear manifolds to represent high-dimensional data. It converts the distance of samples in high-dimensional space to the probability of similarity between samples and maintains high-dimensional space when projecting to low-dimensional space.

PCA. Principal Component Analysis (PCA) [24] is a very widely used unsupervised dimensionality reduction method. Its method is mainly to perform eigendecomposition of the covariance matrix to obtain the principal components (eigenvectors) of the data and their weights (eigenvalues) and preserve the features in the dataset that contribute the most to the variance by retaining the low-dimensional principal components while ignoring the high-dimensional principal components.

FA. Feature Agglomeration (FA) uses agglomerative clustering to group features that look very similar, thus decreasing the number of features.

UMAP. Uniform Manifold Approximation and Projection (UMAP) [25] is constructed from a theoretical framework based on Riemannian geometry and algebraic topology. The UMAP algorithm is competitive with t-SNE for visualization quality, and arguably preserves more of the global structure with superior run time performance. Furthermore, UMAP has no computational restrictions on embedding dimension, making it viable as a general-purpose dimension reduction technique for machine learning.

LLE. Locally Linear Embedding (LLE) [26] tries to maintain the linear relationship between samples in the neighborhood while reducing dimensionality.

MDS. Multidimensional scaling (MDS) [27] seeks a low-dimensional representation of the data in which the distances respect well the distances in the original high-dimensional space.

Isomap. Isometric Mapping (Isomap) [28] uses the same core algorithm as MDS, the difference lies in the calculation of the distance matrix in the original space. A lot of data is non-linear structure, it is not suitable to directly use the PCA algorithm and MDS algorithm.

Among these methods, we use t-SNE to reduce the data to two dimensions, and other methods reduce it to 20 dimensions according to some experience and works of literature.

2.3 Unsupervised Base Classifiers

We implemented 4 unsupervised clustering methods including k-means [29], agglomerative nesting (AGNES) [30], Gaussian Mixture Model (GMM) [31], and spectral clustering [32] on the low dimensional data.

K-means. K-means algorithm selects k points in the data set as the initial center of each cluster according to a certain strategy and then observes the remaining data, divides the data into the clusters closest to the k points, that is to say, divides the data into k clusters. The new clusters formed may not be the best division by dividing only once. Therefore, in the new clusters generated, the center point of each cluster is recalculated, and then the division is performed again until the result of each division remains unchanged.

AGNES. The agglomerative nesting algorithm initially treats each object as a cluster, and then these clusters are merged step by step according to certain criteria. The clustering process is repeated until all objects meet the number of clusters. There are many different calculation methods for the similarity between two clusters, we use 'ward' linkage in our SCEC method.

GMM. The Gaussian Mixture Model is a clustering model that uses k Gaussian models and each Gaussian model refers to a probability distribution of the following form:

$$P(y \mid \theta) = \sum_{k=1}^{K} \alpha_k \phi(y \mid \theta_k)$$

Where $\alpha_k (\alpha_k \geq 0, \sum_{k=1}^{k} \alpha_k = 1)$ is the weight of each sub-model, $\phi(y \mid \theta_k)$ is the Gaussian distribution density function of the sub-model, while the $\theta_k = (\mu_k, \sigma_k^2), \phi(y \mid \theta_k) = \frac{1}{\sqrt{2\pi}\sigma_k} \exp\left(-\frac{(y-\mu_k)^2}{2\sigma_k^2} \right)$ is the k-th sub-model.

Spectral Clustering. The spectral clustering algorithm regards each object in the dataset as a vertex of the graph, and quantifies the similarity between the vertices as the weight of the corresponding vertex connecting edge, so that an undirected weighted graph based on the similarity is obtained, so the clustering problem can be transformed into a problem of dividing the graph. The optimal division criterion based on graph theory is to maximize the internal similarity of the divided sub-graphs and minimize the similarity between the sub-graphs.

Based on 7 dimensionality reduction methods and 4 unsupervised clustering methods, we got $4 \times 7 = 28$ base classifiers. Then we construct an incidence matrix for the prediction results of each clustering method:

$$M_{ij}^m = \begin{cases} 1, & \text{cell } i \text{ and cell } j \text{ belong to the same type} \\ 0, & \text{cell } i \text{ and cell } j \text{ belong to different types} \end{cases}$$

Where $m = 1, 2, \ldots, 28$ represents the index of 28 unsupervised base classifiers, and $i, j = 1, 2, \ldots, n$ represent the cells of the dataset. M_{ij}^m indicates whether cell i and cell j belong to the same type in the result of the m th base classifier.

Besides, we also construct a true incidence matrix based on the true labels of all cells:

$$M_{ij}^{true} = \begin{cases} 1, & \text{cell } i \text{ and cell } j \text{ truly belong to the same type} \\ 0, & \text{cell } i \text{ and cell } j \text{ truly belong to different types} \end{cases}$$

2.4 Ensemble Learning

First, we construct an indicator vector for each pair of cells according to the incidence matrixes of all base classifiers:

$$I_{ij} = \left(M_{ij}^1, M_{ij}^2, \ldots, M_{ij}^m \right)^T$$

For each pair of cell i and cell j, I_{ij} indicates whether they belong to the same type in the results of m base classifiers. Obviously, a dataset of n cells will get $n(n-1)/2$ indicator vectors.

Then we implemented a fully connected neural network (FCNN) with I_{ij} as input, and it will output the probability p_{ij} that cell i and cell j belong to the same type. The structure of FCNN is shown in Fig. 2. The neuron number of the input layer is 32, the neuron numbers of each hidden layer are 32, 64, 32, and 16. One of the hidden layers is activated by the relu function. The output layer of the neural network is activated by the sigmoid function:

$$\sigma(x) = \frac{1}{1 + e^{-x}}$$

It inputs real values and "squeezes" them to the range of 0 to 1, which is suitable for the case where the output is probability.

The loss function is defined by binary cross-entropy:

$$L = -\sum_{l=1}^{s} \hat{y}_l \log y_l + \left(1 - \hat{y}_l\right) \log(1 - y_l)$$

Where l represents a pair of cell i and j in the batch size s, y_l represents the prediction probability that cell pair l belong to the same type, while $\hat{y}_l = M_{ij}^{true}$ represent the true label of whether cell pair l belong to the same type.

We use Adaptive Moment Estimation (ADAM) as the optimizer of the FCNN. The learning rate, batch size, and epoch number are set differently according to the size of the dataset. Datasets are shuffled before training, and each dataset is divided into two parts, training set, and validation set with a ratio of 4:1.

After training, we use the trained FCNN to predict the cell types and get the consensus incidence matrix:

$$M_{ij}^{consensus} = \begin{cases} 1, & \text{cell } i \text{ and cell } j \text{ belong to the same type} \\ 0, & \text{cell } i \text{ and cell } j \text{ belong to different types} \end{cases}$$

In fact, the consensus incidence matrix represents the final prediction result for the probability of each pair of cells belonging to the same cell type, the elements in the matrix are not 1 or 0 but consecutive values between 0 and 1. Indeed, this matrix may be regarded as the similarity matrix of the cells.

Finally, we use the k-means clustering method to cluster the consensus incidence matrix to get the final clustering result.

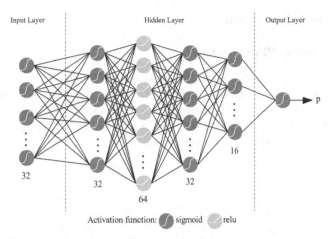

Fig. 2. Structure of the fully connected neural network.

2.5 Evaluation Metrics

Two metrics were used to evaluate the clustering results in this study, including adjusted Rand index (ARI) [33] and normalized mutual information (NMI) [34]. Given the two clustering assignments U and V on a set of n data points, a is the number of pairs of elements that are in the same set in U and the same set in V, b is the number of pairs of elements that are in different sets in U and different sets in V, the Rand index (RI) is computed by:

$$RI = \frac{a+b}{C_n^2}$$

Where C_n^2 is the total number of all possible element pairs in the (unsorted) data set.

However, RI scores cannot guarantee that random label assignments will achieve values close to zero (especially if the number of clusters is the same order of magnitude as the number of samples). To offset this effect, adjusted Rand index (ARI) was defined as:

$$ARI = \frac{RI - E[RI]}{max(RI) - E[RI]}$$

The mutual information (MI) of U and V is given by:

$$MI(U,V) = \sum_{i=1}^{|U|} \sum_{j=1}^{|V|} \frac{|U_i \cap V_j|}{N} log \left(\frac{N|U_i \cap V_j|}{|U_i||V_j|} \right)$$

And the normalized mutual information is defined as:

$$NMI(U,V) = \frac{MI(U,V)}{\sqrt{H(U)H(V)}}$$

$ARI \in [-1, 1]$, $NMI \in [0, 1]$, and the larger the value of them, the more consistent the clustering results are with the real situation.

3 Results and Discussion

3.1 Performance on PBMCs Dataset

In the PBMCs dataset, there are 3694 cells including 6 different cell types: B cell, NK cell, monocyte, CD4+ T cell, CD8+ T cell, and Dendritic cell. The ARI value of SCEC is 0.8640 while the best ARI value of base classifiers is 0.7573 (Spectral clustering with UMAP). The NMI value of SCEC is 0.7430 while the best NMI value of base classifiers is 0.6499 (AGNES with UMAP), showing in Fig. 3.

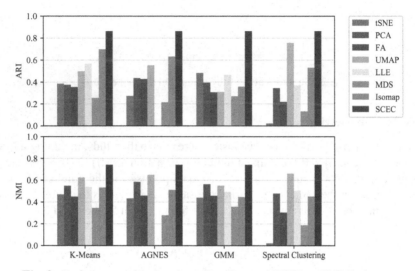

Fig. 3. Performance of various base classifiers and SCEC on PMBCs dataset.

3.2 Performance on Chu Cell Type Dataset

In the Chu cell type dataset, there are 1018 cells including 7 different cell types: H1 embryonic stem cell, H9 embryonic stem cell, human foreskin fibroblast, neuronal progenitor cell, definitive endoderm cell, endothelial cell, and trophoblast-like cell. The ARI value of SCEC is 0.8466 while the best ARI value of base classifiers is 0.7103 (AGNES with MDS). The NMI value of SCEC is 0.8993 while the best NMI value of base classifiers is 0.8317 (AGNES with MDS), showing in Fig. 4.

3.3 Performance on Klein Cell Type Dataset

In the Klein cell type dataset, there are 2717 cells including 4 different cell types. The ARI value of SCEC is 0.9767 while the best ARI value of base classifiers is 0.9190 (Spectral clustering with LLE). The NMI value of SCEC is 0.9536 while the best NMI value of base classifiers is 0.8833 (Spectral clustering with LLE), showing in Fig. 5.

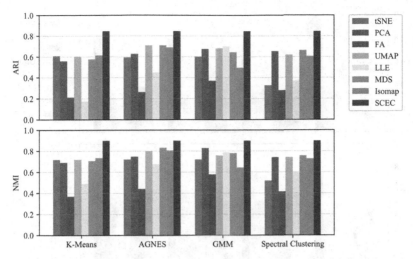

Fig. 4. Performance of various base classifiers and SCEC on Chu cell type dataset.

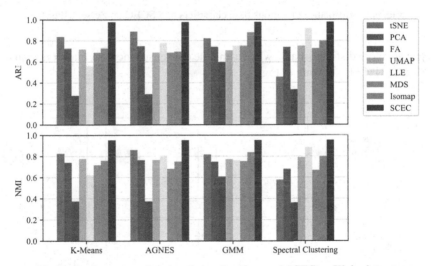

Fig. 5. Performance of various base classifiers and SCEC on Klein dataset.

3.4 Performance on Zeisel Cell Type Dataset

In the Zeisel cell type dataset, there are 3005 cells including 9 different cell types. The ARI value of SCEC is 0.8072 while the best ARI value of base classifiers is 0.7146 (AGNES with LLE). The NMI value of SCEC is 0.7610 while the best NMI value of base classifiers is 0.6442 (AGNES with LLE), showing in Fig. 6.

3.5 Visualization by Consensus Incidence Matrix

In our method SCEC, the consensus incidence matrix can be used not only for clustering but also for data visualization. Compared with the original data, data points of the same

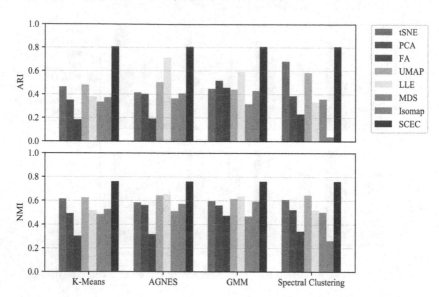

Fig. 6. Performance of various base classifiers and SCEC on Zeisel dataset.

cell type are more distinguishable when using the consensus incident matrix to visualize by t-SNE or UMAP, showing in Fig. 7.

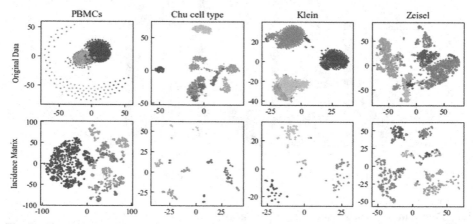

Fig. 7. Comparison of 2D visualization between original data and consensus incidence matrix. The data points of datasets are embedded by t-SNE. The distinct colors of the points represent the true labels.

3.6 Discussion

In this study, we have proposed an ensemble learning based single-cell classifying approach based on learning the cell-pair relationship. We evaluated the proposed SCEC method in a collection of scRNA-seq datasets with predefined cell types. We demonstrate that the SCEC method effectively improved clustering compared with basic clustering methods. Besides, we also tested the performance of data visualization based on the consensus incidence matrix generated by SCEC and found that the data points of the same cell type are more concentrated. There may be some further opportunities to build on SCEC: The ensemble learning part of SCEC only focuses on the clustering results of different unsupervised clustering methods and the personalization characteristics of the dataset are excluded to a certain extent. Therefore, SCEC may be used for single-cell clustering across different datasets.

Acknowledgment. This work was supported by the National Nature Science Foundation of China under Grant No. 12001408, the Science Foundation of Wuhan Institute of Technology under Grant No. K201746, and by Graduate Innovative Fund of Wuhan Institute of Technology under Grant No. CX2020292.

References

1. Qi, R., et al.: Clustering and classification methods for single-cell RNA-sequencing data. Brief. Bioinform. **21**(4), 1196–1208 (2020)
2. Grun, D., et al.: Single-cell messenger RNA sequencing reveals rare intestinal cell types. Nature **525**(7568), 251–255 (2015)
3. Kiselev, V.Y., Andrews, T.S., Hemberg, M.: Challenges in unsupervised clustering of single-cell RNA-seq data. Nat. Rev. Genet. **20**(5), 273–282 (2019)
4. Luecken, M.D., Theis, F.J.: Current best practices in single-cell RNA-seq analysis: a tutorial. Mol. Syst. Biol. **15**(6), e8746 (2019)
5. Yang, L., et al.: SAIC: an iterative clustering approach for analysis of single cell RNA-seq data. BMC Genomics **18**(Suppl 6), 689 (2017)
6. Kiselev, V.Y., et al.: SC3: consensus clustering of single-cell RNA-seq data. Nat. Meth. **14**(5), 483–486 (2017)
7. Grun, D., et al.: De Novo prediction of stem cell identity using single-cell transcriptome data. Cell Stem Cell **19**(2), 266–277 (2016)
8. Herman, J.S., Sagar, G.D.: FateID infers cell fate bias in multipotent progenitors from single-cell RNA-seq data. Nat. Meth. **15**(5), 379–386 (2018). https://doi.org/10.1038/nmeth.4662
9. Lin, P., Troup, M., Ho, J.W.: CIDR: ultrafast and accurate clustering through imputation for single-cell RNA-seq data. Genome Biol. **18**(1), 59 (2017)
10. Zeisel, A., et al.: Cell types in the mouse cortex and hippocampus revealed by single-cell RNA-seq. Science **347**, 1138–1142 (2015)
11. Guo, M., et al.: SINCERA: a pipeline for single-cell RNA-Seq profiling analysis. PLOS Comput. Biol. **11**(11), e1004575 (2015)
12. Blondel, V.D., Guillaume, J.-L., Lambiotte, R., Lefebvre, E.: Fast unfolding of communities in large networks. J. Stat. Mech. Theor. Exp. **2008**(10), P10008 (2008). https://doi.org/10.1088/1742-5468/2008/10/P10008
13. Ester, M., et al.: A density-based algorithm for discovering clusters in large spatial databases with noise. In: Proceedings of the 2nd International Conference on Knowledge Discovery and Data Mining, Portland, Oregon, pp. 226–231. AAAI Press (1996)
14. Wang, B., et al.: Visualization and analysis of single-cell RNA-seq data by kernel-based similarity learning. Nat. Meth. **14**(4), 414–416 (2017)

15. Zheng, R., et al.: SinNLRR: a robust subspace clustering method for cell type detection by non-negative and low-rank representation. Bioinformatics **35**(19), 3642–3650 (2019)
16. Li, X., et al.: Deep learning enables accurate clustering with batch effect removal in single-cell RNA-seq analysis. Nat. Commun. **11**(1), 2338 (2020)
17. Wang, D., Gu, J.: VASC: dimension reduction and visualization of single-cell RNA-seq data by deep variational autoencoder. Genomics Proteomics Bioinf. **16**(5), 320–331 (2018)
18. Lin, Y., et al.: scClassify: hierarchical classification of cells. bioRxiv (2019)
19. Gierahn, T.M., et al.: Seq-Well: portable, low-cost RNA sequencing of single cells at high throughput. Nat. Meth. **14**(4), 395–398 (2017)
20. Chu, L.-F., et al.: Single-cell RNA-seq reveals novel regulators of human embryonic stem cell differentiation to definitive endoderm. Genome Biol. **17**(1), 1–20 (2016)
21. Klein, A.M., et al.: Droplet barcoding for single-cell transcriptomics applied to embryonic stem cells. Cell **161**(5), 1187–1201 (2015)
22. Zeisel, A., et al.: Cell types in the mouse cortex and hippocampus revealed by single-cell RNA-seq. Science **347**(6226), 1138–1142 (2015)
23. Van der Maaten, L., Hinton, G.: Visualizing data using t-SNE. J. Mach. Learn. Res. **9**(11), 2579–2605 (2008)
24. Wold, S., Esbensen, K., Geladi, P.: Principal component analysis. Chemom. Intell. Lab. Syst. **2**(1–3), 37–52 (1987)
25. McInnes, L., Healy, J., Melville, J.: UMAP: uniform manifold approximation and projection for dimension reduction. arXiv preprint arXiv:1802.03426 (2018)
26. Kramer, M.A.: Nonlinear principal component analysis using autoassociative neural networks. AIChE J. **37**(2), 233–243 (1991)
27. Cox, M.A.A., Cox, T.F.: Multidimensional scaling. In: Chen, C., Härdle, W., Unwin, A. (eds.) Handbook of Data Visualization, pp. 315–347. Springer, Heidelberg (2008). https://doi.org/10.1007/978-3-540-33037-0_14
28. Tenenbaum, J.B.: A global geometric framework for nonlinear dimensionality reduction. Science **290**(5500), 2319–2323 (2000)
29. Hartigan, J.A.: Clustering Algorithms. Wiley (1975)
30. Ward Jr., J.H.: Hierarchical grouping to optimize an objective function. J. Am. Stat. Assoc. **58**(301), 236–244 (1963)
31. Reynolds, D.: Gaussian mixture models. In: Li, S.Z., Jain, A. (eds.) Encyclopedia of Biometrics, pp. 659–663. Springer, Boston (2009). https://doi.org/10.1007/978-0-387-73003-5_196
32. Von Luxburg, U.: A tutorial on spectral clustering. Stat. Comput. **17**(4), 395–416 (2007)
33. Hubert, L., Arabie, P.: Comparing partitions. J. Classif. **2**(1), 193–218 (1985)
34. Strehl, A., Ghosh, J.: Cluster—a knowledge reuse framework for combining multiple partitions. J. Mach. Learn. Res. **3**, 583–617 (2002)

ICNNMDA: An Improved Convolutional Neural Network for Predicting MiRNA-Disease Associations

Rui-Kang Ni, Zhen Gao$^{(\boxtimes)}$, and Cun-Mei Ji$^{(\boxtimes)}$

School of Cyber Science and Engineering, Qufu Normal University, Qufu, China
jicm2015@mail.qfnu.edu.cn

Abstract. An increasing number of works have validated that the expression of miRNA is associated with human diseases. miRNA expression profiles may become an indicator for clinical diagnosis, classification, grading and even prognosis of tumors and other diseases, and provide new targets for treatment. In this work, we presented an improved convolutional neural network model to predict miRNA-disease association (ICNNMDA). For capturing more feature of miRNAs and diseases, we designed feature cell to train ICNNMDA, which contains miRNA-disease associations information and three kinds of miRNAs and diseases similarity information. In addition, an improved convolutional neural network was presented which consists of three convolutional layers, three pooling layers and two fully-connected layers, where dropout mechanism was adopted in the first fully-connected layers. Finally, 5CV and a case study were conducted to validate the effectiveness of the proposed model. The results showed that ICNNMDA can effectively identify disease-related miRNAs.

Keywords: Convolutional neural network · Matrix completion · miRNA-disease associations

1 Introduction

miRNAs (~22 nt), short for microRNAs, are a kind of non-coding RNAs, which play a vital role in cell proliferation, apoptosis and cell differentiation [1–3]. By comparing the expression profiles of different miRNAs in cancer cells and normal cells, the researchers found that some miRNAs can inhibit the occurrence and development of malignant tumors [4–8], such as chronic lymphoid leukemia [9], breast cancer [10] and prostate cancer [11]. Hence, discovering disease-associated miRNAs is helpful for prevention and treatment of human diseases. Notice that although identifying interested miRNAs via biological experiment is precise, this method is also time-consuming and money-consuming. Naturally, in recent years, researchers have developed a great number of computational algorithms for predicting miRNA-disease associations and acquired moderate performance [12–17].

We divided approaches into two categories namely similarity-based models and machine learning-based models. Jiang et al. [18] have proposed and verified an assumption that miRNAs which are similar in function are easily to connected with diseases

© Springer Nature Switzerland AG 2021
D.-S. Huang et al. (Eds.): ICIC 2021, LNAI 12838, pp. 445–457, 2021.
https://doi.org/10.1007/978-3-030-84532-2_40

which are similar in phenotype. Also, they have developed an approach for predicting disease-related miRNAs on the basis of cumulative hypergeometric distribution. Since then, most researchers have based their predictions on this assumption.

There are also many fantastic ideas about similarity measurement. Yang et al. [19] have presented a novel algorithm entitled MiRGOFS to measure semantic similarity and miRNA similarity on the basis of Go terms. Chen et al. [20] have introduced lncRNA into miRNA-disease prediction. They have constructed miRNA-lncRNA-disease heterogeneous network, and applied label propagation to identify disease-associated miRNAs. For obtaining more dense similarity, Qu et al. [21] have employed sparse neighborhood to reconstruct miRNA and disease similarity. Then the label propagation was utilized for discovering potential miRNA-disease associations. In addition, Qu et al. [22] also have developed Locality-constrained Linear Coding (LLC) to reconstruct miRNA and disease similarity network. Similarly, the label propagation was implemented for predicting disease-associated miRNAs.

As a popular recommendation system technology, matrix factorization has been widely used in the field of bioinformatics and acquired moderate performance. Chen et al. [23] have applied inductive matrix completion (IMC) into miRNA-disease association prediction. Yu et al. [24] have used MC as a pre-processing step for completing miRNA and disease similarity matrix. And label propagation was used to uncover potential miRNA-disease association. Zhong et al. [25] have constructed a bilayer network consists of miRNA network, disease network and relationships between two networks, and then built models for above three networks based on non-negative matrix factorization (NMF), respectively. Finally, they integrated three models for predicting disease-related miRNAs. Xiao et al. [26] have introduced graph Laplacian regularization and Tikhonov regularization into NMF to predict miRNA-disease association. Stimulated this, Gao et al. [27] have added $L_{2,1}$-norm into their algorithm, and built a dense similarity for miRNAs and diseases, respectively.

To date, a great number of machine learning-based models have been developed for miRNA-disease association prediction or target gene-drug association prediction and so on. Gong et al. [28] have implemented random forest (RF) to predict disease-related miRNAs. In addition, they have employed structural deep network embedding (SDNE) on miRNA-disease association matrix to extract features, and then combined it with other biological features. Wu et al. [13] have first utilized hypergraph learning as technology for discovering disease-connected miRNAs. Then, they have improved it and obtained MSCHLMDA [29]. MSCHLMDA have constructed three kind of features from three perspectives, namely statistic perspective, graph theory and matrix factorization. Then KNN and K-Means were adopted to build hypergraph. Finally, combinative hypergraph learning was implemented for predicting disease-associated miRNAs. Ji et al. [12] have utilized two regression models for building dense feature vector of miRNAs and diseases, respectively. Then, deep autoencoder (AE) was adopted for discovering disease-related miRNAs. Xuan et al. [30] have used gradient boosting decision trees to obtain prediction scores of target gene-drug associations. Li et al. [31] have used graph convolutional neural network (GCN) to extract features for miRNAs and diseases, respectively. Then, a neural IMC have been proposed for prediction. Convolutional neural network (CNN) is a popular model, which is often used in the field of computer vision. Peng et al.

[32] have built a three-layer network composed of miRNA, gene and disease network. After extracting features, AE model was adopted to reduce dimension. Then, a simple CNN model was presented for prediction. Xuan et al. have proposed two models named CNNMDA [33] and CNNDMP [34] both based on CNN. Two models were both adopted dual CNN, left embedding layers both utilized miRNA and disease original biological information, what was different was the right embedding layer. CNNDMP used RWR to acquired network topology information, and CNNMDA utilized matrix factorization to obtain low-dimensional features.

At present, although an increasing number of CNN-based models have been developed for solving association prediction in bioinformatics, these models have imperfect prediction performance. Thus, we design an improved CNN model called ICNNMDA for identifying disease-associated miRNAs. The major work is list as follows:

- Similarity information. We calculate disease and miRNA similarities via three strategies (namely biology similarity, Gaussian kernel interaction profile similarity and low-rank recovery similarity), respectively.
- Feature cell. We design feature cell for training ICNNMDA which contains disease similarity, miRNA similarity and miRNA-disease association information.
- ICNNMDA model. ICNNMDA set up three convolutional layers, three pooling layers and two fully-connected layers. We utilize RMSProp optimizer and cross-entropy loss function to train ICNNMDA model.
- Performance evaluation. We adopt five-fold cross validation (5CV) to validate effectiveness of ICNNMDA model. In addition, a case study is implemented to further evaluate ICNNMDA model.

2 Feature Cell

In this section, we elaborated training samples, entitled feature cell (see Fig. 1), for training ICNNMDA. There were 24068 feature cells in a whole composed of 12034 positive samples and 12034 negative samples. And the corresponding labels were 1 or 0. If a disease d_i was validated to be associated with a miRNA m_j, the label was 1 which means it was a positive sample. All positive feature cells were constructed based on HMDD v3.2 [5], and 12034 unknown associations were randomly selected from all unknown associations.

Specifically, each feature cell contained miRNA similarity information, disease similarity information and experimentally validated miRNA-disease association information downloaded from HMDD v3.2. Each feature cell c_{ij} represented a sample between a disease d_i and a miRNA m_j. So, feature cell c_{ij} included i th row of disease similarity matrix, j th row of miRNA similarity matrix as well as i th row of miRNA-disease association matrix or j th column of miRNA-disease association matrix. Since we used 495 miRNAs and 383 diseases, the size of feature cell of every miRNA-disease pair is 2×878.

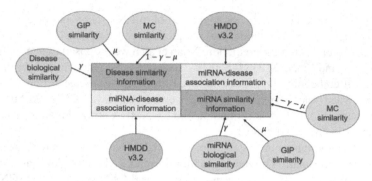

Fig. 1. Feature cell for training ICNNMDA

2.1 Human MiRNA-Disease Associations

HMDD [4, 5] is a database which provides experimental verified evidence for miRNA-disease associations. At present, most studies have utilized known miRNA-disease association from HMDD v2.0, which contains 5430 known associations between 495 miRNAs and 383 diseases. HMDD v3.2 includes 35547 known associations between 1206 miRNAs and 893 diseases. Thus, in this study, we downloaded data from HMDD v3.2 and implemented a series of pre-processing steps. Firstly, we continued the previous 495 miRNAs and 383 diseases. Secondly, we unified disease names referring to the disease mapping file (http://www.cuilab.cn/static/hmdd3/data/) and miRNA names based on previous outstanding study [35]. For instance, has-mir-1a-1 and has-mir-1a-2 were unified as has-mir-1a. After removing the redundant data, at last, we acquired 12034 observed associations between 495 miRNAs and 383 diseases for training ICNNMDA. In addition, an adjacency binary matrix $Y \in R^{n \times m}$ were constructed, where n denotes the number of miRNAs and m is the number of diseases. $Y_{ij} = 1$ denoted that the known association between disease d_i and miRNA m_j exist, otherwise $Y_{ij} = 0$.

2.2 Disease Similarity

In this study, we adopted three types of disease similarity, namely disease biological similarity, Gaussian kernel interaction profile similarity (GIP similarity) and low-rank recovery similarity (MC similarity) [24, 36].

- Disease biological similarity

The hierarchical directed acyclic graphs (DAG) of 383 diseases were downloaded from the National Library of Medicine (http://www.nlm.nih.gov/), representing the relationship between diseases. Based on the previous studies [13, 35, 36], we calculated disease semantic similarity as disease biological similarity via two strategies. Matrix $DES \in R^{m \times m}$ was defined to represent the disease biological similarity [27].

- GIP similarity

Due to the lack of hierarchical DAG, the disease biological similarity matrix *DES* was sparse. So, we also calculated GIP similarity of diseases in order to reduce sparsity of disease similarity to some extent. The ith column of miRNA-disease association matrix $Y \in R^{n \times m}$ denotes interaction profile between a disease d_i and all miRNAs. Based on this, we can calculate the GIP similarity of all diseases [23]. Finally, matrix $DGS \in R^{m \times m}$ was constructed for storing GIP similarity of all diseases [27].

- MC similarity

Although there were disease biological similarity and disease GIP similarity, the similarity matrix was far from perfect. Thus, we adopted MC algorithm stimulated by ref [24]. Matrix completion is a technology which can recover a low-rank matrix, and have been applied in many studies [24, 38]. Similarly, we define $DMS \in R^{m \times m}$ as MC similarity of diseases.

- Integrated disease similarity

Finally, disease biological similarity, GIP similarity of diseases and MC similarity of diseases were integrated into the final disease similarity (as shown in Eq. (1)), where γ as well μ are balance parameter.

$$SD = \gamma * DES + \mu * DGS + (1 - \gamma - \mu) * DMS \tag{1}$$

2.3 miRNA Similarity

Similar as disease similarity measurement, miRNA similarity was set three kinds of similarity, namely miRNA biological similarity *MES*, GIP similarity *MGS* and low-rank recovery similarity *MMS* [24, 36].

- miRNA biological similarity

miRNA functional similarity was regarded as miRNA biological similarity in this paper. Based on an assumption that functionally similar miRNAs are more likely to be associated with diseases which are phenotypically similar [35, 39], we downloaded the miRNA functional similarity information directly from http://www.cuilab.cn/files/images/cuilab/misim.zip. Then, matrix $MES \in R^{n \times n}$ was defined to represent miRNA functional similarity.

- GIP similarity

Like GIP similarity of diseases, we also computed GIP similarity of all miRNAs aim to reduce the sparsity of miRNA similarity. Matrix $MGS \in R^{n \times n}$ was constructed to denote GIP similarity of all miRNAs [27].

- MC similarity

MC similarity of all miRNAs were obtained in a same way as MC similarity of diseases [24]. Finally, $MMS \in R^{n \times n}$ was set as MC similarity of all miRNAs.

- Integrated miRNA similarity

Three similarity matrices were integrated into a final miRNA similarity matrix $SM \in R^{n \times n}$ (as shown in Eq. (2)), where γ as well μ are balance parameter.

$$SM = \gamma * MES + \mu * MGS + (1 - \gamma - \mu) * MM \tag{2}$$

3   ICNNMDA

3.1   Overview for ICNNMDA

Convolutional Neural Network (CNN) [40, 41] is a class of Convolutional Neural Network with deep structure that contains convolutional computation and is a class of classical deep learning model with representational learning ability. In ICNNMDA framework (see Fig. 2), three convolutional layers (Conv) as well as three pooling layers (MaxPooling) were added to extract features and implement feature reduction. In the end, two fully-connected layers were adopted to classify samples.

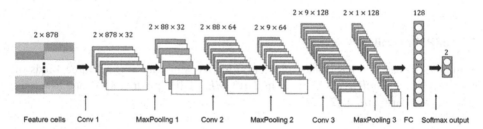

Fig. 2. Flow chart of ICNNMDA for miRNA-disease association prediction

3.2   Convolutional Layer

Convolutional layer (Conv layer) uses the information of adjacent areas in the network to extract features by means of sparse connection and weight sharing. In ICNNMDA framework, three convolution layers are set up, and 32, 64 and 128 convolution kernels with size 1×20 and step size 1 were respectively used for convolution operation. In addition, the ReLU activation function was used in this experiment, which effectively reduced the computation, increased the sparsity of the network, and alleviated the occurrence of overfitting problems.

If the ith layer is convolutional layer, the training parameters contained in the layer network are weight matrix W and offset vector B. The output of the convolutional layer is expressed as:

$$F_i = f(W_i * F_{i-1} + b_i) \tag{3}$$

where $*$ denotes convolution operation between W_i and F_{i-1}, $f(x)$ is ReLU activation function: $f(x) = \max(0, x)$.

3.3 Pooling Layer

Pooling layer can reduce the dimension of feature space by extracting the most prominent feature. In the ICNNMDA model, each convolutional layer was followed by a max pooling layer (MaxPooling). Specifically, in the ICNNMDA model, the second, fourth and sixth layers are the max pooling layers, and the sliding window parameters are uniformly set as size 1×10 and step size 1. If the ith layer is a pooling layer, the output of the layer is expressed as:

$$F_i = Maxpool(F_{i-1}) \tag{4}$$

where $Maxpool()$ denotes max pooling operation.

3.4 Fully-Connected Layer

In ICNNMDA framework, after the max pooling layer is the full connection layer with ReLU activation function, and the previously extracted features are integrated and input to the next fully-connected layer (softmax). In order to reduce the risk of overfitting and enhance the generalization ability of the model, dropout mechanism was added to the first fully-connected layer (FC) to randomly discard some weights and reduce the amount of computation. The output layer uses the softmax activation function as the classifier.

3.5 Model Training

In this paper, the cross-entropy loss function was used to measure the difference between two different probability distributions in the same random variable, which is expressed as the difference between the real probability distribution and the predicted probability distribution in machine learning. The smaller the cross entropy is, the better the prediction effect of the model will be. In addition, the RMSProp optimizer was adopted in this paper to adjust the weight W and offset vector b of the convolution kernel in the CNN model to make them approximate or reach the optimal value, thus minimizing the loss function.

$$Loss(W, b) = -\frac{1}{N} \sum_{i=1}^{N} y_t^{(i)} \log\left(y_p^{(i)}\right) + \left(1 - y_t^{(i)}\right) \log\left(1 - y_p^{(i)}\right) \tag{5}$$

where N is the number of training samples, $y_t^{(i)}$ denotes the true label of miRNA-disease association, and $y_p^{(i)}$ is the prediction score of one sample.

4 Experiments and Results

4.1 Parameter Setting

The hyper-params setting of ICNNMDA model are set as Table 1. The network params are set as Table 2. The size of input for training ICNNMDA model is 2×878, ICNN-MDA model contained three convolutional layers and three max pooling layers. Three convolutional layers have 32, 64 and 128 convolutional kernels with size of 1×20 and step of 1. The sizes of slide windows in three max pooling layers were 1×10 and the steps were 1.

Table 1. ICNNMDA model hyper-params

Parameter	Value
Batch size	512
RMSProp learning rate	0.0001
Epochs	200
Dropout rate	0.5

Table 2. ICNNMDA model network params

Layer (type)	Filter size/stride	Output shape	Param #
conv2d_1	$1 \times 20/1$	(None, 2, 878, 32)	672
max_pooling2d_1	$1 \times 10/1$	(None, 2, 88, 32)	0
conv2d_2	$1 \times 20/1$	(None, 2, 88, 64)	41024
max_pooling2d_2	$1 \times 10/1$	(None, 2, 9, 64)	0
conv2d_3	$1 \times 20/1$	(None, 2, 9, 128)	163968
max_pooling2d_3	$1 \times 10/1$	(None, 2, 1, 128)	0
flatten_1 (Flatten)	–	(None, 256)	0
dropout_1 (Dropout)	–	(None, 256)	0
dense_1 (Dense)	–	(None, 128)	32896
dense_2 (Dense)	–	(None, 2)	258
Total params	–	–	238818
Trainable params	–	–	238818
Non-trainable params:	–	–	0

4.2 Performance Evaluation Based on 5CV

To evaluate the prediction performance of ICNNMDA, we compared ICNNMDA with two other state-of-the-art models based on 5CV. We first introduce the ROC curve and AUC value, then elaborate on 5CV, and give the experimental results.

Since there is no true label for all unknown associations in the problem of disease-related miRNA prediction, thresholds need to be set to identify whether the sample is positive or not. After the prediction model obtains the prediction score of a sample, it will be compared with the threshold value. If it is higher than the threshold value, it will be a positive sample. Otherwise, the model will predict the sample to be a negative sample. Then we can acquire confusion matrix as follows:

Table 3. Confusion matrix

True results	Prediction results	
	Positive samples	Negative samples
Positive samples	True positive (TP)	True negative (TN)
Negative samples	False positive (FP)	False negative (FN)

Based on Table 3, it can be concluded that $TP + FP + TN + FN = $ *the num of all samples*, and the true positive rate (TPR, sensitivity) and false positive rate (FPR, 1-specificity) can be computed according to Eq. (6) and Eq. (7), respectively.

$$\text{TPR} = \frac{TP}{TP + FN} \tag{6}$$

$$\text{FPR} = \frac{FP}{TN + FP} \tag{7}$$

The predicted scores of all m test samples were sorted, and then the samples were divided into positive and negative samples as the threshold value by turns, and then the m pairs of TPR and FPR could be calculated. Then, taking TPR as the vertical axis and FPR as the horizontal axis, ROC curve can be drawn. The area under the ROC curve is defined as AUC value. The higher AUC value, the better the prediction performance of model.

The first step in the five-fold cross validation (5CV) is to divide the entire data set into five equal parts, four subsets for training and one subset for testing. Each subset of the data is then taken as a test set in turn, requiring five sessions of training and testing. Finally, the test results of the five times were averaged, and the test results of the five times of cross-validation were obtained. We conducted 5CV 50 times and plot corresponding ROCs for ICNNMDA, HGMDA [13] and MSCHLMDA [29], and the experimental results are shown in Fig. 3. Their corresponding AUCs are 0.9342, 0.9146 and 0.9263. Results showed that ICNNMDA was apparently superior to several other models, suggesting that ICNNMDA could be an effective tool to predict disease-related miRNAs.

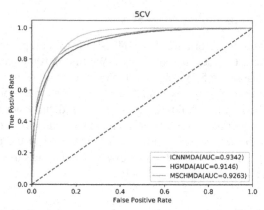

Fig. 3. ICNNMDA and other classic machine learning-based prediction models (HGMDA and MSCHLMDA) were compared in ROC curve and AUC performance for 5CV.

Table 4. Top-30 predicted prostate neoplasms-associated miRNAs

miRNA	Evidence	miRNA	Evidence
hsa-mir-106b	D	hsa-mir-1	D
hsa-mir-200c	D	hsa-mir-133b	D
hsa-mir-628	**unconfirmed**	**hsa-mir-1296**	**unconfirmed**
hsa-mir-765	D	hsa-mir-205	M; D
hsa-mir-92	M; D	hsa-mir-572	D
hsa-mir-519d	D	hsa-mir-198	M; D
hsa-mir-145	M; D	hsa-mir-21	M; D
hsa-mir-513c	M	hsa-mir-616	D
hsa-mir-15a	M; D	hsa-mir-10a	M; D
hsa-mir-154	M	hsa-mir-152	D
hsa-mir-373	M; D	hsa-mir-100	M; D
hsa-mir-203	M	hsa-mir-381	D
hsa-mir-32	M; D	hsa-mir-497	D
hsa-mir-371	D	hsa-mir-144	D
hsa-mir-708	D	hsa-mir-330	M

M: miR2Disease database; D: dbDEMC v2.0 database.

4.3   A Case Study on Prostate Neoplasm

For further evaluate the effectiveness of ICNNMDA model, we implemented a case study on prostate neoplasm. Specifically, all manually validated miRNA-disease associations were train via ICNNMDA model, and other unknown associations were regarded as candidate samples to be evaluated. We predicted prostate neoplasm based on ICN-NMDA, then obtained prediction scores and ranked them from highest to lowest. This paper utilized two famous miRNA-disease associations database, namely, miR2Disease [7] and dbDEMC v2.0 [6], in order to validate disease-related potential miRNAs. The ICNNMDA model was used to predict and obtained the top 30 miRNAs of the prostate neoplasm. Experimental results (see Table 4) showed that 28 miRNAs were associated with prostate neoplasm.

5   Discussion and Conclusion

This study aimed to design a CNN-based model to identify disease-associated miRNAs. ICNNMDA model contained three convolutional layers and three max pooling layers, then followed two fully-connected layers and the last layer for classification. In addition, we constructed feature cell for training samples. Besides, in order to capture more features of miRNAs and diseases, we measured three types of similarity including biology similarity, GIP similarity and low-rank recovery similarity. Furthermore, 5CV and a case study on prostate neoplasm were implemented to evaluate ICNNMDA model.

There is also a state-of-the-art CNN-based model MDA-CNN [32] which reached AUC of 0.8961. Different from ICNNMDA, MDA-CNN model has one convolutional layer, one max pooling layer, two fully-connected layers. In addition, MDA-CNN extract features of miRNA-gene associations and gene-disease associations, which bring us inspiration in the next research. What's more, ICNNMDA model still has room for improvement. More reliable CNN-based model and more outstanding training samples are in need in the future study.

Acknowledgment. This study was supported by the Natural Science Foundation of Shandong Province (grant number ZR2020KC022).

References

1. Victor, A.: The functions of animal microRNAs. Nature **431**, 350–355 (2004)
2. Bartel, D.P.: MicroRNAs: genomics, biogenesis, mechanism, and function. Cell **116**, 281–297 (2004)
3. He, L., et al.: A microRNA polycistron as a potential human oncogene. Nature **435**, 828–833 (2005)
4. Li, Y., et al.: HMDD v2.0: a database for experimentally supported human microRNA and disease associations. Nucleic Acids Res. **42**(D1), D1070–D1074 (2014). https://doi.org/10.1093/nar/gkt1023
5. Huang, Z., et al.: HMDD v3.0: a database for experimentally supported human microRNA–disease associations. Nucleic Acids Res. **47**(D1), D1013–D1017 (2018). https://doi.org/10.1093/nar/gky1010
6. Yang, Z., et al.: dbDEMC 2.0: updated database of differentially expressed miRNAs in human cancers. Nucleic Acids Res. **45**(D1), D812–D818 (2016). https://doi.org/10.1093/nar/gkw1079
7. Jiang, Q., et al.: miR2Disease: a manually curated database for microRNA deregulation in human disease. Nucleic Acids Res. **37**, D98–104 (2009)

8. Manikandan, J., Aarthi, J.J., Kumar, S.D., Pushparaj, P.N.: Oncomirs: the potential role of non-coding microRNAs in understanding cancer. Bioinformation **2**, 330–334 (2008)
9. Calin, G., et al.: Frequent deletions and down-regulation of micro- RNA genes miR15 and miR16 at 13q14 in chronic lymphocytic leukemia. Proc. Natl. Acad. Sci. U.S.A. **99**, 15524–15529 (2002)
10. Blenkiron, C., et al.: MicroRNA expression profiling of human breast cancer identifies new markers of tumor subtype. Genome Biol. **8**, R214 (2007)
11. Garzon, R., Fabbri, M., Cimmino, A., Calin, G., Croce, C.: MicroRNA expression and function in cancer. Trends Mol. Med. **12**, 580–587 (2006)
12. Ji, C., Gao, X.Z., Ma, Q.W., Ni, J., Zheng, C.: AEMDA: inferring miRNA–disease associations based on deep autoencoder. Bioinformatics **37**(1), 66–72 (2020). https://doi.org/10.1093/bioinformatics/btaa670
13. Wu, Q.-W., Wang, Y.-T., Gao, Z., Zhang, M.-W., Ni, J.-C., Zheng, C.-H.: HGMDA: hypergraph for predicting MiRNA-disease association. In: Huang, D.-S., Jo, K.-H., Huang, Z.-K. (eds.) ICIC 2019. LNCS, vol. 11644, pp. 265–271. Springer, Cham (2019). https://doi.org/10.1007/978-3-030-26969-2_25
14. Chen, X., Xie, D., Zhao, Q., You, Z.H.: MicroRNAs and complex diseases: from experimental results to computational models. Brief. Bioinform. **20**, 515–539 (2019)
15. Zhao, Y., Chen, X., Yin, J.: Adaptive boosting-based computational model for predicting potential miRNA-disease associations. Bioinformatics **35**, 4730–4738 (2019)
16. Zhang, X., Zou, Q., Rodriguez-Paton, A., Zeng, X.: Meta-path methods for prioritizing candidate disease miRNAs. IEEE/ACM Trans. Comput. Biol. Bioinform. **16**, 283–291 (2019)
17. Xuan, P., Shen, T., Wang, X., Zhang, T., Zhang, W.: Inferring disease-associated microRNAs in heterogeneous networks with node attributes. IEEE ACM Trans. Comput. Biol. Bioinf. **17**, 1019–1031 (2020)
18. Jiang, Q., Hao, Y., Wang, G.: Prioritization of disease microRNAs through a human phenome-microRNAome network. BMC Syst. Biol. **4**, S2 (2010)
19. Yang, Y., Fu, X., Qu, W., Xiao, Y., Shen, H.-B.: MiRGOFS: a Go based functional similarity measurement for miRNAs, with applications to the prediction of miRNA subcellular localization and miRNa disease association. Bioinformatics **34**, 3547–3556 (2018)
20. Chen, X., Zhang, D.H., You, Z.H.: A heterogeneous label propagation approach to explore the potential associations between miRNA and disease. J. Transl. Med. **16**, 348 (2018)
21. Qu, Y., Zhang, H., Liang, C., Ding, P., Luo, J.: SNMDA: A novel method for predicting microRNa disease associations based on sparse neighbourhood. J. Cell Mol. Med. **22**, 5109–5120 (2018)
22. Yu, Q., Zhang, H., Lyu, C., Liang, C.: LLCMDA: a novel method for predicting miRNA gene and disease relationship based on locality-constrained linear coding. Front. Genet. **9**, 576 (2018). https://doi.org/10.3389/fgene.2018.00576
23. Chen, X., Wang, L., Qu, J., Guan, N.N., Li, J.Q.: Predicting miRNA-disease association based on inductive matrix completion. Bioinformatics **34**, 4256–4265 (2018)
24. Yu, S.P., et al.: MCLPMDA: a novel method for miRNA-disease association prediction based on matrix completion and label propagation. J. Cell Mol. Med. **23**, 1427–1438 (2018)
25. Zhong, Y., Xuan, P., Wang, X., Zhang, T., Li, J.: A non-negative matrix factorization based method for predicting disease-associated miRNAs in miRNA-disease bilayer network. Bioinformatics **34**, 267–277 (2018)
26. Xiao, Q., Luo, J., Liang, C., Cai, J., Ding, P.: A graph regularized non-negative matrix factorization method for identifying microRNA-disease associations. Bioinformatics **34**, 239–248 (2018)
27. Gao, Z., Wang, Y.-T., Qing-Wen, W., Ni, J.-C., Zheng, C.-H.: Graph regularized L2,1-nonnegative matrix factorization for miRNA-disease association prediction. BMC Bioinformatics **21**(1), 61 (2020). https://doi.org/10.1186/s12859-020-3409-x

28. Gong, Y., Niu, Y., Zhang, W., Li, X.: A network embedding-based multiple information integration method for the MiRNA-disease association prediction. BMC Bioinf. **20**(1), 468 (2019). https://doi.org/10.1186/s12859-019-3063-3

29. Qingwen, W., Wang, Y., Gao, Z., Ni, J., Zheng, C.: MSCHLMDA: multi-similarity based combinative hypergraph learning for predicting MiRNA-disease association. Front. Genet. **11**, 354 (2020)

30. Xuan, P., Sun, C., Zhang, T., Ye, Y., Shen, T., Dong, Y.: Gradient boosting decision tree-based method for predicting interactions between target genes and drugs. Front. Genet. **10**, 459 (2019)

31. Li, J., et al.: Neural inductive matrix completion with graph convolutional networks for miRNA-disease association prediction. Bioinformatics **36**, 2538–2546 (2020)

32. Peng, J., et al.: A learning-based framework for miRNA-disease association identification using neural networks. Bioinformatics **35**(21), 4364–4371 (2019)

33. Xuan, P., Sun, H., Wang, X., Zhang, T., Pan, S.: Inferring the disease-associated miRNAs based on network representation learning and convolutional neural networks. Int. J. Mol. Sci. **20**, 3648 (2019)

34. Xuan, P., Dong, Y., Guo, Y., Zhang, T., Liu, Y.: Dual convolutional neural network based method for predicting disease-related miRNAs. Int. J. Mol. Sci. **19**, 3732 (2018)

35. Wang, D., Wang, J.Y., Lu, M.: Inferring the human microRNA functional similarity and functional network based on microRNA-associated diseases. Bioinformatics **26**, 1644–1650 (2010)

36. Gao, Z., et al.: A new method based on matrix completion and non-negative matrix factorization for predicting disease-associated miRNAs. IEEE/ACM Trans. Comput. Biol. Bioinf. (2020)

37. Xuan, P., et al.: Prediction of microRNAs associated with human diseases based on weighted K most similar neighbors. PLoS ONE **8**, e70204–e70204 (2013)

38. Tang, C., Zhou, H., Zheng, X., Zhang, Y., Sha, X.: Dual Laplacian regularized matrix completion for microRNA-disease associations prediction. RNA Biol. **16**, 601–611 (2019)

39. Ding, X., Xia, J.-F., Wang, Y.-T., Wang, J., Zheng, C.-H.: Improved inductive matrix completion method for predicting MicroRNA-disease associations. In: Huang, D.-S., Jo, K.-H., Huang, Z.-K. (eds.) ICIC 2019. LNCS, vol. 11644, pp. 247–255. Springer, Cham (2019). https://doi.org/10.1007/978-3-030-26969-2_23

40. Krizhevsky, A., Sutskever, I., Hinton, G.E.: ImageNet classification with deep convolutional neural networks. Commun. ACM **60**, 84–90 (2017)

41. Abdel-Hamid, O., et al.: Convolutional neural networks for speech recognition. IEEE-ACM Trans. Audio Speech Lang. Process. **22**, 1533–1545 (2014)

42. Jiang, Y., Liu, B., Yu, L., Yan, C., Bian, H.: Predict MiRNA-disease association with collaborative filtering. Neuroinformatics **16**(3–4), 363–372 (2018)

43. Shao, B., Liu, B., Yan, C.: SACMDA: MiRNA-disease association prediction with short acyclic connections in heterogeneous graph. Neuroinformatics **16**(3–4), 373–382 (2018)

DNA-GCN: Graph Convolutional Networks for Predicting DNA-Protein Binding

Yuhang Guo[1], Xiao Luo[1,2], Liang Chen[1], and Minghua Deng[1(✉)]

[1] School of Mathematical Sciences, Peking University, Beijing, China
{yuhangguo,xiaoluo,clandzyy,dengmh}@pku.edu.cn
[2] Damo Academy, Alibaba Group, Hangzhou, China

Abstract. Predicting DNA-protein binding is an important and classic problem in bioinformatics. Convolutional neural networks have outperformed conventional methods in modeling the sequence specificity of DNA-protein binding. However, none of the studies has utilized graph convolutional networks for motif inference. In this work, we propose to use graph convolutional networks for motif inference. We build a sequence k-mer graph for the whole dataset based on the k-mer co-occurrence and k-mer sequence relationship and then learn DNA Graph Convolutional Network(DNA-GCN) for the whole dataset. Our DNA-GCN is initialized with a one-hot representation for all nodes, and it then jointly learns the embeddings for both k-mers and sequences, as supervised by the known labels of sequences. We evaluate our model on 50 datasets from ENCODE. DNA-GCN shows its competitive performance compared with the baseline model. Besides, we analyze our model and design several different architectures to help fit different datasets.

Keywords: Bioinformatics · DNA-protein binding · Graph convolutional network · Motif inference

1 Introduction

DNA-binding proteins play an important role in gene regulation. It's well-known that the transcription of each gene is controlled by a regulatory region of DNA relatively near the transcription start site. There are two fundamental components in transcription, the short DNA regulatory element, and its corresponding gene regulatory proteins. DNA binding sites are small but highly variable, which makes them difficult to detect. Several experimental methods were developed (e.g. ChIP-seq [31]) to solve this problem, but they are usually costly, and each has its artifacts, biases, and limitation. Based on sequence-based data, the problem of predicting DNA-protein binding is to model the sequence specificity of protein binding (i.e. connect a relationship between sequence-based data and binary labels of data). Specifically, the task is a classification problem given training DNA sequences and their binary labels to predict labels of given testing sequences in the

---

Y. Guo and X. Luo—Equal Contribution. This work was done when Xiao Luo interned in Alibaba Group.

dataset. Recent work on motif inference includes conventional machine learning-based methods (e.g. SVM, Random Forest) [8, 11, 16] and deep learning-based methods (e.g. CNN, RNN) [2, 24, 25, 30]. CNN's and RNNs have shown their superiority compared with conventional machine learning-based methods. However, when it comes to small datasets, the performance of the models is often limited. Besides, the models of CNN's usually learn truncated motifs that aren't desired [4].

On the other hand, the binary labels of the sequences are up to whether they have some specific regions called a motif. If we regard the "A", "C", "G" and "T" as special kinds of characters, k-mer can be treated as words and DNA sequences can be viewed as sentences. The k-mer related to given motifs can be viewed as keywords and predicting DNA-protein binding is transformed into the problem of text classification.

In this paper, we propose a novel method based on Graph Convolutional Networks [15] – DNA-GCN for predicting DNA-protein binding. In DNA-GCN, firstly we construct a single large graph from the whole dataset, and then GCN is utilized to obtain neighborhood information. By this, predicting DNA-protein binding is turned into a semi-supervised node classification problem. We choose a lot of different datasets with limited samples to evaluate our model. The model shows competitive performance on the task of predicting TF binding sites. All code is public in https://github.com/Tinard/dnagcn.

In summary, our contributions in this paper are twofold. (1) We propose a novel graph convolutional network for predicting DNA-protein binding. To the best of our knowledge, we are the first to model the sequence specificity with a graphical model and utilize GCN to learn the sequences and k-mer embeddings. (2) The empirical results show that our proposed model has a competitive performance compared with the baseline models on many datasets with limited sequences. We suppose that our method could contribute to the study of DNA sequence modeling and other biological models.

2 Related Work

2.1 Deep Learning for Motif Inference

The deep learning method for motif inference can be categorized into two groups – CNN-based and RNN-based methods. As for the CNN based model (may contain RNN), Deep-Bind [2] is the first CNN-based model to predict DNA-protein binding and since then deep learning has been widely utilized in this field for its great performance. [30] shows that deploying more convolutional kernels is always beneficial. iDeepA [23] applies an attention mechanism to automatically search for important positions. DeeperBind [13] and iDeepS [21] add an LSTM layer on DeepBind to learn long dependency within sequences to further improve the prediction performance. As for the RNN-based model, KEGRU [25] identifies TF binding sites by combining Bidirectional Gated Recurrent Unit (GRU) network with k-mer embedding. Besides model selection, CONCISE [3] and iDeep [22] integrate other information (e.g. structured information) into predicting RBP-binding sites and preference. Other work includes data augmentation [5], circular filters [4] and convolutional kernel networks [6, 18, 19] (Fig. 1).

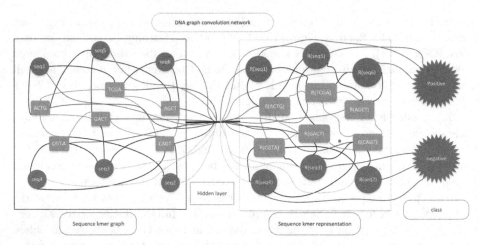

Fig. 1. Architecture of DNA-GCN.

2.2 Graph Convolutional Networks

In the past few years, graph convolutional network [15] has attracted wide attention for its learning hierarchical information on graphs [7, 12, 17]. It has been shown that the GCN model is a special form of Laplacian smoothing which makes the features of nodes similar to their neighbors and makes the subsequent classification task much easier. The layer-wise propagation rule is formulated as:

$$H^{(k+1)} = \phi\left(\tilde{D}^{-\frac{1}{2}}\tilde{A}\tilde{D}^{-\frac{1}{2}}H^{(k)}W^{(k)}\right)$$

where $H^{(k)}$ is the node representation matrix, $W^{(k)}$ is the trainable parameter matrix of the k-th layer, $H^{(0)} = X$ is the origin feature matrix, $\tilde{A} = A+I$ is the adjacency matrix with increased self-connection, $\tilde{D}$ is the degree matrix of $\tilde{A}$ (i.e. $\tilde{D}_{ii} = \sum j\tilde{A}_{ij}$), and ϕ is the activation function, such as $RELU(\cdot)$. In addition, there are many variants of GCN, focusing on improving the performance of GCN and coping with the storage bottleneck of GCN [7, 12, 26, 28, 32]. In recent years, GCN has been used to handle many tasks, such as text classification, drug recommendation and laboratory test classification [29], and has shown better performance than baseline on different tasks.

2.3 Heterogeneous Graph

The heterogeneity is an intrinsic property of a heterogeneous graph, i.e., various types of nodes and edges. Apparently, different types of nodes have different features which fall in different feature space. However, if we utilize Laplacian smoothing directly, different feature space is mixed which seems unreasonable. HAN [27] utilizes an attention mechanism to generate node embedding by aggregating features from meta-path-based neighbors in a hierarchical manner. MedGCN [20] assumes that there is no edge between nodes in the same type and the propagation rule is rewritten as:

$$H_i^{(k+1)} = \phi\left(\sum_{j=1}^{n} A_{ij} \cdot H_j^{(k)} \cdot W_j^{(k)}\right)$$

We assume that the number of types is n, A_{ij} is the adjacency matrix between nodes type i and j. $W_j^{(k)}$ is the learnable weight matrix for type i nodes in layer k.

3   DNA-GCN

3.1   Sequence k-mer Graph

First of all, we construct a large and heterogenous graph $G = (\mathcal{V}, \mathcal{E})$ where $\mathcal{V}, \mathcal{E}$ are sets of nodes and edges respectively to describe the relationship between sequences and k-mers. As shown in Fig. 2, nodes in the graph have two types: sequences nodes and k-mers nodes. The number of nodes in sequence k-mer graph $|\mathcal{V}|$ is the number of sequences including training set, validation set, and testing set plus the number of possible k-mers. The weight of the edge between sequences and k-mers is the number of occurrences of k-mer multiplied by inverse sequence frequency (ISF) in the sequence. ISF is the logarithmically scaled inverse fraction of the number of sequences that contain the k-mer. We test two models with or without ISF and found that the former is better. We suppose that some common k-mers which isn't related to the motif in real-world data may disrupt the performance and ISF can ease the effect of irrelevant k-mers. Pointwise mutual information (PMI) is utilized to calculate weights between two k-mers.

Above all, the adjacent matrix of sequence k-mer graph is formulated as:

$$A_{ij} = \begin{cases} \text{PMI}(i, j) & i, j \text{ are } k - \text{mers, PMI}(i, j) > 0 \\ O * \text{ISF}_{ij} & i \text{ is sequence}, j \text{ is } k - \text{mer} \\ 0 & \text{otherwise} \end{cases}$$

We can computed $PMI(i, j)$ as:

$$\text{PMI}(i, j) = \log \frac{p(i, j)}{p(i)p(j)}$$

$$p(i, j) = \frac{\#W(i, j)}{\#W}$$

$$p(i) = \frac{\#W(i)}{\#W}$$

where $\#W(i)$ is the number of sequences that contain k-mer i, $\#W(i, j)$ is the number of sequences that contain both k-mer i and j, and $\#W$ is the total number of sequences in the dataset. We set k to be 4, and because a motif length is between 6 and 20, the information of a motif may be spitted into several k-mers. We believe that if two k-mers co-occur in a sequence frequently, they are probably to co-decide whether a sequence contains a motif. From the formulation above, a positive PMI value indicates a high correlation of k-mers while a negative PMI value indicates little or no correlation. From the analysis, we set positive PMI values to be the weights of edges between k-mers.

3.2 DNA-GCN

After constructing the sequence k-mer graph, we feed the graph into GCN. Because the information of sequences is embedded into the graph, we set the feature matrix $X = I$ for simplicity. At first, we feed the graph into a two-layer GCN, and the second layer node embeddings only have one dimension and then are fed into a softmax classifier for classification.

$$Z = softmax\left(\hat{A}\text{ReLU}\left(\hat{A}XW_0\right)W_1\right)$$

Where $\tilde{A} = \tilde{D}^{\frac{1}{2}}\tilde{A}\tilde{D}^{\frac{1}{2}}$ and $softmax(x_i) = \frac{1}{Z}\exp(x_i)$ with partition function $\mathcal{Z}$ (i.e. $\mathcal{Z} = \sum_i exp(x_i)$).

The model has transformed into a semi-supervised model this time and the cross-entropy error over all labeled sequences determines loss function.

$$\mathcal{L} = -\sum_{d\in\mathcal{Y}_D} Y_d \ln Z_d$$

Where $\mathcal{Y}_D$ is the set of sequence indices that have labels and Y is the label indicator vector.

We give an ideal example. For the dataset with a specific protein, its positive samples contain the motif "AACGTC" while negative samples don't contain it. AACG, ACGT, CGTC are the key 4-mers which guide classification, the three k-mers is connected to all the positive sample. By training guided by labeled sample, the three k-mers can be trained to have the features that point to positive label, and then the model can predict the label of a testing sequence by whether the key k-mers is connected to target sequences (i.e. Features of key k-mers can be transferred to testing sequences or not). Overall, the information is transferred from labeled samples to k-mers, and then from k-mers to unlabeled sequences. From the analysis above, we need at least two times of Laplacian smoothing (i.e. two-layer GCN) to construct our DNA-GCN. By experiments and experience that too many layers lead to over-smoothing features, we set the number of layers to be two.

We also notice that the sequence k-mer graph is a heterogeneous graph. As a result, feeding our graph into GCN directly seems to be unreasonable. The layer-wise propagation rule can be rewritten as:

$$H^{(k+1)} = \phi\left(\hat{A}\left(H^{(k)}W^{\{(k)\}}\right)\right).$$

The formulation above means we feed every node into an identical single-layer perceptron, and from this point of view, we can feed each type of node into a specific perception. We assume that n_1 nodes represent sequences, n_2 nodes represent k-mers and $n = n_1 + n_2$. $\tilde{A}$ can be partitioned into two blocks, $\left(\tilde{A}_1\right)_{n_1\times n}$ and $\left(\tilde{A}_2\right)_{n_2\times n}$ according to node type. W_1^k and W_2^k are weight matrices with the same shape. The layer-wise propagation rule for a heterogeneous graph is formulated as:

$$H^{(k+1)} = \phi\left(\tilde{A}_1\left(H^{(k)}W_1^{(k)}\right) + \tilde{A}_2\left(H^{(k)}W_2^{(k)}\right)\right).$$

We call the second method DNA-HGCN. It's evident that in DNA-HGCN, the number of parameters doubles. As a result, DNA-HGCN is easier to overfit. We also utilize Simple Graph Convolutional Network (SGC) [28] to build our model. SGC removes non-linearities and collapses weight matrices between consecutive layers to reduce excess complexity while keeping the model's performance.

3.3 Implementation of DNA-GCN

Our model is trained using Adam [14] optimizer with a learning rate of 0.001 for 10000 epochs. 20% sequences are chosen from the labeled set to construct the validation set. We chose the best model according to the performance in the validation set. We set the embedding size of the first convolution layer as 100.

We utilized the area under the ROC (AUC) [9, 10] to assess the prediction performance of prediction. Our model is implemented using Tensorflow [1] for Python.

4 Result

4.1 Datasets

To evaluate the performance of our model, we chose the 50 ChIP-seq ENCODE datasets. Each of these datasets corresponds to a specific DNA-binding protein (e.g., transcription factor); its positive samples are 101bp DNA sequences which were experimentally confirmed to bind to this protein, and its negative samples were created by shuffling these positive samples. All these datasets were downloaded from http://cnn.csail.mit.edu/. We didn't test our performance in all available datasets for two reasons. On one hand, there is a tendency that when training sets contain more samples, better performance can be obtained by DeepBind. From this view, raising performance on these large datasets with high performance (i.e. AUC is about 99%) is useless. On the other hand, our model needs to be learned with the presence of both training and test data. Moreover, the recursive neighborhood expansion across layers poses time and memory challenges for training with large graphs (i.e. large datasets). As a result, We selected 50 datasets with limited samples to test the performance of our model.

4.2 Baselines

- *Gkm-SVM* [11] introduces alternative feature sets using gapped k-mers and develops an efficient tree data structure for computing the kernel matrix. Compared to original kmer-SVM and alternative approaches, gkm-SVM predicts functional genomic regulatory elements and tissue-specific enhancers with significantly improved accuracy.
- *CNN-based model* [30] is similar to the architecture of DeepBind. We utilize their best model with 128 convolutional kernels as our baseline. The overall performance of the CNN-based model is better than DeepBind in ENCODE datasets. Model 1 and model 2 refer to CNN-based models with 1 and 128 convolutional kernels, respectively.

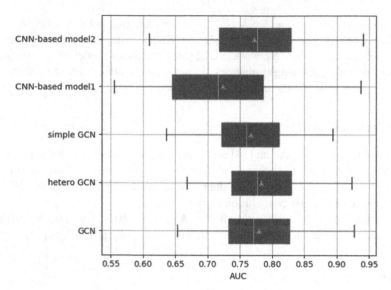

Fig. 2. Overall performance of DNA-GCN.

4.3 Our Model Outperforms on Many Datasets

From Fig. 2, the performance of DNA-HGCN among the datasets is slightly better than the best baseline. DNA-GCN-based three different models have close performance. DNA-GCN based on SGC sacrifices a little performance for its least calculation while DNA-HGCN has better performance with doubled parameters.

As for specific datasets [Fig. 3], we found that the performance among the CNN-based model and GCN-based model is inconsistent, which shows that GCN and CNN predict DNA-protein binding from different views. The performance of the same kind

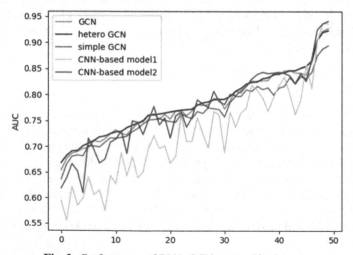

Fig. 3. Performance of DNA-GCN on specific datasets.

of model is consistent, regardless of the GCN-based model or CNN-based model. We believe if two methods can be combined, the best performance can be achieved.

5 Conclusion

In this paper, a novel method named DNA-GCN is proposed to predict DNA-protein binding. We build a heterogeneous sequence k-mer graph for the whole dataset and turn the DNA-protein binding prediction problem into a node classification problem. Our DNA-GCN can transmit information from labeled sequences to key k-mers and predict labels of unlabeled sequences. By experiments, we show that a simple two-layer GCN brings up promising results by comparing numerous models on many datasets with a limited number of sequences.

On the other hand, we believe that we haven't made the best use of GCN to predict DNA-protein binding. Much improvement may be achieved by adjusting the architectures and hyper-parameters on a given dataset. Although DNA-GCN can't arrive at motif logos like the CNN-based model, it can provide us with information about which k-mers are important in the classification. Above all, our model gives a brand new perspective to study motif inference.

Acknowledgements. This work was supported by The National Key Research and Development Program of China (No. 2016YFA0502303) and the National Natural Science Foundation of China (No. 31871342).

References

1. Abadi, M., et al.: Tensorflow: a system for large-scale machine learning. In: OSDI, vol. 16, pp. 265–283 (2016)
2. Alipanahi, B., Delong, A., Weirauch, M.T., Frey, B.J.: Predicting the sequence specificities of DNA-and RNA-binding proteins by deep learning. Nature Biotech. **33**(8), 831 (2015)
3. Avsec, Z., Barekatain, M., Cheng, J., Gagneur, J.: Modeling positional effects of regulatory sequences with spline transformations increases prediction accuracy of deep neural networks. Bioinformatics **34**(8), 1261–1269 (2017)
4. Blum, C.F., Kollmann, M.: Neural networks with circular filters enable data efficient inference of sequence motifs. Bioinformatics (2019)
5. Cao, Z., Zhang, S.: Simple tricks of convolutional neural network architectures improve DNA–protein binding prediction. Bioinformatics (2018)
6. Chen, D., Jacob, L., Mairal, J.: Biological sequence modeling with convolutional kernel networks. Bioinformatics (Oxford, England) (2019)
7. Chen, J., Ma, T., Xiao, C.: Fastgcn: fast learning with graph convolutional networks via importance sampling. arXiv preprint arXiv:1801.10247 (2018)
8. Corrado, G., Tebaldi, T., Costa, F., Frasconi, P., Passerini, A.: Rnacommender: genome-wide recommendation of RNA–protein interactions. Bioinformatics **32**(23), 3627–3634 (2016)
9. Davis, J., Goadrich, M.: The relationship between precision-recall and ROC curves. In: Proceedings of the 23rd international conference on Machine learning, pp. 233–240. ACM (2006)

10. Fawcett, T.: ROC graphs: notes and practical considerations for researchers. Mach. Learn. **31**(1), 1–38 (2004)

11. Ghandi, M., Lee, D., Mohammad-Noori, M., Beer, M.A.: Enhanced regulatory sequence prediction using gapped k-mer features. PLoS Comput. Boil. **10**(7), e1003711 (2014)

12. Hamilton, W., Ying, Z., Leskovec, J.: Inductive representation learning on large graphs. In: Advances in Neural Information Processing Systems, pp. 1024–1034 (2017)

13. Hassanzadeh, H.R., Wang, M.D.: Deeperbind: enhancing prediction of sequence specificities of DNA binding proteins. In: 2016 IEEE International Conference on Bioinformatics and Biomedicine (BIBM), pp. 178–183. IEEE (2016)

14. Kingma, D.P., Ba, J.: Adam: a method for stochastic optimization. arXiv preprint arXiv:1412.6980 (2014)

15. Kipf, T.N., Welling, M.: Semi-supervised classification with graph convolutional networks. arXiv preprint arXiv:1609.02907 (2016)

16. Lee, D.: LS-GKM: a new gkm-SVM for large-scale datasets. Bioinformatics **32**(14), 2196–2198 (2016)

17. Li, Q., Han, Z., Wu, X.-M.: Deeper insights into graph convolutional networks for semi-supervised learning. In: Thirty-Second AAAI Conference on Artificial Intelligence (2018)

18. Luo, X., Chi, W., Deng, M.: Deepprune: Learning efficient and interpretable convolutional networks through weight pruning for predicting dna-protein binding. Front. Genet. **10**, 1145 (2019)

19. Luo, X., Tu, X., Ding, Y., Gao, G., Deng, M.: Expectation pooling: an effective and interpretable pooling method for predicting DNA–protein binding. Bioinfor- matics **36**(5), 1405–1412 (2020)

20. Mao, C., Yao, L., Luo, Y.: Medgcn: Graph convolutional networks for multiple medical tasks. arXiv preprint arXiv:1904.00326 (2019)

21. Pan, X., Rijnbeek, P., Yan, J., Shen, H.-B.: Prediction of RNA-protein sequence and structure binding preferences using deep convolutional and recurrent neural networks. BMC Genomics **19**(1), 511 (2018)

22. Pan, X., Shen, H.-B.: RNA-protein binding motifs mining with a new hybrid deep learning based cross-domain knowledge integration approach. BMC Bioinformatics **18**(1), 136 (2017)

23. Pan. X., Yan, J.: Attention based convolutional neural network for predicting rna-protein binding sites. arXiv preprint arXiv:1712.02270 (2017)

24. Quang, D., Xie, X.: Danq: a hybrid convolutional and recurrent deep neural network for quantifying the function of DNA sequences. Nucleic Acids Res. **44**(11), e107–e107 (2016)

25. Shen, Z., Bao, W., Huang, D.-S.: Recurrent neural network for predicting transcription factor binding sites. Sci. Rep. **8**(1), 15270 (2018)

26. Veličkovič, P., Cucurull, G., Casanova, A., Romero, A., Lio, P., Bengio, Y.: Graph attention networks. arXiv preprint arXiv:1710.10903 (2017)

27. Wang, X., et al.: Heterogeneous graph attention network. arXiv preprint arXiv:1903.07293 (2019)

28. F. Wu, T. Zhang, A. H. d. Souza Jr, C. Fifty, T. Yu, and K. Q. Weinberger. Simplifying graph convolutional networks. arXiv preprint arXiv:1902.07153, 2019.

29. Yao, L., Mao, C., Luo, Y.: Graph convolutional networks for text classification. arXiv preprint arXiv:1809.05679 (2018)

30. Zeng, H., Edwards, M.D., Liu, G., Gifford, D.K.: Convolutional neural network architectures for predicting DNA–protein binding. Bioinformatics **32**(12), i121–i127 (2016)

31. Zhang, Y., et al.: Model-based analysis of chip-seq (macs). Genome Biol. **9**(9), R137 (2008)

32. Zhuang, C., Ma, Q.: Dual graph convolutional networks for graph-based semi-supervised classification. In: Proceedings of the 2018 World Wide Web Conference on World Wide Web, pp. 499–508. International World Wide Web Conferences Steering Committee (2018)

Weighted Nonnegative Matrix Factorization Based on Multi-source Fusion Information for Predicting CircRNA-Disease Associations

Meineng Wang[1], Xuejun Xie[1], Zhuhong You[2(✉)], Leon Wong[3,4], Liping Li[3], and Zhanheng Chen[3,4]

[1] School of Mathematics and Computer Science,
Yichun University, Yichun Jiangxi 336000, China
[2] School of Computer Science, Northwestern Polytechnical University, Xi'an 710072, China
zhuhongyou@nwpu.edu.cn
[3] Xinjiang Technical Institutes of Physics and Chemistry, Chinese Academy of Sciences,
Urumqi 830011, China
[4] University of Chinese Academy of Sciences, Beijing 100049, China

Abstract. Evidences increasingly have shown that circular RNAs (circRNAs) involve in various key biological processes. Because of the dysregulation and mutation of circRNAs are close associated with many complex human diseases, inferring the associations of circRNA with disease becomes an important step for understanding the pathogenesis, treatment and diagnosis of complex diseases. However, it is costly and time-consuming to verify the circRN-disease association through biological experiments, more and more computational methods have been proposed for inferring potential associations of circRNAs with diseases. In this work, we developed a novel weighted nonnegative matrix factorization algorithm based on multi-source fusion information for circRNA-disease association prediction (WNMFCDA). We firstly constructed the overall similarity of diseases based on semantic information and Gaussian Interaction Profile (GIP) kernel, and calculated the similarity of circRNAs based on GIP kernel. Next, the circRNA-disease adjacency matrix is rebuilt using K nearest neighbor profiles. Finally, nonnegative matrix factorization algorithm is utilized to calculate the scores of each pairs of circRNA and disease. To evaluate the performance of WNMFCDA, five-fold cross-validation is performed. WNMFCDA achieved the AUC value of 0.945, which is higher than other compared methods. In addition, we compared the prediction matrix with original adjacency matrix. These experimental results show that WNMFCDA is an effective algorithm for circRNA-disease association prediction.

Keywords: circRNA-disease association · Nearest neighbor · Gaussian interaction profile kernel · Semantic information · Matrix factorization

1 Introduction

CircRNA is a type of non-coding RNA with closed loop structure [1, 2]. Recently, a large number of circRNAs have been uncovered and have attracted more and more

© Springer Nature Switzerland AG 2021
D.-S. Huang et al. (Eds.): ICIC 2021, LNAI 12838, pp. 467–477, 2021.
https://doi.org/10.1007/978-3-030-84532-2_42

attention. As early as 1976, Sanger *et al.* [3] discovered and demonstrated the existence of circRNAs in plants. In 1993, circRNA was first discovered in human cells [4]. Unlike traditional linear RNAs such long non-coding RNAs (lncRNAs) and microRNAs (miRNAs), circRNAs have a closed loop structure, which is not affected by RNA exonuclease, and has biological stability, temporal and spatial specificity, and evolutionary conservatism [5, 6]. Recently studies have shown that circRNA plays an important regulatory role in many human diseases by interacting with miRNAs associated with diseases [7–9]. Especially, circRNAs can be used as biomarkers and therapeutic targets for various human diseases [10–13]. For example, the expression of hsa-circ-0005075 is significantly different in normal cells and hepatocellular carcinoma, its expression level is closely related to tumor size, and can be used as a diagnostic marker and therapeutic target for Hepatocellular carcinoma [14, 15]. Thus, inferring potential associations of circRNA with disease not only contributes to comprehend the pathogenesis of complex diseases, but also helps in the prevention, diagnosis and treatment of diseases [16, 17]. However, identifying the relationships between circRNA and disease through traditional biological experiments is time-consuming and expensive. Therefore, it is an urgent need to exploit fast and effective calculation methods to predict circRNA-disease potential associations.

Recently, many computational methods have been developed for predicting drug-target interactions [18, 19], lncRNA-disease associations [20, 21], protein-protein interactions [22–24] and miRNA-disease associations [25–27]. At the same time, based on the existing databases, some calculation methods are also proposed to infer the circRNA-disease potential associations, such as machine learning, random forest and deep walk embedding etc. For example, DWNN-RLS calculated the circRNA-disease association possibility scores pairs based on Regularized Least Squares of Kronecker product kernel [28]. GAN-CDA predicted associations of circRNA with disease by constructing a deep Generative Adversarial Network [29]. Although these methods have achieved encouraging results, there are still challenges in improving the performance of predicting circRNA-disease association. Previous studies have shown that nonnegative matrix factorization (NMF) is widely used in collaborative filtering for recommender systems [30, 31] and has been successfully applied in bioinformatics [32, 33]. Therefore, we can convert the prediction of the relationship between cicrRNA and disease into a recommendation task and use the NMF method to solve it.

In this work, we propose a computational method, called WNMFCDA, which calculate the circRNA-disease pair scores using weighted nonnegative matrix factorization. Firstly, WNMFCDA calculate the Gaussian interaction profile (GIP) kernel similarities of circRNA and disease based on the known circRNA-disease association. Secondly, we calculate the disease sematic similarity and construct the overall similarity of disease based on sematic similarity and GIP similarity. Finally, nonnegative matrix factorization is used to calculate the association scores between circRNA and disease. Furthermore, to improve the predictive performance of WNMFCDA, the weighted K nearest neighbor as a preprocessing step is performed to rebuild the circRNA-disease association adjacency matrix. To assess the WNMFCDA performance, five-fold cross validation is conducted. Our proposed method achieved the AUC value is 0.945, which is higher than other four competing methods. In addition, the prediction ability of WNMFCDA is further confirmed by comparing the predicted matrix with original adjacency matrix.

2 Materials and Methods

2.1 Dataset

The database of CircR2Disease [34] used in this work includes experimentally verified associations between circRNA and disease. These circRNA-disease associations are accessible to academic users at http://bioinfo.snnu.edu.cn/CircR2Disease/. After removing the duplicated association records, 725 associations between 661 circRNAs and 100 diseases were obtained, which is utilized to construct circRNA-disease association adjacency matrix $M^{m \times n}$. m and n denote the number of circRNA and disease, respectively. If the association of circRNA i with disease j is verified, the entry $M(i, j)$ is set 1, otherwise is 0.

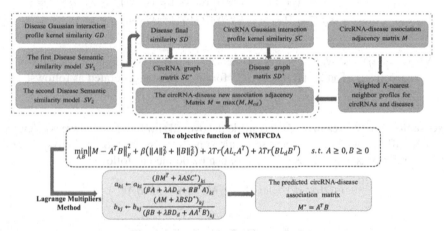

Fig. 1. The flowchart of WNMFCDA

2.2 Method Overview

In this study, weighted nonnegative matrix factorization is used to infer the circRNA-disease potential associations, which contains the following steps as shown in Fig. 1. First, we measure the circRNA-circRNA similarity based on GIP kernel, and measure the disease-disease similarity according to GIP kernel and sematic information, respectively. Second, a preprocessing step is performed to reformulate the circRNA-disease adjacency matrix. Finally, nonnegative matrix factorization algorithm is used to infer the circRNA-disease associations.

2.3 Similarity Measures

CircRNA Similarity Measure. According to the assumption that function similar circRNAs are more likely to be associated with similar diseases [35, 36], we use GIP kernel to calculate the similarity of circRNAs based on circRNA-disease associations matrix [37–39]. The GIP kernel similarity between circRNA c_i and c_j can be defined as follows:

$$SC(c_i, c_j) = GC(c_i, c_j) = \exp\left(-\gamma_c \|M(c_i) - M(c_j)\|^2\right) \tag{1}$$

$$\gamma_c = \frac{1}{\frac{1}{m}\sum_{i=1}^{m} \|M(c_i)\|^2} \tag{2}$$

where $M(c_i)$ is the ith row vector of M, m is the number of circRNAs.

Based on manifold learning and spectral graph theories, p-nearest neighbor graph can be used to model local geometric structure for circRNA [40–42]. Therefore, the weight matrix g^c is calculated based on the circRNA similarity matrix SC as follows:

$$g_{ij}^c = \begin{cases} 1 & i \in N_p(c_j) \& j \in N_p(c_j) \\ 0 & i \notin N_p(c_j) \& j \in N_p(c_j) \\ 0.5 & otherwise \end{cases} \tag{3}$$

Where $N_p(c_i)$ and $N_p(c_j)$ represent the sets of p-nearest neighbors of circRNA c_i and c_j, respectively. The graph matrix SC^* for circRNAs is generated as follows:

$$\forall i, j SC_{ij}^* = g_{ij}^c * SC_{ij} \tag{4}$$

Disease Similarity Measure. In this work, the overall similarity of disease is calculated based on GIP kernel similarity and semantic similarity. Similar to circRNAs, The GIP kernel similarity between disease d_i and d_j can be defined as follows:

$$GD(d_i, d_j) = \exp\left(-\gamma_d \|M(d_i) - M(d_j)\|^2\right) \tag{5}$$

$$\gamma_d = \frac{1}{\frac{1}{n}\sum_{i=1}^{n} \|M(d_i)\|^2} \tag{6}$$

where $M(d_j)$ is the jth column vector of M, n is the number of diseases.

In addition, the hierarchical directed acyclic graph (DAG) is used to measure the semantic similarity of diseases [43–45]. We can obtain the DAGs=(d, N_d, E_d) of diseases from MeSH database. The semantic contribution of disease t to disease d can be denoted as follows:

$$\begin{cases} D_d(t) = 1 & if t = d \\ D_d(t) = max\{\rho * D_d(t') | t' \in childrenoft\} & if t \neq d \end{cases} \tag{7}$$

where N_d denotes the set of parent nodes of disease d including itself, E_d represents the set of links in DAGs. ρ is the semantic contribution factor ($\rho = 0.5$) [46]. So, the first semantic similarity SV_1 of disease d_i with d_j can be determined as follows:

$$SV_1(d_i, d_j) = \frac{\sum_{t \in N_{d_i} \cap N_{d_j}}(D_{d_i}(t) + D_{d_j}(t))}{\sum_{t \in N_{d_i}} D_{d_i}(t) + \sum_{t \in N_{d_j}} D_{d_j}(t)} \tag{8}$$

Considering that the contribution of each disease is inversely proportional to the number of diseases in the DAGs [47]. The second semantic similarity SV_2 is constructed as follows:

$$SV_2(d_i, d_j) = \frac{\sum_{t \in N_{d_i} \cap N_{d_j}} (D'_{d_i}(t) + D'_{d_j}(t))}{\sum_{t \in N_{d_i}} D_{d_i}(t) + \sum_{t \in N_{d_j}} D_{d_j}(t)} \tag{9}$$

$$D'_d(t) = -\log\left(\frac{\text{sum(DAGs(t))}}{\text{sum(diseases)}}\right) \tag{10}$$

where sum(diseases) and sum(DAGs(t)) are the number of all diseases and DAGs including disease t, respectively. $D_{d_i}(t)$ denotes the semantic contribution value of disease t to d_i.

Thereafter, the final similarity of diseases is calculated by:

$$SD(d_i, d_j) =$$

$$\begin{cases} \frac{SV_1(d_i,d_j)+SV_2(d_i,d_j)}{2} & \text{if } d_i \text{ and } d_j \text{ has semantic similarity} \bullet \langle \not\times \not\!\!f " \langle \rightarrow \\ GD(d_i, d_j) & \text{otherwise} \end{cases} \tag{11}$$

Similar to circRNAs, the graph matrix SD^* for diseases can be calculated based on similarity SD of diseases.

$$\forall i, jSD^*_{ij} = g^c_{ij} * SD_{ij} \tag{12}$$

2.4 Weighted K Nearest Neighbor Profiles for CircRNAs and Diseases

Due to Many of the non-associations (the values are 0) in M are unknown cases that may be potential true associations. Thus, Weighted K nearest neighbor is used to calculate the association likelihoods for these unknown cases. For each disease d_l, we sort disease d_j to d_K in descending order based on the similarity with d_l, the corresponding K interaction profile for disease d_l is obtained as follows:

$$M_d(d_l) = \frac{1}{F_d} \sum_{j=1}^{K} \theta^{j-1} * SD(d_j, d_l) * M(d_j) \tag{13}$$

$$E_d = \sum_{1 \leq j \leq K} SD(d_j, d_l) \tag{14}$$

where $\theta \in [0, 1]$ and E_d denote the decay term and normalization term, respectively.

Similar to disease, the new interaction profile $M_c(c_q)$ for corcRNA c_q can be obtained based on the circRNA similarity matrix SC.

Then, we update the original adjacency matrix M by replacing $M_{ij} = 0$ using the average of M_c and M_d as follows:

$$M = \max(M, M_{cd}) \tag{15}$$

$$M_{cd} = \frac{M_c + M_d}{2} \tag{16}$$

2.5 WNMFCDA

According to the idea of nonnegative matrix factorization (NMF), we decomposed the circRNA-disease association matrix $M^{m \times n}$ into two low-dimensional nonnegative latent feature matrices $A^{k \times m}$ and $B^{k \times n}$ ($k < \min(m, n)$). The objective function of NMF for circRNA-disease association prediction is defined as follows:

$$\min_{A,B} \|M - A^T B\|_F^2 s.t. A \geq 0, B \geq 0 \tag{17}$$

where k is subspace dimensionality and $\|\cdot\|_F^2$ is the Frobenius norm.

Previous studies have shown that the standard NMF fails to uncover intrinsic geometrical of circRNA and disease space [48]. To address this problem and prevent overfitting, we introduced Tikhonov (L_2) and graph Laplacian regularization terms into the NMF. The objective function can be expressed as:

$$\min_{A,B} \left\|M - A^T B\right\|_F^2 + \lambda \left(\sum_{i \leq j}^{m} \|a_i - a_j\|^2 SC_{ij}^* + \sum_{i \leq j}^{n} \|b_i - b_j\|^2 SD_{ij}^* \right)$$
$$+ \beta \left(\|A\|_F^2 + \|B\|_F^2 \right) \qquad s.t. A \geq 0, B \geq 0 \tag{18}$$

where a_i and b_j are the ith column of A and jth column of B, respectively. λ and β denote the regularization coefficients. In which, the graph matrices SC^* and SD^* are used to avoid the influence of noisy information on prediction performance. The Eq. (16) can be rewritten as follows:

$$\min_{A,B} \|M - A^T B\|_F^2 + \beta \left(\|A\|_F^2 + \|B\|_F^2 \right) + \lambda Tr \left(AL_c A^T \right) + \lambda Tr \left(BL_d B^T \right)$$
$$s.t. A \geq 0, B \geq 0 \tag{19}$$

where $L_c = D_c - SC^*$ and $L_d = D_d - SD^*$ represent the graph Laplacian matrices with respect to SC^* and SD^*. $D_c(i, i) = \sum_t SC_{it}^*$ and $D_d(j, j) = \sum_r SD_{jr}^*$ are the diagonal matrices. $Tr(\cdot)$ is the trace of a matrix.

In this work, Lagrange multipliers [49] and Karush–Kuhn–Tucker (KKT) [50] conditions are used to solve the optimization problem of Eq. (17). We can obtain the updating rules for a_{ki} and b_{kj} as follows:

$$a_{ki} \leftarrow a_{ki} \frac{(BM^T + \lambda ASC^*)_{ki}}{(\beta A + \lambda AD_c + BB^T A)_{ki}} \tag{20}$$

$$b_{kj} \leftarrow b_{kj} \frac{(AM + \lambda BSD^*)_{kj}}{(\beta B + \lambda BD_d + AA^T B)_{kj}} \tag{21}$$

The feature matrices A and B are updated by Eq. (18) and Eq. (19) until convergence. Then, the predicted matrix for circRNA-disease associations is calculated by $M = A^T B$, and infer whether cicrRNA is related to the disease according to the element value in M.

3   Results

To investigate the performance of WNMFCDA, we conduct five-fold cross-validation and compare it with the previous models: GAN-CDA, DWNN-RLS, K-Nearest Neighbor (KNN) and Support Vector Machine (SVM). There are six parameters in our method, and the values of parameters θ and K are set 0.5 and 5 based on the previous studies. The optimum parameter values are $k = 60$, $p = 8$, $\lambda = 0.1$ and $\beta = 0.1$ based on five-fold cross-validation.

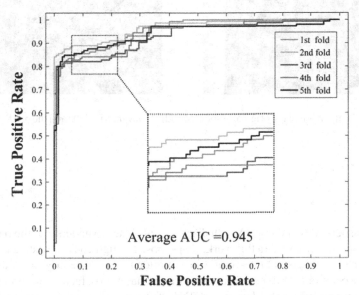

Fig. 2. The ROC curves for WNMFCDA under the five-fold cross validation.

Table 1. The average AUC values among different methods.

Methods	WNMFCDA	GAN-CDA	DWNN-RLS	SVM	KNN
AUC	0.945	0.906	0.885	0.842	0.833

In this study, we draw the Receiver Operating Characteristic (ROC) curve and calculate the area under the ROC curve (AUC) as the evaluation index. As shown in Fig. 2 and Table 1, WNMFCDA achieves the AUC value of 0.945, while the AUC values of KNN, SVM, DWNN-RLS and GAN-CDA are 0.833, 0.842, 0.885 and 0.906, respectively. The results show that the performance of WNMFCDA outperforms other compared methods. To systematically evaluate the predictive performance of our method, Brier score is also used as the measurements in this study. In general, the prediction performance of the model is better if the Brier score is lower. The Brier score obtained by WNMFCDA is 0.0446. In addition, the lager element values of predicted matrix denote that the circR-NAs are more possible to be associated with the corresponding diseases. The original circRNA-disease adjacency matrix and predicted matrix by WNMFCDA are shown in Fig. 3. These experiment results further demonstrated that WNMFCDA is an effective method for inferring circRNA-disease associations.

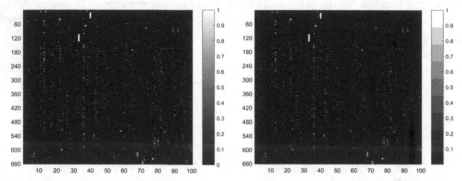

Fig. 3. The comparison of the original association adjacency matrix (left) and the predicted matrix (right).

4   Conclusions

Inferring associations of circRNA with disease contributes to understand the pathogenesis of the complex diseases. In this work, we propose a weighted nonnegative matrix factorization method based on Multi-Source information fusion to identify circRNA-disease potential associations. Different from other traditional matrix factorization methods, in order to reduce the effect of unknown circRNA-disease pairs on prediction performance, a processing step is conducted to construct the new interaction profiles both for circRNA and disease before implementing matrix factorization. The proposed method achieves the best performance compared with other models under 5-fold CV. The experiment results demonstrate that WNMFCDA is an effective tool for identifying associations of circRNA with disease. Furthermore, WNMFCDA also can be used to predict associations among different biomolecules, such as circRNA-miRNA interactions, lnRNA-miRNA interactions, etc. In future work, we will integrate more effective information to improve the predictive performance of our model.

5   Competing Interests

The authors declare no conflict of interest.

Acknowledgements. This work was supported in part by the NSFC Excellent Young Scholars Program, under Grant 61722212, in part by the National Natural Science Foundation of China, under Grant 62002297, in part by the Science and Technology Project of Jiangxi Provincial Department of Education, under Grants GJJ190834, GJJ201605.

References

1. Memczak, S., et al.: Circular RNAs are a large class of animal RNAs with regulatory potency. Nature **495**(7441), 333–338 (2013)
2. Jeck, W.R., Sharpless, N.E.: Detecting and characterizing circular RNAs. Nat. Biotechnol. **32**(5), 453–461 (2014)
3. Sanger, H.L., Klotz, G., Riesner, D., Gross, H.J., Kleinschmidt, A.K.: Viroids are single-stranded covalently closed circular RNA molecules existing as highly base-paired rod-like structures. Proc. Natl. Acad. Sci. **73**(11), 3852–3856 (1976)
4. Nigro, J.M., et al.: Scrambled exons. Cell **64**(3), 607–613 (1991)
5. Wang, F., Nazarali, A.J., Ji, S.: Circular RNAs as potential biomarkers for cancer diagnosis and therapy. Am. J. Cancer Res. **6**(6), 1167 (2016)
6. Wang, Y., et al.: Circular RNAs in human cancer. Mol. Cancer **16**(1), 1–8 (2017)
7. Luo, J., Xiao, Q.: A novel approach for predicting microRNA-disease associations by unbalanced bi-random walk on heterogeneous network. J. Biomed. Inform. **66**, 194–203 (2017)
8. Chen, M., Lu, X., Liao, B., Li, Z., Cai, L., Gu, C.: Uncover miRNA-disease association by exploiting global network similarity. PloS one **11**(12), e0166509 (2016)
9. Fan, C., Lei, X., Pan, Y.: Prioritizing CircRNA-disease associations with convolutional neural network based on multiple similarity feature fusion. Front. Genet. **11**, 1042 (2020)
10. Chen, J., et al.: Circular RNA profile identifies circPVT1 as a proliferative factor and prognostic marker in gastric cancer. Cancer Lett. **388**, 208–219 (2017)
11. Wang, L., You, Z.-H., Huang, Y.-A., Huang, D.-S., Chan, K.C.: An efficient approach based on multi-sources information to predict circRNA–disease associations using deep convolutional neural network. Bioinformatics **36**(13), 4038–4046 (2020)
12. Guo, S., et al.: Microarray expression profile analysis of circular RNAs in pancreatic cancer. Mol. Med. Rep. **17**(6), 7661–7671 (2018)
13. Chen, B., Huang, S.: Circular RNA: an emerging non-coding RNA as a regulator and biomarker in cancer. Cancer Lett. **418**, 41–50 (2018)
14. Shang, X., et al.: Comprehensive circular RNA profiling reveals that hsa_circ_0005075, a new circular RNA biomarker, is involved in hepatocellular carcinoma development. Medicine **95**(22), e3811 (2016)
15. Hao, Q., Han, Y., Xia, W., Wang, Q., Qian, H.: Systematic review and meta-analysis of the utility of circular RNAs as biomarkers of hepatocellular carcinoma. Can. J. Gastroenterol. Hepatol. 2019 (2019)
16. Wang, L., You, Z.-H., Li, J.-Q., Huang, Y.-A.: IMS-CDA: prediction of CircRNA-disease associations from the integration of multisource similarity information with deep stacked autoencoder model. IEEE Trans. Cybern. (2020)
17. Lei, X., Fang, Z., Chen, L., Wu, F.-X.: PWCDA: path weighted method for predicting circRNA-disease associations. Int. J. Mol. Sci. **19**(11), 3410 (2018)
18. Chen, Z.-H., You, Z.-H., Guo, Z.-H., Yi, H.-C., Luo, G.-X., Wang, Y.-B.: Prediction of drug-target interactions from multi-molecular network based on deep walk embedding model. Front. Bioeng. Biotech. **8**, 338 (2020)
19. Cui, Z., Gao, Y.-L., Liu, J.-X., Wang, J., Shang, J., Dai, L.-Y.: The computational prediction of drug-disease interactions using the dual-network L 2, 1-CMF method. BMC Bioinf. **20**(1), 1–10 (2019)
20. Guo, Z., You, Z., Wang, Y., Yi, H., Chen, Z.: A learning-based method for LncRNA-disease association identification combing similarity information and rotation forest. iScience **19**, 786–795 (2019)

21. Fu, G., Wang, J., Domeniconi, C., Yu, G.: Matrix factorization-based data fusion for the prediction of lncRNA–disease associations. Bioinformatics **34**(9), 1529–1537 (2018)
22. Chen, Z.-H., You, Z.-H., Li, L.-P., Wang, Y.-B., Qiu, Y., Hu, P.-W.: Identification of self-interacting proteins by integrating random projection classifier and finite impulse response filter. BMC Genomics **20**(13), 1–10 (2019)
23. Chen, Z.-H., Li, L.-P., He, Z., Zhou, J.-R., Li, Y., Wong, L.: An improved deep forest model for predicting self-interacting proteins from protein sequence using wavelet transformation. Front. Genet. **10**, 90 (2019)
24. Chen, Z., You, Z., Zhang, W., Wang, Y., Cheng, L., Alghazzawi, D.: Global vectors representation of protein sequences and its application for predicting self-interacting proteins with multi-grained cascade forest model. Genes **10**(11), 924 (2019)
25. Guo, Z., Yi, H., You, Z.: Construction and comprehensive analysis of a molecular association network via lncRNA–miRNA–disease–drug–protein graph. Cells **8**(8), 866 (2019)
26. You, Z., et al.: PRMDA: personalized recommendation-based MiRNA-disease association prediction. Oncotarget **8**(49), 85568–85583 (2017)
27. Chen, M., et al.: A novel information diffusion method based on network consistency for identifying disease related microRNAs. RSC Adv. **8**(64), 36675–36690 (2018)
28. Yan, C., Wang, J., Wu, F.-X.: DWNN-RLS: regularized least squares method for predicting circRNA-disease associations. BMC Bioinf. **19**(19), 73–81 (2018)
29. Wang, L., You, Z.-H., Li, L.-P., Zheng, K., Wang, Y.-B.: Predicting circRNA-disease associations using deep generative adversarial network based on multi-source fusion information. In: 2019 IEEE International Conference on Bioinformatics and Biomedicine (BIBM). IEEE (2019)
30. Luo, X., Zhou, M., Li, S., You, Z., Xia, Y., Zhu, Q.: A nonnegative latent factor model for large-scale sparse matrices in recommender systems via alternating direction method. IEEE Trans. Neural Netw. Learn. Syst. **27**(3), 579–592 (2015)
31. Wang, Y.-X., Zhang, Y.-J.: Nonnegative matrix factorization: a comprehensive review. IEEE Trans. Knowl. Data Eng. **25**(6), 1336–1353 (2012)
32. Wang, M.-N., You, Z.-H., Li, L.-P., Chen, Z.-H., Xie, X.-J.: WGMFDDA: a novel weighted-based graph regularized matrix factorization for predicting drug-disease associations. In: Huang, D.-S., Premaratne, P. (eds.) ICIC 2020. LNCS (LNAI), vol. 12465, pp. 542–551. Springer, Cham (2020). https://doi.org/10.1007/978-3-030-60796-8_47
33. Zou, L., Chen, X., Wang, Z.J.: Underdetermined joint blind source separation for two datasets based on tensor decomposition. IEEE Signal Process. Lett. **23**(5), 673–677 (2016)
34. Fan, C., Lei, X., Fang, Z., Jiang, Q., Wu, F.-X.: CircR2Disease: a manually curated database for experimentally supported circular RNAs associated with various diseases. Database 2018 (2018)
35. Chen, M., Zhang, Y., Li, A., Li, Z., Chen, Z.: Bipartite heterogeneous network method based on co-neighbor for MiRNA-disease association prediction. Front. Genet. **10**, 385 (2019)
36. van Laarhoven, T., Nabuurs, S.B., Marchiori, E.: Gaussian interaction profile kernels for predicting drug–target interaction. Bioinformatics **27**(21), 3036–3043 (2011)
37. Yi, H.-C., You, Z.-H., Wang, M.-N., Guo, Z.-H., Wang, Y.-B., Zhou, J.-R.: RPI-SE: a stacking ensemble learning framework for ncRNA-protein interactions prediction using sequence information. BMC Bioinf. **21**(1), 60 (2020)
38. Chen, X., Huang, Y.-A., You, Z.-H., Yan, G.-Y., Wang, X.-S.: A novel approach based on KATZ measure to predict associations of human microbiota with non-infectious diseases. Bioinformatics **33**(5), 733–739 (2017)
39. Yan, C., Wang, J., Ni, P., Lan, W., Wu, F.-X., Pan, Y.: DNRLMF-MDA: predicting microRNA-disease associations based on similarities of microRNAs and diseases. IEEE/ACM Trans. Comput. Biol. Bioinf. **16**(1), 233–243 (2017)

40. You, Z.-H., Lei, Y.-K., Gui, J., Huang, D.-S., Zhou, X.: Using manifold embedding for assessing and predicting protein interactions from high-throughput experimental data. Bioinformatics **26**(21), 2744–2751 (2010)

41. Ezzat, A., Zhao, P., Wu, M., Li, X.-L., Kwoh, C.-K.: Drug-target interaction prediction with graph regularized matrix factorization. IEEE/ACM Trans. Comput. Biol. Bioinf. **14**(3), 646–656 (2016)

42. Wang, M.-N., You, Z.-H., Wang, L., Li, L.-P., Zheng, K.: LDGRNMF: LncRNA-disease associations prediction based on graph regularized non-negative matrix factorization. Neurocomputing **424**, 236–245 (2020)

43. Zheng, K., You, Z.-H., Wang, L., Zhou, Y., Li, L.-P., Li, Z.-W.: MLMDA: a machine learning approach to predict and validate MicroRNA–disease associations by integrating of heterogenous information sources. J. Transl. Med. **17**(1), 260 (2019)

44. Zheng, K., You, Z.-H., Li, J.-Q., Wang, L., Guo, Z.-H., Huang, Y.-A.: iCDA-CGR: identification of circRNA-disease associations based on chaos game representation. PLOS Comput. Biol. **16**(5), p. e1007872 (2020)

45. Chen, M., Liao, B., Li, Z.: Global similarity method based on a two-tier random walk for the prediction of microRNA–disease association. Sci. Rep. **8**(1), 1–16 (2018)

46. Xiao, Q., Luo, J., Liang, C., Cai, J., Ding, P.: A graph regularized non-negative matrix factorization method for identifying microRNA-disease associations. Bioinformatics **34**(2), 239–248 (2018)

47. Yan, X., Wang, L., You, Z.-H., Li, L.-P., Zheng, K.: GANCDA: a novel method for predicting circRNA-disease associations based on deep generative adversarial network. Int. J. Data Min. Bioinform. **23**(3), 265–283 (2020)

48. Cai, D., He, X., Han, J., Huang, T.S.: Graph regularized nonnegative matrix factorization for data representation. IEEE Trans. Pattern Anal. Mach. Intell. **33**(8), 1548–1560 (2010)

49. Wang, M.-N., You, Z.-H., Li, L.-P., Wong, L., Chen, Z.-H., Gan, C.-Z.: GNMFLMI: graph regularized nonnegative matrix factorization for predicting LncRNA-MiRNA interactions. IEEE Access **8**, 37578–37588 (2020)

50. Facchinei, F., Kanzow, C., Sagratella, S.: Solving quasi-variational inequalities via their KKT conditions. Math. Program. **144**(1–2), 369–412 (2013). https://doi.org/10.1007/s10107-013-0637-0

ScSSC: Semi-supervised Single Cell Clustering Based on 2D Embedding

Naile Shi[1], Yulin Wu[1], Linlin Du[1], Bo Liu[2], Yadong Wang[1,2], and Junyi Li[1(✉)]

[1] School of Computer Science and Technology, Harbin Institute of Technology (Shenzhen), Shenzhen 518055, Guangdong, China
lijunyi@hit.edu.cn
[2] Center for Bioinformatics, School of Computer Science and Technology, Harbin Institute of Technology, Harbin 150001, Heilongjiang, China

Abstract. In recent years, with the development of single-cell RNA sequencing (scRNA-seq) technology, more and more scRNA-seq data has been generated. Corresponding analysis methods such as clustering analysis are also proposed, which effectively distinguish the cell types and reveal the cell diversity. However, due to more than ten thousand genes for normal species, the dimension of scRNA-seq data is very high. Meanwhile, there exist many zero counts in scRNA-seq data. They all increase the difficulty of clustering analysis of scRNA-seq data. This paper proposes ScSSC, a semi-supervised clustering method based on 2D embedding. ScSSC uses the autoencoder for pre-training to construct the network and applies the community discovery algorithm to label cells. Then a semi-supervised network is used to clustering the data after training. The clustering results of three public data sets show that ScSSC has better performance than other clustering methods.

Keywords: Single-cell clustering · Semi-supervised learning · 2D embedding · Autoencoder · Community discovery

1 Introduction

The analysis of single-cell RNA sequencing (scRNA-seq) helps to understand diversity and heterogeneity of biological tissues. Effective analysis methods can distinguish different cells in single-cell data, classify similar cells, and find the potential relationship between them. scRNA-seq RNA data is often used to find genes associated with diseases. Especially for complex diseases, single-cell data is more conducive to find the potential causes of these diseases [1–4]. Clustering analysis is the most important one in single-cell data analysis method. The commonly used and classic clustering algorithms are k-means clustering and spectrum clustering [5]. However, due to more than ten thousand genes for normal species, the dimension of scRNA-seq data is very high. Meanwhile, there exist many zero counts in scRNA-seq data. Therefore, current high dimension, high divergence of scRNA-seq data bring great challenges to data analysis.

N. Shi and Y. Wu—Contributed equally to this work.

© Springer Nature Switzerland AG 2021
D.-S. Huang et al. (Eds.): ICIC 2021, LNAI 12838, pp. 478–489, 2021.
https://doi.org/10.1007/978-3-030-84532-2_43

With the continuous development of scRNA-seq sequencing technology, corresponding analysis methods are proposed [6]. Aiming at the high dimension problem of scRNA-seq data, the concept of shared nearest-neighbour is proposed a clustering method called SNNClip [7]. When traditional distance measurement methods such as vector similarity is not applicable, a multi-kernel-based spectral clustering method (SIMLR) has also been proposed, which combines multiple cores to learn and is suitable for scRNA data [8]. When the amount of sequencing data is large, the storage and calculation of the Laplacian matrix face huge challenges for the computer. With the improvement of modern sequencing technology, the number of sequenced cells and the number of genes are continuously increasing, which makes it difficult to apply Laplacian matrix-based methods to large-scale data. In view of the many zero-value problems in scRNA-seq data, many researchers have also developed some methods, such as CIDR [9], DeepImpute [10], scDeepCluster [11], ZINB [12], scScope [13], ScGSLC [14], etc. CIDR focuses on dimension reduction and its clustering method is based on more representative coordinates. DeepImpute uses a neural network to predict the missing value of genes and estimates the ratio of gene and clusters as improved input data. ScDeepCluster mainly uses the autoencoder of the deep neural network (DNN) to learn the main features and it add a certain Gaussian noise to the coding part to simulate the error of single-cell data. ScScope uses the nesting of multiple auto-encoders, and it uses the output of the previous auto-encoder as the input of the next auto-encoder. ScGSLC combines scRNA-seq data with protein data and uses graph convolutional network to convert the similarity between cells to the similarity of sub-graphs, finally use the similarity matrix to complete the clustering. Gregory [15] proposed a tree structure for visualization in order to intuitively reflect the relationship between the cells in the scRNA-seq data.

Some methods use model data errors to optimize single-cell data, and then use less complex methods for data clustering. However, these methods are not designed for clustering models. Therefore, the clustering results are not able to fully reflect the potential form of data. Compared with PCA, which can only do simple linear dimensionality reduction, DNN has a stronger ability to learn data characteristics [16]. It can use linear or non-linear transformation to map high-dimensional data to low-dimensional space. Therefore, DNN has a excellent performance for dimension reduction for single-cell data. Studies have shown that DNN can reduce the amount of scRNA-seq data on a large scale, and it effectively extract low-dimensional features in scRNA-seq as well [17, 18]. Convolutional neural network (CNN) also has good performance in labeled classification tasks such as image classification [19, 20].

In this paper, we design a semi-supervised neural network model based on 2D embedding to learn the effective features of scRNA-seq data to complete the final clustering. This method will use an unsupervised method to label part of the data, then use a semi-supervised neural network to train the entire data set to extract features, and finally use the feature data for clustering. Our contributions are mainly as follows: First, we design a new semi-supervised model based on convolutional neural network. Secondly, we synthesize the genetic data of each cell into a gray-scale image to realize the transformation of the scRNA-seq data to two-dimensional data, so that it can be convolved later. Third, each gene in the cell has its own biological significance, and they are related to each other rather than individual individuals. Although we don't know the specific correlations, we can calculate the correlation size of genes and group them. The sequence of genes has a certain influence on the synthesis of pictures.

2 Dataset

With the rise of single-cell sequencing technology, a large amount of single-cell data is used for research and analysis. The original sequencing data is DNA sequence data composed of bases. After a series of statistics, single-cell gene expression profile data is finally obtained. This article selects three more commonly used data sets. Selected single-cell data sets Goolam [21], Polle [22], Kolod [23] data sets. In Table 1, the basic information of the single-cell data set is counted.

Table 1. Statistics related to the original data set

Dataset	Organism	Number of cells	Number of genes	Number of cell types
Goolam	Mouse	124	41480	5
Polle	Human	301	23730	11
Kolodziejczyk	Mouse	704	38653	9

3 Methods

We designed a novel scRNA-seq clustering model ScSSC. First, a series of preprocessing is performed on the data, and the processed data set is transformed into an image set. Then the image set is used as input to the autoencoder model for pre-training and preliminary clustering. After that, we combined dozens of rounds of preliminary clustering results into a network and used the community discovery algorithm to tag some of the data. Finally, use all the data to train the neural network and get the final clustering results and evaluate the performance of the model. The flowchart of ScSSC is shown in Fig. 1:

3.1 Data Pre-processing

First, there are some genes whose expression values are all 0 in the cell, and we will remove these genes. Secondly, the gene expression gap of each cell in the single-cell data may be large. We need to normalize the entire data so that the total amount of genes expressed by each cell is the same. Third, single-cell data generally includes tens of thousands of genes, but many genes have little effect on cluster analysis but will greatly increase the computer's storage and calculation load. Therefore, we select the top n genes with the largest variance as feature genes, where the value of n is between 5929 and tens of thousands.

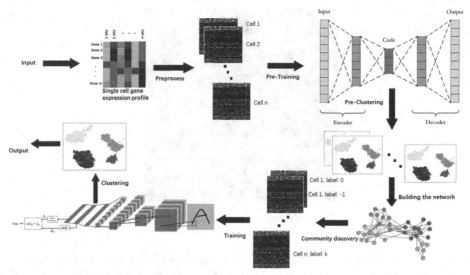

Fig. 1. Overall framework of ScSSC. The gene expression profile is converted into two-dimensional image data as input data and used as the input of the autoencoder. After the training is stabilized, the pre-clustering is performed dozens of times, and the pre-clustering results are used to construct the network and the community discovery algorithm is used to partially label data. The convolutional neural network is used for semi-supervised training of the data, and finally the trained network is used for feature extraction and clustering to obtain the final result.

3.2 Image Synthesis

The 2D embedding method used in this paper maps single-cell data into 2D images. We use "Fill-up" [24] to arrange the gene expression data of each cell into a two-dimensional matrix of a certain size, and then determine the gray value of the pixel according to the amount of gene expression corresponding to each pixel. Since the sequence of genes is different, different images can be obtained, so we need to sort the genes. First of all, this paper needs to calculate the Pearson correlation coefficient matrix of characteristic genes and use spectral clustering to group the characteristic genes, and adjust the order of the genes according to the results so that the cells of the same group are arranged together. Finally, the entire single-cell data is converted into an image set, that is, the one-dimensional vector representing each cell is converted into a grayscale image. For example, a 1*10000 vector will be converted into a 100*100 two-dimensional image as shown in Fig. 2 is a composite Grayscale image:

3.3 Pre-training with Autoencoder

Autoencoder [25] is a powerful tool in unsupervised deep neural network. It effectively solves the problem of dimension reduction. Compared with the traditional dimensionality reduction method such as PCA, the autoencoder normally lose fewer features on the nonlinear data. The autoencoder is a DNN which has same input and output. It aims to make the difference between the output and the input as small as possible. The function f

Fig. 2. Grayscale image synthesized by 2D embedding

is to transform the given input space $X \in \mathcal{X}$ to the feature space $h \in \mathcal{F}$, and the function g is to transform the feature space $h \in \mathcal{F}$ is transformed to the given input space $X \in \mathcal{X}$, and finally the function f and the function g are obtained to minimize the reconstruction error.

$$f : \mathcal{X} \rightarrow \mathcal{F} \tag{1}$$

$$g : \mathcal{F} \rightarrow \mathcal{X} \tag{2}$$

$$f, g = \underset{f,g}{\operatorname{argmin}} \|X - g[f(X)]\|^2 \tag{3}$$

In this autoencoder, we use the more commonly used MSE loss function,

$$\operatorname{loss}(X, g[f(X)]) = (X - g[f(X)])^2 \tag{4}$$

After the training is relatively stable, we will take out tens (such as 20) times in a row and only pass the input through the coding part to achieve the purpose of dimensionality reduction, and then use the spectral clustering method to cluster and record the clustering results.

3.4   Build a Network and Use Community Discovery Algorithms to Classify Data

We use the pre-training clustering results to obtain the clustering matrix $S(n * n)$ in which the cells are clustered into the same category through statistics, where n represents the number of cells contained in the data set, and S_{ij} represents that cell i and cell j are clustered. The number of times of class to the same class (for example, if we count the clustering results 20 times, cell i and cell j are classified into the same class 18 times, then $S_{ij} = 18$, $\max(S_{ij}) = 20$, $\min(S_{ij}) = 0$, And then we will use the matrix S to build the network G. The network contains a total of n nodes, and a minimum threshold k is set. If $S_{ij} \geq k$, an undirected edge with weight S_{ij} is added between node i and node j.

After traversing the matrix S, the network G is established. After that, we will use the Louvain algorithm to divide the community of the network G and record the result of the division. We define the division reliability of cell i as L_i, and define the number of cells i divided into the same category as n_i,

$$L_i = \frac{\sum_{i,j \, in \, the \, same \, category} S_{ij}}{n_i - 1} \tag{5}$$

When the classification reliability L_i of cell i is low, we change the category of cell i to -1. Finally, the labels of all cells are obtained. If the reliability of the division of cell i is high, its label is the result of the division of Louvain [26] algorithm, otherwise its label is -1.

3.5 Semi-supervised Neural Network Model

We construct a semi-supervised neural network suitable for this article based on the convolutional neural network model. We will train the image data and use the trained model to extract features from all cell image data, and finally use the extracted features for clustering. The convolutional neural network used in this article contains a total of 3 convolutional layers, 3 pooling layers, and 3 fully connected layers. 3 fully connected layers are used for training, but only 2 fully connected layers are used for clustering. The layer allows each cell image data to be converted into a feature vector. We use the cross entropy function [27] as the loss function for the labeled data to get the loss $\mathcal{L}_s$ First, you need to use the Sigmoid function to adjust the data size between 0 and 1 for the output result, and then pass it into the cross entropy function.

$$S(x) = \frac{1}{1 + e^{-x}} \tag{6}$$

$$loss(x, class) = -log\left(\frac{e^{x[class]}}{\sum_j e^{x[j]}}\right) = -x[class] + log(\sum_j e^{x[j]}) \tag{7}$$

Where x represents the features extracted from the cell image data after passing through the convolutional neural network, and class represents the category of x. For unlabeled data, we will only pass two fully connected layers after passing the convolutional layer, and use the MSE as the loss function to get the loss $\mathcal{L}_u$. In the end, the loss of the entire network is loss $= \omega\mathcal{L}_u + \mathcal{L}_s$.

3.6 Evaluation Index

The evaluation indicators used in this article include ARI (Adjusted Rand index) and NMI [28]. The Rand index [29] is a measure of agreement between two cluster results U and V. The ARI is used to correct the lack of a constant value of the Rand index when the cluster results are selected randomly [30]. NMI is defined as mutual information between U and V divided by the entropy of the clustering U and V.

$$ARI = a_{11} - \frac{\frac{(a_{11}+a_{01})(a_{11}+a_{10})}{a_{00}}}{\frac{(a_{11}+a_{01})+(a_{11}+a_{10})}{2} - \frac{(a_{11}+a_{01})(a_{11}+a_{10})}{a_{00}}} \tag{8}$$

where the clustering results U and V have C_u and C_v clusters respectively. And a_{11} represents the number of sample pairs in the same category in the real category and the clustering result, a_{00} represents the number of sample pairs in the same category in both the real category and the clustering result, and a_{10} represents the number of sample pairs in the same category in the real category. The clustering result is the number of sample pairs of different categories, a_{01} represents the number of sample pairs of different categories in the real category and the same category in the clustering result.

If one contains n data and has two clustering results C_u and C_v, then

$$NMI = \frac{\sum_{p=1}^{C_u}\sum_{q=1}^{C_v}|U_p \cap V_q|log\frac{n|U_p \cap V_q|}{|U_p|\times|V_q|}}{max\left(-\sum_{p=1}^{C_U}|U_p|log\frac{|U_p|}{n}, \; -\sum_{q=1}^{C_V}|V_q|log\frac{|V_q|}{n}\right)} \qquad (9)$$

4   Results

4.1   Similarity Heat Map

In this paper, we use the similarity between cells when clustering the obtained feature vectors. In order to show the similarity of the cell feature vectors more intuitively, we draw a heat map based on the cell similarity matrix, as shown in Fig. 3:

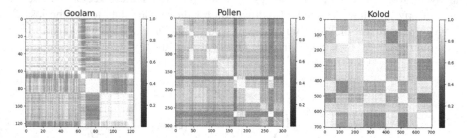

Fig. 3. Heat map of cell similarity obtained after training by ScSSC model

It can be seen from Fig. 3 that the higher the degree of similarity between cells, the closer the color of their corresponding places is to white. The white rectangle can be easily found in the figure, indicating that the similarity between these cells is very high, and they will basically be grouped into the same category in the end. For example, in the data set Kolod, this data set contains more cells, so the white matrix is more obvious. We can easily find 8 white rectangles, so this data set is roughly divided into 8 categories.

4.2   Results of Clustering Performance Indicators (ARI and NMI)

We show the final performance index results in the form of a histogram in Fig. 4. From Fig. 4, we can easily find that our method is significantly better than other methods in terms of performance indicators, including PCA [31] +K-means [32], NMF [33] +K-means, SIMLR [34], SC3 [35], RAFSIL [36], PM(Pyramid Match Kernel) [37], VH(Vertex histogram kernel) [38].

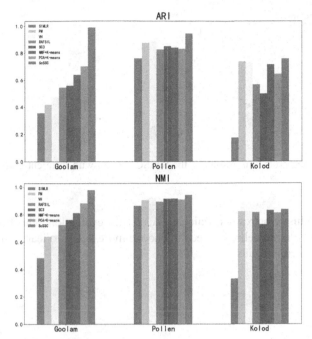

Fig. 4. The performance index of ScSSC is compared with other clustering methods. The higher the value, the higher the consistency between the predicted label and the real label.

4.3 Visualization of Results

The visualization of two-dimensional results in single-cell clustering analysis can be considered as an indispensable method for displaying clustering results. T-SNE [39] is mostly used for two-dimensional or three-dimensional visualization. It is a nonlinear dimension reduction method and has a strong ability to find the most suitable mapping from high dimension to low-dimension.

In order to make the clustering effect more intuitive, this paper visualizes the high-dimensional feature vector obtained by ScSSC, we use T-SNE to reduce the feature vector to 2 dimensions, and the result is shown in Fig. 5. In the figure, each scattered point represents a cell, and the cluster to which the cell belongs is labeled according to the clustering result of the corresponding feature vector. We can see that in these three data sets, the division of cells is more obvious, that is, cells of the same type are more compact, and cells of different types are more scattered (Fig. 5).

4.4 Parameter Sensitivity

Here we will analyze the influence of the number of selected genes on the final evaluation index of the experiment under the same other conditions. As shown in Fig. 6, we can see that when fewer genes are selected, our model will not learn enough features, so that the clustering effect does not reach the highest value. When the number of genes we select is close to the total number of genes, our model will learn too many features that have

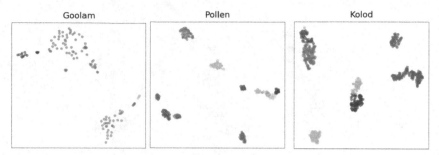

Fig. 5. Visualize the prediction results of the ScSSC model, with different colors representing different cell types

no effect on the clustering results, which will cause the evaluation index to drop sharply. For a data set with more cells, we need to choose more genes to learn enough features to get better clustering results.

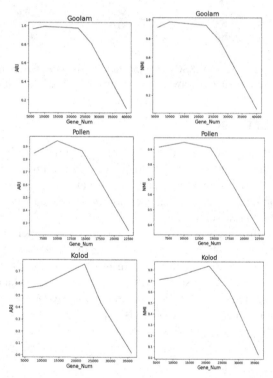

Fig. 6. Line chart of ARI and NMI changes with the number of genes

5   Conclusion

Using the 2D embedding method to synthesize single-cell data into images can more intuitively present the gene expression of each cell. At the same time, the data has a certain two-dimensional structure, and the connection between genes can be better explored through the convolutional layer. The advantage of unsupervised neural networks is that they can be trained on a large number of unlabeled data in the world and can effectively extract features, while semi-supervised neural networks have unmatched accuracy in other methods.

In this paper, ScSSC effectively combines the advantages of these three methods, turning the unsupervised clustering problem into a semi-supervised problem with partial labels, and discovering the hidden relationships between different genes through the convolutional layer. These pairs ultimately The improvement of clustering accuracy has a great effect. At the same time, we visualize the results in two dimensions so that the clustering effect can be displayed more intuitively. The results on the current 3 data sets show that ScSSC is a very competitive clustering method. At the same time, with the rapid increase in the size of single-cell sequencing data, ScSSC can use only part of the data for training, and then perform feature extraction and clustering on all data after obtaining network parameters, which can effectively shorten the training time on large-scale data. Therefore, ScSSC is a promising method for cluster analysis of large-scale scRNA-seq data.

Acknowledgements. This work was supported by the grants from the National Key Research Program (2017YFC1201201, 2018YFC0910504 and 2017YFC0907503), Shenzhen Science and Technology Program the university stable support program (20200821222112001) from JL.

Authors' Contributions. NS, YW and JL designed the study, performed bioinformatics analysis and drafted the manuscript. All of the authors performed the analysis and participated in the revision of the manuscript. JL conceived of the study, participated in its design and coordination and drafted the manuscript. All authors read and approved the final manuscript.

Competing Interests. The authors declare that they have no competing interests.

Additional Files. All additional files are available at: https://github.com/NaiLeShi/-ScSSC.

References

1. Kulkarni, A., Anderson, A.G., Merullo, D.P., Konopka, G.: Beyond bulk: a review of single cell transcriptomics methodologies and applications. Curr. Opin. Biotechnol. **58**, 129–136 (2019)
2. Lake, B., Chen, S., Hoshi, M., Plongthongkum, N., Jain, S.: A single-nucleus RNA-sequencing pipeline to decipher the molecular anatomy and pathophysiology of human kidneys. Nat. Commun. **10**(1), 2832 (2019)
3. Lee, E.J., et al.: A validated single-cell-based strategy to identify diagnostic and therapeutic targets in complex diseases. Genome Med. **11**, 47 (2019). https://doi.org/10.1186/s13073-019-0657-3

4. Zhang, P., Yang, M., Zhang, Y., Xiao, S., Li, S.: Dissecting the single-cell transcriptome network underlying gastric premalignant lesions and early gastric cancer. Cell Rep. **27**(6), 1934-1947.e1935 (2019)
5. Mereu, E., Lafzi, A., Moutinho, C., Ziegenhain, C., Heyn, H.: Benchmarking single-cell RNA sequencing protocols for cell atlas projects. Nature Biotech. **38**(6), 747–755 (2020)
6. Jla, B., Wca, B., Zsa, C.: Single-cell sequencing technologies: current and future. J. Genet. Genomics **41**(10), 513–528 (2014)
7. Xu, C., Su, Z.: Identification of cell types from single-cell transcriptomes using a novel clustering method. Bioinformatics **12**, 1974–1980 (2015)
8. Wang, B., Zhu, J., Pierson, E., Ramazzotti, D., Batzoglou, S.: Visualization and analysis of single-cell RNA-seq data by kernel-based similarity learning. Nat. Methods **14**(4), 414 (2017)
9. Lin, P., Troup, M., Ho, J.: CIDR: ultrafast and accurate clustering through imputation for single-cell RNA-seq data. Genome Biol. **18**(1), 59 (2017)
10. Arisdakessian, C., Poirion, O., Yunits, B., Zhu, X., Garmire, L.X.: DeepImpute: an accurate, fast, and scalable deep neural network method to impute single-cell RNA-seq data. Genome Biol. **20**(1), 1–14 (2018)
11. Tian, T., Wan, J., Song, Q., Wei, Z.: Clustering single-cell RNA-seq data with a model-based deep learning approach. Nature Mach. Intell. **1**(4), 191 (2019)
12. Williamson, J.M., Lin, H.M., Lyles, R.H., Hightower, A.W.: Power calculations for ZIP and ZINB models. J. Data Sci. **5**(4), 519–534 (2007)
13. Yue, D., Feng, B., Dai, Q., Wu, L., Altschuler, S.: Massive single-cell RNA-seq analysis and imputation via deep learning (2018)
14. Li, J., Jiang, W., Han, H., Liu, J., Liu, B., Wang, Y.: ScGSLC: an unsupervised graph similarity learning framework for single-cell RNA-seq data clustering. Comput. Biol. Chem. **90**, 107415 (2021)
15. Schwartz, G.W., Zhou, Y., Petrovic, J., Fasolino, M., Faryabi, R.B.: TooManyCells identifies and visualizes relationships of single-cell clades. Nature Methods **17**(4), 1–9 (2020)
16. Bengio, Y., Courville, A., Vincent, P.: Representation learning: a review and new perspectives. IEEE Trans. Pattern Anal. Mach. Intell. **35**(8), 1798–1828 (2013)
17. Ding, J., Condon, A., Shah, S.P.: Interpretable dimensionality reduction of single cell transcriptome data with deep generative models. Nat. Commun. **9**(1), 2002 (2018)
18. Lin, C., Siddhartha, J., Hannah, K., Ziv, B.J.: Using neural networks for reducing the dimensions of single-cell RNA-Seq data. Nucleic Acids Res. **2017**(17), e156 (2017)
19. Guo, X., Long, G., Liu, X., Yin, J.: Improved deep embedded clustering with local structure preservation. In: IJCAI (2017)
20. Xie, J., Girshick, R., Farhadi, A.: Unsupervised deep embedding for clustering analysis. Computer Science (2015)
21. Goolam, M., et al.: Heterogeneity in Oct4 and Sox2 targets biases cell fate in 4-cell mouse embryos. Cell **165**(1), 61–74 (2016)
22. Pollen, A., et al.: Low-coverage single-cell mRNA sequencing reveals cellular heterogeneity and activated signaling pathways in developing cerebral cortex. Nat. Biotechnol. **32**, 1053–1058 (2014)
23. Kolodziejczyk, A.A., et al.: Single cell RNA-sequencing of pluripotent states unlocks modular transcriptional variation. Cell Stem Cell **17**(4), 471–485 (2015)
24. Nguyen, T.H., Prifti, E., Chevaleyre, Y., Sokolovska, N., Zucker, J.D.: Disease classification in metagenomics with 2D embeddings and deep learning (2018)
25. Hinton, G.E., Salakhutdinov, R.R.: Reducing the dimensionality of data with neural networks. Science **313**(5186), 504–507 (2006)
26. Blondel, V.D., Guillaume, J.L., Lambiotte, R., Lefebvre, E.: Fast unfolding of communities in large networks. J. Stat. Mech. Theor. Exp. **2008**(10), P10008 (2008)

27. Rubinstein, R.: The cross-entropy method for combinatorial and continuous optimization. Methodol. Comput. Appl. Probab. 1(2), 127–190 (1999)
28. Strehl, A., Ghosh, J.: Cluster ensembles - a knowledge reuse framework for combining multiple partitions. J. Mach. Learn. Res. 3(3), 583–617 (2002)
29. William, M.: Rand: objective criteria for the evaluation of clustering methods. J. Am. Stat. Assoc. 66(336), 846–850 (1971)
30. Hubert, L., Arabie, P.: Comparing partitions. J. Classif. 2(1), 193–218 (1985)
31. Todorov, H., Fournier, D., Gerber, S.: Principal components analysis: theory and application to gene expression data analysis. Genomics Comput. Biol. 4(2), 100041 (2018)
32. Macqueen, J.: Some methods for classification and analysis of MultiVariate observations. In: Proceedings of Berkeley Symposium on Mathematical Statistics & Probability (1965)
33. Warren, A.G., Brorson, H., Borud, L.J., Slavin, A.M.D.: A comprehensive review. Ann. Plast. Surg. 59(4), 464–472
34. Wang, B., Ramazzotti, D., De Sano, L., Zhu, J., Pierson, E.: SIMLR: a tool for large-scale genomic analyses by multi-kernel learning. Proteomics 11(3), 333 (2018)
35. Kiselev, V.Y., et al.: SC3: consensus clustering of single-cell RNA-seq data. Nature Methods 14(5), 483–486 (2017)
36. Baran, P.M., Dennis, K.: Random forest based similarity learning for single cell RNA sequencing data. Bioinformatics 13, i79–i88 (2018)
37. Pyramid Match Kernels: Discriminative Classification with Sets of Image Features (2006)
38. Grauman, K., Darrell, T.: The pyramid match kernel: discriminative classification with sets of image features. In: Tenth IEEE International Conference on Computer Vision (2005)
39. Laurens, V.D.M., Hinton, G.: Visualizing data using t-SNE. J. Mach. Learn. Res. 9(2605), 2579–2605 (2008)

SNEMO: Spectral Clustering Based on the Neighborhood for Multi-omics Data

Qi Guan[1], Jianping Zhao[1($\boxtimes$)], and Chunhou Zheng[1,2]

[1] College of Mathematics and System Sciences, Xinjiang University, Urumqi, China
[2] School of Computer Science and Technology, Anhui University, Hefei, China

Abstract. In this paper, we proposed spectral clustering based on the neighborhood for multi-omics data (SNEMO). Firstly, the similarity matrix of each genome is established by using the neighbor-based approach. Secondly, the index function is added and the relative similarity matrix between samples is established. Thirdly, for multi-omics data, SNEMO used cross-view tensor product graphs (TPGs) to integrate multiple similarity matrices. Finally, given the final relative similarity matrix, we provide two solutions to determine the number of clusters K. In addition to define the K value, the user can also estimate the K value according to eigengap heuristic. Gaussian mixture model (GMM) was used to cluster the final feature matrix. The performance of SNEMO was tested on four cancer datasets. Experimental results showed that our approach avoids iterative optimization, so it is faster and simpler than state-of-art techniques.

Keywords: Clustering · Multi-omics · TPGs · Eigengap heuristic

1 Introduction

Cancer is a disease caused by the disorder of genes. Within the same type of cancer, different subtypes can be subdivided according to the pathogenic genes. At the same time, for each specific cancer patient, individual differences and different prognostic responses to surgery or drugs are more challenging for the current clinical treatment of cancer [1]. The clustering method based on a single genomic data type is relatively simple, but it is difficult to obtain results with biological significance. So researchers began to explore the clustering methods based on multiple sets of scientific data. Then, the methods of SNF [2], low-rank approximation (LRAcluster) [3], PINS [4], NEMO [5], and Spectrum [6] have also been published.

In this study, we proposed a new spectral clustering method based on the neighborhood for multi-omics data (SNEMO). The method was inspired and built on the previous domain-based and spectral clustering based on multi-group clustering methods. Our contributions are as follows. First, tensor product graph (TPG) data consolidation, merge different data sources and denoising them. Second, different methods were used to determine the number of clusters. Third, additional omics can be supported, as well as more complex feature types.

© Springer Nature Switzerland AG 2021
D.-S. Huang et al. (Eds.): ICIC 2021, LNAI 12838, pp. 490–498, 2021.
https://doi.org/10.1007/978-3-030-84532-2_44

2 Materials and Methods

SNEMO can be divided into four phases. Firstly, establishing patient-to-patient similarity matrices for each genome. Secondly, integrating different omics matrices. Thirdly, selecting cluster number K. Finally, clustering. The flowchart of SNEMO is shown in Fig. 1.

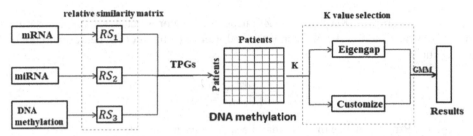

Fig. 1. Schematic overview of SNEMO. (A) Establishing patient-to-patient relative similarity matrices for each genome. (B) Using the cross-view tensor product graphs to integrate the relative similarity matrix of multi-omics. (C) K value selection uses two methods, one is eigengap heuristic, the other is custom. (D) Gaussian mixture model to cluster the final eigenvector matrix

2.1 Similar Matrix

On a set of data matrices of n samples (patients), given L omics, X_l with size $p_l \times n$ represents the data matrix of omics, where p_l is the number of features of omics l. Let X_{li} represents the section of sample I in omics l (column i in X_l). For omics l, a similarity matrix S_l of $n \times n$ is defined as follows:

$$S_l(i,j) = \frac{1}{\sqrt{2\pi}\sigma_{ijl}} \exp\left(-\frac{\|x_{li} - x_{lj}\|^2}{2\sigma_{ijl}^2}\right) \tag{1}$$

$$\sigma_{ijl}^2 = \frac{1}{3} \cdot \left(\frac{1}{k}\sum_{r\in\eta_{li}}\|x_{li} - x_{lr}\|^2 + \frac{1}{k}\sum_{r\in\eta_{lj}}\|x_{lj} - x_{lr}\|^2 + \|x_{li} - x_{lj}\|^2\right) \tag{2}$$

Next, we define the relative similarity matrix RS_l for each omics l:

$$RS_l(i,j) = \frac{S_1(i,j)}{\sum\limits_{r\in\eta_{li}} S_1(i,r)} \cdot I(j \in \eta_{li}) + \frac{S_1(i,j)}{\sum\limits_{r\in\eta_{lj}} S_1(r,j)} \cdot I(i \in \eta_{lj}). \tag{3}$$

where I is the indicator function. For convenience, we denote $A_{ij} = RS_l(i,j)$.

2.2 Similarity Matrix Integration

Next, our aim is to combine L omics' relative similarity matrix (graph). We calculate cross-view tensor product graphs (TPGs) from each pair of individual graphs, where each graph is a Kronecker product of a pair of single views. Cross-view TPGs are integrated into a simple diagram using a linear combination and the effective diagram diffusion process on TPG is performed. The process is listed as follows:

Step 1. A group of relative similarity matrices obtained by combining (3):

$$A = \sum_{i=1}^{L} A_{ij} \qquad (4)$$

Step 2. Sparsify A. Keep only the Zth nearest neighbor for each sample and set the rest of the values to 0. A kNN graph is formed. Let R_i be the set of Z nearest neighbors for x_i, then:

$$A_{ij} = \begin{cases} A_{ij}, \ j \in R_i \\ 0, \ otherwise \end{cases} \qquad (5)$$

Step 3. Row normalize of A. So that the sum of each line is 1:

$$A_{ij} = A_{ij} / \sum_j A_{ij} \qquad (6)$$

Step 4. Perform graph diffusion iterations. Let $Q^1 = A$, I is the identity matrix of A. Then for the tth iteration from 2; …; iters:

$$Q^t = AQ^{t-1}A^T + I \qquad (7)$$

Step 5. Let $A^* = Q^T$. A is the final similarity matrix.
In this study, we set the parameters $Z = 10$ and iters $= 5$ according to the experience.

2.3 K Value Selection and Clustering

Given the average relative similarity matrix A^*, SNEMO finally used the Ng spectral clustering method [7], but with the eigengap heuristic to estimate the number of clusters, and GMM is used to cluster the final eigenvector matrix. The steps are as follows:

Step 1. Using the diagonal matrix D, whose (i, i) element is the sum of the ith row, to construct the normalized graph Laplace L:

$$L = D^{-1/2} A^* D^{-1/2} \qquad (8)$$

Step 2. Eigenvector $x_1, x_2, …, x_n$ and eigenvalue $\lambda_1, \lambda_2, …, \lambda_{n+1}$ of L are extracted by eigen-decomposition of L.

Step 3. Evaluate the difference eigengap between the eigenvalues. Starting from the second eigenvalue n = 2, select the optimal k, represented by k^*, to maximize the eigengap.

$$k^* = \underset{n}{argmax}(\lambda_n - \lambda_{n+1}) \qquad (9)$$

Step 4. Get the $x_1, x_2, ..., x_{k^*}$, k^* largest eigenvectors of L, then form the matrix $X = [x_1, x_2, ..., x_{k^*}] \in \mathbb{R}^{n \times k^*}$ by stacking the eigenvectors in columns.

Step 5. By re-normalizing each row of X, the unit length is obtained, and the matrix Y is obtained from X:

$$Y_{ij} = \frac{X_{ij}}{(\sum_j X_{ij}^2)^{1/2}}. \tag{10}$$

Step 6. Each row of Y is treated as a sample s_i, then all the points are clustered into k^* clusters using GMM.

If the value of K is defined by itself, then step 4–6 are performed after specifying the value of K.

2.4 Datasets

We applied our approach to 4 cancer datasets through TCGA: glioblastoma multiforme (GBM), breast invasive carcinoma (BIC), kidney renal clear cell carcinoma (KRCCC), and lung squamous cell carcinoma (LSCC). The DNA methylation, mRNA, and miRNA expression data for these cancers vary in sample size (BIC is 105, LSCC is 106, GBM is 215, KRCCC is 122) and a number of measurements as well as heterogeneity. These data can be obtained from the literature [2].

3 Results

3.1 The Results of Eigengap Heuristic

We performed a survival curve analysis of the p-values of the Cox proportional hazard model on four datasets, which used a logarithmic rank test to test the significance of differences in survival time between clusters. The execution results of all methods on all datasets are shown in Table 1, p-values of SNEMO in LSCC and GBM datasets (0.0035, 0.00097) are all significantly superior to the original heuristic method. Under the same data set, different clustering methods select different K values according to the eigengap heuristic method and the clustering effect is also different.

3.2 The Result of Custom K Value

When customizing K, we took the evaluation results on the BIC dataset as an example. We evaluated the p-value of the Cox proportional hazard model and plotted the survival curve analysis diagram when the number of clusters K was consistent with the NEMO and Spectrum methods (5 clusters, 3 clusters), as shown in Fig. 2. The experiment shows that the performance of SNEMO is significantly higher than the other two methods.

In the case of customizing the number of clusters K, we evaluated SNEMO with the other four methods on the four datasets. The p-values of the Cox proportional hazard model corresponding to each method are shown in Table 2. In addition, we also compared the concordance index and running time of NEMO, Spectrum and SNEMO in the four

Table 1. Spectral clustering based on neighborhood performance relative to original algorithms

Dataset	Data types	N	NEMO	Spectrum	SNEMO
BIC	mRNA, miRNA, DNA methylation	105	**2.5e−03(5)**	0.74(3)	0.72(2)
LSCC	mRNA, miRNA, DNA methylation	106	**2.8e−04(8)**	0.054(2)	**3.5e−03(5)**
GBM	mRNA, miRNA, DNA methylation	215	0.057(6)	0.037 (5)	**9.7e−04(2)**
KRCCC	mRNA, miRNA, DNA methylation	122	0.26(5)	0.31 (2)	**0.13(2)**

Note: The number of clusters K obtained by using the eigengap heuristic algorithm in parentheses.

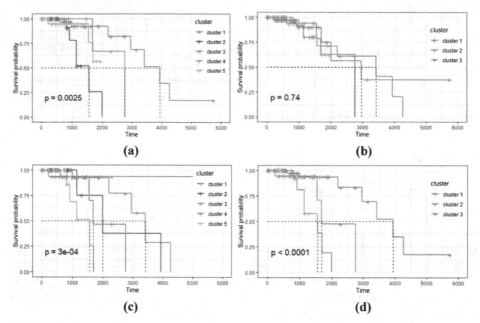

(a)   (b)

(c)   (d)

Fig. 2. BIC data were used to find the survival curve analysis results of the Cox proportional hazard models with p-values on different methods under 5 and 3 clusters. (a) Survival curve analysis results of five clusters on BIC dataset by NEMO method; (b) Analysis results of three clusters of survival curves clustered by Spectrum method on BIC dataset; (c) The survival curve analysis results of the SNEMO method aggregated into 5 clusters on BIC dataset; (d) The survival curve analysis results of the BIC dataset clustered into 5 clusters.

data sets (Fig. 3). Experimental results show that although our method is simple, SNEMO is superior to other methods in terms of clustering effect, consistency and running speed.

Table 2. Results of applying the five algorithms on cancer datasets

Dataset	SNF	MOCOM	NEMO	Spectrum	SNEMO
GBM (3 clusters)	0.002	0.0019	0.0053	0.0025	**0.0018**
BIC (5 clusters)	0.0011	0.0016	0.0012	0.21	**0.0003**
KRCCC (3 clusters)	0.029	0.39	**0.0032**	0.83	0.32
LSCC (4 clusters)	0.02	0.54	0.018	0.017	**0.016**

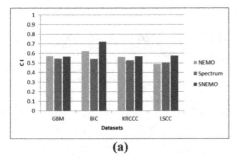 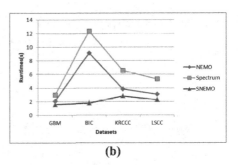

(a)   (b)

Fig. 3. CI and runtimes of NEMO, spectrum and SNEMO methods on four datasets GBM, BIC, KRCCC and LSCC. (a) Concordance index (CI). (b) The running time for each method.

Based on the aforementioned experiments, we can find SNEMO is comparable to several leading multi-omics clustering algorithms. SNEMO has obvious advantages in running time, whether using the eigengap heuristic method or custom K value.

3.3 A Case Study: Subtype Analysis in GBM

In this study, we took GBM data as an example. We downloaded its clinical data from the cBio Cancer Genomics Portal (https://www.cbioportal.org/) [8], including expression subtype, diagnosis age, and therapy class information. We further analyzed the heterogeneity of GBM data containing 215 samples.

In Table 3, we observed that under the gene expression subtype, Proneural samples were mainly distributed in clusters 1 and 3, Neural, Classical and Mesenchymal samples were mainly distributed in clusters 1 and 2. G-CIMP samples were mainly distributed in clusters 2 and 3. Under DNA methylation subtype, G-CIMP samples were mainly distributed in clusters 2 and 3, Non-G-CIMP samples were mainly distributed in clusters 1 and 2. In addition, the mean age of diagnosis in groups 1, 2, and 3 was 60, 52, and 47 (Fig. 4(a)), respectively, with group 3 having the youngest age at diagnosis and longer overall survival than group 1 and group 2. This shows that, in this case, our method strongly confirms that the neural presubtype can be defined as two subtypes based on G-CLMP methylation and expression data together. Comparatively, SNF [2] could not analyze the Proneural subtype conferred by the non-G-CLMP on the same data of 215 GBM samples.

Table 3. Comparison of clusters identified by SNEMO to gene expression and DNA methylation subtypes of GBM

		Clusters 1	Clusters 2	Clusters 3
Gene expression subtypes	G-CIMP	0	2	16
	Mesenchymal	32	34	0
	Classical	48	9	1
	Neural	22	10	2
	Proneural	16	7	16
DNA methylation subtypes	G-CIMP	0	2	17
	Non-G-CIMP	118	60	18

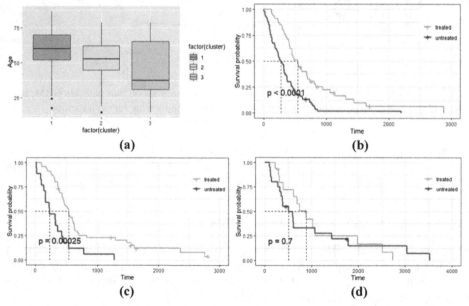

Fig. 4. (a) The box chart describes the distribution of age at diagnosis for each patient in each of the three GBM subtypes and the mean age for each cluster. The average age of each class was 60, 52 and 47, respectively. (b) Survival analysis of GBM patients for treatment with TMZ in cluster 1. (c) Survival analysis of GBM patients for treatment with TMZ in cluster 2. (d) Survival analysis of GBM patients for treatment with TMZ in cluster 3. The specified P values were calculated using the Cox log-rank test. Comparing with the P values, we confirmed that cluster 1 had a favorable response to TMZ.

We further investigated the response of individual clusters to temozolomide (TMZ), a commonly used drug for the treatment of GBM. Three survival curves (Fig. 4(b), 4(c), and 4d)) indicated that TMZ-treated samples had different drug responses compared with those without the drug. For cluster 3 (15 patients treated versus 20 patients not treated with TMZ, P value using Cox log-rank test 7e−01), we found that patients who were treated lived significantly longer than those who were not. However, patients belonging to cluster 1 (45 patients treated versus 73 patients not treated with TMZ, P value using Cox log-rank test 1.476e−05) and cluster 2 (45 patients treated versus 17 patients not treated with TMZ, P: 2.5e−04), survival time was significantly increased after TMZ treatment. Therefore, we confirmed that cluster 1, and cluster 2 have a favorable response to TMZ.

4 Discussion

In this paper, we developed a new method for cancer genome data clustering based on the classical clustering algorithm [9]. The proposed SNEMO is much simpler and has better performance than the existing multi-group clustering algorithm. The simplicity of SNEMO makes it more flexible and easier to adapt to different environments. It only needs to define a distance between two samples within omics, so it can support additional omics, numerical, discrete, and ordinal features, even more complex feature types.

Due to the inherent defects of computational biology in the research of cancer subtype identification [10], this paper has discussed some related issues and obtained some research conclusions, but with the continuous deepening of the research in related fields, the clustering research of cancer subtype identification based on genome data needs to be further improved and perfected. There are also some defects in our method, which are also the problems we need to solve in the future.

Acknowledgements. This work was supported by grants from the Xinjiang Autonomous Region University Research Program (XJEDU2019Y002), and the National Natural Science Foundation of China (Nos. U19A2064, 61873001).

References

1. Ozsolak, F., Milos, P.M.: RNA sequencing: advances, challenges and opportunities. Nat. Rev. Genet. **12**(2), 87–98 (2011)
2. Wang, B., Mezlini, A.M., Demir, F., Fiume, M., Tu, Z.W., et al.: Similarity network fusion for aggregating data types on a genomic scale. Nat. Methods **11**(3), 333–337 (2014)
3. Wu, D.M., Wang, D.F., Zhang, M.Q., Gu, J.: Fast dimension reduction and integrative clustering of multi-omics data using low-rank approximation: application to cancer molecular classification. BMC Genomics **16**(1), 1022 (2015)
4. Nguyen, T., Tagett, R., Diaz, D., Draghici, S., Diaz, D.: A novel approach for data integration and disease subtyping. Genome Res. **27**(12), 2025–2039 (2017)
5. Nimrod, R., Ron, S.: Nemo: cancer subtyping by integration of partial multi-omics data. Bioinformatics **35**(18), 3348–3356 (2019)
6. John, C.R., Watson, D., Barnes, M.R., Pitzalis, C., Lewis, M.J.: Spectrum: fast density-aware spectral clustering for single and multi-omic data. Bioinformatics **36**(4), 1159–1166 (2019)
7. Ng, A.Y.: On spectral clustering: analysis and an algorithm. Adv. Neural. Inf. Process. Syst. **14**(1), 849–856 (2002)
8. Ge, S.G., Xia, J., Sha, W., Zheng, C.H.: Cancer subtype discovery based on integrative model of multigenomic data. IEEE/ACM Trans. Comput. Biol. Bioinf. **14**(5), 1115–1121 (2016)

9. Rappoport, N., Shamir, R.: Multi-omics and multi-view clustering algorithms: review and cancer benchmark. Nucleic Acids Res. **46**(20), 10546–10562 (2018)

10. Wang, D., Gu, J.: Integrative clustering methods of multi-omics data for molecule-based cancer classifications. Quant. Biol. **4**(1), 58–67 (2016)

Covid-19 Detection by Wavelet Entropy and Jaya

Wei Wang(✉)

Informatics Building, School of Informatics, University of Leicester,
University Road, Leicester LE1 7RH, UK
ww152@leicester.ac.uk

Abstract. The past year has seen a global pandemic of COVID-19, with extremely high transmission and mortality rates causing worldwide alarm and a significant negative impact on the global economy and human security. The asymptomatic COVID-19 patients have also made epidemic control very difficult. Using artificial intelligence technology to analyse CT images can locate infected patients quickly and precisely. Our research proposed a machine learning model based on wavelet entropy, single hidden layer feedforward neural network and Jaya algorithm, use K-fold cross-validation to report unbiased performance, which obtained a promising performance. The mean sensitivity was 73.31% ± 2.26%, specificity was 78.11% ± 1.92%, precision was 77.03% ± 1.35%, accuracy was 75.71% ± 1.04% and F1 score was 75.10% ± 1.23%. Matthews correlation coefficient of 51.51 ± 2.07%, and feature mutual information of 75.14% ± 1.22%. Our research proved the importance of AI technology for the medical field to a certain extent.

Keywords: COVID-19 · Wavelet entropy · Jaya algorithm · K-fold cross-validation · Feedforward neural network

1 Introduction

Coronavirus disease 19 (COVID-19) is an acute atypical respiratory disease caused by a new coronavirus named Severe Acute Respiratory Syndrome Coronavirus-2 (SARS-CoV-2, 2019-nCoV), which first identified in December 2019. COVID-19 is spreading at a highly rapid global epidemic between 2020 and 2021 [1]. The World Health Organization (WHO) declared COVID-19 a global epidemic and defined it as a Public Health Emergencies of International Concern (PHEIC). This new coronavirus has a high structural similarity (79.5%) to the SARS virus, a global epidemic between 2002 and 2003, affecting the respiratory system with concurrent effects on other body organ systems [2].

The incubation period of COVID-19 is usually 3–7 days, with a maximum of 14 days [3]. Patients during the incubation period have no apparent symptoms but are still infectious. After the incubation period, patients usually develop a persistent cough, fever, loss of taste, and life-threatening symptoms such as respiratory distress [4]. According to surveys, a certain number of people with COVID-19 do not show any symptoms

© Springer Nature Switzerland AG 2021
D.-S. Huang et al. (Eds.): ICIC 2021, LNAI 12838, pp. 499–508, 2021.
https://doi.org/10.1007/978-3-030-84532-2_45

(asymptomatic patients) but are still as infectious as other patients [5]. Therefore, an accurate and rapid test is essential for the prevention and treatment of COVID-19.

The most common standard way to detect COVID-19 is by reverse-transcription polymerase chain reaction (RT-PCR) [6]. However, this method is time-consuming, taking up to two days to produce a single run result. Also, it has a high proportion of false negatives, requiring multiple tests to finalise the result. In this context, the characteristic presentation of disease on chest CT images of COVID-19 patients has attracted several sources [6]. However, manual-based imaging can be subjective and inefficient, especially when the number of patients is high, making it difficult to become a mainstream detection method. More scholars believe that the application of artificial intelligence in medical image analysis is potentially valuable for the diagnosis of COVID-19 [7].

Yao and Han (2020) [8] proposed a wavelet entropy (WE) and biogeography-based optimisation (BBO) based method (WE-BBO) to classify CT images of COVID-19 patients and healthy people and achieved good performance. They used WE to effectively reduce the feature dimension and BBO to reduce the model computational cost and improve the model performance. Lu (2016) [10] used a radial basis function (RBF) to identify brain disease. His method can be applied to COVID-19 recognition. Chen (2020) [11] combined the grey-level co-occurrence matrix (GLCM) and support vector machine (SVM).

Rao (2016) [9] proposed an evolutionary algorithm called the Jaya algorithm in 2016, which can solve constrained and unconstrained optimisation problems by staying away from the worst solution while getting as close to the optimal solution as possible. Compared to other algorithms, the Jaya algorithm has achieved awe-inspiring results without constraints specific to the algorithm's parameters. Our model combined the Jaya algorithm with Yao and Han (2020) [8]'s research and achieved a better performance, which is also the first algorithm that combines the Jaya algorithm and WE to classify COVID-19 CT images. The contributions include the following aspects: (i) explored a medical image classification model combining Jaya and WE. (ii) validated the possibility of training a COVID-19 diagnostic aid model on a small data set. (iii) demonstrated the promise of artificial intelligence for the COVID-19 CT image recognition task.

In the rest of the paper, the second section describes the data set used in the experiment. The third section briefly describes the methodology used. The fourth section discusses the results of the experiment and compared them with start-of-the-art methods.

2   Dataset

The dataset consists of 132 subject samples, each sample containing a complete chest CT image with a corresponding nucleic acid test result. The subjects were 132 individuals ranging in age from 24 to 91 years, in which there are 77 males and 55 females. The entire dataset divided into two groups, the observation group, and the control group, with the observation group containing 66 data samples from 66 COVID-19 infected patients admitted to the Fourth People's Hospital in Huai'an, China, including 39 men and 27 women with a mean age of 48 years. The control group of the dataset contains 66 data samples, obtained by random sampling from the health check-up results of 159 people who did not infect COVID-19. The final selected data samples of the control group belong to 38 males and 28 females with a mean age of 38.44 years. The Fig. 1 show two image samples of the dataset.

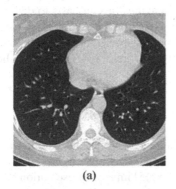
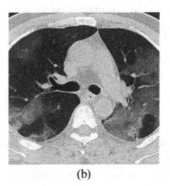

(a)   (b)

Fig. 1. CT Image sample of Health Control (a) and COVID Patient (b).

To ensure the professionalism and rigour of the data, two specialist chest radiologists simultaneously reviewed all CT images uploaded to the Picture Archiving and Communication System (PASC), recorded the distribution, size, and shape of the lesions in the CT images and selected 1 to 4 CT images for each subject. Preference is given to CT images with larger volumes and more lesions while randomly selecting CT images of healthy subjects. There is a senior physician to supervise the complete identification, recording and selection process.

3   Methodology

3.1   Wavelet Entropy

The Fourier Transform (FT) is a crucial tool in facilitating the development of image processing techniques. FT can transform image signals in the time and frequency domains utilising a linear integral transform to obtain information about the image in terms of spatial frequency, thus helping to select the appropriate filter for image processing and analysis tasks. The Eq. (1) shows the transformation of FT.

$$F(\omega) = \int_{-\infty}^{\infty} f(t)e^{-i\omega t}dt \qquad (1)$$

Where ω refers to frequency, t refers to time.

In real world, most of smooth signals are artificial, and signals in nature are almost always non-stationary. However, FT is flawed in dealing with non-smooth signals in that it can only obtain the frequencies contained in a segment of the signal but not the time at which each frequency occurs. In such a case, signals that differ significantly in the time domain may be the same in spectral domain after FT. Furthermore, the image representation provided by FT based only on the frequency of the image, and is not spatially localised [12]. Therefore, FT is often not an appropriate option for the medical image analysis.

The wavelet transform effectively addresses FT's shortcomings by replacing the infinitely long triangular basis in FT with a finite decaying wavelet basis to define the entropy of time evolution [13], thus eliminating the relying on the assumption of signal smoothness. Besides, the wavelet transform can decompose the signal into multiple scale levels, thus providing different resolution image representations [14]. The Eq. (2) shows the wavelet transform.

$$W(a, \tau) = \frac{1}{\sqrt{a}} \int_{-\infty}^{\infty} f(t)\psi * \left(\frac{t - \tau}{a}\right) dt \tag{2}$$

Where a represents scale, τ represents translation, ψ represents parent wavelet function, and t represents time.

Although the wavelet transform's multi-resolution [15] image representation retains more image information, the redundant features are laced with much useless information, resulting in significant space and time costs [16]. Therefore, we introduced entropy to reduce the dimensionality of the features.

Entropy is a statistic that characterises the randomness of the texture features of an input image and is a measure of the uniformity of the distribution. Simply put, the more uniformly distributed an image is, the higher the entropy [17]. The different probabilities of grey levels in the image can approximately define the entropy of an image [18]. The Eq. (3) defines the Entropy.

$$S(\alpha) = -\sum_i P(\alpha_i) log_b P(\alpha_i) \tag{3}$$

Where α refers to grey levels and P refers to probabilities of grey levels [19].

3.2 Feedforward Neural Network

Feedforward neural network [20] is a classical neural network model. As a classifier, a feedforward neural network maps the input x to $y = f(x; \theta)$, and by learning the value of the parameter θ, derives the function that yields the output that most closely approximates the target value, i.e., the function with the lowest loss value [21].

We feed the features extracted and reduced from the CT images into a feedforward neural network for classification. Feedforward neural networks [22] consist of an input layer, an output layer and one or more hidden layers, each layer consisting of numbers of neurons (perceptron) [23]. The Fig. 2 shows the structure of feedforward Neural Network. Deep neural network [24–26] and transfer learning [27, 28] will be out future research directions (Fig. 2).

3.3 Jaya Algorithm

The Jaya algorithm is a relatively new evolutionary algorithm [29]. Compared to traditional evolutionary algorithms, the Jaya algorithm does not require algorithm-specific

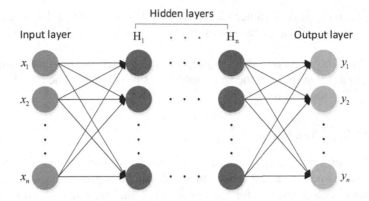

Fig. 2. Structure of feedforward neural network

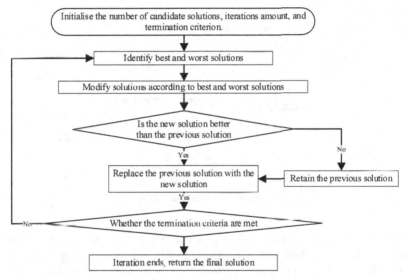

Fig. 3. Flowchart of the Jaya algorithm

parameters [30], reducing computational cost and avoiding local optima due to inappropriate parameter tuning. The Jaya algorithm is more user-friendly, requiring only one phase [31].

For an objective function $f(x)$ to be optimised that have candidate solutions $\mathbf{X} = \{X_1, X_2, \cdots, X_n\}$, the number of candidate solutions is n, the number of iterations is i, and the corresponding dimension is d, The Eq. (4) shows the basic equation of Jaya algorithm [32].

$$X'_{j,k,i} = X_{j,k,i} + r_{1,j,i}\left(X_{j,best,i} - \left|X_{j,k,i}\right|\right) - r_{2,j,i}\left(X_{j,worst,i} - \left|X_{j,k,i}\right|\right) \qquad (4)$$

Where r_1 and r_2 are two subjective random number between 0 and 1, $X_{j,best,i}$ refers to the best solution, $X_{j,worst,i}$ refers to the worst solution, $k = 1, 2, \cdots, n$, and $j = 1, 2, \cdots, d$.

The idea of Jaya algorithm's is to keep trying to reach the optimal solution [33] while staying as far away from the worst solution as possible [9]. The Fig. 3 shows the flowchart of Jaya algorithm.

3.4 K-fold Cross Validation

In general, to ensure higher robustness of the model, researchers usually divide the dataset into a training set and a test set to test the model's performance when dealing with unknown data. However, for smaller datasets, the number of training sets can significantly affect the model performance. K-fold cross-validation [34] is a widely used method to solve this problem.

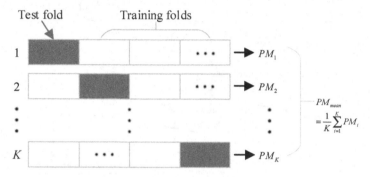

Fig. 4. K-fold cross validation

K-fold cross-validation divides the data set into K groups, selects one of them as the test set each time without repeating, uses the remaining K-1 group as the training set, and finally calculates the mean of performance metrics (PM) to evaluate the model, where K is an arbitrary integer, and its value usually depends on the size of the dataset. A higher K value can better mitigate the adverse effects of a small data set but lead to higher computational costs [35]. The Fig. 4 illustrates the K-fold cross validation.

4 Experiment Results and Discussions

4.1 WE Results

We use WE as the feature extraction method. Figure 5 shows an image representation of the four-level discrete wavelet transform (left) and an image sample (right). The original image signal was decomposed to obtain one low-frequency component and three high-frequency components, where LL1 represents the low-frequency component obtained after the first level of the wavelet decomposition.

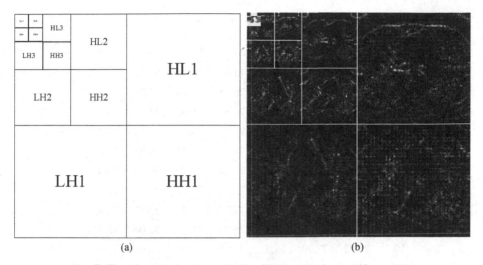

Fig. 5. Four-level discrete wavelet transform (a) and sample image (b).

HL1, HH1 and LH1 represent the high-frequency components obtained after the first level of decomposition. The final LL4 is obtained by decomposing the LL components at multiple-levels wavelet decomposition, the low-frequency component of the fourth level of the wavelet decomposition.

4.2 Statistical Results

The experiments used a single hidden layer feedforward neural network as the classifier, the Jaya algorithm as the training algorithm, and K-fold cross-validation to report unbiased performance. The experiments ultimately achieved good performance (shown in Table 1) with an average sensitivity of 73.31% ± 2.26%, specificity of 78.11% ± 1.92%, precision of 77.03% ± 1.35%, accuracy of 75.71% ± 1.04%, and F1 score of 75.10% ± 1.23%, Matthews correlation coefficient of 51.51 ± 2.07%, and feature mutual information of 75.14% ± 1.22%.

4.3 Comparison to State-of-the-Art Approaches

Compare to the other state-of-art approaches in CT image classification of COVID-19, our model shows significant improvement in all aspects, as shown in Table 2 for numerical comparison. The results also demonstrate the proposed method is a promising method for the CT image classification task of COVID-19.

Table 1. 10 runs of 4-fold cross-validation.

Run	Sen	Spc	Prc	Acc	F1	MCC	FMI
1	70.95	80.41	78.36	75.68	74.47	51.58	74.56
2	71.62	81.08	79.10	76.35	75.18	52.94	75.27
3	77.03	75.68	76.00	76.35	76.51	52.71	76.51
4	71.62	78.38	76.81	75.00	74.13	50.11	74.17
5	74.32	75.00	74.83	74.66	74.58	49.33	74.58
6	71.62	79.05	77.37	75.34	74.39	50.82	74.44
7	70.95	77.03	75.54	73.99	73.17	48.06	73.21
8	76.35	79.05	78.47	77.70	77.40	55.43	77.40
9	74.32	77.70	76.92	76.01	75.60	52.06	75.61
10	74.32	77.70	76.92	76.01	75.60	52.06	75.61
Mean	73.31 $\pm$ 2.26	78.11 $\pm$ 1.92	77.03 $\pm$ 1.35	75.71 $\pm$ 1.04	75.10 $\pm$ 1.23	51.51 $\pm$ 2.07	75.14 $\pm$ 1.22

(Sen = Sensitivity; Spc = Specificity; Prc = Precision; Acc = Accuracy; F1 = F1 Score; MCC = Matthews correlation coefficient; FMI = Feature Mutual Information).

Table 2. Performance comparison to other methods

Method	Sen	Spc	Prc	Acc	F1	MCC	FMI
RBFNN [10]	66.89 $\pm$ 2.43	75.47 $\pm$ 2.53	73.23 $\pm$ 1.48	71.18 $\pm$ 0.80	69.88 $\pm$ 1.08	42.56 $\pm$ 1.61	69.97 $\pm$ 1.04
WE-BBO [8]	72.97 $\pm$ 2.96	74.93 $\pm$ 2.39	74.48 $\pm$ 1.34	73.95 $\pm$ 0.98	73.66 $\pm$ 0.98	47.99 $\pm$ 2.00	73.66 $\pm$ 1.33
GLCM-SVM [11]	72.03 $\pm$ 2.94	78.04 $\pm$ 1.72	76.66 $\pm$ 1.07	75.03 $\pm$ 1.12	74.24 $\pm$ 1.57	50.20 $\pm$ 2.17	74.29 $\pm$ 1.53
Ours	73.31 $\pm$ 2.26	78.11 $\pm$ 1.92	77.03 $\pm$ 1.35	75.71 $\pm$ 1.04	75.10 $\pm$ 1.23	51.51 $\pm$ 2.07	75.14 $\pm$ 1.22

(Sen = Sensitivity; Spc = Specificity; Prc = Precision; Acc = Accuracy; F1 = F1 Score; MCC = Matthews correlation coefficient; FMI = Feature Mutual Information).

5   Conclusions

Artificial intelligence-based diagnostic methods for COVID-19 chest CT hold considerable promise and will provide a considerable boost to the response to the global COVID-19 pandemic. The performance of our WE and Jaya algorithm-based model also supports this view to some extent. In the meantime, our method is theoretically applicable to other medical image studies based on CT images, but further experiments are needed to demonstrate its performance. We are confident that we can achieve better performance in the future with more optimisation and improvement of the model [36].

References

1. Hotez, P.J., Fenwick, A., Molyneux, D.: The new COVID-19 poor and the neglected tropical diseases resurgence. Infect. Dis. Poverty **10**(1), 3 (2021)

2. Yuki, K., Fujiogi, M., Koutsogiannaki, S.: COVID-19 pathophysiology: a review. Clinical Immunology, p. 108427 (2020)

3. Long, C., et al.: Diagnosis of the Coronavirus disease (COVID-19): rRT-PCR or CT? Europ. J. Radiol. **126**, 108961 (2020)

4. Struyf, T., et al.: Signs and symptoms to determine if a patient presenting in primary care or hospital outpatient settings has COVID-19 disease. Cochrane Database of Systematic Reviews 2020(7) (2020)

5. Zhao, H., et al.: COVID-19: asymptomatic carrier transmission is an underestimated problem. Epidemiology & Infection, 2020. **148** (2020)

6. Fang, Y., et al.: Sensitivity of chest CT for COVID-19: comparison to RT-PCR. Radiology **296**(2), E115–E117 (2020)

7. Wehbe, R.M., et al.: DeepCOVID-XR: an artificial intelligence algorithm to detect COVID-19 on chest radiographs trained and tested on a large US clinical data set. Radiology **299**(1), E167–E176 (2021)

8. Yao, X., Han, J.: COVID-19 detection via wavelet entropy and biogeography-based optimization. In: Santosh, K.C., Joshi, A. (eds.) COVID-19: Prediction, Decision-Making, and its Impacts. LNDECT, vol. 60, pp. 69–76. Springer, Singapore (2021). https://doi.org/10.1007/978-981-15-9682-7_8

9. Rao, R.: Jaya: a simple and new optimization algorithm for solving constrained and unconstrained optimization problems. Int. J. Ind. Eng. Comput. **7**(1), 19–34 (2016)

10. Lu, Z.: A pathological brain detection system based on radial basis function neural network. J. Med. Imaging Health Inf. **6**(5), 1218–1222 (2016)

11. Chen, Y.: Covid-19 classification based on gray-level co-occurrence matrix and support vector machine. In: Santosh, K.C., Joshi, A. (eds.) COVID-19: Prediction, Decision-Making, and its Impacts. LNDECT, vol. 60, pp. 47–55. Springer, Singapore (2021). https://doi.org/10.1007/978-981-15-9682-7_6

12. Saravanan, N., Ramachandran, K.: Incipient gear box fault diagnosis using discrete wavelet transform (DWT) for feature extraction and classification using artificial neural network (ANN). Expert Syst. Appl. **37**(6), 4168–4181 (2010)

13. Quiroga, R.Q., et al.: Wavelet entropy in event-related potentials: a new method shows ordering of EEG oscillations. Biol. Cybern. **84**(4), 291–299 (2001)

14. Saritha, M., Joseph, K.P., Mathew, A.T.: Classification of MRI brain images using combined wavelet entropy based spider web plots and probabilistic neural network. Pattern Recogn. Lett. **34**(16), 2151–2156 (2013)

15. Phillips, P.: Intelligent facial emotion recognition based on stationary wavelet entropy and Jaya algorithm. Neurocomputing **272**, 668–676 (2018)

16. El-Dahshan, E.-S.A., Hosny, T., Salem, A.-B.M.: Hybrid intelligent techniques for MRI brain images classification. Digital Signal Process. **20**(2), 433–441 (2010)

17. Gorriz, J.M.: Multivariate approach for Alzheimer's disease detection using stationary wavelet entropy and predator-prey particle swarm optimization. J. Alzheimers Dis. **65**(3), 855–869 (2018)

18. Wang, S., Du, S., Atangana, A., Liu, A., Lu, Z.: Application of stationary wavelet entropy in pathological brain detection. Multimed. Tools Appl. **77**(3), 3701–3714 (2016). https://doi.org/10.1007/s11042-016-3401-7

19. Yildiz, A., et al.: Application of adaptive neuro-fuzzy inference system for vigilance level estimation by using wavelet-entropy feature extraction. Expert Syst. Appl. **36**(4), 7390–7399 (2009)

20. Jansen-Winkeln, B., et al.: Feedforward artificial neural network-based colorectal cancer detection using hyperspectral imaging: a step towards automatic optical biopsy. Cancers **13**(5), 13 (2021)

21. Venkata, R.R.: Abnormal breast detection in mammogram images by feed-forward neural network trained by Jaya algorithm. Fund. Inform. **151**(1–4), 191–211 (2017)
22. Calvo-Pardo, H., Mancini, T., Olmo, J.: Granger causality detection in high-dimensional systems using feedforward neural networks. Int. J. Forecast. **37**(2), 920–940 (2021)
23. Svozil, D., Kvasnicka, V., Pospichal, J.: Introduction to multi-layer feed-forward neural networks. Chemom. Intell. Lab. Syst. **39**(1), 43–62 (1997)
24. Cheng, X.: PSSPNN: PatchShuffle stochastic pooling neural network for an explainable diagnosis of COVID-19 with multiple-way data augmentation. Comput. Math. Methods Med. **2021**, 6633755 (2021)
25. Guttery, D.S.: Improved breast cancer classification through combining graph convolutional network and convolutional neural network. Inf. Process. Manage. **58** (2021)
26. Wang, X., et al.: A comprehensive survey on convolutional neural network in medical image analysis. Multimed. Tools Appl., 1–45 (2020)
27. Wang, S.-H.: COVID-19 classification by CCSHNet with deep fusion using transfer learning and discriminant correlation analysis. Inf. Fusion **68**, 131–148 (2021)
28. Karaca, Y., et al.: Glomerulus classification via an improved GoogLeNet. IEEE Access **8**, 176916–176923 (2020)
29. Cheng, H., Multiple sclerosis identification based on fractional Fourier entropy and a modified Jaya algorithm. Entropy **20**(4), 254 (2018)
30. Han, L.: Identification of Alcoholism based on wavelet Renyi entropy and three-segment encoded Jaya algorithm. Complexity **2018**, 1–13 (2018)
31. Satapathy, S.C., Rajinikanth, V.: Jaya algorithm guided procedure to segment tumor from brain MRI. J. Optim. **2018**, 12 (2018)
32. Zhao, G.: Smart pathological brain detection by synthetic minority oversampling technique, extreme learning machine, and jaya algorithm. Multimed. Tools Appl. **77**(17), 22629–22648 (2018)
33. Degertekin, S.O., Bayar, G.Y., Lamberti, L.: Parameter free Jaya algorithm for truss sizing-layout optimization under natural frequency constraints. Comput. Struct. **245**, 29 (2021)
34. Rajasekaran, S., Rajwade, A.: Analyzing cross-validation in compressed sensing with Poisson noise. Signal Process. **182**, 9 (2021)
35. Moore, A.W.: Cross-validation for detecting and preventing overfitting. School of Computer Science Carneigie Mellon University (2001)
36. Wang, S.-H.: Covid-19 classification by FGCNet with deep feature fusion from graph convolutional network and convolutional neural network. Inf. Fusion **67**, 208–229 (2021)

An Ensemble Learning Algorithm for Predicting HIV-1 Protease Cleavage Sites

Zhenfeng Li[1], Pengwei Hu[2], and Lun Hu[2(✉)]

[1] School of Computer Science and Technology, Wuhan University of Technology, Wuhan, China
[2] Xinjiang Technical Institute of Physics and Chemistry, Chinese Academy of Sciences, Urumqi, China
hulun@ms.xjb.ac.cn

Abstract. Understanding the substrate specificity of human immunodeficiency virus 1 (HIV-1) protease plays a significance role in the design of effective HIV-1 protease inhibitors. During the past two decades, a variety of machine learning models have been developed to predict the existence of HIV-1 protease cleavage sites. However, since the acquisition of cleavable octapeptides requires expensive and time-consuming experiments, and uncleavable octapeptides are usually generated by artificial strategies, the number of cleavable octapeptides in the existing data set is far less than that of uncleavable octapeptides. This phenomenon of unbalanced datasets may cause the prediction performance of the classification model to be inaccurate. In this work, we combine the idea of asymmetric bagging and the support vector machine (SVM) classifier to propose an ensemble learning algorithm, namely AB-HIV, for an effective treat the dataset imbalance problem in predict HIV-1 protease cleavage sites. In order to make full use of the information of the substrate sequence, AB-HIV uses three different coding schemes (amino acid identities, chemical properties and variable length coevolutionary patterns) to construct the feature vector. By using asymmetric bagging to resample a set of balanced training subsets from the training set, and then a set of SVM classifiers can be built for integration to complete the prediction task. Experiments on three independent benchmark datasets indicate that the proposed ensemble learning method outperforms the existing prediction methods in terms of AUC, PR AUC and F-measure evaluation criteria. Therefore, AB-HIV can be regarded as an effective method to deal with the dataset imbalance problem in predict HIV-1 protease cleavage sites.

Keywords: Cleavage sites prediction · Asymmetric bagging · Imbalance dataset

1 Introduction

As the pathogen of acquired immunodeficiency syndrome (AIDS), HIV-1 destroys the immune system by affecting several types of cells in the body [22]. According laboratory-based experiments, HIV-1 protease plays a vital role in the entire life cycle of HIV [27]. HIV-1 protease generates infectious virus particles by cutting HIV polyproteins at

© Springer Nature Switzerland AG 2021
D.-S. Huang et al. (Eds.): ICIC 2021, LNAI 12838, pp. 509–521, 2021.
https://doi.org/10.1007/978-3-030-84532-2_46

multiple sites [31, 35]. Hence, for the purpose of HIV treatment, an efficient way is to prevent the HIV-1 replication by inhibiting the activity of corresponding HIV-1 protease.

Understanding the substrate specificity of HIV-1 protease is of great significance for reducing the side effects of HIV-1 PI. In the early stages of the study, many researchers claimed that the prediction of HIV-1 PR cleavage sites was a non-linear problem [25]. Therefore, they focused on using different classification models to perform prediction tasks. In particular, Thompson et al. [33] applied an ANN to the prediction of HIV-1 protease cleavage sites for the first time. They used a standard feed-forward multilayer perceptron (MLP) to test on a small number of octapeptides, and the classification accuracy reached 82%. Cai et al. [2] repeated the work of [33] on an extended data sets using a standard MLP with eight hidden units, and concluded that MLP has superior performance in dealing with non-linear problems, such as predicting HIV-1 protease cleavage sites. Narayanan et al. [23] tried using decision trees to extract rules for HIV-1 protease cleavage sites prediction, but found that decision tree was never able to predict cleavage sites as well as ANN. Cai et al. [3] applied SVM to this problem and tried to use different kernel functions combined with SVM. The experimental results showed that the performance of Gaussian kernel function is the best. Moreover, Cai et al. [3] pointed out that SVM had a powerful ability to predict non-linear problems such as HIV-1 protease cleavage sites. HIVcleave established the first web server for predicting the HIV-1 protease cleavage site by combining the discriminant function algorithm and the vectorized sequence-coupling model [28].

With more and more experimental data were collected, You et al. [25] found that the prediction of HIV-1 protease cleavage site should be a linear problem, and using a linear classifier like the simple perceptron or linear support vector machine (LSVM) can solve the problem. Therefore, the problem of how to extract linearly separable features from octapeptides had attracted the attention of many researchers. Li et al. [18] mapped the amino acid sequence corresponding to the octapeptide region to the local kernel space, and reduced the dimensionality of the linear SVM classifier. They pointed out that using cross-validation for evaluation is better than other methods. Gök et al. [8] studied several different coding schemes, and proposed an OETMAP coding scheme based on amino acid features and linear classifiers. Cross-validation was performed on two larger data sets. The experimental results showed that the prediction performance of using OETMAP encoding was better than standard amino acid encoding. Rögnvaldsson et al. [26] pointed out that LSVM with orthogonal coding scheme may be the best predictor of HIV-1 protease cleavage site. The experimental results proved that it had better performance than currently available predictive models. PROSPERous [29] was developed as a function-based integrated system to prediction cleavage site by using different scoring functions of the substrate sequence and structure to construct feature vectors. As the advanced version of PROSPER, iProt-Sub [30] integrated heterogeneous features and structural features, and used a two-step feature selection procedure to eliminate redundant and irrelevant features. The experimental results showed that iProt-Sub was able to achieves better prediction performance than several existing prediction tools. Recently, Hu et al. [11] proposed a novel feature extraction method, namely Evocleave, which used the co-evolution information of the substrate sequence to identify the coevolutionary patterns from the substrate sequence with the ability of providing some evidence to support or refute the existence of cleavage site in the substrate [10, 15]. Based on the Evocleave was able to only extract the coevolutionary patterns of paired amino acids, and may not make full use of the co-evolution information of the substrate, Li and Hu [19] proposed to use a variable-length coevolutionary patterns, namely Evocleave V2.0, to build a prediction model. The cross-validation experiment result showed that Evocleave V2.0 further improves the prediction performance.

Since cleavable octapeptides are often obtained via expensive and time-consuming experiments, while uncleavable octapeptides were artificially generated by using different strategies [20, 26]. Obviously, this situation usually causes data imbalance in datasets, i.e., the number of cleavable octapeptides is much smaller than the uncleavable octapeptides. Therefore, when we apply the machine learning algorithm to an imbalanced dataset to predict the HIV-1 protease cleavage site, the trained classifier is mostly derived from the uncleavable octapeptides. In addition, the trained classifier may miss or ignore the information from the cleavable octapeptides, which results in poor prediction performance for the cleavable octapeptide because the classifier is mainly biased towards uncleavable octapeptides. However, for the prediction of HIV-1 protease cleavage site, we are more interested in the prediction of cleavable octapeptides.

To this end, we adopt ensemble learning methods to improve the prediction performance of training classifiers on skewed datasets. In this work, we proposed an ensemble learning prediction model, namely AB-HIV, which combines asymmetric bagging [32] with SVM to build a more accurate classifier to predict HIV-1 protease cleavage sites. Instead of re-sampling from the training set, asymmetric bagging keeps the positive dataset fixed and re-samples only from the negative dataset to balance the training subset of the basic classifier. Furthermore, in order to make full use of the sequence information of the substrate, AB-HIV uses three different coding schemes (amino acid identities, chemical properties and variable length coevolutionary patterns) to construct feature vectors. The experimental results showed that AB-HIV yielded the best evaluation scores on almost all datasets, which proves that the combination of Asymmetric bagging and SVM could greatly improve the predictive performance of HIV-1 protease cleavage sites.

2   Materials and Methods

2.1   Feature Vector Construction

Each octapeptide is a sequence composed of eight amino acids. In particular, given an alphabet set $\Lambda = \{\lambda_i\}(1 \leq i \leq n_\Lambda, n_\Lambda = 20)$ representing a set of 20 distinct amino acids, $\Gamma = \{\beta_j | \beta_j = \alpha_m \alpha_n\}(1 \leq j \leq n_\Gamma^2, 1 \leq m, n \leq n_\Gamma)$ consisting of 400 amino acid sequences with length 2, and an octapeptide is represented as $P = P_1 P_2 P_3 P_4 P_5 P_6 P_7 P_8$ where $P_i \in \Lambda (1 \leq i \leq 8)$. The cleavage site is located between P_4 and P_5. In order to predict whether there is a cleavage site in the substrate, each substrate is represented as an N-dimensional feature vector. By using the sequence information of the octapeptide, we extracted three different features, namely amino acid identities, chemical properties and variable length coevolutionary patterns. A detailed description of these features is presented below.

Amino Acid Identities. In order to map octapeptide to the feature space, the octapeptide is represented adopting an orthogonal coding scheme where each amino acid by a 20 bits vector with 19 bits set to -1 and one bit set to 1. By this way, each octapeptide is mapped to an 8 by 20 matrix, which is transformed into a 160-dimensional vector in the feature space. However, since each position must be composed of one amino acid (the last value of the orthogonal vector is restricted by other elements), the dimension of this problem can be simplified to 152 dimensions.

Chemical Properties. Apart from amino acid identities, the chemical properties of amino acids are also considered for feature vector construction. According to the chemical structure properties of amino acids, Λ can be divided into eight different chemical groups [5]. The detailed grouping is given in Table 1. Then, similar to the process of extracting amino acid identities features, the orthogonal coding scheme is used to map each amino acid into an 8-dimensional feature vector. Since each amino acid can only belong to one chemical group, the last amino acid in the octapeptide is restricted by other positions, which can reduce the dimension to 7 dimensions. The total number of dimensions of the chemical properties features is $8 \times 7 = 56$(for any octapeptide).

Table 1. The chemical classes to which the 20 amino acids belong.

Chemical group	Amino acids
Sulfur-containing	C, M
Aliphatic 1	A, G, P
Aliphatic 2	I, L, V
Acidic	D, E
Basic	H, K, R
Aromatic	F, W, Y
Amide	N, Q
Small hydroxy	S, T

Variable Length Coevolutionary Patterns. According to the research on HIV envelope protein [34], it was found that the amino acid change of one residue might cause the amino acid change of another residue. Inspired by this observation, Hu et al. [11] proposed a coevolutionary patterns called Evocleave, which used the mutual evolutionary knowledge between paired amino acids to provide some evidence to support or refute the existence of cleavage site in substrates by HIV-1 PR [9, 16]. Since Evocleave only provides the limitation of a coevolutionary pattern composed of a single amino acid, Li and Hu [19] considered using a variable-length coevolutionary pattern to improve Evocleave. The experiment result had shown that Evocleave V2.0 can further improve the prediction performance of Evocleave. The variable length coevolutionary pattern is divided into three types, A_A, A_AB and AB_A. Take A_AB as an example, $(\alpha_i, \beta_j)_k$

denotes that α_i is followed by β_j at k-1 positions later, EvoCleave V2.0 determines whether $(\alpha_i, \beta_j)_k$ is a coevolutionary pattern by (1).

$$diff((\alpha_i, \beta_j)_k) = \frac{p((\alpha_i, \beta_j)_k) - p((\alpha_i, *)_k)p((*, \beta_j)_k)}{\sqrt{\frac{p((\alpha_i, *)_k)p((*, \beta_j)_k)}{n_1}(1 - p((\alpha_i, *)_k))(1 - p((*, \beta_j)_k))}} \qquad (1)$$

Among them, $p((\alpha_i, \beta_j)_k), p((\alpha_i, *)_k)$ and $p((*, \beta_j)_k)$ are the respective probabilities that $(\alpha_i, \beta_j)_k, (\alpha_i, *)_k$, and $(*, \beta_j)_k$ are observed in the octapeptide, and n_1 is the number of octapeptides. It should be noted that the octapeptide here only means the cleavable octapeptide, because the experimental results show that only the coevolutionary model of cleavable octapeptide can also complete the prediction task well. Since the value of diff follows a normal distribution, we reason that $(\alpha_i, \beta_j)_k$ is considered as a coevolutionary pattern in n_1 at a confidence level of 95% if $diff((\lambda_i, \lambda_j)_k) \geq 1.96$. Next, Evocleave V2.0 further uses (2) to quantify the amount of evidence provided by each coevolutionary pattern from the perspective of mutual information [12, 14].

$$weight((\alpha_i, \beta_j)_k) = \log\frac{p((\alpha_i, \beta_j)_k)}{p((\alpha_i, *)_k)p((*, \beta_j)_k)} - \log\frac{p((\alpha_i, *)_k) - p((\alpha_i, \beta_j)_k)}{p((\alpha_i, *)_k)(1 - p((*, \beta_j)_k))} \qquad (2)$$

2.2 Asymmetric Bagging SVM Classifier

Support Vector Machines. The Support vector machines (SVM) proposed by Vapnik [4] was a popular classification model and were used in many fields, such as text mining, image classification, and bioinformatics [13, 21]. The basic model of SVM is a linear classifier with the largest interval defined in the feature space, which effective handling to high dimensional datasets and nonlinear classification using kernel functions. For binary classification, a classic SVM classification constructs a hyperplane in the feature space to distinguish between positive and negative examples.

For a given training set $D = \{(x_i, y_i)\}(1 \leq i \leq n)$ the aim of the classification is to find a hyperplane $(\omega^T x_i + b = 0)$ that correctly distinguish the training data, where x_i denotes the N-dimensional feature vector of P_i and $y_i \in \{-1, 1\}$ is its label. In the real training data, there may be no separable hyperplane because of noisy data in both positive training set and negative training set, the soft margin SVM is proposed, which is defined by (3).

$$Minimize : \tfrac{1}{2}\omega^T\omega + C_1 \sum_{i=1}^{m-1} \xi_i + C_2 \sum_{i=m}^{n} \xi_i$$
$$s.t. \, y_i(\omega^T x_i + b) \geq 1 - \xi_i, \xi_i \geq 0, i = 1, 2, \ldots, n \qquad (3)$$

The above ω is the normal vector of the SVM hyperplane, ξ refers to the corresponding slack variable used to calculate the error cost, b represents the offset of the hyperplane from the origin along the normal vector ω, and C controls the amount of training errors allowed. Based on the soft margin SVM, we incorporate the linear kernel function defined by (4) into (3) for the case of HIV-1 PR cleavage site prediction.

$$kernel(x_i, x_j) = x_i^T \cdot x_j \qquad (4)$$

Regarding the implementation of SVM with linear kernel function, the svm.SVC library of sklearn package [24] was adopted to train and test SVM classifier. During the fine-tuning phase, by varying the value of hyperparameter C from the set $\{0.03123, 0.0625, 0.125, 0.25, 0.5, 1, 2, 4, 8, 16, 32\}$, so as to optimize the prediction performance of the SVM classifier.

Asymmetric Bagging. Bagging is one of the traditional integration methods, which includes the benefits of bootstrapping and aggregation [1]. The Bagging algorithm selects multiple training subsets from the training set that are replaced, i.e., bootstrapping, and multiple classifiers can be generated by training on these training subsets, then the aggregation of multiple groups of classifiers is realized by averaging and majority voting. Experimental results have shown that bagging can improve the stability of a single classifier, but the unbalanced training data also reduce its generalization performance. However, directly use bagging to predict the HIV-1 protease cleavage site is not suitable since we only have a small number of cleavable octapeptide samples. Therefore, we propose to use asymmetric bagging strategy to handle the problem of dataset imbalance. The bootstrapping of asymmetric bagging is executed only on negative sample data since the number of uncleavable octapeptides is much larger than the cleavable octapeptides. In this way, each classifier of asymmetric bagging is generated on an equal number of positive and negative samples, thus solve the problem of imbalanced data sets. Combining asymmetric bagging strategy can solve the unstable problem of single SVM classifier and the imbalance problem of training set.

Algorithm 1. AB-HIV

Input: P, N, T, F = number of bootstraps

Output: a score s:$T \rightarrow \mathbb{R}$

1: Initialize $\forall x \in T, f(x) \leftarrow 0$

2: **for** t $= 1$ to F **do**

3: Extract a training subset N_t from N by using bootstrapping, the size of N_t is equal to P

4: Train an individual model f_t on the training subset $P \cup N_t$ by using SVM clas- sifier

---

5: For $x \in T$, update:

6: $f(x) \leftarrow f(x) + f_t(x)$
7: **end for**
8: **return** $s(x) = f(x)/F$ for $x \in T$

In summary, the detailed process of combining asymmetric bagging with SVM is introduced in Algorithm 1. We call it AB-HIV when asymmetric bagging and SVM are used to predict HIV-1 protease cleavage sites. Among, P is the positive example data in the training datasets, N is the negative example data in the training datasets, and T is the testing datasets. The number F of iteratively generated classifiers is a user-defined parameter. Intuitively, the larger the value of F the better prediction performance, but there is almost no improvement after the observation that F is greater than 30 during the experiment. Finally, we use a simple average method to summarize these classifiers, and other summary rules can be easily be used.

3   Experiment Results

To evaluate the performance of AB-HIV, we compared it with several well-known predictive models, including Evocleave, [26], PROSPERous, HIVcleave and iProt-Sub. A detailed description of several methods be given in the section of introduction. Among them, EvoCleave, [26], HIVcleave, PROSPERous all use sequences to design prediction models, while iProt-Sub integrates different biological information to build prediction models.

3.1   Experimental Datasets

Regarding the performance evaluation of the experiment, we selected three independent benchmark datasets to avoid any bias caused by the selection of training and testing sets. The statistics of the three data sets are given in Table 2. All datasets could be downloaded from the UCI machine learning repository [7]. We noticed that these datasets are all unbalanced datasets, because the number of cleavable octapeptides in the dataset is much smaller than that of uncleavable octapeptides. Generally, this imbalance between the positive set and negative set will affect the training process of the classification model, thus affecting the accuracy of the prediction model. These three benchmark data sets were collected from the work of [17, 26] on human protein, the details of how the three datasets were collected are described in the references.

Table 2. Detailed descriptions of three datasets. The column of Source gives the original source of corresponding dataset. The column of Octapeptides is the number of all octapeptides in the dataset. The columns of Cleaved and Uncleaved are the sizes of positive and negative sets respectively.

Dataset	Source	Octapeptides	Cleaved	Uncleaved
1625Dataset	[17]	1625	347	1251
impensDataset	[26]	947	149	798
schillingDatasct	[26]	3272	434	2838

3.2   Evaluation Metrics

In the experiment, we use three different evaluation metrics, i.e., ROC analysis, Precision-Recall analysis and F-measure to compare the prediction performance of each method. In particular, ROC analysis considers predictive performance as a trade-off between sensitivity and specificity. By setting different threshold parameters, a curve of true positive versus false positive rate can be obtained, i.e., ROC curve. As the area under the ROC curve, AUC is a widely accepted performance comparison index. The value of the AUC score is between 0 and 1. If the algorithm predicts the HIV-1 cleavage site more accurately, its corresponding AUC value is closer to 1. Similar to ROC analysis, Precision-Recall analysis focuses on the trade-off between precision and recall. The PR

AUC score is the area under the PR curve calculated by trapezoidal integration. The reason why we used Precision-Recall analysis is that according to Table 2, most of the datasets were unbalanced data sets, i.e., the number of cleaved octapeptides was much less than uncleaved octapeptides. For unbalanced datasets, using PR ROC analysis was better than ROC analysis [6].

F-measure is the harmonic mean of precision and recall, and it is computed as:

$$\text{Precision} = \frac{TP}{TP + FP}$$
$$\text{Recall} = \frac{TP}{TP + FN} \tag{5}$$
$$\text{F - measure} = \frac{2 \times Precison \times Recall}{Precision + Recall}$$

where TP (True Positive) is the number of correctly predicted octapeptides in the set of cleaved octapeptides, FP (False Positive) is the number of incorrect predictions in the negative set, and FN (False Negative) is the number of incorrect predictions in the positive set. In the experiment, we calculated F-measure at a threshold of 50%. That is to say, if the probability that AB-HIV predicts that the octapeptide is cleavable is greater than 0.5, then the octapeptide is declared as a cleavable category.

3.3 10-Fold Cross Validation

In this part, we conducted the 10-fold cross-validation (CV) experiment, and the results are given in Table 3. In particular, each data was first randomly divided into 10 equal parts, we then alternatively used 9 parts (training data) to train AB-HIV and evaluate it based on the rest part (testing data).

Comparing AB-HIV with other methods in terms of AUC, we notice that AB-HIV yields the largest score in all the datasets. To put it more specific, the average AUC score obtain by AB-HIV is improved by 11.01%, 2.16%, 13.14%, 53.75% and 33.29% than EvoCleave, [26], PROSPERous, HIVcleave and iProt-Sub respectively. One should note that the performance of AB-HIV never performed worse than that of Evocleave and [26]. Evocleave and [26] utilize coevolutionary pattern and orthogonal coding to construct feature vectors respectively while AB-HIV combines these two methods. This could be an indicator that the combination of multiple features improves the prediction accuracy. Another point worth to noting that the AUC scores of Evocleave and [26] are different from the results reported in [11] and [26], because of the training set and testing set use in the 10-fold cross-validation are different due to the strategy of applying a random division to the original datasets in our experiments. Moreover, the performance of AB-HIV has never been worse than PROSPERous and iProt-Sub that both PROSPERous and iProt-Sub integrate multiple information sources including sequence and structural features.

The experimental results in Table 3 indicate that AB-HIV shows a bigger margin in the PR AUC scores when compared with the AUC scores. The possible reason for this phenomenon is that the datasets we use in the experiment are all imbalanced, i.e., the number of cleavable octapeptides is much smaller than that of uncleavable octapeptides.

Table 3. Experiment results of 10-fold CV.

Dataset	Model	AUC	PR AUC	F-measure		
				Precision	Recall	F-measure
1625Dataset	AB-HIV	**0.98**	**0.94**	0.8	0.93	**0.86**
	EvoCleave	0.93	0.84	0.85	0.74	0.8
	[14]	0.97	0.9	0.85	0.8	0.83
	PROSPERous	0.82	0.33	0.23	1	0.38
	HIVcleave	0.73	0.61	0.69	0.67	0.68
	iProt-Sub	0.68	0.41	0.41	0.26	0.32
impendsDataset	AB-HIV	**0.92**	**0.73**	0.49	0.85	0.62
	EvoCleave	0.88	0.64	0.77	0.42	0.54
	[14]	0.9	0.7	0.69	0.62	**0.65**
	PROSPERous	0.83	0.17	0.16	1	0.27
	HIVcleave	0.56	0.29	0.29	0.45	0.35
	iProt-Sub	0.72	0.36	0.43	0.34	0.38
schillingDataset	AB-HIV	**0.96**	**0.8**	0.53	0.91	**0.67**
	EvoCleave	0.78	0.36	0.5	0.2	0.28
	[14]	0.93	0.68	0.66	0.66	0.66
	PROSPERous	0.88	0.15	0.14	0.95	0.24
	HIVcleave	0.59	0.34	0.31	0.41	0.35
	iProt-Sub	0.75	0.37	0.39	0.34	0.37

*For each dataset, the best results are bolded.

Recall that PR ROC analysis measures the performance of each algorithm on imbalanced datasets is better than ROC analysis. The excellent performance of AB-HIV in terms of PR AUC further proved that AB-HIV is more robust to processing imbalanced datasets. Therefore, we believe that the strong performance of AB-HIV in terms of PR AUC shows that from the perspective of the imbalance of the dataset, AB-HIV is more promising in predicting HIV-1 protease cleavage sites.

We also notice that the powerful performance of AB-HIV in terms of F-measure is not obvious, and the best performance is only obtained in 1625Dataset and schillingDataset. To explain the reason for the performance of AB-HIV in F-measure, we conduct an in-depth study to the prediction results of AB-HIV. We found that the prediction probability of some uncleavable octapeptides was greater than 0.5, which yielding a smaller score of Precision and a higher score of Recall. This may indicate that AB-HIV is more interested in predicting the cleavable octapeptide when predicting the HIV-1 protease cleavage site. Simultaneously, the score of Recall is improved greatly, which indicates that AB-HIV is a suitable method to solve the imbalance problem.

In summary, experimental results demonstrated a strong performance of AB-HIV in predicting HIV-1 protease cleavage site, as it yields the best average performance in all datasets.

3.4 Analysis of Feature Significance and Contribution

Table 4. Experiment Results of feature analysis. Three different types of features are used in different combinations to construct feature vectors, and then cross-validation is performed on three independent data sets. The experimental result is the average of three independent data sets.

Feature	AUC	PR AUC	F-measure
AAI	0.94	0.78	0.68
CheP	0.91	0.69	0.63
VLCoP	0.82	0.58	0.55
AAI + CheP	0.94	0.81	0.7
AAI + VLCoP	0.94	0.79	0.7
CheP + VLCoP	0.93	0.75	0.67
AAI + CheP + VLCoP	0.95	0.82	0.72

Recall that we chose three different feature sets (amino acid identities, chemical properties and variable length coevolutionary patterns) to construct feature vectors since they can provide sufficient informative information for AB-HIV to predict HIV-1 protease cleavage sites. To evaluate the contribution of these features to the prediction model, we constructed an experiment to analysis the importance of the individual feature and their combinations for improving the prediction performance of AB-HIV.

For simplicity, the feature sets of amino acid identities, chemical properties and variable length coevolutionary patterns were denoted as AAI, CheP and VLCoP respectively. Then, we used the individual feature and their combinations to construct feature vector, and perform a 10-fold cross-validation experiment in three independent datasets. The average AUC, PR AUC and F-measure scores on the three datasets are given in Table 4. Among the three individual features set, we found that the AB-HIV model that only used AAI achieved the best performance on all metrics. This is able to indicate that the orthogonal encoding of amino acid identities the effective predictor of the HIV-1 protease cleavage site, which is consistent with the results of [26]. Compared with an individual feature set, when multiple feature sets were combined, the performance of AB-HIV would be further improved. In addition, we filter out a feature from the combined feature set each time. The experimental results in rows 3–5 showed that using the combined feature set without VLCoP can achieve better performance than those of other two kind of combined feature sets. We also noticed that AB-HIV showed the best performance when combining all three feature sets, but the difference in the performance of AB-HIV between AAI + CheP + VLCoP and AAI + CheP was small. This phenomenon may indicate that VLCoP has little influence on improving the prediction performance of AB-HIV. The prediction performance of VLCoP was not as prominent as claimed in [19]. A possible reason for this phenomenon may be that AB-HIV only used the variable length coevolutionary patterns extracted from the cleavable octapeptide to construct the feature vector. In sum, for these three feature sets, the consideration of AAI was more important for improve the prediction performance of AB-HIV while VLCoP contributed the least to the prediction task.

4 Conclusion

In this work, an efficient prediction algorithm, namely AB-HIV, is proposed to predict HIV-1 protease cleavage site. The main idea of AB-HIV is to use ensemble learning method to solve the problem of existing data imbalance, as the trained classifier is mostly derived from the uncleavable octapeptide if we train directly the classification model on the imbalanced dataset, which leads to the poor prediction performance of cleavable octapeptide. Therefore, by using the idea of asymmetric bagging, AB-HIV extracts multiple training subsets with equal numbers of positive and negative samples from the training set to train a series of classifiers, and then integrated a final model to predict HIV-1 protease cleavage site. The experiment results demonstrate that AB-HIV yielded a promising performance when applied to predict HIV-1 protease cleavage site, as it achieved better results than the state-of-the-art prediction methods for most cases. In future work, we will start from the following aspects. First, there may be different effects from using different feature encoding schemes on the performance of AB-HIV. We plan to explore more complex machine learning methods for feature extraction to better describe the features that distinguish cleavable and uncleavable octapeptides. Secondly, we would to embed the feature selection method in the training process of AB-HIV. On the one hand, this can not only eliminate some redundant and useless features, but also improve the generalization ability of a single classifier. On the other hand, different feature selection for different training subsets, which makes more diversity of bagging and improves the overall performance of AB-HIV.

Acknowledgements. This work has been supported by the National Natural Science Foundation of China [grant number 61602352] and the Pioneer Hundred Talents Program of Chinese Academy of Sciences.

References

1. Breiman, L.: Bagging predictors. Mach. Learn. **24**(2), 123–140 (1996)
2. Cai, Y.D., Chou, K.C.: Artificial neural network model for predicting hiv protease cleavage sites in protein. Adv. Eng. Softw. **29**(2), 119–128 (1998)
3. Cai, Y.D., Liu, X.J., Xu, X.B., Chou, K.C.: Support vector machines for predicting hiv protease cleavage sites in protein. J. Comput. Chem. **23**(2), 267–274 (2002)
4. Cortes, C., Vapnik, V.: Support-vector networks. Mach. Learn. **20**(3), 273–297 (1995)
5. Dang, T.H., Van Leemput, K., Verschoren, A., Laukens, K.: Prediction of kinasespecific phosphorylation sites using conditional random fields. Bioinformatics **24**(24), 2857–2864 (2008)

6. Davis, J., Goadrich, M.: The relationship between precision-recall and roc curves. In: Proceedings of the 23rd International Conference on Machine Learning, pp. 233–240 (2006)
7. Dua, D., Graff, C.: UCI machine learning repository (2017). http://archive.ics.uci.edu/ml 7(1) (2019)
8. Gök, M., Ozcerit, A.T.: A new feature encoding scheme for hiv-1 protease cleavage ¨ site prediction. Neural Comput. Appl. **22**(7), 1757–1761 (2013)
9. Hu, L., Chan, K.C., Yuan, X., Xiong, S.: A variational bayesian framework for cluster analysis in a complex network. IEEE Trans. Knowl. Data Eng. **32**(11), 2115–2128 (2019)
10. Hu, L., Chen, Q., Qiao, L., Du, L., Ye, R.: Automatic detection of melanins and sebums from skin images using a generative adversarial network. Cognitive Computation, pp. 1–10 (2021)
11. Hu, L., Hu, P., Luo, X., Yuan, X., You, Z.H.: Incorporating the coevolving information of substrates in predicting hiv-1 protease cleavage sites. IEEE/ACM Trans. Comput. Biol. Bioinf. **17**(6), 2017–2028 (2019)
12. Hu, L., Pan, X., Yan, H., Hu, P., He, T.: Exploiting higher-order patterns for community detection in attributed graphs. Integrated Computer-Aided Engineering (Preprint), 1–12 (2020)
13. Hu, L., Wang, X., Huang, Y.A., Hu, P., You, Z.H.: A survey on computational models for predicting protein–protein interactions. Briefings in Bioinformatics (2021)
14. Hu, L., Yang, S., Luo, X., Zhou, M.: An algorithm of inductively identifying clusters from attributed graphs. IEEE Trans. Big Data (2020)
15. Hu, L., Yuan, X., Liu, X., Xiong, S., Luo, X.: Efficiently detecting protein complexes from protein interaction networks via alternating direction method of multipliers. IEEE/ACM Trans. Comput. Biol. Bioinf. **16**(6), 1922–1935 (2018)
16. Hu, L., Zhang, J., Pan, X., Yan, H., You, Z.H.: HISCF: leveraging higher-order structures for clustering analysis in biological networks. Bioinformatics (2020)
17. Kontijevskis, A., Wikberg, J.E., Komorowski, J.: Computational proteomics analysis of hiv-1 protease interactome. Proteins: Structure Function Bioinform. **68**(1), 305–312 (2007)
18. Li, X., Hu, H., Shu, L.: Predicting human immunodeficiency virus protease cleavage sites in nonlinear projection space. Mol. Cell. Biochem. **339**(1), 127–133 (2010)
19. Li, Z., Hu, L.: The identification of variable-length coevolutionary patterns for predicting hiv-1 protease cleavage sites. In: 2020 IEEE International Conference on Systems, Man, and Cybernetics (SMC), pp. 4192–4197. IEEE (2020).
20. Li, Z., Hu, L., Tang, Z., Zhao, C.: Predicting hiv-1 protease cleavage sites with positive-unlabeled learning. Front. Genet. **12**, 456 (2021)
21. Luo, X., Zhou, Y., Liu, Z., Hu, L., Zhou, M.: Generalized nesterov's accelerationincorporated non-negative and adaptive latent factor analysis. IEEE Trans Services Comput. (2021)
22. Martin, M.P., et al.: Epistatic interaction between kir3ds1 and hla-b delays the progression to aids. Nat. Genet. **31**(4), 429–434 (2002)
23. Narayanan, A., Wu, X., Yang, Z.R.: Mining viral protease data to extract cleavage knowledge. Bioinformatics **18**(suppl_1), S5–S13 (2002)
24. Pedregosa, F., et al.: Scikit-learn: machine learning in python. J. Mach. Learn. Res. **12**, 2825–2830 (2011)
25. R¨ognvaldsson, T., You, L.: Why neural networks should not be used for hiv-1 protease cleavage site prediction. Bioinformatics **20**(11), 1702–1709 (2004)
26. R¨ognvaldsson, T., You, L., Garwicz, D.: State of the art prediction of hiv-1 protease cleavage sites. Bioinformatics **31**(8), 1204–1210 (2015)
27. Sadiq, S.K., Noé, F., De Fabritiis, G.: Kinetic characterization of the critical step in hiv-1 protease maturation. Proc. Natl. Acad. Sci. **109**(50), 20449–20454 (2012)
28. Shen, H.B., Chou, K.C.: Hivcleave: a web-server for predicting human immunodeficiency virus protease cleavage sites in proteins. Anal. Biochem. **375**(2), 388–390 (2008)

29. Song, J., et al.: Prosperous: high-throughput prediction of substrate cleavage sites for 90 proteases with improved accuracy. Bioinformatics **34**(4), 684–687 (2018)
30. Song, J., et al.: iprot-sub: a comprehensive package for accurately mapping and predicting protease-specific substrates and cleavage sites. Brief. Bioinform. **20**(2), 638–658 (2019)
31. Sundquist, W.I., Kräusslich, H.G.: Hiv-1 assembly, budding, and maturation. Cold Spring Harbor perspectives in medicine **2**(7), a006924 (2012)
32. Tao, D., Tang, X., Li, X., Wu, X.: Asymmetric bagging and random subspace for support vector machines-based relevance feedback in image retrieval. IEEE Trans. Pattern Anal. Mach. Intell. **28**(7), 1088–1099 (2006)
33. Thompson, T.B., Chou, K.C., Zheng, C.: Neural network prediction of the hiv-1 protease cleavage sites. J. Theor. Biol. **177**(4), 369–379 (1995)
34. Travers, S.A., Tully, D.C., McCormack, G.P., Fares, M.A.: A study of the coevolutionary patterns operating within the env gene of the hiv-1 group m subtypes. Mol. Biol. Evol. **24**(12), 2787–2801 (2007)
35. Wang, X., Hu, P., Hu, L.: A novel stochastic block model for network-based prediction of protein-protein interactions. In: International Conference on Intelligent Computing, pp. 621–632. Springer, Cham (2020). https://doi.org/10.1007/978-3-030-60802-6_54

RWRNCP: Random Walking with Restart Based Network Consistency Projection for Predicting miRNA-Disease Association

Ming-Wen Zhang[1], Yu-Tian Wang[1], Zhen Gao[1], Lei Li[1], Jian-Cheng Ni[1(✉)], and Chun-Hou Zheng[1,2(✉)]

[1] School of Cyber Science and Engineering, Qufu Normal University, Qufu, China
[2] School of Computer Science and Technology, Anhui University, Hefei, China

Abstract. The prediction of association between disease and microRNAs is playing an increasing important role for understanding disease etiology and pathogenesis. So far, many various computational methods have been proposed by researchers to predict the potential associations between microRNAs and diseases. Considering that the past methods have many limitations, we developed Random Walking with Restart based Network Consistency Projection for Predicting miRNA-disease Association to uncover the relationship between diseases and miRNAs. Based on diverse similarity measures, the proposed model constructed the topological similarity of miRNAs and diseases by random walking with restart (RWR) algorithm on the similarity network, which took full advantage of the network topology information, and introduced the Gaussian interaction profile kernel similarity to get the integrated similarity of miRNA and disease, respectively. Then, we projected miRNA space and disease space on the miRNA-disease interaction network, respectively. Finally, we can obtain the predicted miRNA-disease association score matrix by combining the above two space projection scores. Simulation results showed that RWRNCP can efficiently infer miRNA-disease relationships with high accuracy, obtaining AUCs of 0.9479 and 0.9274 in leave-one-out cross validation (LOOCV) and five-fold cross validation (5CV), respectively. Furthermore, a case study also suggested that RWRNCP is promising for discover new miRNA-disease interactions.

Keywords: miRNA-disease association · Random walk with restart · Network consistency projection

1 Introduction

A short class of non-coding RNAs called miRNAs, whose length is generally 19 to 25 nt. They usually regulate gene expression and protein production [1–5]. It is worth noting that with the development of bioinformatics, more researches start to focus on the function of miRNAs. In addition, miRNAs begin to play an important role in biological processes such as proliferation, cell differentiation, viral infection, and signal

© Springer Nature Switzerland AG 2021
D.-S. Huang et al. (Eds.): ICIC 2021, LNAI 12838, pp. 522–535, 2021.
https://doi.org/10.1007/978-3-030-84532-2_47

transduction. Moreover, some miRNAs are closely related to human diseases. Considering the strong association between miRNA and disease, all their potential associations should be explored. In medicine, the advantage is that it can promote the diagnosis and treatment of some complex diseases [6–9]. However, predicting miRNA-disease associations (MDAs) is time-consuming and expensive. Therefore, it is necessary to use computational methods instead of traditional experimental methods. In previous studies, functionally similar miRNAs tend to connect with similar diseases, and vice versa [10]. Based on such theory, more and more computational methods and models are proposed for identifying potential MDAs.

Researchers have already developed some computational methods in predicting miRNA-disease associations. For example, Chen et al. reviewed 20 state-of-the-art computational models of predicting miRNA–disease associations from different perspectives [11]. Finally, they summarized four important factors for the difficulties of predicting potential disease-related miRNAs, the framework of constructing powerful computational models to predict potential miRNA–disease associations including five feasible and important research schemas, and future directions for further development of computational models. Chen et al. proposed a method HGIMDA (Heterogeneous Graph Inference miRNA-Disease Association) to predict novel MDAs [12]. It is worth noting the known miRNA-disease associations, miRNA functional similarity, disease semantic similarity, and Gaussian interaction profile kernel similarity for diseases and miRNAs are integrated into this method. The benefit is that the accuracy of the algorithm is improved to some extent. The functional relationship between miRNA targets and disease genes in PPI (Protein–Protein Interaction) networks are considered by researchers. Chen et al. developed a computational model of Matrix Decomposition and Heterogeneous Graph Inference for miRNA-disease association prediction (MDHGI) to discover new miRNA-disease associations by integrating the predicted association probability obtained from matrix decomposition through sparse learning method, the miRNA functional similarity, the disease semantic similarity, and the Gaussian interaction profile kernel similarity for diseases and miRNAs into a heterogeneous network [13]. Chen et al. proposed a novel computational method named Ensemble of Decision Tree based MiRNA-Disease Association prediction (EDTMDA) [14], which innovatively built a computational framework integrating ensemble learning and dimensionality reduction. For each miRNA-disease pair, the feature vector was extracted by calculating the statistical measures, graph theoretical measures, and matrix factorization results for the miRNA and disease, respectively. Then multiple base learnings were built to yield many decision trees (DTs) based on random selection of negative samples and miRNA/disease features. Chen et al. presented a computational model named Laplacian Regularized Sparse Subspace Learning for MiRNA-Disease Association prediction (LRSSLMDA) [15], which projected miRNAs/diseases' statistical feature profile and graph theoretical feature profile to a common subspace. It used Laplacian regularization to preserve the local structures of the training data and a L1-norm constraint to select important miRNA/disease features for prediction. Chen et al. proposed a novel computational model of Bipartite Network Projection for MiRNA-Disease Association prediction (BNPMDA) based on the known miRNA-disease associations, integrated miRNA similarity and integrated disease similarity [16].

Chen et al. proposed a new method of ranking-based KNN called RKNNMDA to identify potential MDAs [17]. These previously similarity-based sorted neighbors were re-ranked to get better prediction results. Recently, matrix factorization algorithms have been used to identify novel MDAs. The advantage is that these methods can better handle missing associations. Li et al. proposed a novel method using deep collaborative filtering called DCFMDA to predict miRNA-disease potential associations [18]. Li et al. proposed a novel diffusion-based computational method DF-MDA for predicting miRNA-disease association based on the assumption that molecules are related to each other in human physiological processes [19]. Chen et al. developed a computational model of ELLP-MDA (Ensemble Learning and Link Prediction for miRNA-Disease Association) to predict novel MDAs [20]. They constructed a similarity network and utilized ensemble learning to combine rank results given by three classic similarity-based algorithms. To evaluate the performance of ELLPMDA, they exploited global and local Leave-One-Out Cross Validation (LOOCV), 5-fold Cross Validation (5CV) and three kinds of case studies.

Although existing methods have made great contributions to uncover disease-related miRNAs, a great number of methods are ignoring the topological network structure information of disease similarity network and miRNA similarity network and difficult to mine internal relationships from multiple kinds of data. In this paper, we propose a novel prediction method based on Walking Random with Restart based Network Consistency Projection for predicting miRNA-disease association and refer it as RWRNCP. To make full use of network topology information between disease similarity network and miRNA similarity network, two pre-processing methods, namely random walking with restart and Gaussian interaction profile kernel similarity, were used. Finally, we develop an improved network consistent projection to predict miRNA-disease associations. To evaluate the

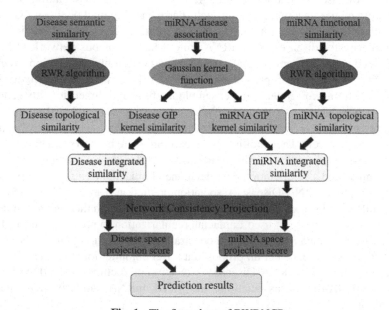

Fig. 1. The flow chart of RWRNCP

effectiveness and performance of RWRNCP, we implement 5CV, global LOOCV and a case study. Overall, we find that RWRNCP could reliably and effectively predict disease-associated miRNAs (Fig. 1).

2 Materials and Methods

2.1 Human miRNA-Disease Association

The data of known human miRNA–disease associations, which used in this work were retrieved from the HMDD v2.0 database. After sorting and standardizing the downloaded data, we obtained 5430 experimentally verified human miRNA–disease associations between 383 diseases and 495 miRNAs. An $nd \times nm$ adjacency matrix A is defined as:

$$\begin{cases} A(d(i),\ m(j)) = 1 & disease\ d(i)\ has\ association\ with\ miRNA\ m(j) \\ A(d(i),\ m(j)) = 0 & disease\ d(i)\ has\ no\ association\ with\ miRNA\ m(j) \end{cases} \quad (1)$$

2.2 miRNA Function Similarity

The miRNA functional similarity was calculated based on a basic assumption that functionally similar miRNAs tend to connect with similar diseases, and vice versa [21–23]. The miRNA functional similarity was calculated based on a basic assumption that functionally similar miRNAs tend to connect with similar diseases, and vice versa. Thanks to the excellent work of Wang et al. [23], we can download the miRNA functional similarity data from http://www.cuilab.cn/files/images/cuilab/misim.zip. With these data, we constructed a $nm \times nm$ matrix FS to represent the miRNA functional similarity. The element $FS(m(i), m(j))$ denotes the functional similarity between miRNA $m(i)$ and $m(j)$.

2.3 Disease Semantic Similarity

Disease Semantic Similarity Model 1
A Directed Acyclic Graph (DAG) was constructed to describe a disease based on the MeSH descriptors downloaded from the National Library of Medicine [24]. The DAG of disease D included not only the ancestor nodes of D and D itself but also the direct edges from parent nodes to child nodes. The semantic score of disease D could be defined by the following equation:

$$DV1(D) = \sum_{d \in T(D)} D_D1(d) \quad (2)$$

where $D_D1(d)$ denotes the contribution score of disease d in $DAG(D)$ to the disease D, and is defined as follows:

$$\begin{cases} D_D1(d) = 1 & if\ d = D \\ D_D1(d) = \max\{\Delta * D_D1(d') | d' \in children\ of\ d\} & if\ d \neq D \end{cases} \quad (3)$$

Here, Δ is the semantic contribution factor ($\Delta = 0.5$) [23]. The contribution score of disease is decreased as the distance between D and other diseases increases. Based on the assumption that two diseases with larger shared area of their DAGs may have greater similarity score, the semantic similarity score between disease $d(i)$ and disease $d(j)$ could be defined by the following equation:

$$SS1(d(i), d(j)) = \frac{\sum\limits_{t \in T(d(i)) \cap T(d(j))} \left(D_{d(i)}1(t) + D_{d(j)}1(t)\right)}{DV1(d(i)) + DV1(d(j))} \tag{4}$$

Disease Semantic Similarity Model 2
Supposing for two diseases in the same layer, if one disease appears in less disease DAGs than the other disease, obviously we can conclude that the first disease would have a greater contribution to the semantic value of disease D than the second disease. In conclusion, different disease terms in the same layer of $DAG(D)$ may have the different contribution to the semantic value of disease D. Considering about the above factor, we used a new method to describe the contribution of a disease d in $DAG(D)$ to the semantic value of disease D:

$$D_D2(d) = -\log\left[\frac{the\ number\ of\ DAGs\ including\ d}{the\ number\ of\ disease}\right] \tag{5}$$

The semantic value of disease D is defined as follows:

$$DV2(D) = \sum_{d \in T(D)} D_D2(d) \tag{6}$$

Based on the assumption that two diseases with larger shared area of their DAGs may have higher similarity score, we define the semantic similarity score between disease $d(i)$ and disease $d(j)$ as following:

$$SS2(d(i), d(j)) = \frac{\sum\limits_{t \in T(d(i)) \cap T(d(j))} \left(D_{d(i)}2(t) + D_{d(j)}2(t)\right)}{DV2(d(i)) + DV2(d(j))} \tag{7}$$

$$S_d(d(i), d(j)) = \frac{SS1(d(i), d(j)) + SS2(d(i), d(j))}{2} \tag{8}$$

2.4   Topological Similarity of Disease and miRNA

To improve the prediction accuracy, instead of directly using the similarity, the topological similarity of a disease and miRNA was constructed via implementing the RWR algorithm on the similarity network, that is,

$$S^{t+1} = (1 - \varepsilon)S^t W + \varepsilon S^0 \tag{9}$$

$$W(i,j) = \begin{cases} \frac{Sim(i,j)}{\sum_{p=1}^{n} Sim(p,j)} & if \sum_{p=1}^{n} Sim(p,j) \neq 0 \\ 0 & f \sum_{p=1}^{n} Sim(p,j) = 0 \end{cases} \tag{10}$$

where S^t represents the relevance matrix and $S^t(i,j)$ indicates the probability that the $i-th$ node reaches the $j-th$ node after t iterations. S^0 denotes the initial distribution matrix, which is the identity matrix consistent with the dimensions of similarity matrix Sim. The parameter ε is the restart probability that affects the interaction between nodes in the weighted fully connected network with miRNA as the node. The corresponding restart probability for disease is denoted by the parameter δ. W is the probability transition matrix obtained by normalizing each column of the integrated similarity matrix Sim for the miRNA and disease.

After several iterations, a stable matrix S^∞ will be obtained if the difference between S^{t+1} and S^t is less than 10^{-10} based on the L_1 norm. Then, S^∞ is denoted as M_{MT} and M_{DT} when Sim is M_{MS} and M_{DS}, respectively. Namely, M_{MT} is the miRNA topological similarity, and M_{DT} is the disease topological similarity.

2.5 Gaussian Interaction Profile Kernel Similarity for Diseases and miRNA

Based on the basic assumption that similar diseases tend to be associated with functionally similar miRNAs and vice versa [21–24], we calculated Gaussian interaction profile (GIP) kernel similarity to represent the miRNA similarity and disease similarity. Firstly, we used vector $IP(d(i))$ to represent the interaction profile of disease $d(i)$ by observing whether there is known association between disease $d(i)$ and each miRNA or not. Then, GIP kernel similarity between disease $d(i)$ and $d(j)$ was calculated as follows.

$$KD(d(i), d(j)) = \exp\left(-\gamma_d ||IP(d(i)) - IP(d(j))||^2\right) \tag{11}$$

where γ_d is used to control kernel bandwidth which is obtained by normalizing a new bandwidth parameter γ_d by the average number of associations with miRNAs for all the diseases. γ_d is defined as follows:

$$\gamma_d = \gamma_d / \left(\frac{1}{nd} \sum_{i=1}^{nd} ||IP(d(i))||^2\right) \tag{12}$$

Similarly, GIP kernel similarity between miRNA $m(i)$ and $m(j)$ is defined in a similar way:

$$KM(m(i), m(j)) = \exp\left(-\gamma_m ||IP(m(i)) - IP(m(j))||^2\right) \tag{13}$$

$$\gamma_m = \gamma_m / \left(\frac{1}{nm} \sum_{i=1}^{nm} ||IP(m(i))||^2\right) \tag{14}$$

2.6   Integrated Similarity for Diseases and miRNAs

In fact, we could not get DAGs for all diseases. That is to say, for the specific disease without DAG, we could not calculate the semantic similarity score between the disease and other diseases. Therefore, for those disease pairs with semantic similarity score, we used the semantic similarity score to denote the disease similarity, for the others, the Gaussian interaction profile kernel similarity score was used to denote the disease similarity. The disease similarity matrix between disease $d(i)$ and disease $d(j)$ is constructed as follows:

$$S_d(d(i), d(j)) = \begin{cases} M_{DT}(d(i), d(j)) & \begin{array}{l} d(i) \ and \ d(j) \ has \\ semantic \ similarity \end{array} \\ KD(d(i), d(j)) & otherwise \end{cases} \tag{15}$$

Similarly, the miRNA similarity matrix between miRNA $m(i)$ and miRNA $m(j)$ is constructed as follows:

$$S_m(m(i), m(j)) = \begin{cases} M_{MT}(m(i), m(j)) & \begin{array}{l} m(i) \ and \ m(j) \ has \\ functional \ similarity \end{array} \\ KM(m(i), m(j)) & otherwise \end{cases} \tag{16}$$

2.7   Network Consistency Projection of miRNA-Disease Association

In accordance with the assumption that diseases associated with highly related miR-NAs are more similar (and vice versa) and that miRNAs associated with highly related diseases are more similar (and vice versa), we developed the random walking with restart-based Network Consistency Projection for Predicting miRNA-disease Association (RWRNCP). RWRNCP calculates the potential miRNA-disease association score consisting of two network consistency projection scores, miRNA space projection score and disease space projection score, separately. The network consistency mentioned here refers to the higher the spatial similarity of miRNA $m(i)$ associated miRNAs in miRNA-miRNA similarity network and disease $d(j)$ associated miRNAs in the known miRNA-disease network, the greater the association of miRNA $d(i)$ with disease $d(j)$. We use vector space projection to represent it and named miRNA space projection. Similarly, disease space projection measures the association of miRNA $m(i)$ and disease $d(j)$ in disease space. Considering the miRNA-disease associations not verified by experiment cannot confirm that there is no association and to avoid having 0 as the denominator, we replace 0 in matrix A to ε. In our experiments, ε is set to 10^{-30}. Simultaneously, we use $|C|$ to represent the length of vector C (the norm of vector C). The miRNA space projection score is calculated as

$$NCP\_m(i, j) = \frac{S_{Mi} \times A_j}{|A_j|} \tag{17}$$

where S_{Mi} is the i - th row of matrix S_M and a vector consisting of the similarities between miRNA $m(i)$ and all other miRNAs. Similarly, A_j is the $j-th$ column of matrix A and the vector consisting of the associations of disease $d(j)$ and all miRNAs. Matrix

NCP_m is the network consistency projection score of the miRNA similarity network S_M on the known miRNA-disease association network, A; the variable $NCP\_m(i,j)$ in row i and column j is the network consistency projection of S_{Mi} on A_j. Notably, the smaller angle between S_{Mi} and A_j, the more miRNAs associated with disease $d(j)$, and the more similar miRNAs and miRNA $m(i)$ are, the greater the network consistency projection score $NCP\_m(i,j)$ is. Similarly, the disease space projection score is calculated as follows:

$$NCP\_d(i,j) = \frac{A_j \times S_{Dj}}{|A_i|} \tag{18}$$

where S_{Dj} is the j - th column of matrix S_D, the vector comprising the similarities of disease $d(j)$ and all other diseases. Similarly, A_i is the i - th row of matrix A, which consists of the associations of miRNA $m(i)$ and all diseases. Matrix NCP_d is the projection of the disease similarity network, S_D, on the known miRNA-disease association network A; $NCP\_d(i,j)$ in row i and column j is the network consistency projection of S_{Dj} on A_i. Remarkably, the smaller angle between SD_j and A_i, the more diseases are associated with miRNA $m(i)$, and the more similar these diseases and disease j are, the greater the network consistency projection score $NCP\_d(i,j)$ is.

Finally, the miRNA space projection score and disease space projection score are combined and normalized as shown below:

$$NCP(i,j) = \frac{NCP\_m(i,j) + NCP\_d(i,j)}{|S_{Mi}| + |S_{Dj}|} \tag{19}$$

where $NCP(i,j)$ is the final score of network consistency projection of miRNA $m(i)$ and disease $d(j)$; $NCP\_m(i,j)$ and $NCP\_d(i,j)$ are the miRNA space projection score and disease space projection score of miRNA $m(i)$ and disease $d(j)$, respectively. The final score is used to predict miRNA-disease association. If only RWRNCP in miRNA space projection (remove $NCP\_d(i,j)$ and $|S_{Dj}|$) is considered, the final score of miRNA $m(i)$ and disease $d(j)$ is the cosine similarity of space vector S_{Mi} and A_j. Similarly, the cosine similarity of space vector S_{Dj} and A_i is the final score of miRNA $m(i)$ and disease $d(j)$ when considering RWRNCP in disease space projection only.

3 Experiments and Results

3.1 Performance Evaluation

To validate the prediction performance of RWRNCP, the three state-of-art models, namely IMCMDA [25], ICFMDA [26], and SACMDA [27] were compared via two different cross validation methods, including five-fold cross-validation (5CV) and global leave-one-out cross-validation (global LOOCV).

In the 5CV method, all known interactions between miRNAs and diseases were randomly divided into five sections: one section was for the test, and other four sections were for training in turn. Interactions among all sections were manually validated, and other unknown interactions were regarded as candidate samples. Similarly, in the global LOOCV method, all manually validated miRNA-disease associations were considered as the test samples in turn, and the rest of the miRNA-disease associations were considered as the training set. The interactions without known evidence were considered as the candidate set.

After all datasets were divided, by either the 5CV method or the global LOOCV method, RWRNCP was carried out to obtain the predicted score for all associations. The ranks of the test samples in relative to those of the candidate samples were then calculated. Subsequently, the receiver operating characteristics (ROC) curves at different thresholds were plotted using the false positive rate (FPR, 1-specificity) as the abscissa and the true positive rate (TPR, sensitivity) as the ordinate. Sensitivity is the percentage of the test samples that are ranked above the threshold, and 1-specificity is the percentage of the test samples that are ranked below the threshold. Finally, the areas under the ROC curve (AUC) were determined: the higher the AUC value, the better the prediction performance of the model. In this work, the 5CV method was conducted 100 times, and the average AUC values of RWRNCP, IMCMDA, ICFMDA, and SACMDA reached 0.9274, 0.8330, 0.9046, and 0.8773, respectively (see Fig. 2). When the global LOOCV was conducted, the average AUC values of RWRNCP, IMCMDA, ICFMDA, and SACMDA were 0.9479, 0.8384, 0.9072, and 0.8777, respectively (see Fig. 2). These data show that RWRNCP has better performance in predicting miRNA-disease associations among above mentioned methods.

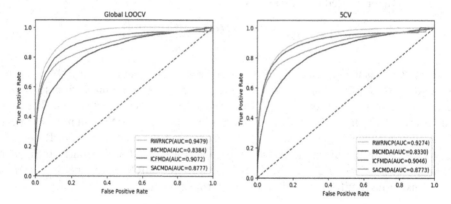

Fig. 2. Performance comparisons between RWRNCP and other prediction models.

3.2   A Case Study

A case study is conducted to further verify the capability of RWRNCP to predict miRNA-disease association. Case study for colon neoplasms was conducted as follows: based on HMDD v2.0 database, we regarded the miRNAs without known association with colon neoplasms as candidate miRNAs; after RWRNCP finished the prediction work, we prioritized the candidate miRNAs according to the predicted scores by RWRNCP. Consequently, 27 out of top 30 predicted colon neoplasms related miRNAs were confirmed by dbDEMC (db) [28] and miR2Disease (miR) [29] (See Table 1).

We took hepatocellular carcinoma as the second kind of case study, in which we removed all the known hepatocellular carcinoma related miRNA to simulate a new disease as input of RWRNCP. Then, we verified the predicted potential hepatocellular carcinoma related miRNAs generated by the model. Finally, all 30 miRNAs were experimentally confirmed by HMDD v2.0, dbDEMC and miR2Disease (See Table 2).

According to the previous paper [27], with the model of SACMDA, we found that 26 out of top 30 predicted colon neoplasms related miRNAs were confirmed by dbDEMC (db) [28] and miR2Disease (miR) [29] (See Table 3) and 28 out of top 30 predicted hepatocellular carcinoma related miRNAs were confirmed (See Table 4).Obviously, the model RWRNCP has higher accuracy.

Table 1. The top 30 predict miRNAs associated with Colon Neoplasms by RWRNCP

miRNA	Evidence	miRNA	Evidence
has-mir-21	miR; db	has-mir-16	db
has-mir-155	miR; db	has-mir-127	miR; db
has-mir-19b	miR; db	has-mir-29b	miR; db
has-mir-18a	miR; db	**has-mir-146b**	**unconfirmed**
has-mir-20a	miR; db	**has-mir-101**	**unconfirmed**
has-let-7a	miR; db	**has-mir-92b**	**unconfirmed**
has-mir-19a	miR; db	has-mir-9	miR; db
has-mir-143	miR; db	has-mir-214	db
has-mir-125b	db	has-mir-1	miR; db
has-mir-34a	miR; db	has-mir-30c	miR; db
has-let-7e	db	has-mir-181b	miR; db
has-let-7d	db	has-mir-191	miR; db
has-mir-223	miR; db	has-mir-222	db
has-let-7c	db	has-let-7g	miR; db
has-let-7b	miR; db	has-mir-106b	miR; db

Table 2. The top 30 predict miRNAs associated with Hepatocellular Carcinoma by RWRNCP

miRNA	Evidence	miRNA	Evidence
has-mir-21	HMDD; miR; db	has-mir-200b	HMDD; miR; db
has-mir-17	HMDD; miR	has-mir-221	HMDD; miR; db
has-mir-155	HMDD; miR; db	has-mir-141	HMDD; miR; db

(continued)

Table 2. (*continued*)

miRNA	Evidence	miRNA	Evidence
has-mir-19b	HMDD; db	has-mir-29b	HMDD; miR; db
has-mir-145	HMDD; miR; db	has-mir-16	HMDD; db
has-mir-18a	HMDD; miR; db	has-mir-146b	HMDD; miR; db
has-mir-20a	HMDD; miR	has-mir-127	HMDD; miR; db
has-let-7a	HMDD; miR; db	has-mir-92b	db
has-mir-19a	HMDD; db	has-mir-9	HMDD; miR; db
has-let-7e	HMDD; db	has-mir-101	HMDD; miR; db
has-mir-34a	HMDD; db	has-mir-106a	db
has-mir-125b	HMDD; miR	has-leg-7g	HMDD; db
has-mir-223	HMDD; db	has-mir-106b	HMDD; db
has-mir-126	HMDD; miR; db	has-mir-210	HMDD; miR; db
has-mir-92a	HMDD	has-mir-191	HMDD; miR; db

Table 3. The top 30 predict miRNAs associated with Colon Neoplasms by SACMDA

miRNA	Evidence	miRNA	Evidence
has-mir-199a	**unconfirmed**	has-let-7f	miR; db
has-mir-221	miR; db	**has-mir-92a**	**unconfirmed**
has-mir-19a	miR; db	has-mir-141	miR; db
has-mir-19b	miR; db	**has-mir-101**	**unconfirmed**
has-let-7i	db	has-mir-29b	miR; db
has-let-7d	db	has-mir-34c	miR
has-mir-31	miR; db	has-mir-222	db
has-mir-9	miR; db	has-let-7g	miR; db
has-mir-196a	miR; db	has-mir-125a	miR; db
has-mir-203	miR; db	has-mir-1	miR; db
has-mir-218	db	has-mir-34b	miR; db
has-mir-10b	miR; db	has-mir-127	miR; db
has-mir-191	miR; db	has-mir-210	db
has-mir-142	**unconfirmed**	has-mir-106b	miR; db
has-mir-205	db	has-mir-132	miR

Table 4. The top 30 predict miRNAs associated with Hepatocellular Carcinoma by SACMDA

miRNA	Evidence	miRNA	Evidence
has-mir-103a	HMDD	has-mir-106a	HMDD; miR; db
has-mir-10b	HMDD	has-mir-126	HMDD; miR; db
has-mir-135a	HMDD	has-mir-151a	HMDD
has-mir-152	HMDD; miR	has-mir-17	HMDD; miR
has-mir-181b	HMDD; miR; db	has-mir-182	HMDD; miR
has-mir-183	HMDD; miR	has-mir-191	HMDD; db
has-mir-192	HMDD; miR	**has-mir-193b**	**unconfirmed**
has-mir-194	miR; db	has-mir-195	HMDD; miR; db
has-mir-200a	HMDD; miR; db	has-mir-200b	HMDD; miR
has-mir-200c	HMDD;	has-mir-203	HMDD; miR
has-mir-204	**unconfirmed**	has-mir-205	HMDD; miR
has-mir-20a	HMDD; miR; db	has-mir-210	HMDD; db
has-mir-215	miR	has-mir-221	HMDD; miR; db
has-mir-223	HMDD; miR	has-mir-25	HMDD; miR; db
has-mir-26b	HMDD; db	has-mir-31	HMDD; miR

4   Discussion

In this study, we proposed a model of random walking with restart-based Network Consistency Projection for Predicting miRNA-disease Association (RWRNCP). The better performance of our model can be analyzed from two aspects. First, similarity network topology information of miRNA and disease were obtained by algorithm of random walking with restart. Second, the model was based network consistency projection, which can completely represent the complex relationships among miRNA-disease pairs.

This method still has some limitations. For example, the materials we used including human miRNA-disease associations, disease semantic similarity and miRNA functional similarity possibly contains noise and outliers. Therefore, we believe that our model would perform even better in future research.

Acknowledgement. This work was supported by the National Natural Science Foundation of China (Nos. 61873001, U19A2064, 61872220, 11701318), Natural Science Foundation of Shandong Province (grant number ZR2020KC022), and the Open Project of Anhui Provincial Key Laboratory of Multimodal Cognitive Computation, Anhui University, No. MMC202006.

References

1. Ambros, V.: microRNAs: tiny regulators with great potential **107**(7), 823–826 (2001)

2. Ambros, V.: The functions of animal microRNAs. Nature **431**(7006), 350–355 (2004)
3. Ibrahim, R., Yousri, N.A., Ismail, M.A., Elmakky, N.M.: miRNA and gene expression based-cancer classification using self-learning and co-training approaches. In: IEEE International Conference on Bioinformatics and Biomedicine, pp. 495–498 (2014)
4. Katayama, Y., Maeda, M.: Identification of pathogenesis-related microRNAs in hepatocellular carcinoma by expression profiling. Oncol. Lett. **4**(4), 817–832 (2012)
5. Meister, G., Tuschl, T.: Mechanisms of gene silencing by double-stranded RNA. Nature **431**(7006), 343–349, 16–19 (2004)
6. Zheng, C.H., Huang, D.S.: Tumor clustering using nonnegative matrix factorization with gene selection. IEEE Trans. Inf Technol. Biomed. **13**(4), 599–607 (2019)
7. Sethupathy, P., Collins, F.S.: MicroRNA target site polymorphisms and human disease. Trends Genet. **24**(10), 489–497 (2008)
8. Li, J., et al.: Evidence for positive selection on a number of MicroRNA regulatory interactions during recent human evolution. Plos Genet. **8**(3), e1002578–e1002590 (2012)
9. Chen, K., Rajewsky, N.: Natural selection on human microRNA binding sites inferred from SNP data. Nat. Genet. **38**(12), 1452–1456 (2006)
10. Wang, D., Wang, J.: Inferring the human microRNA functional similarity and functional network based on microRNA-associated diseases. Bioinformatics **26**(13), 1644–1650 (2010)
11. Chen, X., Xie, D.: MicroRNAs and complex diseases: from experimental results to computational models[J]. Brief. Bioinform. **20**(2), 515–539 (2019)
12. Chen, X., Yan, C.C.: HGIMDA: Heterogeneous graph inference for miRNA-disease association prediction. Oncotarget **7**(40), 65257–65269 (2016)
13. Chen, X., Yin, J.: MDHGI: matrix decomposition and heterogeneous graph inference for miRNA-disease association prediction. PLoS Comput. Biol. **14**(8), e1006418–e1006442 (2018)
14. Chen, X., Zhu, C.C.: Ensemble of decision tree reveals potential miRNA-disease associations. PLoS Comput. Biol. **15**(7), e1007209–e1007219 (2019)
15. Chen, X., Huang, L.: LRSSLMDA: laplacian regularized sparse subspace learning for MiRNA-disease association prediction. PLoS Comput. Biol. **20**(2), 515–539 (2017)
16. Chen, X., Xie, D., Wang, L., Zhao, Q., You, Z.-H., Liu, H.: BNPMDA: bipartite network projection for MiRNA–disease association prediction. Bioinformatics **34**(18), 3178–3186 (2018)
17. Chen, X., Wu, Q.F., Yan, G.Y.: RKNNMDA: ranking-based KNN for MiRNA-disease association prediction. RNA Biol. **14**(7), 11–20 (2017)
18. Li, W., Cheng, Z.: Prediction of miRNA-disease association using deep collaborative filtering. Biomed. Res. Int. **2021**, 1–16 (2021)
19. Li, H.Y., You, Z.H.: DF-MDA: an effective diffusion-based computational model for predicting miRNA-disease association from heterogeneous biological network. Mol. Ther. **26**(13), 1644–1650 (2021)
20. Chen, X., Xing, Z., Zhou, Y.: ELLPMDA: ensemble learning and link prediction for miRNA-disease association prediction. Rna Biology **16**, 363–372 (2018)
21. Goh, K.I., Cusick, M.E.: The human disease network. Proc. Natl. Acad. Sci. **104**(21), 8685–8690 (2007)
22. Lu, M., Zhang, Q.: An analysis of human MicroRNA and disease associations. PLoS ONE **3**(10), e3420–e3432 (2008)
23. Wang, D.: Inferring the human microRNA functional similarity and functional network based on microRNA-associated diseases. Bioinformatics **26**, 1644–1650 (2010)
24. Lipscomb, C.E.: Medical subject headings (MeSH). Bull. Med. Libr. Assoc. **88**, 265–266 (2000)
25. Chen, X., Wang, L.: Predicting miRNA-disease association based on inductive matrix completion. Bioinformatics **24**, 4256–4265 (2018)

26. Jiang, Y., Liu, B., Yu, L.: Predict MiRNA-disease association with collaborative filtering. Neuroinformatics **16**, 363–372 (2018)
27. Shao, B., Liu, B., Yan, C.: SACMDA: MiRNA-disease association prediction with short acyclic connections in heterogeneous graph. Neuroinformatics **20**(2), 515–539 (2018)
28. Zhen, Y., Fei, R., Liu, C., et al.: dbDEMC: a database of differentially expressed miRNAs in human cancers. BMC Genomics **11**(Suppl 4), 1–8 (2010)
29. Jiang, Q., Wang, Y., Hao, Y.: miR2Disease: a manually curated database for microRNA deregulation in human disease. Nucleic Acids Res. **37**(Database), D98–D104 (2009)

MELPMDA: A New Method Based on Matrix Enhancement and Label Propagation for Predicting miRNA-Disease Association

Zhen-Wei Zhang[1], Zhen Gao[1], Chun-Hou Zheng[1,2], Yu-Tian Wang[1(✉)], and Su-Min Qi[1(✉)]

[1] School of Cyberspace Security, Qufu Normal University, Qufu, China
[2] School of Computer Science and Technology, Anhui University, Hefei, China

Abstract. MicroRNAs (miRNAs) play a vital role in regulating various cellular processes, and involving the occurrence of various complex diseases. The association prediction between miRNAs and diseases provides a reference for exploration of the underlying pathogenesis of diseases. Some published prediction methods cleverly alleviate the inherent noise and incompleteness of biological data sets, and greatly improve the accuracy of prediction, but these methods still have room for optimization. In this research, we presented a novel method called MELPMDA, which is based on matrix enhancement and label propagation to infer the potential association between miRNAs and diseases. In order to enhance the most reliable similarity information, we established a similarity reward matrix based on three cases of strong connection, weak connection and negative connection. Then, a self-adjusting method was constructed to extract effective similarity information, which can enhance the association matrix to reduce its sparsity. In addition, label propagation was utilized as predictive model to further discover unobvious associations. Finally, the AUC obtained by 5-fold Cross-Validation (5CV) was 0.9550, which proved the rationality and effectiveness of our method. Furthermore, the predictive reliability of MELPMDA was further validated by the positive results in a case study of hepatocellular carcinoma.

Keywords: Matrix enhancement · Label propagation · miRNA-disease association predicting

1 Introduction

Human cells contain a large number of microRNAs (miRNAs), which are non-coding RNAs with a length of about 22 nt. They are involved in the regulation of a variety of biological processes and play an invaluable role in living organisms [1, 2]. Many studies have found that there are many close associations between miRNAs and human tumors [3–6]. miRNA is of extraordinary significance to life, and cracking the secrets of miRNA will enable human beings to further understand the truth of nature, which will have an important and far-reaching impact on human exploration of the pathogenesis of diseases as well as targeted prevention, diagnosis and treatment. Many scholars

© Springer Nature Switzerland AG 2021
D.-S. Huang et al. (Eds.): ICIC 2021, LNAI 12838, pp. 536–548, 2021.
https://doi.org/10.1007/978-3-030-84532-2_48

have used biological experimental methods to identify miRNAs related to diseases and obtained reliable results. However, the biological experiment method requires a lot of time and consumes a lot of manpower, financial resources and material resources. With the rapid development of biotechnology, many publicly available miRNAs or disease-related databases have been released. These databases provide experimental supporting evidence for humans to understand the relationship between miRNA and disease, which also provides a huge opportunity for using these data resources to discover the potential relationship between disease and miRNA.

In recent years, in order to infer the interaction between miRNA and disease, many researchers have introduced a variety of biological information and integrated them organically, thus obtaining relatively reliable prediction results, which also brings us inspiration. Jiang et al. [7] introduced the functional similarity of miRNAs, and ranked the associations between miRNAs and diseases based on the human phenotype-miRNAome network, and inferred the most likely potential associations based on the ranking sequence. Li et al. [8] proposed to infer miRNAs that may be related to the disease by calculating the functional consistency between the disease gene and the target gene, and has verified it. Xu et al. [9] determined the priority of disease-related miRNAs by fusing human disease genes with miRNA-target interactions, and inferred miRNAs related to human diseases. Mork et al. [10] used the miRNA-protein interaction and the disease-protein interaction to calculate the miRNA-disease associations. Chen et al. [11] calculated and used a variety of biological information, such as the functional similarity of miRNAs, the semantic similarity of diseases, and the kernel similarity of Gaussian interaction profiles (GIP), and relied on the iterative model to calculate the size of the association.

In addition, there are many machine learning algorithms that have been widely used in this field. Xu et al. [12] used SVM classifier to identify positive miRNA-disease associations from negative samples. Chen et al. [13] used random walk with restart to predict the disease-related microRNAs. Chen et al. [14] used the random forest model to discover the most stable attributes in the known information, and based on these attributes to identify possible disease-related microRNAs. Yu et al. [15] proposed MCLPMDA, which combined a variety of biological information to fill the similarity matrix, and then carried out label propagation on the heterogeneous network. Xiao et al. [16] imported the WKNNP into GRNMF as preprocessing, which improved the sparsity of the miRNA-disease association matrix. Chen et al. [17] restored missing miRNA-disease associations based on known miRNA disease associations and integrated disease (miRNA) similarities.

For the task of miRNA-disease association prediction, it is very important to construct similarity information reasonably. Some of the aforementioned methods improve the problems of the lack of similarity information (such as the GIP kernel similarity) and the sparsity of miRNA-disease association matrix (such as WKNNP), but these methods still have the possibility of improvement.

In this research, we proposed a calculation algorithm to predict disease-associated miRNAs based on matrix enhancement and label propagation. First, we construed an algorithm called matrix enhancement, which controls the existing similarity matrix through known associations. Then, for reducing the sparsity of adjacency matrix, we processed it through extracting the most reliable information from similarity interaction profile of each miRNA and disease. Finally, we carried out label propagation in a heterogeneous network composed of similarity networks and associated networks. In the 5CV experiment, we obtained an AUC value of 0.9550. In addition, a case study of hepatocellular carcinoma (HCC) showed that MELPMDA has reliable performance and value.

2   Materials

2.1   Human miRNA-Disease Associations

In the HMDD v2.0 (H2) database, $A \in R^{383 \times 495}$ is an adjacency matrix composed of 495 miRNAs and 383 diseases, and 5430 associations have been experimentally verified. Specifically, if the disease d_i is related to miRNA m_j, then the element $A(d_i, m_j)$ is 1, otherwise it is 0. Therefore, the ith row $A(d_i)$ of A represents the association between disease d_i and all miRNAs, and the jth column $A(m_j)$ of A represents the association between miRNA m_j and all diseases.

2.2   Disease Semantic Similarity

MeSH database includes many disease descriptions. Directed acyclic graphs (DAG) are used to calculate disease semantic similarity. For node D, we define $DAG(D) = (T(D), E(D))$, where $T(D)$ and $E(D)$ are the node set and edge set, respectively. $T(D)$ includes node and its ancestor nodes, and $E(D)$ represents the direct connections between parent nodes and child nodes. $SD \in R^{383 \times 383}$ is the disease semantic similarity matrix composed of 383 diseases, where $SD(d_i, d_j)$ is the similarity between disease d_i and disease d_j.

2.3   miRNA Functional Similarity

Based on the idea that miRNAs with similar functions have similar performance to similar diseases, the functional similarity of miRNAs is calculated. $FM \in R^{495 \times 495}$ is composed of 495 miRNAs, where $FM(m_i, m_j)$ is the similarity between miRNA m_i and miRNA m_j.

3   MELPMDA

Due to the inherent noise of existing datasets, the obtained similarity matrix may lose useful information or have a lot of redundancy, which greatly limits the prediction accuracy. Therefore, how to design a reasonable way based on current data to reduce noise and make full use of useful information becomes very important. In this work, we developed a new method called MELPMDA, which makes full use of the most reliable similarity information to predict potential associations and obtain good prediction results in subsequent experiments. The overall workflow of MELPMDA is shown in Fig. 1.

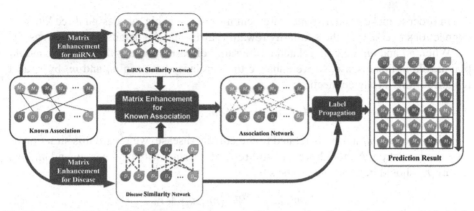

Fig. 1. MELPMDA can be divided into three steps: (1) we regulate the similarity network through known associations; (2) we preprocess the incidence matrix to reduce its sparsity; (3) label propagation is used as the final predictive model

3.1 Enhance the Similarity Matrix Through Similarity Reward Matrix (ESSRM)

Since the similarity information in the current datasets is not complete, and the known association is real and has been verified, it may be more credible if we use the known association to adjust the similarity network.

Similarity Reward Matrix

Each miRNA in the known association corresponds to 383 diseases, so we can regard 383 associations between miRNA m_i and 383 diseases as the expression feature of miRNA m_i, and the expression feature of miRNA m_j can be obtained in a similar way. The closer their expression features are, the more similar they are (Fig. 2).

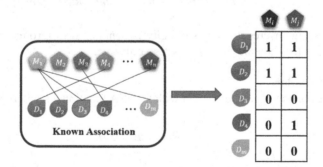

Fig. 2. Examples of the associations between miRNAs and disease

In the association matrix $A \in R^{383 \times 495}$, 5430 elements are definite associations, and the remaining elements are unknown associations. These unknown associations may or may not be potential associations. Certain things should play a more important role and should not be in the same position as unknown things.

In order to make similarity measurement more reasonable, we design three kinds of connections to construct the similarity reward matrix, and the details are as follows:

When m_i and m_j are both related to the same disease, it means that both m_i and m_j play a role in this disease, so we enhance the similarity between m_i and m_j by r_s as a reward for this strong connection:

$$RM\left(m_i, m_j\right) = RM\left(m_i, m_j\right) + r_s \tag{1}$$

When neither m_i nor m_j is related to the current disease, we regard this situation as a weak connection. Although we will still reward the similarity between m_i and m_j, this reward r_w should be controlled to be small:

$$RM\left(m_i, m_j\right) = RM\left(m_i, m_j\right) + r_w \tag{2}$$

When m_i and m_j have different associations for the same disease, we are more confident to judge that their functions are different. We regard this situation as a negative connection, so we penalize their similarity:

$$RM\left(m_i, m_j\right) = RM\left(m_i, m_j\right) - r_n \tag{3}$$

We define the credibility of known association as σ, and the credibility of unknown association as 1, where e is greater than 1. Based on the above three situations, the following definitions can be made:

$$r_s = \delta r_n = \delta^2 r_w = \delta^2 \tag{4}$$

Next, the matrix RM is normalized to a value between 0 and 1 as a similarity reward matrix:

$$RM\left(m_i, m_j\right) = \exp(\delta\left(\frac{RM\left(m_i, m_j\right) - \min_{1 \leq s \leq n}\{RM\left(m_i, m_s\right)\}}{\max_{1 \leq s \leq n}\{RM\left(m_i, m_s\right)\} - \min_{1 \leq s \leq n}\{RM\left(m_i, m_s\right)\}} - 1\right)) \tag{5}$$

Such processing ensures that any similarity is configured to zero to one. And as δ increases, the gap between the similarity is also enlarged.

Integration of Similarity

After RM were obtained, we integrated it with miRNA functional similarity matrices as follows:

$$MS = \frac{\alpha \times RM + \beta \times FM}{\alpha + \beta} \tag{6}$$

where α and β are used to control the fusion ratio (α and β were simply set to 0.5 in this paper). In the same way, the similarity reward matrix RD can be used to enhance disease similarity:

$$DS = \frac{\alpha \times RD + \beta \times SD}{\alpha + \beta} \tag{7}$$

3.2   Enhance the Association Matrix Through Self-adjusting Nearest Neighbor Method (EASNN)

There are only 5430 known associations in matrix $A \in R^{383 \times 495}$, which accounting for only about 2.86% of the total 189585 associations. The lack of known information is not conducive to the effective functioning of the predictive model, so how to enhance matrix A becomes particularly important.

Basic Method
WKNNP can be used to enhance matrix A by constructing a new interaction profile. For each m_i, it uses the similarity of the K most similar miRNAs and their interaction profile to obtain the following interaction profile:

$$A_m(m_i) = \frac{1}{N_{mi}} \sum\nolimits_{j=1}^{K} w_j A(m_j)$$

(8)

where m_1 to m_K are sorted in descending order by their similarity to m_i; w_j is defined by $w_j = r^{j-1} * M(m_i, m_j)$, where $r \in [0, 1]$ controls the weight attenuation factor. As j increases, the weight decreases exponentially; $N_{mi} = \sum_{j=1}^{K} M(m_i, m_j)$ is normalization term, which controls $A_m(i, j)$ between zero and one. Naturally, we can construct interaction profile for each miRNA in the same way:

$$A_d(d_i) = \frac{1}{N_{di}} \sum\nolimits_{j=1}^{K} w_j A(d_j)$$

(9)

Next, we combine the matrices A_m and A_d obtained from the miRNAs space and diseases space:

$$A_{md} = \frac{\mu A_m + v A_d}{\mu + v}$$

(10)

$$A = max(A, A_{md})$$

(11)

WKNNP uses the K nearest neighbor (KNN) information in each similar interaction profile to preprocess the association matrix, so that continuous adjustment is needed to determine the most suitable K. Although it is possible to find the optimal K through adjustment, this can only make the overall optimal, and it cannot guarantee that the most suitable effective information can be found from every similarity interaction profile. Sometimes there are more than K valid information in $M(m_i)$ or $D(d_j)$, and the extra valid information will be discarded; sometimes less than K, then useless information will be used. These two situations will cause the loss of effective information and the increase of ineffective noise respectively.

In Fig. 3, it is reasonable for miRNA1 and miRNA2 to select the two largest and three largest similarity nodes respectively. If K is defined as 2, then case 2 will lose a valid message; if K is defined as 3, then case 1 will introduce unnecessary noise.

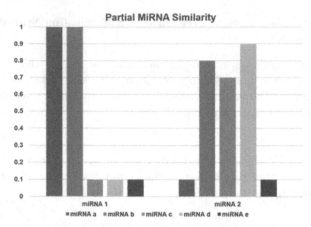

Fig. 3. Example of miRNA similarity distribution

Self-adjusting Method to Select Nearest Neighbor (SNN)
In order to improve this problem, we hope to automatically find out a flexible K instead of a fixed K. Specifically, the aim of this self-adjusting method is to find a different number of the most reliable information for similarity interaction profile of each disease or miRNA. Among them, the self-adjusting method we designed to find a suitable nearest neighbor is referred to as SNN.

First, we sorted the similarity interaction profile Si in descending order, and then search backward from the first point until a position k is found meets the following conditions:

$$Si(k) - Si(k + l) < Si(k + l) - Si(k + 3l) \tag{12}$$

where l is the step length, which is generally set at one-fifth of the length of Si. In order to further ensure that enough information is obtained, we usually start the search from one-fifth of Si and end at one-half of Si at the latest.

The rate of decrease of continuous information after k is significantly lower than the rate of decrease of previous continuous information. That is, the numerical value of the information reaches a certain stable state from this position. Although the next steady state may appear after this steady state, it is enough for our purpose of extracting the most reliable information (Fig. 4).

Through this operation, each similarity interaction profile has found its appropriate amount of relabeled information, and the searched information is retained, while other information is set to zero:

$$M\left(m_i, m_j\right) = \begin{cases} MS\left(m_i, m_j\right) & MS\left(m_i, m_j\right) \in SNN\left(m_i\right) \\ 0 & MS\left(m_i, m_j\right) \notin SNN\left(m_i\right) \end{cases} \tag{13}$$

$$D\left(d_i, d_j\right) = \begin{cases} DS\left(d_i, d_j\right) & DS\left(d_i, d_j\right) \in SNN\left(d_i\right) \\ 0 & DS\left(d_i, d_j\right) \notin SNN\left(d_i\right) \end{cases} \tag{14}$$

The resulting matrices M and D will be used by Eqs. (8) and (9) to fill the known association matrix. Our treatment of the association matrix is essentially a prediction

Algorithm 1. The Procedure of SNN

Input:	Similarity sequence $S_i \in R^{n \times 1}$, step length l.

Output:	End point k.

Sort S_i in descending order.

Repeat:

$$k = k + 1$$

Until:

$$Si(k) - Si(k+l) < Si(k+l) - Si(k+3l)$$

Return	k

Fig. 4. The procedure of SNN

of the potential association, and it can be seen that good results have been obtained in subsequent experiments. However, when this model is applied to other directions or data sets, it is not ruled out that some special situations will occur that will limit the prediction effect. In addition, our processing of the matrix has not undergone any iterations, so there is no guarantee that the results after processing will be stable.

3.3 Label Propagation (LP)

In this section, we choose an iterative model to make predictions again to ensure convergence and stability of the prediction results. Label propagation is a graph-based semi-supervised learning algorithm. The basic idea is to predict unlabeled node label information from labeled node label information, and use the relationship between samples to establish a complete graph model, which is suitable for undirected graphs.

In this experiment, we took miRNA similarity and disease similarity as transmission coefficients respectively to carry out label propagation on the association network, and finally integrated them together to obtain the final prediction result:

$$F_D^{t+1} = \mu \times D \times F_D^t + (1 - \mu) \times A \qquad (15)$$

$$F_M^{t+1} = \mu \times M \times F_M^t + (1 - \mu) \times A^T \qquad (16)$$

where F_M and F_D represent the propagation results in miRNA and disease space respectively, μ is the coefficient of control propagation and is set to 0.1 in this experiment. After multiple iterations, the iteration results on each space have reached a stable state and the final prediction result is:

$$F = \nu \times F_M + (1 - \nu) \times (F_D)^T \qquad (17)$$

Since we regarded the results obtained by the two heterogeneous networks as equally important, ν is set as 0.5.

4 Experiments

4.1 Performance Evaluation

In this section, we used multiple groups of experiments to assess the performance of the model. We adjusted different parameters to observe their impact on the model, thereby evaluating the stability of the model. After parameter optimization, we randomly divided the training set and test set several times to measure the performance of the model. In addition, we carried out experiments to compare with other methods.

Hyperparametric Experiment
In this section, we fixed the model for better performance by debugging two main hyperparameters. Where σ is the known association credibility, and Si/l is the ratio of sequence length to step length in SNN. The following table shows the impact of these two parameters for model performance. For the evaluation of the effect, we mainly used 5-fold Cross-Validation and global Leave-One-Out Cross-Validation (global LOOCV).

Table 1. .

σ	Si/l	5-CV	Global LOOCV
2	30	0.9411	0.9633
2	40	0.9427	0.9641
2	50	0.9452	0.9672
2	60	0.9433	0.9643
3	30	0.9501	0.9701
3	40	0.9531	0.9716
3	50	0.9549	0.9723
3	60	0.9522	0.9712
4	30	0.9438	0.9659
4	40	0.9463	0.9669
4	50	0.9490	0.9698
4	60	0.9441	0.9653

After multiple debugging, the hyperparameters with good effects were determined. In order to verify the stability of the model, we repeated experiments and re-divided the training set and test sets in each experiment (Table 2).

Table 2. 5CV results of different training sets.

Testing set	1	2	3	4	5	Average
Accuracy	0.9543	0.9561	0.9550	0.9547	0.9551	0.9550

Comparison with Other Methods

In this section, we used 5430 known associations in the H2 database for the 5CV experiment. For each Cross-Validation, we randomly selected 80% of the positive samples as the training set and the remaining 20% positive samples and all negative samples as the test set. Finally, the performance of MELPMDA is evaluated based on the test results. After estimating the correlation probability of the test sample, the sample is ranked by its association score. The higher the ranking of the node pair of the positive sample, the better the performance of MELPMDA.

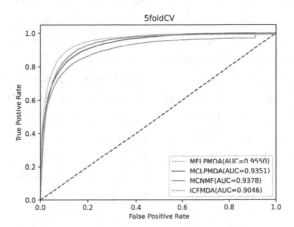

Fig. 5. The 5CV results of MELPMDA and the other methods.

As shown in Fig. 5, MELPMDA obtained a reliable AUC verification of 0.9550 in the 5CV, which has been greatly improved compared with other methods [15, 18, 19], thus demonstrating the good performance of our method.

4.2 Case Study

In this section, we took HCC as an example to conduct experiments and used higher version data as verification to illustrate the effectiveness of MELPMDA. HCC ac-counts for 80% to 90% of primary liver cancer. If the patient does not receive special treatment, then the patient's health will be fatally threatened. Although liver cancer has been taken seriously as a major health problem worldwide, we still have no clear method to prevent or cure it, and there are still 500,000 to 1 million new cases occur-ring every year worldwide. Therefore, it is necessary for the case study of HCC. For the diseases investigated, we listed the top 50 miRNAs calculated by our method based on H2. Subsequently, the two other databases D2 and miR2D were used to verify the prediction results. Experimental results (see Table 1) showed that 45 miR-NAs were associated with HCC (Table 3).

4.3 Ablation Study

In order to further explore the effectiveness of MELPMDA, we removed some of the modules in the model, and then observed the changes in its performance through the

Table 3. THE TOP 50 HCC-related candidates.

miRNA	Evidence	miRNA	Evidence
hsa-mir-21	miR2D	hsa-mir-1	D2; miR2D
hsa-mir-155	D2; miR2D	hsa-mir-199a	D2; miR2D
hsa-mir-17	miR2D	hsa-mir-210	D2;
hsa-mir-20a	D2; miR2D	hsa-let-7f	D2 miR2D
hsa-mir-145	D2; miR2D	hsa-mir-222	D2; miR2D
hsa-mir-34a	D2; miR2D	hsa-let-7i	D2; H3
hsa-mir-146a	D2; miR2D	hsa-mir-200a	D2; miR2D
hsa-mir-18a	D2; miR2D	hsa-mir-146b	D2
hsa-mir-19b	miR2D	hsa-mir-106b	D2; miR2D
hsa-let-7a	D2; miR2D	**hsa-mir-34c**	**unconfirmed**
hsa-mir-126	D2; miR2D	hsa-mir-15a	miR2D
hsa-mir-92a	miR2D	hsa-mir-29c	D2;
hsa-mir-125b	D2; miR2D	hsa-let-7g	miR2D
hsa-mir-221	D2; miR2D	hsa-mir-181a	D2; miR2D
hsa-mir-19a	miR2D	hsa-mir-181b	miR2D
hsa-let-7b	D2; miR2D	hsa-mir-205	miR2D
hsa-mir-223	miR2D	hsa-mir-125a	miR2D
hsa-mir-16	miR2D	hsa-mir-10b	miR2D
hsa-let-7c	D2; miR2D	hsa-mir-142	miR2D
hsa-mir-29b	**unconfirmed**	hsa-mir-214	D2; miR2D
hsa-let-7e	D2; miR2D	hsa-mir-30a	miR2D
hsa-mir-200b	miR2D	**hsa-mir-218**	**unconfirmed**
hsa-mir-29a	**unconfirmed**	hsa-mir-24	miR2D
hsa-mir-200c	**unconfirmed**	hsa-mir-101	D2; miR2D
hsa-let-7d	D2; miR2D	hsa-mir-203	miR2D

5CV to determine how much the key parts of the entire process play a role. Where ESSRM is the abbreviation to similarity enhancement, and EASNN is the abbreviation to association enhancement. Where LP represent the method of label propagation (Fig. 6).

It can be seen from the experimental results of ESRSM + LP that the effect of directly using the reconstructed similarity network for label propagation is not ideal. Although the similarity network reconstructed by our method obviously enhances the reliable information, a large amount of unnecessary information still exists. Therefore, if the label propagation is directly carried out, it will not play an active role. However, due to our reconstruction method, the obtained similarity network is easier to filter out noise

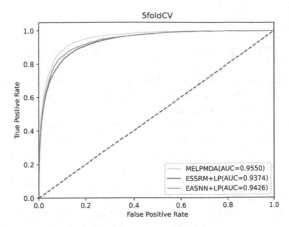

Fig. 6. The 5CV results of ablation experiments

and extract more reliable similarity information in the subsequent processing, which is a vital part of our entire method.

The experimental results of EASNN + LP show that the AUC value after using EASNN is 0.0075 higher than that of MCLPMDA, indicating that EASNN is effective. When the similarity distribution is significantly unbalanced, the performance of EASNN will be more reflected.

Through the comparison of the above experiments, it is shown that our method ESRSM and EASNN correspond to two excellent functions respectively: under the processing of ESRSM, the useful information in the similarity matrix is enhanced, and the invalid noise is easier to remove. EASNN can find the most critical information in each similarity interaction profile according to its different distribution. The two methods are combined to give better play to their advantages.

5 Conclusions

Predicting the association between miRNAs and diseases can help us discover the mechanism of action at the biological level, and can help us explore the nature of diseases. The computational method we proposed, called MELPMDA, can make full use of the available information in the existing data set to discover potential associations between diseases and miRNAs. The main innovation of our method is to effectively enhance the similarity information through the definition of strong, weak and negative connections, and improve the solution to the problem of sparse known correlations, thereby improving the performance of predicting unknown correlations. Our method has been verified by 5CV and case studies, which shows that MELPMDA has good performance and value. This work is only our starting point, and how to rationally integrate various biological data sets is the focus of our next research.

Acknowledgements. This work was supported by the National Natural Science Foundation of China (Nos. U19A2064, 61873001).

References

1. Bartel, D.P.: MicroRNAs: genomics, biogenesis, mechanism, and function. Cell **116**, 281–297 (2004)
2. Victor, A.: The functions of animal microRNAs. Nature **431**, 350–355 (2004)
3. Li, Y., et al.: HMDD v2.0: a database for experimentally supported human microRNA and disease associations. Nucleic Acids Res. **42**, D1070-4 (2014)
4. Huang, Z., et al.: HMDD v3. 0: a database for experimentally supported human microRNA–disease associations. Nucleic Acids Res. **47**, D1013–D1017 (2018)
5. Yang, Z., et al.: dbDEMC 2.0: updated database of differentially expressed miRNAs in human cancers. Nucleic Acids Res. **45**, D812–D818 (2016)
6. Jiang, Q., et al.: miR2Disease: a manually curated database for microRNA deregulation in human disease. Nucleic Acids Res. **37**, D98-104 (2009)
7. Jiang, Q., et al.: Prioritization of disease microRNAs through a human phenome-microRNAome network. BMC Syst. Biol. **4**, S1–S2 (2010)
8. Li, X., et al.: Prioritizing human cancer microRNAs based on genes' functional consistency between microRNA and cancer. Nucleic Acids Res. **39**(22), e153 (2011)
9. Xu, C., et al.: Prioritizing candidate disease miRNAs by integrating phenotype associations of multiple diseases with matched miRNA and mRNA expression profiles. Mol. BioSyst. **10**(11), 2800–2809 (2014)
10. Mork, S., et al.: Protein-driven inference of miRNA-disease associations. Bioinformatics **30**(3), 392–397 (2014)
11. Chen, X., et al.: HGIMDA: heterogeneous graph inference for miRNA-disease association prediction. Oncotarget **7**(40), 65257–65269 (2016)
12. Xu, J., et al.: Prioritizing candidate disease miRNAs by topological features in the miRNA target-dysregulated network: case study of prostate cancer. Mol. Cancer Ther. **10**(10), 1857–1866 (2011)
13. Chen, X., et al.: RWRMDA: predicting novel human microRNA-disease associations. Mol. BioSyst. **8**(10), 2792–2798 (2012)
14. Chen, X., Wang, C., Yin, J., You, Z.: Novel Human miRNA-disease association inference based on random forest. Molecular Therapy-Nucleic Acids **13**, 568–579 (2018)
15. Yu, S., et al.: MCLPMDA: a novel method for miRNA-disease association prediction based on matrix completion and label propagation. J. Cell Mol. Med. **23**(2), 1427–1438 (2019)
16. Xiao, Q., et al.: A graph regularized non-negative matrix factorization method for identifying microRNA-disease associations. Bioinformatics **34**(2), 239–248 (2018)
17. Chen, X., Sun, L., Zhao, Y.: NCMCMDA: miRNA-disease association prediction through neighborhood constraint matrix completion. Brief Bioinform. **22**(1), 485–496 (2021)
18. Jiang, Y., Liu, B., Yu, L., Yan, C., Bian, H.: Predict MiRNA-disease association with collaborative filtering. Neuroinformatics **16**(3–4), 363–372 (2018). https://doi.org/10.1007/s12021-018-9386-9
19. Gao, Z., et al.: A new method based on matrix completion and non-negative matrix factorization for predicting disease-associated miRNAs. IEEE/ACM Trans. Comput. Biol. Bioinform. PP (2020)

Prognostic Prediction for Non-small-Cell Lung Cancer Based on Deep Neural Network and Multimodal Data

Zhong-Si Zhang[1], Fei Xu[1], Han-Jing Jiang[1(✉)], and Zhan-Heng Chen[2]

[1] Key Laboratory of Image Information Processing and Intelligent Control of Education Ministry of China, Institute of Artificial Intelligence, School of Artificial Intelligence and Automation, Huazhong University of Science and Technology, Wuhan 430074, China
jianghanjing@hust.edu.cn

[2] Institute of Machine Learning and Systems Biology, School of Electronics and Information Engineering, Tongji University, No. 4800 Caoan Road, Shanghai 201804, China

Abstract. Non-small-cell lung cancer (NSCLC) is the most common lung cancer with poor prognosis. Prognostic prediction is significant in improving the prognosis of NSCLC patients. Clinical information and multi-omics data including gene expression, miRNA, copy number variations, and DNA methylation are closely related to NSCLC prognosis. In this study, we propose a deep neural network to conduct prognostic prediction for NSCLC patients based on all five types of data. Given the high dimensional features of the omics data, past works reduce the feature dimension by regression analysis or correlation sorting algorithms. A shortcoming of these methods is that only a small number of features are considered. To overcome it, we propose a convolution neural network-based feature transformation method, which considers all features and extracts the abstract representations of the omics data. Based on the representations, we predict the five-year survival status of NSCLC patients. The results show that our method achieves a more precise prediction than previous work, with the areas under the curve improved from 0.8163 to 0.8508 and the accuracy improved from 0.7544 to 0.8096.

Keywords: Cancer prognosis · Non-small-cell lung cancer · Convolution neural network · Multi-omics

1 Introduction

Lung cancer is the most commonly diagnosed cancer with the highest mortality rate[1]. As the main category, non-small-cell lung cancer (NSCLC) accounts for more than 85% of lung cancers while the predicted five-year survival rate of NSCLC is merely 15.9% [2]. Prognostic analyses are helpful for physicians to improve the overall survival of non-small-cell lung patients [3]. Clinical information and multi-omics data including gene expression (mRNA), miRNA, copy number variations (CNV), and DNA methylation (DNAm) are closely associated with NSCLC prognosis [4]. However, previous works use only part of those data to the researches. It is essential to conduct a comprehensive prognostic analysis for NSCLC patients based on all five types of data.

© Springer Nature Switzerland AG 2021
D.-S. Huang et al. (Eds.): ICIC 2021, LNAI 12838, pp. 549–560, 2021.
https://doi.org/10.1007/978-3-030-84532-2_49

During the past two decades, extensive research has been devoted to prognostic stratification for NSCLC patients. Beer et al. proposed a method that used the Kaplan Meier (KM) estimation [5] and the Cox proportional hazards (CPH) regression [6] to predict the survival of patients based on mRNA data [7]. Similarly, by using KM estimation and CPH regression, Sandoval et al. found five gene markers associated with NSCLC prognosis based on DNAm profiles [8]. Yanaihara et al. identified two gene signatures correlated with the survival of NSCLC patients based on miRNA expression profiles [9]. Another two gene markers were proved to be associated with the prognosis of NSCLC based on CNV data [9, 10]. These works show the strong relationships between the omics data and prognosis of NSCLC but only consider a single type of data.

With the rapid advances of artificial intelligence technologies, methods based on machine learning have been successfully applied to prognostic prediction. Chen et al. constructed an artificial neural network for prognostic risk classification on NSCLC patients by integrating the mRNA and clinical features [13]. Lai et al. developed an integrative deep neural network-based model to predict the five-year survival status of NSCLC patients based on mRNA markers and clinical features [15]. Yang et al. built random forest and support vector machine models to predict prognosis-related molecular subtypes based on mRNA and DNAm profiles [16]. These researches demonstrate that integrating the machine learning method and multimodal data could improve the prognostic stratification while ignoring other types of available profiles.

When developing a prognostic prediction model based on omics data, the first problem is that the feature dimension of omics data is too high to fed to the model directly. Therefore, it is especially necessary to reduce the feature dimension. Previous dimensionality reduction methods can be divided into two main categories: gene markers selection based on regression analysis [7–9] and correlation sorting algorithm [13–15]. In terms of the former, the dimension reduction process relies on the CPH regression and the KM estimation, and the size of the selected features is often small. As for the latter, the correlations between features and NSCLC prognosis were ranked, and the higher-ranked features are used as the final features. Both types of methods use only a few important features and ignore a large number of seemingly less important features.

In this paper, we propose an efficient convolution neural network-based feature transformation method, which considers all features and distills the abstract feature representations. With this feature transformation method, we obtain the low-dimensional and precise representation of omics data. For consistency, we build a deep neural network-based feature transformation model for clinical data. Finally, we conduct prognostic prediction for NSCLC patients based on the deep neural network (DNN) and the feature representations.

2   Materials and Methods

2.1   Dataset and Data Processing

We obtained all the data from publicly available cancer genomics dataset, namely The Cancer Genome Atlas (TCGA, https://portal.gdc.cancer.gov/), which contained multimodal data including mRNA, miRNA, CNV, DNAm, and clinical data. The datasets used in this study were extracted from two TCGA projects: Lung Adenocarcinoma (TCGA-LUAD) and Lung Squamous Cell Carcinoma (TCGA-LUSC). We filtered the datasets by adhering to the following principles: for censored samples, the days to last follow up of each case must exist and be greater than 1825 (five years); otherwise, the days to death should exist and be not less than 0. Finally, we collected 492 cases consist of 225 LUAD and 267 LUSC, in which 161 cases with missing data were packed as the additional set (Table 1). Among the rest standard set (163 LUAD and 168 LUSC), 94 cases with a longer survival time than five years are labeled as 1, other 237 cases were labeled as 0.

Table 1. The properties of the datasets and features.

Data category	Addition set	Standard set	Dimension	Feature size
Clinical	161	331	7	20
mRNA	156	331	60483	246 × 246
miRNA	139	331	1881	44 × 44
CNV	144	331	60516	246 × 246
DNAm	61	331	487755	700 × 700

For clinical data processing, we removed all the characteristics existing missing value and finally identified seven features including the extent of the tumor (T), the extent of spread to the lymph nodes (N), the presence of metastasis (M), tumor stage, gender, prior malignancy, and age at index. Among them, categorical features containing T, M, N, and tumor stage were transformed into integer features (detailed in Table 2), then converted to one-hot encoding [17]. For omics data, we filled the missing value with -1 and utilized min-max normalization to transform the value into the range [0, 1]. The feature sequence of each patient was reshaped to a matrix that was similar to the single-channel image (the insufficient positions were filled with -1). More information could be found in Table 1.

Table 2. Integer encoding for categorical clinical features.

Feature	Category (Label)
T	T1 (0), T1a (0), T1b (0), TX (1), T2 (1), T2a (1), T2b (1), T3 (2), T4 (3)
M	M0 (0), MX (1), M1 (2), M1b (2), M1a (2)
N	NX (0), N0 (0), N1 (1), N2 (2), N3 (3)
Tumor stage	IB (0), IA (1), I (1), IIB (2), IIA (3), II (3), IIIB (4), III (5), IIIA (5), IV (6)

2.2 Feature Transformation

Omics data are characterized by small sample collection yet large feature quantity. To use omics data in prognostic prediction, dimension reduction is a primary and critical step. Traditional dimension reduction methods are almost selecting a certain number of features depending on expertise or specific relevance ranking algorithms. An obvious shortcoming is that the feature set identified by these methods is a proper subset of the initial with numerous latent features excluded. To overcome the shortcoming, we propose a convolution neural network-based transformation method. Convolution neural network (CNN) is a specialized type of neural network that uses convolution in place of general matrix multiplication in at least one of their layers [12]. CNN is skilled in extracting abstract representations that in traditional algorithms are dependent on prior knowledge and human intervention. By using the CNN-based transformation method, we obtain low-dimensional and precise representations of omics data.

Given the heterogeneity of omics data, we design personalized feature transformation models for four types of omics datasets used in this study. Four kinds of excellent CNNs including ResNet [18], SENet [19], EfficientNet [20], and ResNeXt [21] are utilized and tested on each omics dataset separately. These models are slightly revised on the first layer to fit the input size. And a fully collected (FC) layer with a fixed size (128) is inserted into the last but one layer for feature extraction. We suppose that the model performing better on the prediction task would extract a more precise feature representation. Therefore, the optimal architectures are identified according to the prediction performance. For consistency, we construct a DNN-based feature transformation model to extract feature representations from clinical information. The model consists of an input layer, an output layer, and three hidden FC layers. To extract the same size features as omics data, we fix the output size of the third hidden FC layer to 128. For the other two hidden layers, we identify the number of units by using the grid search strategy among 64, 128, 256, 512, and 1024.

To identify the optimal architectures for each model, we divide the standard set into a training set (80%) and a validating set (20%). The additional set is also added to the training set. We train and validate CNN models on each type of omics dataset, and the DNN model is trained and validated on the clinical dataset. The architectures are identified according to the prediction performance of models. After that, we train and test the models again with five-fold cross-validation. The standard set is randomized into five subsets. In every round, four of five subsets are used for training while the rest for validating. The better parameters are saved during iterative training and reloaded to the model at the end. Finally, we conduct inference on the whole standard set to extract the feature representations. For all CNN and DNN models, we use the AdamW [24] optimizer with a constant learning rate and minimize the weighted cross-entropy loss l_{CE} defined as:

$$l_{CE} = \frac{-1}{N * (1 + w)} \sum_{i=0}^{N-1} [w * y_i \log(\widehat{y_i}) + (1 - y_i) \log(1 - \widehat{y_i})], \tag{1}$$

where N denotes the size of the dataset, $y_i, \widehat{y_i}$ are the target label and predictive probability for the i_{th} sample, and w is the weight parameter. The rectified linear unit (ReLU)

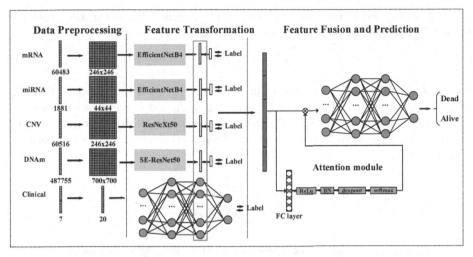

Fig. 1. The framework of the proposed prognostic prediction model.

activation function [22], batch normalization (BN) [23], and dropout are adopted to optimize the parameters and accelerate model training.

2.3 Fusion Deep Neural Network

The integration and analysis of multi-omics datasets is a crucial and critical step to gain actionable knowledge in a precision medicine framework [25]. Given the difference among heterogeneous data, it is necessary to find a model that can fully integrate and exploit the available information. In this work, we develop a fusion deep neural network that fuses the feature representations extracted from mRNA, miRNA, CNV, DNAm, and clinical data for prognostic prediction. An overview of the proposed method is shown in Fig. 1. The framework is composed of three core modules: 1) a data preprocessing module where omics microarrays are reshaped as matrices and clinical data is encoded as one-hot features; 2) a feature transformation module that transforms the omics matrices and clinical features into the fix-sized feature representations; 3) a feature fusion module that integrates the representation and presents the final prediction of five-year survival status for NSCLC patients.

In the last module, we construct a deep neural network that contains an input layer, an output layer, and three hidden FC layers. The numbers of units in hidden layers are identified by using the grid search among 128, 256, 512, 1024, and 2048. Following all layers but the last one, we use ReLU as our activation function, which is followed by BN and dropout.

To force the model to focus on more significant features, we introduce the attention mechanism into the fusion model. Given the feature representation of the i_{th} sample as $X_{i,mRNA}, X_{i,miRNA}, X_{i,CNV}, X_{i,MBV}$, and $X_{i,clinical}$ for the five types of datasets separately, the integrated feature X_i can be expressed as:

$$X_i = X_{i,\mathrm{mRNA}} \oplus X_{i,\mathrm{miRNA}} \oplus X_{i,\mathrm{CNV}} \oplus X_{i,MBV} \oplus X_{i,\mathrm{clinical}}, \tag{2}$$

where $\oplus$ is an operator that connects two inputs in the second dimension. X_i is presented to the FC layer first, the output F_i can be expressed as:

$$F_i = W * X_i + B, \tag{3}$$

where W, B is the weight and bias of the FC layer. F_i is fed to the ReLU, BN, and dropout. We obtain a vector $Z_i = \{z_{i,0}, z_{i,1}, ..., z_{i,D-1}\}$, and D represents the number of dimensions of X_i. Then Z_i is normalized into a probability distribution consisting of probabilities proportional to the exponentials of $z_{i,j}$ ($j = 0, 1, ..., D-1$) with the softmax function [26].

$$a_{i,j} = \frac{\exp(z_{i,j})}{\sum\limits_{j=0}^{D-1} \exp(z_{i,j})}, \tag{4}$$

where $a_{i,j}$ is the j_{th} element of the attention weight A_i. Finally, we obtain the weighted feature $\widehat{X}_i$ by multiplying the attention weight A_i and input feature X_i.

$$\widehat{X}_i = X_i \otimes A_i, \tag{5}$$

where $\otimes$ is an element-wise multiplication. To optimize the parameters of the fusion models, we use the AdamW optimizer and the weighted cross-entropy loss defined in Eq. (1).

3 Experiments and Results

For model evaluation, we consider multiple criteria including precision, recall, accuracy (ACC), and F1-score. Given the label imbalance in our dataset, we record the receiver operating characteristic (ROC) curve and the area under the curve (AUC) because they are insensitive to data imbalance in model validating. All models used in the experiments were built on the Pytorch platform.

3.1 Performance of Feature Transformation Models

To identify the optimal architecture for omics data, we choose four CNN models including ResNet50, ResNeXt50, SE-ResNet50, and EfficientNetB4 as candidates. We train each model on each omics dataset separately and the results are recorded in Table 3. According to AUC and ACC values, we find that the EfficientNetB4 obtains the best performance on mRNA (AUC: 0.6513, ACC: 0.7164) and miRNA (AUC: 0.75, ACC: 0.7164). ResNeXt50 presents a superior performance on CNV (AUC: 0.7094, ACC: 0.7761). And SE-ResNet50 performs better than others on DNAm (AUC: 0.7588, ACC: 0.7463). Therefore, these CNNs are identified as optimal architectures for the feature transformation models of mRNA, miRNA, CNV, and DNAm. For the clinical dataset, the DNN-based feature transformation models are evaluated and the number of units in the first two hidden layers was determined by grid search to be 256 and 512.

Table 3. Results of the convolution neural network-based models trained on the single datasets.

Model	Profile	Precision	Recall	ACC	AUC	F1-score
ResNet50	mRNA	0.5000	0.1579	0.7164	0.6042	0.2400
	miRNA	0.5000	0.2632	0.7164	0.6404	0.3448
	CNV	0.6000	0.3158	0.7463	0.6590	0.4138
	DNAm	**0.6667**	0.2105	**0.7463**	0.6250	0.3200
SE-ResNet50	mRNA	**0.5714**	0.2105	**0.7313**	0.6118	0.3077
	miRNA	**0.6250**	0.5263	**0.7761**	0.6650	**0.5714**
	CNV	**0.7143**	0.2632	0.7612	0.6272	0.3846
	DNAm	0.5556	**0.5263**	**0.7463**	**0.7588**	**0.5405**
EfficientNetB4	mRNA	0.5000	**0.3684**	0.7164	**0.6513**	**0.4242**
	miRNA	0.5000	**0.6316**	0.7164	**0.7500**	0.5581
	CNV	0.4667	0.3684	0.7015	0.6557	0.4118
	DNAm	0.6000	0.1579	0.7313	0.7116	0.2500
ResNeXt50	mRNA	0.5000	0.1579	0.7164	0.6261	0.2400
	miRNA	0.4800	**0.6316**	0.7015	0.6743	0.5455
	CNV	0.6667	**0.4211**	**0.7761**	**0.7094**	**0.5161**
	DNAm	0.4286	0.1579	0.7015	0.7237	0.2308

After architecture optimization, we train each model with five-fold cross-validation while training on four of five subsets and validating on the rest in each round. We observe that the performance of these models varies, but seems to be similar between each round (Table 4). For example, the model trained on miRNA (mean AUC: 0.7342) tends to perform better than others according to AUC. The model trained on DNAm has a great accuracy (mean ACC: 0.728). The model trained on clinical data shows to be more sensitive to true positive samples (mean Recall: 0.7561). These results demonstrate the heterogeneities among different profiles and indicate that we might obtain a better result by combining the advantages of individual models.

3.2 Performance of the Fusion Deep Neural Network

Until the features transformation model training is complete, the optimal parameters of each model are reloaded to the model, we conduct inference on the whole standard set to obtain the feature representations. Then, the feature representations generated from the same patient are fused in each round. Next, the fusing feature representations are present to the deep neural network for the final prognostic prediction.

The fusion DNN and attention-based DNN (ADNN) models are trained and validated on fusing feature representations with five-fold cross-validation. By observing the results present in Fig. 2b and Table 4, we find that the fusion DNN model performs generally better than feature transformation models trained on the single dataset. Although the

Table 4. Performance of feature transformation models based on different profiles with 5-fold cross-validation.

Profile	Fold	Precision	Recall	ACC	AUC	F1-score
mRNA	0	0.5000	0.3684	0.7164	0.6261	0.4242
	1	0.5455	0.3333	0.7424	0.6701	0.4138
	2	0.6364	0.3684	**0.7576**	0.6764	0.4667
	3	0.4545	0.5263	0.6818	0.6226	0.4878
	4	0.4737	0.4737	0.6970	0.6853	0.4737
miRNA	0	0.5238	0.5789	0.7313	0.7357	0.5500
	1	0.5330	0.4444	0.7424	0.7535	0.4848
	2	0.5000	0.3158	0.7121	0.6881	0.3871
	3	0.5294	0.4737	0.7273	0.7212	0.5000
	4	0.4516	0.7368	0.6667	**0.7727**	0.5600
CNV	0	0.4000	0.6316	0.6269	0.7007	0.4898
	1	0.4500	0.5000	0.697	0.647	0.4737
	2	0.4167	0.5263	0.6515	0.7055	0.4651
	3	0.5455	0.6316	0.7424	0.7301	0.5854
	4	0.5333	0.4211	0.7273	0.7021	0.4706
DNAm	0	0.5625	0.4737	0.7463	0.7248	0.5143
	1	0.4615	0.3333	0.7121	0.706	0.3871
	2	0.4667	0.3684	0.6970	0.6405	0.4118
	3	**0.6667**	0.2105	0.7424	0.6865	0.3200
	4	0.5714	0.4211	0.7424	0.6820	0.4848
Clinical	0	0.4615	**0.9474**	0.6716	0.7478	**0.6207**
	1	0.4545	0.8333	0.6818	0.7078	0.5882
	2	0.4286	0.6316	0.6515	0.6383	0.5106
	3	0.5000	0.5789	0.7121	0.7413	0.5366
	4	0.4412	0.7895	0.6515	0.7251	0.5660

mean Recall (0.3836) and F1-score (0.506) seem not good, the mean Precision (0.7784), ACC (0.7916), and AUC (0.8250) increase 44.1%, 8.7%, and 12.4% separately when compared to the best single dataset-based models. These results show the DNN model has successfully learned the reliable correlation between fusing feature and NSCLC prognosis. In contrast to DNN, the attention-based DNN performs much better. In Fig. 2a and Table 5, we find that the ROC curves of ADNNs are almost all on top of DNN models. Among five folds, the mean ACC (0.8096), AUC (0.8508), F1-score (0.6578), and Recall (0.6503) of ADNN increase 30%, 2.2%, 2.5%, 69.5% by comparing to DNN. In each round, the improvement brought by the attention mechanism is obvious too. Taking the first round for example, except the Precision (0.75 to 0.7, improved by −6.7%), the AUC (0.8816 to 0.9024, improved by 2.4%), ACC (0.7761 to 0.8358, improve by 7.6%), F1-score (0.4444 to 0.7179, improved by 61.5%) and Recall (0.3158 to 0.7368, improved by 133%). Moreover, the results presented by DNN and ADNN outperform the previous work [15] (AUC: 0.8163, ACC: 0.7544). The performances of ADNN strongly demonstrate that the attention-based fusion deep neural network could further improve the accuracy of prognostic prediction for NSCLC.

Table 5. Results of (A)DNN models trained on the fusing feature.

Fold	Model	Precision	Recall	ACC	F1-score
0	DNN	**0.7500**	0.3158	0.7761	0.4444
	ADNN	0.7000	**0.7368**	**0.8358**	**0.7179**
1	DNN	**0.7273**	0.4444	0.8030	0.5517
	ADNN	0.5600	**0.7778**	0.7727	**0.6512**
2	DNN	**0.8333**	0.2632	0.7727	0.4000
	ADNN	0.7059	**0.6316**	**0.8182**	**0.6667**
3	DNN	**0.8889**	0.4211	**0.8182**	0.5714
	ADNN	0.7333	**0.5789**	**0.8182**	**0.6471**
4	DNN	0.6923	0.4737	0.7879	0.5625
	ADNN	**0.7143**	05263	**0.803**	**0.6061**

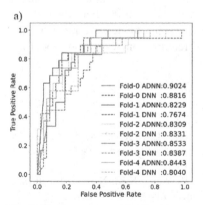

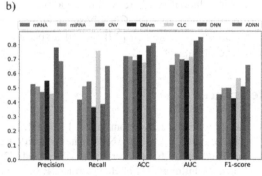

Fig. 2. Performance comparison between the single dataset-based models, the fusion deep neural network (DNN), and the attention-based fusion deep neural network (ADNN). (a) ROC curves and AUC values of the fusion models. (b) The average results of five folds for models trained on the single dataset and multimodal dataset.

4 Discussion and Conclusion

NSCLC is the most common type of lung cancer and poses a great threat to human health with a low five-year survival rate. Precise prognosis prediction of the patients is extremely significant for doctors to design a proper clinical treatment plan. In this work, we propose prognostic prediction model based on fusion deep neural network and multimodal data to predict the five-year survival status of NSCLC patients. Given the high-dimensional features of omics data, we develop CNN and DNN-based feature transformation models to extract abstract representations of mRNA, miRNA, CNV, DNAm, and clinical data. The feature representations are fused and fed to a fusion deep neural network for model training and prognostic prediction. To improve the efficiency of fusion, we introduce an attention mechanism to the fusion network and evaluate the model again. The experiment results show that the fusion deep neural network successfully fuses the representations from the different datasets. With an average accuracy of 0.8096 and an average AUC of 0.8508, the model based on the attention mechanism achieves more accurate predictions than previous research [15] (accuracy:0.7544, AUC: 0.8163). This demonstrates that we can improve the fusion DNN by forcing the model to focus on important features.

In the future, we will go a step further in the following aspects: 1) another type of data such as whole slide histopathological whole slide images might be introduced into the multimodal dataset. Pathological examination of histopathological slides is a basis for lung cancer assessment such as prognostic stratification [27, 28]. Previous research has demonstrated that the histopathological images contain several prognosis-related features and could be utilized to conduct survival analysis [29]; 2) we might try to testify the efficiency of our method on another disease like breast cancer, and there is a large amount of publicly available data online. Take the TCGA dataset for example, it provides diverse profiles including mRNA, miRNA, CNV, DNAm, whole slide images, and clinical data of 1098 breast cancer cases; 3) designing more personalized deep neural architecture including the CNN-based feature transformation model. We might utilize neural architecture search [30] to find a specialized feature transformation model for each type of dataset.

References

1. Bray, F., Ferlay, J., Soerjomataram, I., Siegel, R.L., Torre, L.A., Jemal, A.: Global cancer statistics 2018: GLOBOCAN estimates of incidence and mortality worldwide for 36 cancers in 185 countries. CA Cancer J. Clin. 68(6), 394–424 (2018)
2. Chen, Z., Fillmore, C.M., Hammerman, P.S., Kim, C.F., Wong, K.K.: Non-small-cell lung cancers: a heterogeneous set of diseases. Nat. Rev. Cancer 14(8), 535–546 (2014)
3. Taugner, J., et al.: Survival score to characterize prognosis in inoperable stage III NSCLC after chemoradiotherapy. Transl. Lung Cancer Res. 8(5), 593 (2019)
4. Woodard, G.A., Jones, K.D., Jablons, D.M.: Lung cancer staging and prognosis. Lung Cancer 170, 47–75 (2016)
5. Kaplan, E.L., Meier, P.: Nonparametric estimation from incomplete observations. J. Am. Stat. Assoc. 53(282), 457–481 (1958)
6. Cox, D.R.: Regression models and life-tables. J. Roy. Stat. Soc.: Ser. B (Methodol.) 34(2), 187–202 (1972)

7. Beer, D.G., et al.: Gene-expression profiles predict survival of patients with lung adenocarcinoma. Nat. Med. **8**(8), 816–824 (2002)
8. Sandoval, J., et al.: A prognostic DNA methylation signature for stage I non-small-cell lung cancer. J. Clin. Oncol. **31**, 4140–4147 (2013)
9. Yanaihara, N., et al.: Unique microRNA molecular profiles in lung cancer diagnosis and prognosis. Cancer Cell **9**(3), 189–198 (2006)
10. Okuda, K., Sasaki, H., Yukiue, H., Yano, M., Fujii, Y.: Met gene copy number predicts the prognosis for completely resected non-small cell lung cancer. Cancer Sci. **99**(11), 2280–2285 (2008)
11. Yin, J., et al.: Copy-number variation of MCL1 predicts overall survival of non-small-cell lung cancer in a Southern Chinese population. Cancer Med. **5**(9), 2171–2179 (2016)
12. Goodfellow, I., Bengio, Y., Courville, A., Bengio, Y.: Deep Learning, vol. 1, no. 2. MIT press, Cambridge (2016)
13. Chen, Y.C., Ke, W.C., Chiu, H.W.: Risk classification of cancer survival using ANN with gene expression data from multiple laboratories. Comput. Biol. Med. **48**, 1–7 (2014)
14. Sun, D., Wang, M., Li, A.: A multimodal deep neural network for human breast cancer prognosis prediction by integrating multi-dimensional data. IEEE/ACM Trans. Comput. Biol. Bioinf. **16**(3), 841–850 (2018)
15. Lai, Y.H., Chen, W.N., Hsu, T.C., Lin, C., Tsao, Y., Wu, S.: Overall survival prediction of non-small-cell lung cancer by integrating microarray and clinical data with deep learning. Sci. Rep. **10**, 1–11 (2020)
16. Yang, K., Wu, Y.: A prognosis-related molecular subtype for early-stage non-small-cell lung cell carcinoma by multinomics integration analysis. BMC Cancer **21**(1), 1–8 (2021)
17. Categorical Encoding Using Label-Encoding and One-Hot-Encoder. https://towardsdatascience.com/categorical-encoding-using-label-encoding-and-one-hot-encoder-911ef77fb5bd, Accessed 21 Mar 2021
18. He, K., Zhang, X., Ren, S., Sun, J.: Deep residual learning for image recognition. In: Proceedings of the IEEE Conference on Computer Vision and Pattern Recognition, Las Vegas, pp. 770–778 (2016)
19. Hu, J., Shen, L., Sun, G.: Squeeze-and-excitation networks. In: Proceedings of the IEEE Conference on Computer Vision and Pattern Recognition, Salt Lake City, pp. 7132–7141 (2018)
20. Tan, M., Le, Q.: Efficientnet: Rethinking model scaling for convolutional neural networks. In: Proceedings of International Conference on Machine Learning, Long Beach, pp. 6105–6114 (2019)
21. Xie, S., Girshick, R., Dollár, P., Tu, Z., He, K.: Aggregated residual transformations for deep neural networks. In: Proceedings of the IEEE Conference on Computer Vision and Pattern Recognition, Hawaii, pp. 1492–1500 (2017)
22. Nair, V., Hinton, G.E.: Rectified linear units improve restricted boltzmann machines. In: International Conference on Machine Learning, Haifa (2010).
23. Ioffe, S., Szegedy, C.: Batch normalization: accelerating deep network training by reducing internal covariate shift. In: International Conference on Machine Learning, pp. 448–456. PMLR, Lille (2015)
24. Loshchilov, I., Hutter, F.: Decoupled weight decay regularization (2017). arXiv preprint arXiv:1711.05101
25. Nicora, G., Vitali, F., Dagliati, A., Geifman, N., Bellazzi, R.: Integrated multi-omics analyses in oncology: a review of machine learning methods and tools. Front. Oncol. **10**, 1030 (2020)
26. Bridle, J.S.: Probabilistic interpretation of feedforward classification network outputs, with relationships to statistical pattern recognition. In: Neurocomputing, pp. 227–236. Springer, Heidelberg (1990). https://doi.org/10.1007/978-3-642-76153-9_28

27. Campanella, G., et al.: Clinical-grade computational pathology using weakly supervised deep learning on whole slide images. Nat. Med. **25**(8), 1301–1309 (2019)
28. Luo, X., et al.: Comprehensive computational pathological image analysis predicts lung cancer prognosis. J. Thorac. Oncol. **12**(3), 501–509 (2017)
29. Wang, H., Xing, F., Su, H., Stromberg, A., Yang, L.: Novel image markers for non-small-cell lung cancer classification and survival prediction. BMC Bioinf. **15**(1), 1–12 (2014)
30. Elsken, T., Metzen, J.H., Hutter, F.: Neural architecture search: a survey. J. Mach. Learn. Res. **20**(55), 1–21 (2019)

Drug-Target Interactions Prediction with Feature Extraction Strategy Based on Graph Neural Network

Aoxing Li[1], Xiaoli Lin[1(✉)], Minqi Xu[1], and Haiping Yu[2]

[1] Hubei Key Laboratory of Intelligent Information Processing and Real-Time Industrial System, School of Computer Science and Technology, Wuhan University of Science and Technology, Wuhan 430065, China
linxiaoli@wust.edu.cn
[2] School of Computer, Huanggang Normal University, Huanggang 438000, China

Abstract. The binding of drug compounds with their targets affects the physiological functions and metabolic effects of the body, as well as the pharmacological effects leading to phenotypic effects. Studying drug-target interactions can facilitate the evaluation or identification of new targets for existing drugs. In order to better extract drug-target features and further improve the progress of model prediction, this paper investigates and analyzes a variety of graphical neural network models to predict drug-target interaction. In these models, compounds are represented as two-dimensional molecular graphs and SMILES sequences are algorithmically encoded as graph structures, which can better learn the characteristics of compound molecules. Three feature extraction strategies are experimented on the basis of two loss functions. The experimental results show that GROAN has the best results with binary cross-entropy. Compared to other methods, GROAN-based prediction model achieves better results on the benchmark dataset.

Keywords: Drug-target interactions · Graph neural network · Feature extraction

1 Introduction

Drugs are substances that affect the physiological functions and metabolism of the body, which are generally recognized as molecule compounds. A drug binds to a specific biomolecule in order to achieve its effect on the body, and its site of action on the biomolecule is the drug target. Drug discovery is the process of identifying new candidate compounds with potential therapeutic effects, and the prediction of drug-target interactions is an indispensable step in the drug discovery process [1]. Discovering drug-target interactions effectively and accurately can facilitate the efficiency of drug development and reduce research costs [2]. In addition, the discovery of drug-target interactions can expose the potential function of drug molecules or target proteins, and reveal the disease-causing mechanisms [3]. The organism is a highly complex biological system, and the influence of drugs on biological systems is multilayered. Exploring a compound that selectively binds to a potential target is a very challenging task during

© Springer Nature Switzerland AG 2021
D.-S. Huang et al. (Eds.): ICIC 2021, LNAI 12838, pp. 561–569, 2021.
https://doi.org/10.1007/978-3-030-84532-2_50

drug research. In fact, only a small number of candidate compounds have been determined to be usable drugs, while the interaction of a large number of compounds with proteins remains unknown. With the advancement of biotechnology, the existing computational methods can to some extent discern drug-target interactions, but a large number of undiscovered interactions are still possible. Thus, predicting drug-target interactions is significant for the identification of potential new drugs and contributes to narrowing down the universe of possible drug candidates [4].

Biomedical data are growing in large quantities, and genomic structure and compound activity information required for drug development are more easily accessible. At the same time, with the enhancement of computer performance, the computer-aided design is gradually becoming a powerful aid to biological research [5–7], which has also facilitated the development of drug discovery technologies [8]. Machine learning assists in revealing the underlying link between massive drug molecules and target proteins, and exploiting never-before-seen insights in drug-target interactions [9].

In addition to machine learning methods, an increasing number of researchers have focused their attention on deep learning in recent years to explore the adaptability of deep learning methods for drug-target interaction prediction [10–12]. Wen [13] developed the DeepDTI algorithm framework based on deep confidence networks, which applied deep learning to learn features from ECFP drug fingerprints and PSC protein descriptors to achieve interaction prediction of drug-target pairs. Hu [14] proposed a deep learning prediction model based on drug target descriptors to distinguish potential associations between drugs and target proteins. Ozkirimli [15] proposed a deep learning model based on protein and ligand sequences to predict the binding affinity of protein-ligand interactions for the Davis Kinase binding affinity dataset [16] and KIBA large-scale kinase inhibitor bioactivity data [17, 18].

Bioinformatics data are multifaceted and strongly correlated. There are complex relationships between different biological features that affect each other. Therefore, the structured presentation of graphs is well suited for the representation of biological information, especially for molecular structures and functional relationships between molecules. In recent years, graph neural networks have attracted attention in the field of bioinformatics. It can effectively handle non-ordered and non-Euclidean spatial data, and extract information from the nodes themselves as well as the dependencies between nodes, and realize the recognition and prediction of vertices or edges.

In the last two years, graph neural network approaches have achieved some excellent results in the field of bioinformatics. It can be used to more accurately represent molecular information and effectively obtain the relationships between molecules. Thus, more accurate molecular features can be extracted using graph neural networks, and the accuracy of drug-target interaction prediction can be further improved. For example, Hao et al. [20] proposed a new active semi-supervised graph neural network (ASGN) framework to predict the properties of molecules by merging labeled and unlabeled molecules in chemical space.

As mentioned above, researchers have conducted a lot of research in the field of drug-target interaction prediction and have achieved certain results. The research of the machine learning methods and the exploration of the latest graph neural network methods applied in the field of molecular biology have provided a solid foundation for our researches.

This paper uses the feature extraction strategy based on graph neural network to encode the drug molecules. SMILES is encoded as a graph, and the information of atoms and atomic bonds is used as nodes and edges of the graph. The obtained drug graph information is then fed into the drug feature extraction module. It trained model in four datasets of Gold Standard Datasets.

2   Method

The most important issue in drug-target interactions is to obtain the characteristics that can be validly expressed for the target and the drug. In this paper, the SMILES sequences of the drugs and the amino acid sequences of the target proteins were selected for the study, respectively.

Drugs and proteins are vastly different. In terms of one-dimensional sequence, the average sequence length of proteins in the enzyme dataset is longer than that of drugs. Compared with proteins, which have complex folding structures and are difficult to determine [19], drugs can be easily represented in two-dimensional structural form. The focus of this paper describes the extraction strategies of drug features.

2.1   Graph-Based Feature Extraction

Graph Neural Network (GNN) [23], has already achieved some results in drug-related fields, such as drug discovery, ab initio molecular design, drug side effect prediction, and drug similarity measurement. To select the most suitable graph neural network, the parameters were compared among several graph neural algorithms, and the experiments proved that the GROAN (GRaph cOnvolutional and Attention Network) drug feature extraction strategy performed the best in the drug-target interaction prediction. The drug feature extraction strategies based on graph neural network are described in detail below.

Graph convolutional network (GCN) was proposed by Thomas in 2017, which provides a new way of processing the graph structured data. The GCN layer is defined as [24]

$$\tilde{D}^{-\frac{1}{2}}\tilde{A}\tilde{D}^{-\frac{1}{2}}X\Theta \tag{1}$$

$$\tilde{D}_{ii} = \sum_{j}\tilde{A}_{ii} \tag{2}$$

where $\tilde{A}$ is the graph adjacency matrix with self-loop, X is a signal with C-dimensional feature vector for every node, and Θ is the matrix of filter parameter.

GCN relies on Laplacian matrix and cannot be directly used in directed graphs. Model training relies on the entire graph structure and cannot be used in dynamic graphs. There is no way to assign different weights to neighboring nodes during convolution. Graph Attention Network (GAT) [25] was proposed to solve the problems of GCN.

GAT takes the set of nodes of the graph as input. x is the node feature vector, and each node is linearly transformed by the weight matrix W. The attention coefficient between node i and its nearest neighbor node j is calculated as

$$\alpha\left(Wx_i, Wx_j\right) \tag{3}$$

This attention coefficient represents the importance of the node j for the node i. The attention coefficient is then regularized by the softmax function, which is used in calculating the output features of the node i. The calculation procedure is shown below.

$$\sigma\left(\sum\nolimits_{j\in N(i)} a_{ij}Wx_j\right) \tag{4}$$

Where $\sigma(\bullet)$ is the nonlinear activation function and a_{ij} is the regularized attention coefficient.

2.2 GROAN-Based Feature Extraction Strategy

The experiments on GAT-based feature extraction strategy reveal that compared with the deeper GCN-based graph structure, the graph learning structure using exclusively GAT layers is more likely to overfit the training data. That is, it will produce the reverse upward of the validation set loss value in fewer training rounds and higher loss points, and more dropout layers are needed to discard certain features to avoid the overfitting. However, reducing the depth of the GAT structure will result in insufficient learning and high training curves. Therefore, the second GAT layer is replaced with a GCN structure to reduce the model's excessive focus on the subset of the training data. This strategy is known as GROAN (GRaph cOnvolutional and Attention Network). Experimental results demonstrate that GROAN strategy is slightly more effective than relying exclusively on GCN or exclusively on GAT.

The GROAN-based feature extraction module mainly consists of one GAT layer and one GCN layer which are both activated by the ReLU function. In this strategy, the molecular graph features are first extracted by the graph attention mechanism, and the more important substructural features are grasped by assigning corresponding weights to the different neighboring nodes of each node. Next graph features are then learned by GCN for the whole graph to update the overall structural information of the graph. The obtained graph features are then subjected to global maximum pooling and global average pooling, respectively. The former reinforces the effective substructure features, while the latter integrates the full graph structure features and obtains the complete graph features by fusion.

3 Experiments

3.1 Dataset

There is a wide variety of target proteins, including enzymes, ion channels, receptors, gene loci, transporters, nucleic acids and other biological proteins. The most important of them are receptors, followed by enzymes. Among the receptors, G protein-coupled receptors are the most important. In this paper, drug-target interactions were explored mainly on four benchmark datasets introduced by Yamanishi et al. [21], which comes from SuperTarget [26], KEGG [27], DrugBank [28] and BRENAD [29]. These four benchmark datasets provide a well-defined classification of interaction by target type and are commonly used in drug-target interaction studies. The datasets are shown in Table 1.

Table 1. The datasets of the drug-target interactions

	Enzymes	GPCRs	Ion channels	Nuclear receptors
Target proteins	664	95	204	26
Drug compounds	445	223	210	54
Interaction pairs	2926	635	1476	90

When the datasets are unbalanced, the evaluation results may be biased. However, in this example, the targets with higher number of interactions and those with lower number of interactions were separately assessed, which implies that there were only targets having similar unbalanced properties assessed together. Furthermore, unbalanced does not affect the validity of the AUC for each method. AUC can simply and intuitively reflect the ability of the classifier to rank the samples. AUC takes into account the classification ability of the learner for both positive samples and negative samples, and can still make a reasonable evaluation of the classifier in the case of sample imbalance. Therefore, AUC is selected as the evaluation metric in this paper.

3.2 Experimental Results

Experimental Results of Different Drug Feature Extraction Strategy
In order to select a better drug feature extraction strategy, this paper analyzes the optimization effect of two commonly used loss functions on the drug-target interaction prediction model, and the experimental comparison results are listed in Fig. 1.

Figure 1 shows the results of three different feature extraction strategies under two different loss functions (Cross-entropy and Binary cross-entropy). The AUC of GAT was higher than that of GCN, but slightly lower than that of GROAN with cross-entropy. For binary cross-entropy, the AUC of GAT was slightly lower than that of GCN, but obviously lower than that of GROAN. Also, the AUC of GCN was lower than that of GROAN. So the results of the GROAN-based drug feature extraction strategy were both optimal under the two different loss functions. Based on the analysis of the above experimental results, the subsequent experiments are based on the drug feature extraction strategy of GROAN with binary cross-entropy.

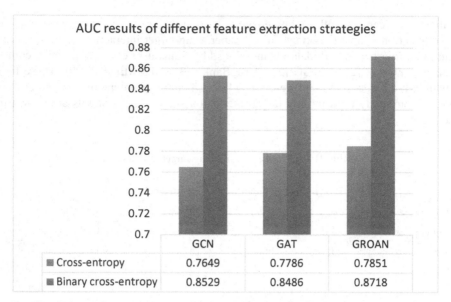

Fig. 1. AUC results of different feature extraction strategies with different loss functions

Comparison and Analysis of Experimental Results

To fully evaluate the performance of the proposed model, it was then compared with prediction results obtained from other state-of-the-art work on the same dataset. Cross-validation was performed on all four datasets. Table 2 presents the AUC values obtained by the different methods, where the best results are in bold. It can be seen that the classification performance of the model proposed in this paper is improved over the other methods on the three datasets. The GROAN-based model obtained better results on the enzyme, ion channel and G protein-coupled receptor datasets. The results show that the model proposed in this paper is a reliable model compared with other methods, which are promising in drug-target interaction prediction.

Table 2. Results of AUC comparison with other advanced models on four benchmark datasets

Method	E	IC	GPCR	NR
Yamanishi [22]	0.892	0.812	0.827	0.835
KBMF2K [30]	0.832	0.799	0.857	0.824
AM-PSSM [31]	0.843	0.722	0.839	0.767
Wang [32]	0.943	0.911	0.874	**0.817**
MLCLE [33]	0.842	0.795	0.850	0.790
GROAN	**0.947**	**0.936**	**0.879**	0.756

4   Conclusion

In this paper, feature extraction strategies based on graph neural networks are analyzed, including GCN, GAT and GROAN. Among them, GROAN is a hybrid method that combines the advantages of GCN and GAT. The SMILES sequence of the drug is encoded as a graph, while the information of atoms and atomic bonds is encoded as nodes and edges of the graph. The experimental results show that GROAN can better retain the compositional and structural information of compounds by learning their properties through graphs. There are great differences and diversity among different targets and drugs, which makes drug-target interaction prediction models susceptible to bias toward drug and target features that occur more frequently. In addition, there are difficulties in making valid predictions for completely new drugs or targets. In the next re-study, we will focus on more available biochemical features and further investigate the performance of different types of graph neural networks in drug-target interaction prediction.

Acknowledgment. The authors thank the members of Machine Learning and Artificial Intelligence Laboratory, School of Computer Science and Technology, Wuhan University of Science and Technology, for their helpful discussion within seminars. This work was supported in part by Hubei Province Natural Science Foundation of China (No. 2019CFB797), by National Natural Science Foundation of China (No. 61972299, 61702385).

References

1. Kim, I.W., Jang, H., Hyunkim, J., et al.: Computational drug repositioning for gastric cancer using reversal gene expression profiles. Sci. Rep. **9**, 2660 (2019)
2. Ganotra, G.K., Wade, R.C.: Prediction of drug-target binding kinetics by comparative binding energy analysis. ACS Med. Chem. Lett. **9**(11), 1134–1139 (2018)
3. Kingsmore, K.M., Grammer, A.C., Lipsky, P.E.: Drug repurposing to improve treatment of rheumatic autoimmune inflammatory diseases. Nat. Rev. Rheumatol. **16**, 32–52 (2020)
4. Williams, G., Gatt, A., Clarke, E., et al.: Drug repurposing for Alzheimer's disease based on transcriptional profiling of human iPSC-derived cortical neurons. Transl. Psychiatry **9**, 220 (2019)
5. Lin, X.L., Zhang, X.L., Xu, X.: Efficient classification of hot spots and hub protein interfaces by recursive feature elimination and gradient boosting. IEEE/ACM Trans. Comput. Biol. Bioinf. **17**(5), 1525–1534 (2020)
6. Lin, X.L., Zhang, X.L.: Identification of hot regions in hub protein-protein interactions by clustering and PPRA optimization. BMC Med. Inform. Decis. Mak. **21**, S1 (2021)
7. Lin, X.L., Zhang, X.L.: Prediction of hot regions in PPIs based on improved local community structure detecting. IEEE/ACM Trans. Comput. Biol. Bioinf. **15**(5), 1470–1479 (2018)
8. Stokes, J.M., Yang, K., Swanson, K., et al.: A deep learning approach to antibiotic discovery. Cell **180**(4), 668–702 (2020)
9. Zhang, W., Lin, W., Zhang, D., Wang, S., Shi, J., Niu, Y.: Recent advances in the machine learning-based drug-target interaction prediction. Curr. Drug Metab. **20**(3), 194–202 (2019)
10. Zong, N., Kim, H., Ngo, V., Harismendy, O.: Deep mining heterogeneous networks of biomedical linked data to predict novel drug-target associations. Bioinformatics **33**(15), 2337–2344 (2017)

11. Pliakos, K., Vens, C., Tsoumakas, G.: Predicting drug-target interactions with multi-label classification and label partitioning. IEEE/ACM Trans. Comput. Biol. Bioinf. (2019)
12. Pliakos, K.: Mining biomedical networks exploiting structure and background information. KU Leuven, Belgium (2019)
13. Wen, M., et al.: Deep-learning-based drug-target interaction prediction. J. Proteome. **16**(4), 1401–1409 (2017)
14. Hu, S., Zhang, C., Chen, P., et al.: Predicting drug-target interactions from drug structure and protein sequence using novel convolutional neural networks. BMC Bioinformatics **20**(Suppl 25), 689 (2019)
15. Öztürk, H., Özgür, A., Ozkirimli, E.: DeepDTA: deep drug-target binding affinity prediction. Bioinformatics **34**(17), i821-i829 (2018)
16. Davis, M.I., Hunt, J.P., Herrgard, S., et al.: Comprehensive analysis of kinase inhibitor selectivity. Nat. Biotechnol. **29**(11), 1046–1051 (2011)
17. He, T., Heidemeyer, M., Ban, F., et al.: SimBoost: a read-across approach for predicting drug-target binding affinities using gradient boosting machines. J. Cheminf. **9**(1), 24 (2017)
18. Tang, J., Szwajda, A., Shakyawar, S., et al.: Making sense of large-scale kinase inhibitor bioactivity data sets: a comparative and integrative analysis. J. Chem. Inf. Model. **54**(3), 735–743 (2014)
19. Lin, X., Zhang, X., Zhou, F.: Protein structure prediction with local adjust tabu search algorithm. BMC Bioinf. **15**(Suppl 15), S1 (2014). https://doi.org/10.1186/1471-2105-15-S15-S1
20. Hao, Z., Lu, C., Huang, Z., et al.: ASGN: an active semi-supervised graph neural network for molecular property prediction. In: The 26th ACM SIGKDD Conference on Knowledge Discovery and Data Mining (2020)
21. Yamanishi, Y., Araki, M., Gutteridge, A., et al.: Prediction of drug-target interaction networks from the integration of chemical and genomic spaces. Intell. Syst. Molec. Biol. **24**(13), 232–240 (2008)
22. Yamanishi, Y., Masaaki, K., Minoru, K., et al.: Drug-target interaction prediction from chemical, genomic and pharmacological data in an integrated framework. Bioinformatics **26**(12), 246–254 (2010)
23. Scarselli, F., Gori, M., Tsoi, A.C., et al.: The graph neural network model. IEEE Trans. Neural Netw. **20**(1), 61–80 (2009)
24. Kipf, T.N., Welling, M.: Semi-supervised classification with graph convolutional networks. In: Proceedings of the International Conference on Learning Representations (ICLR) (2017)
25. Velic̆kovic̆, P., Cucurull, G., Casanova, A., et al.: Graph attention networks. In: Proceedings of the International Conference on Learning Representations (ICLR) (2018)
26. Gunther, S., Kuhn, M., Dunkel, M., Campillos, M., Senger, C., Petsalaki, E., et al.: SuperTarget and matador: resources for exploring drug-target relationships.Nucleic Acids Res. **36**, 919–922 (2007)
27. Kanehisa, M., Goto, S., Hattori, M., et al.: From genomics to chemical genomics: new developments in KEGG. Nucleic Acids Res. **34**(90001), 354–357 (2006)
28. Wishart, D.S., Knox, C., Guo, A.C., et al.: Drugbank: a knowledgebase for drugs, drug actions and drug targets. Nucleic Acids Res. **36**(suppl 1), D901–D906 (2008)
29. Jeske, L., Placzek, S., Schomburg, I., et al.: BRENDA in 2019: a European ELIXIR core data resource. Nucleic Acids Res. **47**, 542–549 (2019)
30. Gonen, M.: Predicting drug-target interactions from chemical and genomic kernels using Bayesian matrix factorization. Bioinformatics **28**(18), 2304–2310 (2012)

31. Mousavian, Z., Khakabimamaghani, S., Kavousi, K., et al.: Drug-target interaction prediction from PSSM based evolutionary information. J. Pharmacol. Toxicol. Methods **78**, 42–51 (2016)
32. Wang, L., You, Z., Chen, X., et al.: A computational-based method for predicting drug–target interactions by using stacked autoencoder deep neural network. J. Comput. Biol. **25**(3), 361–373 (2018)
33. Pliakos, K., Vens, C., Tsoumakas, G.: Predicting drug-target interactions with multi-label classification and label partitioning. IEEE/ACM Trans. Comput. Biol. Bioinf., 1 (2019)

CNNEMS: Using Convolutional Neural Networks to Predict Drug-Target Interactions by Combining Protein Evolution and Molecular Structures Information

Xin Yan[1,2], Zhu-Hong You[3(✉)], Lei Wang[3,4(✉)], and Peng-Peng Chen[1(✉)]

[1] School of Computer Science and Technology, China University of Mining and Technology, Xuzhou, China
chenp@cumt.edu.cn
[2] School of Foreign Languages, Zaozhuang University, Zaozhuang, China
[3] Guangxi Academy of Science, Nanning, China
{zhuhongyou,leiwang}@ms.xjb.ac.cn
[4] College of Information Science and Engineering, Zaozhuang University, Zaozhuang, China

Abstract. Emerging evidences shown that drug-target interactions (DTIs) recognition is the basis of drug research and development and plays an important role in the treatment of diseases. However, the recognition of interactions among drugs and targets by traditional biological experiments is usually blind, time-consuming, and has a high false negative rate. Therefore, it is urgent to use computer simulation to predict DTIs to help narrow the scope of biological experiments and improve the accuracy of identification. In this study, we propose a deep learning-based model called CNNEMS for predicting potential interrelationship among target proteins and drug molecules. This method first uses the Convolutional Neural Network (CNN) algorithm to deeply excavate the features contained in the target protein sequence information and the drug molecule fingerprint information, and then the Extreme Learning Machine (ELM) is used to predict the interrelationship among them. In experiments, we use 5-fold cross-validation method to verify the performance of CNNEMS on the benchmark datasets, including enzymes, ion channels, G-protein-coupled receptors (GPCRs) and nuclear receptors. The cross-validation experimental results show that CNNEMS achieved 94.19%, 90.95%, 87.95% and 86.11% prediction accuracy in these four datasets, respectively. These prominent experimental results indicate that CNNEMS as a useful tool can effectively predict potential drug-target interactions and provide promising target protein candidates for drug research.

Keywords: Drug-target interactions · Position-Specific Scoring Matrix · Convolutional Neural Network · Deep learning · Extreme Learning Machine

1 Introduction

The validation and identification of drug-target interactions (DTIs) as an initial part in drug development and design is of great significance to its research [1]. According to statistics, there are approximately 6,000 to 8,000 pharmacological targets in the

© Springer Nature Switzerland AG 2021
D.-S. Huang et al. (Eds.): ICIC 2021, LNAI 12838, pp. 570–579, 2021.
https://doi.org/10.1007/978-3-030-84532-2_51

human genome, but the number of target proteins currently identified as associated with approved drugs is only a small percentage [2]. Since the experimental method of identifying DTI is usually expensive, laborious, high error rate and limited to a small range [3], the computational methods are urgently needed to predict DTIs quickly and accurately in the whole genome [4].

Recently, several sequence-based computational methods have been designed for predicting potential DTIs. Since the target protein sequence contains a wealth of information and it does not involve the 3D structure of protein information, and thus has a wide range of applicability [5]. Lan et al. designed the PUDT method for predicting DTIs based on the information of drug structure and protein sequence. In the experiment, PUDT achieved good results through the weighted support vector machine classifier [6].

In this study, based on the hypothesis that proteins similar to a ligand target may interact with this ligand, and vice versa, we designed a new deep learning-based called CNNEMS to predict potential drug-target interactions. Firstly, CNNEMS transforms the target protein amino acid sequence into the Position-Specific Scoring Matrix (PSSM) which contain the biological evolutionary properties; secondly, converting the drug compound into a molecular fingerprint and paired with the target protein to form a numerical descriptor; then using the deep learning CNN algorithm to mine their hidden abstract features; finally, utilizing the Extreme Learning Machine (ELM) classifier to predict DTIs rapidly and accurately. We validated CNNEMS in the four benchmark datasets, including enzymes, ion channels, G protein-coupled receptors (GPCRs) and nuclear receptors, and achieved competitive results. These excellent results show that CNNEMS can accurately predict the drug-target interactions and provide guidance for the development and design of drugs.

2 Materials and Methods

2.1 Benchmark Datasets

In this paper, we use the four classes of DTIs benchmark datasets, including enzyme, ion channel, G-protein-coupled receptor (GPCR) and nuclear receptor, collected from DrugBank [7], SuperTarget [8], KEGG [9] and BRENDA [10] which are introduced by Yamanishi et al. [11]. These datasets can be downloaded at http://web.kuicr.kyoto-u.ac. jp/supp/yoshi/drugtarget/. After careful inspection, the total number of DTI pairs was 5127, of which 2926 were enzyme, 1467 were ion channel, 635 were GPCR, and 90 were nuclear receptor.

2.2 Drug Represented by Molecular Fingerprint Descriptor

The fingerprint is one of the commonly used methods to describe the structures of drug compounds. It transforms the drug molecular into a set of binary fingerprint sequences by detecting the absence or presence of certain substructures (i.e., molecular structure fragments) in the molecular structure. The core idea of the molecular fingerprint is to describe molecules based on molecular fragments. Here, we use molecular fingerprints from the PubChem database to effectively represent pharmaceutical compounds. In this molecular fingerprint, the molecular substructure is represented by an 881-dimensional vector. The corresponding bit is coded as 1 or 0 depending on the presence or absence of the molecular substructure. This fingerprint is encoded by Base64, and the text description is provided by binary data. Those data can be obtained at the PubChem website (https://pubchem.ncbi.nlm.nih.gov/).

2.3 Representing Target Protein with PSSM

The Position-Specific Scoring Matrix (PSSM) was originally proposed to detect distantly related protein [12, 13], and now it has been widely used in the disordered regions prediction [14], protein secondary structure prediction [15] and protein binding site prediction [16] fields. The PSSM matrix consists of H rows and 20 columns, in which H represent the length of the protein sequence, and 20 represent the 20 kinds of amino acids. Assuming $Pssm = \{\Theta_{i,j} : i = 1 \cdots H \text{ and } j = 1 \cdots 20\}$, then a PSSM matrix can be represented as:

$$Pssm = \begin{bmatrix} \Theta_{1,1} & \Theta_{1,2} & \cdots & \Theta_{1,20} \\ \Theta_{2,1} & \Theta_{2,2} & \cdots & \Theta_{2,20} \\ \vdots & \vdots & \vdots & \vdots \\ \Theta_{H,1} & \Theta_{H,2} & \cdots & \Theta_{H,20} \end{bmatrix} \tag{1}$$

where $\Theta_{i,j}$ in i row and j column in matrix means that the ith residue is mutated to the j-type probability of 20 amino acids during protein evolution from multiple sequence alignments.

2.4 Feature Extraction Using CNN

In this study, we use the deep learning Convolution neural network (CNN) algorithm to extract the features of protein data. Deep learning is one of the directions of machine learning. The motivation of it is to emulate the neural network mechanism of the human brain to interpret data and to discover the high-level features of data. CNN has a prominent performance compared to other depth learning models in mining deep features of data. Therefore, we use CNN to mine the deep features of DTIs data in order to improve the accuracy of the prediction.

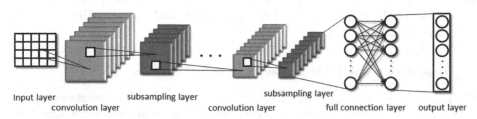

Input layer   subsampling layer   subsampling layer
   convolution layer   convolution layer   full connection layer   output layer

Fig. 1. CNN structure diagram

The CNN is the multi-layer network, which consists of the input layer, the convolution layer, the subsampling layer, the full connection layer and the output layer. Its output value is calculated by forward propagation, and the weight and bias are adjusted by backward propagation. The neuronal units between adjacent layers are partially connected in CNN, that is, the perceptual region of a neural unit comes from the part of the neural unit of the upper layer. Figure 1 shows the structure of the CNN. Suppose that C_i represents the feature map of the *ith* layer, which can be expressed by the following formula:

$$C_i = g(C_{i-1} \cdot W_i + b_i) \tag{2}$$

where $g(x)$ represents the activation function, W_i denotes the weight matrix of the *ith* layer convolution kernel, b_i denotes the offset vector and operator · represents convolution operations. The subsampling layer is usually behind the convolution layer and samples the feature map based on specific rules. Assuming C_i is the subsampling layer, which sampling rules are as follows:

$$C_i = subsampling(C_{i-1}) \tag{3}$$

After several convolution and sampling operations, the fully connected layer is used to classify the features and obtain the probability distribution Γ of the original input data. Essentially, CNN is a mathematical model, which converts the original input matrix C_0 into a new feature representation Γ through multi-level data transformation or dimension.

$$\Gamma(i) = Map(P = p_i | C_0; (W, b)) \tag{4}$$

where C_0 indicates the original input matrix, p_i represents the *ith* label class, and Γ indicates the feature representation.

The purpose of CNN training is to minimize the loss function $H(W, b)$. In training, in order to alleviate the problem of over-fitting, CNN usually uses the norm control the final loss function $L(W, b)$, and adjusts the over-fitting intensity through parameter θ.

$$L(W, b) = H(W, b) + \frac{\theta}{2} W^T W \tag{5}$$

In the training process, the gradient descent method is usually used to update the network layer parameters (W, b) of CNN layer by layer, and adjust the intensity of back propagation by learning rate ε.

$$W_i = W_i - \varepsilon \frac{\partial E(W, b)}{\partial W_i} \tag{6}$$

$$b_i = b_i - \varepsilon \frac{\partial E(W, b)}{\partial b_i} \tag{7}$$

2.5 Classification by ELM

Extreme learning machine (ELM) is used in our model to classify the extracted feature data. The ELM is a supervised learning algorithm to solve neural network problem [17].

The algorithm has the merits of less training parameters and faster speed. Therefore, we use it as a classifier for predicting drug-target interactions.

Assuming there are L tagged input samples (X_i, P_i), and the ELM containing N neurons can be represented as:

$$\sum_{i=1}^{N} V_i g(W_i \cdot X_j + b_i) = O_j, j = 1, \ldots, L \tag{8}$$

where $X_i = [x_{i1}, x_{i2,\ldots,}x_{iL,}]^T \in \mathbb{R}^L$, $P_i = [P_{i1}, P_{i2}, \ldots, P_{im}]^T \in \mathbb{R}^m$, V_i is the output weight matrix, $g(x)$ is the activation function, b_i indicates the offset of the ith neurons, $W_i = [w_{i1}, w_{i2}, \ldots, w_{iL}]^T$ indicates the input weight matrix, and $W_i \cdot X_j$ indicates the inner product of W_i and X_j.

The training objectives of the ELM is to minimize the output error, that is $\sum_{j=1}^{L} \|O_j - P_j\| = 0$, To accomplish this, the extreme learning machine needs to adjust the parameters so that

$$\sum_{i=1}^{N} V_i g(W_i \cdot X_j + b_i) = P_j, j = 1, \ldots, L \tag{9}$$

This formula can be represented in matrix form

$$SV = P \tag{10}$$

$$S = \begin{bmatrix} g(W_1 \cdot X_1 + b_1) & \cdots & g(W_N \cdot X_1 + b_N) \\ \vdots & \vdots & \vdots \\ g(W_1 \cdot X_L + b_1) & \cdots & g(W_N \cdot X_L + b_N) \end{bmatrix}_{L \times N} \quad V = \begin{bmatrix} V_1^T \\ \vdots \\ V_N^T \end{bmatrix}_{N \times m} \quad P = \begin{bmatrix} P_1^T \\ \vdots \\ P_L^T \end{bmatrix}_{L \times m} \tag{11}$$

where S represents the hidden layer neurons output, P represents the expected output, and V represents the output weight. In order to make ELM learning the best results, we want to obtain $\widehat{W_i}, \widehat{b_i}$ and $\widehat{V_i}$, which makes

$$\left\| S\left(\widehat{W_i}, \widehat{b_i}\right)\widehat{V_i} - P \right\| = \min_{W,b,V} \|S(W_i, b_i)V_i - P\| \quad i = 1, 2, \cdots, N \tag{12}$$

This is equal to minimizing the loss function

$$E = \sum_{j=1}^{L} \left(\sum_{i=1}^{N} V_i g(W_i \cdot X_j + b_i) - P_j \right)^2 \tag{13}$$

According to the extreme learning machine design framework, when the offset b_i and the input weight W_i of the hidden layer are determined, we can uniquely calculate the output matrix of the hidden layer. Thus, the training of ELM is converted to solving a linear equation $SV = P$, and the solution of this equation is unique and minimal.

3 Results

3.1 Evaluation Criteria

To facilitate the comparison of performance between different methods, we used the 5-fold cross-validation (CV) method and calculated the common evaluation criteria. In this paper, we use generic evaluation criteria, including accuracy (Accu.), sensitivity (Sen.), specificity (Spec.), precision (Prec.) and Matthew correlation coefficient (MCC), which are expressed as follows:

$$Accu. = \frac{TP + TN}{TP + TN + FP + FN} \tag{14}$$

$$Sen. = \frac{TP}{TP + FN} \tag{15}$$

$$Spec. = \frac{TN}{TN + FP} \tag{16}$$

$$Prec. = \frac{TP}{TP + FP} \tag{17}$$

$$MCC = \frac{TP \times TN - FP \times FN}{\sqrt{(TP + FP)(TP + FN)(TN + FP)(TN + FN)}} \tag{18}$$

where TP, FP, TN and FN indicate the true positive, false positive, true negative and false negative. Furthermore, we also calculated the receiver operating characteristic (ROC) curve and its area under the ROC curve (AUC) [18, 19].

3.2 Evaluate Prediction Performance

In this paper, we estimate the performance of the CNNEMS on the DTIs benchmark datasets, including enzymes, ion channels, GPCRs and nuclear receptors. Table 1 illustrates the accuracy, sensitivity, precision, Matthew correlation coefficient and AUC of CNNEMS on enzyme dataset, which is 94.19%, 91.91%, 96.33%, 88.51% and 94.37%, respectively. And their standard deviations are 0.41%, 1.41%, 1.81%, 0.89% and 0.59%. The accuracy of CNNEMS on icon channel dataset is 90.95%, sensitivity is 90.31%, precision is 91.76%, MCC is 81.95% and AUC is 90.88%. The standard deviations of these evaluation criteria are 1.10%, 1.23%, 2.36%, 2.24% and 0.97%, respectively. Table 1 also summarizes the 5-fold CV results of CNNEMS on GPCR dataset. The accuracy, sensitivity, precision, MCC and AUC are 87.95%, 94.16%, 83.69%, 76.41% and 88.02%, respectively, and the standard variance is 1.51%, 1.45%, 2.22%, 2.88% and 2.88%, respectively. The 5-fold CV results of CNNEMS for predicting the interaction of drug targets on nuclear receptor dataset are also summarized in the table. We can see from the table, the accuracy, sensitivity, precision, MCC and AUC of CNNEMS is 86.11%, 85.53%, 85.92%, 72.46% and 86.63%, and the standard variance is 4.39%, 1.45%, 11.56%, 8.97% and 4.77% respectively. The eventual 5-flod CV results demonstrated that CNNEMS combining biological information and deep learning performs well. Figures 2, 3, 4 and 5 exhibit the ROC curves plotted by CNNEMS on these four benchmark datasets.

Table 1. The performance of CNNEMS on enzyme dataset

Dataset	Accu. (%)	Sen. (%)	Prec. (%)	MCC (%)	AUC (%)
Enzyme	94.19 ± 0.41	91.91 ± 1.41	96.33 ± 1.81	88.51 ± 0.89	94.37 ± 0.59
Icon channel	90.95 ± 1.10	90.31 ± 1.23	91.76 ± 2.36	81.95 ± 2.24	90.88 ± 0.97
GPCR	87.95 ± 1.51	94.16 ± 1.45	83.69 ± 2.22	76.41 ± 2.88	88.02 ± 2.88
Nuclear receptor	86.11 ± 4.39	85.53 ± 1.45	85.92 ± 11.56	72.46 ± 8.97	86.63 ± 4.77

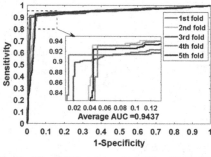

Fig. 2. The ROC curves plotted by CNNEMS on enzyme dataset

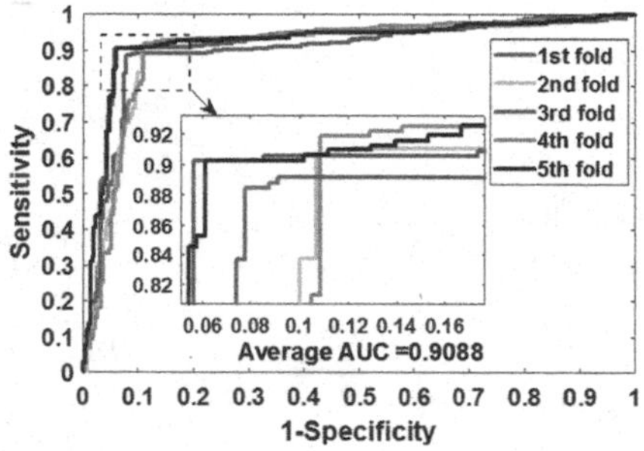

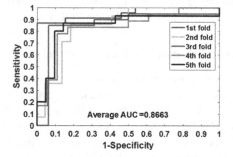

Fig. 3. The ROC curves plotted by CNNEMS on icon channel dataset

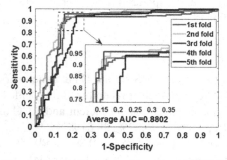

Fig. 4. The ROC curves plotted by CNNEMS on GPCR dataset

Fig. 5. The ROC curves plotted by CNNEMS on nuclear receptor dataset

3.3 Comparison with Other Outstanding Methods

In order to evaluate the performance of CNNEMS more clearly, we compared it with other outstanding methods. Here we chose the method of computing AUC on four benchmark datasets. These methods are SIMCOMP [20], NLCS [20], Temerinac-Ott [21], Yamanishi [3], KBMF2K [22], WNN-GIP [23], DBSI [24] and NetCBP [25], respectively. Table 2 summarizes the AUC values calculated by these methods, and we show them in percentage terms for easy viewing. It can be seen that CNNEMS obtains the best results in the four benchmark datasets. This suggests that the CNN algorithm combined with the ELM classifier can effectively improve the prediction performance of CNNEMS.

Table 2. The AUC obtained by the other outstanding methods and CNNEMS on four benchmark datasets

Method	Enzymes	Icon channels	GPCRs	Nuclear receptors
SIMCOMP	0.8630	0.7760	0.8670	0.8560
NLCS	0.8370	0.7530	0.8530	0.8150
Temerinac-Ott	0.8320	0.7990	0.8570	0.8240
Yamanishi	0.8210	0.6920	0.8110	0.8140
KBMF2K	0.8320	0.7990	0.8570	0.8240
WNN-GIP	0.8610	0.7750	0.8720	0.8390
DBSI	0.8075	0.8029	0.8022	0.7578
NetCBP	0.8251	0.8034	0.8235	0.8394
CNNEMS	0.9437	0.9088	0.8802	0.8663

4   Conclusion

In this study, we propose a new deep learning-based approach called CNNEMS to predict potential DTIs based on protein sequence and drug molecular fingerprint information. In order to effectively mine the abstract features hidden in the data, the deep learning CNN algorithm and ELM are introduced into the model. We apply CNNEMS to the benchmark drug-target interactions datasets that include enzymes, ion channels, GPCRs and nuclear receptors. The 5-fold CV experimental results indicate that CNNEMS performs well in these four benchmark datasets. To verify the predictive ability of model of CNN algorithm combined with ELM classifier, we compare it with the 2DPCA descriptor model and the SVM classifier model. Besides that, we compare CNNEMS with other outstanding methods based on the same datasets. In these comparisons, CNNEMS also yielded competitive results. These experimental results indicated that CNNEMS is suitable for predicting drug-target interactions and contributing to improving predictive performance. In future research, we will try to improve the deep learning algorithm to improve the performance of the model to predict potential drug-target interactions.

Acknowledgements. This work is supported is supported in part by the National Natural Science Foundation of China, under Grants 61702444, 62002297, in part by the West Light Foundation of The Chinese Academy of Sciences, under Grant 2018-XBQNXZ-B-008, in part by the Chinese Postdoctoral Science Foundation, under Grant 2019M653804, in part by the Tianshan youth - Excellent Youth, under Grant 2019Q029, in part by the Qingtan scholar talent project of Zaozhuang University. The authors would like to thank all anonymous reviewers for their constructive advices.

References

1. Xuan, P., Sun, C., Zhang, T., et al.: Gradient boosting decision tree-based method for predicting interactions between target genes and drugs. Front. Genet. **10**, 459 (2019)
2. Landry, Y., Gies, J.-P.: Drugs and their molecular targets: an updated overview. Fundam. Clin. Pharmacol. **22**, 1–18 (2008)
3. Yamanishi, Y., Kotera, M., Kanehisa, M., et al.: Drug-target interaction prediction from chemical, genomic and pharmacological data in an integrated framework. Bioinformatics **26**, i246–i254 (2010)
4. Wang, L., You, Z.H., Chen, X., et al.: An ensemble approach for large-scale identification of protein-protein interactions using the alignments of multiple sequences. Oncotarget **8**, 5149 (2017)
5. Wang, L., You, Z.H., Chen, X., et al.: RFDT: a rotation forest-based predictor for predicting drug-target interactions using drug structure and protein sequence information. Curr. Protein Pept. Sci. **19**, 445–454 (2018)
6. Lan, W., Wang, J., Li, M., et al.: Predicting drug-target interaction based on sequence and structure information. IFAC-PapersOnLine **48**, 12–16 (2015)
7. Wishart, D.S., Knox, C., Guo, A.C., et al.: DrugBank: a knowledgebase for drugs, drug actions and drug targets. Nucleic Acids Res. **36**, D901–D906 (2008)
8. Gunther, S., Kuhn, M., Dunkel, M., et al.: SuperTarget and Matador: resources for exploring drug-target relationships. Nucleic Acids Res. **36**, D919–D922 (2008)
9. Kanehisa, M., Goto, S., Furumichi, M., et al.: KEGG for representation and analysis of molecular networks involving diseases and drugs. Nucleic Acids Res. **38**, D355–D360 (2009)
10. Schomburg, I., Chang, A., Ebeling, C., et al.: BRENDA, the enzyme database: updates and major new developments. Nucleic Acids Res. **32**, D431–D433 (2004)
11. Yamanishi, Y., Araki, M., Gutteridge, A., et al.: Prediction of drug-target interaction networks from the integration of chemical and genomic spaces. Bioinformatics **24**, I232–I240 (2008)
12. Gao, Z.G., Wang, L., Xia, S.X., et al.: Ens-PPI: a novel ensemble classifier for predicting the interactions of proteins using autocovariance transformation from PSSM. Biomed Res. Int. **2016**, 1–8 (2016)
13. Wang, L., et al.: An improved efficient rotation forest algorithm to predict the interactions among proteins. Soft. Comput. **22**(10), 3373–3381 (2017). https://doi.org/10.1007/s00500-017-2582-y
14. Jones, D.T., Ward, J.J.: Prediction of disordered regions in proteins from position specific score matrices. Proteins-Struct. Func. Bioinf. **53**, 573–578 (2003)
15. Jones, D.T.: Protein secondary structure prediction based on position-specific scoring matrices. J. Mol. Biol. **292**, 195–202 (1999)
16. Chen, X.-W., Jeong, J.C.: Sequence-based prediction of protein interaction sites with an integrative method. Bioinformatics **25**, 585–591 (2009)
17. Huang, G.B., Wang, D.H., Lan, Y.: Extreme learning machines: a survey. Int. J. Mach. Learn. Cybern. **2**, 107–122 (2011)
18. Wang, L., You, Z.-H., Yan, X., et al.: Using two-dimensional principal component analysis and rotation forest for prediction of protein-protein interactions. Sci. Rep. **8**, 12874 (2018)
19. Ghadermarzi, S., Li, X., Li, M., et al.: Sequence-derived markers of drug targets and potentially druggable human proteins. Front. Genet. **10**, 1075 (2019)
20. Öztürk, H., Ozkirimli, E., Özgür, A.: A comparative study of SMILES-based compound similarity functions for drug-target interaction prediction. BMC Bioinf. **17**, 1–11 (2016)
21. Temerinac-Ott, M., Naik, A.W., Murphy, R.F.: Deciding when to stop: efficient stopping of active learning guided drug-target prediction. Comput. Sci. (2015)

22. Gonen, M.: Predicting drug-target interactions from chemical and genomic kernels using Bayesian matrix factorization. Bioinformatics **28**, 2304–2310 (2012)
23. Van, L.T., Marchiori, E.: Predicting drug-target interactions for new drug compounds using a weighted nearest neighbor profile. Plos One **8**, e66952 (2013)
24. Cheng, F., et al.: Prediction of drug-target interactions and drug repositioning via network-based inference. PLoS Comput. Biol. **8**(5), e1002503 (2012). https://doi.org/10.1371/journal.pcbi.1002503
25. Chen, H., Zhang, Z.: A semi-supervised method for drug-target interaction prediction with consistency in networks. Plos One **8** (2013)

A Multi-graph Deep Learning Model for Predicting Drug-Disease Associations

Bo-Wei Zhao[1,2,3], Zhu-Hong You[1,2,3](✉), Lun Hu[1,2,3], Leon Wong[1,2,3], Bo-Ya Ji[1,2,3], and Ping Zhang[4]

[1] The Xinjiang Technical Institute of Physics and Chemistry, Chinese Academy of Sciences, Urumqi 830011, China
zhuhongyou@nwpu.edu.cn
[2] University of Chinese Academy of Sciences, Beijing 100049, China
[3] Xinjiang Laboratory of Minority Speech and Language Information Processing, Urumqi 830011, China
[4] College of Informatics, Huazhong Agriculture University, Wuhan 430070, China

Abstract. Computational drug repositioning is essential in drug discovery and development. The previous methods basically utilized matrix calculation. Although they had certain effects, they failed to treat drug-disease associations as a graph structure and could not find out more in-depth features of drugs and diseases. In this paper, we propose a model based on multi-graph deep learning to predict unknown drug-disease associations. More specifically, the known relationships between drugs and diseases are learned by two graph deep learning methods. Graph attention network is applied to learn the local structure information of nodes and graph embedding is exploited to learn the global structure information of nodes. Finally, Gradient Boosting Decision Tree is used to combine the two characteristics for training. The experiment results reveal that the AUC is 0.9625 under the ten-fold cross-validation. The proposed model has excellent classification and prediction ability.

Keywords: Computational drug repositioning · Multi-graph deep learning · Drug-disease associations

1 Introduction

Drug discovery and development have become more and more important to a human healthy life. The huge market demand makes the pharmaceutical industry continuously increase investment [1]. However, the clinic-used of drugs can be counted on one's fingers. According to an investigation, the development of a new drug is divided into three stages: drug discovery, clinical trials, and marketing approval. Of these, more than 90% of these drug candidates fail in the first stage and usually put up at least several billion dollars and 8 to 12 years to get to market, and finally, less than 10% of the drugs are successful [2, 3]. Therefore, it is urgent to effectively improve the process of drug development, shorten the time and reduce the cost [4]. To address this challenge, drug

© Springer Nature Switzerland AG 2021
D.-S. Huang et al. (Eds.): ICIC 2021, LNAI 12838, pp. 580–590, 2021.
https://doi.org/10.1007/978-3-030-84532-2_52

repositioning has attracted extensive attention from the pharmaceutical industry and clinical researchers. Drug repositioning is the restudy of an existing drug to discover new effects. This approach can fill the gap in the discovery and development of new drugs.

In general, the discovery of potential effects of drugs can be divided into two main categories, including computational-based methods and activity-based methods [5]. Activity-based methods need a large number of drug trial data to be screened and are a laboratory approach. Furthermore, the lack of clarity about the underlying function of drug molecules makes it difficult to search for hidden mechanisms of drugs [6]. Consequently, the computation-based method can reduce the manpower and material resources while ensuring the accuracy of drug relocation, it has become the main direction. The main reason for the success of computational drug repositioning is the enormous amount of medical and biological data being collected and the improvement of computer-related algorithms.

Computational drug repositioning has been widely used to explore drug hiding mechanisms, including machine learning-based methods, matrix factorization-based methods, and deep learning-based methods [7–21]. For example, drug-drug similarity and disease-disease similarity were used to construct features by Gottlieb et al. [22], who proposed the PREDICT model, a logistic regression classifier used to predict potential drug-disease associations. Wang et al. [23] constructed drug similarity and disease similarity metrics by collecting molecular structure, molecular activity and phenotype data, and SVM is used to train the feature of drugs and diseases. Dai et al. [24] used a matrix factorization model to uncover unknown drug-disease interactions by integrating drug-gene interactions, disease-gene interactions and gene-gene interactions. Yang et al. [25] calculated drug-disease association scores by constructing a causal network connecting drugs, targets, pathways, genes and diseases, and learned the probability matrix factorization of known drug-disease associations to predict unknown drug-disease associations. Zeng et al. [26] built a heterogeneous network containing multiple drug correlations, and a multi-modal deep autoencoder was used to extract low-dimensional characteristics of drugs. Then the resulting characteristics along with the drug-disease interactions are then used by a collective variational autoencoder to discover the hidden drug-disease interactions. At present, the prediction of drug-disease associations is basically to construct drug-related networks and explore the characteristics of drugs and diseases. However, this approach separates the network from the characteristic information and does not consider the network from the perspective of graph data. From a graph point of view, the structure information and the attribute information are learned together. Therefore, the study of methods suitable for the actual drug molecular association networks is indispensable for the discovery of potential drug expression.

Recently, graph neural networks have received much attention in graph-structured data. It can well solve the problem of data processing in non-Euclidean space, where some related studies have been applied in biological data [27–37]. Huang et al. [38] proposed that for predicting miRNA-disease associations with the GCMDR model, the features of each node in the graph can be learned from the graph convolutional network. Yu et al. [39] applied the graph convolutional network to the heterogeneous network of drugs and diseases and applied what they learned about the embeddings to the prediction of drug-diseases. Inspired by the recent success of the graph-based neural network approach [40–46], we propose a multi-graph deep learning method to predict undiscovered drug-disease interactions based on graph attention network (GAT) and graph embedding algorithm.

In this paper, graph representation learning is applied to explore novel drug-disease associations, and our method can be divided into three stages. Firstly, the characteristics of drugs and diseases are calculated. Specifically, the drug-drug similarity network and disease-disease similarity network are constructed and calculated, and then the input characteristics of Graph Attention Network are obtained by using the autoencoder dimensionality reduction. Secondly, the characteristics of graph representation learning were obtained. Graph Attention Network is utilized to learn the local structure information, and a graph embedding algorithm is exercised to learn the global structure information. Finally, machine learning classifiers are used to predict potential drug-disease associations. The experimental results indicate that our method has excellent predictive capability under ten-fold cross-validation. Meanwhile, our model has high superiority compared with the latest methods.

2   Materials and Methods

2.1   Experimental Dataset

In this study, the gold standard dataset is obtained from Luo et al., which included 663 drugs and 409 diseases, and 2532 drug-disease interactions. In addition, drug information is extracted from the DrugBank database [47] and disease information is obtained from the OMIM database [48]. Specifically, the drug-drug similarity network and disease-disease similarity network are constructed by the calculation method of Luo et al. [6].

2.2   The Input Feature Extraction of Graph Attention Network

For the processing of high-dimensional data, there are many mainstream methods, including PCA (Principal Component Analysis), t-SNE (t-distributed stochastic neighbor embedding), SVD (Singular Value Decomposition) and Autoencoder [49, 50]. In the nonlinear structure data, Autoencoder has a great performance. Therefore, the Autoencoder is used in this dataset. It is mainly divided into two steps, encoding and decoding, respectively. The function of the Autoencoder is to compress the input data into the hidden layer and then restore the data at the output. The relationship between the output layer and the input layer of the self-coding network is as follows:

$$\hat{x}_i \approx x_i \tag{1}$$

where the output of neurons is only between 0 and 1, and the input needs to be averaged normalized.

Autoencoder can be thought of as compressing data and then recovering it when needed with as little loss as possible. Firstly, the Autoencoder is to restore the compressed data with the following parameters:

$$h_{W,b} \approx X \tag{2}$$

Secondly, the loss should be minimized to restore the data, and the objective function is defined as:

$$J(W, b) = \frac{1}{m} \sum_{i=1}^{m} \left(\hat{X} - X \right)^2 \tag{3}$$

Finally, the hidden layer of the trained Autoencoder is extracted as the input feature of GAT.

2.3 Graph Attention Network

Graph Attention Network (GAT) [51] is an algorithm that can learn information about the neighbors of nodes. Let us assume that we are given a graph $G(N, H)$ contains N nodes, the eigenvector of each node is h_i, and the dimension is F:

$$H = [h_1, h_2, h_3, \cdots, h_N], h_i \in \mathfrak{R}^F \tag{4}$$

A linear transformation is carried out on the node's eigenvector H to obtain a new eigenvector h_i, whose dimension is F', as shown below:

$$h_i' = W h_i \quad W \in \mathfrak{R}^{F' \times F} \tag{5}$$

$$H' = \left[h_1', h_2', h_3', \cdots, h_N' \right] h_i' \in \mathfrak{R}^{F'} \tag{6}$$

where W is the matrix of linear transformation. If node j is a neighbor of node i, the Attention mechanism can be used to calculate the importance of node j to node i, i.e., the Attention Score:

$$e_{ij} = Attention(W h_i, W h_j) \tag{7}$$

$$\alpha_{ij} = \text{softmax}_j(e_{ij}) = \frac{\exp(e_{ij})}{\sum_{k \in N_i} \exp(e_{ik})} \tag{8}$$

Specifically, the Attention approach is to join the eigenvectors h_i' and h_j' of nodes i and j, and then calculate the inner product with a vector an of $2F'$ dimension. The activation function takes LeakyRelu with the following formula:

$$\alpha_{ij} = \frac{\exp(\text{LeakyReLU}(a^T[W h_i || W h_j]))}{\sum_{k \in N_i} \exp(\text{LeakyReLU}(a^T[W h_i || W h_j]))} \tag{9}$$

where $||$ is represented as splicing. Ultimately, the eigenvector of node i after Attention is as follows:

$$h_i' = \sigma \left(\sum_{j \in N_i} \alpha_{ij} W h_j \right) \tag{10}$$

2.4 Graph Embedding Algorithm

Graph Embedding is a process to transform complex graph data into low-dimensional dense vectors [41]. In general, the input is the topology of the graph and the output is the spatial representation of the nodes. In this section, node2vec [52] is used to calculate the global structure information of each node in the graph. Let $f(u)$ be the mapping function that maps vertex u to the embedding vector. For each vertex u in the graph, $N_S(u)$ is defined as the set of adjacent vertices of vertex u by sampling strategy S. The optimization objective function of node2vec is:

$$\max_f \sum_{u \in V} logPr(N_s(u)|f(u)) \tag{11}$$

in which. $f(u)$ is represented as the current node, and $N_s(u)$ is denoted as the neighbor node.

In order to find the optimal solution, two conditions are assumed, the conditional independence assumption and the eigenspace symmetry assumption. In the conditional independence hypothesis, the probability of the occurrence of a given vertex's nearest neighbor vertices is independent of the rest of the vertices in the nearest neighbor set.

$$Pr(N_s(u)|f(u)) = \prod_{n_i \in N_s(u)} Pr(n_i|f(u)) \tag{12}$$

In the eigenspace symmetry hypothesis, a vertex is shared with the embedding when it is the source vertex and when it is the neighbor vertex. Hence, the conditional probability formula can be expressed as:

$$Pr(n_i|f(u)) = \frac{\exp f(n_i) \cdot f(u)}{\sum_{v \in V} \exp f(v) \cdot f(u)} \tag{13}$$

Consequently, the final objective function is expressed as:

$$\sum_{u \in V} logPr(N_s(u)|f(u)) \tag{14}$$

$$= \sum_{u \in V} \log \prod_{n_i \in N_x(u)} Pr(n_i|f(u) \tag{15}$$

$$= \sum_{u \in V} \sum_{n_i \in N_s(u)} logPr(n_i|f(u)) \tag{16}$$

$$= \sum_{u \in V} \sum_{n_i \in N_s(u)} \log \frac{\exp(f(n_i) \cdot f(u))}{\sum_{u \in V} \exp(f(v) \cdot f(u))} \tag{17}$$

$$= \max_f \sum_{u \in V} \left[-\log Z_u + \sum_{n_i \in N_s(u)} f(n_i) \cdot f(u) \right] \tag{18}$$

The sampling strategy of node2vec is to use a biased random walk to get the nearest neighbor sequence of vertices. Given the current vertex v, the probability of accessing the next vertex x is:

$$P(c_i = x|c_{i-1} = v) = \begin{cases} \frac{\pi_{vx}}{Z} & \text{if } (v, x) \in E \\ 0 & \text{otherwise} \end{cases} \tag{19}$$

where π_{vx} is the unnormalized transition probability between vertices v and x, and Z is the normalized constant. Two super parameters p and q are introduced to control the random walk strategy. Suppose the current random walk goes through the edge (t, v) to vertex v. Let $\pi_{vx} = \alpha_{pq}(t, x) \cdot w_{vx}$, w_{vx} is the weight of the edge between vertex v and x.

$$\alpha_{pq}(t, x) = \begin{cases} \frac{1}{p} & \text{if } d_{tx} = 0 \\ 1 & \text{if } d_{tx} = 1 \\ \frac{1}{q} & \text{if } d_{tx} = 2 \end{cases} \tag{20}$$

where d_{tx} is the shortest distance between vertex t and vertex x.

3 Results and Discussion

3.1 The Evaluation Performance of the Proposed Model

For binary classification, ROC (Receiver Operating Characteristic) curve, whose abscissa is False Positive Rate (FPR) and the ordinate is True Positive Rate (TPR), can be seen directly from the changes of the test set of the model. AUC is represented as the area covered by the ROC curve. The precision-recall (PR) curve reflects whether the number of positive and negative samples is balanced. The higher the AUC value, the better the classifier classification effect. The true-positive rate (TPR) is calculated as follows:

$$TPR = TP/(TP + FN) \tag{21}$$

where TP (True Positive) is the correctly predicted positive sample, and FN (False Negative) is the incorrectly predicted positive sample. The false-positive rate (FPR) is calculated as follows:

$$FPR = FP/(FP + TN) \tag{22}$$

where TN (True Negative) is the correctly predicted negative sample, and FP (False Positive) is the incorrectly predicted negative sample.

Moreover, cross-validation is employed to evaluate the performance indicators of our model. The whole data set is divided into two parts, one for training and the other for validation. In this experiment, ten-fold cross-validation is exploited, the GDBT (Gradient Boosting Decision Tree) classifier is exploited to implement the presentation of the proposed features, as shown in Fig. 1.

The proposed model achieves a higher AUC of 96.25% under ten-fold cross-validation. Meanwhile, each fold has outstanding performance and has stability and reliability. In our model, positive and negative samples are applied for training and testing. Positive samples are denoted as known drug-disease associations, while negative samples are obtained according to unsupervised clustering algorithm (k-means). Specifically, unsupervised learning is conducted on both known and unknown relationships in the association matrix of drugs and diseases. Clusters are generated through clustering, and then unknown relationship pairs are randomly selected for each cluster [53, 54]. Conclusively, the negative samples are got for binary training need. There may be too many

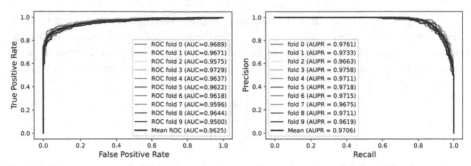

Fig. 1. The ROC and PR curves of the proposed model under ten-fold cross-validation.

potential associations in the previous random sampling, and these associations are called false-negative samples, but this practice can greatly reduce the potential associations and select more real negative samples. Experiments have confirmed the effectiveness of our model.

3.2   The Proposed Model Compares with Other Methods

To reflect the advantages of the proposed method, we compare five latest methods, while BNNR [55], DRRS [6], MBiRW [56], DrugNet [57], HGBI [58], respectively, as shown in Table 1. The AUC value is compared with other methods. Under the benchmark data set, the AUC of our model is significantly higher than that of other advanced methods, among which, our method is 0.0145 higher than the best method and 0.0155, 0.0295, 0.0595, and 0.1045 higher than DRRS, MBiRW, DrugNet, and HGBI, respectively. This fully shows that our model has an excellent performance in predicting the relationships between drugs and diseases, and it proved that our feature extraction method can discover more hidden features of drugs and diseases.

Table 1. The AUC value is compared with other methods

Models	AUCs
The proposed model	0.9625
BNNR	0.948
DRRS	0.947
MBiRW	0.933
DrugNet	0.903
HGBI	0.858

4   Conclusions

Computational drug repositioning plays a fundamental role in discovering the underlying mechanisms and functions of drugs. In this paper, we established a multi-graph deep learning model to explore potential drug-disease interactions. In evaluation, experiments demonstrate our model has a remarkable performance, where the fusion of multiple graph representation learning enhances the characteristics of drugs and diseases and effectively explores the deep characteristics of the drug-disease networks. Furthermore, the selection of negative samples is particularly important for the performance of the model, we can get excellent negative samples by the clustering algorithm, so as to improve the prediction ability of the proposed model. Therefore, we believe that the proposed model can provide a powerful aid for biomedical experiments.

Acknowledgement. This work is supported in part by the major science and technology projects in Xinjiang Uygur Autonomous Region, under Grant 2020A03004–4, The authors would like to thank all the guest editors and anonymous reviewers for their constructive advices.

References

1. Jarada, T.N., Rokne, J.G., Alhajj, R.: A review of computational drug repositioning: strategies, approaches, opportunities, challenges, and directions. J. Cheminf. **12**(1), 1–23 (2020). https://doi.org/10.1186/s13321-020-00450-7
2. Paul, S.M., et al.: How to improve R&D productivity: the pharmaceutical industry's grand challenge. Nat. Rev. Drug Disc. **9**, 203–214 (2010)
3. Adams, C.P., Brantner, V.V.: Estimating the cost of new drug development: is it really $802 million? Health Aff. **25**, 420–428 (2006)
4. DiMasi, J.A., Hansen, R.W., Grabowski, H.G.: The price of innovation: new estimates of drug development costs. J. Health Econ. **22**, 151–185 (2003)
5. Luo, H., Li, M., Yang, M., Wu, F.-X., Li, Y., Wang, J.: Biomedical data and computational models for drug repositioning: a comprehensive review. Brief. Bioinf. **22**, 1604 (2019)
6. Luo, H., Li, M., Wang, S., Liu, Q., Li, Y., Wang, J.: Computational drug repositioning using low-rank matrix approximation and randomized algorithms. Bioinformatics **34**, 1904–1912 (2018)
7. Chen, Z.-H., You, Z.-H., Guo, Z.-H., Yi, H.-C., Luo, G.-X., Wang, Y.-B.: Prediction of drug-target interactions from multi-molecular network based on deep walk embedding model. Front. Bioeng. Biotechnol. **8**, 338 (2020)
8. Chen, Z.-H., You, Z.-H., Li, L.-P., Wang, Y.-B., Qiu, Y., Hu, P.-W.: Identification of self-interacting proteins by integrating random projection classifier and finite impulse response filter. BMC Genomics **20**, 1–10 (2019)
9. Ji, B.-Y., You, Z.-H., Jiang, H.-J., Guo, Z.-H., Zheng, K.: Prediction of drug-target interactions from multi-molecular network based on LINE network representation method. J. Transl. Med. **18**, 1–11 (2020)
10. Jiang, H.-J., Huang, Y.-A., You, Z.-H.: SAEROF: an ensemble approach for large-scale drug-disease association prediction by incorporating rotation forest and sparse autoencoder deep neural network. Sci. Rep. **10**, 1–11 (2020)
11. Jiang, H.-J., Huang, Y.-A., You, Z.-H.: Predicting drug-disease associations via using gaussian interaction profile and kernel-based autoencoder. BioMed Res. Int. **2019**, 1–11 (2019)
12. Jiang, H.-J., You, Z.-H., Huang, Y.-A.: Predicting drug– disease associations via sigmoid kernel-based convolutional neural networks. J. Transl. Med. **17**, 382 (2019)
13. Hu, L., Wang, X., Huang, Y.-A., Hu, P., You, Z.-H.: A survey on computational models for predicting protein–protein interactions. Brief. Bioinf. (2021)

14. Hu, L., Pan, X., Yan, H., Hu, P., He, T.: Exploiting higher-order patterns for community detection in attributed graphs. Integr. Comput.-Aided Eng. **28**, 1–12 (2020)
15. Hu, L., Yang, S.: A fast algorithm to identify coevolutionary patterns from protein sequences based on tree-based data structure. In: 2019 IEEE International Conference on Systems, Man and Cybernetics (SMC), pp. 2273–2278. IEEE (2019)
16. Zhao, B.-W., Zhang, P., You, Z.-H., Zhou, J.-R., Li, X.: Predicting LncRNA-miRNA interactions via network embedding with integrated structure and attribute information. In: Huang, D.-S., Jo, K.-H. (eds.) ICIC 2020. LNCS, vol. 12464, pp. 493–501. Springer, Cham (2020). https://doi.org/10.1007/978-3-030-60802-6_43
17. Jiang, H.-J., You, Z.-H., Hu, L., Guo, Z.-H., Ji, B.-Y., Wong, L.: A highly efficient biomolecular network representation model for predicting drug-disease associations. In: Huang, D.-S., Premaratne, P. (eds.) ICIC 2020. LNCS (LNAI), vol. 12465, pp. 271–279. Springer, Cham (2020). https://doi.org/10.1007/978-3-030-60796-8_23
18. Wang, L., You, Z.-H., Li, L.-P., Yan, X., Zhang, W.: Incorporating chemical sub-structures and protein evolutionary information for inferring drug-target interactions. Sci. Rep. **10**, 1–11 (2020)
19. Wang, L., You, Z.-H., Chen, X., Yan, X., Liu, G., Zhang, W.: Rfdt: a rotation forest-based predictor for predicting drug-target interactions using drug structure and protein sequence information. Curr. Protein Pept. Sci. **19**, 445–454 (2018)
20. Wang, L., et al.: A computational-based method for predicting drug–target interactions by using stacked autoencoder deep neural network. J. Comput. Biol. **25**, 361–373 (2018)
21. Zhang, P., Zhao, B.-W., Wong, L., You, Z.-H., Guo, Z.-H., Yi, H.-C.: A novel computational method for predicting LncRNA-disease associations from heterogeneous information network with SDNE embedding model. In: Huang, D.-S., Jo, K.-H. (eds.) ICIC 2020. LNCS, vol. 12464, pp. 505–513. Springer, Cham (2020). https://doi.org/10.1007/978-3-030-60802-6_44
22. Gottlieb, A., Stein, G.Y., Ruppin, E., Sharan, R.: PREDICT: a method for inferring novel drug indications with application to personalized medicine. Mol. Syst. Biol. **7**, 496 (2011)
23. Wang, Y., Chen, S., Deng, N., Wang, Y.: Drug repositioning by kernel-based integration of molecular structure, molecular activity, and phenotype data. PloS one **8**, e78518 (2013)
24. Dai, W., et al.: Matrix factorization-based prediction of novel drug indications by integrating genomic space. Comput. Math. Methods Med. **2015**, 1–9 (2015)
25. Yang, J., Li, Z., Fan, X., Cheng, Y.: Drug–disease association and drug-repositioning predictions in complex diseases using causal inference–probabilistic matrix factorization. J. Chem. Inf. Model. **54**, 2562–2569 (2014)
26. Zeng, X., Zhu, S., Liu, X., Zhou, Y., Nussinov, R., Cheng, F.: deepDR: a network-based deep learning approach to in silico drug repositioning. Bioinformatics **35**, 5191–5198 (2019)
27. Wang, L., You, Z.-H., Li, Y.-M., Zheng, K., Huang, Y.-A.: GCNCDA: a new method for predicting circRNA-disease associations based on Graph Convolutional Network Algorithm. PLOS Comput. Biol. **16**, e1007568 (2020)
28. Li, J., Zhang, S., Liu, T., Ning, C., Zhang, Z., Zhou, W.: Neural inductive matrix completion with graph convolutional networks for miRNA-disease association prediction. Bioinformatics **36**, 2538–2546 (2020)
29. Jiang, M., et al.: Drug–target affinity prediction using graph neural network and contact maps. RSC Adv. **10**, 20701–20712 (2020)
30. Wang, B., Lyu, X., Qu, J., Sun, H., Pan, Z., Tang, Z.: GNDD: a graph neural network-based method for drug-disease association prediction. In: 2019 IEEE International Conference on Bioinformatics and Biomedicine (BIBM), pp. 1253–1255. IEEE (2019)
31. Sun, M., Zhao, S., Gilvary, C., Elemento, O., Zhou, J., Wang, F.: Graph convolutional networks for computational drug development and discovery. Brief. Bioinf. **21**, 919–935 (2020)
32. Zhao, T., Hu, Y., Valsdottir, L.R., Zang, T., Peng, J.: Identifying drug–target interactions based on graph convolutional network and deep neural network. Briefings in Bioinformatics (2020)

33. Torng, W., Altman, R.B.: Graph convolutional neural networks for predicting drug-target interactions. J. Chem. Inf. Model. **59**, 4131–4149 (2019)
34. Hu, L., Chan, K.C., Yuan, X., Xiong, S.: A variational Bayesian framework for cluster analysis in a complex network. IEEE Trans. Knowl. Data Eng. **32**, 2115–2128 (2019)
35. Guo, Z.-H., You, Z.-H., Wang, Y.-B., Huang, D.-S., Yi, H.-C., Chen, Z.-H.: Bioentity2vec: attribute-and behavior-driven representation for predicting multi-type relationships between bioentities. GigaScience **9**, giaa032 (2020)
36. Yi, H.-C., You, Z.-H., Huang, D.-S., Guo, Z.-H., Chan, K.C., Li, Y.: Learning representations to predict intermolecular interactions on large-scale heterogeneous molecular association network. Iscience **23**, 101261 (2020)
37. Wong, L., You, Z.-H., Guo, Z.-H., Yi, H.-C., Chen, Z.-H., Cao, M.-Y.: MIPDH: a novel computational model for predicting microRNA–mRNA interactions by DeepWalk on a heterogeneous network. ACS Omega **5**, 17022–17032 (2020)
38. Huang, Y.-A., Hu, P., Chan, K.C., You, Z.-H.: Graph convolution for predicting associations between miRNA and drug resistance. Bioinformatics **36**, 851–858 (2020)
39. Yu, Z., Huang, F., Zhao, X., Xiao, W., Zhang, W.: Predicting drug–disease associations through layer attention graph convolutional network. Brief. Bioinf. (2020)
40. Guo, Z.-H., Yi, H.-C., You, Z.-H.: Construction and comprehensive analysis of a molecular association network via lncRNA–miRNA–disease–drug–protein graph. Cells **8**, 866 (2019)
41. Yue, X., et al.: Graph embedding on biomedical networks: methods, applications and evaluations. Bioinformatics **36**, 1241–1251 (2020)
42. Guo, Z.-H., You, Z.-H., Huang, D.-S., Yi, H.-C., Chen, Z.-H., Wang, Y.-B.: A learning based framework for diverse biomolecule relationship prediction in molecular association network. Commun. Biol. **3**, 1–9 (2020)
43. Zhao, B.-W., et al.: A novel method to predict drug-target interactions based on large-scale graph representation learning. Cancers **13**, 2111 (2021)
44. Guo, Z.-H., et al.: MeSHHeading2vec: a new method for representing MeSH headings as vectors based on graph embedding algorithm. Brief. Bioinform. **22**, 2085–2095 (2021)
45. Guo, Z.-H., You, Z.-H., Yi, H.-C.: Integrative construction and analysis of molecular association network in human cells by fusing node attribute and behavior information. Molec. Therapy-Nucleic Acids **19**, 498–506 (2020)
46. Zhao, B.-W., You, Z.-H., Wong, L., Zhang, P., Li, H.-Y., Wang, L.: MGRL: predicting drug-disease associations based on multi-graph representation learning. Front. Genet. **12**, 491 (2021)
47. Wishart, D.S., et al.: DrugBank 5.0: a major update to the DrugBank database for 2018. Nucl. Acids Res. **46**, D1074-D1082 (2017)
48. Hamosh, A., Scott, A.F., Amberger, J., Bocchini, C., Valle, D., McKusick, V.A.: Online mendelian inheritance in man (OMIM), a knowledgebase of human genes and genetic disorders. Nucl. Acids Res. **30**, 52–55 (2002)
49. Van Der Maaten, L., Postma, E., Van den Herik, J.: Dimensionality reduction: a comparative. J Mach. Learn. Res. **10**, 13 (2009)
50. Wang, Y., Yao, H., Zhao, S.: Auto-encoder based dimensionality reduction. Neurocomputing **184**, 232–242 (2016)
51. Veličković, P., Cucurull, G., Casanova, A., Romero, A., Lio, P., Bengio, Y.: Graph attention networks (2017). arXiv preprint arXiv:1710.10903
52. Grover, A., Leskovec, J.: node2vec: scalable feature learning for networks. In: Proceedings of the 22nd ACM SIGKDD International Conference on Knowledge Discovery and Data Mining, pp. 855–864 (2016)
53. Manoochehri, H.E., Nourani, M.: Drug-target interaction prediction using semi-bipartite graph model and deep learning. BMC Bioinf. **21**, 1–16 (2020)

54. Zhang, Y., Qiao, S., Lu, R., Han, N., Liu, D., Zhou, J.: How to balance the bioinformatics data: pseudo-negative sampling. BMC Bioinf. **20**, 1–13 (2019)
55. Yang, M., Luo, H., Li, Y., Wang, J.: Drug repositioning based on bounded nuclear norm regularization. Bioinformatics **35**, i455–i463 (2019)
56. Luo, H., et al.: Drug repositioning based on comprehensive similarity measures and bi-random walk algorithm. Bioinformatics **32**, 2664–2671 (2016)
57. Martinez, V., Navarro, C., Cano, C., Fajardo, W., Blanco, A.: DrugNet: network-based drug–disease prioritization by integrating heterogeneous data. Artif. Intell. Med. **63**, 41–49 (2015)
58. Wang, W., Yang, S., Li, J.: Drug target predictions based on heterogeneous graph inference. In: Biocomputing 2013, pp. 53–64. World Scientific (2013)

Predicting Drug-Disease Associations Based on Network Consistency Projection

Qiang Zhang[1,2], Zonglan Zuo[1], Rui Yan[2], Chunhou Zheng[1(✉)], and Fa Zhang[2(✉)]

[1] College of Computer Science and Technology, Anhui University, Hefei, China
[2] High Performance Computer Research Center, Institute of Computing Technology, Chinese Academy of Sciences, Beijing, China
zhangfa@ict.ac.cn

Abstract. With the increasing cost of traditional drug discovery, drug repositioning methods at low cost have attracting increasing attention. The generation of large amounts of biomedical data also provides unprecedented opportunities for drug repositioning research. However, how to effectively integrate different types of data is still a challenge for drug repositioning. In this paper, we propose a computational method using **N**etwork **C**onsistency **P**rojection for **D**rug-**D**isease **A**ssociation (NCPDDA) prediction. First of all, our method proposes a new method for calculating one type of disease similarity. Moreover, since effective integration of data from multiple sources can improve prediction performance, the NCPDDA integrates multiple kinds of similarities. Then, considering that noise may affect the prediction performance of the model, the NCPDDA uses the similarity network fusion method to reduce the impact of noise. Finally, the network consistency projection is used to predict potential drug-disease associations. NCPDDA is compared with several classical drug repositioning methods, and the experimental results show that NCPDDA is superior to these methods. Moreover, the study of several representative drugs proves the practicality of NCPDDA in practical application.

Keywords: Drug repositioning · Drug-disease association · Network consistency projection · Similarity network fusion

1 Introduction

In the traditional drug development, the successful development of a completely new drug is behind the high investment of more than 800 million dollars and more than a decade of continuous efforts of researchers [1]. Even so, usually only one in ten drugs are approved by the FDA (Food and Drug Administration) for actual treatment each year [2]. Given these challenges, drug repositioning, which is the discovery of new indications for existing drugs, has attracted increasing attention. Compared with traditional drug development strategies, the computational drug repositioning methods have advantages in terms of time, cost, and risk reduction because the repositioned drug has already passed some preclinical trials. There are many typical examples of drug repositioning:

© Springer Nature Switzerland AG 2021
D.-S. Huang et al. (Eds.): ICIC 2021, LNAI 12838, pp. 591–602, 2021.
https://doi.org/10.1007/978-3-030-84532-2_53

for example, the sildenafil, developed for individuals with heart diseases, repositioned for erectile dysfunction [3]. Besides, the aspirin, developed for mild or moderate pain and repositioned for inhibit thrombosis. These successful drug repositioning cases have further promoted the development of drug repositioning.

Recently, many methods for computational drug repositioning have been proposed, including machine learning-based methods and network-based methods. By integrating drug similarities and disease similarities, Gottlieb et al. proposed a machine learning model that uses logistic regression classifiers to infer drug repositioning [4]. Liang et al. integrated multiple types of similarities and proposed Laplacian regularized sparse subspace learning (LRSSL) method to predict new indications for drugs [5]. Based on the drug similarity and disease similarity, Yang et al. proposed a bounded nuclear norm regularization (BNNR) method that is robust to the noise in the data and makes the prediction scores of all drug-disease associations within the range of (0, 1) [6]. Adding target information into the BNNR model leads to a significant increase in the calculation cost of BNNR. Yang et al. further proposed a method based on overlap matrix completion [7]. Besides, based on known drug-disease associations, disease similarity and five types of drug similarities, Zhang et al. proposed a similarity constrained matrix factorization method to predict potential drug-disease associations [8]. Moreover, with the advent of the era of big data and the progress of science and technology, a large number of biological and clinical data that can be processed by computer technology have been produced. Because the network has ability to integrate data from multiple sources, network-based approaches are widely used in drug repositioning. Wang et al. proposed a three-layer heterogeneous network model using an iterative algorithm to achieve drug repositioning [9]. Martínez et al. proposed a network-based prioritization approach to infer new relationships between drugs and diseases [10]. Luo et al. proposed a drug repositioning method based on comprehensive similarity measures and Bi-Random walk algorithm [11]. Even though the above methods have accelerated the speed of drug repositioning, there are still some limitations. Some approaches are limited to a single type of data, such as considering only phenotype similarity of diseases and chemical structure similarity of drugs. Since different types of data reflect different aspects of drugs or diseases, the mechanism of action of drugs or diseases can be understood more clearly by integrating multi-source data. In addition, drug or disease data may contain noise, which can reduce the accuracy of prediction.

In this work, we propose a method using network consistency projection for drug-disease association (NCPDDA) prediction. Firstly, a method for calculating disease similarity based on drug characteristics is proposed. Secondly, the NCPDDA uses the similarity network fusion method to integrate four kinds of drug similarities and three kinds of disease similarities respectively, because the similarity network fusion method can effectively fuse different types of data and reduce noise. Finally, based on drug-disease association network and the integrated drug similarity network and disease similarity network, the network consistency projection is used to obtain the prediction scores of all drug-disease associations. The overall framework of the NCPDDA method is depicted in Fig. 1. The experimental results show that our method has better prediction performance than other three classical methods. In the case studies section, the new indications for

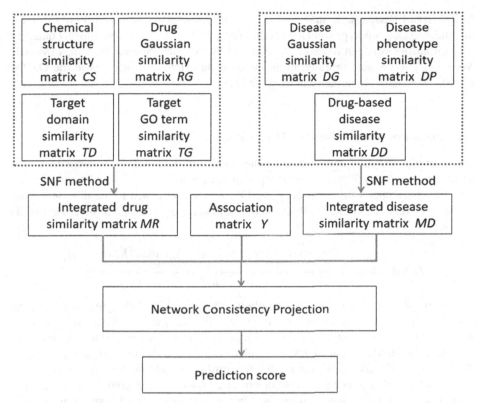

Fig. 1. The overall framework of the NCPDDA method.

four drugs are validated, and the experimental results further confirms the practicality of our method.

2 Materials and Methods

2.1 Dataset

Drug-disease Associations. The LRSSL dataset including 763 drugs, 681 diseases and 3,051 known drug-disease associations is used by our method. A binary matrix $Y \in R^{m \times n}$ is used to represent drug-disease associations, where m and n are the number of drugs and diseases, respectively. If the drug r_i is associated with the disease d_j, then $Y(i, j) = 1$, otherwise it is 0.

Similarities of Drugs. The drug data includes drug chemical structure, drug target proteins domain and gene ontology (GO) term of drug targets. Based on the chemical fingerprints extracted from PubChem database [12], the Jaccard coefficient is used to calculate similarity, and the drug chemical structure similarity matrix $CS \in R^{m \times m}$ is obtained. Similarly, based on the drug target domain and drug target gene ontology term extracted from InterPro database [13] and UniProt database [14], the drug target domain similarity matrix TD and the drug target GO term similarity matrix TG are calculated.

Similarity of Diseases. MimMiner [15] is used to calculate the similarity of diseases, and the disease phenotype similarity matrix $DP \in R^{n \times n}$ is obtained. MimMiner quantify the similarities between diseases according to the Medical Subject Headings (MeSH) Vocabulary terms that appeared in the medical descriptors of diseases in the OMIM (Online Mendelian Inheritance in Man) database.

2.2 Disease Similarity Based on Drug Characteristics

Since similar diseases are often associated with similar drugs, we calculate a type of disease similarity based on three types of drug similarities. According to [16 and 17], we firstly obtain the drug sets r_a and r_b, which are related to the disease d_a and d_b, respectively. Then, the similarity between disease d_a and d_b can be computed as follows:

$$DD(d_a, d_b) = \frac{\sum_{i=1}^{u} \max_{1 \leq j \leq v} \left(RS\left(r_{ai}, r_{bj}\right)\right) + \sum_{j=1}^{v} \max_{1 \leq i \leq u} \left(RS\left(r_{bj}, r_{ai}\right)\right)}{u + v} \quad (1)$$

Where $RS(r_{ai}, r_{bj})$ is the drug similarity of r_{ai} and r_{bj} belonging to r_a and r_b, respectively; u and v are the number of drugs included by r_a and r_b. We use the similarity network fusion (SNF) method [18] to integrate the above three drug similarity matrices into the drug similarity matrix RS to calculate the disease similarity matrix DD, $DD \in R^{n \times n}$. The flow chart for calculating disease similarity based on drug characteristics is shown in Fig. 2. It is important to note that in the cross-validation, some diseases may not have associated drugs, making it impossible to calculate the disease similarity matrix. Therefore, we initialize $Y' = Y$, and update the matrix Y' as follows:

$$Y'(i) = \frac{1}{\sum_{d_j \in N_{d_i}} DP(i,j)} \sum_{d_j \in N_{d_i}} DP(i,j) Y(j) \quad (2)$$

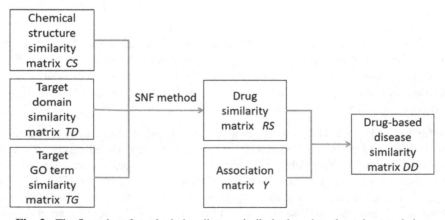

Fig. 2. The flow chart for calculating disease similarity based on drug characteristics.

Where i represents the index of disease d_i, which has no associated drug in Y'; N_{d_i} denotes the set of k neighbor nodes of d_i; $Y'(i)$ and $Y(j)$ represent the i-th column of Y' and the j-th column of Y, respectively; $DP(i, j)$ denotes the disease phenotype similarity between disease d_i and disease d_j. Then, the similarity matrix DD is recalculated based on the updated matrix Y'.

2.3 Gaussian Similarity of Drugs and Diseases

Since the more the number of common diseases (or drugs), the more similar the drugs (or diseases), the Gaussian similarity of drugs and diseases can be calculated according to the association matrix Y. Firstly, i-th row of the association matrix Y is used to represent the association profile of drug r_i. The association profile is a binary vector, and a value in the association profile indicates whether the drug (or disease) is association with a certain disease (or drug). Similarly, we can obtain association profile of drug r_j. Then, the Gaussian similarity between drug r_i and drug r_j can be calculated as follows:

$$RG(r_i, r_j) = exp\left(-r_r \|Y(i, :) - Y(j, :)\|^2\right) \tag{3}$$

$$r_r = 1 / \left(\frac{1}{m} \sum\nolimits_{i=1}^{m} \|Y(i, :)\|^2\right) \tag{4}$$

Where r_r is responsible for controlling the bandwidth of Gaussian kernel and is the ratio of the number of drugs to the average number of diseases associated with each drug.

Similarly, the disease Gaussian similarity can be calculated as follows:

$$DG(d_i, d_j) = exp\left(-r_d \|Y(:, i) - Y(:, j)\|^2\right) \tag{5}$$

$$r_d = 1 / \left(\frac{1}{n} \sum\nolimits_{i=1}^{n} \|Y(:, i)\|^2\right) \tag{6}$$

Where r_d is computed similarly to r_r. Similar to the similarity matrix DD, the similarity matrix RG and DG need to be recalculated in the cross-validation.

2.4 Integrated Similarity for Drugs and Diseases

In this section, the similarity matrices of drugs and diseases are respectively integrated to implement the network consistency projection algorithm. By using the similarity network fusion (SNF) method [18], the above four drug similarity matrices are integrated into the drug similarity matrix MR, and the above three disease similarity matrices are integrated into the disease similarity matrix MD. SNF, which updates the similarity network corresponding to each similarity matrix in each iteration to make it closer to other networks, is a nonlinear method based on message passing theory. In the above way, SNF can capture common and complementary information between different networks and reduce noise.

Taking the integration of three disease similarity networks as an example, the main process of similarity network fusion is introduced. Firstly, the matrices $W^{(1)}$, $W^{(2)}$ and $W^{(3)}$ are used to represent three different disease similarity networks, and the correspondingly state matrices $P^{(1)}$, $P^{(2)}$ and $P^{(3)}$ are obtained as follows:

$$P(i,j) = \begin{cases} \frac{W(i,j)}{2\sum_{k \neq i} W(i,k)}, j \neq i \\ 1/2, j = i \end{cases} \tag{7}$$

Where $W(i, j)$ denotes the similarity of node i and node j.

Secondly, the correspondingly kernel matrices $S^{(1)}$, $S^{(2)}$ and $S^{(3)}$ are calculated by using the matrices $W^{(1)}$, $W^{(2)}$, and $W^{(3)}$ as follows:

$$S(i,j) = \begin{cases} \frac{W(i,j)}{\sum_{k \in N_i} W(i,k)}, j \in N_i \\ 0, otherwise \end{cases} \tag{8}$$

Where N_i represents the set of K (empirically set to 20) neighbors of node i.

Then, the key step of the similarity network fusion approach is to iteratively update the state matrices, and the updating process is represented as follows:

$$P_{t+1}^{(1)} = S^{(1)} \times \left(\frac{P_t^{(2)} + P_t^{(3)}}{2} \right) \times \left(S^{(1)} \right)^T \tag{9}$$

$$P_{t+1}^{(2)} = S^{(2)} \times \left(\frac{P_t^{(1)} + P_t^{(3)}}{2} \right) \times \left(S^{(2)} \right)^T \tag{10}$$

$$P_{t+1}^{(3)} = S^{(3)} \times \left(\frac{P_t^{(1)} + P_t^{(2)}}{2} \right) \times \left(S^{(3)} \right)^T \tag{11}$$

Where $P_{t=0}^{(1)} = P^{(1)}, P_{t=0}^{(2)} = P^{(2)}$ and $P_{t=0}^{(3)} = P^{(3)}$. After each iteration, we normalize the state matrices. After t (empirically set to 20) iterations and updates, the integrated similarity matrix P is finally obtained by taking the mean of the state matrices as follows:

$$P = \frac{P_t^{(1)} + P_t^{(2)} + P_t^{(3)}}{3} \tag{12}$$

2.5 Network Consistency Projection Method

Through the above section, the integrated drug similarity matrix MR and disease similarity matrix MD are obtained. In this section, MR and MD are also used to represent the integrated drug similarity network and disease similarity network, respectively. Moreover, the association matrix Y is also regarded as drug-disease association network. We perform the network consistency projection method on the integrated drug similarity network and the disease similarity network respectively, and obtain two projection scores, namely the drug space projection score and the disease space projection score.

The drug space projection score and the disease space projection score are combined and normalized to obtain the final prediction score.

The projection of the drug similarity network on the drug-disease association network is the drug space projection, which can be calculated as follows:

$$RSP(i,j) = \frac{MR(i,:) \times Y(:,j)}{|Y(:,j)|} \qquad (13)$$

Where $MR(i,:)$ is the i-th row of the matrix MR, representing the similarities between drug r_i and all drugs; $Y(:,j)$ is the the association profile of disease d_j; $|Y(:,j)|$ represents the length of the association profile $Y(:,j)$.

Similarly, the disease space projection can be computed as follows:

$$DSP(i,j) = \frac{Y(i,:) \times MD(:,j)}{|Y(i,:)|} \qquad (14)$$

Where $MD(:,j)$ represents the similarities between disease d_j and all diseases.

The final prediction score of drug r_i and disease d_j can be calculated as follows:

$$NCP(i,j) = \frac{RSP(i,j) + DSP(i,j)}{|MR(i,:)| + |MD(:,j)|} \qquad (15)$$

3 Experiments

3.1 Evaluation Metrics

To evaluate the ability of our method to predict potential drug-disease associations, a fivefold cross-validation is performed. All known drug-disease associations in the LRSSL data set are randomly divided into 5 roughly equal subsets, each of which is used as the test set in turn, and the remaining subsets are used as the training set. After the performing prediction, the prediction scores of all drug-disease associations are ranked in descending order. If the ranking of the drug-related disease is higher than a specific threshold, it is considered a True Positive (TP) sample; otherwise, it is considered a False Negative (FN) sample. Moreover, if the ranking of a disease not associated with the drug is higher than a specific threshold, it is considered a False Positive (FP) sample; otherwise, it is considered a True Negative (TN) sample. According to different ranking thresholds, the number of samples in each of the above four categories can be calculated to construct receiver operating characteristic (ROC) curve and precision-recall (PR) curve. The area under ROC curve (AUC) and the area under PR curve (AUPR) are used to evaluate the overall performance of the prediction methods.

3.2 Parameter Analysis

Different values of the hyperparameter can produce different prediction performance, so it is necessary to determine the optimal value of the hyperparameter to achieve the best performance. In our method, the optimal value of hyperparameter k is determined within the range [0, 24]. As shown in Fig. 3, as the value of k changes, the AUC value does not change significantly, while the AUPR value changes more significantly. In addition, when $k = 2$, the AUPR value reaches the maximum and decreases gradually with the increase of k. Therefore, we set the value of k to 2 as the optimal parameter value, and then the AUC value and AUPR value of NCPDDA are 0.9733 and 0.4871, respectively.

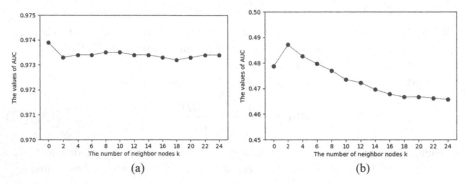

(a)   (b)

Fig. 3. The predicted results under different number neighbor nodes settings. (a) AUC values for various settings. (b) AUPR values for various settings.

3.3 Comparison with Other Methods

To evaluate the performance of NCPDDA, we compare it with other three classical approaches: OMC2 [7], BNNR [6], and MBiRW [11]. In order to make a fair comparison, the best hyperparameter values of the other methods are selected according to their publications. As depicted Fig. 4, the AUC value and AUPR value of NCPDDA are superior to those of other methods. Specifically, NCPDDA obtain the best AUC value of 0.9733, while OMC2, BNNR and MBiRW are 0.9342, 0.9101 and 0.9122, respectively. Moreover, NCPDDA also achieve the best AUPR value of 0.4871, which are 8.83%, 9.19% and 17.21% higher than OMC2, BNNR and MBiRW, respectively. The other three methods only use one type of drug similarity and disease similarity, while NCPDDA integrates four types of drug similarities and three types of similarities. The experimental results indicate that the integration of multiple types of similarities can improve the performance of the prediction methods.

3.4 Comparison of Different Similarity Network Fusion Methods

In the process of similarity information fusion, many methods adopt linear fusion methods (for example, mean fusion), while our proposed method uses similarity network fusion (SNF) method. Compared with mean fusion method, SNF can integrate common information and complementary information of various types of data. Besides, the similarities of drugs and diseases may be incomplete or noisy, and SNF can effectively reduce noise.

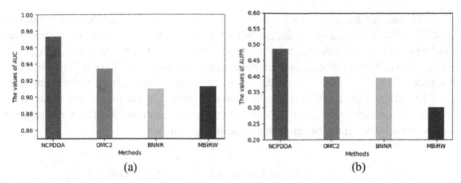

Fig. 4. The predicted results of all methods. (a) AUC values for the various methods. (b) AUPR values for various methods.

We set up two groups of comparative experiments to illustrate the effect of similarity network fusion method. NCPDDA_DrugMean represents that the mean fusion method is used to integrate three types of drug similarities to calculate one type of disease similarity, and NCPDDA_Mean represents that four kinds of drug similarities and three kinds of disease similarities are integrated into one kind of drug similarities and disease similarities respectively by mean fusion method. As shown in Fig. 5, the AUC values of NCPDDA and NCPDDA_DrugMean are approximately equal, while the AUPR value of NCPDDA is 3% higher than NCPDDA_DrugMean. Moreover, the AUC value of NCPDDA is 2.48% higher than NCPDDA_Mean and the AUPR value of NCPDDA is 4.25% higher than NCPDDA_Mean.

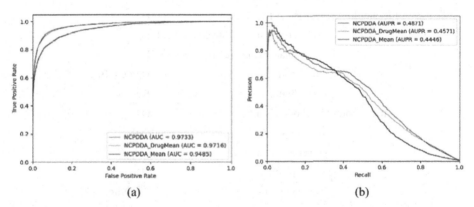

Fig. 5. The performance of different similarity fusion methods. (a) ROC curves of different methods. (b) precision-recall curves of different methods.

3.5 Case Studies

Through the previous experiments, the excellent predictive performance of NCPDDA has been confirmed. In this section, we further validate the ability of the NCPDDA to predict potential associations between drugs and diseases. All known associations in the LRSSL dataset are treated as the training set to train the NCPDDA model, and the trained NCPDDA is used to get the prediction score of all unknown associations. The candidate diseases for each drug are then ranked according to the predicted scores.

The top 5 candidate diseases for four representative drugs, Levodopa, Capecitabine, Flecainide and Amantadine, are validated by searching authoritative public databases, such as DrugBank [19] and CTD [20]. As shown in Table 1, more than 3 new indications are validated for each representative drug. It further suggests that NCPDDA can be used to predict new indications for drugs in practical applications.

Table 1. The top 5 candidate diseases for the four representative drugs.

Drugs	Top 5 candidate diseases	Evidences
Levodopa	Hyperprolactinemia	CTD
	Psychotic disorders	
	Dyskinesia, drug-induced	CTD
	Schizophrenia	CTD
	Tourette syndrome	
Capecitabine	Stomach neoplasms	CTD
	Carcinoma, basal cell	CTD
	Rectal neoplasms	CTD
	Folic acid deficiency	
	Anemia, megaloblastic	
Flecainide	Ventricular fibrillation	CTD
	Tachycardia, supraventricular	CTD
	Ventricular premature complexes	CTD
	Atrial fibrillation	CTD/DrugBank
	Atrial flutter	CTD
Amantadine	Psychotic disorders	CTD
	Tourette syndrome	CTD
	Hyperprolactinemia	
	Schizophrenia	CTD
	Huntington disease	CTD/DrugBank

Besides, our approach has also identified some novel drug-disease associations, including: Levodopa for psychotic disorders and tourette syndrome; Capecitabine for folic acid deficiency and anemia, megaloblastic; Amantadine for hyperprolactinemia. Although these associations are not recorded in the database, it does not necessarily mean that they do not exist.

4   Conclusion

In this work, we develop a method based on the network consistency projection to achieve drug repositioning. In order to accurately predict potential drug-disease associations, our proposed approach effectively integrates information from multiple sources. In addition, the similarity network fusion is used to integrate the data to reduce the influence of noise. Compared with three classical prediction methods, our method is proved to have excellent performance. In the case studies section, four representative drugs are studied to further prove the effectiveness of our method.

However, although our method has achieved some results, we must acknowledge some limitations of our method. First, our method of calculating the similarities of drugs and diseases may not be optimal, and there may be better methods of calculating the similarities. Second, we should integrate more types of information to further improve prediction performance. In the future research, we will conduct further research on the two points mentioned above.

Acknowledgement. This paper is supported by National Key Research and Development Program of China (No. 2017YFE0103900 and 2017YFA0504702), the NSFC projects Grant (No. 61932018, 62072441 and 62072280), Beijing Municipal Natural Science Foundation Grant (No. L182053).

References

1. Emmert-Streib, F., Tripathi, S., Simoes, R.D.M., Hawwa, A.F., Dehmer, M.: The human disease network: opportunities for classification, diagnosis, and prediction of disorders and disease genes. Syst. Biomed. **1**(1), 20–28 (2013)
2. Weng, L., Zhang, L., Peng, Y., Huang, R.S.: Pharmacogenetics and pharmacogenomics: a bridge to individualized cancer therapy. Pharmacogenomics **14**(3), 315–324 (2013)
3. Ghofrani, H.A., Osterloh, I.H., Grimminger, F.: Sildenafil: from angina to erectile dysfunction to pulmonary hypertension and beyond. Nat. Rev. Drug Discov. **5**(8), 689–702 (2006)
4. Gottlieb, A., Stein, G.Y., Ruppin, E., Sharan, R.: PREDICT: a method for inferring novel drug indications with application to personalized medicine. Mol. Syst. Biol. **7**(1), 496 (2011)
5. Liang, X., et al.: LRSSL: predict and interpret drug-disease associations based on data integration using sparse subspace learning. Bioinformatics **33**(8), 1187–1196 (2017)
6. Yang, M., Luo, H., Li, Y., Wang, J.: Drug repositioning based on bounded nuclear norm regularization. Bioinformatics **35**(14), i455–i463 (2019)
7. Yang, M., Luo, H., Li, Y., Wu, F.-X., Wang, J.: Overlap matrix completion for predicting drug-associated indications. PLoS Computat. Biol. **15**(12), e1007541 (2019)
8. Zhang, W., et al.: Predicting drug-disease associations by using similarity constrained matrix factorization. BMC Bioinformatics **19**(1), 1–12 (2018)
9. Wang, W., Yang, S., Zhang, X., Li, J.: Drug repositioning by integrating target information through a heterogeneous network model. Bioinformatics **30**(20), 2923–2930 (2014)
10. Martínez, V., Navarro, C., Cano, C., Fajardo, W., Blanco, A.: DrugNet: network-based drug-disease prioritization by integrating heterogeneous data. Artif. Intell. Med. **63**(1), 41–49 (2015)
11. Luo, H., et al.: Drug repositioning based on comprehensive similarity measures and Bi-Random walk algorithm. Bioinformatics **32**(17), 2664–2671 (2016)

12. Wang, Y., Xiao, J., Suzek, T.O., Zhang, J., Wang, J., Bryant, S.H.: PubChem: a public information system for analyzing bioactivities of small molecules. Nucleic Acids Res. **37**(suppl_2), W623–W633 (2009)
13. Mitchell, A., et al.: The InterPro protein families database: the classification resource after 15 years. Nucleic Acids Res. **43**(D1), D213–D221 (2015)
14. UniProt Consortium, U.: The universal protein resource (UniProt) in 2010. Nucleic Acids Res. **38**(suppl_1), D142–D148 (2010)
15. Van Driel, M.A., Bruggeman, J., Vriend, G., Brunner, H.G., Leunissen, J.A.: A text-mining analysis of the human phenome. Eur. J. Hum. Genet. **14**(5), 535–542 (2006)
16. Wang, D., Wang, J., Lu, M., Song, F., Cui, Q.: Inferring the human microRNA functional similarity and functional network based on microRNA-associated diseases. Bioinformatics **26**(13), 1644–1650 (2010)
17. Xuan, P., Cao, Y., Zhang, T., Wang, X., Pan, S., Shen, T.: Drug repositioning through integration of prior knowledge and projections of drugs and diseases. Bioinformatics **35**(20), 4108–4119 (2019)
18. Wang, B., et al.: Similarity network fusion for aggregating data types on a genomic scale. Nat. Methods **11**(3), 333 (2014)
19. Wishart, D.S., et al.: DrugBank: a knowledgebase for drugs, drug actions and drug targets. Nucleic Acids Res. **36**(suppl_1), D901–D906 (2008)
20. Davis, A.P., et al.: The comparative toxicogenomics database: update 2019. Nucleic Acids Res. **47**(D1), D948–D954 (2019)

An Efficient Computational Method to Predict Drug-Target Interactions Utilizing Matrix Completion and Linear Optimization Method

Xinguo Lu$^{(\boxtimes)}$, Fang Liu, Jinxin Li, Keren He, Kaibao Jiang, and Changlong Gu

College of Computer Science and Electronic Engineering, Hunan University, Changsha, China

Abstract. The experimental determination of drug-target interaction is time-consuming and expensive. Therefore, a continuous demand for more effective prediction of drug-target interaction using computing technology. Many algorithms have been designed to infer potential interactions. Most of these algorithms rely on drug similarity and target similarity as auxiliary information in modeling, but they ignore the problem that there are a lot of missing auxiliary data of existing drugs or targets, which affects the prediction performance of the model and fails to achieve the expected effect. Here, we propose a calculation model named MCLO, which is based on the matrix completion and linear optimization technology to predict novel drug-target interactions. First, the proposed method calculate the side effect similarity of drugs and protein-protein interaction similarity of targets. Then we utilize the idea of linear neighbor representation learning to predict the potential drug-target interaction. It is worth mentioning that our method uses the idea of matrix completion technology to complete the imperfect similarity before drug-target interactions prediction. To evaluate the performance of MCLO, we carry out experiments on four gold standard datasets. The experimental results show that MCLO can be effectively applied to identify drug-target interactions.

Keywords: Drug-target interaction · Linear optimization · Matrix completion

1 Introduction

Discovering to determine the potential medical uses of a novel drug is a long process. Including target identification, target verification, compound cues to be identified, verified and optimized, as well as the initial stages of different types of preclinical and clinical trials until the final approval by the US Food and Drug Administration (FDA) [1]. In terms of time and cost, bringing new drugs to market is a challenging and complex process [2]. Despite the increasing investment of government departments in drug development and design. In fact, drugs are rarely only combined with the expected target, and non-target effects are also very common and may even cause unnecessary side effects [3], which is another important reason for the declining number of new drugs on the market every year. This phenomenon also promotes the research in the field of drug reuse, that is, finding new targets for existing drugs or developing new drugs on the basis of existing

© Springer Nature Switzerland AG 2021
D.-S. Huang et al. (Eds.): ICIC 2021, LNAI 12838, pp. 603–614, 2021.
https://doi.org/10.1007/978-3-030-84532-2_54

drugs to accelerate drug research and development [4]. With the continuous improvement of public biomedical databases, it is possible to develop a practical computational method, which overcomes the limitations of traditional experimental approaches and helps to find novel interaction between existing drugs and off-target effects. However, due to the potential unknown complexity of pharmacology and biology, drug reuse is full of challenges.

Early attempts to calculate and predict drug-target interaction (DTI) are mainly divided into two categories: docking simulation [5] and ligand-based [6] approaches. The docking method relies on the known three-dimensional (3D) structure of the chemical ligand and the protein target. However, this approach is very time-consuming, and the three-dimensional structure of most drugs is difficult to obtain [7]. The ligand-based method compares the query ligand with a group of known target protein ligands, but when the type and quantity of known ligands in the target protein are insufficient, it is difficult to build a virtual screening model to predict potential targets for the drug [8].

To overcome these challenging problems, computer intelligent algorithms for computational prediction of DTIs have become more and more popular in recent years. These methods make full use of the potential correlation between drug-related properties and targets, and provide an effective way for the prediction of drug-target interaction. Yamanishi et al. developed a new framework that integrates chemistry, genome, and pharmacological space to improve the research efficiency of genomic drug discovery [9]. It is clarified that the similarity of pharmacological action is more important than the similarity of chemical structure in the prediction of unknown drug-target interactions. Wang et al. proposed a method based on a heterogeneous network [10]. The method first obtains diffusion characteristics from the heterogeneous network, then directly uses the obtained diffusion distribution to derive the predicted score of drug-target interaction. However, the direct use of the diffusion state as a characteristic to make predictions is susceptible to noise and high-dimensional data bias, which leads to inaccurate prediction of drug-target interactions [11]. Luo et al. proposed a new prediction approach DTINet, which extracts low-dimensional feature information from the heterogeneous network and uses the inductive matrix completion algorithm to predict the DTI score [11]. Since these methods are difficult to predict interactions involving new drugs (without any known targets) or unknown targets (without any known therapeutic drugs), many missing edges in the network are actually unknown interactions, Ezzat et al. proposed a drug-target interaction prediction method called GRMF [12], which developed a preprocessing step to enhance the prediction of "new drugs" and "new targets" by adding edges with intermediate interaction likelihood scores, so as to realize the interaction prediction of new drugs or new targets. Moreover, considering that the comprehensive fusion of multiple data may introduce noise into the data, in order to better utilize multiple biological information to assist the prediction of drug-target interactions, Olayan et al. proposed a DTIs algorithm called DDR [1]. DDR makes full use of multiple auxiliary information of drugs and multiple auxiliary information of the target, which is different from the previous method that directly integrates all similarity information. The DDR algorithm constructs a heuristic similarity selection algorithm, which first selects the best combination of similarities to achieve the purpose of retaining effective information and removing redundant information, thereby increasing the abundance of comprehensive similarity information.

Most of these existing studies rely on drug similarity and target similarity as auxiliary information in modeling, but they ignore the problem that there are a large number of missing auxiliary data of existing drugs or targets, which leads to the prediction performance of the model is affected and fails to achieve the expected effect. Therefore, in view of the shortcomings of existing methods, we propose a novel method, named MCLO, for DTI prediction (Fig. 1). This method firstly calculates the side effect similarity of drugs and protein-protein interaction (PPI) similarity of targets based on the side effects of the drug and the PPI of the target. Then, the idea of matrix completion technology was introduced to complete the similarity of drug side effects similarity and the target PPI similarity to enhance their information abundance. Next, the potential drug-target interaction is predicted by using the linear optimization method according to the completed drug similarity, completed target similarity and known drug-target interaction. The experimental results show that our approach can effectively predict the DTIs in the 5-fold cross-validation and obtain better performance than the previous model.

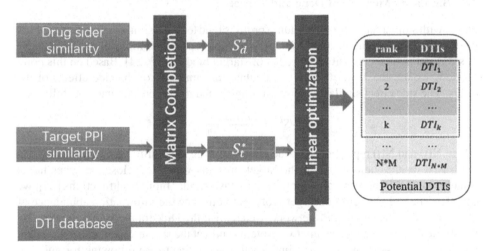

Fig. 1. Overall workflow of MCLO for discovering potential DTIs.

2 Materials and Methods

2.1 Datasets

The known drug-target interactions are obtained from [13] to evaluate the prediction models of drug-target interactions. The dataset is originally collected by Yamanishi et al. and used as a reference in many studies [14–16]. This dataset contains observed DTIs as retrieved from KEGG BRITE databases [17], SuperTarget [18], DrugBank [19] and BRENDA [20]. The DTIs information in the dataset is divided into four groups according to different target protein class: (i) enzymes (E); (ii) ion-channels(IC); (iii) G-protein-coupled receptors (GPCR) and (iv) nuclear receptors(NR). Table 1 shows the statistics of these four data types. Moreover, the side effects of the drugs are obtained from the SIDER2 database [21]. Protein-protein interaction of the targets is obtained from the HIPPIE database [22].

Table 1. Summary of the DTI datasets in this study.

Datasets	Drugs	Targets	DTIs	Sparsity of the interaction matrix
IC	210	204	1476	96.55%
GPCR	223	95	635	97.00%
NR	54	26	90	93.59%
E	445	664	2926	99.01%

2.2 Similarity Measure of Drug and Target

Drugs with similar target protein binding profiles tend to cause similar side effects, which means that there is a direct correlation between target protein binding and the similarity of side effects, so it is possible to predict off-target binding [23, 24]. Based on this point of view, we use the Jaccard score to calculate the similarity of the side effects of the drugs. The side effect similarity between drug d_1 and d_2 can be calculated as follows:

$$S_d^s = \frac{|N(i) \cap N(j)|}{|N(i) \cup N(j)|} \tag{1}$$

where N(i) and N(j) represents the side effects of drug i and drug j, respectively.

Based on the viewpoint that the target proteins which are closer to other target proteins in the PPI network are more likely to have similar biological functions [25], we calculate the PPI similarity of target proteins to enhance the information abundance of DTI network. For a given PPI network, we can use the Dijkstra algorithm to calculate the shortest distance between any two proteins and get the shortest path matrix D. Then, the distance can be converted to a similar value according to the following formula.

$$S_t^p = \alpha e^{-bD(t_i, t_j)} \tag{2}$$

where $D(t_i, t_j)$ is the shortest path between target protein i and j in the PPI network, α and b is a variable parameter. In this study, we set both the parameter α and b to 1 according to the previous studies.

2.3 Enhancing the Information of Similar Network

Although there is more and more information about drugs and targets, the current data is far from complete, which means that part of the data set will be incorrect or missing [26]. For example, the side effect of a drug refers to the symptoms that appear after the drug is used, which is discovered and collected manually. However, not all the side effects information can be obtained. Therefore, the similarity matrix of drug side effects will be very sparse, which cannot fully reflect the real similarity between drugs. To solve this problem, we reconstruct the similarity matrix S_d^* to take the place of the original drug side effect similarity matrix. The incomplete similarity matrix S_d^s can be decomposed into two parts. The first part is the linear combination SR of S_d^s, which is low rank and essentially is the projection of noise data S_d^s onto a lower-dimensional space. The second part is a noise matrix E separated from the original similarity matrix S_d^s. According to the above definition, S_d^s can be decomposed as follows:

$$S_d^s = SR + E \tag{3}$$

Obviously, formula (3) has an infinite number of solutions, but based on the expectation that the rank of the low-rank matrix S is low enough and the noise matrix E is sparse enough. The kernel norm constraint matrix SR can be added, and the $L_{1,2}$ norm can be used to constrain the error term E. Specifically, a low-rank restoration matrix D can be obtained by solving the following convex optimization problem.

$$\min_{S,E} \|S\|_* + \omega \|E\|_{2,1} \quad s.t. \quad S_d^s = SR + E \tag{4}$$

where ω is the coefficient used to balance the proportions of S and E ($\omega > 0$).

Existing research has proposed many algorithms to solve the above models. In this study, the Augmented Lagrange Multiplier model [27] is used to solve the above problems. According to the Augmented Lagrange Multiplier algorithm, Eq. (4) could be transformed to the following:

$$\min_{S,E,X} \|X\|_* + \omega \|E\|_{2,1} \quad s.t. \quad S_d^s = SR + N, S = X \tag{5}$$

The augmented Lagrangian function of Eq. (5) is

$$L(X,S,E,Y_1,Y_2) = \|X\|_* + \omega \|E\|_{2,1} + Tr\left(Y_1^T\left(S_d^s - SR - E\right)\right) + Tr\left(Y_2^T(S-X)\right)$$
$$+ \frac{\mu}{2}\left(\left\|S_d^s - SR - E\right\|_F^2\right) + \frac{\mu}{2}\left(\|S-X\|_F^2\right) \tag{6}$$

where Y_1^T and Y_2^T is Lagrange multiplier, μ is a penalty parameter ($\mu > 0$).

Then, alternately update and calculate X_{k+1}, S_{k+1} and E_{k+1} by fixing other variables. We can obtain

$$X_{k+1} = \arg\min \frac{1}{\mu}\|X\|_* + \frac{1}{2}\left\|X_k - \left(S_k + Y_{2_k}/\mu\right)\right\|_F^2 \tag{7}$$

$$S_{k+1} = \left(I + S_d^{sT} S_d^s\right)^{-1}\left(S_d^{sT} S_d^s - S_d^{sT} E_k + X_{k+1} + \left(S_d^{sT} Y_{1_k} - Y_{2_k}\right)/\mu\right) \tag{8}$$

$$E_{k+1} = \arg\min \frac{\omega}{\mu}\|E_k\|_{2,1} + \frac{1}{2}\left\|E_k - \left(S_d^s - SR + Y_{1_k}/\mu\right)\right\|_F^2 \tag{9}$$

After obtaining X_{k+1}, S_{k+1} and E_{k+1}, the Lagrangian multipliers $Y_{1_{k+1}}$ and $Y_{2_{k+1}}$ can be updated as follows:

$$Y_{1_{k+1}} = Y_{1_k} + \mu\left(S_d^s - SR - E_{k+1}\right) \tag{10}$$

$$Y_{2k+1} = Y_{2k} + \mu(S_{k+1} - X_{k+1}) \qquad (11)$$

The data matrix S^* and the noise matrix E^* during their reaching the convergence can be expressed as $\|S_d^s - SR - E_\infty\| < \varepsilon$ and $\|S - X_\infty\| < \varepsilon$ ($\varepsilon \ll 1$), respectively. The complete drug side effect similarity matrix S_d^* is calculated by $S_d^s \times S^*$. Similarly, the complete target PPI similarity matrix S_t^* can be obtained by $S_t^p \times S^*$.

2.4 Construction of the Heterogeneous Network

We construct a heterogeneous drug-target network using DT, S_d^* and S_t^*. The matrix DT represents the observed DTIs network, if drug i and target j are connected, the element $DT(i, j) = 1$; otherwise, $DT(i, j) = 0$. Therefore, the heterogeneous drug-target network could be expressed by a K × K (K = M + N is the total number of drugs and targets in the network) undirected adjacency matrix $A_{K \times K}$.

$$B = \begin{bmatrix} S_d^* & DT \\ DT^T & S_t^* \end{bmatrix} \qquad (12)$$

2.5 Linear Optimization Model for Drug-Target Interactions Prediction

The possibility of the existence of a link between two nodes can usually be obtained based on the linear summation of the neighbors nodes' contributions [28]. That is, assuming that the possibility of a connection from i to j is p, then p can be unfolded by the linear sum of the contributions from the neighbors between i and j.

$$p_{ij} = \sum_k a_{ik} w_{kj} \qquad (13)$$

where w_{kj} is the contribution from node i to node j. According to the above definition, after obtaining the adjacency matrix A of the heterogeneous network, the possibility of interaction between the drug and the target can be written as a linear combination of a and the weighting matrix W, i.e. P = AW. Since P and W are unknown, formula (13) has infinitely many solutions, but based on the principle of self-consistency, the rating matrix A and matrix P should be highly consistent, and the magnitude of W should be small. Therefore, the determination of the likelihood matrix P can be simply transformed into the following optimization problem.

$$\min_W \alpha \|A - AW\|_F^2 + W_F^2 \qquad (14)$$

Equation (14) can be unfolded as follows:

$$M = \alpha Tr\left[(A - AW)^T (A - AW)\right] + Tr\left(W^T W\right) \qquad (15)$$

Then take partial derivative of M with respect to W as follows:

$$\frac{\partial M}{\partial W} = \alpha\left(-2A^T A + 2A^T AW\right) + 2W \qquad (16)$$

Set $\frac{\partial M}{\partial W} = 0$, the optimal solution of W can be obtain:

$$W^* = \alpha(\alpha A^T A + I)^{-1} A^T A \tag{17}$$

where I is an identity matrix, α is a variable parameter and it can be set by cross-validation. In our study, α is set to 0.5, 0.15, 0.15, 0.07 for NR, GPCR, E, IC datasets respectively, the MCLO model achieves the best performance. After obtaining W^*, the possibility matrix P can be obtained as follows:

$$P = BW^* \tag{18}$$

Then, we extract the DTI network in the upper right of the likelihood matrix P to obtain the final prediction matrix P'. All unobserved links are sorted in descending order according to their corresponding scores in the prediction matrix P'. The higher the score of these links, the more likely is potential drug-target interaction.

3 Result

3.1 Experimental Setting and Evaluation Metrices

We use 5-fold cross-validation (5-CV) based on the known DTIs in Yamanishi_08 dataset to evaluate the predictive performance of the MCLO approach. The drug-target pairs in DT are randomly divided into 5 equal-sized subsets. In each fold, a single subset is used as the probe set for testing the method, and the remaining four subsets together with the S_d^* and S_t^* are used as training sets. To avoid the bias in data split, the cross-validation process is run independently 5 times, and each of the 4 subsets is only used once as the probe set. Then, we average the calculated 5 results to obtain the final estimate.

Here, for each prediction algorithm, at each in case of cross-validation, we adopt four evaluation metrics to measure performances of prediction models, i.e., recall, F-measure, area under the ROC curve (AUC) and the area under the precision-recall curve (AUPR). We define true negative (TN), false negative (FN), true positive (TP) and true negative (TN). The AUC is achieved according to the area under ROC curve constructed by recall and false positive rate (FPR) under different threshold settings, and the AUPR is achieved according to area under the precision recall curve constructed by precision and recall under different threshold settings. The recall, precision, FPR and F-measure are calculated as follow:

$$recall = \frac{TP}{TP+FN} \tag{19}$$

$$precision = \frac{TP}{TP+FP} \tag{20}$$

$$FPR = \frac{FP}{FP+TN} \tag{21}$$

$$F - measure = 2 * \frac{precision*recall}{precision+recall} \tag{22}$$

3.2 Overall Performance

Table 2 and Table 3 show the AUC and AUPR values achieved with various variant models from different views of the overall framework. The Model_A means not to complete any similarity matrix before prediction, Model_B represents to complete only the PPI similarity of target, Model_C indicates only to complete the side effects similarity of drug, MCLO is the method we proposed, that is, the side effects similarity of drug and the PPI similarity of target are complemented before prediction. As shown in Table 2 and Table 3, the performance of Model C is better than Model B, which indicates that the side effect network of the drug provides more information than the PPI network of the target. In addition, after complementing both drug similarity and target similarity, the model achieve the best performance than other models, and the Model_A obtained the worst results both for AUC and for AUPR. In particular, the AUPR is only 0.137 in the NR dataset, which is predictable. Because the NR dataset is very small, the known side effects of drugs and PPI of targets are very rare, so the prediction performance is very poor. In summary, based on our prediction results, it is necessary to complete the similarity of missing information before prediction.

Table 2. The AUC of MCLO and different variant models.

Dataset	Model_A	Model_B	Model_C	MCLO
IC	0.939	0.963	0. 979	0.994
GPCR	0.843	0.886	0.951	0.979
NR	0.693	0.784	0.941	0.950
E	0.895	0.957	0.938	0.982
Avg.	0.843	0.898	0.952	0.976

Table 3. The AUPR of MCLO and different variant models.

Dataset	Model_A	Model_B	Model_C	MCLO
IC	0.667	0.746	0.749	0.901
GPCR	0.310	0.375	0.639	0.822
NR	0.137	0.350	0.713	0.820
E	0.587	0.799	0.704	0.919
Avg.	0.425	0.568	0.701	0.866

3.3 Comparison with Other Existing Methods

We evaluate our model on the Yamanishi_08 database, and compare the MCLO with five widely applied DTIs prediction approaches: WNN-GIP [29], MSCMF [30], NRLMF

[31], DDR [1] and DLapRLS [32] under the same conditions for all algorithms, i.e. under the 5-CV based on same datasets, we set the parameters of these algorithms as the same of these best setting provided in original paper.

We show that MCLO, using 5-CV, achieve better performance than other approaches. Figure 2 and Fig. 3 show the overall results of AUC values and AUPR values for MCLO and all compared algorithms. The results show that the MCLO model is superior to all other methods in the terms of AUC and AUPR on all datasets. It is worth noting that our approach get a better AUPR value with a margin of 4%, 3%, 9% on NR, E and GPCR datasets, respectively.

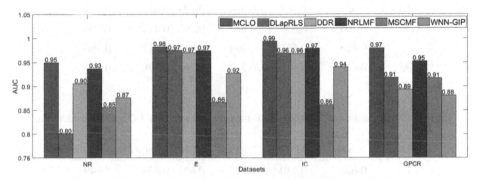

Fig. 2. The AUCs averaged over 10 runs by different methods.

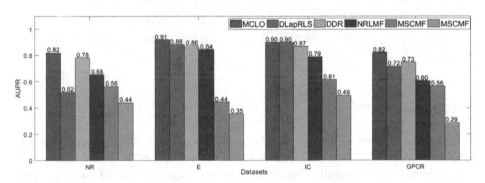

Fig. 3. The AUPRs averaged over 10 runs by different methods.

In addition, Table 4 and Table 5 show the Recall and F-measure. Our method achieves the best Recall scores over three datasets (i.e., GPCR, NR, E) and obtains the third-best Recall values on the ion-channels dataset, where DDR and DLapRLS outperform MCLO. The average Recall obtained by MCLO is 0.811, which is 5% higher than that obtained by the second-best approach DDR. In addition, the average F-measure by MCLO is 0.822, which is 6.3% higher than the second method DDR. Moreover, it is worth noting that different from other approaches, our model is also very useful for small data, and it has also obtained superior performance on the nuclear receptors dataset. This may be because MCLO first complete the imperfect similarity before predicting, which greatly improve the information abundance of the training data. In summary, based on our prediction results (Figs. 2 and 3, Tables 4 and 5), the MCLO is powerful in discovering potential drug-target interactions.

Table 4. Performance comparison with Recall between MCLO and other methods in 5-CV based on IC, GPCR, NR and E datasets.

Dataset	WNN-GIP	MSCMF	NRLMF	DDR	DLapRLS	MCLO
IC	0.753	0.693	0.822	0.829	0.827	0.780
GPCR	0.525	0.608	0.694	0.703	0.622	0.754
NR	0.564	0.534	0.657	0.702	0.444	0.804
E	0.623	0.630	0.794	0.811	0.817	0.906
Avg.	0.616	0.616	0.742	0.761	0.678	0.811

Table 5. Performance comparison with F-measure between MCLO and other methods.

Dataset	WNN-GIP	MSCMF	NRLMF	DDR	DLapRLS	MCLO
IC	0.633	0.730	0.803	0.804	0.854	0.849
GPCR	0.378	0.599	0.658	0.654	0.687	0.784
NR	0.493	0.553	0.652	0.739	0.516	0.769
E	0.464	0.633	0.839	0.838	0.855	0.884
Avg.	0.492	0.629	0.738	0.759	0.728	0.822

4 Conclusions

In this article, we propose a novel model to predict potential DTIs. Considering that in addition to drug-target interactions, the auxiliary information of drugs and targets used to assist in prediction is usually imperfect. Therefore, we use the idea of matrix completion technology to conduct imperfect similarities before making predictions. Then use the idea of linear neighbor representation learning to predict the potential drug-target interactions. We have analyzed MCLO and different variant models, and the experimental results show that it is very effective to complete the imperfect similarity data before prediction, which greatly improves the prediction performance. In addition, we compared MCLO with WNN-GIP, MSCMF, NRLMF, DDR and DLapRLS. The results show that our model is powerful in discovering potential drug-target interactions.

Acknowledgements. This work was supported by Natural Science Foundation of China (Grant No. 61972141) and Natural Science Foundation of Hunan Province, China (Grant No. 2020JJ4209).

References

1. Olayan, R.S., Ashoor, H., Bajic, V.B.: DDR: efficient computational method to predict drug–target interactions using graph mining and machine learning approaches. Bioinformatics **34**(7), 1164–1173 (2017)
2. Goh, K.I., Cusick, M.E., Valle, D., et al.: The human disease network. Proc. Natl. Acad. Sci. **104**(21), 8685–8690 (2007)
3. Avorn, J.: The $2.6 billion pill--methodologic and policy considerations. New Engl. J. Med. **372**(20), 1877–1879 (2015)
4. Ming, H., Bryant, S.H., Wang, Y.: Predicting drug-target interactions by dual-network integrated logistic matrix factorization. Sci. Rep. **7**, 40376 (2017)
5. Malina, D., Greene, J.A., Loscalzo, J.: Putting the patient back together - social medicine, network medicine, and the limits of reductionism. New Engl. J. Med. **377**(25), 2493 (2017)
6. Guo, L., Yan, Z., Zheng, X., et al.: A comparison of various optimization algorithms of protein–ligand docking programs by fitness accuracy. J. Mol. Model. **20**(7), 2251 (2014). https://doi.org/10.1007/s00894-014-2251-3
7. Liu, Y., et al.: Neighborhood regularized logistic matrix factorization for drug-target interaction prediction. PLoS Comput. Biol. **12** (2016)
8. Peng, J., Li, J., Shang, X.: A learning-based method for drug-target interaction prediction based on feature representation learning and deep neural network. BMC Bioinform. **21**(Suppl 13), 394 (2020)
9. Yamanishi, Y., Kotera, M., Kanehisa, M., Goto, S.: Drug-target interaction prediction from chemical, genomic and pharmacological data in an integrated framework. Bioinformatics **26**(12), 246–254 (2010)
10. Huang, Y., et al.: Predicting drug-target on heterogeneous network with co-rank. In: The 8th International Conference on Computer Engineering and Networks, pp. 571–81 (2020)
11. Cheng, F., et al.: Prediction of drug-target interactions and drug repositioning via network-based inference. PLoS Comput. Biol. **8**(5), 1002503 (2012)
12. Zzat, A.E., Zhao, P., Min, W., et al.: Drug-target interaction prediction with graph regularized matrix factorization. IEEE/ACM Trans. Comput. Biol. Bioinform. **14**(3), 1 (2016)
13. Yamanishi, Y., Araki, M., Gutteridge, A., Honda, W., Kanehisa, M.: Prediction of drug–target interaction networks from the integration of chemical and genomic spaces. Bioinformatics **24**(13), i232–i240 (2008)
14. Mei, J.-P., Kwoh, C.-K., Yang, P., Li, X.-L., Zheng, J.: Drug–target interaction prediction by learning from local information and neighbors, Bioinformatics **29**(2), 238–245 (2013)
15. Ba-Alawi, W., et al.: DASPfind: new efficient method to predict drug-target interactions. Cheminform **8**(1), 15 (2016)
16. Daminelli, S., et al.: Common neighbours and the local-community-paradigm for topological link prediction in bipartite networks. New J. Phys. **17**(11), 113037 (2015)
17. Kanehisa, M., et al.: From genomics to chemical genomics: new developments in KEGG. Nucleic Acids Res. **34**, D354–D357 (2006)
18. Gunther, S., et al.: Super target and matador: resources for exploring drug-target relationships. Nucleic Acids Res. **36**, D919–D922 (2008)
19. Wishart, D.S., et al.: DrugBank: a knowledgebase for drugs, drug actions and drug targets. Nucleic Acids Res. **36**, D901–D906 (2008)
20. Schomburg, I.: BRENDA, the enzyme database: updates and major new developments. Nucleic Acids Res. **32**, D431–D433 (2004)
21. Kuhn, M., Letunic, I., Jensen, L.J., et al.: The SIDER database of drugs and side effects. Nucleic Acids Res. **44**(D1), D1075–D1079 (2016)

22. Alanis-Lobato, G., Andrade-Navarro, M.A., Schaefer, M.H.: HIPPIE v2.0: enhancing mean-ingfulness and reliability of protein–protein interaction networks. Nucleic Acids Res. **45**(D1), D408–D414 (2017)
23. Campillos, M., Kuhn, M., Gavin, A.C., et al.: Drug target identification using side-effect similarity. Science **321**(5886), 263–266 (2008)
24. Vilar, S., Hripcsak, G.: The role of drug profiles as similarity metrics: applications to repur-posing, adverse effects detection and drug-drug interactions. Brief. Bioinform. **18**(4), bbw048 (2016)
25. Deng, M., et al.: Prediction of protein function using protein-protein interaction data. In: Proceedings IEEE Computer Society Bioinformatics Conference EE (2002)
26. Shen, C., Luo, J., Lai, Z., et al.: Multiview joint learning-based method for identifying small-molecule-associated MiRNAs by integrating pharmacological, genomics, and network knowledge. J. Chem. Inf. Model. (2020)
27. Lin, Z., Chen, M., Ma, Y.: The augmented Lagrange multiplier method for exact recovery of corrupted low-rank matrices. eprint arxiv:9 (2010)
28. Pech, R., Hao, D., Lee, Y.L., et al.: Link prediction via linear optimization. Phys. A: Stat. Mech. Appl. **528** (2019)
29. van Laarhoven, T., Marchiori, E.: Predicting drug-target interactions for new drug compounds using a weighted nearest neighbor profile. PLoS ONE **8**(6), e66952 (2013)
30. Zheng, X., Ding, H., Mamitsuka, H., Zhu, S.: Collaborative matrix factorization with mul-tiple similarities for predicting drug-target interactions. In: KDD 2013: Proceedings of the 19th ACM SIGKDD International Conference on Knowledge Discovery and Data Mining, pp. 1025–1033 (2013)
31. Liu, Y., et al.: Neighborhood regularized logistic matrix factorization for drug-target interaction prediction. PLoS Comput. Biol. **12** e1004760 (2016)
32. Ding, Y., Tang, J., Guo, F.: Identification of drug-target interactions via dual Laplacian regularized least squares with multiple Kernel fusion. Knowl.-Based Syst. **204**, 106254 (2020)

Protein Structure and Function
Prediction

Protein-Protein Interaction Prediction by Integrating Sequence Information and Heterogeneous Network Representation

Xiao-Rui Su[1,2,3], Zhu-Hong You[1,2,3(✉)], Zhan-Heng Chen[1,2,3], Hai-Cheng Yi[1,2,3], and Zhen-Hao Guo[1,2,3]

[1] The Xinjiang Technical Institute of Physics and Chemistry, Chinese Academy of Sciences, Urumqi 830011, China
[2] University of Chinese Academy of Sciences, Beijing 100049, China
[3] Xinjiang Laboratory of Minority Speech and Language Information Processing, Urumqi 830011, China

Abstract. Protein-protein interaction (PPI) plays an important role in regulating cells and signals. PPI deregulation will lead to many diseases, including pernicious anemia or cancer. Despite the ongoing efforts of the bioassay group, continued data incompleteness limits our ability to understand the molecular roots of human disease. Therefore, it is urgent to develop a computational method that accurately and quickly detects PPIs. In this paper, a highly efficient model is proposed for predicting PPIs through heterogeneous network by combining local feature with global feature. Heterogeneous network is collected from several valuable datasets, containing five types of nodes and nine interactions among them. Local feature is extracted from protein sequence by k-mer method. Global feature is extracted from heterogeneous network by LINE (Large-scale Information Network Embedding). Protein representation is obtained from local feature and global feature by concatenation. Finally, random forest is trained to classify and predict potential protein pairs. The proposed method is demonstrated on STRING dataset and achieved an average 86.55% prediction accuracy with 0.9308 AUC. Extensive contrast experiments are performed with different protein representations and different classifiers. Obtained experiment results illustrate that proposed method is economically viable, which provides a new perspective for future research.

Keywords: Protein-protein interaction · Protein sequence · LINE · Network representation learning

1 Introduction

Protein-protein interactions (PPIs) constitute a major component of cell biochemical reaction network. Studying PPIs not only reveals the function of proteins at the molecular level. Moreover, it is essential for the rules of life activities such as growth, development, differentiation and apoptosis. The previous works show that the deregulation

© Springer Nature Switzerland AG 2021
D.-S. Huang et al. (Eds.): ICIC 2021, LNAI 12838, pp. 617–626, 2021.
https://doi.org/10.1007/978-3-030-84532-2_55

of PPIs may lead to many diseases, including pernicious anemia, cancers, cardiovascular disease and neurodegenerative disorders [1]. In order to detect the interactions between proteins, some high-throughput experiments have been proposed, including yeast two-hybrid screens [2], tandem affinity purification [3] and mass spectrometric protein complex identification [4]. Despite the ongoing efforts of these high-throughput experiments, continued data incompleteness limits our ability to detect more PPIs. In addition, these methods are not only time-consuming, but waste money and labor. Therefore, it is very meaningful to propose a low-cost, high-efficiency computing method to identify PPIs.

In recent years, a large number of machine learning methods are widely applied to bioinformatics applications [5–14]. The protein attributes which used to extract features are protein structures, phylogenetic profiles, literature knowledge, network topology and genome [15–20]. However, the methods based on these attributes are hard to apply without pre-existing information. Besides, sequence data of protein is the most available information. Hence, computational methods based on protein amino acid sequence attract widely attention and interests. A number of existing works show that sequence information is enough to predict PPIs due to the well performance. Romero et al. [21] predicted the protein-protein interactions using SVM only based on the sequence of proteins. The feature was extracted by the general-purpose numerical codification of polypeptides, which transformed pairs of amino acid sequences into a machine learning-friendly vector, whose elements represented numerical descriptors of residues in proteins. It achieved an average accuracy of 66.1% under 10-fold cross-validation on 3did, iPfam and Negatome 2.0 databases. Shen et al. [22] developed a novel computational method for inferring PPIs using protein sequence. A conjoint-triad feature was extracted from protein amino acids to represent protein. When applied this method to a data set containing 16,000 diverse PPI pairs, it achieved a very high predictive accuracy of 83.90%. Chen et al. [23] used a hybrid feature representation including three different protein-pair representations and a stacked generalization scheme integrating five learning algorithms to predict PPIs. Wang et al. [24–26] explored the protein evolutionary features from the angle of the image processing techniques in order to open a new way of researching protein sequences. Sequence-based approaches typically represent protein sequences as a vector by feature representation methods, which as input to a classification algorithm.

However, existing methods mentioned above all discussed PPIs at protein level, without considering the relationship between protein and other small molecules such as miRNA, lncRNA, diseases and drug. Therefore, it is feasible to predict PPIs on a larger scale. When considering other molecules, more complicated the protein associations are, more potential information is obtained. Potential interactions between protein researched by this network is very advanced, but also from the microscopic point of view to have a deeper understanding of human life activities.

In this paper, we proposed a systematic and comprehensive model to predict PPI based on protein sequence and network embedding. Firstly, nine proven small-molecular associations have been collected for heterogeneous network construction, called molecular associations network. After de-redundancy and repetition, five molecules are obtained and combined together throughout cellular level view, comprising protein, lncRNA, miRNA, drug and disease. After pre-processing dataset, local feature and global feature are extracted, respectively. Local feature is extracted from protein sequence by 3-mer. Global feature is extracted by LINE (Large-scale Network Embedding), which is a neural network-based network embedding method. It can capture first-order and second-order similarity efficiently and accurately. Then, the last part of model is to classify samples. Random Forest is integrated to proposed model as classifier. The construction of systematic and complex heterogeneous network offers a new view, which can help us better understand biology and disease pathologies.

2 Materials and Methods

2.1 Dataset Collecting

Proposed model predict PPI interaction based on a heterogeneous network, which is a systematically and holistically biomolecular relationship network. As a result, the first task is to collect data to construct network.

Thanks to many researches have studied the interactions between individual small molecules well, providing a few valuable datasets of molecular interactions. Nine databases [27–36] containing nine kinds of individual biological small molecule associations were collected. Finally, the network was constructed, owning 105546 associations with five types of nodes and nine associations of individual small molecules after performing the inclusion of identifier unification, de-redundancy, simplification and deletion of the irrelevant items. The statistic of heterogeneous network is shown in Table 1.

Table 1. The statistic of heterogeneous network.

Heterogeneous network properties	Sources	Number
#Protein	-	1,649
#LncRNA	-	769
#miRNA	-	1,023
#Disease	-	2,062
#Drug	-	1,025
#miRNA-LncRNA	lncRNASNP2	8,374
#miRNA-Disease	HMDD	16,427
#miRNA-Protein	miRTarBase	4,944
#LncRNA-Disease	LncRNADisease, lncRNASNP2	1,264
#Protein-Protein	STRING	19,237
#Protein-Disease	DisGeNET	25,087
#Drug-Protein	DrugBank	11,107
#Drug-Disease	CTD	18,416
#LncRNA-Protein	LncRNA2Target	690

2.2 Local Feature Extraction from Protein Sequence by K-mer

Previous studies have proven that protein sequence is useful to PPI prediction task. As a result, protein sequence downloaded from STRING is collected to extract protein basic information.

Before extracting protein local feature, protein original embedding is needed. According to the polarity of the side chain, Shen et al. [22] has divided 20 amino acids into four groups, comprising (Ala, Val, Leu, Ile, Met, Phe, Trp, Pro), (Gly, Ser, Thr, Cys, Asn, Gln, Tyr), (Arg, Lys, His) and (Asp, Glu). Inspired by Shen, we simplied the sequences of proteins to a 64 (4 × 4 × 4) dimensional vector using the method of 3-mer. Each dimension of vector is initialized to 0. Then setting a sliding window, whose length is 3, to scan the whole protein sequence in step of 1. In each slide, the amino acid sequence possessed in the window is recorded to the corresponding position of the vector. After sliding completed, the vector is normalized, and each dimension in the vector is the frequency at which the amino acid sequence appears in the original protein sequence. The reason for constructing 64-dimensional vectors is that there are 64 possible sorts of amino acids in four. Finally, the vector obtained by 3-mer is attribute feature.

2.3 Global Feature Extraction from Network by LINE

In the entire biomolecular network, the protein nodes include not only self-basic local feature but also global feature. Global feature describes network structure for each protein node.

Network embedding can be regarded as the process of converting the representation of nodes from an original high-dimensional space into a low-dimensional vector space. With the computer science development, a lot of network embedding methods are proposed. They can be grouped into three categories, which are Matrix Factorization-based model [37], Random Walk-based model [38, 39], and Neural Network-based model [40, 41]. Considering both efficiency and model complexity, LINE [40] is integrated into proposed model to learn low-rank representations of each node. LINE maps the nodes in a large network to the vector space according to the density of their relationships, so that the closely connected nodes are projected into similar locations, and the tightness of the two nodes is measured in network.

LINE designs two objective functions attempting to address the local and global network structures, respectively, instructing researchers to consider network structures at both the local and global levels. LINE defines the First-order proximity (see Fig. 1A) and the Second-order proximity (see Fig. 1B). The first-order proximity in the network is the self-similarity between the two nodes (regardless of other nodes). For each undirected edge (i, j), the joint probability between node v_i and v_j is defined as follows:

$$p_1(v_i, v_j) = \frac{1}{1 + \exp(-\overrightarrow{v_i}^T \cdot \overrightarrow{v_j})} \tag{1}$$

The second-order proximity between a pair of nodes (u, v) in a network is the similarity between their neighboring network structures. In mathematics, let $P_u =$

$(W_{u,1}, W_{u,2}, W_{u,3}, \ldots, W_{u,|V|})$ denotes the first-order similarity between u and all other nodes, then the second-order similarity between u and v is determined by P_u and P_v. The second-order proximity assumes that the nodes of the shared neighbor are similar to each other. Each node plays two roles: the node itself and the neighbors of other nodes. Thus, the probability that v_i is a neighbor of v_j is defined as:

$$p_2(v_i|v_j) = \frac{\exp(-\vec{v_i}^T \cdot \vec{v_j})}{\sum_{k=1}^{|V|} \exp(\vec{v_k}^T \cdot \vec{v_j})} \tag{2}$$

Accordingly, the results of LINE can be regarded as a global feature of nodes, called global feature.

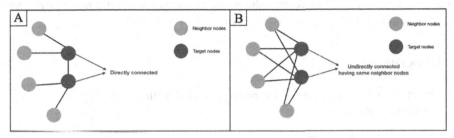

Fig. 1. An illustration of First-order proximity and Second-order proximity in LINE. A) First-order proximity and B) Second-order proximity.

2.4 Protein Representation

Local feature focus on protein sequence information and global feature learns heterogeneous network structure. In order to represent protein nodes both locally and globally, an aggregation method is applied to form final protein representation. More specificity, the final representation called aggregated feature is the concatenation of local feature and global feature, which can be formulated by:

$$Agg_{concat} = \sigma \left(W \cdot \left(e_l^{d_i}; e_g^{d_i} \right) + b \right) \tag{3}$$

Where $e_l^{d_i}$ represents node d_i local feature and $e_g^{d_i}$ denotes node d_i global feature. W and b are trainable parameters.

2.5 Performance Evaluation Indicators

Five-fold cross-validation is used to test proposed model. The entire dataset is divided into five equal subsets randomly, each taking one part as the test set and the remaining four parts as training set, cycle 5 times in turn, taking the average of ten times as the final performance.

Several criteria are used to evaluate proposed method, including accuracy (Acc.), sensitivity (Sen.) and precision (Prec.), Receiver operating characteristic (ROC), Area

Under Curve (AUC) and Area Under Precision-Recall (AUPR). These criteria are sufficient to measure the quality, robustness, and predictability of the model from different perspectives.

$$\text{Acc.} = \frac{TN + TP}{FP + TP + FN + TN} \tag{4}$$

$$\text{Sen.} = \frac{TP}{TN + TP} \tag{5}$$

$$\text{Prec.} = \frac{TP}{TP + FP} \tag{6}$$

Where FP, TP, FN and TN represent false positive, true positive, false negative and true negative, respectively.

3 Experiments

3.1 Prediction Performance of Proposed Method with Three Types of Representations

In order to exploit the discriminative features of nodes, each node has two features, including local and global feature in our study. To explore the impact of network embedding and node attributes on final classification result, we evaluate and compare the network embedding alone and individual node attributes and the combination of the two under five-fold cross validation, respectively. As shown in Table 2.

Table 2. Predictive performance of three kinds of node representations on STRING dataset.

Representation	Acc.	Sen.	Prec.	AUC	AUPR
Local feature	0.7491 ± 0.0090	0.6945 ± 0.0109	0.7797 ± 0.0103	0.8206 ± 0.0080	0.8185 ± 0.0181
Global feature	0.8570 ± 0.0045	0.8130 ± 0.0105	0.8916 ± 0.0099	0.9240 ± 0.0046	0.9238 ± 0.0093
Aggregated feature	**0.8655 ± 0.0050**	**0.8249 ± 0.0085**	**0.8979 ± 0.0088**	**0.9301 ± 0.0050**	**0.9308 ± 0.0045**

The nodes represented by local feature achieved an average accuracy of 0.7491, an average sensitivity of 0.6945, an average precision of 0.7797 and the average AUC value is 0.8206, the average AUPR is 0.8185. Compared with local feature, the model adopted global feature had a better performance with an average accuracy of 0.8570, an average sensitivity of 0.8130, an average precision of 0.8916 and the average AUC value is 0.9240, the average AUPR is 0.9238. Though global feature is more representative than local feature, the model with aggregated feature achieved the best performance on STRING dataset with the highest accuracy of 0.8655 and AUC and AUPR value. Moreover, aggregated feature achieved smaller standard deviations, making the model stable and robust.

3.2 Comparison of Different Machine Learning Classifiers

For the purpose of evaluating the performance of classifier, we compared Random Forest (RF) with AdaBoost, SVM, Logistic Regression (LR), Naïve Bayes (NB) and XGBoost [42–45] under five-fold cross validation in same evaluation criteria. In order to avoid bias, every classifier uses default parameters in our experiment. The results are shown in Table 3.

Table 3. Predictive performance under various classifiers on STRING dataset.

Classifier	Acc.	Sen.	Prec.	AUC	AUPR
SVM	0.7103 ± 0.0078	0.7577 ± 0.0113	0.6921 ± 0.0074	0.7747 ± 0.0077	0.7686 ± 0.0074
LR	0.7056 ± 0.0072	0.7452 ± 0.0119	0.6905 ± 0.0067	0.7733 ± 0.0078	0.7667 ± 0.0076
NB	0.6772 ± 0.0084	0.7392 ± 0.0098	0.6578 ± 0.0090	0.7563 ± 0.0071	0.7827 ± 0.0075
AdaBoost	0.6946 ± 0.0088	0.7306 ± 0.0115	0.6816 ± 0.0090	0.7669 ± 0.0094	0.7713 ± 0.0086
XGBoost	0.8600 ± 0.0081	**0.8867 ± 0.0063**	0.8419 ± 0.0109	**0.9326 ± 0.0051**	0.9240 ± 0.0048
RF	**0.8655 ± 0.0050**	0.8249 ± 0.0085	0.8979 ± 0.0088	0.9301 ± 0.0050	**0.9308 ± 0.0045**

SVM and LR are belonging to liner model. Both of them are not performing well. SVM achieved an average accuracy of 0.7103, AUC value of 0.7747 and AUPR value of 0.7686. LR achieved an average accuracy of 0.7056, AUC value of 0.7733 and AUPR value of 0.7827. Owning to the interactions between proteins are diverse, not a single linear relationship, these two models are not suitable for this dataset.

NB is a generation model. NB achieved an average accuracy of 0.6772, AUC value of 0.7563, and AUPR value of 0.7827. However, NB classifiers assumed that each feature of the sample is not related to other features. Due to the global feature describing the relationship between different nodes, this method is also not suitable.

AdaBoost, XGBoost and Random Forest are belonging to integrated model. Among the three models, AdaBoost got the worst results with an average accuracy of 0.6946, an average AUC value of 0.7669 and an average AUPR value of 0.7713. XGBoost performed well on datasets, achieving the highest AUC of 0.9326. However, the accuracy of XGBoost was 0.8600, which was lower than Random Forest. Moreover, XGBoost had a higher standard deviation of 0.0081 meaning the model was not stable under five-fold cross validation. Random Forest achieved the best results on accuracy with a high AUC value of 0.9309 and a high AUPR value of 0.9311. Simultaneously, Random Forest had small standard deviation 0.0051 proving the method was stable and robust. Therefore, Random Forest was selected as final classifier as the result of its excellent performance in experiment.

4 Conclusion

In conclusion, a computational sequence and network representation learning based model is proposed for PPI prediction. Protein attribute feature is extracted from protein sequence by 3-mer, called local feature. Another feature is extracted from heterogeneous network called global feature, which aims to capture network structure and obtain potential link information. Proposed method integrates local feature with global feature to represent protein node. By this way, the protein feature contains both protein attribute and network structure information. Experiment results also prove that this combined feature is helpful to improve model performance. These good results show that proposed method can be used as a new way to predict PPIs from a global view. In future work, we will consider incorporating more small molecules to increase the potential link between proteins, thereby improving the accuracy of predictions.

Funding. This work was supported in part by Awardee of the NSFC Excellent Young Scholars Program, under Grant 61722212, in part by the National Natural Science Foundation of China, under Grants 61702444, in part by the Chinese Postdoctoral Science Foundation, under Grant 2019M653804, in part by the National Natural Science Foundation of China under Grant 62002297, in part by the West Light Foundation of The Chinese Academy of Sciences, under Grant 2018-XBQNXZ-B-008.

References

1. Kotlyar, M., et al.: In silico prediction of physical protein interactions and characterization of interactome orphans. Nat. Methods **12**, 79 (2015)
2. Fields, S., Song, O.-k.: A novel genetic system to detect protein–protein interactions. Nature **340**, 245 (1989)
3. Gavin, A.-C., et al.: Functional organization of the yeast proteome by systematic analysis of protein complexes. Nature **415**, 141 (2002)
4. Ho, Y., et al.: Systematic identification of protein complexes in Saccharomyces cerevisiae by mass spectrometry. Nature **415**, 180 (2002)
5. An, J.-Y., Meng, F.-R., You, Z.-H., Fang, Y.-H., Zhao, Y.-J., Zhang, M.: Using the relevance vector machine model combined with local phase quantization to predict protein-protein interactions from protein sequences. BioMed Res. Int. **2016**, (2016)
6. Huang, D.-S., Zhang, L., Han, K., Deng, S., Yang, K., Zhang, H.: Prediction of protein-protein interactions based on protein-protein correlation using least squares regression. Curr. Protein Pept. Sci. **15**, 553–560 (2014)
7. Huang, Y.-A., Chen, X., You, Z.-H., Huang, D.-S., Chan, K.C.: ILNCSIM: improved lncRNA functional similarity calculation model. Oncotarget **7**, 25902 (2016)
8. Luo, X., Ming, Z., You, Z., Li, S., Xia, Y., Leung, H.: Improving network topology-based protein interactome mapping via collaborative filtering. Knowl.-Based Syst. **90**, 23–32 (2015)
9. Wong, L., You, Z.-H., Ming, Z., Li, J., Chen, X., Huang, Y.-A.: Detection of interactions between proteins through rotation forest and local phase quantization descriptors. Int. J. Mol. Sci. **17**, 21 (2016)
10. You, Z.-H., Lei, Y.-K., Gui, J., Huang, D.-S., Zhou, X.: Using manifold embedding for assessing and predicting protein interactions from high-throughput experimental data. Bioinformatics **26**, 2744–2751 (2010)

11. You, Z.-H., Yin, Z., Han, K., Huang, D.-S., Zhou, X.: A semi-supervised learning approach to predict synthetic genetic interactions by combining functional and topological properties of functional gene network. BMC Bioinf. **11**, 343 (2010)
12. You, Z.-H., Zhou, M., Luo, X., Li, S.: Highly efficient framework for predicting interactions between proteins. IEEE Trans. Cybern. **47**, 731–743 (2016)
13. Zheng, C.-H., Zhang, L., Ng, T.-Y., Shiu, C.K., Huang, D.-S.: Metasample-based sparse representation for tumor classification. IEEE/ACM Trans. Comput. Biol. Bioinf. **8**, 1273–1282 (2011)
14. Zheng, C.-H., Zhang, L., Ng, V.T.-Y., Shiu, C.K., Huang, D.-S.: Molecular pattern discovery based on penalized matrix decomposition. IEEE/ACM Trans. Comput. Biol. Bioinf. (TCBB) **8**, 1592–1603 (2011)
15. An, J.-Y., et al.: Identification of self-interacting proteins by exploring evolutionary information embedded in PSI-BLAST-constructed position specific scoring matrix. Oncotarget **7**, 82440 (2016)
16. Deng, S., Yuan, J., Huang, D., Zhen, W.: SFAPS: an R package for structure/function analysis of protein sequences based on informational spectrum method. In: IEEE International Conference on Bioinformatics & Biomedicine (2014)
17. Deng, S.-P., Zhu, L., Huang, D.-S.: Mining the bladder cancer-associated genes by an integrated strategy for the construction and analysis of differential co-expression networks. BMC Genomics **16**, S4 (2015). BioMed Central
18. Guo, Y., Yu, L., Wen, Z., Li, M.: Using support vector machine combined with auto covariance to predict protein–protein interactions from protein sequences. Nucleic Acids Res. **36**, 3025–3030 (2008)
19. Sun, J., et al.: Refined phylogenetic profiles method for predicting protein–protein interactions. Bioinformatics **21**, 3409–3415 (2005)
20. Zhang, Q.C., et al.: Structure-based prediction of protein–protein interactions on a genome-wide scale. Nature **490**, 556 (2012)
21. Romero-Molina, S., Ruiz-Blanco, Y.B., Harms, M., Münch, J., Sanchez-Garcia, E.: PPI-Detect: a support vector machine model for sequence-based prediction of protein–protein interactions. J. Comput. Chem. **40**, 1233–1242 (2019)
22. Shen, J., et al.: Predicting protein–protein interactions based only on sequences information. Proc. Natl. Acad. Sci. **104**, 4337–4341 (2007)
23. Chen, K.-H., Wang, T.-F., Hu, Y.-J.: Protein-protein interaction prediction using a hybrid feature representation and a stacked generalization scheme. BMC Bioinf. **20**, 308 (2019)
24. Wang, Y., You, Z., Li, X., Chen, X., Jiang, T., Zhang, J.: PCVMZM: using the probabilistic classification vector machines model combined with a Zernike moments descriptor to predict protein–protein interactions from protein sequences. Int. J. Mol. Sci. **18**, 1029 (2017)
25. Wang, Y.-B., You, Z.-H., Li, L.-P., Huang, Y.-A., Yi, H.-C.: Detection of interactions between proteins by using legendre moments descriptor to extract discriminatory information embedded in PSSM. Molecules **22**, 1366 (2017)
26. Wang, Y.-B., et al.: Predicting protein–protein interactions from protein sequences by a stacked sparse autoencoder deep neural network. Mol. BioSyst. **13**, 1336–1344 (2017)
27. Szklarczyk, D., et al.: The STRING database in 2017: quality-controlled protein–protein association networks, made broadly accessible. Nucleic Acids Res. **45**(D1), D362D368 (2016). gkw937
28. Chen, G., et al.: LncRNADisease: a database for long-non-coding RNA-associated diseases. Nucleic Acids Res. **41**, D983–D986 (2012)
29. Cheng, L., et al.: LncRNA2Target v2. 0: a comprehensive database for target genes of lncRNAs in human and mouse. Nucleic Acids Res. **47**, D140-D144 (2018)
30. Chou, C.-H., et al.: miRTarBase update 2018: a resource for experimentally validated microRNA-target interactions. Nucleic Acids Res. **46**, D296–D302 (2017)

31. Davis, A.P., et al.: The comparative toxicogenomics database: update 2019. Nucleic Acids Res. **47**, D948–D954 (2018)
32. Huang, Z., et al.: HMDD v3. 0: a database for experimentally supported human microRNA–disease associations. Nucleic Acids Res. **47**, D1013-D1017 (2018)
33. Kozomara, A., Birgaoanu, M., Griffiths-Jones, S.: miRBase: from microRNA sequences to function. Nucleic Acids Res. **47**, D155–D162 (2018)
34. Miao, Y.-R., Liu, W., Zhang, Q., Guo, A.-Y.: lncRNASNP2: an updated database of functional SNPs and mutations in human and mouse lncRNAs. Nucleic Acids Res. **46**, D276–D280 (2017)
35. Piñero, J., et al.: DisGeNET: a comprehensive platform integrating information on human disease-associated genes and variants. Nucleic Acids Res. **45**(D1): D833D839 (2016). gkw943
36. Wishart, D.S., et al.: DrugBank 5.0: a major update to the DrugBank database for 2018. Nucleic Acids Res. **46**, D1074-D1082 (2017)
37. Belkin, M., Niyogi, P.: Laplacian Eigenmaps for Dimensionality Reduction and Data. Neural Comput. **15**, 1373–1396 (2003)
38. Perozzi, B., Al-Rfou, R., Skiena, S.: DeepWalk: online learning of social representations. In: Proceedings of the 20th ACM SIGKDD International Conference on Knowledge Discovery and Data Mining, pp. 701–710. Association for Computing Machinery, New York (2014)
39. Grover, A., Leskovec, J.: node2vec: scalable feature learning for networks. In: ACM SIGKDD International Conference on Knowledge Discovery & Data Mining (2016)
40. Tang, J., Qu, M., Wang, M., Zhang, M., Yan, J., Mei, Q.: Line: large-scale information network embedding. In: Proceedings of the 24th International Conference on World Wide Web, pp. 1067–1077. International World Wide Web Conferences Steering Committee (2015)
41. Wang, D., Cui, P., Zhu, W.: Structural deep network embedding. In: Proceedings of the 22nd ACM SIGKDD International Conference on Knowledge Discovery and Data Mining, pp. 1225–1234. ACM (2016)
42. Chen, T., Guestrin, C.: Xgboost: a scalable tree boosting system. In: Proceedings of the 22nd ACM SIGKDD International Conference on Knowledge Discovery and Data Mining, pp. 785–794. ACM (2016)
43. Hosmer, D.W., Jr., Lemeshow, S., Sturdivant, R.X.: Applied Logistic Regression. Wiley, New York (2013)
44. Suykens, J.A., Vandewalle, J.: Least squares support vector machine classifiers. Neural Process. Lett. **9**, 293–300 (1999)
45. Rätsch, G., Onoda, T., Müller, K.-R.: Soft margins for AdaBoost. Mach. Learning **42**, 287–320 (2001)

DNA-Binding Protein Prediction Based on Deep Learning Feature Fusion

Shixuan Guan, Tengsheng Jiang, Weizhong Lu, Qiming Fu, Haiou Li,
and Hongjie Wu[✉]

School of Electronic and Information Engineering, Suzhou University of Science
and Technology, Suzhou 215009, China

Abstract. DNA-binding protein is a special kind of protein. It can interact with DNA, play an important role in various gene-related life activities, and is closely related to many diseases. Therefore, it is of great significance to study the identification methods of DNA-binding proteins. However, traditional biological experiment methods require a lot of human resources and material resources. It cannot meet the trend of rapid increase in protein sequences. In this article, a tool for DNA-binding protein prediction based on Convolutional Neural Networks (CNN) and Bidirectional Long Short-Term Memory (BiLSTM) neural networks is proposed. It can not only extract features from the original sequence of a protein, but also extract related features from the co-evolution relationship of the protein. Compared with other methods, the experimental results of this model are more accurate.

Keywords: DNA-binding protein · CNN · BiLSTM · Multi-feature fusion

1 Introduction

DNA-binding proteins (DBPs) are those proteins that interact with DNA. They are related to many DNA-related life activities in biological cells, including control of transcription and translation, DNA repair, splicing, apoptosis and mediating stress responses [1, 2] and so on. In 2004, Shanahan et al. [3] discovered the structure patterns of three DNA-binding proteins through a protein structure comparison method, which provided the necessary foundation for the subsequent prediction of DNA-binding proteins. With the development of high-throughput technologies, such as ChIP-seq [4] and HT-SELEX [5], the resolution of specific protein-DNA interaction determinations has been improved. However, the cost of traditional biological experiment methods is still relatively high [6]. Therefore, many calculation-based DNA binding protein prediction methods have been proposed continuously. Commonly used algorithms include Random Forest (RF) [7], Support Vector Machine (SVM) [8], Naive Bayes (NB) [9] and so on. Traditional machine learning algorithms require too much human participation in the feature extraction stage, while deep learning can automatically learn useful features. This makes deep learning algorithms gradually applied to the field of protein [10, 11]. In 2015, Alipanahi et al. [12] first used Convolutional Neural Networks to predict DNA-binding

© Springer Nature Switzerland AG 2021
D.-S. Huang et al. (Eds.): ICIC 2021, LNAI 12838, pp. 627–633, 2021.
https://doi.org/10.1007/978-3-030-84532-2_56

proteins, which greatly improved the accuracy of prediction. In this article, a deep learning framework is constructed, which can not only extract useful information from the original protein sequence, but also extract useful information from the co-evolutionary information of the protein. After that, the extracted features are fused to improve the accuracy of prediction.

2   Data Set and Data Representation

2.1   Data Set

In this article, the protein sequence used is from the Protein Data Bank (website: http://www.rcsb.org/pdb/home/home.do) [13]. The protein sequence similarity in the data set is limited to 25%. The length of the sequence is limited to between 50 and 2000 amino acids. And we deleted all protein sequences with irregular amino acids ("X" and "Z"). The training set contains 1075 pieces of data, the validation set contains 594 pieces of data, and the independent test set contains 186 pieces of data. The training set contains 550 positive samples and 525 negative samples. The number of positive and negative samples in the validation set and test set each account for 50%. This data set is a relatively classic data set in the field of DNA-binding proteins, which is convenient for comparison and analysis with other methods.

2.2   Data Representation

The original protein sequence is represented by One-hot encoding. One-Hot encoding is a universal encoding method. It is extremely easy to generate while effective for protein function prediction associated problems [14]. For each residue in the protein sequence, a One-Hot code corresponds to a 20-dimensional vector. It contains 19 "0"s and 1 "1". The "1" corresponds to the amino acid at the index of a certain protein sequence. As shown in Fig. 1.

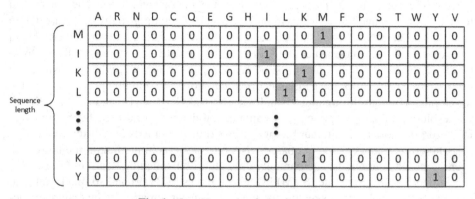

Fig. 1. One-Hot code of protein residues

Co-evolution information is expressed using a position-specific scoring matrix (PSSM). The PSSM [15] is an important form of expressing protein co-evolution information. PSSM is generated by iteratively searching protein databases using query sequences. It can reflect the evolutionary characteristics of protein sequences. According to research [16], conserved regions are functional regions during evolution. Therefore, PSSM has been widely used in biological information problems. In our research, we use PSSM as part of the input to extract relevant features. For a given protein sequence, the PSSM matrix is an L × 20 matrix, where L represents the length of the protein sequence. As shown in Fig. 2.

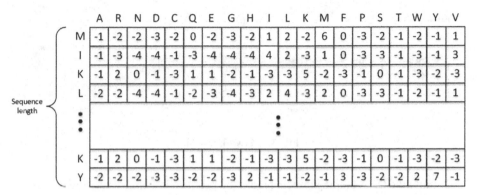

Fig. 2. Position-specific scoring matrix of protein residues

3 Methods

3.1 Model Description

In this section, a novel composite deep learning network will be introduced. Figure 3 shows the specific model structure. Most existing methods only use protein sequences or features derived from protein sequences to predict DNA binding proteins [17, 18]. Unlike these methods, we not only use the original sequence of the protein, but also the co-evolutionary information of the protein. The original protein sequence is input into the BiLSTM network [19], and the co-evolution information (PSSM) is input into the CNN network. We use these two networks to extract the features in the sequence and co-evolution information respectively. Then they are combined into a feature vector to represent the protein. Finally, input the extracted multi-scale features into the fully connected layer network to predict the protein.

The Sigmoid activation function is used after the last fully connected layer. This ensures that the output is a positive number between 0 and 1 [20]. The calculation formula of the Sigmoid function is as follows:

$$\sigma(x) = \frac{1}{1 - e^{-x}} \tag{1}$$

In this article, we interpret the positive number of this output as the probability that the protein is predicted to be a DNA binding protein. When the output is greater than 0.5, we treat it as a DNA binding protein.

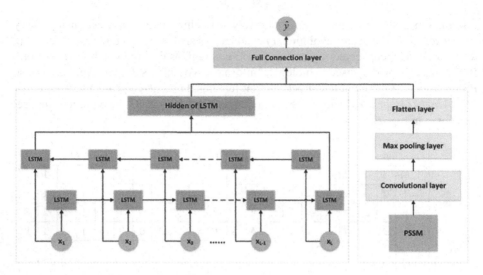

Fig. 3. Network model

Because the DNA binding protein prediction problem is a binary classification problem, in this article, we use binary cross entropy as the loss function. It can be a good measure of the degree of fit between the predicted data and the real data [21]. In the N protein sequences, y_i represents the true category of the ith sequence, and $\hat{y}_i$ represents the predicted probability of the ith sequence. The binary cross entropy loss is calculated as follows:

$$L(\theta) = -\sum_{i=1}^{N} \left(y_i \log \hat{y}_i + (1 - y_i) \log(1 - \hat{y}_i) \right) \tag{2}$$

3.2 Model Parameters

The network models designed in this paper are all implemented by Python language combined with the deep learning framework Pytorch. This article uses backpropagation algorithm to update model parameters. Optimization algorithm uses Adam. Loss function uses binary cross entropy loss. Batch_size is set to 64, and iterative training is performed for 150 rounds. As shown in Table 1, it is the pseudo code of the program.

Table 1. Pseudo code of the model

Algorithm: A method to predict DNA binding protein

Input: Training data

1   Initialize weights with randomly generated values

2   Iteration n = 1; Begin training stage:

3   for n < max iteration OR lost function criteria met, do:

4   for train_input_data x1 to xL, do:

5   a. PSSM data forward propagate through convolution, pooling

6   b. Protein sequence data forward propagate through BiLSTM network

7   c. Fuse co-evolutionary characteristics and sequence feature, and enter the fully connected layer together

8   d. Calculate loss function value for the input

9   e. Calculate the gradient of the parameters

10   f. Backpropagation to update the parameters of the network

Output: Trained network parameters

4   Results and Discussion

In this article, we use the most commonly used evaluation indicators: accuracy (ACC), Matthews correlation coefficient (MCC), sensitivity (SN), and specificity (SP) to evaluate the performance of the model. Their calculation formula is as follows:

$$ACC = \frac{TP}{TP + FN} \tag{3}$$

$$MCC = \frac{TP \times TN - FP \times FN}{\sqrt{(TP + FN) \times (TP + FP) \times (TN + FP) \times (TN + FN)}} \tag{4}$$

$$SN = \frac{TP}{TP + FN} \tag{5}$$

$$SP = \frac{TN}{TN + FP} \tag{6}$$

Among them, TP represents the number of positive samples predicted correctly. TN represents the number of negative samples predicted correctly. FP is the number of positive samples predicted incorrectly. And FN is the number of negative samples predicted incorrectly.

In order to prove the effectiveness of our model, we compared it with some existing classic models, including DNA-Prot [22], iDNA-Prot [23] and iDNA-Protldis [24]. The experimental results of each model are shown in Table 2.

Table 2. Performance comparisons between different methods

Method	ACC (%)	MCC	SN (%)	SP (%)
DNA-Prot	72.55	0.44	82.67	59.75
iDNA-Prot	75.40	0.50	83.81	64.73
iDNA-Protldis	77.30	0.54	79.40	75.27
Our method	80.57	0.61	85.11	76.10

It can be seen from Table 2 that our prediction model is better in terms of ACC, MCC, SN and SP, where MCC is the overall index for evaluating the two types of models. The ACC, MCC, SN and SP of our method are 80.57%, 0.61, 85.11% and 76.10%, respectively. These results intuitively show that the integration of sequence features and co-evolution information can improve the accuracy of prediction. In addition, the experimental results are obtained on standard data. Therefore, the effectiveness of the neural network for feature extraction is verified, and it proves once again that our proposed method is an effective prediction method.

5 Conclusion

In this paper, using the original protein sequence and PSSM matrix as input, we build a DNA binding protein prediction tool based on deep learning. This method uses a deep learning-based method to automatically learn rich features from the input data. This method has been experimented on the collected data sets, and a large number of experimental results have been obtained. The excellent results prove the effectiveness of our method.

Acknowledgement. This paper is supported by the National Natural Science Foundation of China (62073231, 61772357, 61902272, 61876217, 61902271), National Research Project (2020YFC2006602) and Anhui Province Key Laboratory Research Project (IBBE2018KX09).

References

1. Hudson, W.H., Ortlund, E.A.: The structure, function and evolution of proteins that bind DNA and RNA. Nat. Rev. Mol. Cell Biol. **15**(11), 749–760 (2014)
2. Iftode, C., Daniely, Y., Borowiec, J.A.: Replication protein A (RPA): the eukaryotic SSB. Crit. Rev. Biochem. Mol. Biol. **34**(3), 141–180 (1999)
3. Shanahan, H.P., Garcia, M.A., Jones, S., et al.: Identifying DNA-binding proteins using structural motifs and the electrostatic potential. Nucleic Acids Res. **32**(16), 4732–4741 (2004)
4. Furey, T.S.: ChIP–seq and beyond: new and improved methodologies to detect and characterize protein–DNA interactions. Nat. Rev. Genet. **13**(12), 840–852 (2012)
5. Jolma, A., Kivioja, T., Toivonen, J., et al.: Multiplexed massively parallel SELEX for characterization of human transcription factor binding specificities. Genome Res. **20**(6), 861–873 (2010)

6. Du, X., Diao, Y., Liu, H., et al.: MsDBP: exploring DNA-binding proteins by integrating multiscale sequence information via Chou's five-step rule. J. Proteome Res. **18**(8), 3119–3132 (2019)

7. Nimrod, G., Szilágyi, A., Leslie, C., et al.: Identification of DNA-binding proteins using structural, electrostatic and evolutionary features. J. Mol. Biol. **387**(4), 1040–1053 (2009)

8. Ho, S.Y., Yu, F.C., Chang, C.Y., et al.: Design of accurate predictors for DNA-binding sites in proteins using hybrid SVM–PSSM method. Biosystems **90**(1), 234–241 (2007)

9. Yan, C., Terribilini, M., Wu, F., et al.: Predicting DNA-binding sites of proteins from amino acid sequence[J]. BMC Bioinform. **7**(1), 1–10 (2006)

10. Min, S., Lee, B., Yoon, S.: Deep learning in bioinformatics. Brief. Bioinform. **18**(5), 851–869 (2017)

11. Li, S., Chen, J., Liu, B.: Protein remote homology detection based on bidirectional long short-term memory. BMC Bioinf. **18**(1), 1–8 (2017)

12. Alipanahi, B., Delong, A., Weirauch, M.T., et al.: Predicting the sequence specificities of DNA-and RNA-binding proteins by deep learning. Nat. Biotechnol. **33**(8), 831–838 (2015)

13. Sussman, J.L., Lin, D., Jiang, J., et al.: Protein Data Bank (PDB): database of three-dimensional structural information of biological macromolecules. Acta Crystallogr. D Biol. Crystallogr. **54**(6), 1078–1084 (1998)

14. Ding, H., Li, D.: Identification of mitochondrial proteins of malaria parasite using analysis of variance. Amino Acids **47**(2), 329–333 (2015)

15. Altschul, S.F., Madden, T.L., Schäffer, A.A., et al.: Gapped BLAST and PSI-BLAST: a new generation of protein database search programs. Nucleic Acids Res. **25**(17), 3389–3402 (1997)

16. Jeong, J.C., Lin, X., Chen, X.W.: On position-specific scoring matrix for protein function prediction. IEEE/ACM Trans. Comput. Biol. Bioinf. **8**(2), 308–315 (2010)

17. Mishra, A., Pokhrel, P., Hoque, M.T.: StackDPPred: a stacking based prediction of DNA-binding protein from sequence. Bioinformatics **35**(3), 433–441 (2019)

18. Chauhan, S., Ahmad, S.: Enabling full-length evolutionary profiles based deep convolutional neural network for predicting DNA-binding proteins from sequence. Proteins Struct. Funct. Bioinf. **88**(1), 15–30 (2020)

19. Lample, G., Ballesteros, M., Subramanian, S., et al.: Neural architectures for named entity recognition. arXiv preprint arXiv:1603.01360 (2016)

20. Yam, J.Y.F., Chow, T.W.S.: A weight initialization method for improving training speed in feedforward neural network. Neurocomputing **30**(1–4), 219–232 (2000)

21. Ho, Y., Wookey, S.: The real-world-weight cross-entropy loss function: modeling the costs of mislabeling. IEEE Access **8**, 4806–4813 (2019)

22. Kumar, K.K., Pugalenthi, G., Suganthan, P.N.: DNA-Prot: identification of DNA binding proteins from protein sequence information using random forest. J. Biomol. Struct. Dyn. **26**(6), 679–686 (2009)

23. Lin, W.Z., Fang, J.A., Xiao, X., et al.: iDNA-Prot: identification of DNA binding proteins using random forest with grey model. PloS One, **6**(9), e24756 (2011)

24. Liu, B., Xu, J., Lan, X., et al.: iDNA-Prot| dis: identifying DNA-binding proteins by incorporating amino acid distance-pairs and reduced alphabet profile into the general pseudo amino acid composition. PloS One **9**(9), e106691 (2014)

Membrane Protein Identification via Multiple Kernel Fuzzy SVM

Weizhong Lu[1,2](✉), Jiawei Shen[1], Yuqing Qian[1](✉), Hongjie Wu[1,2], Yijie Ding[1,2], and Xiaoyi Chen[1]

[1] School of Electronic and Information Engineering, Suzhou University of Science and Technology, Suzhou 215009, China
luwz@usts.edu.cn
[2] Suzhou Key Laboratory of Virtual Reality Intelligent Interaction and Application Technology, Suzhou University of Science and Technology, Suzhou 215009, China

Abstract. Membrane proteins are an important part of daily life activities in biological information. Predicting membrane proteins can improve drug targeting accuracy and artificial intelligence-assisted drug progression. Traditional methods such as X-ray and MRI are more accurate but consume huge human and material resources, and as science progresses, traditional experimental methods have become more and more difficult to match the needs of experts. In this paper, from the perspective of machine learning, pseudo-PSSM (PsePSSM), averaging block (AvBlock), discrete cosine transform (DCT), discrete wavelet transform (DWT) and histogram of oriented gradients (HOG) are used, and then features are extracted via position scoring matrix (PSSM). An evolutionary feature and fuzzy support vector machine based membrane protein prediction model is proposed. The results show that this method has better prediction and higher accuracy than other methods on two benchmark data sets, TRAIN1 and TRAIN2, reaching 90.6% and 89.7% accuracy, respectively.

Keywords: Membrane proteins · Evolutionary features · PSSM · Fuzzy support vector machine

1 Introduction

Every cell has a membrane composed of proteins and lipids. Researchers refer to the basic proteins embedded in the lipid bilayer as membrane proteins. Membrane proteins can be classified into (1) type 1 single-span type; (2) type 2 single-span type; (3) type 3 single-span type; (4) type 4 single-span type; (5) multi-span type; (6) lipid-anchored type; (7) GPI-anchored type and (8) peripheral type.

With the development of the world, human medical treatment is getting higher and higher, and membrane proteins are an important part of the medical field, so we need to classify the structures of membrane proteins to contribute to contemporary biomedical and other research fields, and how to predict the types efficiently by virtue of protein sequences is an important challenge on the path of current biological research. Although

© Springer Nature Switzerland AG 2021
D.-S. Huang et al. (Eds.): ICIC 2021, LNAI 12838, pp. 634–646, 2021.
https://doi.org/10.1007/978-3-030-84532-2_57

traditional physical chemistry-based experiments can predict protein types more accurately to some extent, there are inevitably some drawbacks, such as the need to invest huge human and financial resources and the harsh requirements on the surrounding experimental environment, so it is unrealistic to determine all membrane proteins simply by traditional methods.

In the post-genetic era, many scientific prediction methods based on machine learning have emerged [1–6], most of which use Chou's PseAAC algorithm, which has a good performance in predicting membrane protein types, but it has room for further improvement. From a machine learning perspective, the type prediction problem of membrane proteins is a traditional multiclassification problem. Therefore, machine learning was used to build predictive models of membrane proteins after extracting the effective features we needed from the protein sequences. In this paper, we use pseudo-PSSM (PsePSSM) [15], average block (AvBlock) [18], discrete cosine transform (DCT) [16], discrete wavelet transform (DWT) [14], and histogram of oriented gradients (HOG) to extract features from the PSSM [17] matrix that are useful to us, and then combine them with an FSVM classifier to predict the types of membrane proteins.

2 Materials and Methods

The research process of membrane protein prediction method can be completed in three stages, namely, model building, training and protein prediction. In the modeling phase, the baseline dataset is first processed using BLAST and the features are extracted by applying the Average Block (AvBlock), Discrete Cosine Transform (DCT), Discrete Wavelet Transform (DWT), Histogram of Oriented (HOG) and Pse-PSSM (PsePSSM). These five PSSM-based features are used to construct five kernels. Then integrating the above five kernels, we proposed a multi-kernel method based on FSVM(MKFSVM):

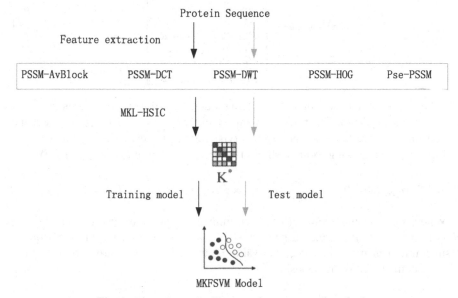

Fig. 1. The schematic diagram of our proposed method.

Hilbert-Schmidt independence criterion (MK-HSIC) [19] to predict membrane protein types. To illustrate the whole process, the method framework diagram is given in Fig. 1.

2.1 Data Set

To evaluate the performance, we tested the model on two datasets, named Dataset 1, and Dataset 2. These two datasets (Dataset 1, 2) consist of 8 membrane proteins. Dataset 1 was obtained by removing the redundant sequences from Chou's data [15]. To update and expand the size of the dataset, Chen et al. constructed a new dataset 2 [13].

2.2 Extracting Evolutionary Conservatism Information

The PSSM, the Position-Specific Score Matrix, stores the sequence information of amino acids. To reflect the evolutionary information, we use the PSSM in our protein prediction method. For a protein sequence Q, its PSSM can be generated by performing three iterations of PSI-BLAST search (PSI-BLAST finds the best result by multiple iterations, which uses the first search result to form the position specificity score matrix and uses it for the second search, the second search result for the third search, and so on until the best result is found. The second search result is used for the third search, and so on, until the best search result is found, and the best search result is found in three iterations, so it is set to three PSI-BLAST iterations), and its E threshold is set to 0.001. Suppose the sequence $Q = q_1q_2q_3 \dots q_L$, and the length of the sequence is L, then the protein of PSSM can be expressed as a matrix of L × 20 (L rows and 20 columns), and the matrix representation is as follows:

$$PSSM_{original} = \begin{bmatrix} p_{1,1} & p_{1,2} & \cdots & p_{1,20} \\ p_{2,1} & p_{2,2} & \cdots & p_{2,20} \\ \vdots & \vdots & \cdots & \vdots \\ p_{i,1} & p_{i,2} & \cdots & p_{i,20} \\ \vdots & \vdots & \vdots & \vdots \\ p_{L,1} & p_{L,2} & \cdots & p_{L,20} \end{bmatrix}_{L \times 20} \qquad (1)$$

Where L denotes the length of the protein sequence, 20 denotes the number of amino acid types, and $p_{i,j}$ denotes the fraction of amino acids at position i in the protein sequence that have been converted to amino acids of type j during the evolutionary process.

Besides, the following formula shows the representation of $PSSM_{original}(i, j)$:

$$PSSM_{original}(i, j) = \sum_{k=1}^{20} \omega(i, k) \times D(k, j), i = 1, \dots, L.j = 1, \dots, 20 \qquad (2)$$

Where $\omega(i, k)$ is the frequency of $k - th$ amino acid type at the position i and $D(k, j)$ refers to the mutation rate that turns from $k - th$ amino acid to the in protein sequence of substitution matrix. The larger the value is, the more conservative its position is. Otherwise, the result is the opposite.

2.2.1 PsePSSM

PsePSSM feature was usually used for membrane protein prediction. It was inspired by Chou's pseudo amino acid (PseAAC). PSSM matrix is widely used in protein description. The original PSSM of proteins should be further normalized for later calculation and work.

$$f_{i,j} = \frac{p_{i,j} - \frac{1}{20}\sum_{k=1}^{20} p_{i,k}}{\sqrt{\frac{1}{20}\sum_{l=1}^{20}\left(p_{i,l} - \frac{1}{20}\sum_{k=1}^{20} p_{i,k}\right)^2}}, i = 1, \ldots, L; j = 1, \ldots, 20 \qquad (3)$$

The Pnormalized is as follows:

$$P_{normalized} = \begin{bmatrix} f_{1,1} & \cdots & f_{1,20} \\ \vdots & \ddots & \vdots \\ f_{i,1} & \cdots & f_{i,20} \\ \vdots & \ddots & \vdots \\ f_{L,1} & \cdots & f_{L,20} \end{bmatrix}_{L \times 20} \qquad (4)$$

where $f_{i,j}$ is the score of the normalized PSSM; the average of 20 amino acids is 0. $p_{i,j}$ is the original score. The positive score refers to the occurrence of the corresponding homologous mutations, is more frequent in multiple permutations, and is higher than that by accident, and the negative score is opposite to positive score.

2.2.2 Average Blocks

The full name of the AB method is the Average Block method that was first presented by Huang et al. Because the amount of amino acids in each protein is different, the size of the feature vector is diverse when PSSM is transformed into the feature vector immediately. For this problem, average features over the local region in PSSMs, and this method is referred to as the AB method. Every block contains a 5% protein sequence. Here, the AB method is used in PSSM without regard to the length of the protein sequence. Divide each matrix into 20 blocks by row, and the size of every block is N/20. Therefore, the protein sequence will be divided into 20 blocks, and every block is composed of 20 features that originated from 20 columns in PSSMs. Its expression is as follows:

$$AB(k) = \frac{20}{N}\sum_{p=1}^{\frac{N}{20}} Mt\left(p + (i-1) \times \frac{20}{N}, j\right), i = 1, \ldots, 20; j = 1, \ldots, 20; k = j + 20 \times (i-1) \qquad (5)$$

where N/20 is the size of j blocks and $Mt\left(p + (i-1) \times \frac{20}{N}, j\right)$ is one vector with the size of 1×20 extracted from position i of j th block in PSSMs.

2.2.3 Discrete Wavelet Transform

DWT is a discrete wavelet transform. Nanni et al. first put forward the concept that reflects the information of frequency and location. Looking upon the protein sequence as a picture that is particular and then using different matrices to express the sequence, the matrix is decomposed into coefficients with different levels by DWT.

Furthermore, wavelet transform (WT) is the projection of signal $f(t)$ that casts onto the wavelet function. The formulation is as follows:

$$T(a, b) = \frac{1}{\sqrt{a}} \int_0^t f(t) \psi\left(\frac{t-b}{a}\right) dt \tag{6}$$

where a denotes the scale variable, b is the translation variable, and $\psi\left(\frac{t-b}{a}\right)$ means the wavelet analysis function. $T(a, b)$ refers to the transform coefficients that can be found in a specific wavelet period and specific position of signal. An effective DWT algorithm was proposed by Nanni et al.; they presumed that discrete signal $f(t)$ is x[n] to perform DWT. The coefficients are calculated as follows:

$$y_{j,low}[n] = \sum_{k=1}^{N} x[k]g[2n-k] \tag{7}$$

$$y_{j,high}[n] = \sum_{k=1}^{N} x[k]h[2n-k] \tag{8}$$

where N is the length of the discrete signal and g and h denote the low-pass filter and high-pass filter. $y_{j,low}[n]$ means the approximative coefficient of signal while and $y_{j,high}[n]$ is the coefficient that is elaborate. The former is low-frequency components, and the latter is the opposite. Their value of maximum, minimum, mean and standard deviation is calculated by 4-level DWT in this study. In addition, the discrete signals of PSSM over level 4 of discrete wavelet transform are analyzed, which is composed of 20 discrete signals.

2.2.4   Discrete Cosine Transform

Discrete Cosine Transform (DCT) is a linear separable transformation for converting a signal into elementary frequency components. It has been widely used in image compression. Here, we use 2 dimensions DCT (2D-DCT) to compress PSSM of protein. The 2D-DCT transformation is defined as follows:

$$F_{PSSM-DCT} = \alpha_i \alpha_j \sum_{m=0}^{M-1} \sum_{n=0}^{N-1} PSSM(m, n) \cos\frac{\pi(2m+1)i}{2M} \cos\frac{\pi(2n+1)j}{2N} \tag{9}$$

$$\alpha_i \begin{cases} \sqrt{\frac{1}{M}}, i = 0 \\ \sqrt{\frac{2}{M}}, 1 \leq i \leq M-1 \end{cases}, \alpha_j \begin{cases} \sqrt{\frac{1}{N}}, j = 0 \\ \sqrt{\frac{2}{N}}, 1 \leq j \leq N-1 \end{cases} \tag{10}$$

A major characteristic of DCT is the conversion of information density from evenly to unevenly distribution. Most of natural signals are concentrated in the low-frequency part of the compressed PSSM, which distribute in the upper left corner.

Finally, we extract the feature vector FPSSM − DCT by retaining first 20 × 20 = 400 dimensions.

2.2.5   Histogram of Oriented Gradient

Histogram of Oriented Gradient (HOG) is a feature descriptor used for pedestrian detection in computer vision. Here, PSSM is regarded as a special image matrix, which can be processed by HOG. First, we calculate the gradient magnitude matrix and gradient direction matrix by the horizontal and vertical gradient values of PSSM. Second, we divide gradient magnitude and gradient direction matrix into 25 sub-matrices, respectively. Each sub-matrix includes both gradient magnitude and direction. Then, we create 10 different histogram channels based on the gradient direction. Each submatrix is produced in 10 histogram channels.

Finally, we extract the feature vector FPSSM − HOG with $25 \times 10 = 250$ dimensions.

2.3 Support Vector Machine

Support Vector Machine (SVM) is a popular classifier [20], which was developed by Cortes and Vapnik [21]. Data examples labeled positive or negative are projected into a high dimensional feature space, and the hyper plane of feature space is optimized by maximizing the margin of positive and negative data.

Given a training dataset of instance-label pairs $\{x_i, y_i\}, i = 1, 2, ..., N$, the classification decision function implemented by SVM is represented as follows:

$$f(x) = sign\left[\sum_{i=1}^{N} y_i\alpha_i \cdot K(x, x_i) + b\right] \tag{11}$$

where $x_i \in R^{1 \times d}$ and $y_i \in \{+1, -1\}$. The coefficient αi is obtained by solving the following convex Quadratic Programming (QP) problem as follows:

$$Maximize \sum_{i=1}^{N} \alpha i - \frac{1}{2}\sum_{i=1}^{N}\sum_{j=1}^{N} \alpha i \alpha j \cdot y i y j \cdot K(x_i, x_j) \tag{12}$$

$$\sum_{j=1}^{N} \alpha_i y_i = 0, i = 1, 2, ..., N \tag{13}$$

where C is a regularization parameter that controls the trade-off between margin and misclassification error, and x_j is called pup port vector only if the corresponding $\alpha_j > 0$.

We implemented one SVM model using LIBSVM [22]. Because the prediction of membrane protein types is the multi-class problem (single-label), LIBSVM can construct several individual one-vs-rest binary classifiers to deal with multi-task classification.

2.4 Fuzzy Support Vector Machine

Support Vector Machine (SVM) is a generalized model for binary classification of data according to supervised learning. The decision boundary is to solve the maximum margin hyperplane for the learning samples. Lots of researchers had employed SVM in bioinformatics. However, noise sample points are generally present in training samples. The standard SVM algorithm may be over-fitting. And Lin [38,39] developed a Fuzzy SVM (FSVM) algorithm to overcoming the effects of outliers via membership values.

For FSVM model, one training sample is a set of $\{x_i, y_i, s_i\}$, $i = 1, 2, ..., N$, where $x_i \in R^{d \times 1}$ denotes the input, $y_i \in \{+1, -1\}$ is the label and $s_i \in [0, 1]$ denotes the value of membership, respectively. Similar to standard SVM, the optimization problem for finding hyperplane can be defined as follows:

$$min\frac{1}{2}\|\omega\|^2 + C\sum\nolimits_{i=1}^{N} s_i\xi_i \tag{14}$$

$$s.t.y_i\left(\omega^T\varphi(x) + b\right) \geq 1 - \xi_i \tag{15}$$

$$\xi_i \geq 0, i = 1, 2, ..., N \tag{16}$$

where ξ_i is an error measure of point x_i, C is the regularization parameter for imposing a trade-off between the training error and generalization, si is fuzzy membership value for point i. In FSVM, different samples should have different regularization parameters. So, $s_i\xi_i$ can be regarded as an error measure with different weights. Unimportant points have lower cost and important samples have a higher cost.

The objective function of FSVM is denoted as follows:

$$max \sum\nolimits_{i-1}^{N} \alpha_i - \frac{1}{2} \sum\nolimits_{i=1}^{N} \sum\nolimits_{j=1}^{N} \alpha_i\alpha_j \cdot y_iy_j \cdot K\left(x_i, x_j\right) \tag{17}$$

$$s.t.0 \leq \alpha_i \leq s_iC \tag{18}$$

$$\sum\nolimits_{i=1}^{N} \alpha_iy_i = 0, i = 1, 2, ..., N \tag{19}$$

The decision function of FSVM is represented as follows:

$$f(x) = sign\left[\sum\nolimits_{i=1}^{N} y_i\alpha_i \cdot K(x, x_i) + b\right] \tag{20}$$

Neighboring samples often reflect many commonalities, we try to use nearest neighbor samples of a sample i to represent itself. In our previous research, we employed Sparse Representation (SR) of nearest neighbor samples and calculated reconstruction residuals to build FSVM-based on Linear Neighborhood Representation (FSVM-LNR). However, it is only the linear neighborhood representation of original input space. The original input space often cannot fully express the spatial distribution of the data. So, we further propose the Kernelized Neighborhood Representation-based membership function (KNR).

In the case of LNR, sample x_i can be represented by linear combination of neighboring samples $\left(x_i^j, j = 1, 2, ..., k\right)$ and the optimization function is defined as follows:

$$\hat{\beta}_i = \arg min\|\beta_i\|_1 \tag{21}$$

$$s.t.\|x_i - X_i\beta_i\|_2^2 \leq \epsilon \tag{22}$$

$$i = 1, 2, ..., N \tag{23}$$

The reconstruction error r_i of sample x_i as follows:

$$r_i = \|x_i - X_i\hat{\beta}_i\|_2^2 \tag{24}$$

In kernelized neighborhood representation, essentially approach is to map original input in the high dimensional feature space and solve Eq. by the kernel trick. We let xi mapped to g_i (by $\varphi: \chi \to G$), KNR can be performed by solving the following:

$$\hat{\beta}_i = argmin\|\varphi(x_i) - \varphi(X_i)\beta_i\|_2^2 \tag{25}$$

where $\varphi(X_i) \triangleq \{\varphi(x_i^1), \varphi(x_i^2), ..., \varphi(x_i^k)\}$.

And the new reconstruction error r_i for sample $\varphi(xi)$ as follow:

$$
\begin{aligned}
r_i &= \|\varphi(x_i) - \varphi(X_i)\hat{\beta}_i\|_2^2 = \varphi(x_i)^T\varphi(x_i) + \hat{\beta}_i^T\varphi(X_i)^T\varphi(X_i)\hat{\beta}_i - 2\varphi(x_i)^T\varphi(X_i)\hat{\beta}_i \\
&= K(x_i, x_i) + \hat{\beta}_i^T K(X_i, X_i)\hat{\beta}_i - 2K(x_i, X_i)\hat{\beta}_i
\end{aligned}
\tag{26}
$$

where $K(X_i, X_i) \in R^{k\times k}$ is a positive semidefinite Gram matrix.

In the positive (or negative) class, we select the nearest neighbor samples with $D(\varphi(x_i), \varphi(x_j)) \leq \varepsilon$, ($\varepsilon \in [0, 1]$), respectively. The larger reconstruction residual of sample, the more likely is an outlier.

The reconstructed error can be mapped to 0–1 and the membership function as follows:

$$
s_i = \begin{cases}
\left(1 - \frac{r_i - r_{min}}{r_{max} - r_{min}}\right)^2 + 0.01, R < ri \leq r_{max} \\
1 - \frac{r_i - r_{min}}{r_{max} - r_{min}}, r_{min} < r_i \leq R
\end{cases}
\tag{27}
$$

where $R = (r_{max} + r_{min})/2$ denotes average value of r_{max} and r_{min}. $r_{min} = min(r_i|i = 1, 2,..., N)$ and $r_{max} = max(r_i|i = 1, 2,..., N)$ are the minimum and maximum value of the reconstruction residuals, respectively. s_i is the membership score of samples i in training set.

2.5 Multiple Kernel Support Vector Machine Classifier

Based on five related PSSM-based feature extraction, we employ the Radial Basis Function (RBF) and five types of features to construct the corresponding kernel, respectively.

The RBF kernel is defined as follows:

$$K_{ij} = K(x_i, x_j) = exp(-\gamma\|x_i - x_j\|^2), i, j = 1, 2, ..., N \tag{28}$$

where x_i and x_j are the feature vectors of samples i and j, N denotes the number of samples. In addition, γ is the bandwidth of Gaussian kernel.

A kernel set K as follows:

$$K = \{K_{PSSM-AvBlock}, K_{PSSM-DCT}, K_{PSSM-DWT}, K_{PSSM-HOG}, K_{PsePSSM}\} \tag{29}$$

3   Results

In this section, we analyze the performance between different kernels with FSVM and different classifiers (e.g. logistic regression, random forest and decorrelated neural network ensembles). In addition, we compare the performance between our method and other existing methods on independent test sets.

3.1   Evaluation Measurements

There are several parameters: overall prediction accuracy (ACC), individual sensitivity (S_{in}), individual specificity (S_{ip}) and Matthew's correlation coefficient (MCC_i), which are defined as follows:

$$
\begin{cases}
SN = \frac{TP}{TP+FN} \\
SP = \frac{TN}{TN+FP} \\
ACC = \frac{TP+TN}{TP+FP+TN+FN} \\
MCC = \frac{TP \times TN - FP \times FN}{\sqrt{(TP+FN) \times (TN+FP) \times (TP+FP) \times (TN+FN)}}
\end{cases}
\tag{30}
$$

Where, TP denotes the number of correctly predicted positive samples, TN denotes the number of correctly predicted negative samples, FP denotes the number of incorrectly predicted positive samples, and FN denotes the number of incorrectly predicted negative samples. SN denotes the percentage of correctly predicted samples among positive samples, SP denotes the percentage of correctly predicted samples among negative samples, and ACC denotes the percentage of correctly predicted samples among all samples. MCC is used to reflect the prediction quality of the model and takes values in the range of $[-1,1]$, when MCC $= -1$, it means that all samples are misclassified; when MCC $= 0$, it means that the prediction performance is the same as random selection; when MCC $= 1$, it means that all samples are correctly predicted [23–25].

3.2   Prediction on Dataset 1

To reduce potential prediction bias caused by the overrepresented of homologous sequences in the datasets, Chen and Li [13] conducted an additional performance analysis using Dataset 1. Dataset 1 is a homology-reduced version of the Zhou's data. The results can be seen in Table 1. Our method obtains accuracy increase of 5.1% (84.6% over 79.5%), 10.0% (90.0% over 80.0%) and 4.2% (100.0% over 95.8%) in types 2, 4 and 7, respectively. Our model achieves best overall ACC of 90.6% on the testing set of Dataset 1.

Table 1. The comparison of prediction accuracy among different predictors on the testing set of Dataset 1.

Specific types	$MemType-2L^a(\%)$	$predMPT^b(\%)$	$Ave-WT^c(\%)$	$Our\ method^*$
Single-span type 1	76.7(171/223)	**91.5**(204/223)	89.2(199/223)	89.2(199/223)
Single-span type 2	66.7(26/39)	74.4(29/39)	79.5(31/39)	**84.6**(33/39)
Single-span type 3	**33.3**(2/6)	16.7(1/6)	**33.3**(2/6)	**33.3**(2/6)
Single-span type 4	70.0(7/10)	80.0(8/10)	**90.0**(9/10)	**90.0**(9/10)
Multi-span type 5	91.4(1529/1673)	**92.8**(1552/1673)	91.1(1524/1673)	92.3(1545/1673)
Lipid-anchor type 6	23.1(6/26)	**53.8**(14/26)	30.8(8/26)	34.6(9/26)
GPI-anchor type 7	70.8(17/24)	95.8(23/24)	91.7(22/26)	**100.0**(24/24)
Peripheral type 8	68.2(208/305)	82.6(252/305)	**88.9**(271/305)	88.2(269/305)
Overall	85.3(1966/2306)	90.3(2083/2306)	89.6(2066/2306)	90.6(2090/2306)

∗: MKFSVM-HSIC.
a: Results excerpted from [15].
b: Results excerpted from [13].
c: Average weights-based MKSVM.

3.3 Prediction on Dataset 2

To address the potential obsoleteness problem, Chen and Li [13] also created a completely new set (Dataset 3) of protein data using more updated SwissProt annotation. The results of Dataset 2 are list in Table 2. Comparing with predMPT, the overall accuracy has been improved by nearly 1.4% (89.6% over 88.2%). The accuracy of our method increases 2.5% (87.8% over 85.3%), 2.5% (67.1% over 64.6%), 0.5% (93.0% over 92.5%) and 6.7% (87.0% over 80.3%) in types 1, 2, 5 and 8, respectively. Although predMPT uses 3D structure feature (such as Largest cationic patches from protein 3D structure), our prediction performance is slightly better than predMPT. Moreover, our method is totally better than the MKSVM.

Table 2. The comparison of prediction accuracy among different predictors on the testing set of Dataset 2.

Specific types	$MemType - 2L^a(\%)$	$predMPT^b(\%)$	$Ave - WT^c(\%)$	Our method*
Single-span type 1	69.0(169/245)	85.3(209/245)	82.5(202/245)	**87.8**(215/245)
Single-span type 2	58.2(46/79)	64.6(51/79)	55.7(44/79)	**67.1**(53/79)
Single-span type 3	**55.6**(5/9)	22.2(2/9)	11.1(1/9)	0.11(1/9)
Single-span type 4	52.9(9/17)	**58.8**(10/17)	47.1(8/17)	47.1(8/17)
Multi-span type 5	90.7(2247/2478)	92.5(2293/2478)	92.0(2280/2478)	**93.0**(2305/2478)
Lipid-anchor type 6	33.3(12/36)	**50.0**(18/36)	16.7(6/36)	25.0(9/36)
GPI-anchor type 7	65.9(27/41)	**85.4**(35/41)	65.9(27/41)	75.6(31/41)
Peripheral type 8	43.9(307/699)	80.3(561/699)	86.7(606/699)	**87.0**(610/699)
Overall	78.3(2822/3604)	88.2(3179/3604)	88.1(3174/3604)	89.7(3232/3604)

*: MKFSVM-HSIC.
a: Results excerpted from [15].
b: Results excerpted from [13].
c: Average weights-based MKSVM.

4 Conclusion and Discussion

PseAAC [3] has been widely used to identify membrane protein types in previous works [3, 4, 7–13, 15], and shows excellent performance in other studies of protein classification. Inspired by Chou's work [15] for extracting features from PSSM, we use PsePSSM, HOG, DCT, DWT and AvBlock to extract features from PSSM. To further improve the performance of prediction, we employ MKFSVM-HSIC to integrate the multiple features and construct a predictive model. Our method obtains better predictive performance on different data sets of membrane protein.

On the independent test set of Dataset 1–2, our proposed method produces higher overall accuracies of 90.6%, and 89.7%, respectively. However, there are still some proteins that fail to be predicted. Besides some of the prediction performance is not as satisfactory due to the affiliation of small sample types.

To improve the performance, in the future, we will enhance our method to improve the prediction performance by improving the feature representation and classification algorithms. For the former, combining some other biologically relevant features is considered; for the latter, techniques such as deep learning will be used to optimize the prediction performance.

Acknowledgement. This paper is supported by the National Natural Science Foundation of China (62073231, 61772357, 61902272, 61876217 and 61902271), National Research Project (2020YFC2006602) and Anhui Province Key Laboratory Research Project (IBBE2018KX09).

References

1. Cedano, J., Aloy, P., Perezpons, J., et al.: Relation between amino acid composition and cellular location of proteins. J. Mol. Biol. **266**(3), 594–600 (1997)
2. Feng, Z., Zhang, C.: Prediction of membrane protein types based on the hydrophobic index of amino acids. J. Protein Chem. **19**(4), 269–275 (2000)
3. Chou, K.: Prediction of protein subcellular attributes using pseudo-amino acid composition. Proteins Struct. Funct. Bioinform. **43**(6), 246–255 (2001)
4. Cai, Y., Ricardo, P., Jen, C., Chou, K.: Application of SVM to predict membrane protein types. J. Theoret. Biol. **226**(4), 373–376 (2004)
5. Zou, Q., Li, X., Jiang, Y., Zhao, Y., Wang, G.: Binmempredict: a web server and software for predicting membrane protein types. Curr. Proteom. **10**(1), 2–9 (2013)
6. Wei, L., Tang, J., Zou, Q.: Local-DPP: an improved DNA-binding protein prediction method by exploring local evolutionary information. Inf. Sci. **384**, 135–144 (2017)
7. Chou, K., Elrod, D.: Prediction of membrane protein types and subcellular location. Proteins Struct. Funct. Bioinform. **34**(1), 137–153 (1999)
8. Wang, M., Yang, J., Liu, G., Xu, Z., Chou, K.: Weighted-support vector machines for predicting membrane protein types based on pseudo-amino acid composition. Protein Eng. Des. Sel. **17**(16), 509–516 (2004)
9. Liu, H., Wang, M., Chou, K.: Low-frequency Fourier spectrum for predicting membrane protein types. Biochem. Biophys. Res. Commun. **336**(3), 737–739 (2005)
10. Hayat, M., Khan, A.: Predicting membrane protein types by fusing composite protein sequence features into pseudo amino acid composition. J. Theoret. Biol. **271**(1), 10–17 (2010)
11. Han, G., Yu, Z., Anh, V.: A two-stage svm method to predict membrane protein types by incorporating amino acid classifications and physicochemical properties into a general form of Chou's PseAAC. J. Theoret. Biol. **344**(7), 31–39 (2014)
12. Wang, S., Yang, J., Chou, K.: Using stacked generalization to predict membrane protein types based on pseudo-amino acid composition. J. Theoret. Biol. **242**(4), 941–946 (2006)
13. Chen, Y., Li, K.: Predicting membrane protein types by incorporating protein topology, domains, signal peptides, and physicochemical properties into the general form of Chou's pseudo amino acid composition. J. Theoret. Biol. **318**(1), 1–12 (2013)
14. Nanni, L., Brahnam, S., Lumini, A.: Wavelet images and Chous pseudo amino acid composition for protein classification. Amino Acids **43**(2), 657–665 (2012)
15. Chou, K., Shen, H.: MemType-2L: a web server for predicting membrane proteins and their types by incorporating evolution information through Pse-PSSM. Biochem. Biophys. Res. Commun. **360**(2), 339–345 (2007)
16. Ahmed, N., Natarajan, T., Rao, K.: Discrete cosine transform. IEEE Trans. Comput. **23**(1), 90–93 (1974)
17. Boeckmann, B., Bairoch, A., Apweiler, R., et al.: The SWISS-PROT protein knowledgebase and its supplement TreMBL in 2003. Nucleic Acids Res. **31**(1), 365–370 (2003)
18. Jeong, J., Lin, X., Chen, X.: On position-specific scoring matrix for protein function prediction. IEEE/ACM Trans. Comput. Biol. Bioinform. **8**(2), 308–315 (2011)
19. Gretton, A., Bousquet, O., Smola, A., Schölkopf, B.: Measuring statistical dependence with Hilbert-Schmidt norms. In: Jain, S., Simon, H.U., Tomita, E. (eds.) Algorithmic Learning Theory, ALT 2005. LNCS, vol. 3734, pp. 63–77. Springer, Heidelberg (2005)
20. Ding, Y., Tang, J., Guo, F.: Identification of drug-target interactions via multiple information integration. Inf. Sci. **418–419**, 546–560 (2017)
21. Cortes, C., Vapnik, V.: Support-vector networks. Mach. Learn. **20**(3), 273–297 (1995)
22. Chang, C., Lin, C.: LIBSVM: a library for support vector machines. ACM Trans. Intell. Syst. Technol. **2**(3), 389–396 (2011)
23. Chou, K., Wu, Z., Xiao, X.: iLoc-Euk: a multi-label classifier for predicting the subcellular localization of singleplex and multiplex eukaryotic proteins. PLoS ONE **6**(3), e18258 (2011)

24. Chou, K., Wu, Z., Xiao, X.: iLOC-Hum: using the accumulation-label scale to predict sub-cellular locations of human proteins with both single and multiple sites. Mol. Biosyst. **8**(2), 629–641 (2011)
25. Chou, K.: Some remarks on predicting multi-label attributes in molecular biosystems. Mol. Biosyst. **9**(6), 1092–1100 (2013)

Golgi Protein Prediction with Deep Forest

Yanwen Yao, Yujian Gu, Wenzheng Bao, Lei Zhang[(✉)], and Yonghong Zhu

School of Information Engineering (School of Big Data), Xuzhou University of Technology,
Xuzhou 221018, China
459932264@qq.com

Abstract. Golgi proteins are encapsulated in membrane system. The main function of the Golgi is to process, sort, and transport proteins, synthesized by the endoplasmic reticulum, and then to be sorted into specific parts of the cell or secreted outside the cell. The Golgi apparatus is the site for the final processing and packaging of cell secretions, such as proteins. In this paper, we use Deep Forest to classify 2 different types of protein by 406 features. Deep Forest achieves more simply and more efficient process compared to traditional KNN classifier.

Keywords: Golgi proteins · Deep forest · Classification

1 Introduction

Golgi is one of the components of the intimal system in eukaryotic cells. It was first found by Italian cytologist Camilo Gorky in nerve cells by staining with silver nitrate. It consists of three basic components: saccules, vacuoles, and vesicles. Golgi proteins are encapsulated in membrane system. The main function of the Golgi is to process, sort, and transport proteins, synthesized by the endoplasmic reticulum, and then to be sorted into specific parts of the cell or secreted outside the cell. The Golgi apparatus is the site for the final processing and packaging of cell secretions, such as proteins. A vesicle from the endoplasmic reticulum fuses with the Golgi membrane and delivers the inclusions into the Golgi cavity, where the newly synthesized protein peptide chain continues to complete the modification and packaging. Golgi apparatus also synthesizes some polysaccharides secreted outside the cell and modifies the cell membrane materials.

Disorders of protein are the core factor which leads to many neurodegenerative diseases. The Golgi apparatus is a basic organelle in the material metabolic pathway, and should be closely related to it. In order to understand the mechanism of Golgi function, the important step is to find a Golgi-resident, and use the types and functions of the Golgi-resident protein to determine the principles of the disease.

After several years' effort, the prediction of the Golgi type has become one of the hottest subjects in the field of computational biology and bioinformatics. It is currently known that whether a protein is a Golgi resident protein is not enough to fully explain the function of the Golgi body. Further analysis of the specific type of Golgi-resident protein is needed.

In this paper, we use Deep Forest to classify 2 different types of protein by 406 features. Deep Forest achieves more simply and more efficient process compared to traditional KNN classifier.

© Springer Nature Switzerland AG 2021
D.-S. Huang et al. (Eds.): ICIC 2021, LNAI 12838, pp. 647–653, 2021.
https://doi.org/10.1007/978-3-030-84532-2_58

2 Methods and Materials

2.1 Data

The experiment uses a data set which consists of 1600 records of 2 types of protein, and each record has 406 features. The radio of the 2 types samples is 1:1. To know more about the model, We also use data sets which consists of 2400 records of 2 types of protein whose radio of the two types is 1:2 and data sets which consists of 3200 records of 2 types of protein whose radio of the two types is 1:3.

2.2 Construction of Classification

The experiment uses a classifier named Deep Forest. Deep Forest was first proposed by professor Zhi-Hua Zhou and Dr. Ji Feng. This model is a series structure which features multi granularity scanning. What's more, it is a model based on tree integration. Its representation learning ability can be enhanced by multi granularity scanning of high-dimensional input data. The number of layers in series can also be determined adaptively, so that the model complexity does not need to be a custom super parameter, but a parameter which sets automatically according to the data situation instead.

The classifier's construction mainly consists of two parts: cascaded forest and multi granularity scanning. Our cascaded forest consists of 4 random forests in each training layer. Our four random forests are composed of two random forests of which the max_features equal "sqrt" and two random forests of which the max_features equal 1. The min_samples_mgs of them are all 0.03. The split nodes are selected by Gini coefficient in a random feature subspace. Cascaded forest adopts the layer structure in DNN. The input data and output result data of the former layer are concatenated as the input of the next layer. This vector is then spliced with the original eigenvector input to the next level of the cascade. In this way, we make a feature change and keep the original features for subsequent processing. This is true for each layer. In the last layer, the 406-dimensional vectors of all random forest outputs are added and averaged to calculate the largest one-dimensional as the final output. As for the training layer, it stops growing while there is no further improvement.

In order to reduce the risk of over fitting, the class vectors generated by each forest are generated by 8-fold cross validation, that is, each sample is trained 7 times as training data to generate 7 similarly 406-dimension-feature vectors, and then the average value is the final feature vector of the forest, and then the 406-dimension-feature vectors are connected together as the enhanced feature vectors of the next layer. After extending a new layer, the performance of the whole cascade will be evaluated on the verification set. If there is no performance improvement, the training process will be terminated. Therefore, the number of cascade layers is automatically determined.

In front of the cascade forest lies in the multi granularity scanning area to enhance the deep forest's performance as features could have relations. Our multi-grained scanning is realized by two random forest classifiers. One's max_features equal "sqrt", while the other's equals 1. Their min_samples_mgs equal 0.05. We use sliding windows of 47 dimensions to obtain more feature sub samples. Since our input feature number is 1600 and the scanning window size is 47, we can get 1554 * 47 dimensions feature vectors in total, and each 47 dimensions feature vector corresponds to a 2 dimensions class vector. Finally, after classified by the 2 random forest, cascade forest will get 9133 * 2 dimensional characteristic variables from them.

2.3 Evaluation Methods

As for the performance measurement, we choose ACC for evaluation. For a binary classification problem, the predicted results will only have two values of 0 and 1. If an instance is a positive class and is predicted to be a positive class, it is a true positive (TP) class. If it is a negative class, it is predicted to be a positive class, and it will be called a false positive (FP) class. If it is a negative class, it is predicted to be a negative class. Then it is called true negative (TN) class. What's more, we call it false negative (FN) class when a positive class is predicted to be negative. We also do 8, 5 and 4 fold cross validations on the samples whose radio of the two types of protein are 1:1 and 1:2 to test the stability of the model.

$$Accuracy = \frac{TP + TN}{TP + FP + TN + FN} \tag{1}$$

3 Results and Discussion

In this section, we mainly describe the result and further discussion of the records' classification in the Deep Forest.

3.1 Results

To get the most accurate classification when the running time is acceptable, we change the number of trees in random forest during multi grain scanning and number of trees in a single Random Forest in a cascade layer in the inter [50.300], of which the interval is 50. The radio of the 2 types samples is 1:1. The results are shown in Figs. 1 and 2.

3.2 Discussion

From Figs. 1 and 2, we draw the conclusion that the accuracy reaches the top when the number of trees in random forest during multi grain scanning is around 100, and the number of trees in a single Random Forest in a cascade layer is around 200. What's more, we find the trend of ACC becomes much flatter as the number of trees growing. Variance data also proves the conclusion. We calculate variances and standard deviations of the first half ACC data and the second half in which the former is higher than the latter, and the data is shown in Table 1. But on a whole, the wave of ACC is small, which shows not only the stabilization of the model but the relatively good performance at a small cost.

Then we train the model to get results when the radio of the 2 types samples is 1:2, 1:3 to check the usability when the positive and negative samples are imbalanced. Together

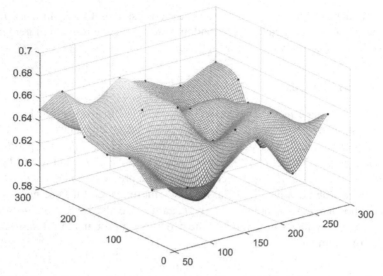

Fig. 1. 3D surface of the number of trees in random forest during multi grain scanning, number of trees in a single Random Forest in a cascade layer and Corresponding ACC.

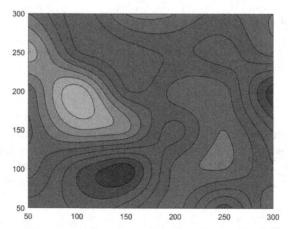

Fig. 2. Contour map of the number of trees in random forest during multi grain scanning, number of trees in a single Random Forest in a cascade layer and Corresponding ACC.

Table 1. Variances and standard deviations of the first half ACC data and the second half.

Location	Variance	Standard deviation
The first half ACC	0.000591	0.024306
The second half ACC	0.000233	0.01528

Table 2. The data of varies radio of the two types.

Radio of 2 types	ACC	TP	FP	TN	FN
1:1	0.6875	53	23	57	27
1:2	0.6833	12	8	152	68
1:3	0.7469	2	3	237	78

with the data when the radio of the 2 types samples is 1:1 from previous training, the results are shown in Table 2.

From Table 2, it is clear that Deep Forest is good at classifying 2 types of protein even when the positive and negative samples are relatively imbalanced (1:2, 1:3). At the same time, since TP, FP, TN and FN are both not zero, the classification is still effective.

What's more, we also do 8-fold, 5-fold and 4-fold cross validations on the samples whose radio of the two types of protein are 1:1 and 1:2, since the data are relatively small. Results of the cross validations together with the result of 10-fold cross validation above are shown in Table 3. The results are similar, which proves the stability of Deep Forest, and it is good at prediction.

Table 3. Data of 10-fold, 8-fold, 5-fold and 4-fold cross validations

Radio of 2 types	ACC	TP	FP	TN	FN
1:1	0.6875	53	23	57	27
	0.6600	66	34	66	34
	0.6281	91	50	110	69
	0.6250	130	80	120	70
1:2	0.6833	12	8	152	68
	0.6833	15	10	190	85
	0.6973	26	13	307	134
	0.6802	34	26	374	166

4   Conclusion

In this article, we use Deep Forest to classify two types of protein. We use ACC and N-fold cross validations to evaluate the model, and adjust the structure of the random forests in Deep Forest to achieve the best result when classify the data set. What's more, we found the more random trees used in the model, the flatter the result is, despite of the high cost. We also draw the conclusion that Deep Forest is also good at classifying 2 types of protein even when the positive and negative samples are relatively imbalanced (1:2, 1:3). We do multi-fold cross validations as well, and the result shows stability and awesome prediction ability of the model when the training data scale are small and imbalanced as well.

Acknowledgement. This work was supported by the Natural Science Foundation of China (No. 61902337), Natural Science Fund for Colleges and Universities in Jiangsu Province (No. 19KJB520016), Jiangsu Provincial Natural Science Foundation (No. SBK2019040953), Young talents of science and technology in Jiangsu and the Xuzhou Science and Technology Plan Funded Project - Research on Key Technologies for Three-dimensional Monitoring of Lake Water Environment Based on 5G Internet of Things (KC19208).

References

1. Marengo, A., Rosso, C., Bugianesi, E.: Liver cancer: connections with obesity, fatty liver, and cirrhosis. Annu. Rev. Med. **67**, 103–117 (2016)
2. Altekruse, S.F., McGlynn, K.A., Reichman, M.E.: Hepatocellular carcinoma incidence, mortality, and survival trends in the united states from 1975 to 2005. J. Clin. Oncol. **27**, 1485–1491 (2009)
3. Choi, J.M., et al.: HepG2 cells as an in vitro model for evaluation of cytochrome p450 induction by xenobiotics. Arch. Pharm. Res. **38**, 691–704 (2015)
4. Jantamat, P., Weerapreeyakul, N., Puthongking, P.: Cytotoxicity and apoptosis induction of Coumarins and Carbazole alkaloids from Clausena harmandiana. Molecules **24**, 3385 (2019)
5. Wang, L., et al.: Trilobatin, a novel SGLT1/2 inhibitor, selectively induces the proliferation of human hepatoblastoma cells. Molecules **24**, 3390 (2019)
6. Weng, Z.B., et al.: Positive skeletal effect of two ingredients of Psoralea corylifolia I. on estrogen deficiency-induced osteoporosis and the possible mechanisms of action. Mol. Cell Endocrinol. **417**, 103–113 (2015)
7. Haraguchi, H., Inoue, J., Tamura, Y., Mizutani, K.: Antioxidative components of Psoralea corylifolia (Leguminosae). Phytother. Res. PTR **16**, 539–544 (2002)
8. Wu, C., Sun, Z., Ye, Y., Han, X., Song, X., Liu, S.: Psoralen inhibits bone metastasis of breast cancer in mice. Fitoterapia **91**, 205–210 (2013)
9. Bera, T.K., Ali, K.M., Jana, K., Ghosh, A., Ghosh, D.: Protective effect of aqueous extract of seed of Psoralea corylifolia (Somraji) and seed of Trigonella foenum-graecum l. (methi) in streptozotocin-induced diabetic rat: a comparative evaluation. Pharmacogn. Res. **5**, 277–285 (2013)
10. Li, H.N., Wang, C.Y., Wang, C.L., Chou, C.H., Leu, Y.L., Chen, B.Y.: Antimicrobial effects and mechanisms of ethanol extracts of psoralea corylifolia seeds against listeria monocytogenes and methicillin-resistant staphylococcus aureus. Foodborne Pathog. Dis. **16**, 573–580 (2019)
11. Latha, P.G., Evans, D.A., Panikkar, K.R., Jayavardhanan, K.K.: Immunomodulatory and antitumour properties of Psoralea corylifolia seeds. Fitoterapia **71**, 223–231 (2000)
12. Zhang, Z., Zhang, W., Ji, Y.P., Zhao, Y., Wang, C.G., Hu, J.F.: Gynostemosides ae, megastigmane glycosides from gynostemma pentaphyllum. Phytochemistry **71**, 693–700 (2010)
13. Bapat, K., et al.: Preparation and in vitro evaluation of radioiodinated bakuchiol as an anti tumor agent. Appl. Radiat. Isotopes **62**, 389–393 (2005)
14. Chen, Z., et al.: Anti-tumor effects of bakuchiol, an analogue of resveratrol, on human lung adenocarcinoma a549 cell line. Eur. J. Pharmacol. **643**, 170–179 (2010)

15. Han, Y., Xu, B.L., Guo, Y.H.: A novel chaetomugilin from cullen corylifolium (l.) medik. Lat. Am. J. Pharm. **38**, 7 (2019)

16. Chopra, B., Dhingra, A.K., Dhar, K.L.: Psoralea corylifolia l. (Buguchi) - folklore to modern evidence: review. Fitoterapia **90**, 44–56 (2013)

17. Lu, H., Zhang, L., Liu, D., Tang, P., Song, F.: Isolation and purification of Psoralen and Isopsoralen and their efficacy and safety in the treatment of osteosarcoma in nude rats. Afr. Health Sci. **14**, 641–647 (2014)

18. Wang, X., et al.: Effects of Psoralen as an anti-tumor agent in human breast cancer MCF-7/ADR cells. Biol. Pharm. Bull. **39**, 815–822 (2016)

19. Wu, D., et al.: Pharmacological inhibition of dihydroorotate dehydrogenase induces apoptosis and differentiation in acute myeloid leukemia cells. Haematologica **103**, 1472–1483 (2018)

20. Marx, D., et al.: Differential expression of apoptosis associated genes bax and bcl-2 in ovarian cancer. Anticancer Res. **17**, 2233–2240 (1997)

21. Knudson, C.M., Korsmeyer, S.J.: Bcl-2 and bax function independently to regulate cell death. Nat. Genet. **16**, 358–363 (1997)

22. Du, L., Fei, Z., Song, S., Wei, N.: Antitumor activity of lobaplatin against esophageal squamous cell carcinoma through caspase-dependent apoptosis and increasing the bax/bcl-2 ratio. Biomed. Pharmacother. **95**, 447–452 (2017)

23. Stepien, A., Izdebska, M., Grzanka, A.: The types of cell death. Postepy Hig. Med. Dosw. **61**, 420–428 (2007)

24. Joseph, E.K., Levine, J.D.: Caspase signalling in neuropathic and inflammatory pain in the rat. Eur. J. Neurosci. **20**, 2896–2902 (2004)

25. Peng, X., Zhang, Y.Y., Wang, J., Ji, Q.: Ethylacetate extract from tetrastigma hemsleyanum induces apoptosis via the mitochondrial caspase-dependent intrinsic pathway in HepG2 cells. Tumor Biol. **37**, 865–876 (2016)

Prediction of Protein-Protein Interaction Based on Deep Learning Feature Representation and Random Forest

Wenzheng Ma[1], Wenzheng Bao[2(✉)], Yi Cao[1], Bin Yang[3], and Yuehui Chen[1]

[1] School of Information Science and Engineering, University of Jinan, Jinan 250024, China
[2] School of Information and Electrical Engineering, Xuzhou University of Technology, Xuzhou 221018, China
baowz55555@126.com
[3] School of Information Science and and Engineering, Zaozhuang University, Zaozhuang 277160, China

Abstract. As the basis and key of cell activities, protein plays an important role in many life activities. Protein usually does not work alone. Under normal circumstances, most proteins perform specific functions by interacting with other proteins, and play the greatest role in life activity. The prediction of protein-protein interaction (PPI) is a very basic and important research in bioinformatics. PPI controls a large number of cell activities and is the basis of most cell activities. It provides a very important theoretical basis and support for disease prevention and treatment, and drug development. Because experimental methods are slow and expensive, methods based on machine learning are gradually being applied to PPI problems. We propose a new model called BiLSTM-RF, which can effectively predict PPI.

Keywords: Protein-protein interaction · Deep learning · Machine learning · Bi-directional long short-term memory · Random forest

1 Introduction

As an important component of living organisms, protein maintains the operation of their lives and participates in various important life activities. With the continuous in-depth study of protein [1], many impressive results have been produced in the study of protein at the micro level [2, 3]. People gradually discovered that proteins usually do not perform their functions alone. They form a protein complex with other proteins to participate in some important life activities [4]. A protein complex is composed of two or more proteins interacting through the formation of chemical bonds. PPI is the basis of cell activities and plays an important role in many processes such as signal transduction, transportation and metabolism [5–8]. The interaction between proteins is also the key to the realization of cell functions, and also plays an important role in the development of biocatalysts and cell regulatory network construction.

© Springer Nature Switzerland AG 2021
D.-S. Huang et al. (Eds.): ICIC 2021, LNAI 12838, pp. 654–662, 2021.
https://doi.org/10.1007/978-3-030-84532-2_59

PPI is a very important research field in bioinformatics, and there are many methods and techniques for predicting PPI [9]. In the early stages of the development of the PPI field, high-throughput laboratory methods were the mainstream methods for studying this problem, such as yeast two-hybrid technology, plasmon resonance technology, and immunoprecipitation [10–13]. The initial laboratory methods have the disadvantages of slow and expensive prediction, and they cannot guarantee high accuracy and stability. Later, some methods based on prior biological knowledge, such as phylogenetic profiles, appeared, which was time-consuming and labor-intensive [14]. Although the previous methods have many flaws, it is undeniable that they laid the foundation for our later research and provided a large number of available databases. With the rapid development of machine learning, people have focused their attention on machine learning, and there have been many effective methods based on machine learning [15]. In 2008, Burger et al. proposed a new Bayesian network method to achieve effective prediction of PPI [16]. In 2014, You et al. used the mRMR method to extract sequence features, combined with support vector machines (SVM), to achieve an average prediction accuracy of 84.91% for brewing yeast [17–21]. In addition to basic machine learning methods, many researchers have also tried to integrate basic classifiers and have achieved good results. Yi et al. proposed a model based on k-mer sparse matrix and integrated basic classifier in 2020, which effectively predicted the interaction between ncRNA and protein [22]. With the advent of the deep learning boom, researchers dedicated to deep learning also use deep learning to study PPI. Du et al. proposed DeepPPI model, which was trained and tested on the PPI dataset of brewing yeast through a deep neural network, achieving an accuracy of 92.50% and an AUC value of 97.43% [23–26].

In this paper, we propose the BiLSTM-RF model to extract the features of protein pair sequences through deep learning. After the feature is reconstructed, it is used as the input of the random forest classifier. We use ten-fold cross validation to train the model. After the model is trained, we test it on the human PPI independent test dataset. Finally, we use Area Under Curve (AUC), Accuracy (ACC), Matthew Correlation Coefficient (MCC), Specificity (Sp) And Sensitivity (Sn) to evaluate the performance of the model.

2 Materials and Methods

We first extracted the features of the human PPI dataset with BiLSTM, then reconstructed the feature of the protein pair on the dataset, and constructed multiple datasets for experimental comparison. Finally, Acc, AUC, Sp, Sn and MCC are used to evaluate the performance of the model. Our workflow is shown in Fig. 1.

2.1 Datasets

In order to train and test our proposed BiLSTM-RF model, we obtained a non-redundant human dataset. After downloading the dataset from the DIP database, Kong et al. used the cd-hit tool to cluster the sequences based on sequence similarity to remove redundancy, and finally established a non-redundant human PPI dataset [26]. This dataset contains 4262 interacting protein pairs and 3899 non-interacting protein pairs.

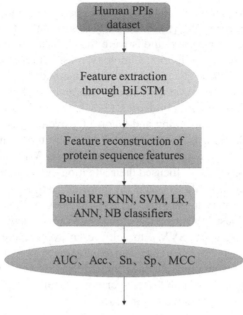

Fig. 1. Work flow

2.2 Feature Extraction

2.2.1 Extracting Sequence Features Based on Deep Learning

Since the research in the field of PPIs entered the era of machine learning, the research on this problem has been transformed into the analysis and research of protein sequences, describing the protein sequence as a matrix or vector. There are many basic feature extraction methods, such as one-hot encoding, PSSM matrix, etc., all of which can describe protein sequences as matrices or vectors. Many researchers themselves have proposed some feature extraction methods based on mathematics or amino acid properties, such as EAAC and so on. Including before, we have improved the feature extraction method proposed by Kong et al. and finally proposed a new feature extraction method ACT, which also has a good performance on the human dataset [27]. When we wanted to combine the ACT method with the long and short-term memory (LSTM) network to predict PPI, we found that the features extracted by the previous ACT method had lost part of the protein sequence information, so we thought of using BiLSTM to extract features, and construct a basic classifier to compare with the previous method. We found that the effective information retained based on the features extracted by deep learning is more comprehensive.

2.2.2 BiLSTM

BiLSTM is composed of forward LSTM and backward LSTM. Compared with LSTM, BiLSTM can not only encode front-to-back information, but also encode back-to-front information. A typical BiLSTM model is shown in Fig. 2.

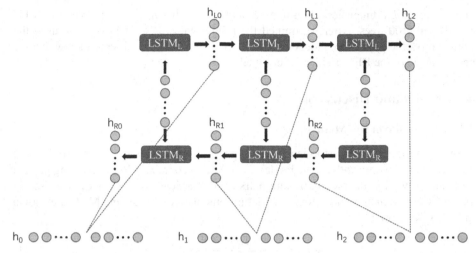

Fig. 2. Typical BiLSTM model

For protein sequences, front-to-back and back-to-front information is very important. The type, number, arrangement order and positional relationship of amino acids together determine the PPI problem. We constructed a typical BiLSTM model to extract features of protein pairs in the human database, including 4262 pairs of non-interacting proteins and 3899 pairs of interacting proteins. In the end, what we get is two feature matrices with shape (4262,3605) and two feature matrices with shape (3899,3605).

2.2.3 Refactoring Features

After we extracted the features of the protein sequence through BiLSTM, we obtained the feature representations of four single protein datasets. We combine the features of a single non-interacting protein into the feature of a non-interacting protein pair, and combine the features of a single interacting protein into the feature of an interacting protein pair to express the relationship between protein pairs. Finally, a non-interacting protein pair dataset feature with a size of (4262,7210) and an interacting protein pair dataset feature with a size of (3899,7210) are obtained.

After the feature reconstruction is completed, the training set and the test set are divided according to the ratio of 1:1, and finally a training set with a size of (4081,7210) and a test set with a size of (4080,7210) are obtained, which are used to train and test our model.

3   Building a Random Forest Classifier

Random forest (RF) classifier is a highly flexible machine learning algorithm with good accuracy, broad application prospects, and have good performance on classification problems. We use the features extracted by BiLSTM to reconstruct the training set size (4081,7210). Since RF can effectively run on big data and can process input samples of high-dimensional features, and does not require dimensionality reduction, we can directly use high-dimensional training set features as the input of RF. We built a RF model with 100 trees. After we trained the model with the training set, we used the trained model to predict the independent test set. The experimental results show that the performance of the RF classifier is very well.

4   Results and Discussion

4.1   Evaluation of the Method

In order to evaluate the performance of our proposed model, we use a non-redundant human dataset to train and test the model. This dataset contains 4262 interacting protein pairs and 3899 non-interacting protein pairs. In this article, we use AUC, Acc, Sn, Sp and MCC as evaluation indicators. The definitions of Acc, Sn, Sp and MCC are shown in Eq. (1–4) shows:

$$Acc = \frac{TP + TN}{TP + TN + FP + FN} \tag{1}$$

$$Sn = \frac{TP}{FN + TP} \tag{2}$$

$$Sp = \frac{TN}{FP + TN} \tag{3}$$

$$MCC = \frac{TP \times TN - FP \times FN}{\sqrt{(TP + FP) \times (TP + FN) \times (TN + FP) \times (TN + FN)}} \tag{4}$$

The AUC value refers to the area under the ROC curve. The larger the value, the better the prediction effect of the model.

4.2   BiLSTM-RF Shows Better Performance

For a classification prediction model, the choice of classifier is very important. Our BiLSTM-RF model constructed an RF classifier including 100 trees, which showed good prediction performance and stability. RF can handle the high-dimensional features that we previously acquired with BiLSTM well, and there is no need for dimensionality reduction processing. And its essence is integrated learning, and its main idea is to integrate multiple decision trees. The basis of RF is a decision tree, and each decision tree is a classifier. The RF model we built integrates 100 decision trees, and each decision tree will produce a classification result. RF uses a voting strategy to integrate the 100 results, and finally gets the prediction result of the RF model. We also built five basic classifiers: K nearest neighbor (KNN), support vector machine (SVM), artificial neural network (ANN), logistic regression (LR) and naive Bayes (NB) for comparison. The experimental results are shown in the Table 1 shown.

In Table 1, the bolded data is the maximum value of each column. From Table 1, we can see that the Acc value of RF has reached 0.8676, which has a high accuracy, and the MCC has reached 0.8355. The values of Sn and Sp are also high and similar. It can be seen that the RF is also relatively high. Has good stability. From Fig. 3 we can see the superior performance of RF more intuitively.

Table 1. Performance comparison of different classifiers

Classifier	AUC	Acc	MCC	Sn	Sp
KNN	0.9080	0.8316	0.6712	0.7286	**0.9259**
LR	0.8568	0.8000	0.7007	0.7615	0.8352
RF	0.8919	**0.8676**	**0.8355**	**0.8497**	0.8840
NB	0.8166	0.7733	0.5453	0.7455	0.7987
SVM	0.7908	0.7169	0.4374	0.7563	0.6809
ANN	**0.9119**	0.8427	0.6870	0.7821	0.8982

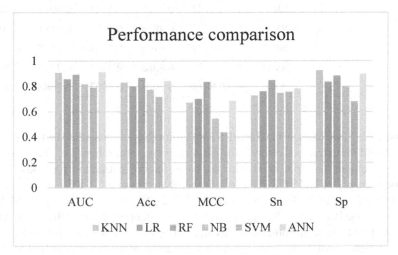

Fig. 3. Comparison of classifier performance

4.3 The Feature Information Extracted by Deep Learning is More Comprehensive

In a predictive model that solves classification problems, the feature extraction method is very critical. Especially for protein sequences, the sequence and position information of amino acids is particularly important. The sequence and position of the biological information in the protein sequence are closely related to the final prediction result, so we thought of using BiLSTM for feature extraction, as far as possible to retain the protein sequence from front to back and back to front information. ACT is a new feature extraction method proposed by us after improving the feature extraction method of Kong et al. In the same classifier, the improved ACT method is more accurate than the feature extraction method of Kong et al. Promote. We use the same data set, the same training set and test set, reconstruct the features represented by the ACT method and the BiLSTM feature extraction method in the same way, and put them in the same basic classifier for training and testing. Experiments The results show that more important information is retained in the features extracted by BiLSTM. The experimental comparison results are shown in Table 1.

Table 2. Comparison of different feature extraction methods

Feature extraction method	Classifier	AUC	Acc	MCC	Sn	Sp
BiLSTM	KNN	0.9080	0.8316	0.6712	0.7286	**0.9259**
	LR	0.8568	0.8000	0.7007	0.7615	0.8352
	RF	0.8919	**0.8676**	**0.8355**	**0.8497**	0.8840
	NB	0.8166	0.7733	0.5453	0.7455	0.7987
	SVM	0.7908	0.7169	0.4374	0.7563	0.6809
	ANN	**0.9119**	0.8427	0.6870	0.7821	0.8982
ACT	KNN	0.9165	0.8118	0.6444	0.6575	**0.9531**
	LR	0.8177	0.7505	0.5001	0.6915	0.8046
	RF	0.8875	0.7849	0.5812	0.6511	0.9073
	NB	0.6089	0.6105	0.2642	0.2527	0.9378
	SVM	0.8938	**0.8388**	**0.6791**	0.7774	0.8950
	ANN	0.8819	0.8008	0.6007	**0.7883**	0.8122

From Table 1, we can see that the BiLSTM feature extraction method is more effective than ACT, and the extracted feature information is more comprehensive. The two feature extraction methods are combined with six basic feature extraction methods. Among them, the accuracy of BiLSTM-RF is 6% higher than that of ACT-RF, and the accuracy of BiLSTM-NB is 16.28% higher than that of ACT-NB. In addition, BiLSTM-KNN, BiLSTM-LR and BiLSTM-ANN all have relatively better performance. In addition to the support vector machine, the other five classifiers are combined with the BiLSTM method to produce higher indicators, and all have been greatly improved. The BiLSTM feature extraction method is combined with the random forest model, and the Acc value can reach 0.8676. It can be seen that the feature extraction method based on BiLSTM is better and can more fully capture the bidirectional position information. Our BiLSTM-RF model has high predictive ability and good stability.

5 Conclusion

Protein is the material basis, and PPI is a common form of protein to perform its important functions and the basis of biological biochemical reactions. Therefore, studying PPI can further reveal the function of protein and the laws of many life activities, which has great biological significance. Since humans entered the post-genome era, the field of PPI has gradually developed into a research hotspot and difficulty in molecular biology. In the development process of the PPIs field, predecessors have made great contributions, laid the research foundation for us and guided our future research directions. Since the rise of PPI deep learning, many researchers have applied it to the field of PPIs and achieved extraordinary results. In this article, we propose the BiLSTM-RF model, which uses BiLSTM for feature capture of protein sequences, which more comprehensively retains the positional features of the sequence. Subsequently, we carried out feature reconstruction on the features, and divided the training set and independent test set. At the same time, we constructed a random forest classifier, using non-redundant human data sets for training and testing. It can be seen from the experimental results that our proposed model has a good predictive effect on the human PPIs data set. We will continue to use deep learning in depth in the future to provide more reliable support for research in the field of PPIs.

Acknowledgments. This work was supported in part by the University Innovation Team Project of Jinan (2019GXRC015), and in part by Key Science &Technology Innovation Project of Shandong Province (2019JZZY010324), the Natural Science Foundation of China (No. 61902337), the talent project of "Qingtan scholar" of Zaozhuang University, Natural Science Fund for Colleges and Universities in Jiangsu Province (No. 19KJB520016), Jiangsu Provincial Natural Science Foundation (No. SBK2019040953), Young talents of science and technology in Jiangsu.

References

1. Brohee, S., Van Helden, J.: Evaluation of clustering algorithms for protein-protein interaction networks. BMC Bioinf. **7**(1), 1–19 (2006)
2. Sugaya, N., Ikeda, K.: Assessing the druggability of protein-protein interactions by a supervised machine-learning method. BMC Bioinf. **10**(1), 263 (2009)
3. Shen, J., et al.: Predicting protein–protein interactions based only on sequences information. Proc. Nat. Acad. Sci. **104**(11), 4337–4341 (2007)
4. Zhang, Q.C., et al.: Structure-based prediction of protein–protein interactions on a genome-wide scale. Nature **490**(7421), 556–560 (2012)
5. Wu, J., et al.: Integrated network analysis platform for protein-protein interactions. Nat. Meth. **6**(1), 75–77 (2009)
6. De Las Rivas, J., Fontanillo, C.: Protein–protein interactions essentials: key concepts to building and analyzing interactome networks. PLoS Comput. Biol. **6**(6), e1000807 (2010)
7. Zhang, Y.P., Zou, Q.: PPTPP: a novel therapeutic peptide prediction method using physicochemical property encoding and adaptive feature representation learning. Bioinformatics **36**(13), 3982–3987 (2020)
8. Shen, Z., Lin, Y., Zou, Q.: Transcription factors–DNA interactions in rice: identification and verification. Brief. Bioinform. **21**(3), 946–956 (2019)
9. Liu, G.-H., Shen, H.-B., Dong-Jun, Y.: Prediction of protein–protein interaction sites with machine-learning-based data-cleaning and post-filtering procedures. J. Membr. Biol. **249**(1–2), 141–153 (2016)
10. Sato, T., et al.: Interactions among members of the Bcl-2 protein family analyzed with a yeast two-hybrid system. Proc. Nat. Acad. Sci. **91**(20), 9238–9242 (1994)
11. Schwikowski, B., Uetz, P., Fields, S.: A network of protein–protein interactions in yeast. Nat. Biotechnol. **18**(12), 1257–1261 (2000)
12. Coates, P.J., Hall, P.A.: The yeast two-hybrid system for identifying protein–protein interactions. J. Pathol. J. Pathol. Soc. Great Brit. Irel. **199**(1), 4–7 (2003)
13. Free, R.B., Hazelwood, L.A., Sibley, D.R.: Identifying novel protein-protein interactions using co-immunoprecipitation and mass spectroscopy. Curr. Protoc. Neurosci. **46**(1), 5–28 (2009)

14. Kim, Y., Subramaniam, S.: Locally defined protein phylogenetic profiles reveal previously missed protein interactions and functional relationships. Proteins Struct. Funct. Bioinform. **62**(4), 1115–1124 (2006)

15. Zhang, S.-W., Hao, L.-Y., Zhang, T.-H.: Prediction of protein–protein interaction with pairwise kernel Support Vector Machine. Int. J. Mol. Sci. **15**(2), 3220–3233 (2014)

16. Burger, L., Van Nimwegen, E.: Accurate prediction of protein–protein interactions from sequence alignments using a Bayesian method. Mol. Syst. Biol. **4**(1), 165 (2008)

17. You, Z.-H., Zhu, L., Zheng, C.-H., Hong-Jie, Y., Deng, S.-P., Ji, Z.: Prediction of protein-protein interactions from amino acid sequences using a novel multi-scale continuous and discontinuous feature set. BMC Bioinform. **15**(Suppl. 15), S9 (2014)

18. Cui, G., Fang, C., Han, K.: Prediction of protein-protein interactions between viruses and human by an SVM model. BMC Bioinform. **13**(Suppl. 7), S5 (2012)

19. Bradford, J.R., Westhead, D.R.: Improved prediction of protein–protein binding sites using a support vector machines approach. Bioinformatics **21**(8), 1487–1494 (2005)

20. Guo, Y., et al.: Using support vector machine combined with auto covariance to predict protein–protein interactions from protein sequences. Nucleic Acids Res. **36**(9), 3025–3030 (2008)

21. Koike, A., Takagi, T.: Prediction of protein–protein interaction sites using support vector machines. Protein Eng. Des. Sel. **17**(2), 165–173 (2004)

22. Yi, H., You, Z., Wang, M., et al.: RPI-SE: a stacking ensemble learning framework for ncRNA-protein interactions prediction using sequence information. BMC Bioinform. **21**, 60 (2020)

23. Du, X., et al.: DeepPPI: boosting prediction of protein–protein interactions with deep neural networks. J. Chem. Inf. Model. **57**(6), 1499–1510 (2017)

24. Sun, T., et al.: Sequence-based prediction of protein protein interaction using a deep-learning algorithm. BMC Bioinform. **18**(1), 1–8 (2017)

25. Zhang, L., et al.: Protein–protein interactions prediction based on ensemble deep neural networks. Neurocomputing **324**, 10–19 (2019)

26. Kong, M., et al.: FCTP-WSRC: protein-protein interactions prediction via weighted sparse representation based classification. Front. Genet. **11**, 18 (2020)

27. Ma, W., et al.: ACT-SVM: prediction of protein-protein interactions based on support vector basis model. Sci. Program. **2020**, 8866557:1–8866557:8 (2020)

Author Index

Printed in the United States
by Baker & Taylor Publisher Services